# The Talmudic Anthology

# The
# TALMUDIC
# Anthology

TALES AND TEACHINGS OF THE RABBIS

A Collection of Parables, Folk-tales, Fables, Apho-
rism, Epigrams, Sayings, Anecdotes, Proverbs and
Exegetical Interpretations

SELECTED AND EDITED BY

## Louis I. Newman

COMPILER OF THE HASIDIC ANTHOLOGY

✡

IN COLLABORATION WITH

## Samuel Spitz

## Behrman House, Inc · Publishers

To

LOUIS BEHRMAN

WITH HIGH REGARD FOR HIS DEVOTED SERVICE
IN THE DISSEMINATION OF
ISRAEL'S LORE

# Contents

NOTE: Page numbers only are indicated throughout Contents.

xi

INTRODUCTION

# The Ethical Message of the Talmud

# INTRODUCTION

## The Ethical Message of the Talmud

T HE ETERNAL PEOPLE OF ISRAEL, to whose God a thousand
years are but as yesterday when it is passed, has, out of the torment and aspiration of its experience in history, evolved two great
monuments in the world's literature. One is the Bible, born out of
more than twelve centuries of travail and vision, and emerging as
the foremost factor in the spiritual and moral life of mankind. The
other—likewise the fruition of many centuries of meditation, discussion, and yearning for the divine—is the Talmud. Both the Bible
and the Talmud are eternal emblems of the creative power of the
eternal people.

To the uninitiated the Talmud is a fabulous world. Sometimes it
is regarded as a bewildering labyrinth wherein the layman, if he
dare seek to penetrate, becomes speedily lost. Some speak of the
"sphinx-like nature of the Talmud"; others are baffled by "its
enormous size, its intricacy and mysterious architecture." Nevertheless this great library of books, for the most part, has been translated
into languages which make them accessible to the modern reader.
There is no reason why an interested person cannot make use of
these materials at hand. This *Anthology*, however, employs this
closely knit and compact literature in such a fashion as to present
a selection of typical items in the Talmudic books, classified under
more than four hundred rubrics. These categories deal with ethical,
spiritual, legal and sociological themes. The editors have striven
for simplicity and intelligibility, endeavoring to act upon the Talmudic dictum: "If I had not removed for thee pieces of clay, how
wouldst thou have found the pearl?"

Talmudic literature is encyclopaedic in character. It is not embraced, as we have said, in a book; it is rather a monumental
library. It is the rich harvest of those powerful intellectual, moral,
judicial and religious forces which moved within the Jewish people
for ten centuries, and carried forward the message of the Bible and
the Apocrypha. In the Academies and Schools of the two chief
centers of Jewish life during this epoch—Palestine and Babylonia—

the teachers and leaders of Israel sought to shape a unified outlook towards the entirety of life, under the aegis of the Hebraic legacy as it had developed until then. Though legal matters in the so-called *Halakah* (the Path, or Way) receive primary attention, about one-third of the Babylonian and one-sixth of the Palestinian Talmud, consists of non-legal matter, or the so-called *Aggadah*. The latter term embraces a wide variety of topics, including ethics, poetry, religious philosophy, theology, folklore, history, mathematics, astronomy and natural science—presenting a panorama of infinite complexity, reflecting the substance and spirit of Jewish life in different lands and under diversified conditions.

In tracing the history and growth of the Talmud, we must inevitably go to its roots, the Bible. The Bible represents a religious and intellectual evolution extending over a thousand years from the days before Moses to the days immediately following the destruction of the Second Temple in the year 70 c.e. Within the library of the Bible books, including the Pentateuch, the Prophets and the Holy Writings, is a majestic body of law, the *Torah*, which became the foundation-stone for Jewish religious life throughout the ages. The concept of *Torah* maintained its supremacy in Jewish life not only in the simple economy of Bible days, but also in the epoch of the Second Hebrew Commonwealth when the needs of a more complex national state demanded its considerable elaboration and development. As an outgrowth of these new forces, the principle of *Torah*, or Teaching, found another expression, with many more facets, in the activity of Study, or *Talmud*. The Talmud is said to have originated with the return of the Judean people from their Babylonian Captivity about 538 B.C.E., and its development before assuming written form was, at some points, coincident with the unfolding of the Bible.

Over a period of several centuries, it eventually developed into two mighty collections of writings, one known as the Palestinian Talmud, edited in Jerusalem about 400 c.e., and the other, the Babylonian Talmud, edited in the Academies of Babylonia about 500 c.e. Within the Talmud, the *Torah* served as the nucleus for the writings of the *Mishnah* (Repetition), the first codification of the Oral Law, compiled and edited by the illustrious Rabbi Judah, known as *ha-Nasi*, or the Prince, about 220 c.e. In its turn it stimulated a vast activity of more Study which created the intricate, far-reaching *Gemara*, or the Completion of the *Mishnah*.

Moreover, on the basis of the Bible, the *Mishnah* and the *Gemara*, there arose a huge edifice of homiletical lore, known as the *Midrash*, and of imaginative, narrative lore, known as the *Aggadah*. Mystical writings appeared also within the same domain. The total collection of these libraries—the *Midrashic, Aggadic* and *Halakic* (writings chiefly legal in character)—representing the creative endeavours of more than a millennium—can be called the *Talmudic-Midrashic* literature.

It is not our purpose here to chronicle the evolution and development of Talmudic literature, or even to define in detail the vocabulary of terms necessary to a technical understanding of it, among them the Oral Law, the Written Law, *Gemara, Midrash,* and the like. Nor will we do more than mention that the architects and builders of the Talmud were the *Soferim* or Scribes; the *Zugot,* or Pairs of Rabbis; the *Tannaim,* the *Amoraim* and the *Sabboraim,* three major groups of Jewish scholars and Sages. For these facts relating to the Talmud, we must direct the reader to any comprehensive article on the subject among the many which are available. Sufficient it is for us to quote from the words of one of the world's greatest living Talmudists, Professor Louis Ginzberg.* "The most contradictory judgments have been passed upon the Talmud— its theology, its ethics, its system of law, and its literary form. There can, however, be only one opinion on its great influence upon Jewish life and thought for almost two thousand years. Biblical Judaism was limited to one small country, and to a time of cultural homogeneity of the Jewish people. The Talmud made it possible for Judaism to adapt itself to every time and place, to every state of society, and to every state of civilization."

In compiling this *Anthology,* we have found ourselves in complete concordance with Emanuel Deutsch, author of a famous essay upon the Talmud. He has declared correctly: "Between the rugged boulders of the law which bestrew the path of the Talmud, there grow the blue flowers of romance—parable, tale, gnome, saga; its elements are taken from heaven and earth, but chiefly and most lovingly from the human heart and from Scripture, for every verse and every word in this latter became, as it were, a golden nail upon which it hung its gorgeous tapestries."

Talmudic literature, while it has its secrets and profundities, is a veritable gold-mine of wisdom—of good common sense, of witty and subtle insight, of inspiration made manifest in terms which even the humblest commoner can grásp. The ethical genius of Israel did not atrophy with the close of the Bible writings; it lived on undimmed

* Introductory Essay, *The Palestinian Talmud,* p. lxix.

in the library of Rabbinic writings, a glimpse into which it is our privilege here to vouchsafe.

We have sought to elicit the ethical and spiritual message of the Talmudic writings, and we believe that the illustrations we have included in this compilation, will have a strong appeal to the imagination and feelings of the reader. Again, we echo the words of the great Emanuel Deutsch: "I have been able to bring before you what proves, as it were, but a drop in the vast ocean of Talmud— that strange, wild, weird ocean, with its leviathans, and its wrecks of golden argosies, and with its forlorn bells that send up their dreamy sounds ever and anon, while the fisherman bends upon his oar, and starts and listens, and perchance the tears may come into his eyes."

### The Rabbis Who Created the Talmud

The Sages who created the Talmudic-Midrashic literature over a period of several hundred years were men of varying backgrounds, origins, experiences and temperaments. The Talmudic passages associated with their names vary, therefore, greatly in content and viewpoint. There is the amiable Hillel whose love embraced all human folk; he taught (p. 10)* that it is better for a man to lose many zuzim than to cause him to lose his temper. There is the tempestuous Shammai, standing at the opposite pole from Hillel, in disposition and legal outlook; Jochanan ben Zakkai who secures from the Roman conqueror permission to found an Academy at Jabneh after the Temple's Fall in Jerusalem; Elisha ben Abuyah, the rebel, self-alienated from Israel and called by his colleagues *Aher* (Other); Simeon ben Yohai, devoted to mystical reveries and to whom so much of the lore of the Kabbalah is attributed. We meet with the wise and valiant Akiba who joins the warrior Bar Kochbah in a vain revolt against Rome, dying a martyr's death; Meir, master of the fable and great exponent of Rabbinic jurisprudence; the scrupulously honest Simeon ben Shetach; Simeon ben Lakisch, renowned for his unusual physical beauty and for his adventurous past before becoming a Sage. It is a remarkable galaxy of scholars and teachers who confront us in the manifold pages of the Talmudic books. To make their acquaintance through their

* Page numbers in parenthesis throughout Introduction refer to pages in text.

aphorisms, legal decisions, expository comments and narratives is a rare and memorable privilege.

It must not be thought for a moment that these were men aloof from their contemporaries, dwelling in an ivory tower of unworldly piety. According to the Rabbis, God says: "In every place where thou findest the prints of a man's foot, there am I before thee." In other words, they moved and lived among their fellow-men. They were, for the most part, practical, statesmanlike personalities, who sought to translate into concrete form the classic message of the Torah, so that it might be valid, not for the aristocracy of the learned alone, but for the democratic masses as well.

The Rabbis esteemed manual labor, and numbers of them engaged in it for their own livelihood, believing that scholarship and physical work formed a happy partnership. Rabbi Sheshet, for example, extolling the work which brought sweat to his brow, carried logs (p. 241); Akiba, at one time in his life, was a shepherd; Rabbi Joseph turned a mill; Abba Joseph was a workman for a builder; Rabbi Hiyya bar Abin was a carpenter; Rabbi Abba ben Abba was a dealer in silk; Rabbi Abba bar Zmina was a tailor; and Rabbi Yitzhak Nafha who was a smith. Thus the Rabbis acted upon their own dictum: "Acquire a trade with the Torah."

It is not surprising, therefore, that throughout the Talmud, we find constant praise of the laborer, and a recognition of the importance of safeguarding his rights. "He who has a trade," said the Rabbis, "is like a woman who has a husband, and a vineyard which has a fence." "The right of the workingman always has precedence," we are told. As soon as the day's work was over, Rab Hamnun would gather his laborers together, and give them their pay, saying: "Here, take your souls." If one of them declined to be paid at that time, the Rabbi would insist, saying: "Thou canst not deposit with me thy body; how much the less thy soul." Again and again we find the injunction to show consideration for serfs and servants. Once Rabbi Jose chided his wife for rebuking her servant unjustly. "But you should not have reproved me in her presence," protested his wife. "Nay," answered the Rabbi. "She ought to know that her rights are not despised." Moreover during an epoch when the world at large sanctioned slavery, the Rabbis, by their numerous restrictions against inhumane treatment of serfs and slaves, did their utmost to discourage the institution of holding fellow-men in bondage. The social compassion of the Rabbis concerning workmen, serfs and slaves has an especial appeal for us today.

The Sages were essentially modest and humble folk, without over-weening pride in themselves as exponents of the law and as masters of homiletical wisdom. We read (p. 372): "He who listens to the Rabbis and remembers their words, is like a Rabbi himself." There are many sharp criticisms of hypocrisy and ostentation in religious practice, together with a healthy self-analysis of Rabbinical char-acter, as is manifested in the saying of Rabbi Benjamin, "There are hypocrites of learning. It is supposed by the people that they are Biblical and Talmudical scholars, but they are not. They wrap their Tallit about them, and have their Tefillin on their head, 'and behold the tears of the oppressed who have no comforter' (Eccl. 4:1)." When Rabbi Eleazar b. R. Simeon is enjoined not to become the police-head of the community, he is told: "Leave it to the Owner of the Vineyard to weed out His thorns Himself." Again and again, the Rabbis are commanded to be humble: witness the rebuke to a proud Rabbi by a hunchback whom he had offended (p. 197). In short, the Sages were very human folk, undergoing the tests and challenges of ordinary experience, but distinguishing themselves because of their lofty ideals and their saintly be-havior.

## The Aggadah and Its Imaginative Lore

The wisdom of the Rabbis comes to the fore, not only in the legal, or *Halakic,* material of the Talmud, but in its *Aggadic,* or imaginative, lore as well. The *Aggadah* (flowing speech), or non-legal, narrative matter, communicates its message through a poet-ical, emotional approach, rather than a purely intellectual one. Con-cerning it, the great Leopold Zunz has written: "The *Aggadah* which is intended to bring heaven down to the earth, and also to lift man up to heaven, appears in this office both as the glorification of God and the comfort of Israel. Hence religious truths, maxims, discussions concerning divine retribution, the incul-cation of laws which attest Israel's nationality, descriptions of the past and future greatness, scenes and legends from Jewish history, comparisons between the divine and Jewish institutions, praises of the Holy Land, encouraging stories and comforting reflections of all kinds, form the important subjects of these discourses." The Tal-mudic writings abound in this imaginative lore. For example, we are given a highly colorful and creative dialogue between Moses and God (p. 37), who finally concedes to the Prophet a glimpse of the Promised Land. Vivid and picturesque imagery marks the literary style of these items.

The *Midrash,* containing most of the *Aggadic,* or narrative material, reflects, as Solomon Schechter has said, the very "life of the Rabbis" and may be compared to a collection of jewels sparkling with myriads of facets. It is replete with word-pictures, similes, metaphors and poetic phraseology in a prose setting. In portraying the role of Israel in the world, we find epigram after epigram of descriptive force and pungency: Israel is likened to a vine, an olive, an apple tree, to glass, a worm, a bird, to dust and the stars.

Rabbi Jonathan, driving home a moral lesson, remarks that the potter in testing the work of the kiln, examines it by striking the well-wrought vessels only. He does not try the more fragile objects in this fashion, for one blow will suffice to break them. Even so does God afflict only those who, in a spirit of piety and resignation, can bear the burden and test of sorrow and suffering.—A pithy phrase suggesting the Rabbis' profound understanding of character: "Offer not pearls for sale to those who deal in vegetables and onions."—Another effective simile is found in Rabbi Levi's words: "The Tabernacle was like a cave that joins the sea. The sea rushes in and floods the cave; the cave is filled, but the sea is in no wise diminished. By the same token, the Tabernacle was filled with the radiance of the Divine Presence, but the world thereby lost nothing of that Presence."—A simple image, typical of many others, serving to bring home a great spiritual concept to the plain folk of Israel, is found in the comparison of God to a mother hen which guards her chicks against all harm. Within the *Aggadah* there are many phrases of homely, salty strength whereby the Rabbis impressed the common people.

We find a wide range of methods employed for the narration of stories containing an ethical or spiritual message. The *Mashal,* or parable, was appreciated as an instrument of great value (p. 35). For example, Rabbi Abbahu comforts R. Hiyya ben Abba, when the populace preferred his *Aggadic* discourse to the latter's *Halakic* or legalistic exposition: "Two men once entered the same town, the one offering for sale precious stones and pearls; the other tinsel. To whom do you think the people throng? Is it not to him who sells the tinsel, which they can afford to purchase?"

The allegory is a favorite Rabbinic device; there is one recounting the conspiracy of Falsehood and Injustice in the days of the Flood (p. 359); another telling of the cooperation of Joy and Gladness (p. 276).—The fable, too, is especially dear to the Sages. We learn of the singing fox (p. 359); of the lion which informs the stork that its only reward for drawing a bone from his royal throat is the right to boast of its safe escape from the exploit; of the dog, which shrewdly snared a loaf from the baker; of the faithful dog which revealed by its own martyrdom the poisoned milk.—It may be of interest to note that while many of the fables attributed to Rabbi Meir are of his own composition, the rest, doubtless, were culled from the literature of other peoples, with Meir serving as a vehicle of transmission.

Proverbs and folk-sayings appear copiously, in the Talmudic books, some of inherently Hebraic origin, and others imported from the folklore of neighboring peoples. For example: "He who has been bitten by a snake is frightened by a rope" (p. 355).—"In a field where there are no mounds, do not tell secrets."—"Better one bird securely bound than a hundred free and flying."—Numerous cryptic utterances, such as "a crow flew by," require explanation in the light of contemporary conditions, but in almost every instance, they will be found to contain a lesson of interest and value even today.

Stories regarding man's friendship for animals and his kindly pity for them are also plentiful. Moses is deemed worthy to shepherd Israel when God perceives him carrying in his arms a lamb which had quenched its thirst at a distant stream.

We find, moreover, a deep interest in the natural world and in early science, expressed sometimes in poetic and symbolic terms. "With what," it is asked, "does God occupy Himself at night?" The answer is: "He rides on the wings of one of His swift Cherubs and visits the eighteen thousand worlds that are His."—The First Man, we are told, had a tail like a monkey, an item, which with others, indicates the Rabbis' discernment of close kinship between man and the higher animals.—A Sage, commenting upon the rainfall, notes that fish fatten and weigh more after a heavy downpour.—Many of the Rabbis were profound mathematicians and it is said of Eleazar Hizma that he could "count the drops in the ocean" (Hor. 10a). Johanan ben Zakkai could compute the courses of the sun and the moon (Suk. 28a) by his knowledge of the solstices and the calendar. In fact, astronomy was a science of the deepest fascination for the Rabbis who combined faith in the *Adon Olam*, the Lord of the Universe, with vast curiosity concerning the laws governing it. There were some who became so well versed in this science that a Rabbi

Shemuel of Nehardea could say of himself that the paths of the heavens were as clear to him as the streets of his native city.

## Psychological Insight in the Rabbinic Writings

Keen psychological insight is to be noted in countless comments by the Rabbis. They were acute students of human nature, and their aphorisms, epigrams, parables and stories amply evidence their power of wise perception. For example: "He who buys a Jewish serf buys a master for himself."—"Thou hast given bread to a child; let its mother know" (p. 354).—Rab Assi's mother, after asking for ornaments, urged her son to find a suitable husband for her, saying: "I wish a man as handsome as thou." Thereupon, the Rabbis tells us, he left her, and went to Palestine, recognizing the unhealthy elements in her character (p. 310).—"A man can quickly die if he has nothing to do."—"A virgin who prays continually; a widow who visits her neighbors too frequently; and an undergraduate who gives decisions in the law—these are the destroyers of the world."—"Can a goat live in the same barn with a tiger? In the same fashion, a daughter-in-law cannot live with her mother-in-law under the same roof."—When witnesses, by a slip of the tongue, declared a certain respected Rabbi to be dishonest, Rabbah b. R. Huna recognizing the error, said: "Surely, when a claimant brings witnesses to testify as to his character, he brings favorable witnesses only."—Rabbi Akiba said: "At the beginning, sin is like a thread of a spider's web, but in the end it is like the cable of a ship" (p. 436).—Rabbi Benaah, when asked to decide which of two sons was illegitimate, instructed both to beat with their staff upon the grave of the father; the son, born through the mother's infidelity, was willing, but the real son refused thus to dishonor his father's grave. He was declared the true heir.—The blind Rab Sheshet, awaiting the cortege of the king, after a band of music and a cavalcade of mounted men had passed by, noted that a carriage followed amid silence. "The king is now passing," he correctly inferred.—Rabbi Simeon ben Yohai visited a rich man, whom he found eating a meal of simple lentils, out of richly appointed dishes. "I eat this food because I like it," said the man of wealth. "The reason, however, I have such fine ornaments and costly plates is that only thus can I win your respect. You Rabbis are admired for your learning, but the rich must depend for respect upon their wealth."

Two daughters were cured of their ailments—one of idleness, the other of kleptomania, by wise psychiatric treatment; but the third daughter, being accustomed to engage in slanderous gossip, proved incurable (p. 460).—A story, revealing the cruelty which the Rabbis attributed to earthly rulers, perhaps more than mere psychological insight on the part of the monarch or of the narrator, tells of the Jew who grew tired of life and deliberately insulted the Emperor. When examined by the sovereign, he said: "My soul wishes food, and cannot obtain it; my wife and my child also are in want." "Let him go," said the Emperor to his attendants. "Life will be a greater punishment for him than death" (p. 521).

## Humor in the Talmudic Books

Humor among the Rabbis is not mere hilarious jesting; it is rather satiric and pointedly instructive. They appreciated the importance of wit, but regarded it chiefly as an educational instrument. We read, for example, that Rabbah would open his discourse with a jest, and let his hearers laugh a little; then he would become serious (p. 343).—The great Judah ha-Nasi, in order to stimulate the waning interest of an audience, suddenly declared: "A woman in Egypt gave birth to 600,000." He explained that it was Jochebed, "for she gave birth to Moses, the equal of all Israel, as it is written: 'Then sang Moses and Israel.' "—Another Rabbi remarked that an egg fell down and drowned sixty towns. It is offered in explanation that the Rabbi had just written the words: "sixty towns," and placed the paper on a table when a chicken jumped up, laid an egg there; it broke, and erased the words.

When Caesar made a Sepphoris tailor the "Duke of Galilee," the latter remarked to his friends: "You are surprised, but I am even more surprised." "In like manner," the Rabbis go on to say; "when the nations of the Levantine countries perceived Israel mustered under flags in brigades and regiments, and divided into four armies, they could not hide their astonishment. They said: 'Yesterday, these were serfs, making bricks out of clay and cement; today, they are a most resplendent nation.' Israel, amazed at its own unexpected prowess, answered: 'You are surprised, but we are even more surprised.' "

The good-for-nothing neighbor of a greybeard whom the Emperor rewarded for his gift of figs, learns to his dismay that the royal soldiers deny him the expected gold-pieces, but pelt him instead with his own fruit. On his return home, he answers his wife's inquiry, saying: "I fared excellently. Had I taken Etrogim (citrons), I would have died from their blows."—King Solomon is told by a tiny ant whom he has taken on his palm: "I am greater than thee, since God has sent thee to carry me."—When Rab was asked by a Persian to whom he was teaching the Hebrew language: "How will you prove to me that this is an 'Aleph,' " the Rabbi pulled his ear, and the Persian exclaimed: "Oh, my ear, my ear!" When asked how he knew it was his ear, he replied: "Everyone knows that this is my ear." Thereupon the Rabbi remarked: "By the same token, everyone knows that this is an 'Aleph.' " The Persian laughed and became a proselyte.

Pert remarks by children are frequently found in the Talmud, and greatly pleased the fancy of the Rabbis. We are told of a precocious lad in Jerusalem, who was asked by an Athenian to whom he had brought cheeses and eggs: "Tell me which cheese comes from the milk of a black cow, and which from a white cow." The lad answered: "You are older; tell me first which eggs are from a white hen, and which from a black."—A saucy little girl tells R. Joshua b. Hananiah, as he walked through a field that the path on which he was treading, had been made by "other trespassers" like him.—The Rabbi is rebuked by a child whom he questions concerning a dish which he is carrying, covered with a cloth: "If my mother had wished everyone to know, she would not have covered it."

## Rabbinic Colloquies with the Mighty

Some of the choicest items in Talmudic literature deal with colloquies, real and imaginary, between leading Rabbis and rulers, chiefly Roman Emperors and Roman officials. In these conversations, the sovereign is taught why the Israelites worship the Invisible God rather than the visible sun; why the laws of Moses receive more complete obedience than the royal edicts; why the Rabbi, since the Emperor does not know exactly where his own son is sojourning overseas, should not be expected to know accurately what happens in Heaven. Antoninus is told by Rabbi Judah ha-Nasi why he enjoyed a second meal less than a previous one. An essential ingredient was absent. "It is the Sabbath which is lacking. Have you the Sabbath in your cellar-stores?" (p. 399)—A disciple explains his failure to note the presence of the Roman governor during his prayers: "Thou standest before a human king who is here today and in his grave tomorrow. Thou couldst not reply to another's greeting. How much the less could I acknowledge thy greeting, when I stood before the King of Kings, who is eternal!'"

Stories about Alexander the Great and his visit to Palestine are full of ethical significance. The conqueror seeks to gain entrance into Paradise by the gift of a human skull weighted with gold. The Sages advise him, however, to place some earth upon the eye, thereby making the gift more appropriate, saying: "A human eye is not satisfied with all the gold that exists until it is covered with the earth of the grave" (p. 257).—Alexander, unsuccessfully trying to arrange marriages by royal decree, is rebuked for his effort to run counter to the ways of man and the universe, in the words: "Surely the sun and rain come to your land for the sake of the innocent beasts, not for the sake of unjust men. In our land, however, the sun shines and the rain descends for the sake of men, and the beasts receive their food for our sake" (p. 227).

The Rabbis did not hesitate to exhibit a strong and daring spirit in their narratives regarding encounters with rulers. This independence and audacity are evident on numerous occasions. It is told that Rabbi Samuel found the jewel-box of the Empress, but returned it on the thirty-first day, instead of on the thirtieth, before which the finder had been commanded to restore it, saying: "I delayed because I wished to show you that I returned the jewel-box not for reward, nor through fear of you, but solely out of fear of God." The Empress thereupon blessed the God of Israel.—A Rabbi, unprepossessing in appearance, who had been offended by an arrogant young princess, taught her a lesson in humility by proving to her that ugly vessels are used to store precious wines, but that expensive vessels turned them to vinegar. The stout-hearted, undaunted Sages who did not hesitate to defy monarchs and teach them according to the dictates of Israel's faith are exemplified by Rabbi Hanina who declared that "in the scheme of God's universe, all the royal legions and regiments are of no more value than the flies" which hover over the fruits in the market-place.

## Israel and the Nations

Contacts between non-Jews and Jews during the Talmudic epoch were steady and continuous. The people of Israel were staunchly loyal to their heritage, but they sought to live in amity with the majority populations, even when they suffered hardships at their hands. That the Rabbis were keenly aware of the complexities in the relationships of non-Jews and Jews is shown by their question: "What caused Israel to be dispersed among the nations?" The answer was: "The friendliness which Israel sought among them" (p. 298). A spirit of good-humored exchange and discussion prevails between Jew and non-Jew, as recorded in the Rabbinic books, but it is crowned by the noble words of the Sages: "The righteous of all the nations of the earth have a share in the World-to-Come." —"Even an idolator who studies the Torah is like the High Priest" (p. 301).

Numerous references occur to newcomers from Gentiledom into Judaism. "There are three kinds of proselytes: one becomes an Israelite because he loves a Jewess; the second, because he receives Jewish charity; the third, because he reveres the Name of God" (p. 348).—There is an amusing tale of the pagan who purchased a cow from an indigent disciple. The animal, however, refused to draw the plough on the Sabbath, thereby so impressing the pagan with the potency of Judaism that he accepted it as his faith. Henceforth he was known as Rabbi Hanina ben Turta, the "Son of a Cow."

A pagan asked Rabbi Joshua ben Karha why Israelites who professed to respect majority vote, did not adopt the majority religion. "Have you sons?" replied the Rabbi. "Yes," said the pagan, "but I am tormented by their conduct. When we are gathered for the family meal, each one says grace in the name of a different divinity, and they quarrel among themselves." "Well," answered the Rabbi, "suppose you decide among your own family the religion you are to accept, and afterwards come to us."

## Fortifying Troubled Israel

It is natural that the Rabbis should direct much of their sympathy and counsel to their own people Israel. They take deeply to heart the sufferings of Jewry, and seek to comfort them. Israel, they say, is like a lamb couched among seventy wolves.—"A synagogue retains its holiness even after it has been desolated" (p. 454).—"As everyone treads on dust, so does every nation tread on Israel. But as dust lasts longer than metal, so shall Israel outlast all nations" (p. 311).—"Israel is like the heart of humanity. As no one can live if the heart stops, so humanity cannot exist without Israel" (p. 205). —Rabbi Jose, with pardonable pride in his own people, informs the Roman matron that just as she selects out of a basket the more tasty figs, so God chooses Israel because of its righteous deeds.

The famous story of the "Fox and the Fishes" teaches Israel that it must not leave its natural element, the Torah, either under threat of danger or beguilement.—The unique ideals of Israel, including the Promise of the Messiah, and the Mission of Israel, are discussed in great detail by the Rabbis. We have one item which tells us that on the very day the Temple was destroyed, the Messiah was born, indicating that God never withdraws hope utterly from his people in tribulation. At the same time, we learn from the parable, that the Messiah disappeared also on this very day, teaching us the lesson that the object of our hopes is ever evanescent, and that, even as Israel was enjoined to fare forth on an eternal pilgrimage to discover the Messiah, so mankind must forever aspire to the fulfilment of its hopes for a better world.

## The Art of Human Relations

The Sages have much to say regarding the art of human relations, and they offer much wise counsel to members of the family of mankind. Children—their education and their place in the home and society—receive tender consideration at the hands of the Rabbis. "The world itself," we are told, "rests upon the breath of the children in the schoolhouse."—"When does a child become especially dear to his father? When he begins to talk?"—The Rabbis restored to an erring Shohet his prized knife "for the sake of his children" (p. 416).—"If one is a person of great learning, even though a mere boy, we must give him the same honor as an elder," said Rabbi Judah, when he met a lad, erudite in Scripture, leading a donkey on the highway.

Rabbinic approval of filial reverence is exemplified by the well-known story of Dama ben Netinah who refused to awaken his father in order to sell a precious gem to the Sanhedrin. Later he declined an additional sum for the transaction, saying: "Shall I sell for profit the honor I pay my parent?" (p. 309).—Rabbinic stories regarding husbands and wives show the profound faith cherished by the Sages in romantic love, in consideration and attentiveness by one spouse to the other, and in fidelity and constancy within the marriage bond. Even the Holy Name of God, we are told, is effaced for the sake of reconciliation between husband and wife. There is a poignant story of the wife, who, on being granted the opportunity to remove that which she most desired before the divorce became effective, took home with her, her cherished husband.

Astute and sagacious advice regarding life and its complex problems is available throughout Talmudic literature for those who seek it. The physician is praised, and sound suggestions are furnished for the healing of diseases (p. 431). We also read: "Reside not in a town, the mayor of which is the community physician. He will be too busy to attend thee in thy illness" (p. 319).—Valuable maxims are presented for the conduct of life, in terms of courtesy, modesty, benevolence and kindness. We read amusing comments upon the addiction of Noah to wine; we are reminded again and again of the power of the tongue for good and evil. "Why did Joseph die before his brothers?" it is asked. "Because he was masterful and ruled over them" (p. 252).—"The stone fell on the pitcher? Woe to the pitcher. The pitcher fell on the stone? Woe to the pitcher."—"The latest bandit," we are told, "is the first one to hang."—Concerning false friends, the Rabbis say, cryptically: "Say to the bee: neither thy honey nor thy sting."

Spiritual guidance is imparted in items such as these: "When a passenger on the deck of a ship falls into the sea, the captain throws him a line, crying: 'Grasp it firmly, and slacken not thy hold upon it, at the peril of thy life!' By the same token, amid the troubled seas of his earthly voyage, man should cling to the precepts of the Torah, and thereby remain attached to God. For thus he may truly live."

## The Letter of the Law and the Spirit

It must not be forgotten that the essence of the two Talmuds—the Jerusalem and the Babylonian—is found in its jurisprudence, for Judaism is basically a religion of law. The "Written Law" and the "Oral Law" were synthesized by the compilers, editors and redactors of the Talmudic books, into the *Halakah*, meaning, literally, the Way or the Path. The *Halakah* came to include a vast array of legal decisions founded upon a body of customs and traditional practices, growing up and evolving for many centuries. The codes of Maimonides in the 12th century and of Joseph Caro in the 16th century were built upon the cornerstone of Talmudic legalism.

Complex and technical as these legal sections of the Talmuds may be, they are at the same time permeated by a deep sense of humanity and justice. The Rabbis, preoccupied with these ideals, demanded the highest attainable standards of character and conduct among judges designated to interpret the law. Mar bar Rab Ashi said: "I cannot try the case of a student of the law, because I love him as myself, and no one can see a fault in himself."—When R. Samuel was crossing a bridge, a man lent him a sustaining hand. "Why so attentive?" inquired the Rabbi. "I have a lawsuit before thee." "In that case," said the Rabbi, "thy attention has disqualified me from judging."—"The law," said the Rabbis, "requires a head as clear as a clear day in the summer."—"The judge who renders a just decision is as though he had collaborated with God in the work of creation."—We learn from the experience of R. Simeon ben Shetach with King Jannai that "no king should be judged or called as a witness; neither shall he act as a judge, nor have witnesses testify against him." The timid will find it impossible, declared the Rabbis, to mete out true justice because of their awe before the monarch.

The Rabbis did not encourage litigation for its own sake. "Disagreements in courts of the law constitute the desolation of the world," they said. "It is a Mitzvah to arbitrate a suit rather than to institute it."—Whenever possible, they sought to temper justice with mercy, saying: "Warning must precede punishment."—"Hunger overtakes the world when justice knows not mercy."—Rabbah b. Bar Hana hired some porters to carry barrels of wine to his home. They were careless and broke them. In restitution, he seized their overgarments. They appealed to Rab, who ordered Rabbah to return the garments. Rabbah inquired: "Is this the law?" And Rab replied: "Yes. It is written (Proverbs 2:20): 'that thou mayest walk in the way of good men.' " The porters thereupon remarked: "We are poor; we have worked all day and we are hungry." Rab commanded Rabbah to pay their hire. Again the latter protested, asking: "Is this the law?" Rab answered: "Yes; it is written in the same passage: 'and keep the path of the righteous.' " Thus we see that the Rabbis, though eager to apply the law wisely, were also eager to mitigate its severity whenever the opportunity presented itself.

Pervading the entire body of Talmudic material is a sublime ethical motivation. No one exploring the treasures of Rabbinic literature can hold the notion that the Rabbis were strict, rigorous legalists. They always sought to judge "on the side of merit," declaring that one should not pass judgment upon his comrade until he had stood in his place. There is a story (p. 225) of the hired man who accepted, without complaint, his employer's failure to pay him his wages, believing that the employer had donated his entire wealth to the Temple Fund; though this impression later proved to be incorrect, the kindly laborer had judged him "in the scale of merit." —"Do not attribute the fault within thee to thy fellow-man," is another injunction.—Once R. Haggai, while walking with R. Zeira, approached a passer-by, carrying a load of wood, asking him for a sliver wherewith to cleanse his teeth. But his comrade reprimanded him, saying: "Do not do this; if everyone took but a sliver, the man's livelihood would be gone." In discussing the query whether R. Zeira was unreasonably scrupulous in this instance, the Sages answered thus: "Nay. Since he was a famous personage, it was incumbent upon him, through his actions, to teach the spirit of our Creator's laws, even though no objection could be taken to the letter thereof."

## The Compassionate Virtues

The gentler virtues are always extolled by the Rabbis. "It is permitted," we read, "to do good to a man without consulting him." Forbearance, patience, compassion, fellow-feeling, charity, kindliness, tenderness, consideration—these are but a few of the higher qualities of character which the Rabbis displayed to their comrades and to their adherents, recommending them, also, as a way of conduct for Israel and the world. "Shall I throw a stone at the one who has fallen?" asks a Rabbi (p. 193).—"Let sin, not sinners, disappear from the earth," says Beruria, the wife of Rabbi Meir, commenting upon a Biblical verse.—"Who is the bravest hero? He who turns his enemy into a friend" (p. 135). "Seek not to take revenge upon the man who has abused thee. Be rather the man who is abused, and humble of spirit" (p. 382).—R. Zeira, on arriving in Palestine, allowed himself to be struck on the cheek by a scoffer who died soon after. To his disciples, the Rabbi said: "I assure you I had no thought in mind to punish. I believed it was the practice here."

Charity in the eyes of the Rabbis is a paramount excellency of character. They had implicit faith in its power to rescue the individual from danger, poverty and death. Charity, we learn, can render a scorpion harmless; it led a Rabbi to advise his wife to give bread to a beggar, saying: "Do this, so that the same may be done to our children." She exclaimed: "You are cursing them." He replied:

"There is a wheel which revolves in the world; the poor become rich, and the rich poor."—"He who entreats aid for his comrade," we are told, "though he himself is in need, is answered first." Thus we see that charity constitutes a cornerstone of Rabbinic teaching.

### The Religious Ideals of the Rabbis

Not only do we encounter a portrayal of Israel and humanity in the pages of the Talmudic writings, but we meet also a detailed description of the God of the Universe, as envisaged by the Jewish sages. He is no transcendental, aloof Deity, removed from the ways and needs of men, but He is, throughout, a Loving Father, Companion and Friend, preoccupied with the most intimate problems and minute vexations of His children. The lowliest acts—ploughing, sowing, reaping and the like—are elevated into a service to Israel's God (p. 406). God, we are told, appeared to Moses in the thornbush, to demonstrate that there is no place on earth, however lowly, void of the Divine Presence.—"When a man smiles at his own shadow, it smiles back at him. By the same token, God is thy shadow; as thou art to Him, so He is to thee."—There are charming stories of the miracles which God sanctions, and numerous tales portraying God's unfailing goodness to men. One of the Talmudic personalities is Nahum Ish Gam-Zu, so-called because he was accustomed to say, whatever transpired: "Also this is for good."

Spiritual intensity marks a multitude of the Rabbinic utterances. "When a man travels a road, let him make it the road to God, and let him invite God to be his companion" (p. 513). "Even a steel door in a prison of stone cannot place an obstacle between Israel and his Father in Heaven."—"The heart's cry to God is the highest form of prayer" (p. 339). "Tears break through the gates and doors of Heaven" (p. 342).—"An arrow carries the width of a field; but repentance carries to the very throne of God" (p. 379).—"Why is repentance likened to the sea? As the sea is open at all times, so is the gate of penitence" (p. 377).

\*　　　\*　　　\*

Thus it can be seen that within the unbounded domain of Talmudic literature there can be uncovered riches of priceless worth. "My face is illumined," said R. Judah, "because I find joy in Torah." It is Torah, in the sense of being a comprehensive presentation of what a great modern teacher calls "Jewish civilization" which we find in the Talmud. "He who loves Torah," we read further, "is never satisfied with Torah" (p. 501). Acting upon this dictum, let the reader who takes this volume in hand to peruse and utilize understand that it does not aspire to be a scholarly work, but aims primarily to make available to the average reader some of the lore of the Sages. Let the great granary of Rabbinic wisdom yield a little nourishment again for those who wish to call upon it.

We are told that the Academy at Sura in Babylonia during the 5th century, presided over by the illustrious Rabbi Ashi, was "a center of learning of the very highest type and of extraordinary proportions. We can almost hear it humming with big crowds seething with great activity. Its fame is unbounded; its influence irresistible. It is the clearing house of all views and problems, on all matters of law from all its contemporaries, and a court from which there is no appeal for all the generations to come." * Out of the historic editorial activity of the men who compiled the Babylonian Talmud about 500 C.E., and their predecessors in Jerusalem, compiling the Palestinian Talmud about a century prior, came the library of literature, to which we are indebted so profoundly. It is our hope that in this *Anthology*, directed to the average reader, we have been able to cull a few of the choicer Rabbinic items, thereby extending its influence a bit further in the field of the humanities of the world's culture.

LOUIS I. NEWMAN.

* Julius Kaplan, *The Redaction of the Babylonian Talmud*, New York, 1933, p. 78.

# Editors' Note

This *Talmudic Anthology* has been compiled at the invitation of Mr. Louis Behrman of Behrman House, for the purpose of presenting to contemporary readers an alphabetically arranged collection of some of the utterances, aphorisms, ethical injunctions, parables and folk-tales found in the vast library of books, known as the Talmud and the Midrash. Despite the difficulty of discovering and gathering such material, we have been encouraged to undertake this task by the interest shown in the *Hasidic Anthology*, which sought to perform the same function for the great literature of Hasidism during the eighteenth and nineteenth centuries.*

There are, to be sure, several works varying in size and value, presenting Talmudic wisdom, but there is no compilation sufficiently comprehensive, we believe, to furnish to the lay and ministerial reader an adequate insight into the wealth of Rabbinic lore. Even the *Rabbinic Anthology,* compiled by the late Claude G. Montefiore and H. Loewe † organizes its material under only thirty-one rubrics. It is our hope, however, that the *Talmudic Anthology* may enable the average reader to acquire easily and rapidly an appreciation of Talmudic ideals on themes of moral, spiritual, ethico-legal and sociological interest. We trust, also, that it will place within the reach of teachers and preachers illustrative items for addresses and sermons.

It must be understood that though it is essential in numerous instances to know the setting for cryptic remarks by the Rabbis, a description of this background has not been the purpose of the compilers. Our aim has been chiefly homiletical, the student being free to pursue to its origin the particular item selected. The subject matter of this *Anthology,* classified under its more than four hundred rubrics, has been translated with considerable freedom. Some items have been abridged; others amplified by the inclusion of brief material from the commentaries, in order to make them more useful for the general reader. In addition to using the original sources, we have sometimes drawn upon items already rendered into

* Compiled by Louis I. Newman and Samuel Spitz; New York, 1934.
† Macmillan, London, 1938.

English by other writers; we have employed three anthologies in the Hebrew language, one of tales, another of sayings and maxims, and a third of tales and maxims from the *Zohar*. Some sources are arranged according to the *Sedrah,* or the Weekly Portion, read from the Scroll of the Law. We caution the reader to avoid the belief that if a theme or utterance is not found under one heading, it will not be found under a synonymous rubric.*

We wish to express our appreciation to Dr. Aharon Kessler, Rabbi Alexander Burnstein and to Miss Dena Behrman for their valuable suggestions. Our readers know, of course, that there is a great plenitude of material which, because of space limitations, we have been unable to include. With this reservation, we present our *Anthology* to the attention of those who are interested in representative selections from the monumental literature of the Talmud and the *Midrash*.

Louis I. Newman and Samuel Spitz.

* Occasional errors or misprints may have crept into the references to the original books from which we have made selections. As far as possible, we have verified the source reference, but, being more interested in presenting the ethical substance, we have left further verification to the technical student.

# The Talmudic Anthology

# 1. ABSTINENCE AND ASCETICISM

### THE PAIN OF ABSTINENCE

One who causes himself pain by abstinence from something he desires is called a sinner.

*Nazir, 19.*

### SELF-IMPOSED ABSTINENCE

Self-imposed abstinence is disapproved by many Rabbis. Rabbi Isaac said:

"Are not the things prohibited you in the Law enough for you, that you wish to prohibit yourself other things?"

*Y. Nedarim, 41b.*

### RENDERING ACCOUNT

Rab said: "A man will have a demerit in his record on Judgment Day for everything he beheld with his eyes and declined to enjoy."

*Y. Kiddushin, 4.*

### A HOLY PROFESSION

Rabbi Johanan visited the school of a certain city, where he found a teacher in a faint. After reviving him, he asked the cause, and was told: "I vowed to fast today."

"Make no such vows henceforth," the Rabbi warned him. "If even a laborer in a profane occupation may not fast, how much the less may one engaged in a holy profession?"

*Y. Demai, 7.*

### THE NAZIRITE'S SIN-OFFERING

Why does the Torah prescribe a sin-offering for a Nazirite? Wherein did he sin? He made a vow that it would be a sin for him to enjoy wine, and hence he castigated his soul. If a man who thus abstained only from wine is called a sinner, how much the more is one who vows to castigate his soul or body in matters far more important?

*Taanit, 11.*

### THE COMELY SHEPHERD

The tale is told by Simeon, the Righteous, that a comely young shepherd took the Nazirite's vow because his beauty, as he saw himself with his flowing locks reflected in water, awakened in him emotions like unto those of Narcissus. Simeon blessed him and made an exception in his case by eating the flesh of his sacrificial animal.

*Nazir, 4b.*

## 2. ABUSE AND INSULT

### APHORISMS

To smite an Israelite is as if one smote the Shekinah.

*Sanhedrin, 58.*

For every sin, a messenger is sent to punish, except the sin of abusing without cause, for which God Himself punishes.

*Baba Metzia, 59.*

If thou sayest a minor word of abuse against another, consider it as if thou hadst said a major word.

*Derek Eretz Zuta, 1.*

Oftentimes a man praises his fellow in a low voice but derides him in a loud.

*Sotah, 32.*

### WRONGING ONE ANOTHER

"And ye shall not wrong one another" (Lev. 25, 17). This injunction, repeated in verses 14 and 17 applies in one instance to money and in the other to words. How to words? If one is a penitent, say not: "Remember thy previous deeds." If one is the son of a proselyte, say not: "Remember thy father's deeds."

*Sifra to Lev. 25, 17.*

### SEEKING PEACE

The Sages have told: Once at the close of Yom Kippur, all the people followed after the High Priest to escort him to his home. But when they observed Shemaiah and Abtalion, they left the High Priest and formed an escort for the Chief Justices. The latter, however, escorted the High Priest to his home, for the sake of peace.

The arrogant High Priest remarked to them: "May the sons of the Gentiles go in peace!"

The Rabbis resented this reminder of their origin and declared: "May the sons of the Gentiles go in peace, for they imitate Aaron in seeking peace! But should the son of Aaron go in peace when he does not imitate his forefather in seeking peace?"

*Yoma, 71.*

## 3. ADULTERY

"Commit no adultery."

Namely, give no profit to the spirit of violence; cause no violence to enter into the world.

Read not: "tin-af," but "ten-af."

R. Simeon b. Lakish said: "One may commit adultery with the eyes."

The adulterer strives to conceal his crime. What does God do?

He fashions the child of sin in the likeness of the adulterer.

R. Isaac said: "In theft, one party gains, and the other loses. In adultery, both parties gain pleasure. Who loses? The Creator. He is compelled to become a party in their crime, and to create their child together with them."

*Pesikta Rabbati, 25, 2.*

## 4. AFTER-LIFE (PARADISE, GEHENNA, OLAM HA-BA)

### SAYINGS

There is a place in Eden and in Gehenna for every soul. The Zaddik (Righteous, Saint) receives his place and the place of a wicked man as well. By the same token, the wicked man receives his own place and the place of a Zaddik.

*Hagigah, 15.*

No one partakes of the enjoyments of the World-to-Come because of his father's merits.

*Midrash Tehillim, 146, 2.*

There are three persons who have a share in the World-to-Come: he who resides in Palestine; he who raises his children to be scholars, and he who honors the Sabbath.

*Pesahim, 113.*

Who is a son of the World-to-Come? He who is included among those concerning whom Isaiah saith: "And before His Elders shall be Glory" (24:23).

*Baba Batra, 10.*

Rab used to say: "The World-to-Come is not like this world. In the World-to-Come there is no eating and drinking, no begetting of children, no bargaining, no jealousy and hatred, and no strife. But the Righteous sit with their crowns on their heads, enjoying the effulgence of the Shekinah."

*Berakot, 17a.*

## Among His Own Kind

Rabbi Simeon ben Lakish was wont to study Torah in a cave in Tiberias. Nearby a potter had his shop, and he was accustomed to place a pitcher in the cave with cool water for the Rabbi to drink.

Once the potter entered the cave and said: "Rabbi, doubtless you recollect that both of us studied together in the same primary school. You were fortunate enough to attain high position, whereas I was unlucky. Will you not promise to endeavour to have me as your companion in Paradise?"

The Rabbi answered: "What wouldst thou do, my friend, among persons of great learning, and how wouldst thou feel among those whom you cannot understand? Let me rather pray that thou take thy place among the pious ones of thine own class. In this fashion wilt thou enjoy thy share in Paradise."

*Kohelet Rabbah, 3 (Amplified).*

## Higher Than His Neighbor

Rabbi Johanan said: "The praises of God that ascend from Gehenna are more than those that ascend from Paradise. For each one who is a step higher than his neighbor praises God, saying: 'Happy am I that I am a step nearer the portal of exit than the one below me.'"

*Yalkut Shimeoni to Psalm 84:7.*

## Neighbors in Paradise

Rabbi Simeon ben Yohai prayed that he might behold his neighbor in Paradise, and was informed in a dream that it would be a certain butcher whose name and place of residence were also given him. The Rabbi paid the butcher a visit and found him to be a wealthy and charitable man. He called him aside and said: "Pray, tell me the good deeds you have performed."

The butcher replied that he distributed meat to the poor without charge. This, however, did not satisfy the Rabbi, and he continued: "Tell me of some unusual deed of goodness you have done."

The butcher bethought himself and said: "I am the collector of the customs at this port. Once the captain of an arriving ship declared to me: 'I have a secret treasure on my vessel; buy it from me for ten thousand gold pieces, sight unseen.' I protested, but he was firm, saying: 'If you do not make the purchase, you will regret it.'

"I counted the money into his hand, and he delivered to me two hundred Jewish prisoners, men and women. I welcomed them, clothed them, gave them shelter, and later presented them with dowries for marriage among themselves, since they were all youths. The most beautiful girl I gave to my own son, and invited them to the wedding feast. Everyone rejoiced, except one young man who could not restrain his tears. On being questioned, he said to me: 'Your son's bride was my betrothed before we were made captives.' I offered him a fortune as a compensation for surrendering her, but he answered: 'She is dearer to me than all the gold of the world.' Thereupon I commanded my son to divorce her, and delivered her in marriage to the youth, together with the money wherewith I had sought to test him."

Rabbi Simeon, on hearing this tale, exclaimed: "I thank the Lord for deeming me worthy to be your neighbor in Paradise."

*Intr. to Tanhuma, Buber, 135.*

Antoninus, the Emperor, once asked Rabbi Judah, the Patriarch: "Will I have a share in the World-to-Come?"

Rabbi Judah replied: "Yes."

"But is it not written," the heathen demanded, " 'And there shall not be any remaining in the house of Esau?' "

"Yes," came the quick reply of Rabbi Judah, "but that applies only to those who commit Esau's acts of violence!"

*Abodah Zarah, 10b.*

This world is only the vestibule to another; you must prepare yourself in the vestibule so that you may enter the banquet hall.

*Abot, 4, 21.*

In Paradise there are seven sections for the various types of pious souls, and a separate division of seven sections for the souls of pious women.

*Hagigah, 12b.*

In Paradise there will be reserved for the righteous a sumptuous banquet, at which the huge leviathan, the mythical fish, will be the principal dish.

*Baba Batra, 74b-75a.*

Rabbi Johanan claimed that a partition of only a handbreadth, the width of four inches, separates Hell and Heaven.

*Kohelet Rabbah, 7.*

Rabbi Simeon ben Lakish said: "In the future that is to be, there will be no Gehenna. But God will take the sun out of its orbit, and in its heat the righteous will be healed and the wicked consumed."

*Nedarim, 8b.*

The Rabbis ask the question: "Whence came this darkness? From where did such a thick darkness emanate?"

Rabbi Judah said: "The darkness came from above."

Rabbi Nehemiah said: "The darkness came from below. Gehenna opened its jaws and let loose part of its own thick darkness."

*Shemot Rabbah, 14.*

The wise ones find rest neither in this world nor in the World-to-Come, but "they shall ascend from strength to strength until they appear before God in Zion." (Psalm 84:8)

*Berakot, 64a.*

Rabbi Simeon ben Eleazar said that in this world the wicked are not punished until the righteous are rewarded,[1] for in the next world "his breath goeth forth, he returneth to his dust!"[2] (Psalm 146:4)

*Abot de-R. Nathan, 32.*

[1] The Flood had to be delayed until Noah was able to save himself.
[2] And is not dependent on others, so there is no need for delaying punishment.

Rabbi Jacob said: "Better is one day of repentance and good deeds in this world than all the life of the World-to-Come!"

*Abot 4, 22.*

Rabbi Johanan said: "All our Prophets foretell only what will happen in the days of the Messiah, in the ideal future state here on earth; but as for the world beyond the grave, no eye hath seen, and no ear hath heard, but God alone knows what He hath prepared for those who wait for Him!"

*Berakot, 34b.*

## 5. THE AGED

### Sayings

The aged man walks as if he seems to seek that which he has not lost.

*Shabbat, 152.*

Even the chirping of a bird awakens the aged.

*Shabbat, 152.*

To the aged man a small mound is comparable to a tall mountain.

*Shabbat, 152.*

Old men sometimes dye their hair, but its roots remain white.

*Nazir, 39.*

An old man in a house is a burden, but an old woman is a treasure.

*Arakin, 19.*

People are accustomed to say: when we were young, we were considered adults in wisdom; now that we are old, we are considered as youths.

*Baba Kamma, 92.*

The unlearned lose the power of clear thinking as they grow old, but scholars gain in it as their years advance.

*Kinnim, end.*

How welcome is old age! The aged are beloved by God.

*Shemot Rabbah, 5, 12.*

## 6. HONORING THE AGED

### The Broken Tablets

Rabbi Joshua ben Levi said: "Honor and respect the aged and saintly scholar, whose physical powers are broken, equally with the young and vigorous one; for the broken Tablets of Stone no less than the whole ones, had a place in the Ark of the Covenant."

*Berakot, 8b.*

### The Hoary Head

"Thou shalt rise up before the hoary head." (Lev. 19:32)

Issi ben Judah said: "Any hoary head is meant, even that of the unlearned or of the non-Jew."

Rabbi Johanan would rise before an aged Gentile, and say: "How many events has he experienced!"

Abbaye would give his hand to an aged man to make it easier for him to walk.

Rabba would send his servant to aid the aged, and so, too, did his Master, Rab Nahman bar Jacob. Rab Nahman would say: "It would be improper for me to neglect my duties and trouble myself with the men of age, for without the Torah, how many Nahmans would there be in the city?"

Rabbi Mana would rise up before an ignorant old man, and would say: "If the man had not performed some worthy deeds, he would not have been rewarded with long life."

Rabbi Hanina would compel people to rise up before him by shouting: "Will ye abrogate a commandment of the Torah by your indolence?"

*Kiddushin, 33; Y. Bikkurim, 3.*

### Two Opinions

Should the aged man or sage endeavor to avoid walking past people and thus compel them to rise up in tribute? There are two opinions.

Rabbi Simeon ben Eleazar held that they should avoid, if possible, placing the multitude at the inconvenience of standing up. To this end the verse says: "Thou, old man and hoary head, shalt fear thy God, and not cause trouble to the many."

Rabbi Abba, the Kohen, bar Papa, said: "When I would see a crowd of people I would make my way by another passage, in order not to inconvenience them. When I mentioned this to Rabbi Jose ben Zabida, he said: 'Thou shouldst pass them by and permit them to see thee and rise up before thee, thus bringing them into the fear of Heaven, as it is said: "Thou shalt rise up . . . and thou shalt fear thy God."'" (Lev. 19:32)

*Kiddushin, 33; Tanhuma, Kedoshim.*

### The Diligent and the Lazy

Emperor Hadrian, on his way to war, rode past a garden where he observed a very old man planting a fig tree. He halted his horse and asked: "Why in your old age do you labor so zealously? Do you expect to eat the fruit of the tree you are planting?"

The old man replied: "If it be the will of God, I shall eat of it; if not, my sons will enjoy it."

Three years later the Emperor passed the garden again. The same old man approached Hadrian with a basket of figs, and, handing it to him, said: "My Master, be good enough to receive this gift. I am the man to whom you spoke three years ago."

The Emperor was touched, and commanded that the basket be filled with gold pieces and given to the diligent old man.

The wife of his neighbor chanced to be in the graybeard's home when he returned with the gold. She heard his story and immediately commanded her husband to take to the Emperor a large basket filled with varied fruits.

"He loves the fruit of this region," she said, "and he may, as a reward, fill your basket with gold pieces."

The husband followed his wife's commands, and, bringing the fruit to the Emperor, said: "Sire, I have heard that you are fond of fruit, and I have brought these for your enjoyment."

On hearing the whole story, the Emperor became incensed at the man's impudence, and gave orders to his soldiery to throw the fruit at his face. Bruised and half-blinded, the schemer returned to his home.

"How did you fare?" asked his wife greedily.

"I fared excellently," replied her husband. "Had I taken etrogim (citrons), I would have died from their blows."

*Wayyikra Rabbah, 25.*


## 7. THE PREMATURELY AGED

Three men become aged before their time: he who lives on an upper floor; he who endeavors to raise poultry for a livelihood; and he who gives orders but is not obeyed.

*Otzar Midrashim, p. 166.*

Four things cause a man to age prematurely: a fright, anger, children, and an evil-natured wife.

*Tanhuma, Hayye Sarah.*

## 8. ANGELS

The names of the months and the names of the angels were brought from Babylon.

*Y. Rosh ha-Shanah, 1, 2.*

In Arabot, the highest heaven, are found: righteousness and judgment, the treasury of life and peace and blessing, the souls of the righteous dead, the souls and spirits that are yet to be created, the dew with which God will revive the dead, the Ophanim and Seraphim, the holy beasts and the ministering angels.

*Hagigah, 12b.*

## 9. ANGER

### SAYINGS

Most angry people in the end allow themselves to be pacified.

*Ekah Rabbah, 1, 23.*

All men of anger are fools.

*Kohelet Rabbah, 12, 14.*

All men of anger are men of pride.

*Kohelet Rabbah, 12, 14.*

The angry man's speech is like the water which overflows from a boiling kettle.

*Kohelet Rabbah, 7, 9.*

Grow not angry, and ye shall not sin; grow not drunk, and ye shall not offend.

*Berakot, 29.*

He who grows angry gives no consideration even to the Shekinah. He forgets his learning and increases folly.

*Nedarim, 22.*

How shall a man know whom to bring near, or whom to keep far from himself? When a man becomes angry, his true character is made manifest.

*Zohar, ii, 182b.*

If a man in his anger breaks something, the broken object represents a sacrifice on the altar of the Satan.

*Zohar, ii, 163b.*

He whose face is inflamed with anger shows that the Sitra Ahara burns within him.[1]

*Zohar, iv, 179a.*

[1] Sitra Ahara: the spirit of evil, or the opposite of the Holy Spirit.

Rabbi Simeon ben Levi said: "A sage who indulges in anger loses his knowledge."

*Pesahim, 66.*

Rabbi Simeon ben Eleazar said: "He who rends his garments, breaks a vessel, or scatters his money in a moment of anger shall be regarded as if he worshipped idols."

*Shabbat, 105.*

The Rabbis have taught that there are three whose lives are not lives: the compassionate, the irritable, and the fastidious. Rab Joseph said: "All three are combined in my person."

*Pesahim, 113.*

## The Gentle Hillel

A man once laid a wager with a friend that he would place Hillel out of temper. If he succeeded he was to receive 400 zuzim, but if he failed he was to forfeit this sum. The Sabbath Eve was approaching, and Hillel was engaged in his ablutions, when a man, passing his door, shouted: "Where is Hillel?"

Wrapping his robe about him, Hillel sallied forth to inquire what the man wished.

"I wish to ask thee a question," was the reply.

"Ask, my son," said Hillel.

"I wish to know why the Babylonians have such round heads," said the man.

"A very important question, my man," said Hillel. "The reason is that their midwives were not clever."

Several times this procedure was repeated. "I have many more inquiries, but you will lose patience with me and become angry," said the questioner.

"Ask whatever you wish," replied Hillel.

The man, in vexation, said: "May there not be many like thee in Israel, O Chief Justice! Through thee I have lost 400 zuzim on a wager that I could harass thee out of temper."

"Be warned for the future," said Hillel. "Better it is that thou shouldst lost 400 zuzim and 400 more after them than have it said of Hillel that he lost his temper."

*Shabbat, 31a.*

## Never Get Angry on a Full Stomach

Elijah said to R. Nathan: "Eat to a third of your capacity, drink to a third, and leave the rest of the space in your stomach so that when you get angry you may not become distressed."

*Gittin, 70a.*

## 10. ANIMALS (BIRDS, INSECTS)

### PARABLES

When a fox has his hour of importance, bow to him. (If the unimportant man has authority, do not dispute it.)

*Megillah, 16.*

When one dog barks, he soon finds other dogs to bark with him.

*Shemot Rabbah, 31, 9.*

Better one bird that is tied than a hundred birds that are flying.

*Kohelet Rabbah, 4, 6.*

When the chicks of a hen are young, she gathers them to her; when they are grown, she drives them away (to shift for themselves).

*Wayyikra Rabbah, 25, 5.*

Why is the stork called Hasidah? Because she practices Hasidut (kindness) among her fellow birds.[1]

*Hullin, 63.*

[1] See *The Hasidic Anthology*, p. 130.

The fox cannot be caught if he has reached his hole.

*Ketubot, 71.*

People are accustomed to say: "When a dog is hungry, he will eat leftovers."

*Baba Kamma, 92.*

Spread out the snare for the wolf before he comes to the flock.

*Bemidbar Rabbah, 22, 5.*

Throw a bone to a dog and he will lick the dust on your feet.

*Zohar, iii, 63.*

If you do not teach the ox to plow in his youth, it will be difficult to teach him when he is grown.

*Midrash Mishle, 22.*

Even concerning snakes, scorpions, spiders and insects which seem to injure the world, it is written: "It is very good."

*Zohar, iii, 107.*

People say: "There are many old camels loaded with the hides of young camels."[1]

*Sanhedrin, 52.*

[1] The old sometimes outlive the young.

Why is the camel's tail short? Because he eats thorns.[2]

*Shabbat, 77.*

[2] This item shows the antiquity of the practice of giving reasons for the physical traits of species.

Lions are before thee, and thou inquirest of foxes! [3]

*Y. Shebiit, 9, 4.*

[3] Instead of asking great authorities, you inquire of minor ones.

A crow flew by! [4]

*Betzah, 21.*

[4] Very often quoted and meaning: Don't annoy me!

The ox fell; sharpen the knife. [5]

*Shabbat, 32.*

[5] Strike while the iron is hot.

When the ox falls, many are ready to slaughter him.

*Ekah Rabbah, 1, 34.*

Courageous is the lamb which grazes among seventy wolves. [6]

*Yalkut to Pentateuch, 923.*

[6] Israel among the nations.

People say if a male dog barks at thee, enter; if a female dog, depart.

*Erubin, 86.*

It is the way of a dog that if he is hit by a stone, he bites a fellow dog. [7]

*Zohar, i, 149.*

[7] The oppressed peasant smites the oppressed Jew.

The gait of the ass is according to the amount of barley he receives.

*Shabbat, 51.*

The donkey feels cold even in July.

*Shabbat, 53.*

It is unseemly for a lion to weep before a fox.

*Eliyahu Rabbah, 17.*

The peacock is born of a white drop, but its adornment is of many colors.

*Bereshit Rabbah, 7, 4.*

In this world he who is a dog can become a lion, and he who is a lion can become a dog.

*Ruth Rabbah, 3, 2.*

In the World-to-Come the wolf will spin silk, and the dog will open gates. [8]

*Kohelet Rabbah, 1.*

[8] Men of wickedness will engage in peaceful pursuits.

To a bee they say: "Neither thy honey nor thy sting."

*Midrash Tehillim, 1, 22.*

A calf may wish to suckle, but the cow wishes even more to give suck.[9]

*Pesahim, 112.*

[9] The teacher wishes to teach even more than the pupil wishes to learn.

Had the Torah not been given, man could have learned from the ant not to rob; from the dove not to commit adultery; from the cat to be modest; from the rooster to have good manners, etc.

*Erubin, 100.*

### STRENGTH IN UNION

Two dogs tending a flock were always quarreling. When the wolf attacked one, however, the other thought: "If I do not help my neighbor today, the wolf may attack me tomorrow."

Thereupon the two dogs settled their differences, and together they killed the wolf.

*Sanhedrin, 105a.*

### THE FOOD OF BIRDS

Rabbi Judah said: "There is one species of bird that must wait for its food until it succeeds in capturing a fish in the sea. Rabbi Johanan once saw this bird, and said: "Harsh is the decree of this creature's fate."

When he saw an ant, however, he said: "A single kernel of grain suffices for its meal and it is easily obtained. Great is the charity which God has displayed to this tiny insect."

*Hullin, 63.*

### THE ZARZIR AND THE CROW

In the days of Rabbi Hiyya Rabbah a new bird came to Palestine. By reason of the sound of its chirp it was called Zarzir. Rabbi Hiyya was asked if it was permitted to use this bird as food. He said: "Watch the sort of bird we know, with which it associates."

It was found that the Egyptian crow kept company with the Zarzir on the roofs of the town. Thereupon Rabbi Hiyya pronounced the Zarzir unclean. Then the saying was born: for good reason the crow went to the Zarzir: because they belonged to the same species.[10]

*Bereshit Rabbah, 65.*

[10] Birds of a feather flock together, or a thief seeks the company of thieves.

### THE LION AND THE STORK

In the days of Rabbi Joshua ben Hananiah the Emperor of Rome issued a decree that the Holy Temple be rebuilt. The Samaritans immediately came forward with the same arguments they had used in the days of Zerubabel. The Emperor's government then issued a decree that the plan must follow the Emperor's measurements, and that the Temple must be built on a new site. The Jews could not consent to the change, and were greatly incensed.

Rabbi Joshua called the people together, and said: "A lion while eating found that a bone had stuck in his throat. He roared out that whosoever would remove the bone would be rewarded. A stork thrust its long bill into the lion's throat and drew forth the bone. He then asked for the reward. 'Your reward,' said the lion, 'is that you will be able henceforth to boast that you are the only creature whose head was in the lion's mouth and came out alive.' So it is with us— it is enough that we have emerged without harm from a decree by the Emperor."

*Bereshit Rabbah, 64.*

### THE GAZELLE

Rabbi Levi in the name of Rabbi Simeon ben Lakish, said: "The gazelle is the animal best beloved of God. When she gives birth to a fawn, God sends an herb to heal her. When she is thirsty, she digs her horns into the ground and moans. God hears her plea and she senses out water in the deep pits. When she goes forth to drink, she is at first in terror of the other beasts, but God imbues her with courage. She stamps with her feet and uses her horns. The beasts then flee from her. Why does God love her? Because she harms and disturbs the peace of no one."

*Midrash Samuel, 9.*
*Midrash Tehillim, 42.*

### THE PHOENIX

There are two myths concerning the Phoenix in the literature of the Rabbis. According to the first myth, the Phoenix alone of all living creatures did not partake of the fruit of the Tree of Knowledge; therefore, he does not die. The second myth recounts the fact that when the Phoenix observed in the Ark that Noah was burdened day and night catering to the wants of the creatures, he alone went off by himself and remained unnoticed for the time being. When Noah finally discovered him half-starved, he appreciated his goodwill and blessed him with eternal life. The Phoenix grows for a thousand years, then passes through flame, and emerges new-born.

*Sanhedrin, 108 (see Job 29, 18).*

### THE SCIENCE OF THE SAGES

A philosopher sought to learn how long a snake requires to bear her offspring. He placed a male and female snake in a box and cared for them. After seven years a baby snake was born. Proud of his newly acquired knowledge, he accosted Rabbi Gamaliel and Rabbi Joshua. He placed the question before them, and Rabbi Joshua gave the correct answer. The philosopher knocked his head against the wall in chagrin, saying: "It cost me infinite pains for many years to discover what the Rabbis have told me offhand."

*Bereshit Rabbah, 20.*

### THE SHREWD DOG

Rabbi Tanhum bar Maryon said: "I observed in Rome some dogs with almost human sagacity. When one of them became hungry, he lay down on the ground before a baker's shop, and pretended to sleep. As soon as the baker began to slumber, the dog overturned the bread on the floor of the shop. Before the baker had time to pick it up, the dog had run away with a loaf. It is in these devious ways that the Satan labors to compel a man to sin."

*Bereshit Rabbah, 22.*

### LOYAL FRIENDS

"When a man's ways please the Lord,
He maketh even his enemies to be at peace."

Proverbs, 16:7.

Rabbi Halafta said: "The snake loves garlic in any form. Once a wandering snake crept into a house, attracted by the odor of garlic. The creature ate it and then spat venom into the plate. A pet snake, however, of the household, observing this, filled the plate with earth, and thereby saved the life of its master."

Rabbi Meir said: "Once some shepherds milked a cow and placed the crock on the ground. A snake drank from it and spat venom into the crock. The shepherd-dog observed this and barked furiously when his masters came to drink the milk. When they paid no attention, he leaped at them and overturned the crock. The venom affected the dog and he died. The shepherds in gratitude placed a monument at his grave telling of his loyalty and martyrdom."

*Y. Terumot, 8, 3.*

The phrase "Za'ar Ba'ale Hayyim" means pity towards a living creature. The Jew was commanded to feed his household animals before he sat down to his own meal.

*Berakot, 40a.*

### JUDGMENT BY THE ANTS

Rabbi Simeon ben Halafta read Proverbs 6:6: "Go to the ant, thou sluggard; consider her ways, and be wise; which having no chief, overseer or ruler, provideth her bread in the summer, and gathereth her food in the harvest."

By nature the Rabbi was fond of discovering things for himself. Knowing that ants dislike sun, he went out to a field and spread his mantle over an anthill. A single ant emerged, and the Rabbi quickly dashed some paint upon it in order to be able to identify it. The ant ran back and soon returned with a considerable company of ants who apparently expected to find shade. Before this, however, the Rabbi had removed his mantle. He saw the group of ants turn against the leader who had lured them out by his promise of shade, and they killed him.

"Had these ants a ruler," thought the Rabbi, "he would have instituted judgment and designated an appropriate form of punishment."

*Hullin, 57.*

The similes of the old Rabbis are, like those of the Bible, drawn from the characteristic habits of animals, birds and fishes, such as the modesty, the gentleness, the chastity and the marital fidelity of the dove, the voracity of fishes, the cunning of the fox, the alertness of the stag, the pride of the lion, the paternal care of the eagle. They are taken from the nature of plants and flowers; they reflect the beauty of the rising dawn, the grandeur of the seas, the majesty of the volcanic eruption of the earth.

*Feldman, p. 16 (see Bibliography).*

## 11. ANIMALS—HOW TO TREAT THEM

### SAYINGS

No man may buy a beast, an animal or a bird until he has provided food for it.

*Y. Yebamot, 15, 3.*

People say: The burden must be according to the camel.

*Ketubot, 67.*

In the World-to-Come God will punish riders who wound their horses with spurs.

*Sefer Hasidim, par. 44, Post-Talmudic.*

### BEASTS BEFORE MEN

Rab Huna and Rab Hisda were seated together. Gneiba passed by, and the one Rabbi said to the other: "Let us rise before him because he is a sage."

The other answered: "Shall we rise up before a quarrelsome person, who torments Mar Ukbah, the Chief Justice?"

Gneiba halted, however, and took his seat near them, and said: "Greetings to you, O Kings!"

The Rabbis asked: "Why do you greet us so?"

Gneiba replied: "Because we read in Proverbs 8:15: 'By me (learning or wisdom) kings reign.'"

They invited him into the house and set food before him. He said: "I have not yet fed my beast, and Rab Judah has said in the name of Rab that a man is forbidden to eat unless he has fed his beasts, as it is written (Deut. 11:15): 'I will give grass in thy fields for thy cattle, and thou shalt eat and be satisfied.'"

*Gittin, 62.*

### AFFLICTION AND CURE

"The Lord is good to all; and His tender mercies are over all His works." (Ps. 145:9)

The Patriarch, Rabbi Judah I, suffered from toothache for many years. Why was he thus punished? Because he once saw a bound calf being taken to the slaughter. The calf bleated and appealed for his aid, but the Rabbi said: "Go, since it is for this that thou hast been created."

And how was the Patriarch cured? He once saw a litter of mice being carried to the river to be drowned. He said: "Let them go free, for it is written that 'His mercies are over all His works.'"

*Y. Kilaim, chap. 9.*

## 12.  ANTONINUS CAESAR AND RABBI JUDAH I

### RABBI JUDAH'S COUNSEL

Antoninus, the Emperor, once said to Rabbi Judah I: "Two things I wish the Senate to do for me: to elect my son, Annias Verus Codemus, as my successor, and to make Tiberias a free city so that students of the Torah may be released from taxes. I know, however, that they will grant me only one of these two favors."

The Rabbi thereupon had one man climb on the other's shoulders, and the man above was handed a dove. He then said to his royal friend: "Command the man below to command the man above to release the dove."

Antoninus then understood the Rabbi's counsel. He was to ask the Senate to ratify the election of Codemus, and Codemus, when Emperor, would make Tiberias free.

The Emperor then said: "The patricians torment me. What shall I do?"

The Rabbi led him to a garden and pulled out a plant. The following day he pulled out another. Antoninus then understood. He should rid himself of his adversaries one by one, and not engage in quarrel with them all at one time.

Antoninus was accustomed also to send to the Rabbi golden coin in sacks of wheat, with some wheat at the top of each sack. Rabbi Judah informed him that he had no need for gold, but the Emperor said: "My successors will doubtless demand much gold from your successors. Hence, in time it will all be returned to its source."[1]

*Abodah Zarah, 10.*

[1] According to Rabbi Solomon Judah Rapoport, the Emperor is Marcus Aurelius (121-180), son-in-law of Antoninus Pius (81-161) and father of Codemus.

### Etiquette before Royalty

Rabbi Judah I asked Rabbi Offas to write a letter to the Emperor Antoninus.[1] Rabbi Offas wrote: "From me, Judah, the Prince, to our Lord, the King Antoninus."

The Rabbi tore up the letter and said: "Write instead, 'From me, thy servant Judah, to our Lord Antoninus."

Rabbi Offas then asked: "Why do you lower your dignity as the Patriarch?"

Rabbi Judah replied: "Did not Jacob send to Esau by messenger: 'Thus saith thy servant Jacob.' Am I better than he?"

*Bereshit Rabbah, 75.*

[1] Marcus Aurelius?

### Praying Every Hour

It is said that Antoninus once asked Rabbi Judah ha-Nasi: "What is your opinion with respect to prayer at every hour?"

"It is forbidden," was the reply, "lest a man become accustomed to calling upon the Almighty falsely."

Antoninus did not appreciate the force of the answer until the Rabbi presented himself once every hour, beginning in the early morning, and greeted him with nonchalant familiarity: "Good morning, O Emperor; your good health, O King!"

The Emperor indignantly exclaimed: "How dare you treat royalty with such disrespect?"

"If you, a mere mortal King, object to being saluted every hour, how much more the Sovereign King!"

*Tanhuma Buber, Miketz, 11.*

## 13. APPRECIATION OF FAVORS—GRATITUDE

### Sayings

Whosoever openeth his door to another and performeth a kind deed in his behalf shall receive honor from the beneficiary equal to the honor paid by the latter to his parents.

*Shemot Rabbah, 4, 2.*

People say: "Throw no stone into the well from which thou drinkest."

*Baba Kamma, 92.*

A man should remember the place from which he has derived a benefit.

*Bereshit Rabbah 79, 6.*

If thy neighbor invite thee to a dinner of lentils, reply with an invitation to a dinner of meat. Why? Because thy neighbor was the first to invite thee.

*Bereshit Rabbah, 38, 3.*

If thou hast harmed thy neighbor a little, let it be in thine eyes as if thou hadst harmed him much; if thou hast done much for thy neighbor, consider it as little; if thy neighbor has done for thee a little good, regard it as considerable.

*Abot de-R. Nathan, 41.*

If a Gentile blesses thee, respond "Amen." Whosoever blesseth thee, respond "Thou, also."

*Y. Berakot 8, end.*
*Megillah, 27.*

When thou comest to ask a favor, converse at first regarding other matters; be not abrupt with thy request.

*Zohar, i, 127b.*

## 14. APPROVAL AND DISAPPROVAL OF GOD AND MEN

### SAYINGS

Three men are beloved by God: he who does not become angry; he who does not become drunken; and he who does not stand upon his dignity.

*Pesahim, 113.*

As men are in duty bound to win the approval of God, so are they in duty bound to win the approval of their fellows.

*Shekalim, 3, 2, Mishnah.*

God loves the pure of heart.

*Bereshit Rabbah, 41, 11.*

What is the prime virtue? To be pure in the eyes of God and men.

*Shekalim, 3.*

He who justifies himself below is justified above.

*Taanit, 8.*

Just as an artisan is proud of work well-performed, so does God take pride in the man of worthy conduct.

*Midrash Tehillim, 119, 24.*

No one is more beloved of God than a messenger sent to perform a good deed who fulfils his errand at the risk of his life. And we know of no messengers who acted more in accordance with this than the two sent by Joshua to Jericho. No one is more disdained by God than the messenger sent to perform a good deed who accomplishes his errand faultily. And we know of no messengers who acted more in accordance with this than those sent by Moses. Joshua and Caleb, however, were worthy of praise.

*Bemidbar Rabbah, to Num. 13, 1.*

## 15. ARGUMENTATION, DEBATE, DISCUSSION

### SAYINGS

When a debater's point is not impressive, he brings forth many arguments.

*Y. Berakot, 2, 3.*

People say: "In a discussion one decisive point is worth many indecisive ones."

*Yoma, 85.*

"Perhaps thou art from Pumbedita, where they attempt to draw an elephant thru the eyes of a needle." (This criticism of casuistry in the academy recalls the well-known saying in the New Testament.)

*Baba Metzia, 38.*

### THE COACHMAN'S REPLY

Rabbi Jonathan was traveling towards Jerusalem. A Samaritan stopped him near Mount Gerizim and inquired: "Why do you go to Jerusalem for prayer? It were better to pray on this blessed mountain."

"Why is it blessed?" the Rabbi asked.

"Because it escaped the flood in Noah's time," was the answer.

The Rabbi was at a loss to reply, but his coachman asked permission to make a retort. He said: "If this be a high mountain, it is included in the Biblical statement that every high mountain was covered with water. If it is a small mountain, there was no necessity to call attention to it, for if high mountains were covered, how much the more the small ones."

Rabbi Jonathan was greatly pleased at his coachman's wit, and exchanged places with him for three miles.

*Bereshit Rabbah, 32.*

### ONE IN TEN

A Samaritan asked Rabbi Meir: "Why did your Patriarch, Jacob, who was an honorable man, consecrate to God's service only the tribe of Levi, when he had vowed to devote to God a tithe of everything?"

Rabbi Meir said: "You wish to know how he kept his vow by two tribes above ten. In reality, however, Jacob added Ephraim and Manasseh to the tribes, so that there were fourteen tribes, or sons."

"You added water; add flour," the Samaritan answered.

Rabbi Meir said: "There are four mothers of Jacob's sons. The law at that time was that the first-born son of a wife was of himself consecrated to God. This left only ten, and, in accordance with his vow, Jacob consecrated Levi to God's service."

*Bereshit Rabbah, 80.*

## 16. ASTROLOGY AND ASTRONOMY

How do we know that it is forbidden to consult astrologers? Because it is written: "Wholehearted shalt thou be with thy God." (Deut. 18:13)

*Pesahim, 113.*

### THE SMALL DONATION

Two Disciples of Rabbi Hanina, who, like their Master, disbelieved in the power of sorcerers, went into the forest to chop some firewood. They met an astrologer, who read their horoscope and predicted that they would not return alive. This, however, did not hinder them from going on their way. They met an old man who accosted them and asked for food. They had only a single loaf of bread, but they divided it with him. When they returned, people who had heard the astrologer's prediction asked him: "Is then the power of your astrology false?"

He invited them to unwrap the bundles of wood which the two Disciples carried. In each of them half a snake was found.

"What did you do," asked the astrologer, "to merit escape from sure death?"

"We know of nothing," they answered, "except that we gave half a loaf of bread to an old man."

"What can I do," the astrologer remarked, "if the God of the Jews is placated with half a loaf of bread?"

*Sanhedrin, 39.*

The man who might study astronomy and will not, sinfully shuts his eyes to the signs of God's working in the universe.

*Shabbat, 75a.*

### THE SIEVE

The Emperor said to Rabbi Gamaliel: "Your Psalmist praises God for knowing the number of the stars. Is this then so great a feat? Cannot a human being count them?"

Rabbi Gamaliel said: "Here is a sieve containing nuts. Can you count them while I make the sieve revolve?"

"Let the sieve rest and I can count them," replied the Emperor.

"Ah, but the stars revolve without rest," was the Rabbi's reply.

*Debarim Rabbah, 8.*

## 17. ATONEMENT—EXPIATION

### OFFERINGS

The rich man, who is usually afflicted with pride, was compelled by the Law to offer as atonement for his sins an ox; the man of moderate means, a sheep or goat; a poor man, who is usually the humblest, a dove.

*Zohar, iii, 8b.*

### THE TROUBLING CONSCIENCE

When can penitence atone for a man's sin? If his conscience still troubles him regarding it. If a man's conscience ceases to trouble him, penitence will not avail.

*Zohar, i, 57a.*

### A MAN'S TABLE

In the days of the Temple the altar atoned for a man; in our day his table atones (if he invites a poor man to share his meal with him).

*Hagigah, 127.*

### THE TORAH AS ATONEMENT

When Moses received the Law regarding sacrifices, he asked: "Lord of the Universe, what shall the people of Israel do when they are in exile?"

God replied: "Let them study the Torah, and it will serve them as atonement more effective than all their sacrifices."

*Midrash ha-Neelam, i, 100a.*

### INADVERTENT SINS

Rabbi Johanan ben Zakkai said: "Happy is the generation whose leader brings an atonement for their inadvertent sins. If the leader does so, surely the commoner will do likewise. If for inadvertent sins they make atonement, how much the more readily will they be penitent for presumptuous sins."

*Horaiyot, 6.*

### EXPIATION AND ATONEMENT

Rabbi Ishmael said: "If a man has transgressed and has failed to perform a positive precept, and then repents of his negligence, he is forgiven immediately.

"If a man has transgressed and has done what he should not have done, and then has repented of his sin, his repentance shields him from punishment, and Yom Kippur atones.

"If a man has transgressed and has done forbidden things, the penalty for which is that he be cut off from his people or executed, and he repents thereof, penitence and Yom Kippur shield him from the penalty and chastisements clear his record.

"But if he has caused the name of God to be profaned and repents thereof, penitence, Yom Kippur and chastisements shield him, and the day of his death makes his record clean."

*Yoma, 86.*

## DEEDS OF MERCY

It is narrated that Rabbi Johanan ben Zakkai was one day going out of Jerusalem, accompanied by his disciple, Rabbi Joshua. At the sight of the Temple in ruins, Joshua exclaimed: "Woe to us, for the place where the iniquities of Israel were atoned for is destroyed!"

Rabbi Johanan replied: "Do not grieve, my son, for we have an atonement which is equally good, namely, deeds of mercy, the charity that has a personal character, as the Scripture says: 'For I desire mercy and not sacrifice.'" (Hosea 6:6)

*Abot de-Rabbi Nathan, 4, 5.*

## THE DISCOMFORTS OF EZEKIEL

A sectary (Min) asked Rabbi Abbahu: "Is then your God one who makes sport of his servants? Why did He command Ezekiel to lie down first on his left side and then on his right?" (4:4)

A disciple entered and said: "Pray, explain, O Master, the reason for the 'Sabbath of solemn rest for the land.'" (Lev. 25:4)

Rabbi Abbahu replied: "I shall give you one answer that will suffice to the questions of both of you. God sayeth to Israel: 'Six years thou shalt sow and the seventh year thou shalt neither sow nor prune,[1] in order that thou shalt know the earth is Mine.' But Israel did not obey and was exiled. It is the way of the world that if a city rebels and the king hath a compassionate heart, he punishes only its foremost leaders. Likewise, God bade Ezekiel undergo discomfort so that the sins of Israel might be erased."

*Yoma, 21.*

[1] Lev. 25:4.

## 18. AUTHORITIES

In the generation of Rabban Gamaliel, do according to the opinions of Rabban Gamaliel; in the generation of Rabbi Jose, do according to the opinions of Rabbi Jose.

*Erubin, 41.*

## THE GREATER AND THE LESSER

Once Rabban Gamaliel and Rabbi Joshua disputed regarding the day on which Rosh ha-Shanah begins. Rabban Gamaliel sent word to his opponent: "Joshua, I, as the Patriarch, order thee to appear before me on the Atonement Day of your calendar with your money and your cane."

Rabbi Joshua went to consult Rabbi Dosa ben Harkinas. Rabbi Dosa said: "It is an accepted axiom that an individual must accept the authority of the majority High Court opinion. Since the majority is of Rabban Gamaliel's opinion, you must obey his order."

Rabbi Joshua came to Rabban Gamaliel as ordered. The latter exclaimed: "Come in peace, my teacher and my pupil. Happy is the generation in which the greater obey the lesser."

According to another version, Rabbi Joshua met Rabbi Akiba, and informed him of the command. Rabbi Akiba asked permission to address his teacher, and it was granted. Rabbi Akiba said: "Inasmuch as the Court of Rabban Gamaliel is recognized in Israel as the Court of the highest instance, it has the authority to proclaim any day it desires as Rosh ha-Shanah, and its proclamation sanctifies the day even if the Court acts wrongly, mistakenly, or is deceived by false witnesses." [1]

Rabbi Joshua replied: "Rabbi Akiba has brought me comfort."

*Rosh ha-Shanah, 24-5.*

[1] Lev. 23:4 says: "which Ye shall proclaim." Rabban Gamaliel also depended upon astronomical calculations; Rabbi Joshua, however, upon actual witnessing of the moon's appearance.

## THE COURT'S DECISION

An agent of Bar Ziza entrusted a pound of gold into the keeping of a trustworthy man. Both the agent and Bar Ziza died, and hence the man went to Rabbi Ishmael ben Jose for instruction. Rabbi Ishmael said: "No one knew that the agent possessed gold of his own; in all likelihood it belonged to his patron. Therefore, give the money to Bar Ziza's heirs."

"But some are minors," said the man.

Rabbi Ishmael replied: "Then give half the money to the adults, and keep half as trustee for the minors."

When the minors came of age, the man again visited the Court. The bench was now occupied by Rabbi Hiyya, who had succeeded the late Rabbi Ishmael. Rabbi Hiyya said: "It is often the practice of people to keep secret their possessions. Therefore, give the money to the agent's heirs."

The man replied: "But I have already given half to Bar Ziza's heirs."

Rabbi Hiyya said: "What you have given by order of the Court, you have given. Now give the balance of the money in accordance with the order of the Court which is sitting now. Since you have been following the direction of a Court of Law, you are not personally responsible."

*Y. Shebuot. 7.*

## A Question at Law

Rabba said to Rab Papa and Rab Huna bar Joshua: "If my written decision in a case at law is brought to you, and you are led to question an item of it, do not destroy the decision. Ask me the question and I shall either give you a better explanation or shall acknowledge my error. If my decision is brought to you after my death, even then do not destroy it. Look into it further and seek to discover my reasons. If you cannot understand the reasons for my decision, you may re-try the case, for then you must abide by your own opinion on the basis of the evidence submitted to you, and not depend upon me." [1]

*Baba Batra, 130.*

[1] This injunction is perhaps the basis of the accepted rule in Jewish law: "Before Abbaye and Rabba, the opinion of the Master outweighs the opinion of the Disciple. After their demise, proceed according to the opinion of the later Rabbi and accept the decision of the latest authority."

## From Zion, the Law

Rabbi Hananiah, the son of Rabbi Joshua's sister, emigrated to Babylonia. Believing himself to be the greatest sage in his generation, he usurped the prerogatives of the Palestinian sages and fixed the calendar for the year according to his own calculations. When this became known in Palestine, two sages were sent to him. When they arrived and declared themselves as disciples, he proclaimed them to be great men in Israel. Determined, however, to decrease his authority, the newcomers continually rendered opinions opposed to his. Rabbi Hananiah thereupon declared them to be men of no merit. They replied: "Thou hast built and canst not destroy; thou hast made fences and canst not now make a breach."

He inquired: "Why do you continually oppose me?"

They answered: "Because thou usurpest the privileges belonging to Palestine."

"But Rabbi Akiba also fixed a calendar outside of Palestine," said he.

They said: "But he left none like him in Palestine."

"Neither did I," rejoined Rabbi Hananiah.

The two sages replied: "The kids thou hast left behind have become goats with horns. They instructed us to tell thee: 'If Rabbi Hananiah gives ear, well and good; if not, we will excommunicate him.' Therefore are we to tell the people: 'If ye care naught for Zion, go ye up on the mountain. Your chief, Ahiah will erect an altar, Hananiah will play before it with a harp, and all will say: "We have no share in the God of Israel." ' "

The populace cried out: "Of surety we have a share in the God of Israel."

"Then follow the law that comes out of Zion, not the laws of each community."

Rabbi Hananiah went to Rabbi Judah ben Beteirah with a complaint. Rabbi Judah replied: "We must follow not thy decisions, but theirs."

He mounted a swift horse, and sought to undo the work of Rabbi Hananiah. Wherever he arrived in time, they celebrated the festivals according to the calendar of Palestine.[1] Where he failed to arrive in time, they observed their holidays that year a month later.

*Berakot, 63.*

[1] Were it not for this protest, the Jews might still have different calendars in different localities.

## 19. AUTHORS, TRANSLATORS, COPYISTS

### Sayings

How many pens are broken, how many ink bottles are consumed, to write about things that have never occurred?

*Tanhuma Shofetim, 18.*

"Wealth and riches are in his house, and his benevolence standeth forever." This describes the man who writes excellent books and makes them easily available to others.

*Ketubot, 50.*

Four payments of money have no blessing within them: the payment made to writers; the payment made to translators; money derived from orphans, and money earned across the sea.

*Pesahim, 50.*

Rabbi Judah ben Ilai said: "He who translates a verse with strict literalness is a falsifier, and he who makes additions to it is a blasphemer."

*Kiddushin, 49a.*

The day on which the Torah was translated into Greek was a mournful day unto Israel. It was like unto the day when the Golden Calf was made. Why? Because the Torah cannot be translated exactly as it ought to be.

*Soferim, chap. 1.*

The Men of the Great Synagogue observed many fasts in order that the writers of the Scrolls of the Torah, of the Tefillin, and of the Mezuzot might not grow rich, lest, in becoming rich, they might be tempted to write no longer.

*Pesahim, 50b.*

## 20. BAN—EXCOMMUNICATION (FOR CONTEMPT OF AUTHORITY)

### DESERVING EXCOMMUNICATION

A person who whispers evil behind the bier of a Disciple of the Wise as well as a person who behaves haughtily towards the Most High truly merit a form of excommunication.

*Berakot, 19a.*

### NO INDISCRIMINATE EXCOMMUNICATION

Rabbi Simeon ben Lakish was a watchman in a fruit-garden. A man approached and stole some fruit, despite the watchman's shout of protest. The Rabbi then pronounced the ban against him. The man retorted: "I am in debt to you for some money, but I am not guilty of contempt of the Court of Law. Thou, however, shouldst rather come under the ban for thou hast pronounced it without authority."

When the Rabbi came to the Court for the confirmation of his edict, he was unpleasantly surprised to learn that his ban was without authority, and that he himself was excommunicated. He was advised to bring the man before the Court and persuade him to give him a release. The Rabbi replied: "But I do not know where to find him."

"Then," said the members of the Court, "go to the Patriarch and he will give thee release."

*Moed Katan, 17.*

### THE LEGEND OF RABBI ELIEZER'S BAN

Rabbi Eliezer once engaged in a heated argument with other sages. Despite the opposition of the majority led by Rabbi Joshua, Rabbi Eliezer clung to his opinion.

Rabbi Eliezer said: "If mine is the correct ruling, let the carob tree near the Academy render the decision."

A miracle occurred, and the tree was uprooted.

Rabbi Joshua said: "The carob tree cannot decide."

Rabbi Eliezer thereupon said: "Let the rivulet decide."

The rivulet thereupon changed its course, but this occurrence was not accepted as decisive.

Rabbi Eliezer then said: "If I am right, let the walls of this Academy decide."

The walls began to recede.

Rabbi Joshua exclaimed: "If the sages have a controversy in law, why do you walls seek to fall?"

They neither fell nor resumed their former position.

Rabbi Eliezer thereupon said: "Let Heaven decide."

A voice came down from Heaven: "Why contradict my son Eliezer, who is always right in his decisions?"

Rabbi Joshua said: "It is written: 'It is not in Heaven.' "

A vote was taken, and it was decided to pronounce the ban against Rabbi Eliezer. Rabbi Akiba attired himself in black garments with a black Tallit and approached.

"Why art thou dressed in black?" asked Rabbi Eliezer.

Rabbi Akiba replied: "Thy comrades are separated from thee."

Rabbi Eliezer removed his shoes, rent his garments, and sat down on the ground. Wherever he looked grievous damage was done. Rabban Gamaliel was travelling by ship on that day, and a wave was about to swallow it up. He cried out: "Thou knowest, O Lord, that our actions were guided only for Thy honor, that Thy Law may be spared many contradictory interpretations." The sea thereupon became calm.

Rabban Gamaliel's sister was the wife of Rabbi Eliezer. She prevented her husband from falling on his face so that he might not pray for the punishment of her brother. Once a poor man asked for a donation. When she returned to her husband's presence she found him praying with his face downward. She said: "Thou hast slain my brother."

Her husband said: "I have not done this at all."

She replied: "I was taught in my father's house that even the thoughts of a man in prayer have effect when he has been abused."

Rabbi Eliezer went on the street and a woman who was weeping threw dust into his face by accident. He commented: "He raiseth the poor out of the dust. I should be forgiven by this time." (Ps. 113:7)

*Baba Metzia, 59.*

## 21. BEADLE

Five things characterize the Beadle: he is usually a tall man, impudent, strong of arm, abundant of strength and lacking manners.

*Otzar Midrashim, p. 147.*

## 22. BEAUTY

### SAYINGS

I am the vessel, Thou art the Master; fashion me in beauty so that Thou mayest receive praise for Thy workmanship.

*Midrash Tehillim, 119.*

Why was Hadassah called Esther? Because the nations declared her to be as beautiful as a star.

*Megillah, 13.*

Solomon was the appropriate person to say: "He hath made everything beautiful in its time." Had another person said this, people would have laughed at him and remarked: "This man knows the world very little and has enjoyed nothing of it, yet he says everything has been made beautiful. But Solomon, who has enjoyed the world and everything in it, may fittingly pronounce it beautiful."

*Kohelet Rabbah, 3.*

## THE POWER OF BEAUTY

Rabbi Johanan ben Nappaha was once swimming in the Jordan. He beheld a powerfully built man come towards him. He said: "How much Torah couldst thou learn with such a splendid physique?"

The other, who was Simeon ben Lakish, looked at his counsellor, and said: "Thy beauty is fit for a woman."

Rabbi Johanan replied: "Come and study as my Disciple, and I shall ask my sister, who is more beautiful than I am, to marry thee."

Thus did beauty attract the brilliant Rabbi Simeon to become a famous scholar.

*Baba Metzia, 84.*

## ADORATION OF IDOLS

Rabbi Simeon ben Yohai and his Disciples entered a town. Some beautiful women passed them. Rabbi Simeon lowered his eyes and said to his Disciples: "Turn ye not unto the idols." (Lev. 19:4)

*Zohar, iii, 80.*

When Rabbi Zeira was ordained Rabbi, he was acclaimed by his colleagues in the words: "Neither powder nor paint nor ornament, but yet how beautiful!" [1]

*Ketubot, 17a.*

[1] They referred, of course, to the fact that the new Rabbi lacked eloquence and oratory, and was even physically deformed, but was nevertheless beautiful because of the saintliness of his character and the greatness of his mind.

The Sages said: "Let the beauty of Japheth abide in the tents of Shem." [1]

*Megillah, 9b.*

R. Zeira said: "The beauty with which a Mitzwah is adorned, is worth a third of the Mitzwah itself!"

*Baba Kamma, 9b.*

"Adorn thyself, make thyself beautiful, before Him when doing Mitzwot."

*Shabbat, 133b.*

[1] As long as you retain the essential elements of your faith you may adapt to your needs the new conceptions of beauty and art, of adornment and attractiveness.

## 23. BEGINNING AND END

All beginnings are difficult.

*Mekilta to Jethro, 19, 5.*

People say: "All is well that ends well."

*Pesikta Zutarta, Bereshit, 47, 28.*

If you have commenced a Mitzwah, continue until you finish it.

*Tanhuma Ekeb, 6.*

## 24. BET HA–MIKDASH (HOLY TEMPLE)

### SAYINGS

The Western Wall shall never be in ruins.

*Bemidbar Rabbah, 11, 2.*

The Shekinah does not depart from the Western Wall.

*Midrash Tehillim, 11, 3.*

Why is the Holy Temple called a forest? Because like the forest, it enchants.

*Yoma, 39.*

Iron is used to shorten life; the altar lengthens life. Therefore iron could not be used to make an altar.

*Middot, 3, 4, Mishnah.*

Why is the Holy Temple called Lebanon (the white)? Because it whitens the sins of Israel.

*Yoma, 39.*

The Temple will be built before the Kingdom of the House of David is restored.

*Y. Maaser Sheni, 5, 2.*

The rebuilding of the Holy Temple will precede the ingathering of the exiled in the Land of Israel.

*Zohar, i, 139a.*

### THE THIRD TEMPLE

Rabbi Simeon ben Yohai was asked by an aged non-Jew: "Why do you Jews await the building of the Third Temple when the Prophet Haggai calls the Second Temple the last Temple?" (2, 9)

The Rabbi replied: "It is the last to have been built by the hands of man, but it is to be followed by a Temple to be built by God Himself, as it is written: 'The Lord doth build up Jerusalem; He gathereth together the dispersed of Israel.'" (Psalm 147:2)

*Zohar, iii, 220.*

From the day on which the Temple was destroyed, God knows not laughter.

*Abodah Zarah, 3b.*

### THE STUDENT IN LOVE

A son of Rabbi was betrothed to a daughter of Rabbi Jose ben Zimra. It was understood that the lad would remain at school twelve years before marrying his bride. When he beheld his betrothed, he said: "I shall return in six years and marry her."

When he beheld her a second time, he said, shamefacedly: "I should like to marry her before I go to school."

His father said: "Thou art of one mind with thy Creator. At first He said that Israel should be brought to his land and implanted therein, and erect a firm house for His dwelling.[1] Afterwards He said: 'Make unto Me a holy place and I shall dwell within ye,'[2] without waiting for the establishment of a dwelling-place."

*Ketubot, 65.*

[1] See Exodus 15:17.
[2] See Exodus 25:8.

### THE ORDER OF SERVICE

We learn: The chief officer of the Temple would say: "Recite a benediction." Those present would recite the benediction and then read the Decalogue, the Sh'ma, and finish with three benedictions: "True and firm . . ." "Accept, O Lord, our service . . ." and the three-fold Blessing of the Priests.

On the Sabbath the officiating Priests of the outgoing watch would say before departing, to the incoming watch: "He who caused His Name to dwell in this house shall cause to dwell among ye love, brotherly feeling, peace and friendship."

Rab Judah, in the name of Samuel, said: "The sages wished at first to institute in the synagogues the reading of the Decalogue, but they decided against it lest the Sectarians say that the Decalogue alone should be observed."

*Berakot, 11.*

### THE TEMPLE'S BEAUTY

He who hath not seen the Temple before its destruction hath never beheld a truly beautiful edifice. How did Herod build it? With blue and creamy-white slabs of marble. Herod wished to add gold between the seams, but the Sages declared: "This is unnecessary since the pattern of the marble suggests the waves of the sea."

*Sukkah, 48.*

## 25. BIBLICAL CRITICISM

### SAYINGS

Ezra, the Scribe, said: "If Elijah, the Prophet, should appear and ask me: 'Why have you written thus in the Torah?' I would reply to him: 'I have indicated by periods (or dots) that I am uncertain as to the exact reading.'"

*Abot de-R. Nathan, 34, 4.*

Rabbi Johanan ben Nappaha said: "In the days of the Messiah the books of the Prophets and the Hagiographa are destined to be abrogated." [1]

*Y. Megillah, 70d.*

[1] Moore, i, 245.

Bar Kappara said: "The seven pillars with which Wisdom built her house (Prov. 9:1) are the seven Books of Moses. The paragraph numbers 10:35–36 constitutes a separate book."

*Wayyikra Rabbah, 11, 3.*

Rabbi Aha bar Hanina said: "If Israel had not sinned, only the Pentateuch and Joshua would have been given."

*Nedarim, 22b.*

The Song of Songs is Wisdom; the Book of Ecclesiastes is Understanding, and the Book of Proverbs is Knowledge.

*Zohar, iii, 64b.*

Rabbi Akiba said: "The whole age altogether is not worth as much as the day on which the Song of Songs was given to Israel. All the Scriptures are holy, but the Song of Songs is the holiest of all."

*Mishnah Yadaim, 3, 5.*

Job was not a real person and was not born, but the Book in his name is only a parable. Rabbi Hai Gaon's version is: "Job served only as a parable;" that is to say, Job did not live and did not come to be born except for the purpose of being a parable.

*Baba Batra, 15.*
*Pahad Isaac on Job.*

Rab Yehuda ben Rab Samuel bar Shilat said in the name of Rab: "The Sages considered putting away the Book of Proverbs because it contradicts itself. Proverbs 26:4 bids: 'Answer not a fool according to his folly;' Verse 5, 'Answer a fool according to his folly.' It was replied: 'There is no difficulty; the former verse refers to discussions of words of the Torah, the latter to secular matters.'"

*Shabbat, 30b.*

The Psalms were composed by David and by ten elders. The last of these was Ezra, the Scribe.

*Kohelet Rabbah, 7, 19.*
*Shir ha-Shirim Rabbah, 5.*

## 26. BIBLICAL EXPOSITION

### SAYINGS

What is the most important verse in the Bible? "In all thy ways know Him." (Prov. 3:6)

*Berakot, 63.*

The words "Living-Waters" are written forty-eight times in the Pentateuch, the same number as are the ways wherewith Torah can be acquired.

*Yalkut to Shir ha-Shirim Rabbah, 988.*

The upper waters are the Torah of the Scripture; the lower waters are the Torah of Tradition.[1]

*Tikkune Zohar, 60b.*

[1] The upper waters are in the rarefied atmosphere which needs to be filled with evaporation from below in order to give forth rain, namely, rules of regulated conduct.

"Is not My word like as fire? said the Lord; and like a hammer that breaketh the rock in pieces?" (Jer. 23:29). As a hammer divideth fire into many sparks, so one verse of Scripture has many meanings and many explanations.

*Sanhedrin, 34a.*

An Emperor asked a Rabbi: "Why is God's Name mentioned in the first Five Commandments and not in the last Five?"

The Rabbi answered: "Your statue is placed in clean places, but not in unclean. By the same token, God did not care to place His Name in the Commandments dealing with thieves, adulterers, murderers, false witnesses and those who covet their neighbors' goods."

*Pesikta Rabbati, Piska, 21. Vide, Hezkuni to Jethro.*

### MERELY FOR EXPOUNDING

R. Simeon said: "And because this lad ate a pound of meat and drank a jug of wine from Italy, his parents shall lead him forth to be stoned?" But this never happened and it will never happen. Why, then, is it written? Expound and receive reward.

Likewise it is taught: "The utter destruction of the misled city (Deut. 13:16 and 17) never happened and never will happen. R. Eliezer gives a reason for this statement, declaring: If there were a single Mezuzah in the entire city it could not be burned, for it is ordained that every whit be placed in fire; a Mezuzah, however, may not be burned, as it is written: 'Ye shall not do the like to the Lord your God.' Therefore the whole chapter is not to be accepted for action, but merely for the purpose of expounding and receiving reward."

*Sanhedrin, 71.*

### THE ARGUMENTS OF KORAH

Korah said to Moses: "Thou declarest in the Name of God that a garment with four corners must have Tzitzit of one thread, sky-blue in color, on each corner. Suppose I have a garment made entirely of sky-blue threads, does it require single threads to hang down from the four corners?"

"Yes," answered Moses.

"Thou sayest that the doorpost of a house must have a Mezuzah with two paragraphs of the Torah inscribed upon it. Suppose I have a house filled with Scrolls of the Law, do I still need a Mezuzah?"

"Yes," answered Moses again.

"Then," continued Korah, "thou art a falsifier and God has told thee nothing."

*Bemidbar Rabbah, 18.*

The historical accounts in the Bible are given to us only because of their interpretative value.

*Wayyikra Rabbah, 1.*

### THE TYRANNY OF MOSES

Korah told his confederates this story as an example of the tyranny of Moses:

A widow lived near by, with two orphaned daughters. She wished to till her field. Moses commanded her: Plow not with an ox and an ass yoked together. She wished to sow, but Moses forbade her to sow two sorts together. She wished to reap, but Moses told her: Reap not the left-overs, the forgotten ones, and the stalks growing near the end. She wished to pile the grain in a storehouse; Moses claimed Terumah and tithe. She sold her field and bought two lambs; when they had their young, Aaron claimed the first-born. She sheared them, and Aaron claimed the first shearing. She said: I cannot abide this man, and she slaughtered the lambs. Aaron came again and required from her the arm, the cheeks and the stomach. She said: I give all the flesh to God. Aaron said: Then I shall take it all, and he left her weeping. Is it right, asked Korah, to do all this to a poor defenseless widow? Yet Moses and Aaron are guilty of all these things and profess that God has enjoined them to do so.[1]

*Shoher Tob, 1.*

[1] The true picture, however, is very different from Korah's description. The property owner was required by Jewish law to give less than 20% to 25% of his income to pay the taxes for charity, religious tuition, and other obligations.

### STEADY PAYMENT

Rabbi Abbahu praised Rabbi Saphra to the Sadduceans in Caesarea as a great scholar. One day they wished to know the meaning of the verse: "You only have I known of all the families of the earth; therefore I will visit upon you all your iniquities" (Amos 3:2).

They visited Rabbi Saphra and asked: "How is this verse to be explained? Would a man vent his anger upon one whom he loveth most?" The Rabbi's explanation failed to satisfy the Sadduceans and they taunted him. Rabbi Abbahu chanced to enter, and said: "I consider Rabbi Saphra a great authority, not in exegetical, but in legal matters." When the questioners pressed him for an explanation, Rabbi Abbahu said: "It is like a man to whom two persons owe money. The one whom he likes, he permits to discharge his debt little by little in frequent payments. But the one whom he disdains he compels to discharge his obligation in one payment."

*Abodah Zarah, 4.*

## THE POWER OF THE MASHAL

The Rabbis said: Let not the Mashal (Parable) be lightly regarded, for by means of it a man can understand the words of Torah. It is like a king who has lost a pearl and finds it with the aid of a candle worth only a centime. Solomon clarified the Law by means of parables. R. Nahman, R. Jose, R. Shila and R. Hanina illustrated the idea thus: The wise king tied a rope at the entrance of a labyrinth-like palace, and was able to find his way out of it; he cut a path in a wild thicket of reeds; he fashioned a handle for a heavy case of fruit so that it could be lifted; he formed a handle for a cask of hot liquid so that it could be moved; he joined rope to rope, and was able to draw water from the deep well. Thus from word to word, from Mashal to Mashal, Solomon attained the uttermost secret of the Torah.

*Kohelet Rabbah on 2, 11, etc.*

## 27. BIBLICAL PERSONALITIES

Concerning three is it written that God found them: Abraham, David and Israel.

*Bereshit Rabbah, 29, 3.*

Ten are called in the Bible: Man of God, namely, Moses, Elkanah, Samuel, David, Shemaiah, Iddu, Elijah, Elisha, Micah and Amoz.

*Seder Olam Rabbah, 20.*

On Sabbath afternoon in the Services we recite three verses beginning with the word: Thy righteousness. These are in honor of three great men who died on Sabbath afternoon: Moses, Joseph and David.

*Zohar, i, 156a.*

Why are the intonations of the Books of Psalms, Proverbs and Job alike, though different from the intonations of the other books of Scripture? Because there is a common thread running through the

life of their authors: Job, David and Solomon. All three saw good
days and later evil days, and all three were restored to their former
prosperity.

*Mayan Ganim, Buber, 11.*

Why is Solomon called Kohelet? Because he spoke in Kahal
(Assembly).

*Kohelet Rabbah, 1, 2.*

Ezra deserved to have received the Torah at Sinai, had not Moses
preceded him.

*Sanhedrin, 21.*

God had the same reason for giving Palestine to Canaan before
it came into the rightful hands of Israel that He had for giving Bath-
sheba in marriage to Uriah, the Hittite, before she became the wife of
David, her rightful mate.

*Zohar, i, 73b*

Judah was selected by God as the Royal Tribe, because God's
Name is included in the name Judah.

*Sitre Torah, i, 89b.*

Four pious kings of Judah prayed unto God in the moment of
battle and each prayed differently. David said: Mayest Thou aid me
in pursuing my enemy and overtaking him. Asa said: I cannot pursue
my enemy as did my father David, and I therefore ask Thy aid in
enabling me to defend myself. Jehoshaphat said: I can neither pursue
the enemy like David, nor defend myself like my father, Asa; I shall
sing to Thee and Thou shalt smite them. Hezekiah said: I can
neither pursue, defend myself, nor sing to Thee; I shall lie in my bed,
and Thou shalt smite the adversary.

*Zohar, i, 198b.*

When David said: Am I not a Hasid? a little frog came to him,
and declared: I am an even greater Hasid, for I praise my Maker the
whole night long, but thou doest this only half the night.

*Zohar, iv, 222b.*

## 28. BIBLICAL PERSONALITIES—MOSES

Rabbi was preaching and the audience seemed to lose interest.
Suddenly he said: "A woman in Egypt gave birth to 600,000."
"Who was this?" they asked.
"Jochebed," he answered, "for she gave birth to Moses, the equal
of all Israel, as it is written: 'Then sang Moses and Israel.'"

*Shir ha-Shirim Rabbah, 1.*

The maxim of Moses was: Let justice pierce the mountain.
Aaron sought to make peace between men, and to recall them
from their evil ways by mildness and persuasion.

*Tosefta Sanhedrin, 1, 2.*

### The Infant Moses

When Moses was three years old, he was seated at the royal table on the lap of the Princess Batia. Suddenly he bent towards the King and, removing his crown, placed it on his own head.

The King wished to test the child's intelligence in order that he might know if the child meant serious mischief by this extraordinary act.

He ordered that a dish with a hot coal and another dish with a bright gem be brought before the child.

Moses was about to take the gem, but an Angel guided his hand into the dish with the hot coal. He seized the coal and placed it to his lips, thereby injuring them permanently. The King was satisfied, and did nothing further to punish the adopted child of his favorite daughter.

*Midrash Wayosa, etc. (see also Josephus: "Antiquities").*

### Moses Argues

Moses wished to know why he must die. God said: "Did not Adam die?"

"Adam brought death through the serpent," replied Moses, "And I brought life through the serpent."

"Did not Noah die?"

"Noah prayed not for his generation, and I prayed for mine."

"Did not Abraham die?"

"Abraham brought up the wicked Ishmael."

"Did not Isaac die?"

"Isaac reared Esau, Thine enemy."

"Did not Jacob die?"

"Jacob did not receive the Torah."

"Thou, O Moses, hast sinned before Me."

"But Thou, O Lord," protested Moses, "offerest forgiveness to others, yet to me Thou wishest to refuse it."

"Thou hast committed, not one, but six sins before Me."

"May I not at least see the Promised Land?" asked Moses.

This was granted unto him.

*Dibre ha-Yamin shel Moshe.*

### The Death of Moses

When Moses was told that his days had ended, he asked God why he must die. God replied: "Because I have assigned Joshua to lead Israel into Canaan." Moses replied: "Let him lead, and I shall be his servant." God gave his consent, but when he announced it to Joshua, the latter was displeased. Moses asked: "Do you not wish me to live?" Joshua then agreed to become the master of Moses. When, however, they were about to enter the Holy Tent, a cloud appeared.

Joshua was within it, but Moses was outside the sacred spot. Moses then said: "A hundred deaths are preferable to one pang of jealousy." And he asked to die.

*Dibre ha-Yamin shel Moshe.*

## 29. THE THREE PATRIARCHS

Our Father Abraham transformed his Evil Impulse into a good impulse.

*Y. Berakot, 9, 5.*

Abraham married three wives: Sarah, a Semite; Hagar, a Hamite, and Keturah, a Japhetite.

*Yalkut to Job, 904.*

Abraham brought blessing to the world, Isaac justice, and Jacob mercy, thereby completing all the Lord wished the world to possess.

*Zohar, i, 87b.*

Upon three things the world rests: on Torah, on sacrifice and on benevolence. Jacob stands for Torah, Isaac for sacrifice, and Abraham for benevolence.

*Zohar, i, 146b.*

"Thine, O Lord, is the greatness, and the power, and the glory, and the victory and the majesty" (I Chronicles 29:11). Abraham stands for greatness; Isaac for power; Jacob for glory; Moses for victory, and Aaron for majesty.

*Zohar Hadash, ii, 44b.*

Abraham established the precedent of prayer in the morning; Isaac, of prayer in the afternoon, and Jacob of prayer in the evening.

*Bemidbar Rabbah, 2, 1.*

When God commanded Abraham to depart for a destination to be later revealed to him, he entered Syria and saw people idling and drinking there. Abraham said: "May my residence not be here." When he came to Palestine and beheld the populace busily at work in the fields, he exclaimed: "May I reside here!"

*Bereshit Rabbah, 39, 10.*

A king planned to erect a palace. He dug in several places seeking firm ground for a foundation. At last he struck rock beneath the surface and said: Here will I build. In the same fashion when God sought to create the world, he examined the generation of Enosh and the generation of the Flood, saying: How can I create the world when these wicked men will rise up and provoke me to anger? When he beheld that Abraham was destined to arise, he said: "Now have I found a rock on which to establish and erect the world." For this reason God calls Abraham a Rock. (Isaiah 51:1 f.)

*Yalkut Shimeoni, par. 766 on Num. 23:9.*

Rabbi Jonathan ben Eliezer infers from Isaiah 63:16: "Abraham acknowledges us not and Israel does not recognize us," that only Isaac interceded for sinful Israel. When God said to him: Thy children have sinned, he replied: Are they not Thy children as much as mine? He reduces the time of man's accountability by subtracting his minority, the part of life spent in sleeping, the hours occupied in praying, eating, etc., from seventy to twelve and a half. Let God bear half and he, Isaac, will bear half. Or if he must bear the whole, lo, he sacrificed himself to God, thus making expiation for his people. Thereupon the Israelites exclaimed: Thou art our father. But Isaac admonished them to praise God rather than himself. Then they lifted their eyes on high, saying: Thou, O Lord, art our Father, our Redeemer; from Eternity is Thy Name!

*Shabbat, 89b.*

### THE SALESMAN OF IDOLS

Once Terah left his son Abram in his shop to sell the idols which he had fashioned. An old man wished to buy a fresh idol for his birthday. Abram said: "Here is a new idol, completed this very day. Do you not think that you are of more importance than a god a day old?" The greybeard left in confusion, and Abram did not sell the idol.

"You are incompetent as a salesman," said Terah. "I shall try you out as a priest." Abram asked his mother to prepare a tasty dish for the idols. He then took a large axe, smashed all the idols with the exception of the largest one, in whose hand he placed the axe. When Terah returned, Abram said: "The large idol became incensed at the presumption of the others in wishing to partake of the food before him, and he smashed them." Terah was angry at this conduct on the part of his son and informed King Nimrod that he had desecrated the temple. Nimrod asked Abram: "Why do you not worship my god?"

"Is it an idol of wood or stone that you mean? If so, how can I worship that which I have seen made before my own eyes?" replied Abram.

"Nay, those are for fools. My god is the consuming fire that gives light and destroys," said Nimrod.

"But how can fire be god if water quenches it?" asked Abram.

"Then worship water," commanded the king.

"But a cloud is mightier, carrying water where it wills."

"Worship the cloud then."

"But wind is stronger, for it disperses the clouds."

"Then worship wind."

"But man withstands wind, and I cannot worship man because death overcomes him."

"I still maintain that fire is god," said Nimrod. "I shall hurl you into a cauldron of fire, and then you may be saved by whatever you worship as god."

Abram was thrown to the flames, but they harmed him not. Nevertheless Nimrod was stubborn in his idolatry.

*Bereshit Rabbah, 38, 19.*

## 30. BLESSINGS AND CURSES

Rab Hamnuna Saba's blessing ran thus: May God keep His eye upon thee.

*Zohar, iv, 147b.*

Thus shall ye bless: thus, in the Holy Tongue; thus, in the fear of Heaven, and thus, in humility.

*Zohar, iv, 145b.*

There are treasures of life, of peace and of blessing.

*Hagigah, 12.*

Israel enjoys blessings in this world because of the blessings of Balaam, but the blessings wherewith the Patriarchs have blessed them are preserved for the World-to-Come.

*Debarim Rabbah, 3, 4.*

Blessing is to be found only in a thing hidden from the eye.

*Taanit, 8.*

Better is the curse of Ahijah, the Prophet, than the blessing of Balaam. Ahijah said: "For the Lord will smite Israel, as a reed is shaken in the water" (I Kings 14:15). A reed bends with every wind, and when the wind departs, it stands erect. But Balaam said: "As cedars beside the waters" (Num. 24:6). When a tempest comes, it uproots the cedar tree.

*Taanit, 20.*

People say: be of the cursed, not of the cursers.

*Sanhedrin, 49.*

Curses curse those who utter them.

*Wayyikra Rabbah, 15, 7.*

He who curses himself brings evil upon himself.

*Hakdamah, 14b.*

God cursed the snake, but it finds sustenance everywhere. God cursed the woman, but all men pursue her.

*Yoma, 75.*

Thy sons and thy daughters shall be given over to a strange nation. Read not "Am" (nation) but "Em" (mother). They will be given over to a stepmother. (Deut. 28:32)

*Berakot, 56.*

He who makes a declaration in the name of one who did not utter it brings a curse into the world.

*Yalkut to Proverbs, 938.*

The first curses in Leviticus (end) have 32 verses, the number of the ways of the Torah which were transgressed. The last curses in Deuteronomy 28 have 53 verses, the number of the Sedrahs of the Pentateuch, which were transgressed.[1]

*Zohar Hadash, v, 59b.*

[1] The 32 ways or Netiboth are a standard form in Jewish mysticism and are mentioned also in Ibn Gabirol. So in Hebrew Encyclopaedia *Otzar Israel.*

He who utters blessings is blessed; he who utters curses is cursed.

*Ruth Rabbah, 1, 3.*

The unrighteous bring down curses upon the world, but the righteous bring blessings.

*Zohar, i, 87b.*

There is little blessing in the possessions a Jew acquires outside of Palestine.

*Bereshit Rabbah, 74.*

With money earned across the sea, a man will never behold an omen of blessing.

*Pesahim, 3.*

He who does not permit a scholar to share in the enjoyment of his property will have no blessing from it.

*Sanhedrin, 92.*

Why was death the consequence of the census of Israel in the time of David? Because blessing does not attend a thing which is counted and numbered. And where there is no blessing, curses enter in.

*Zohar, ii, 187b.*

A Rabbi asked: Why were the blessings that Esau received fulfilled, and those of Jacob unfulfilled? He replied: in the present age Esau receives blessings in this world, and Jacob in the Upper World. But in the Messianic age, Jacob will receive blessings both below and above, and Esau will be the loser in both worlds.

*Zohar, i, 143b.*

## A FATHER'S BLESSINGS

When Rabban Gamaliel gave his daughter in marriage, she asked for his blessing. He said: "May I not see your return." When her son was born, she asked again for her father's blessing, and he said: "May it be God's will that the words: 'Woe is me' cease not out of your mouth."

"Why is it, my father," asked the daughter, "that you curse me on my two days of rejoicing?"

"These are indeed blessings and not curses," responded Rabban Gamaliel. "If peace shall abide in your family life, you will not return to my home to live. And if your son is strong and hearty, you will continually remark: 'Woe is me; the child ate too little; he drank not his milk; he is late for school.'"

*Bereshit Rabbah, 26.*

## A NON-JEW'S BLESSING

A non-Jew encountered Rabbi Ishmael and blessed him. The Rabbi said: "Thy reward hath been recorded." Another non-Jew accosted him and cursed him. The Rabbi said: "Thy reward hath been recorded." The Disciples looked wonderingly on, and he remarked: "Is not their reward recorded in Genesis (27:29): 'Cursed be everyone that curseth thee, and blessed be everyone that blesseth thee'?"

Said Rabbi Tanhuma: "If a non-Jew bless thee, respond Amen, as it is written: 'Thou shalt be blessed by all peoples.'" (Deut. 7:14)

*Y. Berakot, 8.*

## A FAREWELL BLESSING

When the Rabbis took their departure from the School of Rabbi Hanina, they said to him: "Mayest thou see thy world in this life; may thy future be in the World-to-Come; may thy name be remembered for many generations! May thy heart perceive with understanding; may thy mouth speak wisely, thy tongue murmur melodiously, thy eyebrows look straightforwardly, thy eyes be kindled by the light of the Torah; may thy countenance be clear as the sky; thy lips pronounce knowledge; thy reins rejoice uprightly, and may thy steps go speedily to hear the words of the Most Ancient of Days."

*Berakot, 17.*

## BLESSINGS AT LEAVE-TAKING

Rabbi Jonathan ben Akmai and Rabbi Judah ben Gerim studied the laws regarding vows under Rabbi Simeon ben Yohai. On their departure they bade him good-bye, but they lingered until the following day and again bade him adieu. In response to his inquiry, they said: "We did this, O Master, because we heard you teach: he who takes leave of his master and spends the night in town, should again bid him farewell before departing the next morning."

"These are gentlemen and scholars," said Rabbi Simeon to his son. "Go to their inn and ask for their blessing." When the youth had returned, he said to his father: "Instead of blessing, they cursed me. They said: 'May you sow and not reap; may you bring in but not dispense; may you bring out, but not in; may your home be ruined, and your temporary abode be built up; may your bread be consumed, and your year of cheer never arrive.' "

"All these are blessings, not curses," said Rabbi Simeon. "They have these meanings: You shall give birth to children and not behold their death; you shall bring in daughters-in-law and not see them leave your sons and return to their fathers; you shall send out your daughters to their husbands' homes, and not behold them return to live with you; you shall live so long that the space allotted to you in the family burying-ground, your abode for many years, will be destroyed by the passage of time; your temporary home on this earth, however, shall endure for a long period; your bread shall be consumed by the many members of your household. Finally your wife shall live as long as you; you will never remarry and have 'the year of bringing cheer to a new wife,' as prescribed in the Torah."

When Rabbi Simeon ben Halafta took his leave from Rabbi Judah ha-Nasi, the latter sent his son to receive his blessing. Rabbi Simeon said: "May it be God's will that you bring shame to no one and that you yourself be not shamed." "It is a fine blessing," commented his father. "Thus did Joel speak in the very Name of God." (Joel 2:27)

*Moed Katan, 9.*

### OFFSPRING LIKE THYSELF

When Rabbi Isaac parted from Rabbi Nahman, the latter sought his blessing. Rabbi Isaac said: "I will tell thee a parable. A traveller was passing through a desert and he grew hungry, faint and thirsty. He found a tree whose fruit was sweet, whose shade was pleasant, and at whose foot there flowed a stream. After refreshing himself, he was about to take his departure and said: 'O tree, how shall I bless thee? If I say to thee: May thy fruit be sweet, lo, it is so already. That thy shade be pleasant, lo, it is pleasant now. That a stream shall nourish thee, lo, this boon is thine already. But I will say: may all the saplings planted from thee be like unto thyself.' Thus is it, my friend with thee. How shall I bless thee? With Torah? Torah is thine. With wealth? Wealth is thine. With children? Children are thine. But I will say: God grant that thy offspring be like unto thyself!"

*Taanit, 6a.*

### ZEBULUN'S BLESSING

Rabbi Abba and Rabbi Jose sat together one night for study. The son of the owner of the house entered and asked permission before he departed for school to say something. He remarked: "Issachar was older than his brother Zebulun, yet we find that both Jacob and Moses first blessed Zebulun. Why is this? Because we know by tradition that Zebulun engaged in labor and trade and supported his brother Issachar, who was a student of the Torah. I, too, as the son of your patron, deserve the blessing I have come to ask of you."

They embraced him, and prophesied a happy future for him.

*Zohar, i, 241.*

The Rabbis asked: "What is meant by the phrase 'May the Lord bless thee and watch over thee'?"

A Rabbi translated these words: "May He bless thee with sons and may He watch over thy daughters."

*Bemidbar Rabbah, 11, 13.*

Another Rabbi translated these words: "God will bless you with wealth and He will watch over you that with that wealth you shall perform Mitzwot, good and beautiful deeds that shall redound to the glory of our God, to the honor and blessedness of our People!"

*Bemidbar Rabbah, 11, 13.*

## 31. BORROWING AND LENDING

### SAYINGS

If a man is asked for a large vessel which he owns, it is in his eyes as if it were a small vessel. If, however, he is asked for a small vessel, and he has it not, it is in his eyes as if it were a large one.

*Berakot, 30.*

He who makes a loan without stipulating the time of repayment should not ask for it until thirty days have elapsed.

*Makkot, 3.*

A purse and a ring are not to be loaned.

*Baba Metzia, 24*

He who lends without interest is more worthy than he who gives charity; he who invests money in the business of a poor man is most praiseworthy.

*Shabbat, 63.*

A man cannot deny a debt in the face of his creditor.

*Baba Metzia, 3.*

### NO LOAN WITHOUT WITNESSES

Said Rab Judah in the name of Rab: "He who loans money without witnesses transgresses the law: 'Place no stumblingblock (temptation) before the blind.'" (Lev. 19:14)

Rab Ashi, the teacher of Rabina, sent a message to the latter on a Friday afternoon, asking him for a loan as a deposit on a piece of land. Rabina replied to the messenger: "Please prepare the document and have witnesses." When Rab Ashi came, he asked: "Couldst thou not trust even me?"

"Thee especially I could not," answered Rabina. "Thy mind is always full of the Law, and therefore thou art more likely than some one else to forget the loan."

*Baba Metzia, 75.*

## THE OBLIGATION OF LENDING

The same obligation applies to lending as to giving. One should not withhold needed relief through apprehension that if he distributes all his property, he may himself be reduced to want. He should remember the promise of Deuteronomy (15:10): "For because of this thing the Lord thy God will bless thee in all thy work." If a man does his part, God will do His. He has the best of security, for "he who befriends the poor lends to the Lord, and He will repay him for his good deed" (Prov. 19:17). The donor who gives God all he has, becomes a creditor of God.

God says to Israel: "My sons, whenever you give food to the poor, I impute it to you as though you gave Me food."

*Midrash Tannaim, Hoffman, p. 83.*

## 32. BREAD: EARNED AND UNEARNED

He who eats of his own bread is like a child reared at his mother's breast.

*Abot de-R. Nathan, 31.*

If a man makes himself a slave to the soil, he will eat bread to satiety.

*Sanhedrin, 58.*

He who eats of another's bread fears to look at him.

*Y. Arlah, 1, 3.*

What does Ezekiel mean by the words: "And hath not eaten upon the mountains"? (18:6). He hath not eaten by virtue of the merit of his fathers. And what mean the words: "Neither hath come near to a woman in her impurity"? He has not made use of the Charity Fund for himself.[1]

[1] Namely, the collector of charity.

*Sanhedrin, 81.*

## EATING WITH CONTENTMENT

R. Aha b. R. Yashia says: If a man eats of his own bread, his mind is at ease, but if he eats of his father's, when he is grown, or even of his mother's, or of his children's bread, his heart is not contented; all the more so, if he eats of the bread of strangers.

*Abot de-R. Nathan, 31.*

R. Hanan said: The mind is not contented unless one eats of the fruit of his own labor. Even the baker's bread is unpalatable, though a man pay for it with money earned by his own labor.

*Shekalim, 3.*

### EATING HIS OWN BREAD

It was said of Rabbi Phinehas ben Jair that he never ate a slice of bread that did not belong to him by purchase. Even in his father's house, he ate no food, since he had adopted this fixed norm of conduct.

Once Rabbi Judah I invited him to a meal. Out of honor to the Patriarchate, he was prepared to make an exception. He explained that in one instance a man invites a guest even though he must deprive himself; another invites a guest unwillingly even though he can afford the hospitality. Rabbi, however, was both willing and able to afford the courtesy; therefore, no good reason presented itself to decline it. As it happened, Rabbi Phinehas entered through a side door, and beheld in an enclosure several white mules. He said: "These animals are accustomed to injure people severely; a pious man should not possess them." And he refused to enter the house.[1]

*Hullin, 7.*

[1] Some scholars claim that Rabbi Phinehas was an Essene.

## 33. BROTHERS, SISTERS

Honor thy father and thy mother—including, also, thine older brother.

*Ketubot, 103.*

When brothers quarrel, strangers come in to effect peace.
*Yerushalmi, quoted in the book "Hatzi Menasseh."*

A man should not wed a woman in one country, and, after divorcing her, marry another woman in a different country. For it may happen that brother and sister may not know of each other, and enter into marriage.

*Yoma, 18.*

When an offender receives a penalty, he becomes thy brother.
*Megillah, 7.*

## 34. BUSINESS AFFAIRS

When a Sage engages in many business undertakings, they interfere with his wisdom.

*Shemot Rabbah, 6, 2.*

That which causes money to come, is similar to money.
*Pesahim, 29.*

If a customer comes to purchase naphtha, the merchant says: here is the gallon measure; use it yourself. If he comes to buy perfume, the storekeeper says: if you will wait a moment, I will measure it out for you.

*Yoma, 39.*

While the dust is yet on thy feet, sell what thou hast brought to market.

*Pesahim, 113.*

People say: to the place where green vegetables are brought in abundance, bring thine also to sell.

*Menahot, 85.*

It is the custom of merchants to display their worst merchandise first.

*Tanhuma Shelah, 6.*

He who buys from a notorious thief is not repaid by the owner.
*Baba Kamma, 115.*

## 35. FAIR AND UNFAIR METHODS IN BUSINESS

"He performed no evil against his fellow man," [1] namely he began no competitive enterprise or trade where there was no demand for it.

*Makkot, 24.*

[1] Psalm 15:3.

Rabbi Judah ben Ilai declared that a shopkeeper should not give to children-customers sweetmeats to attract their patronage. The other Rabbis permitted this, since the merchant does not prevent his competitor from doing likewise. He also declared that a shopkeeper should not cut prices. The others declared: The public owes him grateful remembrance, since this will prevent high prices on foodstuffs, and will also work against the practice of holding goods back for a higher market.

*Baba Metzia, 4, 12, Mishnah.*

### THE UNWANTED PURCHASE

Rab Gidal was bargaining for a certain piece of ground, but Rab Abba bought it instead. Rab Gidal complained to R. Zeira, and when Rab Abba visited him, R. Zeira inquired: "If a poor man bends down to pick up something that belongs to no one else, and, as he does so, another person snatches it away, what would you call the latter?"

"I would call him a wicked person," replied R. Abba.

"Then why did you snatch the property away from R. Gidal?"

"I did not know that he was bargaining for it."

"Will you sell it to him now?"

"No," answered R. Abba. "It was my first purchase, and I do

not care to admit a mistake in my initial land enterprise. However," he continued, "R. Gidal may have it as a gift from me."

R. Gidal refused to accept it, however, and R. Abba declined to use it; hence it was turned over to the Disciples.

*Berakot, 10.*

## How to Ask

When R. Jonathan needed lentils, a kinsman wrote him the price in his town, and he journeyed there to make the purchase. The kinsman being absent, the Rabbi went to market alone, and was informed: "Lentils are scarce and command a high price, but wheat is cheap." He was compelled to pay a high price for the lentils. His kinsman later said: "You lack experience. Though you wished lentils, you should have asked for something else, and they would have quoted a low price on lentils."

R. Jonathan learned the lesson and later instructed correctly his friend, R. Hiyya of Sepphoris, when the latter went to purchase wheat in Syria.

*Midrash Tehillim, 12.*
*(Midrash Tehillim is also called Midrash Shoher Tob).*

## Regulating Prices

Certain officers of the Exilarch were designated to seal up weights and measures, and also to regulate prices. Samuel said to his Disciple Karna: "Go and tell them they have no right to regulate prices." But they answered: "What is thy name?" And when they were told: Karna, meaning a horn, they laughed at him and said: "Thou shouldst have a horn on thy forehead."

They accepted the opinion of R. Isaac, who favored the regulation of prices in order to obstruct the tactics of swindlers. The latter would wait until the honest merchants had sold at a fair price the bulk of the product, and then they would raise prices.

*Baba Batra, 89.*

## Conspiracies Regarding Trade

R. Zeira would curse those who pretended to seek an article for which they knew others were looking, so that the would-be purchasers would be forced to pay a high price. He also cursed those who conspired with the merchants to raise the price of articles which they knew a bona-fide purchaser was seeking.

R. Abba b. Abba would sell his produce early in the season, thereby establishing a low price.

His son, Samuel, wished to improve upon his father's procedure. He would, therefore, keep his produce until prices were higher, and then he would sell at the season's lowest price.

They sent word from Palestine: "We prefer the father's action

to the son's. The father established a low price at the very beginning, but the son's action did not serve to lessen the price of the
produce, since a higher price had already been established.

*Baba Batra, 90. Y. Kiddushin, 3.*

## 36. CARELESSNESS AND CAREFULNESS

People say: the cat and the mouse both make a feast of the cream
of a careless man.

*Sanhedrin, 105.*

Between the midwife and the mother, the child is sometimes lost.
(Each depends upon the other to care for the baby.)

*Bereshit Rabbah, 60, 3.*

### SHOWING PROPER CARE

If a man entrusts his money for safekeeping with another, who
accepts the responsibility and then, carrying it homeward in a bundle
on his back, is robbed by a thief who cuts the bundle open, the second
man must make repayment. Why? Because he did not guard the
money with ordinary care.

Said R. Isaac: "We learn this from Scripture: 'Bind up the money
in thy hand' (Deut. 14:25); even if it is bound up, keep it in thy
hand."

A shepherd was taking care of his flocks, when a sheep fell into
the stream and could not be recovered. Rabba acquitted him of
negligence, saying: "There is no evidence that he did not safeguard
his charges with less than the customary care of shepherds."

*Baba Metzia, 42.*

## 37. CHARITY

Great is charity. It uplifts the soul.

*Eliyahu Zuta, 1.*

He who closes his eyes against giving to charity is like an idolator.

*Ketubot, 68.*

He who gives to charity reverses the course of the river flowing
out of Eden, that it may water the Garden. (He irrigates Paradise
itself.)

*Tikkune Zohar, 78a. Tikkun, 21.*

He who does charity and justice is as if he had filled the whole
world with kindness.

*Sukkah, 49.*

Better is he who gives little to charity from money honestly earned, than he who gives much from dishonestly gained wealth.

*Kohelet Rabbah, 4.*

He who feeds the needy in a year of famine is linked to the Tree of Life, and brings life thereby to his progeny.

*Zohar, i, 208b.*

Take care that the doors of thy home be not shut against the needy.

*Derek Eretz Zuta, 9.*

Let a man be generous in his charities, but let him beware of giving away all that he has.

*Arakin, 28a.*

A man's benefactions should not go beyond a fifth of his property.

*Ketubot, 50a.*

Let a man also beware of giving indiscriminately, without inquiry into the worth of the applicant.

*Baba Batra, 9a.*

A man may give liberally, and yet because he gives unlovingly and wounds the heart of the poor, his gift is in vain, for it has lost the attribute of charity; a man may give little, but because his heart goes with it his deed and himself are blessed.

*Baba Batra, 9b.*

If one gives only the kind word, and speaks comfortably to the poor, he has done true charity, for doth not Holy Writ say: "Because of this *word* will God bless thee"?

*Sifre Deut., 15:10.*

Draw out thy soul to the hungry.

*Wayyikra Rabbah, 34.*

"It is the sign of *gemilut hasadim* to 'run after the poor.' "

*Shabbat, 104a.*

In three things, *gemilut hasadim* excels mere almsgiving: No gift is needed for it but the giving of oneself; it may be done to the rich as well as to the poor; it may be done not only to the living, but to the dead.

*Sukkah, 49.*

Charity is obligatory, but even charity has its limitations. To give away all of one's possessions and thus to pauperize oneself is prohibited.

*Ketubot, 50a.*

R. Akiba married the daughter of Kalba Sebu'a and they were very poor. Elijah visited them in the form of a man and asked them whether they could give him a little straw for his wife, who, he told them, had given birth, and had nothing on which to lie. When Elijah left, R. Akiba remarked to his wife: "You see there are people that do not possess even a little straw."

*Nedarim, 50a.*

All the merit of fasting lies in the almsgiving which goes with it.

*Berakot, 6b.*

By the side of the poor stands God Himself, pleading for His stricken children.

*Wayyikra Rabbah, chap. 34.*

He that feeds the hungry feeds God also.

*Agadat Shir ha-Shirim.*

He that feeds the hungry feeds himself too, for charity blesses him that gives even more than him that takes.

*Ruth Rabbah, 19.*

Charity knows neither race nor creed.

*Gittin, 61a.*

Charity is the saving salt of wealth.

*Ketubot, 60b.*

The whole virtue of charity is its pity.

*Sukkah, 49b.*

If a poor man comes to thee for aid in the morning, give it to him. If he comes again in the evening, give it to him once more.

*Bereshit Rabbah, 61, 3.*

If a man sees that his income is meagre, let him practice charity.

*Gittin, 7.*

Even a poor man who lives on charity should practice charity.

*Gittin, 7.*

He who gives charity serves the Holy One daily, and sanctifies His Name.

*Zohar, iii, 113b.*

He who says: I give this coin to charity that my son may live, gives charity in perfection.[1]

*Pesahim, 8.*

[1] According to the version of R. Hananel.

May my lot be cast among those who gather charity, and not among those who distribute it.

*Shabbat, 118.*

### Regarding Charity

Ipra Hurmiz, the Queen Mother of Persia, sent a purse to Rab Joseph on behalf of a great Mitzwah. "What is a great Mitzwah?" mused Rab Joseph. Abbaye replied: "Rab Sabuel bar Judah has taught: no charity tax may be levied on the property of orphans, even for the ransoming of captives. This proves that the ransoming of captives is the greatest of charities."

A community must maintain two kinds of charity: a free kitchen and a Chest for the Poor. The free kitchen should be open every day, and should be enjoyed by the poor from out-of-town as well as by the local poor. The Chest shall be open every Friday and is for residents only. Other Rabbis declare: for both residents and non-residents.

Rab Judah said: Investigate before you give a garment to a poor man, but do not investigate before giving him food.

A beggar who goes from door to door should not receive from the Chest more than he secures from an individual.

. . .

Rabbi Assi said: Charity is equal to all Mitzwot.

Rabbi Eleazar said: Greater is he who persuades others to give than him who gives.

Rabba said to the people of Mehuza: Do charity among yourselves so that you will enjoy peace.

Rabbi Eleazar said: When the Temple stood, people voluntarily gave a shekel to it. Give charity now, for if you do not, it will be forcibly taken from you by officials.

Rabba said: Charity is like a suit of mail, in which every link is joined to the other, forming the whole garment. In Charity every penny is joined to every other, forming a large sum.

Said R. Eleazar: He who gives charity in secret is as great as Moses.

R. Isaac said: He who strives to do charity is granted money by God wherewith to do it.

*Baba Batra, 8-9.*

R. Nahman bar Isaac said: He who runs after the Mitzwah of charity, will be granted worthy poor by God, and for their relief he will be rewarded.

R. Joshua ben Levi said: He who gives charity frequently and according to his means will be rewarded with sons—learned, wealthy and popular.

R. Judah ben R. Shalom said: On New Year's Day a man's profits and losses are determined for the year. If he is charitable, the loss is allocated to charity; if not, it goes to expenses without profit.

R. Pappa was climbing a ladder when his foot slipped. Only by chance did he escape injury. He said: "I almost suffered the penalty for idolatry." Rab Hiyya bar Rab said to him: "Thou must have neglected to feed a poor man, for R. Joshua ben Karha teaches: 'He who closes his eyes to charity is like one who worships idols.' "

R. Eleazar ben Jose said: Kind deeds and charity achieve peace between Israel and their Father in Heaven.

R. Judah said: Great is charity for it brings Redemption nearer.

R. Judah said: Come and see how great is charity. Ten strong things exist in the world: a mountain is strong, but iron breaks it; iron is strong, but fire softens it; fire is strong, but water extinguishes it; water is strong, but clouds bear it along; clouds are strong, but the wind spreads them out; the wind is strong, but the body of man withstands it; the body is strong, but fear breaks it; fear is strong, but wine overcomes it; wine is strong, but sleep dispels it; sleep is strong, but death is stronger still. But charity rescueth even from death.

R. Dosetai ben Yannai said: When you bring a gift to a ruler, it may or may not be accepted; if accepted, you may or may not be called to see the monarch. It is different with God. If a man gives a small coin to the poor, he has a satisfaction equal to beholding the Shekinah, as we read: "As for me, I shall behold Thy face in Zedek" (righteousness). (Psalm 17:15)

*Baba Batra, 9-10.*

R. Eliezer would first give a coin in charity and then commence his prayers: "For I shall behold Thy face in Zedek."

Said R. Johanan: "He that is gracious unto the poor lendeth unto the Lord" (Prov. 19:17), and "the borrower is servant to the lender" (Prov. 22:7). We learn that God, if we are permitted to say so, must perform the will of the charitable person.

R. Hiyya bar Abba said: "The best way to give charity is to drop it into the Collection Box. The donor thus knows not to whom he gives, and the poor man knows not who is giver. Care should be taken, however, that the distributor is an excellent person."

*Baba Batra, 10a-b.*

When a beggar stands at your door, the Holy One, Blessed be He, stands at his right hand.

*Wayyikra Rabbah, 34, 9.*

R. Eleazar ben Pedat said: We must give credit to the impostors among the poor; were it not for them, if a man were asked for alms and did not give them at once, he would be incurring punishment.

*Y. Peah, 21b.*

"Blessed is he that considereth the poor" (Psalm 41:1). It refers to a man who considers how the meritorious act can best be carried out.

*Y. Peah, 21b.*

If a man gives with a sullen face, it is as if he gave nothing; but he who receives the needy person with a cheerful countenance, even if he was not able to give him anything, it is as if he gave him a good gift.

*Abot de-R. Nathan, 13.*

"If thou draw out thy soul to the hungry" (Isaiah 58:10),—if you have nothing to give him, comfort him with words. Say to him: "My soul goes out to you because I have nothing to give to you."

*Wayyikra Rabbah, 34, 15.*

A Rabbi saw a man give a zuz to a beggar publicly. He said to him: Better had you given him nothing rather than give him and put him to shame.

*Hagigah, 5a.*

R. Eleazar of Bertota said: Give unto Him of what is His, seeing that thou and what thou hast are His; this is found expressed in David who said: "For all things come from Thee, and of Thine own have we given Thee." (I Chronicles 29:14)

*Abot, 3, 8.*

More than the householder does for the beggar, the beggar does for the householder.

*Wayyikra Rabbah, 34, 8.*

He who prolongs his stay at table prolongs his life; perhaps a poor man will come and he will give him some food.

*Berakot, 55a.*

A Rabbi advised his wife: "When a beggar comes, hand him bread, so that the same may be done to your children." She exclaimed: "You are cursing them!" He replied: "There is a wheel which revolves in the world: the poor become rich and the rich become poor."

*Shabbat, 151b.*

A proverb declares: The door which is not opened for charity will be opened to the physician.

*Shir ha-Shirim Rabbah to 6, 11.*

Whoever practices charity and justice is as though he filled the whole world with loving-kindness.

*Sukkah, 49b.*

Greater is he who practices charity than all the sacrifices.

*Sukkah, 49b.*

The salt that preserves money is its diminution through charity.

*Ketubot, 66b.*

(The above are selections compiled from *Everyman's Talmud* by the Rev. A. Cohen.)

### Begging for Others

People grumbled against R. Zechariah, the son-in-law of R Simeon b. Lakish, saying that he begged, though he needed it not After he had died, however, it was discovered that he gave the money to others.

R. Hiyya b. Abba said: We have amongst us poor people who accept charity only between Rosh ha-Shanah and Yom Kippur. "Such is our custom," they say.

*Y. Peah, 8.*

### A Debt to Society

Rabbah bar Abbuha said: The public Charity Collector has a right to take away a valuable article from a person who refuses to give his share to charity, even on the eve of the Sabbath, and retain it until the man redeems it. The excuse that he is so busy with the Sabbath that he cannot be troubled, is unacceptable.

Rabbah once took away by force 400 zuzim from R. Nathan bar Ammi, to be used for charity.

*Baba Batra, 8.*

### The Learned Beggar

R. Isaac and R. Jose met a man with a child on one arm, and a pail on the other. After receiving food from them, the man said: Why does God request us to offer Him His food (Numb. 28:2)? Because it is God's rule that a man must evoke below the favor he anticipates receiving from above. And if sacrifice drew down sustenance from above, how much the more will the proffer of food to one in need awaken the same favor from God?

The Rabbis marvelled at the learned beggar, and R. Jose remarked: Truly they were wise who taught us to despise no man. In two ways have we profited: we have earned a great Mitzwah and we have learned a beautiful lesson.

*Zohar, i, 164.*

## 38. THE MANNER OF GIVING CHARITY

Had Jonathan given to David two loaves of bread, Nob, the city of the Kohanim would have been spared.[1]

*Sanhedrin, 104.*

[1] The gift of food is often better than the gift of money.

A fast day on which charity has been collected but not immediately distributed is like the shedding of blood.

*Sanhedrin, 35.*

If the funds in the Community Chest are low, the relief of the women takes precedence over the relief of the men.

*Tos. Ketubot, 6, 8.*

## The Adopted Son

Once a man adopted a poor child, reared him well, taught him a trade, helped him to marriage and to wealth. Later the good man became impoverished and informed his adopted son. The latter sent a ragged boy to his benefactor with a gem, saying: "Buy this of me for a dinar." Later he sent to him a well-dressed man, who purchased the gem for a goodly sum. He did this so that his benefactor might feel no shame through receiving a donation, but might receive aid in the form of a business transaction.

*Meil Zedakah, quoting a Midrash.*

## Considering the Poor

When R. Jonah would learn of a man of good family who had become impoverished, he would say: Please accept this loan until you receive the inheritance a kinsman left you across the seas.

*Wayyikra Rabbah, 34.*

R. Eleazar saw R. Simeon bar Abba approaching, and knowing his poverty, R. Eleazar dropped a dinar to the ground. When R. Simeon wished to return it to R. Eleazar, the latter said: "I lost it some time ago and despaired of finding it. It is therefore legally yours."

*Y. Baba Metzia, 2.*

## Secret Almsgiving

Mar Ukba was accustomed to throw four zuzim every day in the hole of his neighbor's door, and walk away unseen. Once the poor recipient wished to know his benefactor, and ran out of his home to detect him, but he was too late.

Rabbi Abba would lose a kerchief with coins among the poor. He was careful, however, to chase away rogues.

*Ketubot, 67; Hagigah, 5.*

## Dainty Taste

Mar Ukba was accustomed to send a sum of money to a poor neighbor before Yom Kippur. Once his son, who took the money, reported: "The poor man was indulging in old wine, and I did not give him the money." His father retorted: "He must have seen better days since he has such dainty tastes. I will double the amount of my gift."

*Ketubot, 67b.*

## How to Give

A man's hand is to be open wide for the relief of the needy; and not once, but a hundred times. Men are not required to enrich a recipient, but to give the poor "whatever he lacks." [1] If he comes from a high social class, his needs are greater than if he had always been poor.

A gift to the poor must be made privately, with no one else present.

If a needy man refuses to accept charity, aid must be given him in the form of a loan, and no attempt should be made to collect it.

*Yalkut Shimeoni on Deut. 15, 7 to 11.*

[1] Deut. 15:8.

Rabbi Ishmael said: If a man is of good family and is ashamed to ask alms, "open" [1] to him with words: "My son, perhaps you require a loan." Hence the authorities say: Alms may be given like a loan.

*Midrash Tannaim, Hoffman, 82.*

[1] Deut. 15:8.


## 39. GIVING FREELY TO CHARITY

He who gives on behalf of a Mitzwah, does not diminish his property.

*Shemot Rabbah, 36, 2.*

If you see a man donating much to charity, be assured that his wealth is increasing.

*Midrash Mishle, 1.*

He who donates much to charity becomes the richer because of it, inasmuch as he opens up a channel for God's blessing to reach him. Therefore say not: if I give so much today, what will I do tomorrow?

*Zohar, iii, 110b.*

He who stints on charity deserves life neither in this world nor the next.

*Zohar, i, 109a.*

Charity promotes peace, and he who gives much charity will bring great peace on earth and above.

*Zohar, i, 200b.*

Great is the privilege of the philanthropist, for he awakens the good in the Jewish community. Inasmuch as charity is the tree of life, it saveth from death.

*Zohar, iii, 111a.*

If a non-Jew donates money on behalf of a special object in a synagogue, it may not be allocated on behalf of a different object.

*Arakin, 6.*

### Stuffed Fowl and Old Wine

A poor man came to Raba and begged for a meal. "On what dost thou usually dine?" asked Raba. "On stuffed fowl and old wine," was the reply. "What!" exclaimed Raba, "art thou not concerned at being so great a burden to the community?"

The poor man answered: "I eat nothing belonging to them, but only what the Lord provides. As we read (Psalm 145:15): 'The eyes of all wait upon Thee, and Thou givest them their meal in his season.' It is not said: 'in their season,' but 'in his season.' Thus we learn that God provides for each individual in his season of need."

While they were thus conversing, Raba's sister entered. She had not visited him for several years, and brought him as a gift a stuffed fowl and some old wine. Raba marvelled at the coincidence, and turning to his poor guest, he said: "I beg thy pardon, friend. Arise, I pray thee, and eat."

*Ketubot, 67b.*

### He Will Not Go Where the Poor Are Not Welcome

There was a pious man with whom Elijah would visit and walk. However, when that man made a watchman's door at the gate of his yard, and thus prevented the poor people from entering the house, Elijah refrained from visiting him.

*Baba Batra, 7b.*

### Treasures for Above

In years of famine, King Monobaz of Adiabene distributed all his treasures to the poor. His kinsmen remonstrated with him: "Your fathers laid up treasures, but you squander them."

He replied: "My fathers laid up treasures for below: a place where force prevails—treasures which bear no fruit; treasures of money, treasures for others to enjoy; treasures of consequence only in this world. I, however, have laid up treasure for Above: a place where no force prevails—treasures bearing fruit; treasures for souls, treasures which I, myself, will enjoy; treasures of value in the World-to-Come."

*Tosefta Peah, 4, 18; Baba Batra, 11a.*

### Economy and Generosity

The Rabbis in their collections for the Academies planned to visit first a certain rich man, named Barbuhin. As they neared his house, they overheard a conversation between the householder and his son, in which the father asked his son to buy "Truksemin" of a cheaper kind for supper. They went away, deciding that such a miser should not head the list of donors. When they had completed their work, they returned to the rich man, who said: "Go to my wife and tell her to give you a measure of gold pieces." She inquired: "Did my husband ask that the measure be planed or the gold given in a heap?"

"He gave no instructions," said the Rabbis.

"Then I shall give it in a heap," she said, "and if he is not agreeable, he may deduct it from my marriage settlement."

"My wife did as I wished," said the man. "But why did you come to me last?" When they had frankly told him the reason, the rich man said to the Rabbis: "By my soul, for myself I have the right to practice economy, but there can be no economy in fulfilling the commandment of my Creator."

*Esther Rabbah, 1.*

## ABBA YUDAN, THE GENEROUS

In the suburbs of Antioch, R. Eliezer, R. Joshua and R. Akiba encountered a good-hearted man, Abba Yudan, as they went forth to collect money for the School. He had lost his fortune and had only one field left. He asked his wife's advice and she answered: "Sell half the field and give your usual donation." The Rabbis blessed him: "May the Lord restore your prosperity."

Abba Yudan went forth to plow the remaining half of his field, and his ox stumbled on a stone and became lame. Beneath the stone Abba Yudan discovered a small chest, filled with coins of the realm. He prospered greatly henceforth, and when the Rabbis came again on their yearly visit, people said: "Abba Yudan is a man of many servants, cattle and camels. Who can expect to merit a sight of this wealthy man's countenance?" When Abba met them, he said: "Your blessing has brought me fruit and the fruit of fruits." They replied: "Though others have given more, your name has always headed the list of donors."

R. Simeon ben Lakish on his collections in Botzrah heard mentioned the name of a wealthy man as Abba Yudan, the Cheater. He was told that this man would add up the donations of every Jew in the city and give as much as all of them together. This prompted people to give more than otherwise, and therefore Abba Yudan cheated them out of money.

*Wayyikra Rabbah, 5.*

## PURCHASING RIGHTEOUSNESS

Rabbi Tarfon was very rich, but did not give enough to charity. Rabbi Akiba asked him for a large sum to purchase a village, but when he received the money, he distributed it among the poor. When Rabbi Tarfon asked for the deed to the village, Rabbi Akiba opened the Psalter to 112:9, and read to him: "He hath scattered abroad; he hath given to the needy; his righteousness endureth forever." "This have I purchased for thee," added Rabbi Akiba, and Rabbi Tarfon embraced him.

*Wayyikra Rabbah, 34, 16; Baraita Kallah.*

### Hardening the Heart

Scripture forbids a man to harden his heart towards his needy brother, or to close his hand. There are men who are perplexed whether to give or not; and there are men who stretch out their hand, and later contract it.

*Yalkut Shimeoni to Deut. 15, 7.*

## 40. CHARITY AND THE HELPING HAND

Not only does man support man, but all nature does so. The stars and the planets, and even the Angels support each other.

*Tikkune Zohar, 122, T. 43.*

"And happy is everyone who supporteth her" (Prov. 3:18). Who are the supporters of the Torah? Those who loan money to students, enabling them to earn their bread by a few hours of trade or handiwork.

*Zohar, iii, 53b.*

The horse does not carry the hero through to victory, but the hero carries through the horse.[1]

*Matnot Kehuna to Bereshit Rabbah, 68, 9, as Yerushalmi.*

[1] Patrons do not support the Zaddik, but the Zaddik supports the patrons.

He who contributes to the livelihood of a just man is as one who observes the laws of the Pentateuch.

*Bereshit Rabbah, 58, 8.*

It is the duty of the Zaddikim to aid the wicked; of the wise to aid the unwise; of the rich to aid the poor. Each man should aid his fellow-man according to his talent.

*Zohar, i, 208a.*

He who maintains the Disciples of the Wise out of his property is accounted by Scripture as if he has cleaved to the Shekinah.

*Ketubot, 111b.*

### The Merit of Zebulun

Nahshon, the Prince of Judah, was the first to leap into the Red Sea and he was the first to bring his offering for the dedication of the Tabernacle.

The second was the Prince of Issachar, for this tribe furnished many learned men.

The third was the Prince of Zebulun, for this tribe aided Issachar with material goods so that Issachar might engage in study without toiling for his sustenance.

*Bemidbar Rabbah, 13.*

## SAVING ONE LIFE

Only one man was created, in order to teach the lesson that if one destroys a single person, the Scripture imputes it to him as if he had destroyed the whole population of the world. And if he saves the life of a single person, the Scripture imputes it to him as though he had saved the whole world.

*Mishnah Sanhedrin, 4, 5.*

## THE SCALE OF CHARITY

In the scale of charity, the highest is to lay hold of a man who is falling, and to keep him from falling and becoming a public charge. by means of a gift, a loan, a partnership, or by finding him work. Such a man is like a load resting on the top of a wall; as long as it is in its place, one man can take hold of it, and keep it there. But once it has fallen to the ground, five men cannot raise it up again.

*Sifra on Lev. 25, 35.*

Greater is he that lends than he that gives, and greater still is he that lends, and, with the loan, helps the poor man to help himself.

*Shabbat, 63a.*

## 41. IMPROPER CHARITY

Worthless charity is given when a woman acquires money dishonestly and then distributes it to the poor and sick.

*Shemot Rabbah, 31 end.*

Is good sometimes bad? Yes, when one gives charity to a man in public or to a woman in secret.

*Hagigah, 5.*

One form of "strange worship" or idolatry, is practiced by those who build synagogues and academies, placing therein Scrolls of the Torah with crowns to adorn them, but whose motive is not service to God but the attainment of public applause and public fame.

*Zohar, i, 25b.*

## "HE WOULD BE UTTERLY CONTEMNED" (SONG OF SONGS, 8:7)

Ulla said: "Not like Azariah who supported his brother Simeon so that the latter might study Torah; not like the Patriarch Judah II who supported Rabbi Johanan, but like Shebna and Hillel."

Rab Dimi explained: "Shebna was a brother of Hillel but he failed to aid him during his student days. When Hillel became famous as a distinguished scholar, Shebna desired to support his brother with the proviso that Hillel promise him half his expected reward in the World-to-Come; moreover Hillel was to make it known that he was indebted for his knowledge of the Torah to his brother's support. Hillel refused to make this arrangement."

It is hard to understand Israel. He is asked to give to the Golden Calf and he gives. He is asked to give to the Tabernacle and he also gives.

*Y. Shekalim, 1, 1.*

## 42. CHARITY: ITS REWARDS AND PENALTIES

R. Eliezer said: "He who ostentatiously gives alms to the poor—for this, God will bring him to judgment."

*Hagigah, 5a.*

He who gives charity to the poor shall see it remembered by God in the hour of the world's calamity.

*Zohar, i, 104a.*

He who gives nothing to Jacob must give to Esau.

*Wayyikra Rabbah, 34, 13.*

Charity is rewarded according to the benevolence it contains. It is requited by God only in proportion to the love within it.

*Sukkah, 49b.*

A drought occurs when pledges to charity are not paid.

*Taanit, 8.*

Collectors of charity receive a reward equivalent to the reward of all those who donate.

*Zohar, i, 208a.*

Rabbah who merely studied the Torah, lived forty years. Abbayi, who studied the Torah and also practiced benevolence, lived sixty.

*Rosh ha-Shanah, 18a.*

### EXAMINING THE VESSEL

A blind beggar accosted two men walking on the road. One of the travelers gave him a selah, but the other gave him nothing. The Angel of Death approached them and said: "He who gave to the beggar need have no fear of me for fifty years; the other shall speedily die."

"May I not return and give charity to the beggar?" asked the condemned man.

"No," replied the Angel of Death, "a boat is examined for holes and fissures before departure, not when it is already at sea."

*Midrash, quoted in "Meil Zedakah."*

### The Harmless Scorpion

Two men, Joseph and Uzziel, saw a boy carrying a bundle of wood on his head as he walked along the road. Said one to the other: "Do you see the scorpion among the wood? It is a marvel that he remains at rest and does no harm to the lad." They walked over to the boy, showed him the reptile and killed it with a piece of wood. They then asked him: "What good deed hast thou done to deserve being saved?"

The boy bethought himself and said: "Yesterday I saw a hungry orphan boy look longingly at my food, and I gave him half of it."

*Midrash, quoted in "Meil Zedakah."*

### Measure for Measure

The plague once raged in Sura but it completely spared a certain family. It was found that the head of the family helped bury the dead without cost, and therefore death had spared him.

A great fire once broke out in Drokrot, but it passed by a certain home. It was found that the woman of the house was accustomed to invite the poor women to come to her fine fire on Fridays, and bake their loaves in her oven. Therefore the great fire had spared her house.

*Taanit, 21.*

### "Cast Thy Bread upon the Waters (Eccl. 11:11)

R. Akiba related: When I was once at sea I witnessed a boat sinking and mourned for a friend of mine on it. When I came to Cappadocia, lo, my friend was safe. I inquired: Who saved thee? He answered: Before my departure I gave a loaf of bread to a beggar, and he blessed me, saying: Thou savest my life; may thy life be saved. When the boat sank, great waves carried me to land. I quoted to him the words from Ecclesiastes.

*Kohelet Rabbah, 11.*

A boat on the Great Sea (the Mediterranean) was becalmed. Several days passed without wind. Finally they fried a goat and hung it at the end of a long pole. A whale came by, snatched at the bait, and dragged the ship to another position where the sails found wind. When they reached port, the Sages said: Cast thy bread upon the waters.

Bar Kappara in the port of Caesarea saw a lifeboat come to shore from a wrecked ship. In it was a naked man. He clothed and fed him, and gave him five selaim. Soon after several Jews were imprisoned, and Bar Kappara was sent as emissary to treat with the government. He arrived at his destination, visited the Governor, and gave him the five hundred denarii asked as ransom. The Governor gazed at him intently, and then, with a joyful cry, embraced him, saying: "Dost thou remember rescuing me in distress? I shall release

the prisoners for the sake of thy good deed, and in place of thy five
selaim I will make thee a gift of the five hundred denarii." When
Bar Kappara reported this to the people, they cried out: "Cast thy
bread upon the waters."

*Kohelet Rabbah, 11.*

### Charity Saves from Death

Samuel saw a man unload his pack, and a poisonous snake fell
from it strangled. Samuel asked: "What good deed have you performed?"

The man replied: "I belong to a group of laborers who agreed
that each was to take turns supplying the noon-day meal. Today I
saw that the man whose turn had come, was downcast. Appreciating
his inability to supply the food, I went out and bought it without making this known."

The daughter of Rabbi Akiba stuck her knitting needle into the
wall. It went into the eye of a snake, and in the morning, she drew
forth her needle with the snake. Rabbi Akiba asked her: "What good
deed hast thou done?" She answered: "While we ate, I noticed a
beggar at the door, and I gave him my portion of the food."

*Shabbat, 156.*

### The Death-Warrant

Benjamin, the Zaddik, was keeper of the Poor Box, and a woman
came to him at famine-time to ask for food. "By the worship of
God," he replied, "there is nothing in the Box!" She exclaimed: "O
Rabbi, if thou dost not feed me, I and my seven children will starve."
He then gave her relief from his private purse.

In the course of time he fell ill and was close to death. Then the
Angels interceded with the Lord, saying: "Lord of the Universe,
Thou hast said that he who preserveth the life of one single soul of
Israel is as if he had preserved the lives of the whole world. Shall
Benjamin, the Zaddik, who preserved a poor woman and her seven
children, die so prematurely?" Instantly the death-warrant which
had gone forth was torn up, and twenty-two years were added to
his life.

*Baba Batra, 11a.*

### In the Hour of Want

If you perform a precept in your hour of want, you will perform
it eventually in your hour of plenty. If you disregard a precept in
your hour of plenty, you will eventually disregard it in your hour of
want.

If you give to charity while you are poor, you will eventually give
in days of wealth; if you do not give while you are rich, you will
eventually abstain from giving because of poverty.

God has willed that there be two hands in the matter of charity:

one that gives and one that receives. Thank God that yours is the hand that gives. The giver has the upper, the receiver the lower hand. Consider how much you ought thank Him for granting you the upper hand.

Open a hand of compassion to the poor, and God will open to you His store of abundance. Say not: I will miss what I give. Be like the sheep who give their wool and have no less the next year because they have given.

*Introd. to Tanhuma, Buber, 123-4.*

## THE POWER OF THE ETROG

Once in a town there were two wealthy brothers, one charitable, and the other miserly. One day, the good man had but ten coins left of all his property; collectors of charity met him on the street, asked for a donation towards the marriage fund of a poor girl, and received from him his last coin. He entered the synagogue to take part in the Services which were for Hoshanah Rabbah when the children gather many Ethrogim and play with them. The man filled a sack with Ethrogim, and after the Holiday, hired himself out as a worker on a Mediterranean boat.

It brought him to a distant country where the king lay ill, apparently beyond the power of his physicians to cure him. When the customs-men saw the strange fruit in the poor man's sack, they brought him to the major domo of the palace. The King gave orders that the juice of the Ethrogim be given him as a medicine, and, behold, it made him well. He filled the sack with gold pieces and sent the man to his home in honor.

The uncharitable brother, who had ridiculed his impractical brother for his generosity, took the lesson deeply to heart.

*Wayyikra Rabbah, 37.*

## SHALL GOD FEED THE POOR?

Turnus Rufus once said to Rabbi Akiba: "If your God is a friend of the poor, why does He not feed them?"

Rabbi Akiba promptly replied: "That we by maintaining them may escape the condemnation of Gehenna."

"On the contrary," said the ruler. "The very fact that you maintain the poor will condemn you to Gehenna. It is as if a King should imprison a servant who has offended him, and command that neither food nor drink be given him; and as if one of his subjects should in spite of the King go and supply the servant with both. When the King hears of this, will he not be angry?"

Rabbi Akiba replied: "It is rather like a King, who being angry at his son, imprisons him with orders that no food or drink be given him. But a subject nevertheless gives him both food and drink. When the King hears of this, will he not handsomely reward the man?"

"True," answered the ruler. "Ye are both sons and servants. But the downfall of your nation shows that you are regarded as servants now."

"Even so," responded the Rabbi, "He says to us: 'Deal thy bread to the hungry, and bring the poor that are cast out to thy house.'" (Isaiah 58:7)

*Baba Batra, 10a.*

### The Millionaire's Daughter

Rabbi Johanan ben Zakkai was once riding out of Jerusalem, and saw a woman picking grain left over on the field. She halted him and said: "Dost thou not recognize me, Rabbi; I am the daughter of Nakdimon ben Gorion." The Rabbi pityingly gazed at her, and queried: "Art thou not the same at whose marriage I was present, and whose Ketubah was that of the daughter of a multi-millionaire? What became of thy riches and of thy father's?"

She answered: "Dost thou not remember warning us that charity preserves riches as salt preserves food? We stinted in our gifts to the poor, not giving according to our wealth, and our wealth was lost through many mishaps."

The Rabbi aided her to establish herself in another town.

*Ketubot, 66b.*

### The Rolling of Fortunes

In the School of Rabbi Ishmael they expounded Deut. 25:10: "Thou shalt surely give him (the poor), and thine heart shall not be grieved when thou givest him; for in the rolling of fortunes (bi-gelal), shall this act of thine bring it to pass that the Lord, thy God, shall bless thee in all thy works and in all that thou puttest thine hand to do."

*Shabbat, 151b.*

### The Shorn Sheep

He who sets aside a portion of his wealth for the relief of the poor will be delivered from the judgment of Purgatory. The following parable is an illustration: two sheep attempted to ford a river; one was shorn of its wool, and the other unshorn; the former succeeded in crossing, but the latter, being heavy-laden, sank in the waters.

*Gittin, 7a.*

### Giving Life

R. Phinehas in the name of R. Reuben said: "If a man gives a perutah (a penny) to a poor man, will God repay him in perutahs?" "Nay, he gave not a perutah to the destitute man, but he verily gave him life. Suppose a loaf of bread sells for ten perutahs, and the poor man has only nine, does not this man enable him to buy life-preserving food by his gift of a perutah? God saith to the giver: "Thou hast saved the life of the poor man; when the time comes for your life to end, I will give it back to you."

*Wayyikra Rabbah, 34.*

## IMMEDIATE HELP

Nahum Ish Gamzu, one of R. Akiba's teachers, narrated the following experience: I was once travelling to the house of my father-in-law, taking with me three donkey-loads of food and drink. A starving man asked me for food. I answered that I would give him some when I unloaded, but before I could do so, he fell dead. I greatly grieved over his death, and prayed that the Lord send sufferings upon me in expiation for my sin. I should not have delayed my help, but should have cut through the load and given him food at once.

*Taanit, 21.*

## GOD CAN REVERSE

To one who has the means but withholds relief from the needy, God says: Keep in mind that it is I who made him poor and thee rich; I can also send reverses upon thee, and make thee poor and him rich.

*Tanhuma, Buber, Mishpatim, par. 8.*

## CHARITY WITHOUT RIGHT

He who takes charity without being entitled to it, will come to want before the day of his death. And if one who is entitled to it, leaves it to others still more needy, he will be able before he dies not only to support himself, but will serve as a prop to others.

*Mishnah Peah, 8, 9.*

R. Simeon said: "By the strength and power of Charity will the dead be resurrected. This we learn from the case of Elijah who wandered from mount to mount and from cave to cave. When he came to Zarephath, a widow received him with great hospitality. Although Elijah, the widow and her son ate from the widow's small store of bread and oil, the food remained plentiful because of Elijah. When, a few days later, her son became ill and died, the widow claimed the life of her boy from Elijah. Elijah then prayed to God: 'Master of the Universe, are not all these sorrows I have experienced enough that I must now bear the burden of the widow's complaint? If you will bring her son to life again the people will know that the dead will be resurrected.' His prayer was answered."

*Pirke d'R. Eliezer, chap. 33.*

## CHARITY AVERTS THE EVIL DECREE

The Sages used to say in the name of the Academy of Elijah, the Prophet: "Charity is important. From the day of creation until the very present day, one that has given charity is indeed praiseworthy and is saved from judgment in Gehenna, as it is said: 'Happy is he that considereth the poor: the Lord will deliver him in the day of evil.' Evil refers to that judgment, as it is said: 'Therefore remove vexation from thy heart, and put away evil from thy flesh. And it further says: 'Happy are they that keep justice, that do righteousness at all times.' "

*Seder Eliyahu Zuta, chap. 1, p. 169.*

## 43. CHARM AND ATTRACTION

There are three chief attractions: the attraction of a woman for her husband; the attraction of a city for its residents, and the attraction of an article purchased for its buyer.

*Sotah, 47.*

Close thine eye against beholding a charming woman, lest thou be caught in her net.

*Yebamot, 63.*

## 44. CHEATING AND MISLEADING

An experienced tradesman cannot protest that he has been cheated.

*Baba Metzia, 51.*

To deceive with words or abuse with the tongue is a greater offense than to cheat in matters of money.

*Baba Metzia, 58.*

Abbaye said: "If a man is asked to show his signature in court, he should ask for a sheet of blank paper, and sign on the very top line. Otherwise a man may find the paper and write above his signature that the signer owes him money. Such a document, even unwitnessed, is sufficient to collect unattached property."

*Baba Batra, 167.*

### Procedure

The Rabbis taught: "If a witness to a document wishes to do so, he may copy the subject of the document and retain it as a memorandum. If he is called upon in later years to acknowledge his signature, he may refer to this memorandum. This would prevent a forger from signing the name of a reputable person to a document."

R. Assi said: "If a witness to a document is dead or unavailable, his signature may not be compared with his signature on another document, unless the other document was contested in court, and the court certified its authenticity."

A document was once contested in court, containing the signatures of Rabba and R. Aha b. Adda. Rabba was called to acknowledge his signature. He looked at it carefully and said: "It seems to be mine, but I signed no paper with R. Aha b. Adda." After much effort the forger was induced to confess. Rabba said: "I understand that you were able to forge my signature with ease. But how were you able to forge R. Aha's aged and trembling signature?" The culprit answered: "I sat on a large leather bottle, and while it swayed under me, I imitated R. Aha's signature."

*Ketubot, 20.*

### Evil Types

Rab Gidal said in the name of Rab: "If a man from Neresh kisses you, count your teeth. If a man from Nehar Pekudah offers to escort you, be careful of your cloak. If a man from Pumbedita offers to guide you to an inn, go elsewhere at once." Rab Pappa said: "An anathema upon Neresh: its tallow, its hide and its tail." (Namely, all classes of people within it.)

*Hullin, 127.*

### The Ways of Jeroboam

Rab Judah said: "It is written (I Kings 12:28): 'Whereupon the king took counsel, and made two calves of gold.' What did Jeroboam do? He placed a righteous man beside a wicked one, and said: 'Will ye be loyal and obedient subjects to me?' Both replied in the affirmative. 'Even if I ask you to worship idols?' 'Of course not,' answered the good man. When the king departed, the wicked man said: 'Do you really expect that such a great sage seriously contemplates adopting idolatry? It is only a test. Let us both promise to obey him in all things.' The righteous man would be persuaded and would sign a pledge. Thus Jeroboam introduced idolatry, and protests were unavailing, since everyone had promised submission to his will. Even the Prophet Ahijah, the Shilonite, was misled into signing."

*Sanhedrin, 101.*

### Nullifying a Promise

A bargain made by words only is not binding, but the Sages say: The learned are not content with a man who nullifies his words. God will exact retribution from a man who does not hold fast to his word.

*Tosefta Baba Metzia, 3, 14.*

### Wronging with Words

Just as a man may wrong another in business transactions, so may he also wrong him by words. One should not say: For how much will you sell me this? when he has no intention of buying. One should not say to a penitent: Remember your former deeds. Nor to a proselyte: Remember the deeds of your fathers.

*Mishnah, Baba Metzia, 4, 10.*

## 45. CHILDREN

A man without children is as if he were dead.

*Nedarim, 64.*

When the children are blessed, the parents by this very token are blessed.

*Zohar, i, 227b.*

True compassion and true love exist only among children and for children.

*Zohar, ii, 276b.*

At three years of age a child is ready to be taught the Alphabet.

*Darke Mosheh, Tur, Yoreh Deah, 245, 4, quoting a Midrash.*

Do not threaten a child. Either punish or forgive him.

*Semahot, 2, 6.*

If thou must strike a child, strike it with the string of a shoe.

*Baba Batra, 21.*

A child in his own mind is inclined to exaggerate his own importance.

*Sukkah, 21.*

A child breaks into crumbs and wastes more than it eats.

*Pesikta Zutarti, Bereshit, 47.*

A man appreciates the love of his grandchildren more than the love of his children.

*Zohar, i, 233a.*

The purchase and sale of things by infants is legal only in small matters.

*Gittin, 59, Mishnah.*

### Even the Younger Children

The little children in Jerusalem were brought to the synagogues in order to be worthy of a reward. And when a lad became thirteen years of age, his father would bring him before each learned Elder for a blessing, that the Sage might encourage him, and might pray for him, that he might be worthy to learn and achieve much. Then the father would take his son before every man greater than himself for prayer. It is clear that the people of Jerusalem were admirable, that their deeds were excellent and their hearts directed to Heaven. And even the younger children would not be left behind when the families went to the synagogue, but they went along as well, in order that they might become accustomed to Mitzwoth.

*Sifre to Deut. 31:12.*

### THE CHILDREN'S SESSION

One stormy day the Sages lacked a quorum to open the session of the Academy. Some children entered and said: "Let us play holding a session." The child presiding called upon every playmate to discuss the theme: the significance of the double letters in the Hebrew Alphabet, namely those which have a different form when they occur at the end of a word. One child said: "We have two forms of the letter 'Mem' to signify that the 'Maamar' (Word) of God proceeded from God to Moses, and he transmitted it at once to Israel. It was then from Maamar to Maamar."

The second said: "The two 'Nuns' signify: from Ne'eman to Ne'eman, namely the Torah was given from the loyal Moses to the loyal Israel."

The third said: "The two 'Tzades' signify: From the Zaddik Moses to the Zaddik (Righteous) Israel."

The fourth said: "The two 'Pe's' are to teach: From Peh to Peh (Mouth to Mouth)."

The fifth said: "The two 'Kaphs' signify: From Kaph to Kaph (Hand to Hand) was the Torah given."

The few Sages present asked the children their names, and recorded their sayings. They grew into great scholars, and there was applied to them the verse: "Even when he is a child, the great man is recognized by his deeds." (Prov. 20:11).[1]

*Bereshit Rabbah, 1.*

[1] The letters may also mean: From God to Moses in each instance, rather than from Moses to Israel.

### THE CARE OF CHILDREN

When Rabbi Hanina was eighty years old, he was still able to stand on one foot and remove the shoe from the other. He said: "My strength in old age comes from the frequent warm baths and anointing in oil given my body during infancy."

When a child is a little older, he should be fed eggs and sour milk.

When he is still older, it is important for his development that he be given things to break. Rabbah often bought imperfect earthenware for his little ones to break if they wished.

*Hullin, 24.*

### ACCEPTABLE SURETIES

Rabbi Meir said: When the Israelites came to receive the Torah, God said to them: "Bring to Me good sureties that you will observe it." They answered: "Our Fathers will be our sureties." God answered: "Your sureties need sureties themselves. I have found fault with them." They answered: "Our Prophets will be our sureties." God replied: "I have found fault with them also."

Then the Israelites said: "Our children will be our sureties." They proved acceptable, and God gave to Israel the Torah.

*Shir ha-Shirim Rabbah, on verse 1:4.*

### COUNSEL REGARDING CHILDREN

We should not say to a child: I will give you something, and later change our mind. For this teaches the child to lie.

*Sukkah, 46.*

Touch not my Messiahs, namely my anointed ones, the children at school.

*Shabbat, 119b.*

Children receive the presence of the Shekinah.

*Kallah Rabbati, Baraita, 8.*

He who denies a child religious knowledge robs him of his inheritance.

*Sanhedrin, 91b.*

The child shall keep the memory green of his parents, and whenever he speaks of them it shall be with words of loving veneration.

*Kiddushin, 31b.*

The world itself rests upon the breath of the children in the schoolhouse.

*Shabbat, 119b.*

## 46. CHRISTIANITY [1]

If a man tell thee: I am God, he lies. If he tell thee, I am the Son of Man. he will end by regretting it. If he says: I shall ascend into Heaven, he merely makes this utterance, but he cannot fulfil it.

*Y. Taanit, 2, 1. See Numbers 23:19.*

I am first; I have no Father. I am last; I have no brother. And beside Me, there is no God; I have no son.

*Shemot Rabbah, 29, 5.*

How foolish of heart are the falsifiers! They say that God has a son. Behold, God permitted not Abraham to sacrifice his son. Does it stand to reason that He would permit His own son to be executed, without turning the world into chaos?

*Aggadat Bereshit, 31. Kimchi's Commentary to Psalm 82. Cambridge Edition.*

R. Simeon ben Lakish said: Why has God's seal the word: Emet (Truth)? Because: Aleph is the first letter, Mem the middle, and Tav, the last; as much as to say: "I the Lord am first," for I did not take over the rule from another; "And beside Me there is no god," for

[1] See Herford, R. Travers: *Christianity in Talmud and Midrash*, London, 1903.

I have no partner; "and with the last I am He" (Isaiah 44:6, and 41:4), for I shall not hand it over to another.

*Y. Sanhedrin, 18a.*

The Kingdom of Edom (Rome) will in the days to come make use of a coinage of clay (perhaps a defective religion).

*Tanhuma Terumah, 6.*

If the priests are without morality, who will donate to their churches?

*Bereshit Rabbah, 26, 5.*

A Galilean Sectary said: "Woe to ye, O Pharisees! Ye write in the Bill of Divorce, first the name of the Emperor and then, at the end, ye mention Moses." They answered: "Woe unto thee, O Galilean Sectary! Thy Bible has the name Pharaoh on the same page as the Name of God, and Pharaoh's name is written first."

*M. Yadaim, chap. 4.*

### THE FOOD LAWS

A Roman soldier asked R. Abba: "Why is it said about God: 'He hath given "tereph" (food) unto them that fear Him' (Psalm 111:5). Should it not be written: 'He hath given Tereph to the dogs'?" R. Abba replied: "Tereph is not the same as Terephah which is given to the dogs. If you ask why this word was chosen to signify food, I will explain it thus: God hath given the laws regarding food, as well as His other laws, to those who reverence Him, not to those who, like yourself, have no regard for them." [1]

*Zohar, i, 121.*

[1] The Zohar doubtless means a Christian soldier, and indicates that those who are unwilling to bear the burden of God's Laws cannot be considered in the same category as those who fear Him. God tests the respect of men for Him by commanding them to obey certain laws, for which they know no reason. See Isaiah 66:17.

### THE INCORRUPTIBLE MAGISTRATE

Ima Shalom, the sister of Rabban Gamaliel, wished to put to the test a certain non-Jewish magistrate who had let it be known that he accepted no bribes. She brought to him a gift of a golden candlestick, and later, appearing before him, said: "I wish to secure an equal share in my father's estate." The judge ordered it thus. Her brother protested: "But according to the Law of Moses, a daughter does not receive an equal share with a son." The judge replied: "Since you have been exiled from Jerusalem, a new law has come into force, whereby a daughter shares equally with a son."

R. Gamaliel sent him a valuable white ass, and asked for a retrial. The magistrate declared: "I have read further in the new law, and find written therein: 'I came not to detract from the Law of Moses, nor to add to it.' And in the Law of Moses, it is written that a daughter may not share equally with a son in the father's estate."

Ima Shalom remarked: "May thy light shine as a candle!"

Rabban Gamaliel retorted: "Nay, the ass kicked the candle over."  [1]

*Shabbat, 116.*

[1] Since R. Gamaliel, the brother-in-law of R. Eliezer ben Hyrcanus, lived at the end of the first century, it is not clear whether at this early time there were Christian judges in Palestine. The "incorruptible" magistrate, however, of this story, may have been an arbitrator, or unofficial judge.


## 47. COMPASSION

My children, fill yourselves with compassion, these upon these, and the Lord will be filled with compassion towards you.

*Bereshit Rabbah, 33, 3.*

He who hath compassion upon his fellow-men may be considered a true descendant of Abraham.

*Betzah, 32.*

He who hath compassion upon others receives compassion from Heaven.

*Shabbat, 151.*

If men have virtues, He gives them of the fruits of their deeds; if they have none, He gives them of His grace. Can there be compassion greater than this?

*Midrash Tehillim, i.*

Whoever takes pity on his fellow-beings, on him God in heaven will also take pity.

*Sifre Deut., 96.*

He who has pity on his fellow-men has the blood of Abraham in his veins.

*Betzah, 32b.*

He who is compassionate when he should be severe, ends by being severe when he should be compassionate.

*Kohelet Rabbah, 7.*

He who hath compassion in his heart for the poor shall have mastery over all creatures.

*Hakdamah—Zohar, 13b.*

He who hath compassion on a poor man and refresheth his soul, shall have it accounted to him as if he had created that soul.

*Zohar, ii, 198a.*

Every time that thou art compassionate, the Compassionate One shall have compassion upon thee.

*Tosefta Baba Kamma, 9.*

He who hath no compassion receives none from above.

*Shabbat, 151.*

He who is cruel to the compassionate ends by being compassionate to the cruel.

*Midrash Shemuel, 18.*

He who is cruel will receive cruelty himself.

*Zohar, iii, 83a.*

When the brethren of Joseph fell into his hands, it is written: "And he knew them." When he fell into their hands, it is written: "They knew him not."

*Bereshit Rabbah, 91, 7.*

### THE MIXED MULTITUDE

Shabbatai b. Marinus came to Babylonia, and asked the Jewish community leaders to lend him merchandise wherewith he might make a living as a peddler. When they refused, he asked them for food, but they refused this also. He then said: "They are descended from the mixed multitude who went forth with Israel from Egypt. For he who hath compassion upon his fellows is known to be descended from Abraham, and he who hath no compassion, is known to be not descended from the Patriarch."

*Betzah, 32.*

## 48. CONDUCT AND MANNERS

A man should accustom himself to be pleasant to people.

*Taanit, 4.*

He who walks in the straight paths of integrity honors God.

*Bemidbar Rabbah, 8.*

Thy good conduct will make thee friends, but thy evil conduct will make thee enemies.

*Eduyot, 5, 6.*

He who ponders upon his conduct brings much good to himself.

*Wayyikra Rabbah, 9, 3.*

He who has the approval of the Rabbis shares in the World-to-Come.

*Shabbat, 153.*

He who knows that his comrade is accustomed to greet him, should greet him first.

*Berakot, 6.*

When a student asks something of another student, the latter should answer to no more than he has been asked.

*Betzah, 20.*

Great is the honor due to men! Even a prohibition in the Torah gives way to it.

*Berakot, 19.*

A man should not enter a house suddenly, without ringing or knocking.

*Derek Eretz Rabbah, 5.*

A man should not enter another's home, until he is given permission to enter.

*Pesikta Zutarta, Wayyikra.*

A man should not drink of a glass, and give it to another to drink from it.

*Derek Eretz Rabbah, 9.*

A man should not bite off a slice, and return the piece into the dish.

*Derek Eretz Rabbah, 9.*

A man should not spit in the presence of another.

*Derek Eretz Rabbah, 10.*

I call heaven and earth to witness that whether it be Jew or Gentile, man or woman, manservant or maidservant, according to their acts does the Divine spirit rest upon them.

*Tana d'be Eliyahu, 207.*

Let a man first lead the good life, and then ask God for religious truth.

*Tana d'be Eliyahu, 162.*

The Divine test of a man's worth is not his theology but his life.

*Baba Kama, 38a.*

A man should not drink his goblet in one gulp. This is unmannerly.

*Betzah, 25.*

If you go to a certain place, conduct yourself in conformity with local usage.

*Zohar, i, 144a.*

Great is etiquette! It is equal to the whole Torah.

*Midrash Gadol u-Gedolah, 2.*

It is not customary for a man to take his sons with him to a banquet.

*Wayyikra Rabbah, 26, 7.*

Hillel said: Among those who stand, do not sit, and among those who sit, do not stand. Among those who laugh, do not weep; and among those who weep, do not laugh.

*Tosefta Berakot, 2.*

Rabbi Akiba said: For three things, I like the Medians. They cut meat only on the table, and not holding it on their hands. They kiss on the hand, and not on the lips. They hold counsel only in the fields, and not in a locked room.

*Berakot, 8.*

## THE SOFT TONGUE

Rabbi wished to teach his Disciples a lesson in good conduct. He invited them to a meal, and served to each, both a soft tongue, well-prepared, and a half-raw, tough tongue. They selected the soft and left the tough. "Let this be a lesson to you," said Rabbi. "The soft tongue is agreeable and the tough disagreeable to all of you. May your tongues be tender towards each other."

*Wayyikra Rabbah, 33.*

## THE WINE, THE CUP AND THE MAN

Rabbi Ishmael bar Jose visited Rabbi Simeon ben Jose ben Lekonya. The host handed him a cup of wine which he swallowed in a single gulp. Rabbi Simeon smiled and said: "It seems that you do not agree with the opinion that he who drinks a cup in one swallow is a drunkard."

Rabbi Ishmael answered: "The opinion does not apply to your wine, which is sweet; to your cup which is small, and to a man like myself, who am stout."

*Pesahim, 86.*

## THE CUSTOMS OF JERUSALEM

If a resident of Jerusalem married a woman from out-of-town, she brought him as a dowry her weight in gold. If a man from the provinces married a girl of Jerusalem, he was expected to give her her weight in gold.

No one of Jerusalem would attend a banquet unless he had been invited twice.

No one of Jerusalem would attend a banquet unless he knew who was seated at his table.

No one gave a banquet in his own home, but held it at a tavern: if aught was unpalatable, the owner was expected to pay a fine.

At a banquet, a flag was nailed to the door of the hall. When no more room was available, the flag was removed, and no one else was permitted to enter.

At a banquet, a menu was distributed, so that each might select according to his individual taste.

*Ekah Rabbah, 4.*

### THE PHILOSOPHER

Rabban Gamaliel and three companions visited a large city, and R. Joshua asked him whether he wished to pay a call on a great philosopher resident there. R. Gamaliel advised them to postpone their visit until the philosopher had time to know of their presence in town. Next forenoon, they went to his home and knocked at his door. The man thought to himself: "I shall wait to see if it is a person of good breeding who has come." When they knocked again, he washed and combed himself. At the third knock, he opened the door. When he beheld his distinguished visitors, he said to himself: "If I greet R. Gamaliel first, it will be a slight upon the others. If I greet all together, it will be a slight upon the Patriarch." Therefore he said: "Greeting, ye Sages in Israel, and R. Gamaliel in particular."

*Wayyikra Rabbah, 21.*

### THE MANNERS OF ANIMALS

R. Johanan said: Had the Torah not been given, we could have learned modesty from the cat, honesty from the ant, marital fidelity from the dove, and good manners from the rooster.

The ants live in a home of three stories. They do not occupy the upper story because of the rainwater; nor the understory because of the mud and the dirt; they occupy the middle story only. Though an ant's life lasts only six months, like all boneless insects, and though her food consists of but a grain and a half, she troubles to prepare her food in the summer for the winter months.

R. Simeon ben Halafta said: Once an ant lost her grain. Though others passed by, they smelled of it, and did not take it. It lay there until the ant who had lost it, returned for it.

What are the good manners of a rooster? Before he approaches a hen, he takes her a present, saying: Come to me and I shall give thee a gown of many colors. Later he says: May I lose my comb if I have the money to buy it, and fail to do so.

*Erubin, 100; Debarim Rabbah, 5.*

### A CIVIL QUESTION

Hillel once saw certain tradesmen bringing wheat to the city. He asked the price and was told: the seah measure for two denarii. He met others who gave the price as: the seah measure for three dinars. He declared: I have just met people who asked one dinar less. Why do you ask more?

They replied: It is obvious by your speech that you are one of the foolish Babylonians. Do you not know that there are various grades of wheat, and those grown with greater trouble command more money?

He said: I have asked you a civil question and you have answered uncivilly. Is this good conduct for gentlemen like yourselves?

They asked his pardon and promised to be courteous henceforth.

*Abot de-R. Nathan, 12.*

## MAKING AN EXPLANATION

Rab Huna bar Nathan visited Rab Nahman bar Isaac, who asked his guest: "What is thy name?"

"Rab Huna," he answered.

"Take a seat." He sat down immediately.

A beaker of wine was given him. Rab Huna accepted it at once, and drank it with one stop and without turning away his face.[1]

These actions were contrary to the manners in Rab Nahman's neighborhood, and he asked his guest: "Why do you style yourself Rab?"

"It is my first name."

"Why did you sit down at the first invitation?"

"Whatever your host invites you to do, we are taught to do."

"Why did you accept the beaker at once?"

"One should not run contrary to the wish of a greater man."

"Why did you drink it in two gulps?"

"We have been taught that he who drinks his cup in one gulp is a drunkard; it is mannerly to drink it in two."

"Why did you not turn away your face?"

"We are taught," answered Rab Huna, " 'A bride should turn her face away when she drinks wine, but not a man.' "

*Pesahim, 86.*

[1] Wine in Talmudic days was strong and usually was mixed with water. The custom of turning away the face was doubtless due to a desire to prevent the host from seeing the grimaces of the guest. Rab Huna believed that a man should take a strong drink like a man, without making grimaces at its strength. The expression: "They mixed him a drink or a cup," is synonymous with: "They handed him a drink or a cup." Raw wine was accounted undrinkable.

## 49. CONFESSION

He who confesses has a share in the World-to-Come.

*Sanhedrin, 43. Mishnah.*

If a man confesses his sins before his Maker, what labor does he leave to the Satan? The Satan can do nothing but depart.

*Zohar, ii, 41a.*

If a man confesses his sins, no Heavenly jury tries him, but he comes for trial before God alone. And God is good.

*Zohar, iv, 231a.*

If a man confesses his sins, he cannot be brought to judgment; for the Law says that a man cannot accuse himself of being wicked; and since he has already confessed his sins, a repetition by the Satan is not permitted.

*Zohar, iv, 231a.*

God says to Judah: I will enter into judgment with thee (namely, punish thee) because thou sayest: I have not sinned.

*Y. Taanit, 65d.*

If a man confesses his guilt in a mortal court, he is punished; if he does not admit it, he is sometimes freed. In the Heavenly Court, however, it is the opposite: if he confesses, he is forgiven; if he fails to confess, he is doomed to punishment.

*Midrash Tehillim, 100, 2.*

"He who conceals his transgressions shall not succeed; but he who confesses them (and then) forsakes them shall obtain mercy" (Prov. 28:13). Confession obtains mercy only on condition that the sinful way is forsaken.

*Pesikta, Buber, 159a.*

"Take with you words and return to the Lord" (Hosea 14:2). Lest one should imagine that empty words suffice, we are taught: For Thou art not a God that likes wickedness; evil cannot abide with Thee (Psalm 5:5); but with the confession and with pleas for mercy and with tears. This is the meaning of the phrase: Take with you words.

*Pesikta, Rabbatai, Friedman, 198b.*

## 50. CONTENTMENT AND COMPLAINT

The Rabbis have taught us who are to be accounted rich. Rabbi Meir said: He who is satisfied with his lot. Rabbi Akiba said: He who has a wife who is becoming in all her ways. Rabbi Jose said: He who is of good health.

*Shabbat, 25b.*

He who has a hundred desires two hundred.

*Kohelet Rabbah, 1, 13.*

He who complains at his chastisements receives a double portion of them.

*Eliyahu Rabbah, 2.*

Keep far from complaint lest thou cause harm to the innocent.

*Derek Eretz Zuta, 1.*

### The City of Birth

A Sophist said to the Emperor Diocletian that no man could be happy except in the place of birth; the same is true, he said, of animals. To substantiate his words, he sent marked stags to Phrygia, and after a few years they returned.

Rabbi Simeon ben Lakish was studying on a porch in Tiberias and he heard two women passers-by say: "How happy we are to leave this accursed climate." Interested, he asked them whence they had come and whither they were going. "We came from Mazega and we are returning," they said. Rabbi Simeon turned to his Disciples and remarked: "I was once in Mazega and found the climate there abominable. Yet the natives are convinced it is the very best of places. Blessed is God who giveth grace to a place in the eyes of its inhabitants."

*Bereshit Rabbah, 34.*

Who is truly rich? He who is happy in his portion.

*Abot, 4, 1.*

## 51.  COUNSEL

He who counsels the just man well, is as if he had observed the whole Decalogue.

*Bereshit Rabbah, 58, 8.*

It is an act of gracious manners on the part of an important man to invite the counsel of a lesser.

*Tikkune Zohar, 182b.*

Beware of him who gives thee advice according to his own interests.

*Sanhedrin, 76b.*

The old have no taste; the young have no power of counsel.

*Shabbat, 89.*

Keep far from marrying a wife who is a minor, from endorsing a loan, and from holding an article in trust.

*Y. Yebamot, 13, 1.*

Shemaiah's motto was: Love labor, shun office, and do not cultivate intimacy with the authorities.

*Abot, 1, 10.*

If aged persons tell thee to pull down, and young men say: build up, then pull down and build not; for the pulling down of the aged is equivalent to building up, and the building up of young men is equivalent to pulling down.

*Megillah, 31b.*

Follow the counsel of the aged, but act not upon the advice of the young.

*Derek Eretz Zuta, chap. 7.*

"Then the elders of the city shall call him and speak unto him" (Deut. 25:8). The elders themselves, and not the common members, shall call him, namely, the man who refuseth to marry his deceased brother's widow, and give the advice most proper in the matter. If he be but a youth and she an old woman, or if he be an aged man and she but a girl, they say: What couldst thou do with such an old woman, or with such a girl? Better far that thou shouldst marry one of thine own age, and so bring no dissension into thine house.

*Yebamot, 44a.*

### LEGAL ADVICE

A woman needed a little money and sold her marriage settlement to a money-lender for a small sum. Later she was divorced and died. Her daughter was heir to the marriage money, but the money-lender demanded it. Rab Nahman said to her: "Since your father is aged and has no sons, you are his heir. You have also the same right as your mother to make the settlement a gift unto your father. Do so, and later inherit his estate."

*Ketubot, 85.*

## 52. THE COVENANT OF CIRCUMCISION

Concerning five things the word: "Covenant" is written: Circumcision, the rainbow, salt, chastisements and the priesthood.

*Zohar Hadash, i, 4b.*

Rome and Byzantium will become but a memory, but the nation which practices circumcision will endure forever.

*Tikkune Zohar, Tikkun, 37, 112b.*

God is the Lord of the Covenant, the Torah is the Book of the Covenant, and the circumcised is the Son of the Covenant.

*Zohar, iii, 73b.*

No sin causes so much anger in the Lord as the sin of abandoning circumcision, as it is written: "And I will bring a sword upon you, that shall execute the vengeance of the covenant." (Lev. 26:25)

*Zohar, i, 66b.*

Happy are the Children of Israel! They willingly offer their male children as a sacrifice to God on the eighth day of their birth. The circumcision brings them into the good estate of God.

*Zohar, i, 93a.*

When Elijah complained that Israel had forsaken God's Covenant, he was commanded to be present in spirit wherever the Holy Covenant is observed for new-born Israelites. The tongue which testified that Israel had forsaken the Covenant must now testify that they are keeping the Covenant.

*Zohar, i, 93a.*

As the Altar outside the Temple was made of earth, so should the vessel containing the blood of the circumcision be filled with earth.

*Zohar, i, 95a.*

### THE BETTER HANDIWORK

Turnus Rufus asked R. Akiba: "If thou sayest that man's handiwork is better than God's, how do you explain that man cannot make the Heavens and the earth?"

"Ask me not concerning things not in man's power to perform, but about that which man can do," said R. Akiba.

"Very well then. Why are males born uncircumcised?" asked the Roman.

"I knew that thou wouldst ask me this, and therefore I said unto thee that man's work is better than God's. Man is required to improve upon nature. For example, God gives wheat to man, but man makes of it loaves. Is not man's work an improvement?"

*Tanhuma to Tazria.*

## 53. COVETOUSNESS

The eye sees and the heart covets.

*Bemidbar Rabbah, 10, 2.*

Let not thine eyes covet the possessions of another.

*Eliyahu Zuta, 17.*

## 54. CREATION AND EVOLUTION

The first man had a tail like an animal.

*Bereshit Rabbah, 14, 10.*

God created nothing in vain.

*Shabbat, 77.*

God revealed the earth in His wisdom, and He prepared the world for His congregation.

*Rosh ha-Shanah, 31.*

The First Man was not created out of the dust of this world, but out of the dust of the Upper Holy Temple.

*Zohar, iii, 83a.*

After all the creatures were made, God said to them: Let us make one more creature in partnership. Each of you shall have a share in him, and I will give him a portion of Myself."

*Zohar, iv, 238b.*

Rabbi Abbahu said "God had created and destroyed many worlds before He fashioned this world, but none satisfied Him except this one."

*Bereshit Rabbah, 3, 7 and 9, 2.*

Rabbi Akiba said: As a house implies a builder, and a garment a weaver, and a door a carpenter, so does the existence of the Universe imply a Creator.

*Midrash Temurah, chab. 5, end.*

There is a fanciful notion that God left unfinished the northern-most point of the earth; for, said He, "Whoever professes to be equal to God, let him come and complete this corner which I have left unfinished, and thus all will know that he is equal to God."

*Pirke de-Rabbi Eliezer, chap. 3.*

Rabbi Berechiah said: When God was about to create man, he reasoned thus with Himself: If I create him, then will the wicked proceed from him; but if I do not create him, how then shall the righteous come forth?" What did God do? He separated the ways of the wicked from before Him, and assuming the attribute of mercy, thus He created him.

*Bereshit Rabbah, 8.*

"The Lord God made earth and heaven" (Genesis 2:4). God deliberated: If I create the Universe in My merciful character alone, sins will abound; if in My just character alone, how can the world endure? I will create in both the just and the merciful character, and may it endure!

*Bereshit Rabbah, 12, 15.*

The greatness of God is infinite; for while with one die, man im-presses many coins, and all are exactly alike, the King of Kings with one die, impresses the same image (of Adam) on all men, and yet not one of them is like his neighbor. Thus it is that every one ought to say: "For myself the Universe is created."

*Sanhedrin, 37a.*

God created the world by a Word, instantaneously, without toil and pains.

*Bereshit Rabbah, 3, 2.*

Everything that God fashioned was perfect, as all His dealings with men are just and right. It is not for men to imagine improve-ments in His creation, or to question His providential rule in the Universe.

*Sifre Deut., par. 397.*

Everything that God fashioned belongs to the completeness of the created Universe.

*Shabbat, 77b.*

## As Beautiful, Always

Rabbi Hama and Rabbi Jonathan said: It is like a king who has built himself a beautiful palace. He gazes at it and is delighted with its appearance; and he says: "Palace, Palace, may I find you as beautiful every time, as I find you now." Thus God says: "My Universe, My Universe, may I find thee good in My eyes at all times, even as I find thee good now."

*Bereshit Rabbah, 9, 4.*

## Man Must Enjoy

Rabbi Aibo said: It is like a king who has filled his palace with enjoyments; if he has no visitors, what pleasure does he derive from them? Thus, when the Angels objected to the creation of man, God replied: "And of what use are all the good things I have created, unless men are there to enjoy them?"

*Bereshit Rabbah, 8, 5.*

## Nothing without Purpose

David said to God: "Thou hast created all things in wisdom, and the greatest thing Thou hast created is the capacity of a human brain to acquire and retain wisdom. But when I behold a witless man on the street with torn shirt and bare chest, with children running after him to torment him, I wonder why Thou hast permitted a human being to become insane. Why is there insanity in the Universe?"

God answered: "David, I created nothing without a purpose. A time will come when thou wilt see the uses of insanity itself."

When David escaped to Achish (I Sam. 21:14), and Achish, the King of Gath wished to slay him, David prayed to God: "Teach me the madness which Thou hast created." God instructed him in feigning madness, and David beheld then that even madness has a purpose.

*Shoher Tob, 34.*

Abnimos Hagardi asked the Sages: "How did the earth originally come into existence?"

Aba Joseph, the builder, replied: "God took some dust from beneath His throne of glory, and cast it over the waters and behold the earth was formed!"

*Shemot Rabbah, 13, 1.*

In answer to the question "How did the earth originally come into existence?" a Rabbi replied: "God shot a stone over the waters and from his shooting stone the earth was formed."

*Yoma, 54b.*

"And there was evening and there was morning the first day."
The Rabbis' interpretation of the words does not read, "Let there be
evening," but "And there was evening," to show "that the division of
days and the order of seasons was already existent before this."

*Bereshit Rabbah, 3, 8.*

R. Judah taught: "Man was first created with a tail like an animal,
but God afterwards removed this tail from him for his honor, not to
put him to shame."

*Erubin, 18a.*

It was said: "Up to the generation of Enosh the faces of the people
were K'kufot—they resembled those of monkeys."

*Bereshit Rabbah, 23, 9.*

The words: "There is yet much more work to be done" mean that
the process of the world's creation is only in its infancy.

*Pesikta Rabbati, 6, 25a.*

### POINTLESS PRIDE

Man was created on the sixth day. If ever he is filled with pride,
it can be said to him: A flea preceded thee in creation.

*Sanhedrin, 37.*

Why was man created a solitary human being, without a companion? So that it might not be said that there are several gods; and
that it might not be said: some races are better than others.

*Sanhedrin, 37.*

### TRUTH CAST DOWN

Rabbi Simeon said: When God wished to create man, Benevolence
advised his creation, on the ground that he would practice charity.
Truth, however, protested, on the ground that man would not adhere
to her. Righteousness favored man's creation, saying that many good
men would descend from him. Peace objected, fearing that man
would forsake her. What did God do? He cast Truth to the ground.

*Bereshit Rabbah, 8, 5.*

### GREATER THAN THE ANGELS

The Soul of Man was created on the first day; the Angels on the
second. If man keeps the Spirit of God dominant within him, he is
told: Thou art greater than the angels.

*Bereshit Rabbah, 8.*

## 55. DAMAGE TO PROPERTY

He who burns another's crop shall leave no son behind him as his heir.

*Sotah, 11.*

A man should destroy nothing of his property of which he may later be able to make use.

*Yebamot, 11.*

## 56. DEATH: THE DEAD

Those who die in the Holy Land, do so through an Angel of Mercy.

*Zohar, ii, 141b.*

Since God judges no one under twenty years of age, why do youths die before their time? Because God has pity upon them and takes them to Him while they are yet in their innocence, and He gives to them a sure reward in the World-to-Come.

*Tikkune Zohar, T. 40, p. 120b.*

People say: before a man is dead, his successor is ready.

*Baba Batra, 91.*

A man cannot say to the Angel of Death: I wish to arrange my affairs before I die.

*Debarim Rabbah, 9, 3.*

The Zaddik's soul is always desirous of leaving this world to enter Paradise.

*Midrash ha-Neelam, i, 98a.*

Rabbi Meir wrote on the margin of his Pentateuch: "And it was very good, namely Death."
Death is very good because it takes man to a sinless world, where the battle with his impulses is ended.

*Bereshit Rabbah, 9 and commentary.*

### ALMS FOR THE ANGEL OF DEATH

When the time came for Rabbi Hiyya to die, the Angel of Death could not approach him. The Angel disguised himself as a beggar, and knocked at the door of Rabbi Hiyya. The Rabbi gave him some bread, and the supposed beggar said: "You pity me as a beggar; why dost thou not pity me as a Messenger of God, commissioned to bring thee before Him?"
The Rabbi gave up his soul without further protest.

*Moed Katon, 28.*

### Bar Kappara's Riddle on Death

When it looketh down from heaven,
It spreadeth a tremor on every side,
E'en flying creatures become craven
When they behold it earthward glide.

The young see it and flee,
The aged rise helplessly,
The escaped shout in glee,
The captured exit sinfully.

*Y. Moed Katan, 3.*[1]

[1] S. Sekles in *Poetry of the Talmud*, p. 38, gives the following version:

High from heaven her eye looks down,
Constant strife excites her frown,
Winged beings shun her sight,
She puts the youth to instant flight.

The aged, too, her looks do scout;
Oh! Oh! the fugitive cries out.
And by her snares who'er is lured,
Can never more from sin be cured.

The original Hebrew has seven lines and does not rhyme. Sekles quotes from Graetz, iv, 158, the answer of Rabbi's Servant Maid or Housekeeper, who tyrannized over the Disciples. A second answer offered is: the Herem or Ban. The answer "Death" is given in Yalkut Sippurim, and is taken from the commentary "Pnei Moshe." The "Korban Ha-Edah" gives two answers: either the Soul or the Sheol. The last word: Sheol may be read in the original and appears to be the correct answer. Dr. Guttman of the Breslau Seminary believes that the "Ban" is correct.

The dead have lost the opportunity of obeying the Divine commands.

*Shabbat, 30a.*

The Rabbis ask: "Why does the Bible in recording David's death, say: 'And David slept with his fathers'? Why does it not say: 'And David died'?

"Because," replied the Sages, "David left a son who walked in the good ways of his father, and who continued his noble deeds; therefore, David was really not dead, but lived on through the good deeds of his son."

*Baba Batra, 116a.*

The mystics conceived of the body as an encumbering garment which falls away at death and leaves the true man free to rise into the light of the heavenly life.

*Zohar to Terumah.*

### In Death a Kind Deed

When King David had completed the Book of Psalms, he felt exceedingly proud, and said: "Lord of the Universe, hast Thou a creature that proclaimeth more praises of Thee than I?"

God thereupon sent to him a frog, which said: "David, take not such pride in thyself. I chant the praises of my Creator more than dost thou. Moreover, I am performing a great Mitzwah. For when my time to expire is at hand, I go to the shore of the sea, and permit myself to be swallowed up by one of its creatures. Thus even my death is a deed of kindness."

*Yalkut Shimeoni, ii, 889.*

## THE FINAL INTEREST

A very old woman came to Rabbi Jose ben Halafta and said: "Rabbi I wish to live no longer. I find no taste in food or drink; my limbs are heavy, and I should rejoice to take my departure from the world."

The Rabbi said: "Have you then no interest left in life? Is there nothing you still perform with a degree of alacrity?"

The old woman answered: "I go daily to the synagogue; this is my sole interest in life."

The Rabbi said: "If you feel too weary to continue living, try giving up this interest as well."

She ceased going to the synagogue, and on the third day, sickened and died.

*Yelamdenu, quoted in Yalkut, i, 871.*

## MUST MAN DIE?

R. Abba asked R. Judah: "We are taught that the Torah was inscribed on High long before man was created. And in the Torah it is written that man shall die, whether he be just or wicked. Is there no difference between the good and the evil in this world?"

R. Judah answered: "We cannot know the ways of God, but perhaps we may discover a difference. Had man been perfect in everything he did, he might never have died, but would merely have been summoned to Heaven alive, as was Elijah."

*Zohar, iii, 159.*

## THE LONG SLEEP

The daughters of Rab Hisda said to him: "Father, why dost thou not lie down for a siesta?"

He replied: "Soon, very soon, the days will come when I shall have my long slumber. Now I ought to increase my knowledge of Torah."

*Erubin, 64.*

## THE TWO VESSELS

Man's exit from the world, as compared to and contrasted with his entry into it, is portrayed by Rabbi Levi thus: Of two vessels sailing on the high seas, the ship which has come into port, is in the eyes of the wise, much more an object of joy than the ship about to leave the harbor. Even thus should we contemplate man's departure from this world without sorrow or fear, seeing that at death he has already entered the harbor—the haven of rest in the World-to-Come.

*Shemot Rabbah, 48, 1.*

## 57. COMFORTING ON DEATH

### WHEN THE FIG IS RIPE

In hot weather, a Rabbi delivered his discourse to his Disciples under the shade of a fig tree. They noticed that each morning the owner would pick his ripened figs. "Perhaps he fears that we will pick his fruit," they thought, and they moved to another place. The owner begged them to return. Believing that they had moved because his presence annoyed them, he resolved not to pick the fruit. In the evening, they beheld the figs dropping from the trees, spoiled by the heat of the sun. The Disciples then appreciated why it was necessary for the owner to pick them in the morning.

The Rabbi said: "The owner of the figs knows when his fruit should be picked, lest it be spoiled. Thus does God know when to summon His righteous children before they are spoiled. This is the reason why many good and gracious persons are sometimes called by God in their early manhood."

*Shir ha-Shirim Rabbah, 6.*

### THE JEWELS

While Rabbi Meir was holding his weekly discourse on Sabbath afternoon, his two beloved sons died suddenly at home. Their mother covered them with a sheet, and forbore to mourn on the sacred day. When Rabbi Meir returned after the evening Services, he asked for his sons, whom he had not seen in the synagogue. She asked him to recite the Habdalah and gave him his evening meal. Then she said: "I have a question to ask thee. A friend once gave me jewels to keep for him; now he wishes them again. Shall I return them?"

"Beyond doubt thou must," said Rabbi Meir.

His wife took him by the hand, led him to the bed and drew back the sheet. Rabbi Meir burst into bitter weeping, and his wife said: "They were entrusted to us for a time; now their Master has taken back His very own."

*Midrash Mishle, 28.*

### REASON FOR TEARS

Rabbi Johanan visited Rabbi Eleazar ben Pedat, who was lying ill. He found him weeping and asked: "Why art thou weeping? Is it because thou hast not mastered the Torah? We have the authority of tradition: it matters not whether much or little, if only a man directs his mind to Heaven."

*Berakot, 5b.*

### Sources of Comfort

A man died in the neighborhood of Rab Judah; the family had no friends in the town, and the Rabbi came to them for seven days with ten people. And he comforted the mourners.

*Shabbat, 152.*

Once a house fell in Usha, and killed the owner's son and daughter. All the young men were stationed on one side, and all the young women on the other. And they bewailed the great loss.

*Semahot, 11.*

Thus did Rabbi Judah: When he would behold a wedding or a funeral procession passing by, he would call the attention of the Disciples to it, and say: Doing takes precedence over learning.

*Semahot, 11.*

### The Death of a Child

When Rabbi Abbahu's child died, he said: "We are taught that after the execution of a person condemned by an earthly Court, where lies, deception, favoritism and bribery may have existed, whose judges are but mortal beings, the kinsfolk come and pleasantly greet the judges and witnesses to demonstrate that they have no grievance in their heart against them, because they have judged truthfully. How much the more then, after a person has surrendered his life according to the decree of the Heavenly Tribunal, where no human defects and shortcomings exist, should we not receive with humility and submission the verdict of Heaven."

*Y. Sanhedrin, 6.*

### A Jewel from the King

When Rabban Johanan ben Zakkai's son died, Rabbi Eliezer ben Arak came to offer consolation. He said: "To whom may I liken you? To a man who has received for safekeeping a jewel from his king. As long as he has it beneath his roof, he is troubled with anxiety regarding it; when the king takes it back in the same good condition, the man rejoices. You, O Master, have received for safekeeping a dear soul. He studied much and well, and died without sin. You have returned it in perfection, and you should find comfort in the knowledge of this."

Rabban Johanan thanked him heartily.

*Abot de-Rabbi Nathan, 14.*

## 58.  FUNERAL ORATIONS

### A Scholar's Death

When R. Simeon b. Zebid died, R. Leia ascended the pulpit and said: "If we lose gold, silver, iron or copper, there is sufficient exactly like it to be obtained; but if we lose a scholar like him who has gone, who can bring us one like him, to take his place?"

R. Levi ascended the pulpit, and said: "When Joseph's brothers found their money, their hearts failed them (Gen. 42:29). We have lost more than our wealth. Shall not our hearts fail us?"

*Y. Berakot, 2.*

### The Sleep of the Diligent

When R. Bun b. R. Hiyya died, R. Zeira ascended the pulpit, and said: "To what is the case of R. Bun like? To a king who has hired workmen for his garden, and observes that one of them works expertly and efficiently. He calls him over and walks with him about the garden. In the evening, when the king pays his workmen, he gives to the capable man the same pay as to the others. The latter protest to the king: 'But he has worked only two hours, and we have worked for eight.' 'True,' answers the king, 'but he has accomplished more in the two hours than you in eight.' Likewise, 'My beloved is gone down to His garden' (Song of Songs 6:2). R. Bun has labored in the Torah during his twenty-eight years more than another fine student in a hundred years. Therefore God summoned him to walk with Him. May 'the sleep of the diligent worker be sweet.'" (Eccl. 5:11)

*Shir ha-Shirim Rabbah, 6.*

## 59.  DEATH AND LAST HONORS

### To Honor the Torah

Two young children of R. Akiba died. Numberless people came to pay them last honors. R. Akiba stood upon a high stool and cried out: "Brethren in Israel, hearken unto me! Even if my sons had been old enough to be bridegrooms, I would feel consoled by the great honor you are showing. But have ye come for the sake of Akiba? Nay, for there are many named Akiba. Ye have said to yourself: 'The Torah of his God is in his heart' (Psalm 37:31). Ye came to honor the Torah and your reward is great. Return to your homes in peace."

*Moed Katon, 21b.*

### As in a Dream

R. Nahum bar Simai would never gaze upon the engraving upon a coin, or at a statue. He was therefore called, Nahum, the Holy of Holies. When he died, the Rabbis ordered that all engravings in the mortuary be covered. Some asked: "Is then a corpse aware of anything?" R. Simeon ben Levi answered: "The difference between us and the holy dead rests solely in the power of speech." And R. Zeira said: "The corpse hears the eulogies delivered at the bier as if in a dream."

*Y. Abodah Zarah, 3.*

### LIFTING THE BURDEN

In times long ago funeral expenses were so high that kinsmen would leave their dead and move away. Rabban Gamaliel ordained in his testament that he be buried in simple linen raiment, and thus the burden was lifted.

*Moed Katon, 27.*

### EQUALITY IN DEATH

The Rabbis have taught: formerly those who came to a wealthy mourner with the first meal after the funeral would bring him the food in golden baskets; to the poor mourners, however, they brought food in wicker baskets. The poor felt humiliated, and therefore it was ordained that food should be brought to all mourners only in wicker baskets.

To wealthy mourners, they brought wine in decanters of white glass; to the poor, in vessels of colored glass. Again the poor felt humiliated, because white glass was more costly. Therefore it was ordained that wine should be brought to all mourners in colored glasses.

Formerly the deceased of the wealthy were buried in fancy caskets, of the poor in cheap coffins. This, too, was altered, and now all who die, whether rich or poor, are buried in inexpensive caskets.

*Moed Katon, 27.*

## 60. DEATH AND THE LAST WORDS

### THE RECORD OF CHARITIES

When Mar Ukba was near death, he asked that his record of charities be added up. It was found that he had distributed 7000 denarii. Mar Ukba sighed and said: "The way before me is long indeed, and the provision I have prepared for myself very little." And he ordered that half his possessions be given to charity.

It was asked: How was he able to do so? Did not Rabbi Elai say that the Great Beth Din (Sanhedrin) at Usha adopted a resolution to the effect that a man give no more than one fifth of his property to charity at one time? The answer was: this resolution applied to one in sound health, lest he become impoverished. It does not apply, however, to a man near death.

*Ketubot, 67.*

## WITH TEN FINGERS

Rabbi, the Holy, when dying, lifted up his ten fingers towards Heaven, and said: "Lord of the Universe, it is open and well-known unto Thee, that with these ten fingers I have labored unceasingly in the Torah; I have never sought after any worldly profit with even so much as my little finger. May it therefore please Thee that there may be peace in my rest."

*Ketubot, 104b.*

## THE FEAR OF MAN

When Rabbi Johanan ben Zakkai was sick unto death, his Disciples came to visit him, and before leaving him, they said: "Master, give us thy farewell blessing." And he said unto them: "Oh that the fear of God may be as much upon you as the fear of man." His Disciples remarked: "Should we not fear the Lord more than man?" He replied: "If you should fear to sin in private where only God is aware of it, as much as you fear to sin in public, it were all that could be desired."

*Berakot, 28b.*

## DYING AWAY FROM ISRAEL'S LAND

Ulla's home was in the Land of Israel, but he died in Babylonia. Before he breathed his last, he wept bitterly. "Cease thy weeping," he was told. "We promise to take your body for burial to the Land of Israel." "Of what avail is this to me?" he replied. "I am losing my jewel in an unclean land. Can ye compare one who gives away his dearest [1] while on the lap of his mother,[2] to one who gives it away in the lap of a strange woman?"

*Y. Kilaim, chap. 9.*

[1] His soul.
[2] Palestine.

## THE WAYS OF LIFE

The Disciples of Rabbi Eliezar gathered about his sick-bed, and asked him: "Master, teach us the ways of life, that by them we may attain eternal life." He answered: "Be careful of the honor of your fellow; restrain your sons from reading superficially; set them between the knees of scholars. And when you pray, know before Whom you stand. Thus will you attain to the life of the World-to-Come."

*Berakot, 28a.*

## SO LITTLE DONE; SO MUCH TO DO

When R. Eliezer was on his death-bed, he was visited by R. Akiba and his companions. R. Eliezer sighed and said: "Much Torah have I learned, yet I have not received from my Teachers any more than a dog who licks the salty water of the sea. Much Torah have I taught, yet my disciples have received from me only as much as a tiny brush absorbs by one dip into a vessel of paint."

When he died, R. Akiba beat his hands against his breasts, and cried out: "Father, Father, I have much money, and there is no banker to change it into small coins."[1]

*Sanhedrin, 68.*

[1] Many difficulties in Torah, and no one to explain them.

## DEATH-BED CONFESSION

The man about to die is exhorted to confess in this formula: "May my death be an expiation for all my wickedness." Confession of the particular offense is not exacted.[1]

*Mishnah Sanhedrin, 6, 2.*

[1] In the Mishnah this applies to one about to be executed for a capital crime. This, however, is the present formula for death-bed confession.

## WHEN RABBI DIED

When Rabbi felt that his last hour had come, he called in his sons and said to them: "Honor your Mother." It was asked: Does not the Torah enjoin this? Answer was made: it was meant for their step-mother.

Rabbi next summoned the Sages of Israel. He said to them: "Re-open the School after thirty days. Though my son Simeon is the most learned among my sons, appoint my eldest Gamaliel as President of the Academy; Hanina bar Hama shall be Chairman." On that day, the Rabbis decreed a fast, and maintained prayer throughout the entire day. His servant-maid went to the roof of the house, and prayed: "Those on High desire Rabbi, and those below desire him. May it be Thy will that the wish of those below prevail." When she beheld Rabbi's agonies, she cried out: "May those on High prevail!" She cast a pitcher down, and the Rabbis halted their prayers for a moment. And in that very moment Rabbi died.

Rab Nahman in the name of R. Mana said: "The day was Fri-day." Nevertheless, though countless people assembled to pay Rabbi the final honors, and the funeral lasted many hours, the people had time to complete their preparations for the Sabbath before it became dark. When they looked at the sky, they grew anxious lest they had desecrated the Sabbath. A Voice from Heaven was heard to say: "Whosoever did not perform with indolence the final honors will have a goodly share in the World-to-Come."

*Ketubot, 103.*

## 61. DEATH AND MOURNING

### Appropriate Food

Why are peas the proper food for mourners? As the pea rolls, so does mourning roll from one person to the other.

*Baba Batra, 16.*

### Weep Not Overmuch

Jeremiah said: "Weep ye not for the dead, neither bemoan him" (Jeremiah 22:10). Weep not overmuch and bemoan not beyond the measure. What is the measure? Three days for weeping; seven days for bemoaning; thirty days for not donning clothes that have been pressed, and for not having the hair cut. From now on, saith the Lord, ye may not feel more compassion over him than I do.

*Moed Katon, 27.*

### The Origin of the Mourner's Kaddish

Some say that the Kaddish for a son who mourns his parent originated in this way. A Tanna dreamed he was walking in a deserted place and encountered a spirit loaded with wood. Answering his inquiry, the spirit said that he had been sentenced to carry the wood to Gehenna for a heinous sin he had committed. "Is there any way I can be of help to you?" asked the Rabbi. "Yes, I left a young son in this town (and he named it), and his name is (and he gave the name). If he should go to the synagogue and declare in public a recitation of praise unto the Lord, my sin will be remitted."

The Tanna searched for and discovered the son, and since he knew no Hebrew, he taught the boy the Kaddish in a mixed Hebrew and Aramaic.

*Midrash on the Decalogue.*

### Mourning Rules and Customs

Samuel said: "When Nadab and Abihu died, God ordered their brothers not to allow their hair to grow long, and not to rend their garments because of their holy office. This teaches that others, who are not officiating priests, in mourning for the death of one of their family, should not cut their hair, and should rend their garments."

*Moed Katon, 24.*

R. Hinna bar Papa came to console Rab Tanhum bar Hiyya, who was a mourner, and saw that his clothes were not rent. R. Tanhum explained: "These are not the garments I wore when the death occurred, and these I need not rend."

*Y. Moed Katon, 3.*

When a Sage dies, all are as his kinsfolk. When Rab Saphra died, the Rabbis did not rend their garments, saying: "He taught us naught." Abbaye replied: "The rule does not mention a teacher, but a Sage; moreover we do repeat his teachings in school indirectly."

*Moed Katon, 24.*

He who sees a Sage die is as if he saw a Sepher-Torah burn. R. Abbahu said: "I fast on such a day."

*Y. Moed Katon, 3.*

One must rend his garments when he hears that Jews have been murdered. Samuel heard that King Sapor ordered many Jews executed, yet he did not rend his garments. It was said: "But Sapor boasted that he did not kill any Jews." The comment was: "They were rebels, and were themselves responsible for their own fate."

*Moed Katon, 26.*

Rab said: "When a man dies in a town, all must halt their work and attend the funeral." Rab Hamnuna came to a town. He heard a Sexton announce that a man had died, but observed that many persons did not lay aside their work. "Why?" he wished to know. "Because we do not belong to the dead man's society." "If this be the case," said the Rabbi, "you may continue your work."

*Moed Katon, 27.*

A mourner may not learn or teach; but if many need his teaching, he may teach. A man who mourns his wife may remarry if small children are left; but others must wait thirty days.

*Moed Katon, 27.*

## 62. REFLECTIONS IN THE HOUR OF DYING

In the day of death, a man considers that he has lived but a single day.

*Zohar, i, 98b.*

A man does not tell lies in the hour of death.

*Y. Baba Kamma, 9, 7.*

A man does not joke in the hour of death.

*Baba Batra, 175.*

### THE PROTECTING WINGS

Rabbah bar Nahmani was so popular a teacher that many thousands visited his School to hear his popular discourses before Pesach and Sukkot. The tax-collectors complained that they did not find the people at home, and the government decreed that Rabbah should be sent to prison. Rabbah escaped and hid himself. In his hiding-place he did not cease from studying, and the Angel of Death, who was to summon him, could not approach him. He, therefore, simulated the noise of a marching regiment, and Rabbah interrupted his studies. He was then overcome by death.

His disciples, led by Abbaye, went in search of him, after appeasing the government, and noticed a great number of birds hovering in the air. They sought out the spot, and found that the birds, by the shadow of their wings, were shielding the dead body of their Master.

*Baba Metzia, 86a.*
*The supernatural portion is omitted.*


## 63. DECISION BY MAJORITY RULE

R. Yannai said: God did not give to Moses the final ruling on the laws. He selected as an example, a certain law, and showed Moses that it could be applied pro and con in actual cases. Moses asked: "But how shall we decide?" God replied: "Place the question to a vote following the discussion, and decide according to the opinion of the majority."

*Shoher Tob, 12.*

Said R. Tanhum: "Had the Torah been given in cut and dried form, the Teachers of the Law would have lost prestige entirely if they had erred. But since final rulings were not given, Teachers who follow reason are not regarded as guilty of errors, since they can find companions to share their opinions. The decision by the majority contrary to the opinion of some Teachers does not stamp the latter as guilty of error."

*Pesikta Rabbati, 21, 6.*


## 64. DEDICATION

He who builds a home should say: "I dedicate it to God and not to the Satan."

*Zohar, iii, 50a.*

There were Seven Dedications: Of Heaven and Earth; of the Wall of Jerusalem, of the Temple of Solomon, of the Temple of Zerubabel, of the Priests, of the Chiefs of Tribes, of the Hasmoneans and of the Future Temple.

*Pesikta Rabbati, Piska, 2.*


## 65. DILIGENCE AND EFFICIENCY

If a Mitzwah comes to you, do not let it sour.

*Mekilta Bo.*

A man should not be wasteful or neglectful of his properties.

*Arakin, 24.*

The eager man sometimes profits and sometimes loses by his eagerness.

*Pesahim, 50.*

Carefulness brings efficiency in its train.

*Abodah Zarah, 20.*

### THE SELAIM OF MAR SAMUEL

Mar Samuel said: "The landowner who visits his field or garden every day finds a selah (coin)."

R. Assi visited his garden daily for a long time. Finally he remarked: "Oh, where are Mar Samuel's selaim?"

One day he noticed a slight break in the irrigation dam, threatening to release too much water, and thereby to damage the garden. He removed his robe and stuffed it into the breach. When he raised a cry, several workmen came running and repaired the dam. "I have found all the selaim of Mar Samuel,'" said R. Assi.

*Hullin, 105.*

## 66. DREAMS

The words of dreams neither benefit nor harm.

*Gittin, 52.*

A dream that is not interpreted is like a letter that is unread.

*Berakot, 55.*

In a dream no one sees a golden tree or an elephant going through the eye of a needle. We see at night in dreams only that of which we were thinking by day.

*Berakot, 55.*

As it is impossible for stalks of grain to be free of straw, so is it impossible for a dream to be entirely without worthless elements.

The interpretation of a dream sometimes determines the actual event. If we interpret a dream beneficently, good may result.

A dream is a prophecy in miniature. A fast helps counteract an evil dream, and it should be observed on the very day, even if it be the Sabbath.[1]

*Berakot, 55; Shabbat 11.*

[1] Dreams in the Bible are full of meaning. But false dreams are recognized. (Zechariah 10:2; Eccl. 5:2)

### TWENTY RAFTERS

A man came to R. Jose ben Halafta and said: "I was told in a dream to go to Cappadocia and secure there my father's savings."

"Did your father ever go to Cappadocia?"

"Nay," answered the man.

"Then count twenty rafters in your house," said R. Jose.

"But there are no twenty rafters," the man answered.

"Then count from the top to the bottom, and after that, count from the bottom to the top. When you reach twenty, remove the rafter, and there you will find the money."

This proved to be correct. How did the Rabbi know? He read the word in its Greek meaning: Kapa is twenty, and Dokia is rafters.

*Bereshit Rabbah, 68.*


## 67. DRESS

People say: Rob thy belly and adorn thy body.

*Baba Metzia, 52.*

The garments of skins which God made for Adam and Eve were from the skin cast off by the serpent.

*Pirke de R. Eliezer, 20.*

Before they sinned Adam and Eve were clothed in garments of Or (Light; spelled with an Aleph); afterwards, they were clothed with garments of 'Or (Skin; spelled with an 'Ayin), the skin of the snake.

*Tikkune Zohar, T. 58, 131a.*

### ACCORDING TO YOUR MEANS

A man came to Rabbi dressed in cheap clothes. R. Ishmael said to Rabbi: "His father is exceedingly wealthy." Rabbi replied: "When you see his father, tell him not to send his son to me in such cheap attire." It was explained that Rabbi implied that if he dressed so poorly, the collectors of charity would not know that he was able to give liberally to charity.[1]

*Erubin, 85.*

[1] See the Hasidic story, "The Meal of Stones," *The Hasidic Anthology,* p. 467.

### THE SAGES OF BABYLONIA

R. Hiyya bar Abba asked R. Assi: "Why do the Sages in Babylonia dress in so distinguished a manner?"

R. Assi replied: "Because they are minor scholars, they desire to be respected because of their attire."

R. Johanan overheard him and said: "Thou art wrong. They dress well because they are emigrants there; and the popular saying runs: 'In my own town I am respected for the name I have achieved; in another town I receive my respect because my clothes lend me distinction.'"

*Shabbat, 145.*

### 68. EARS

Do not permit the ear to hear anything to which it is not able to listen.

*Midrash Tehillim, 1, 4.*

If thou givest thy ear to hear a little, thou wilt end in having heard much. If thou understandest a little, thou wilt end in understanding much.

*Sifre, Reeh, 79.*

Come and see: when a man is sorely injured, the physician must plaster him all over, in order to give him life. But God merely saith: Give Me thine ear, and thou wilt have life.

*Pahad Isaac, quoting a Midrash.*

### 69. EATING AND DINING

People say: Many viands lead to many sins.

*Berakot, 32.*

The palate consumes the gold.[1]

*Wayyikra Rabbah, 18.*

[1] Fancy eating wastes a man's fortune.

He who eats a tenth of an Ephah at a meal is healthy and blessed. He who eats more betrays his greedy character; he who eats less will be afflicted by ills.

*Erubin, 83.*

If a man chews well with his teeth, his feet will find strength.

*Shabbat, 152.*

Food is better for a man up to the age of forty; after forty drink is better.

*Shabbat, 152.*

He who blows at the foam of his glass is not thirsty.

*Sanhedrin, 100.*

He who sees what he eats is different from him who does not see what he eats.

*Yoma, 74.*

He who eats in the street is like a dog.

*Kiddushin, 40.*

In the World-to-Come a man will be asked to give an account for that which, being excellent to eat, he gazed at and did not eat.

*Y. Kiddushin, end.*

He who talks much grows thirsty.

*Bereshit Rabbah, 98, 13.*

People say: a sated man always find room for a delicacy.

*Erubin, 82.*

If you have a fine meal to consume, enjoy it in a good light.

*Yoma, 74.*

More people die from overeating than from undernourishment.

*Shabbat, 33.*

A man can live without spices, but not without wheat.

*Midrash Tehillim, 2, 16.*

Is man vouchsafed a feast without labor? [1]

*Shabbat, 153.*

[1] Can anyone acquire the bliss of Paradise without working for it?

Sixty maladies overtake a man who beholds another man eat without being asked to share.

*Baba Kamma, 92.*

Before a man can pray that the words of the Torah should enter his being, he should pray that delicacies of food may not enter.

*Eliyahu Rabbah, 26.*

Eating small fruits makes a man small.[1]

*Berakot, 44.*

[1] Small fruit is oftentimes unripe and unhealthy.

A healthy man eats what he receives; an ill man seeks delicate food.

*Shir ha-Shirim Rabbah, 2.*

Eat a third, drink a third, and leave empty in your stomach the remaining third. If anger overtakes you, there will be room for the expansion of your stomach, and you will not suffer from apoplexy.[1]

*Gittin, 70.*

[1] Maimonides quotes this counsel.

R. Judah ben Pedayah said: "Who will uncover the veil from thine eyes, O Adam! For a single hour thou couldst not restrain thy desire to eat of a forbidden fruit. Yet thy descendants wait three years, and eat not of the forbidden fruit, as it is written: 'Three years shall it be forbidden unto you; it shall not be eaten.'"

*Bereshit Rabbah, 21.*

When a man sits down at his table, the Shekinah and an Evil Spirit both stand by. If the man says grace, the Shekinah pushes forward to receive the words. If the man says no grace, the Evil Spirit pushes forward to receive the profane talk.

*Zohar, iv, 186b.*

A man is forbidden to eat anything until the King on High receives His share, namely, the words of grace.

*Zohar, iv, 241b.*

Regard thy table as the table before the Lord. Chew well, and hurry not.

*Zohar, iv, 246a.*

Man may win purification and forgiveness at his table, if he does two things: invites the needy to partake of his meal, and speaks words of Torah.

*Zohar, ii, 154a.*

The Talmud uses the expression "Dat" together with Torah, "K'dat Shel Torah," to designate "the directions of the Torah" with regard to the menu of a meal.

*Megillah, 12a.*

If words of the Torah are spoken at a meal, it is as if God has shared in it.

*Zohar, ii, 154a.*

A man's table may bring him merit in the World-to-Come; it may make him worthy to receive abundance in This World; and it may make him worthy to be remembered for good by the Ancient of Days.

*Zohar, ii, 154a.*

A man should be clean within and without before going to his table to eat; this is appropriate for a man; it is healthful and it builds up his body.

*Zohar, ii, 154a.*

The bread of a man may win him the merit of yet other bread, namely, the Bread of Paradise.

*Zohar, ii, 156b.*

Before thou eatest thy piece of bread, remember that ten Mitzwot have been performed in preparing it for thy consumption: it was not sown on the Sabbath day or the Sabbath year; it was not plowed then; the ox's mouth was not tied while he worked in the field; the grower has not gathered the left-over and forgotten sheaves; he has not reaped the ends of the field; he has given the Terumah and the tithe to Levi; the second tithe and the tithe of the poor has he given. And thy wife has separated a piece of the dough as Hallah for the Kohen.

*Y. Hallah, 1.*

Ulla visited Pumbedita and a friend set before him a basket of dates. He enjoyed their taste and inquired the price: "Three baskets for a zuz," was the reply. Ulla remarked: "How fortunate are the Babylonians! Three baskets of dates sweet as honey, for one zuz. It is a wonder that more people do not occupy themselves with the study of the Torah." In the night he suffered from indigestion. Ulla exclaimed: "Three measures of poison for a zuz, and yet the Babylonians engage in the study of the Torah!"

*Pesahim, 88.*

Rab Hisda said: "When I was poor, I ate no vegetables, thinking that they had small food value and did not satisfy me. And when I became rich, I also ate no vegetables, saying: let the place which the greens would occupy be rather occupied by meat and fish."

*Shabbat, 140.*

Ulla said: "In the West (Palestine) they have a proverb: 'He who eats fat meat (Alita) must hide in his garret (Ilita). He who eats vegetables (Kikule) sits in the squares (Kikle) of the town (unafraid of his creditors).' "

*Pesahim, 114.*

## THE POOR AT THE TABLE

R. Simeon said: "He who rejoices in the Festivals and gives not a share to God is a miser; the Satan will hate him and bring upon him all manner of tribulations. What is the share of God? The joy that a man brings to a poor man according to his ability. For in the days of the Festivals, God comes to behold his 'Broken Vessels' (the poor). And when he enters their houses and sees there nothing with which to rejoice, He weeps over them and rises up in anger to destroy the world. Then the members of the Tribunal come forward to plead for mercy towards mankind. And God replies: 'I created the world so that mercy might be practiced in it, and the world can stand only if mercy is performed.' And the Angels reply: 'Only this man and that ate and drank and gave naught though he could afford charity.' At once the Satan received God's permission to pursue those who were hard of heart.

"We are taught: at every joyous meal the Satan comes. If he sees that the poor are present, he is satisfied; otherwise he returns to God and informs him regarding the giver of the meal."

*Preface to Zohar, 10, 11.*

## PREPARING FOR MEALS

R. Jose the Elder would not permit his meal to be prepared until he had first prayed to God for sustenance, and had waited a moment. Then he would say: "Now that the King has sent us sustenance, let us prepare it."

*Zohar, ii, 62.*

Bar Yokni desired to hold a banquet for some Roman patricians and asked the advice of R. Eliezer ben Jose. The latter said: "If you invite twenty persons prepare for twenty-five." The man had a different thought, however, saying: "In all likelihood not everyone will come; therefore nineteen portions will be sufficient." It chanced that everyone invited did come, and one portion was missing. The host wished to placate one of them, who was less wealthy, and gave him some gold at his plate. The guest threw it in his face and left in a rage. When Bar Yokni met the Rabbi again, he confessed his fault, and asked: "Are Rabbis learned also in the matter of giving a banquet?" "Surely," answered R. Eliezer. "You came off easily. What would you have done if some one had asked for a second helping?"

*Esther Rabbah, 2.*

The Torah teaches us that one should eat meat only in the evening (Exodus 16:8). Rab Aha bar Jacob said: "Moses taught Israel to have stated hours for eating, and not to peck all day long like hens."

*Yoma, 75.*

R. Jeremiah was ill. A physician visited him and found him eating pumpkin. He said: "He eats poison, yet wishes me to cure him." We learn from this that pumpkin is unfit food for a sick person.

*Nedarim, 49.*

He who eats overmuch of any food invites sickness. Said R. Pappa: "Even of dates."

*Gittin, 70.*

Said R. Isaac: "It is forbidden to eat raw vegetables before breakfast."

*Berakot, 44.*

One shall not drink from a glass, and then give it to another. But once a man did so, when a thirsty person asked him for a drink. The thirsty man declined it and he died from thirst.

*Derek Eretz Rabbah, 8.*

A man may not give his portion to a child of his host without permission.

*Hullin, 94.*

Said R. Huna: "The waiter should have his portion after the meal is over. But if fat meat or old wine is served, he shall receive it immediately, that he may be spared the pain of longing for it."

*Ketubot, 61.*

R. Johanan gave to his slave a portion of everything he himself ate. He said: "Did not He who made me in the womb make him? Did not One fashion us in the womb?" (Job 31:15)

*Y. Ketubot, 5.*

## 70. EAVESDROPPING

The mountains have eyes and the walls have ears.

*Pirke de Rabbenu ha-Kadosh, 3.*

## 71. ECONOMIZING

Eat vegetables and fear no creditors, rather than eat duck and hide.

*Pesahim, 114.*

## 72. EDUCATION AND ITS COST

Rabbi Simeon ben Yohai said: "If you see cities in the Land of Israel that are destroyed to their very foundation, know that it is because they did not provide pay for teachers of the Bible and of tradition, according to Jeremiah 9, 11 ff., 'because they abandoned My Torah.'"

*Y. Hagigah, 1, 7.*

## 73. EMPLOYER AND EMPLOYEE

(See Labor)

A man should pray for the welfare of him who gives him employment.

*Tanhuma, Wayyesheb, 13.*

### A Servant's Rights

Rabbi Jose chanced to overhear his wife blaming her maidservant for something she did not do.

"How can you blame her if you are not certain of her guilt?" he asked his wife.

"But you should not have reproved me in her presence," said his wife.

"Nay," answered the Rabbi. "She ought to know that her rights are not despised." [1]

[1] See *Hasidic Anthology*, p. 206.

*Bereshit Rabbah, 48.*

### The Best Meals

The son of Rabbi Johanan ben Matthias hired several Jewish laborers and promised them their meals. His father said: "It were better that thou gavest them their full hire in money, and let them buy their own meals. No matter how well thou wilt feed them, thy promise will not be fully kept, for a Jew is entitled to the best fare possible."

*Baba Metzia, 86.*

## 74. ENTHUSIASM AND COOLNESS

The Angel Michael is of snow (he cools passions), and Gabriel is of fire (he creates enthusiasm). A man should admit both Angels into his heart.

*Bemidbar Raddah, 12, 8. (Amplified.)*

People say: if two logs are dry and one is wet, the kindling of the two will kindle the wet log as well.

*Sanhedrin, 93.*

The Torah is a fire that consumeth fire. Enthusiasm for learning subdues enthusiasm for sensual pleasures. Passion for the Torah conquers all other passions.

*Zohar Hadash Tikkunim, 106a.*

R. Abbahu was sitting and arranging Midrashim. He felt as if a fire surrounded him. He said: "This signifies that I am laboring aright. Some are able to delve deeply into a matter, but are unable to arrange their findings acceptably. Others are able to arrange well, but cannot delve deeply into the subject. It seems to me that I am privileged to do both acceptably, and my soul is aflame within me."

*Shir ha-Shirim Rabbah, 1.*

## 75. ERETZ YISRAEL; PALESTINE; THE HOLY LAND

### PALESTINE LACKS NOTHING

Hadrian asked R. Joshua ben Hananiah: "Your Torah describes Palestine as a land 'wherein . . . thou shalt not lack anything' (Deut. 8:9). Are you able to bring me these three things: peppers, pheasants and silk from Palestine?" The Rabbi hunted about, and found peppers in Nazhanah, pheasants in Akbra, and silk in Gush Halab.

*Shir ha-Shirim Rabbah, 4.*

### NOT BETTER

Why did Sennacherib deserve to be recorded in the Bible (Ezra 4:10) as the great and noble Asenappar? Because he did not speak derogatively of Palestine, as it is written: "I shall bring you away to a land like your own land" (Isaiah 36:17) and not better than your land.

*Sanhedrin, 94.*

Why is the Land of Israel compared to a hart? As the hart is the fleetest of animals, so the Land of Israel is the land quickest to ripen her fruits.

*Ketubot, 112.*

More beloved is a small school in Eretz Yisrael than a large Academy outside of it.

*Y. Nedarim, 6, 5.*

A handsome man may wear ugly clothes, and an ugly man handsome. But Israel is fine and Israel's garments are fine. Israel is fine and Israel's land is fine. Israel is suited to the Land of Israel, and the Land of Israel is suited to Israel.

*Tanhuma to Masei.*

Eretz Israel is more beloved by Me than everything else.

*Bemidbar Rabbah, 23, 7.*

He who walks four ells in Palestine is assured of the World-to-Come.

*Ketubot, 111.*

Living in Eretz Yisrael is equal to the weight of all Mitzwot. (Said also of the Sabbath, Charity and the Tzizit.)

*Sifre, Reeh.*

In the future Jerusalem will cover all Eretz Yisrael, and Eretz Yisrael will cover the entire world.

*Yalkut to Isaiah, sec. 503.*

He who resides in Palestine, reads the Sh'ma and speaks Hebrew is a son of the World-to-Come.

*Sifre, Berakah, 13.*

He who resides in Palestine is without sins.

*Ketubot, 111.*

Even the merest talk of the residents of Palestine is Torah.

*Wayyikra Rabbah, 34, 7.*

In your Land (Eretz Yisrael) you can sit in safety, but you cannot dwell in safety in a strange land.

*Sifra, Behukotai.*

In the Diaspora a Jew's livelihood comes to him through non-Jews, but in Palestine, through the Shekinah.

*Zohar, iv, 235a.*

In the days to come Eretz Yisrael will be redeemed little by little.

*See Tanhuma, Debarim, 1, 2.*

Three places belong to Israel by the right of purchase: the Site of the Temple; the Cave of Machpelah, and the Grave of Joseph.

*Bereshit Rabbah, 79, 7.*

Why is the Sea of Tiberias called Kinnereth? Because the fruit which grows around it is sweet, like the melody of a Kinnor (a harp).

*Megillah, 6.*

A man may drown in all waters, but not in the Dead Sea.

*Shabbat, 108.*

## OUTSIDE OF PALESTINE

R. Eleazar b. Shamua and R. Johanan, the Alexandrian, planned to study with R. Judah of the family Ben Beteirah, who resided in Netzibin outside of Palestine. When they reached Sidon, they reminded themselves of Palestine, and their eyes were filled with tears. They said: "To live in the Land of Israel is a duty equal to any other Mitzwah. Why should we leave Palestine and forego one Mitzwah in order to perform another?" They returned to their home.

*Sifre to Deut. 12:29.*

## THE AIR OF PALESTINE

When R. Zeira came to Palestine he understood more clearly the arguments of his opponent, R. Illa, and surrendered his own viewpoint in a certain matter, saying: "This demonstrates that the very air of Palestine makes one's brain clearer."

*Baba Batra, 158.*

Abbaye said: A student in Palestine grasps the reasons of a law twice as quickly as a student in Babylonia.

Rabba added: Even a Babylonian student who goes to Palestine becomes twice as keen as he who has remained in Babylonia. Take the case of Jeremiah. When he was here, he did not understand the teachings of the Rabbis, but since he has been in Palestine, he calls us: Those foolish Babylonians.

*Ketubot, 75.*

There is no Torah like the Torah of Palestine, and no wisdom like the wisdom of Palestine.

*Bereshit Rabbah, 15.*

## A PROPHECY IN THE ZOHAR

R. Jose and R. Hiyya were discussing the birth of Ishmael. Said R. Hiyya: "It was a woeful day for Israel when Abraham begat Ishmael and circumcised him on his thirteenth birthday. For four hundred years, the patron Angel of Ishmael shall say: 'Edom was circumcised, and Thou gavest him the rulership of the Holy Land. Should not Ishmael, too, rule over Palestine because he, also, was circumcised?' And when his importunities annoy God, He shall keep Ishmael far from grace above, and grant him in reward the rulership of Palestine. And Ishmael shall keep Israel out of his Land, and it shall be so until the reward for his circumcision shall have been paid in full. And then Ishmael will become entangled in a fierce war with some nations of Edom, and they will battle once on the sea, once on the dry land, and a third time near Jerusalem. And the Edomites shall govern the Ishmaelites, but the Holy Land shall not be taken over entirely by Edom. And at that time a great nation from the other end of the world will rise up against the evil Empire which has descended from the Roman Empire, and for three months will it battle against it. And all the nations of Edom, even those at the far ends of the world, will assemble together. And God will arise and will cause Ishmael again to be cut off from the Holy Land, and Israel will become powerful in his land once more." [1]

*Zohar, ii, 32.*

[1] This excerpt seems to indicate the lateness of certain parts of the Zohar, since in the time when the Rabbis mentioned in it were alive, Ishmael did not rule Palestine, and it speaks of a four hundred year delaying of the event. It may be a record of the Crusades.

Happy are they who dwell in Palestine, for they have no sin and no transgression either in life or in death.

*Midrash Tehillim, 85, 2.*

Had not Israel sinned, then they would have been given only the five books of Moses and the book of Joshua, which represents the measures of Palestine.

*Nedarim, 22b.*

A Rabbi lamented: "The Shekinah does not dwell outside of Palestine."

*Moed Katon, 25a.*

When the Patriarch Jacob, fleeing from his brother's wrath, slept upon a bed of rocks, those rocks were in truth all of Palestine—"for the Lord folded all Eretz Yisrael like a roll, and placed it as a cushion on which to rest his weary head."

*Bereshit Rabbah, 69, 4.*

God weighed all the nations and found only Israel of the generation of the wilderness worthy to receive the Torah; He measured all mountains and found none so worthy as Mount Sinai to receive that precious gift; He measured all cities, and only Jerusalem was found worthy of the Temple; He measured and weighed all lands, but found none so worthy nor as fitting for Israel as Palestine.

*Wayyikra Rabbah, 13, 2.*

### LOVE FOR PALESTINE

When R. Zeira went up to Palestine he came to the river-boundary. Since there was no ferry, he took hold of a rope, and crossed the river on a narrow board. When asked why he had not waited for the ferry, he answered: "How do I know whether I shall be worthy to enter a place which Moses and Aaron did not merit entering?" When R. Abba reached Acco, he kissed the very stones out of love for Zion.

R. Hanina labored to repair Palestine's roads. R. Ammi and R. Assi moved their School on warm days to the shade, and on cool days, to the sunny spots, so that the students, unaccustomed to the climate, might not complain.

R. Jose b. Haninah said: "Why is the boundary city called Acco? The word is a contraction of 'Ad Ko,' 'until here' is holy."

*Ketubot, 112; Y. Shebiit, 4.*

## LEAVING PALESTINE

From the tribulations of Elimelech (Ruth 1:3-5), we learn that a native of Palestine should not leave the land, even temporarily.

A Kohen is especially forbidden to do so, since the outside is less clean ritually. A Kohen came to R. Hanina and said: "My brother departed for Tyre and died there without child. May I go to Tyre to take his widow as my wife, as I am duty bound?" R. Hanina replied: "Thy brother left his mother's lap to sit in the lap of a strange woman; God punished him, and dost thou wish to receive similar treatment?"

R. Simeon b. Abba asked R. Hanina for a letter of recommendation, since he wished to settle in another country for his livelihood. R. Hanina answered: "Tomorrow if I went to thy parents, they would say to me: 'We left a desirable plant in the Land of Israel, yet thou hast permitted it to be transplanted to a strange land.' "

*Y. Moed Katon, 3.*

## 76. ERRORS AND UNWITTING FAULTS

He who has done an evil thing, but without turning his will and heart to the Sitra Ahara, will not be punished.[1]

*Zohar, v, 261b.*

[1] The Other (or Evil Spirit).

Rabbi Judah ben Ilai said: "Be attentive in learned study, for an unwitting fault in it is reckoned as presumptuous."

*Abot, 4, 13.*

## SAMUEL'S INDIFFERENCE

A woman once halted Samuel and cried out for justice. He paid her no attention. His Disciple, Rab Judah, was perplexed at his indifference, but Samuel explained it as follows: "The punishment will lie at the door of the Exilarch Mar Ukba, not at my door, for I do not hold court here."

*Shabbat, 55a.*

A Disciple of the Geonim, R. Hannanel, transmitted the following tradition of the Geonim concerning this episode: "An Amora became ill, and fell into a deep slumber. When he awoke, he said: 'I was on a visit to the Garden of Eden, and beheld that those who are greater here are smaller there.' He implied, says the tradition, that Samuel is considered in Heaven as a Zaddik, lesser than his Disciple Rab Judah, because of his conduct in this case."

*Tosafot to Baba Batra, 10b.*

### Unwitting and Presumptuous Faults

Rabbi Judah ben Ilai said: " 'Show My people their transgressions, and the House of Jacob their sins' (Isaiah 58:1). 'Show My people their transgressions,' these are the scholars whose unwitting faults are for them equivalent to presumptuous sins; 'and the House of Jacob their sins,' these are the unlearned masses whose presumptuous sins are for them equivalent to unwitting faults."

*Baba Metzia, 33b.*

## 77. EVIL, WICKED PEOPLE

The greatest sinner is he who regrets his previous goodness.

*Zohar, iii, 101a.*

When the wicked are in trouble, they are submissive; but when their trouble is ended, they return to their evil ways.

*Tanhuma, Waera, end.*

There are people whose deeds are like unto the deeds of the Sodomites.

*Kiddushin, 70.*

He who raises his hand against a fellow-man, even though he does not smite him, is called a man of wickedness.

*Sanhedrin, 58.*

Fear not the officer or the ruler; fear, however, the man who has no fear of Heaven.

*Pirke de R. Eliezer, 37.*

I would rather be called a fool all my days than to be wicked before the Lord for a single moment.

*Eduyot, 5, 6.*

Do not good to the evil man, and thou wilt not be repaid by evil.

*Bereshit Rabbah, 22, 8.*

Thou hast done good to the evil? Thou hast done evil.

*Kohelet Rabbah, 8.*

He who aids a fellow-man to do a wicked thing is as if he had murdered him.

*Midrash ha-Gadol, 300.*

Four men are called wicked: he who lifts his hand against his fellow-man to smite him; he who borrows and does not repay; he who is impudent of countenance, and he who is quarrelsome.

*Bemidbar Rabbah, 18, 12.*

And one who despises his blood relations is cruel. This signifies the man who has a family feast and does not invite his poor kinsfolk. (A paraphrase of Proverbs 11:17.)

*Wayyikra Rabbah, 34, 3.*

He who is indifferent to evil deeds transgresses these three injunctions: there shall be no other gods unto thee; thou shalt not make unto thee an image, and thou shalt not bow down to them.

*Zohar, i, 239a.*

He who plans evil against Israel is as if he had planned evil against God.

*Eliyahu Rabbah, 7.*

An evil intent is not accounted as an evil deed, except the intention to become disloyal to the Jewish faith.

*Zohar, ii, 150b.*

Bad indeed is the dough which its baker testifies to be bad.

*Bereshit Rabbah, 34, 9.*

An evil upbringing in the home is worse than the wars of Gog and Magog.

*Berakot, 7.*

## 78. EVIL ASSOCIATES

Join not the scoffers lest thou learn to imitate them.

*Abot de-R. Nathan, 26, 2.*

He who cleaves to sinners, even if he does not imitate them, shares in their punishment.

*Abot de-R. Nathan, 30.*

He who consorts with immoral people is himself immoral.

*Kallah Rabbati, 3.*

## 79. EVIL DECREES

The government issues evil decrees against the Jews and the decrees stand, when the Jews cast the study of the Torah to the ground.

*Ekah Rabbah Petihta, 2.*[1]

[1] This Midrash has several "petihtot," or introductions.

A decree should not issue from a ruler unless it has first issued from God.

*Midrash Mishle, 21.*

Said Rabbi Eleazar ben Pedat: Three things annul a dire decree of God, namely, prayer, charity and repentance. And all of them are found in one verse (II Chronicles 7:14).

*Y. Taanit, 65b.*

## Is God Responsible?

A ruler said to R. Abbahu: "There is a drought in the country now on your account, since it is written in your Torah, that when you disobey God, he shuts off the rain. We should fall upon you Jews and slay all of you, so that we may not suffer on your account."

R. Abbahu replied: "But is it not your evil decrees against us which cause us to sin?"

The ruler answered: "Nay, if you did not sin, God would not prompt our hearts to persecute you."

R. Judah remarked: "Well has the ruler spoken."

*Zohar Hadash to Wayyetze.*

## Denying God

"God said to Israel: I adjure you, if the government imposes harsh decrees upon you, that you do not rebel against it, whatever it decrees. But if the government decrees that you nullify the Torah and the Commandments, do not heed the government, but say unto it: I will keep the king's command in everything necessary to you, but 'on account of the oath of God,'. . .'do not stand in an evil thing' (Eccl. 8:2 and 3). For the government does not keep you from the commandments; they seek to make you deny God."

*Tanhuma, Buber, Noah, par. 10; cf. 15.*

## Five Things That Cancel

We find that five things may cancel the harsh decree of Heaven against a person: almsgiving, prayer, change of name, reformation of conduct, and change of residence.

Of charity it is written (Proverbs 10:2): "But almsgiving saveth from death."

Of prayer it is written: "Then they cried unto the Lord in their trouble, and He delivered them out of their distresses" (Psalm 107:6).

Of change of name we know that after Sarai changed her name to Sarah, her state of barrenness was changed.

Of reformation of conduct, we read in Jonah 3:10: "And God saw their works, that they turned from their evil way; and God repented of the evil, which He said He would do unto them; and He did it not."

Of change of residence, it is written, "And the Lord said unto Abraham, 'Get thee out,'" and then it is said: "I will make of thee a great nation."

*Rosh ha-Shanah, 16b.*

## 80. EVIL IMPULSE, SATAN

The Evil Impulse seduces in this world and accuses in the next.

*Sukkah, 52.*

Evil impulses fear naught but words of Torah.

*Zohar, v, 268a.*

If the Evil Impulse says to thee: Sin and God will forgive, believe it not.

*Hagigah, 16.*

The Evil Impulse desires only that which is not permitted.

*Y. Yoma, 6, 2.*

How difficult is the Evil Impulse. Even its Creator called it Evil.

*Kiddushin, 30.*

Had the Israelites not worshipped the Golden Calf and drawn upon themselves the Evil Impulse, they would have lost the impulse to beget children, and there would have been no other generations henceforth.

*Zohar, i, 61a.*

The Evil Impulse is sweet in the beginning and bitter in the end.

*Y. Shabbat, 14, 3.*

There is no Sitra Ahara (Unclean Spirit) that has not a thin thread of the Sitra Kadisha (Holy Spirit). There is no dream without a kernel of wheat (truth) in the mass of chaff (untruths).

*Zohar, Tosefta, ii, 69b.*

God says: A man fashions a goad for his animal, but he forgets to fashion a goad for his Evil Impulse.

*Pesikta, Buber, 23.*

God says: "My sons, I created for you the Evil Impulse; I created for you the Torah as an antidote."

*Sifre on Deut. 11, 18.*

The Good Impulse is poor and weak, and has nothing tangible to show as a reward for obedience. The Evil Impulse is strong. Whatever the Good Impulse is able to acquire through tireless labor, the Evil Impulse snatches away easily by holding forth the immediate rewards of worldly pleasure.

*Pesikta Rabbati, 9, 2, and commentary.*

Rabbi Johanan ben Nuri said: "This is the art of the Evil Impulse. Today it says to a man: Do this! and tomorrow, Do that! until at last it says: Worship other gods; and man goes and does it."

*Shabbat, 105b.*

The Good Impulse seeks the joy of the Torah; the Evil Impulse, the joy of women, wine and arrogance.

*Zohar, i, 202a.*

He is called a man who subdues his impulses.

*Zohar, ii, 128a.*

The Evil Impulse is like a cake of yeast. The yeast is placed at one spot in the dough, but it ferments throughout it. The Evil Impulse does likewise.

*Zohar, ii, 182a.*

The Evil Impulse is known by many names: Snake, Crooked One, Satan, Angel of Death, Unclean One, Enemy, Stumbling-Stone, Uncircumcised, Evil One, and the Northern. (Tzefoni.) [1]

*Zohar, ii, 263a.*

[1] So alluded to in Joel 2, 20 according to some opinions.

When a man is busy at study, the Evil Impulse whispers to him: Why tarryest thou here. Go and join the men who flirt with pretty women.

*Zohar, ii, 265b.*

In the School of Rabbi Ishmael it was taught: "If the Evil Impulse encounters thee, drag him to the School; if he is stone, he will be worn away as by water; if he is iron, he will be shattered to pieces as by fire and a sledge hammer."

*Kiddushin, 30b; Sukkah, 52b.*

The Midrash Bereshit Rabbah explains the words: "And behold, it was very good," as meaning the Yetzer ha-Ra, the Evil Impulse, for without the Yetzer ha-Ra, no one would marry or build. Another exposition may be offered: the Yetzer ha-Ra is bad, because it is too good, and the parable says: "What is too good is bad."

*Introd. to Tanhuma, Buber, 155.*

What is the Good Impulse? That which is clean, permissible and fitting. What is the Evil Impulse? That which is unclean, forbidden, and immoral.

*Zohar, i, 27b.*

God created the Evil Impulse for the purpose of testing man.

*Zohar, i, 106b.*

Even in the Millennium we can hope only for the weakening of the Evil Impulse, but not for its total extinction.

*Zohar, i, 128b.*

Without the Evil Impulse man would feel no satisfaction in his labor and no joy in his Torah. Without it there would be no progeny and no increase. It is needed in the world just as much as rain, but it can be subdued and made subject to deeds of purity.

*Midrash ha-Neelam, i, 138a.*

Thou shalt have no strange god within thee—namely, the Evil Impulse, which seduces thee to perform the commandments of a strange god.

*Zohar, iii, 106b.*

When the Evil Impulse comes to thee, it is like iron as yet cold. If thou dost not drive him forth, it soon becomes molten within thee, as if transformed into fire.

*Zohar, v, 267b.*

To what may the Yetzer ha-Ra be compared? To a man who comes to a door, opens it, and if no one halts him, enters as if he were an invited guest. If no one still objects, he gives orders as if he were the master of the house.

*Zohar, v, 267b.*

If a man conquers the Evil Impulse, the snake turns into a staff.

*Tikkune Zohar, 132a.*

Two types of impulse beat within a man: one brings health and the other disease. The stronger conquers.

*Tikkune Zohar, 151a.*

When a man has learned to subdue his chief enemy, the Evil Impulse, he finds it easier to conquer all other foes.

*Tikkune Zohar, 178a.*

The Rabbis taught that Satan, the Angel of Death, and Evil Impulse, are one.

*Baba Batra, 16a.*

"God saw everything that He had made, and behold it was very good;" even the Evil Impulse, said the Rabbis, was part of that gracious handiwork.

*Bereshit Rabbah, to Gen. i, 31.*

God created the Evil Impulse, but also the Torah as its antidote.

*Kiddushin, 30a.*

Evil thoughts are more deadly than sin itself.

*Yoma, 29a.*

Man is bound to bless God for the evil, even as he blesses God for the good.

*Mishnah Berakot, 9, 5.*

The evil doers, even while alive, may be termed dead.

*Berakot, 18b.*

Who is the thwarter? the leaven that is in the dough [1] and the servitude inflicted by the Gentile powers.

*Berakot, 17a.*

[1] Evil Impulse.

Upon the heart of man lies the stone of the Evil Inclination.
*Bereshit Rabbah, 70, 8.*

The greater the man, the more powerful his impulses.
*Sukkah, 52a.*

"Lord of the Universe," prayed one of the Sages, "Thou knowest that our desire is to do Thy will; if we fail, it is because of the leaven that works within us."
*Berakot, 17a.*

When does the Satan turn informer? When his victim turns away from him to repentance.
*Zohar Hadash, i, 20a.*

Rabbi Jose, the Galilean, said: There are three classes of people: the righteous, who are ruled by their good impulse (and repent of their sins); the wicked, who are ruled by their Evil Impulse (and do not repent); and the middle class, who are ruled now by the one, now by the other. (Sometimes they repent and at other times fail to do so.)
*Berakot, 61b.*

A king had smitten his son a grievous blow. He bound a bandage upon the wound and said: My son, as long as this bandage is upon your wound, you may eat and drink whatever you like; you may bathe in warm water or in cold, and you will suffer no harm. But if you remove the bandage from it a deep sore will result. Thus God said: My children, I have created for you the Evil Impulse, and I have created for you the Torah as an antidote. As long as you occupy yourselves with it, the Evil Impulse will not have dominion over you.
*Kiddushin, 30b.*

Rabbi Samuel ben Nahman observes: "'And behold it was very good' (Gen. 1:31). This is the Evil Impulse. Is then the Evil Impulse good? Yet were it not for the Evil Impulse, no man would build a house, nor marry a wife, nor beget children, nor engage in trade. Solomon said: 'All excelling work is a man's rivalry with his neighbor.'" (Eccl. 4:4)
*Kohelet Rabbah, on 3, 11.*

"Like iron, out of which, when heated in the forge, man can fashion whatever implements he pleases, the Evil Impulse can be subdued to the service of God, by means of the words of the Torah, which is like fire."
*Abot de-Rabbi Nathan, Perek, 16.*

Rabbi Simeon ben Lakish said: "Man should always rouse his good impulse against the Evil, and he may thus succeed in overcoming it. But if not, more potent means are at his command, such as immersing himself in the study of the Torah."
*Berakot, 5a.*

## 81. EXILE

God exiled Israel among the nations, so that proselytes might cleave to Israel.

*Pesahim, 87.*

Rabbi Eleazar Hakapar said: "The synagogues and schools of Babylonia (name for countries of the Exile) will be transplanted to Palestine in the future."

*Megillah, 29a.*

R. Oshaya said: God was charitable to Israel when he dispersed the Children of Israel among many nations.[1]

*Pesahim, 87.*

[1] When one nation persecutes a community of Israel, those in another nation can aid them.

## 82. EYES

The eye that lusts not shall see God.

*Wayyikra Rabbah, 1.*

Poverty and weeping deepen the eyes.

*Midrash Tehillim, 73.*

Three things weaken the eyesight: combing the hair while it is dry; drinking from a drip and putting on wet shoes.

*Pesahim, 111.*

### SATISFYING THE EYE

R. Hananiah and R. Jonathan asked Menahem Talmia: "Did God then give to Israel in the wilderness manna as an unsatisfying food, as it is written: 'And He afflicted thee and suffered thee to hunger.' " (Deut. 8:3)

Menahem showed the Rabbis two melons, a whole one of small size, and a portion of a large melon. He asked them: "If both of these sell by weight and you find that both weigh alike, which would you prefer to buy?"

"The whole one," they answered, "because it satisfies the eye as well as the stomach."

"This is the reason why manna is called hunger-food. Not being in the form of a loaf it did not satisfy the eye."

*Kohelet Rabbah, 5.*

## 83. FAITHFULNESS

If a man is entrusted with something his ignorance of the thing's whereabouts is accounted as inexcusable carelessness.

*Baba Metzia, 35.*

### The Weasel and the Pit

A beautiful maiden lost her way returning home. She grew thirsty, and coming upon a well with a rope tied at the top, she swung herself to the bottom in order to drink. Too late she realized that she had no means of reaching the top again, since she found it impossible to use the rope for the ascent. She shouted and shouted, and finally heard an answering cry. A young man passing by had discovered her, and instructing her to hold fast to the bucket, he pulled her to the surface. They were smitten with love for each other, and pledged their troth at once, taking as witnesses the pit and a weasel passing by.

The maiden remained faithful to her pledge, but the man did not. He forgot her and married another. His first child was strangled by a weasel and the second was drowned in a well. These misfortunes served to remind him of his first word of troth. He divorced his wife at her suggestion and went to seek his true bride. In the meantime the maiden had been constantly urged by her parents to accept a husband, and to avoid their importunities, she assumed the guise of an epileptic. When her true bridegroom at last appeared, he revealed to her his remembrance of the pledge between them; she recognized him, and they were happily married.[1]

*Taanit, 8 (Indicated).*

[1] This is the plot of the Yiddish opera *Shulamith*.


## 84. FAMILY DESCENT (YICHUS): PEDIGREE

Descend a step (in family rank) and take unto thyself a wife.

*Yebamot, 63.*

The proverb runs: of what good is good birth to a man of evil deeds?

*Sanhedrin, 106.*

Why was the dynasty of Saul so brief in point of years? Because it was of impeccable family pedigree.[1]

*Yoma, 22.*

[1] There was too much pride of family.

A single man only was created in order to keep one man from saying to another: My forefather was greater than yours; to exclude pride of ancestry; to prevent families from quarrelling, and men from assaulting and robbing one another, by virtue of the knowledge that they are all of one stock.

*Mishnah Sanhedrin, 4, 5.*

## 85. FAMILY AND HOME

Every man is king in his own home.

*Abot de-R. Nathan, 28.*

Eat less than you can afford, dress less fittingly, but have a fine dwelling.

*Bereshit Rabbah, 20, 12.*

Anger in a home is like rottenness in fruit.

*Sotah, 3.*

Immorality in a home is like a worm in a fruit.

*Sotah, 3.*

The Torah teaches us a lesson: first, build a home, and then marry.

*Sotah, 44.*

Can a goat live in the same barn as a tiger? In the same fashion, a daughter-in-law cannot live with her mother-in-law under the same roof.

*Maaseh Torah, 4.*

If a man sin against those of his own household, he will inevitably come to sin against his neighbor.

*Tanna de-be Eliyahu, 289.*

A home where Torah is not heard will not endure.

*Intr. Tikkune Zohar, 6a.*

A man rejoices when he dwells in his own home.

*Y. Moed Katon, 2, 4.*

He who loves his wife as himself; who honors her more than himself; who rears his children in the right path, and who marries them off at the proper time of their life, concerning him it is written: "And thou wilt know that thy home is at peace."

*Yebamot, 62.*

### Rabbi Akiba and the Eunuch

A eunuch met R. Akiba on the 9th day of Ab, barefooted. He said: "A patrician rides on a horse, a freeman on a donkey, a commoner walks in his own shoes, but a barefooted person is like one who is dead."

R. Akiba replied: "The beauty of a male is a well-grown beard; a wife is the joy of his heart, and children are an inheritance from the Lord. One who lacks all these is better dead."

*Kohelet Rabbah, 10.*

### Not from His House

Hillel came from the roadway and heard loud shouting coming from a house near his home. He said to his companions: "I am confident this does not issue from my own home." [1]

*Berakot, 60.*

[1] He had taught his household to abstain from loud talking and shouting.

## 86. FASTING AND FAST-DAYS

### When Fast-Days Are Instituted

In the days of R. Zeira, the Palestine government promulgated a harsh decree against the Jews, forbidding them to assemble in the synagogues, so that a fast might not be proclaimed.

R. Zeira said: "We may vow to fast as soon as we are permitted, and this vow will be accepted by God as if we fasted. How do I know this? From Daniel 10:12: 'Fear not, Daniel; for from the first day that thou didst set thy heart to understand and to fast before thy God, thy words were heard.'"

If in the rainy season, forty days should pass without rain, an alarm should be sounded, and a fast-day proclaimed. R. Johanan said: "If money is cheap and products are expensive, we can wait forty days, but if money is rare and produce is cheap, we cannot wait even a day. I remember when flour was very low in price, yet people were starving for lack of money to buy it."

*Taanit, 8, 19.*

### Sounding an Alarm

R. Akiba said: "Not only when war threatens should an alarm be sounded with trumpets (Numbers 10:9), but also when any disaster threatens, such as a drought, a pestilence, a plague or a ship in danger."

*Sifre to Numbers 10:9.*

Once wolves devoured two children, and the Elders decreed a fast-day with the alarm.

*Taanit, 19.*

Rab Judah heard that locusts had come to the country. He decreed a fast-day. The Disciples said: "But they have done no harm." He retorted: "Have they brought with them provisions?"

Samuel heard that in a distant city of the land an epidemic had begun. He decreed a fast-day. He was told: "But it is so far." He replied: "Does a plague require a ferry or a bridge to cross the river?"

Rab Nahman heard of an epidemic in Palestine, and he decreed a fast-day in Babylonia, saying: "If the matron is punished, how much the more likely is it that the servant will be punished?"

*Taanit, 21.*

When a fast-day is decreed to petition God for compassion and the removal of the calamity, we should implore Him for only one thing at a time, as it is written: "So we fasted and besought God for this" (Ezra 8:23); not for these.

R. Haggai in the name of R. Zeira said: "If the locusts and a drought come together, God may be entreated concerning both, since both are a combined menace against the harvest."

*Y. Taanit, 4.*

R. Samuel bar Nahmani in his days faced this dilemma: shall God be entreated concerning a famine or a plague, since both occurred at the same time. Some said: "Let us implore God to remove the plague and we shall somehow endure the famine." The Rabbi said: "Nay, let us pray for the cessation of the famine, and the plague will disappear of itself; for God does not bless the produce for the benefit of the dead, as it is written: 'Thou openest Thy hand, and satisfiest with favor every living thing.'" (Psalm 145:16)

*Taanit, 8.*

## 87. FATHER AND SON

Happy is the son who can fill the place made vacant by his father.

*Pesikta Zutarta, Bereshit, 26.*

The proverb runs: He who is descended from thee often teaches thee.

*Yebamot, 63.*

When does a child become especially dear to his father? When he begins to talk.

*Tanhuma, Tetzaweh.*

As my fathers planted for me, so do I plant for my children.

*Taanit, 23.*

He who brings up the child is to be called its father, not he who gave him birth.

*Shemot Rabbah, 46, 5.*

A man's father is his king.

*Pirke de R. Eliezer, 39*

A son inherits from his father looks, strength, wealth, brains and longevity.

*Ediyot, 2, 9.*

Why does Scripture say: "slept" about David (I Kings 2, 10), and "slain" about Joab? Because David left a son like himself.

*Baba Batra, 116.*

He who rebukes not his son leads him into delinquency.

*Shemot Rabbah, 1.*

A father should not be miserly towards his daughter.

*Y. Ketubot, 4, 12.*

If a man has a son in this world, he does not feel lonely in the World-to-Come.

*Zohar Hadash to Ruth, 84a.*

Gehenna has no power over him who leaves a learned son who practices good deeds.

*Zohar Hadash to Ruth, 89a.*

A man is not a complete man if he has no son and daughter.

*Raia Mehemna, iii, 34a.*

Fathers are often respected because of the merit of their sons.

*Tanhuma Wayyikra, 5.*

He who teaches his son is as if he had taught his son, his son's son, and so on to the end of all generations.

*Kiddushin, 30.*

The merits of the father do not benefit the son.

*Sanhedrin, 104.*

A father is usually lenient to his son in money matters.

*Baba Batra, 136.*

A father is responsible for his son's debt even if the endorsement is faulty.

*Baba Batra, 174.*

He who rears his son to study Torah and takes him twice daily to School is as if he observed the Torah twice daily.

*Zohar, i, 105a.*

A man without children is like a piece of wood, which though kindled does not burn or give out light.

*Zohar, i, 187a.*

The soul of a man who leaves no children has no one to help him enter the Chamber of the Lord.

*Zohar, i, 90a.*

A man with children eats his bread in joy; a man without children eats it in sadness.

*Zohar, i, 187a.*

A man who has labored in the Torah day and night but dies without children is protected by his good deeds and his Torah in the World-to-Come.

*Zohar, i, 187b.*

### Three Generations

Rab Huna gave a sweet-smelling and large date to his son Rab-bah. Abba, the son of Rabbah passed by, and the latter gave the date to his son. Rab Huna remarked: "It is just as people say: a father loves his son, and the son his own son."

*Sotah, 48.*

### "Like as a Father"

When Joab heard King David say the words: "Like as a father hath compassion upon his children" (Psalm 103:13), he said: "It is known that a mother hath more compassion than a father. Why did not the king say: 'like as a mother'?"

He resolved to investigate the matter. He came to a poor man who, despite his age, worked without complaint to earn bread for his wife and twelve children. He said to the old man: "Sell me a son, and I will give you one hundred gold pieces." The father angrily refused.

Later Joab received the mother's consent on the stipulation that if the father became angry at her, Joab should return the boy for the money. Joab took the boy and sat down near by to await developments. The old man returned home and missed a child. When the mother told him of her deed, the father seized an axe, ran to find Joab, crying: "Give me back my boy, or either you or I will be killed."

*Taken from Yalkut Sippurim i, 109-110. Source not stated.*

### Rising for His Own Son

R. Hama bar Bissa left his wife and baby son to study in an Academy. After twelve years he returned, and, going to the House of Study, he beheld a young student diligently at work. When he passed by, the student besought him to clarify a few points. R. Hama did so and found the youth to be of extraordinary acuteness. The Rabbi regretfully said: "Had I remained at home, I might have taught my son to be like this youth."

Later at home, he saw the very same young man entering. He believed he had followed him to receive an answer to a question, and rose from his seat to meet him. His wife laughed heartily, saying: "Should a father rise for his own son?" It was his own son, already known as Rabbi Oshaya ben Hama.

*Ketubot, 62.*

## 88. A FATHER'S DUTIES

If thy son is willing and eager to learn and has a retentive memory, he is to go to the Academy before thee.

*Kiddushin, 29.*

If a man's wife has died and she has left him grown-up children, he should not take another wife before he has married off his children. We learn this from Abraham, who first married off Isaac and after that wedded Keturah.

*Bereshit Rabbah, 60.*

Show no partiality among your sons. Treat all of them alike.

*Shabbat, 10.*

If a man does not teach his son Torah, it is as if he had merely created an image.

*Zohar, ii, 93a.*

### SUPPORTING ONE'S CHILDREN

Ukba received a summons to appear before R. Johanan, who, looking at the complaint, said: "Ukba, go and support thy children." Ukba replied: "Where does it say in the Torah that a father must support his children?"

R. Johanan responded in a menacing voice: "Thou, Ukba the wicked, go and support thy children."

*Y. Ketubot, chap. 4.*

### PATERNAL OBLIGATIONS

The father's obligations to his son are: he must circumcise him, redeem him, teach him Torah, teach him a trade, and help him secure a wife—some also say, to teach him to swim.

Rabbi Judah ben Ilai said: A man who does not teach his son a trade, teaches him robbery.

*Tosefta Kiddushin, 1, 11.*

It was asked: "If a father refuses to fulfil any of his obligations to his son, shall the Jewish Court, where it has authority, compel him to do so? The answer is found in the following case: The son of Terumah came to Rabbi Immi and begged him to persuade his father to make it possible for him to marry. The father refused but no penalty was inflicted upon him. Hence it is not in the province of an earthly court to enforce the parental obligations mentioned."

*Y. Kiddushin, chap. 1.*

### STANDING AT MOUNT SINAI

R. Joshua ben Levi said: "He who teaches his sons and grandsons Torah is as if he had received it himself at Mount Sinai."

R. Hiyya b. Abba saw R. Joshua b. Levi hurrying one morning to take his grandson to school. He asked him: "Why the haste?" and R. Joshua answered: "Is it a small thing to stand at Mount Sinai?"

R. Isaac said: "He who teaches Torah to children abides with the Shekinah."

*Kiddushin, 29; Y. Shabbat, 1.*
*Zohar Hadash to Sedrah Lek Leka.*

## THE FRUIT OF THY BODY

We read (Lec. 23–25): "And when ye shall come into the land, and shall have planted all manner of trees for food . . . three years shall it be forbidden unto you; it shall not be eaten; and in the fourth year all the fruit thereof shall be holy, for giving praise unto the Lord. But in the fifth year may ye eat of the fruit thereof, that it may yield unto you more richly the increase thereof."

We may understand these passages to apply not only to trees, but also to the fruit of the body as well. For the first three years do not trouble your son with instruction; but on the fourth year teach him to share in the Mitzwot, to accompany you to synagogue, to recite the responses, the Sh'ma and Amen. But in his fifth year he is to study the Scriptures and the Prayer Book, so that he may yield unto you more richly the increase thereof.

*Introd. to Tanhuma, Buber, p. 125. (An excellent example of Midrashic exposition.)*

## 89. FEAR

Fear the God-fearing man, for God does His will. Fear the ungodly man, lest thou share in the punishment meted out to him.

*Midrash ha-Gadol, 503.*

Why does a man have fear? Because his sins break his courage and he has no strength left.

*Zohar, i, 202a.*

Do not inspire overmuch fear among the members of thy household.

*Gittin, 6.*

The proverb runs: the man bitten by a snake is afraid of a rope.

*Shir ha-Shirim Rabbah to 2, 3.*

Rabbi Ishmael said: As long as a man does not sin, he is feared; as soon as he sins, he himself is in fear.

*Pesikta, Buber, 44b–45a.*

## 90. FELLOW-FEELING

He who entreats aid for his comrade, though he himself is in need, is answered first.

*Baba Kamma, 92.*

Before a man eats, he has two hearts (he considers another's hunger as well as his own); after he eats he has but one heart (he considers only himself, and does not believe his comrade is really hungry).

*Baba Batra, 12.*

### THE TEMPLE GATES

Solomon erected two gates in the Temple: to the right was one for bridegrooms to enter on the Sabbath, where they would be welcomed with the words: "He who abideth here shall grant thee the joy of fatherhood." To the left was a gate for those in tribulation to enter. If one entered with a black cloth over his head, reaching to his mouth, he would be recognized as a mourner, and greeted thus: "He who abideth here shall grant thee consolation."

If one entered with a black cloth reaching to his forehead, he would be known as one under the ban of the Rabbis, and would be greeted with these words: "He who abideth in this house shall grant thee peace of mind, and shall change thy heart to hearken unto thy comrades, so that they may admit thee again into their fellowship."

If one entered to pray for a sick member of his family, they would say: "May the One who abideth here have compassion upon thee."

Once a woman entered, and before she departed, she had received the glad tidings of her son's improvement.

If one entered to pray that his loss should be returned, they would say to him: "He who abideth here, may He place it in the heart of the finder to restore to thee what thou hast lost." Eliezer ben Hananiah lost a Scroll of the Torah valued at one hundred Mannahs. Before he departed from the Temple, it was brought to him safely.

When the Temple was no more, they would repair to the synagogues instead. Israel would rejoice with the bridegrooms, and mourn and sit on the ground with the mourners. Thus all Israel took part in the Mitzwah of showing human sympathy. And concerning them it is said: Blessed art Thou, O Lord, who givest a goodly reward to those who perform deeds of loving-kindness."

*Pirke de Rabbi Eliezer, 17.*
*Mesikta Semahot, 6.*
*Mesikta Sopherim, 19.*

## 91. FLATTERY

Great is the penalty for flattery. Flattery is equal to the sin of idolatry.

*Midrash Gadol u-Gedolah, 16.*

A man may flatter his wife for the sake of marital peace; his creditor for the sake of obtaining a respite, and his teacher for the sake of obtaining more attention.

*Otzar Midrashin, 224.*

## 92. FOOLS AND FOLLY

He who passes judgment on fools is himself judged to be a fool. (Based on Proverbs 29:9)

*Petiheta Ekah Rabbati, 14.*

There is no remedy for a fool.

*Gittin, 70.*

A fool teaches foolishness to his sons.

*Shabbat, 121.*

What is the sign of a foolish man? He talks too much.

*Zohar, iv, 193b.*

The fool thinks every one else is a fool.

*Kohelet Rabbah, 10.*

It is a shame for a man to send a fool as his messenger.

*Tanhuma Tissa, 25.*

As an ass cannot ascend a ladder, so a fool cannot become wise.

*Otzar Midrashim, 191.*

The only thing to do with an idiot and a thorn is to get rid of them.

*Shemot Rabbah, 6, 5.*

One fool can ask a question that a thousand wise men cannot answer. What one fool spoils, a thousand wise men cannot repair.

*Torat ha-Kenaot, p. 42; Bet Jonathan, p. 8. Both are folk-sayings.*

The Torah was not given to fools.

*Pesikta Zutarti Wayyehi, 49, 5.*

Bring no supporting argument from the experience of fools.

*Shabbat, 104.*

Were all people fools, they would not be known as fools.
"For the Lord will be in thy foolishness"—even in things in which thou art foolish. (Prov. 3, 26; usually translated: "Thy confidence.")

*Y. Peah, 1, 1.*

When you flog a fool, by the time it takes you to lower the whip a second time, he has already forgotten the first blow.

*Tanhuma Noah, 24.*

To the wise a wink, and to the fool a fist.

*Midrash Mishle, 22.*

## 93. FORGIVENESS

It is fitting for a great God to forgive great sinners.

*Wayyikra Rabbah, 5, end.*

Three have their sins forgiven: the proselyte; he who ascends to a great position, and he who marries.

*Y. Bikkurim, 3, 3.*

The sins of him are passed over who passes over his own rights.

*Yoma, 23.*

If a man's sins die with him, he can receive complete pardon; but if the fruit of his sins remains after his death, he cannot be completely forgiven.

*Y. Shabbat, 9, 3.*

When the wrong-doer makes amends (confesses and begs forgiveness), it is the duty of the injured party to forgive him: "When thou hast mercy upon thy fellow, thou hast One to have mercy on thee; but if thou hast not mercy upon thy fellow, thou hast none to have mercy on thee."

*Tanhuma, Buber, Wayyera, par. 30.*

Five have no easy forgiveness of sins: he who sins in many ways; he who repents many times of the same sin; he who sins in a sinless age; he who sins in order to repent; he who causes the Holy Name to be profaned.

*Abot de Rabbi Nathan, chap. 39.*

### FORGETTING INJURIES

Rabba said: "He who passes over (forgets) his wrongs, God forgets his sins, as it is written (Micah 7:18): "Who is a God like unto Thee, that pardoneth the iniquity—of him who passeth by the transgression committed against him."

Rab Huna ben R. Joshua became dangerously ill. When Rab Pappa visited him, he ordered that the funeral preparations should begin. But Rab Huna recovered. It was said that he regained his health because he would always pardon those who had wronged him.

*Rosh ha-Shanah, 17.*

R. Eliezer prayed long for rain, but was not answered. R. Akiba stepped to the Reader's Desk, offered a prayer of a few verses,[1] and rain descended. A Voice from Heaven was heard to say: "Not that the latter is a greater man, but R. Eliezer remembers his wrongs, and R. Akiba forgets them."

*Taanit, 25.*

[1] Beginning with the words: "Abinu, Malkenu" (Our Father, Our King).

R. Nehunya, the Elder, was asked by what merit he deserved long life. He said: "I have never accepted gifts, and I have always forgotten the wrongs done against me."

*Megillah, 28.*

## A Reward for Compassion

A man, travelling on a hot day, grew weary and sat down to rest on a rock. He soon fell asleep. A snake crawled towards him, but a sudden gust of wind blew down a branch from a nearby tree and killed the snake. When the man awoke and stepped off the rock, it swung loose and fell into an abyss.

R. Abba chanced to pass by at this very moment, and he said to the man: "You have been saved from death twice. Tell me: what are your good deeds?"

The man answered: "I never fail to make peace with anyone who harms me. I become his friend and repay good for evil. And before I lay myself down to sleep, I forgive all who require forgiveness."

"Thou art greater than Joseph," said R. Abba. "He forgave his brethren, but thou forgivest strangers as well."

*Zohar, i, 200-201.*

## Another Form of Forgiveness

Once Rabbi Johanan ben Zakkai and Rabbi Joshua were walking in Jerusalem and came upon the ruins of the Temple. R. Joshua lamented: "Woe unto us! The place where our sins were forgiven is no more."

His Master replied: "Let not thy heart be heavy. We have another form of forgiveness which is its equal. It is the performance of kind deeds, as it is written: 'For I desire mercy, and not sacrifice, and the knowledge of God rather than burnt-offerings.'" (Hosea, 6, 6.)

*Abot de-Rabbi Nathan, 4.*

## Asking for Forgiveness

He who has vexed his comrade by words only must also beg his pardon.

*Yoma, 87.*

If a man utters his suspicions against another man and finds them unjustified, he must ask his pardon.

*Berakot, 31.*

### THE BLIND TEACHER

In the home of R. Oshaya, the Elder, there lived a blind man who taught his son. It was customary to call the blind teacher for dinner. Once when there were guests, the summons was delayed. R. Oshaya came to the blind man's chamber and excused himself. The blind teacher replied: "Thou hast asked the pardon of one who is seen and seeth not. May He who sees and is not seen accept thy request for pardon."

*Shekalim, chap. 5.*

### ASKING FAVORS TACTFULLY

A Samaritan beggar came to the door and asked the housewife for an onion. When she gave it to him, he asked: "Is onion to be eaten without bread?" He received bread also, and when he had finished, he asked: "Is eating complete without drinking?" and he received water.

A woman wished to borrow a utensil from her neighbor. The door was open, yet she knocked, and was bidden to enter. She said: "How do you do, neighbor? How are your husband, and your children?" She was invited to take a seat and later was asked her wish. It was granted to her.

Another woman sought to borrow the utensil. She went to the same neighbor, opened the closed door without knocking, and asked for the loan, but the utensil was not given her.

A farmer with a farm on lease found that he needed certain acquisitions to make it pay. He washed himself, combed his hair, changed into clean garments, and went to the owner. The owner welcomed him, saying: "Enter, my good lessee, how is your health?" And from questions regarding the land, its fruits, the beasts and their meat, the conversation led to the subject of the loan of ten denarii which were granted. Another lessee, untidy and boorish, was denied a loan. . . .

When we pray for forgiveness, we should follow the example of those who acted wisely. We should first praise the Lord. Then we should ask Him to forgive us our inadvertent sins, then our secret sins, and finally our presumptuous, open sins.

*Wayyikra Rabbah, 5.*

## 94. FORESIGHT

Be not unready when prosperity comes.

*Tanhuma, Buber, Wayyesheb.*

Run not too far, for thou must then return the same distance.

*Kohelet Rabbah, 11, 9.*

The wise man knows at the commencement of a matter what its end will be.

*Y. Sotah, 5 end.*

The careless man places his money on the horn of a deer. (He will never see it again.)

*Ketubot, 107. Mishnah.*

Who is wise? He who foresees what will transpire.

*Tamid, 32.*

## 95. FORTITUDE

How should tribulations be received by thee? Without complaints, but with petitions for God's mercy.

*Berakot, 62.*

The potter, says Rabbi Jonathan, in testing the work of the kiln, examines it by striking the well-wrought vessels only. He does not try the more fragile thus, for one blow will suffice to break them. Even so God afflicts those only who in a spirit of piety and resignation can bear the test of sorrow and suffering.

*Bereshit Rabbah, 55, 2.*

## 96. FREEMEN

The caged bird says: you see my food, but you do not see my captivity.

*Kohelet Rabbah, 11.*

Rab Hama beheld a blind man sitting and learning by heart. He said: "Greetings, freeman." The blind man retorted: "And whence do you infer that I am the son of a serf?"

The Rabbi replied: "You have mistaken my meaning. I meant that you will be a freeman in the World-to-Come. When an earthly master puts out the eye or knocks out the tooth of his serf, he must give him his freedom. You, who by your Heavenly Master have been deprived of both your eyes, will surely be given freedom in the World-to-Come!"

We learn from this that those who suffer on earth will inherit the World-to-Come.

*Bereshit Rabbah, 92.*

## 97. FREE-WILL

My feet lead me to the place I love.

*Sukkah, 53.*

The eye, the ear and the nose are independent of a man's will.

*Wayyikra Tanhuma, 13.*

Rabbi Aha said: God deliberated how to create man. He said to himself: If I create him like the Angels, he will be immortal. If I create him like the beasts, he will be mortal. God decided to leave man's conduct to his own free choice, and if he had not sinned, he would have been immortal.

*Bereshit Rabbah, 8, 11.*

Rabbi Simeon ben Lakish said: "If a man comes to defile himself, the opportunity is given him (but he is not helped); if to purify himself, he is helped to do it (by God)."

*Shabbat, 104a.*

Rabbi Hanina ben Hama said: "Everything is in the power of Heaven except the fear of Heaven.

"God in His providence determines beforehand what a man shall be and what shall befall him, but not whether he shall be righteous or wicked."

*Niddah, 16b.*

### Before a Child Is Born

Before the soul is given residence in the body of a child about to be born, the kernel of the body is brought to the Heavenly Tribunal, where it receives its fate: whether the child will enjoy riches or poverty; whether it be male or female, heroic or cowardly, tall or short, handsome or homely, fat or thin, respected or ignored. One thing, however, is not subjected to predestination, namely whether the child will be good or bad, since it must have freedom of will.

A soul is given residence despite any protestations in the body to be born. It is then given over to an angel who endows it with the capacity of learning the whole Torah and of performing all the Mitzwot. It is taken to Paradise, and the angel says: "These were souls in bodies like yours, and because they did well in life, they are now enjoying their reward." Next it is taken to Gehenna, and the angel declares: "These were like you, and they did evil. Do not imitate them." Then the soul is returned to the womb.

*Tanhuma to Tazria.*

### The Way of Death

Rabbi Pappos interpreted the word of God in Gen. 3:22: "Behold the man is become as one of us in knowing good and evil," as follows: they mean that man has become in this respect like one of the ministering angels. But Rabbi Akiba interpreted them to mean: God set before him two paths: one the way of death, and the other of life. And man chose the way of death.

*Mekilta on Exodus 14:28.*

### Everything Is Foreseen

Rabbi Akiba said: "Everything is foreseen, and freedom of choice is given, and the world is judged with goodness; and everything depends upon the preponderance of doing."

*Abot, 3, 19.*

Whosoever desires to pollute himself with sin will find all the gates open before him; and whosoever desires to attain the highest purity will find all the forces of goodness ready to help him.

*Shabbat, 104a.*

It can be proved by the Torah, the Prophets and the other sacred writings, that man is led along the road which he wishes to follow.

*Makkot, 10b.*

Everything is foreknown, but man is free.

*Abot, 3, 19.*

Only they are free who give themselves to the religious life.

*Abot, 6, 2.*

Only he is master of himself who lives for God and men; he is free from the power of sorrow, free from the oppressor's yoke, free from death.

*Abodah Zarah, 5b.*

R. Johanan b. Zakkai said: "God can be served only by free moral agents, and not by slaves."

*Kiddushin, 22b.*

## 98. FRIENDS, FRIENDSHIP

People say: either companionship or death.

*Taanit, 23.*

Who is the bravest hero? He who turns his enemy into a friend.

*Abot de-R. Nathan, 23.*

It is easy to acquire an enemy, but difficult to acquire a friend.

*Yalkut Shimeoni on Pent., 845.*

A man has three friends: his sons, his wealth and his good deeds.

*Pirke de R. Eliezer, 34.*

Ascend a step and choose thy friend.

*Yebamot, 43.*

Better he who shows a smiling countenance than him who offers milk to drink.

*Ketubot, 111.*

If one man in a society is removed, it falls apart, as if a stone were removed from a heap.

*Bereshit Rabbah, 100, 7.*

### FALSE FRIENDS

There are many persons who eat and drink together, yet they pierce each other with the sword of their tongues.

*Yoma, 9.*

In choosing a friend, go up a step.

*Yebamot, 63a.*

Get thee a companion, one to whom you can tell your secrets.

*Abot, 4.*

How did Job's companions know of his affliction? Each had a flower which they identified with him, and when it drooped they knew that he was troubled.

*Baba Batra, 16b.*

### TWO LOYAL FRIENDS

The outcome of a war parted two friends who had previously lived in the same country: one was left in one kingdom, and the second in another. Though communication between the two lands was forbidden, the two friends remained in touch with each other, and one of them, visiting his friend by stealth, was captured and sentenced to die as a spy. But the man implored the king who had decreed his penalty: "Your Majesty, give me a month's respite so that I may place my affairs in order lest my family be impoverished; at the end of the month I will return to pay the penalty."

The king said: "And who will be thy surety?" The man answered: "Call in my friend, and he will pay for my life with his, in the event I do not return." To the king's amazement, the friend accepted the condition. On the last day when the sword was about to descend, the first friend returned and placed the sword at his own neck. The second friend begged him: "Let me die in your place." The king was touched, and pardoned them both, asking them to include him as a third in their remarkable friendship.

*Jellinek, Beth ha-Midrash.*

### FRIENDS BETTER THAN MONEY

A rich man promised to leave each one of his ten sons the sum of one hundred dinars. But when his time came to die, he discovered that he possessed only nine hundred and fifty. To each of his older sons he left a hundred dinars apiece, and, calling in his youngest son, he said: "I have only 50 dinars left; 30 are needed for burial expenses, and twenty I leave to you. In addition I shall leave you a letter of recommendation to my ten best friends."

The older sons went their way, and the youngest spent little by little the few dinars bequeathed to him. When only one remained he invited the ten friends of his father to a meal. They consulted together and said: "He is the only one among the ten sons of our friend who still cares for us, and he is poor. Let us aid him in his distress." They established him a dairy, and soon he prospered more than his brothers. He said: "Indeed my father left me more than all my brothers together."

*Maasiot le Rabbi Nissim.*

## 99. GAIN AND LOSS

Come and let us take stock of the accounts of the world: the loss caused through a Mitzwah versus the gain, and the gain through a sin versus the loss.

*Baba Batra, 78.*

## 100. THE APPEAL TO GOD

Thou must redeem us eventually. Why delay?

*Midrash Tehillim, 87.*

I have done my part. Do Thou thine.

*Shemot Rabbah, 23, 8.*

If a tribulation befall a man, let him not cry out unto Michael or Gabriel, but only unto God.

*Y. Berakot, 9, 1.*

### The Child's Prayer

R. Eleazar and his companions heard of the serious illness of R. Jose at Pekiin. When they met the townspeople, they learned he was nigh unto death. In the home of the sick man they saw a little child embracing its father and crying bitterly. Then the little lad prayed: "Thou hast written in Thy Torah, O Lord, that the children may be taken away and the mother must be spared. My father was to me and my younger sister, both father and mother, since my mother died. And now Thou art taking him from us as well. It were better Thou didst take us unto Thee, and leave him on earth, in agreement with Thy law."

The Rabbis had no heart to remain and listen, and went to another room. When the boy had fallen asleep in sheer exhaustion, they took him to his own bed, and again entered the room of the stricken Rabbi. And, lo, he opened his eyes and greeted them. They awoke the child and brought him in to see that his prayer for his father had been heard.

The Rabbis went on their way, and since the day was hot, they entered a cave. There they found a dead robber, with a purse of gold tied to his belt. They took the belt with the purse and remained for a moment to see what would transpire. Soon there came a man, and not observing the Rabbis, he prayed thus: "Thou knowest, O Lord, that I do not bewail for myself the loss of my money which the robber has taken from me. But I have aged parents to sustain; moreover some of the money belonged to a poor man who had saved it for his daughter's dowry." The Rabbis gave him the purse.

*Zohar, iii, 204. Condensed.*

## THE WIDOW'S COMPLAINT

A widow who had a trial with a neighbor, passed by the house of the magistrate and heard him read the verse: "Thou shalt not afflict any widow" (Ex. 22:21). She entered and besought him to hear her complaint. "I am busy now," he replied, "return later." The widow said: "I know that this is not a regular hour for court hearings, but because of the verse I heard you read, I believed you would hear my complaint at once." So saith the community of Israel to God: "Because we heard Thee proclaim: 'For the needy shall not always be forgotten' (Psalm 9:19), we came to Thee, and Thou hast forgotten us."

*Midrash Shoher Tob, 13.*

## DEPENDING ON GOD'S MERCY

R. Jacob in the name of R. Eliezer said: " 'And that thou hide not thyself from thine own flesh?' (Isaiah 58:7). This means: 'From thine own divorced wife.' In the days of R. Tanhuma, Israel was in urgent need of rain. The people implored the Rabbi to proclaim a fast-day. He did so, once, twice, and yet no rain came. The third time he commanded that everyone find a poor person and give him charity. A man went to do so and was approached by his divorced wife. She said to him: "Gain merit through me, for since I have left thee, I have seen no single good day." He took pity on her and gave her the money. An eyewitness informed the Rabbi, saying: "If this man did not mean to offend with his divorced wife, he would not have given her money." The Rabbi summoned the man and received his explanation. The Rabbi thereupon declared: "This man had good cause to refuse pity to this woman, and he was not supposed to support her. Yet he was filled with compassion for her. We, O Lord, the Children of Thy beloved Abraham, Isaac and Jacob, are dependent only upon Thee for our support in life. Since Thou art the All-Compassionate, shouldst Thou not succor us and send us rain?"

At once the world was relieved, and the drought ended.

*Wayyikra Rabbah, 34.*

Rabbi Simeon ben Nathaniel said: Do not make your prayer a fixed task, but a plea to God for grace and mercy.

*Abot, 2, 18.*

Rabbi Eliezer ben Hyrcanus said: If a man makes his prayer a fixed task, his prayer is not, as it should be, a plea for God's grace.

*Mishnah Berakot, 4, 3-4.*

When the prophet Isaiah came to King Hezekiah with the message: "Set thine house in order, for thou shalt die," he replied, "Finish thy message and go; I have received the tradition from my royal ancestor David that, even when the sword already touches the neck, man shall not desist from an appeal to the divine mercy."

*Berakot, 10a.*

Israel saith to the Lord: "Be Thou like unto a deer or a young hart" (Song of Songs 8:14). As a deer sleeps with one eye open and one eye closed, be Thou thus with regard to us."

*Zohar, ii, 14.*

## 101. GOD: BLESSING (GRACE, BENEDICTIONS)

Bless the Lord first and then bless others.

*Zohar, i, 227b.*

Leah was the first to thank God; Abraham was the first to call Him Lord, and Hannah was the first to call Him Lord of Hosts. (I Samuel 1:3)

*Berakot, 7, and 31.*

It is proper for a man to praise the Lord for every breath he takes.

*Bereshit Rabbah, 14, 9.*

He who receives enjoyment in this world without blessing God for it, robs both the Lord and the Congregation of Israel.

*Zohar, iii, 44b.*

He who alters the wording of the Sages in benedictions has not fulfilled his duty.

*Berakot, 40.*

Everything that breathes shall praise the Lord; this also means: for every breath a man breathes he is in duty bound to praise his Maker.

*Debarim Rabbah, 2, 37.*

All whom God created in His world praise Him and sing unto Him.

*Zohar, i, 123a.*

A Rabbi asked: "Why do we recite every day the Eighteen Benedictions?"

R. Samuel bar Nahman replied: "Because eighteen times are the Patriarchs mentioned jointly in the Torah. The first joint mention is in the words: 'But God will surely remember you, and bring you out of this land unto the land which He swore to Abraham, to Isaac and to Jacob!' "

*Tanhuma, Wayera, sec. 1.*

For every single breath that a man draws, let him praise God.

*Bereshit Rabbah, 2, 7.*

He who blesses the Lord is likewise blessed.

*Zohar, i, 250a.*

Say grace after thy meal in a spirit of joy. If thou blessest the Lord with joy, He will bless thee with joy and plenty.

*Zohar, ii, 218a.*

The grace before the meal should be said by the master of the home; the grace after the meal, by the guest.

*Raia Mehemna, iv, 244b.*

In this world he who hears good tidings, recites the blessing: "Blessed be He who doeth good"; when he hears evil tidings, he says: "Blessed be the true Judge." But in the World-to-Come, the only blessing will be: "He Who doeth good."

*Pesahim, 50.*

It is a man's duty to bless God for the untoward events of life, by saying: "Blessed be the faithful Judge," just as he blesses Him for the good.

*Mishnah Berakot, 9, 5.*

### Encouraging God

R. Joshua ben Levi said: When Moses ascended on High, he found God making ornaments for the letters. God said to him: "There cometh no greeting from thee?" Moses replied: "May a serf, then, greet his Master?"

God answered: "But thou mayest encourage Me." Moses responded at once: "And now, I pray Thee, let the power of the Lord be great." (Num. 14:17)

*Shabbat, 29.*

Rabbi Simeon ben Yohai says: " 'Ye are My witnesses, saith the Lord, and I am God' (Isaiah 43:10). When ye are My witnesses, I am God, and when ye are not My witnesses, I am not (your) God."

*Sifre Deut., par. 346; Pesikta Buber, 102b.*

"When Israel is of one counsel on earth, God's great Name is praised in Heaven." Rabbi Simeon ben Yohai illustrates this by the figure of a palace built on two boats lashed together, and the consequence if the boats are separated. Similarly he continues: " 'This is my God, and I will make Him lovely' (Exodus 15:2). When I praise Him, he is lovely, and when I do not praise Him, He is, so to speak, lovely in Himself. . . . Again, when, 'Unto Thee do I lift up my eyes, (then), O Thou that sittest in the Heavens' (Psalm 123:1). Otherwise, (it were as if) He should not be sitting in the Heavens."

*Shabbat, 133b; Mekilta Shirah, 3.*

### DEROGATING GOD

A man ascended the pulpit of the Precentor in the presence of R. Hanina. He recited the words: "The Great, Mighty, Awesome, Exalted, Brave, Strong, True, Fearful, Powerful God." The Rabbi waited until the man had finished, and then said to him: "Hast thou completed the praises of thy maker? As for the first three adjectives, if Moses had not included them in the Torah (Deut. 10:17), and the Men of the Great Assembly in the Amidah, we should not have said them. Yet thou sayest so many. It is like a king who possesses millions of gold pieces, and someone praises him as the possessor of millions of silver pieces. Would this not be a derogation of him?"

*Berakot, 33.*

Excess in recounting the praises of God is explicitly forbidden, for it is written: "Who can utter the mighty acts of the Lord, or proclaim all His praise?"

*Megillah, 18a. (Psalm 106:2) Moore, ii, 229.*

### GOD'S DESIRE FOR MAN'S BLESSING

Rabbi Ishmael ben Elisha, the High Priest, said: "I went into the Holy of Holies to offer incense, and I saw the Crowned Lord of Hosts seated on His Throne. He said unto me: 'Ishmael, My son, bless Me.' I responded: 'Lord of the Universe, may it be Thy will that Thy mercies subdue Thy anger, and that Thy mercies be revealed in all Thy attributes, and that Thou conduct Thyself with Thy sons in the attribute of mercy; and that Thou judge them not according to the strict letter of justice.' And God bowed His head to me. This should teach us that the blessing of an unimportant person be not light in our eyes."

*Berakot, 7.*

### THE WORTH OF A BENEDICTION

One man performed a Mitzwah but a second man recited the benediction. Rabban Gamaliel decreed that the second man pay the first ten guldens for taking away the benediction. It was asked: Is it the Mitzwah or the benediction that is worth ten guldens, inasmuch as the Grace after Meals contains four benedictions, but is a single Mitzwah?

The answer is found in the following story. A Sadducee came to Rabbi and said: "We read in Amos (4:13): 'For, lo, He that formeth the mountains, and createth the wind.' Since of one thing it is said that it was formed, and of the other, that it was created, it appears that there are two makers, one who creates and another who forms." Rabbi said: "Look to the end of the verse: 'The Lord, the God of Hosts, is His Name.' He is Only One." The Sadducee promised to return in three days with a proper rejoinder. On the third day Rabbi's servant announced that a Sadducee wished to enter. Rabbi was reluctant to continue the argument, but since the man was of a prominent family, he consented to see him. The man entered and said: "I came to bring these tidings: thy opponent found no report, and fell from a roof and died." Rabbi invited him to dinner, after which he said to him: "By reason of thy tidings, thou canst choose between the recitation of the Grace after Meals with the glass of wine accompanying it, or the receipt of forty guldens." The man chose the Grace and the Cup of Blessing. Later he received a peerage in Rome. From this you may learn that each benediction is worth ten guldens.

*Hullin, 87.*

### A FIVE-FOLD RECITATION

The words "Bless the Lord, O my soul" (Psalm 103:104) were said five times by David with reference both to God and the soul. As God fills the whole world, so does the soul fill the whole body; as God sees and is not seen, so with the soul; as God nourishes the whole world, so does the soul nourish the whole body; as God is pure, so also is the soul pure; as God dwelleth in secret, so does the soul. Therefore let him who possesses these five properties praise Him to whom these five attributes belong.

*Berakot, 10a.*

### IMPROPER BLESSING

If the leader in prayer says: "Thy mercy extends even to the sparrow's nest, and because of good (namely, benefits bestowed), be Thy Name remembered," he is to be silenced.

*Mishnah Megillah, 4, 9.*

## 102. GOD'S CARETAKING (HASHGAHAH)

He who brings forth a generation clothes it.

*Y. Kilaim, 9, 4.*

A man may cleave to a rich man, as long as he is rich; but when the rich man becomes poor, he is ridiculed. But God cleaves to the poor.

*Y. Berakot, 9, 1.*

The Lord does evil to no one, but when He turns His gaze away from a man, that man thereby goes to ruin.

*Zohar, i, Midrash ha-Neelam, 115a.*

A high-placed man cares to attend to others only if they are of the same rank. But God attends to the lowly.

*Sotah, 5.*

God created and He provides; He made and He sustains.

*Tanhuma, Buber, Wayyera, par. 24.*

### GOD'S WATCHFULNESS

Rabbi Simeon ben Yohai and his Disciples, while walking, came upon a stream with no bridge to cross it. Rabbi Jose complained: "What need was there to place a stream in this deserted place?"

Rabbi Simeon answered: "Such a complaint is sinful. Everything here exists for a purpose and the Creator has found everything to be good." As he spoke a snake coiled swiftly between their feet. "Be not alarmed," said the Master. "It may be vouchsafed to us to receive confirmation of the truth of my words." They then beheld the snake engage in a battle with a viper, and eventually both fell over dead. "Had not God sent the snake," said the Master, "the viper might have wounded us."

*Zohar, Emor.*

### THE THORN

Rab Joseph said: Two men were about to embark upon a mercantile enterprise; one of them, having had a thorn pierce his foot, was compelled to forego his intended journey and bemoaned his lot. Later he learned that the ship in which his companion had sailed, had sunk at sea. He confessed his short-sightedness, and praised God in the words of Isaiah (20:1): "I will praise Thee, O Lord because Thou wast angry with me; Thine anger will depart and Thou wilt comfort me."

*Niddah, 31a.*

### EVERYTHING FOR GOOD

It is taught in the name of R. Akiba: A man should accustom himself to say: all that is done in Heaven is done for the best. R. Akiba was travelling, with an ass, a rooster and a lamp. He reached a town, and sought a place to sleep, but no one would admit him. He therefore slept in the open, on the outskirts of the town. A wild beast consumed the ass, a wildcat devoured the rooster, and a wind extinguished his light. Nevertheless he said: "Surely this must all be for good." In the morning he discovered that bandits had fallen upon the town and had carried the residents into captivity. Akiba said: "Is not everything for the best? If my donkey had brayed, or my rooster had crowed, or my lamp had shown a light, they would have carried me off as well."

*Berakot, 61.*

## GAMALIEL'S SERVICE

R. Eliezer, R. Joshua and R. Zadok were feasting in the house of Rabban Gamaliel; they "leaned" according to usage, but Rabban Gamaliel stood and served them with drink. He extended the beaker to R. Eliezer who declined it; he gave it R. Joshua, who accepted it. They said to him: "How is it, Joshua, that we are seated, while Gamaliel, of the Master, stands and offers us drink?" He replied: "We find that one greater than Gamaliel offered service, namely, Abraham, concerning whom it is written: 'And he stands above them.' They did not appear to him as ministering angels, but as Arabs. Therefore should not Rabban Gamaliel, of the Master, stand and give us drink?"

Rabbi Zadok said to him: "How long will ye ignore the honor of the Omnipresent One, and concern yourselves only with the honor of His creatures? The Holy One, Blessed be He, bloweth the winds and bringeth upwards the clouds; He bringeth down rain and causeth the earth to bring forth plants; He prepareth a table for each and every one of his creatures. Therefore shall not Rabban Gamaliel of the Master, stand and give us drink?" [1]

*Kiddushin, 33.*

[1] The term "Of the Master" remains insufficiently explained in the Commentaries. Rabban Gamaliel was not their Master, but their fellow-student. Rashi explains the phrase as "The son of the Master" or "the great person."

## 103. GOD'S COMPASSION ON THE WICKED

In what is God's strength demonstrated? In His patience with the wicked?

*Yoma, 69.*

When the Egyptians were drowning, the angels wished to sing. But God said: "My handiwork is dying, and you wish to sing?"

*Megillah, 10.*

Were it not that "Thy righteousness is like the mighty mountains," who could stand before "Thy judgments (that) are like the great deep?" (Psalm 36:7)

*Arakin, 8.*

Even the evil which God brings down upon the world, He brings down with wisdom.

*Y. Yebamot, 8, 3.*

. Man is not immediately punished for his evil life. God has more patience with men of evil than with the just.

*Zohar, i, 140a.*

The Gentiles are My handiwork, and the Israelites are My handiwork. Shall I destroy the former for the sake of the latter?

*Sanhedrin, 98.*

"The Lord upholdeth all that fall, and raiseth up those that are bowed down" (Psalm 145:14). It does not say: "Those that stand," but "those that are bowed down"—even the wicked.

*Tanhuma, Buber, Wayyetze, par. 10.*

## Long-Suffering

When Moses ascended on High, he saw God writing the word: "Long-suffering." He said: "Art Thou, O Lord, long-suffering to the righteous?" God answered: "To the righteous and to the unrighteous."

Moses responded: "But the unrighteous, O Lord, deserve immediate punishment."

God replied: "Thou shalt see that thou wilt think differently later."

When Israel sinned, God wished to punish them at once. But Moses said: "Not as I have said, do Thou, O Lord, but act as Thou sayest: 'And now, I pray Thee, let the power of the Lord be great, according as Thou hast spoken.'" (Num. 14:17)

*Sanhedrin, 111.*

## 104. GOD'S CURES

God creates the cure before He sends the malady.

*Zohar, i, 196a.*

When a physician cures, the illness may reappear. When God heals, it never returns.

*Zohar, iii, 303b.*

God heals with the same thing that he uses to strike.

*Mekilta Beshallah.*

God heals bitterness with bitter remedies.

*Mekilta Beshallah.*

## A Sharp Sword

When King Hezekiah in his mortal illness heard the announcement of Isaiah in the name of the Lord that he was to die, he replied: "We have a family tradition from David, that even if a sharp sword is resting at a man's throat, he should not refrain from craving mercy." Thereupon he prayed and was granted fifteen more years of life (Isaiah 38:1-5). R. Johanan and R. Eleazar quote in this connection: "Though He slay me, yet will I trust in Him." (Job 13:15)

*Berakot, 10a.*

## 105. DENYING AND HONORING GOD

A philosopher asked R. Reuben of Tiberias: "Who is the most hated of men?" The reply was: "He who denies his God. A transgression of any one of the Ten Commandments means a denial of God. He who respects his God will not have idols, swear falsely in God's name, desecrate His Sabbath wantonly, forbear from honoring his parents, steal, murder, commit adultery or covet another's property."

*Tosefta Shebuot, 3, 5.*

He who walks in straight paths honors God.

*Bemidbar Rabbah, 8, 3.*

Elijah said: "He who increases the honor of God and diminishes his own honor shall see God's honor and his own increased."

*Bemidbar Rabbah, 4, 21.*

It was Abraham who first brought God down from the heavens to the earth, calling Him the God of the heavens and the God of the earth.

*Sifre, Ha'azinu, 134b.*

## 106. FAITH AND TRUST IN GOD

### AFTER STUDY HONORS

R. Zeira said: "I was privileged to know a man with perfect trust in God. He set aside hours for the study of the Torah, and no matter how much he stood to lose, he would never desist from his period of study. He would say: 'If God desires to send me profit, He can do so after my time of study.'"

*Y. Sotah, 9.*

### PRAYER EVERY DAY

The Disciples asked R. Simeon ben Yohai: "Why did not the Manna descend only once a year in an amount sufficient for an entire year's sustenance?" He replied: "Had the Manna come down but once a year, Israel would have looked to God for sustenance only one day a year. But since Israel received only one day's supply at a time, they looked up to God with prayer and trust daily."

*Yoma, 76a.*

## With Faith Alone

Said Rabbi Nehemiah: "Through faith alone Abraham our Father acquired this world and the World-to-Come, as it is written: 'And Abraham had faith in the Lord.'" (Gen. 15:16)

*Mekilta to Exodus 14:31.*

## The Source of Sustenance

R. Eleazer ha-Modii said: "We learn from the story of the Manna that He who fashioned the day also fashioned sustenance for it. Hence he who has bread for one day and is anxious that he may not have food on the morrow is a man with little trust."

*Mekilta Beshallah.*

A man sat and mused: each pore of the body has its own source of sustenance, and no pore depends upon another's source. His wife thereupon said: "Cease from wandering about to find thine own sustenance. He who has provided nourishment for each cell of the body will find it possible to provide food for thee at home."

*Tanhuma to Tazria.*

R. Meir earned three selaim weekly. One he used for food; one for other necessities, and the third he donated to his School. His Disciples inquired: "Why do you not save for your children?" He replied: "If they are righteous, God will provide for them; if unrighteous, why should I provide for those whom God dislikes?"

*Kohelet Rabbah, 2.*

## Israel's Confidence

God said to Moses: "The faith shown by the Children of Israel in obeying the command to march forward into the Red Sea is sufficient reason for Me to divide the sea for them."

*Mekilta Beshallah, 3.*

The Israelites were delivered from Egypt only as a reward for faith, as it is written: "And the people believed." (Exod. 4:31)

*Mekilta Beshallah, 3.*

R. Eliezer the Great said: "He who has a morsel of bread in his vessel and yet says, 'What shall I eat tomorrow?' is of those of little faith."

*Sotah, 48b.*

## Trust in God

One of the Sages said: "I am a child of God, and my neighbor is His child too. My work is in the town, his in the fields. I rise early to my work, and he rises early to his. He boasts not of his work; I will not boast of mine. And if thou sayest that I do great things, and he small things, I ask: 'Have we not learnt that it matters not whether a man accomplish much or little, if only he fix his heart upon his Father in Heaven?' "

*Berakot, 17a.*

Rabbi Eliezer ben Hyrcanus, in dwelling on the moral degeneration of his age, which betokened the end of time, exclaimed: "In whom, then, shall we find support? In our Father who is in Heaven."

*Sotah, 9, 15.*

### FAITH

The light of faith burned brightly from Sabbath Eve unto Sabbath Eve in the home of Sarah.

*Bereshit Rabbah, 60:15.*

"Why was Abraham so severely punished by God," ask the Rabbis, "that his children were to be enslaved in Egypt so many years?"

And they answered: "Because he showed a lack of faith in God's power, when after He assured him: 'I am the Lord that brought thee out of Ur of the Chaldees, to give unto thee this land, to inherit it,' Abraham said to God: 'How do I know that I shall inherit it?' "

*Nedarim, 32a.*

## 107. THE FATHERHOOD OF GOD

There is no father except God.

*Berakot, 35.*

A son respects his father and a servant his master, but ye, Israel, are ashamed to proclaim that I am your Father, or that ye are My servants.

*Zohar, i, 103a.*

God has compassion like a father, and comforts like a mother.

*Pesikta, Buber, 139a.*

Rabbi Judah ben Temah said: "Be strong as a leopard and swift as an eagle and fleet as a gazelle, and brave as a lion to do the will of Thy Father Who is in Heaven."

*Abot, 5, 23.*

Even a steel door in a prison of stone cannot place an obstacle between Israel and his Father in Heaven.

*Pesahim, 85.*

Rabbi Simeon ben Yohai said: "Man's learning in the Torah rejoices the heart not only of his father who is on earth, but also of his Father Who is in Heaven."

*Sifre Deut., par. 48,*

### ENOUGH THAT YE COME

Rabbi Isaac said: When Jeremiah at God's command bade the Israelites repent, they replied: "How can we repent? With what countenance can we come before Him? Have we not provoked Him, have we not insulted Him? The mountains and hills on which we worshipped other gods, are they not still there? 'Let us lie down in our shame and let our confusion cover us'" (Jer. 3:25). When Jeremiah repeated these words to God, he was commanded to return and say to them: "If you come near me, is it not to your Father in Heaven that you come near? As it is written, 'For I became a father to Israel, and Ephraim is my first-born.'" (Jer. 31:9)

*Pesikta Buber, 165a.*

### GOD IN THE WILDERNESS

Rabbi Judah ben Ilai said: The fatherly care of God for Israel is like a man walking on a journey whose son precedes him; robbers came in front to take the boy captive, but his father placed the lad behind him. A wolf came from behind, but the father placed him in front. If robbers came in front and wolves behind, the father took his son in his arms. If the boy was troubled by the heat of the sun, his father stretched his own garment over him. If he became hungry, he gave him food; thirsty, he gave him drink. Thus did God do on behalf of Israel in the wilderness.

*Mekilta Beshallah, 4.*

Rabbi Meir pointed to Hosea as proof that the backsliders also remain "children of the Living God."

*Sifre Deut., 96.*

Rabbi Eliezer ben Hyrcanus said: From the day of the destruction of the Temple, the learned have deteriorated, and the multitude goes to perdition. Yet no one inquires regarding this. And who is there for us to lean upon? Upon our Father Who is in Heaven.

*M. Sotah, 9, 15.*

### HOW THEY PREVAILED

In the battle with Amalek (Exod. 17:8-13), it was not the uplifted arms of Moses that miraculously brought victory to Israel. Scripture teaches us that when the Israelites looked upward and subjected their mind and will to their Father in Heaven, they prevailed; and when they did not, they fell down slain.

*M. Rosh ha-Shanah, 3, 8.*

### GOD'S SUFFERINGS

God lamented the severe sentence He had to pass on Adam; He mourned for six days before the Flood; the death of Nadab and Abihu was twice as hard for Him as even for their father Aaron. God

Himself suffers in the sufferings of men; "In all their affliction He was afflicted" (Isaiah 63:9). He was with Israel in Egypt; He went into exile with them to Babylon, and was delivered with them.

*Tanhuma, Buber, Bereshit, par. 22, etc.*

### WITHOUT POWER

Rabbi Phinehas said: A king left his country and returned after an absence of several years. When he arrived at his palace, his own sons did not recognize him, but looked at each duke and count, searching their faces in quest of their father. The King said: "They are without power; I am your father." Thus saith God: "Turn not unto the angels and saints. They are powerless to avail in your behalf. Turn unto Me; I am your Father."

*Pesikta Rabbati, 21, 11.*

## 108. GOD'S GIFTS TO MAN

Three fine gifts were given to the world: wisdom, strength and wealth.

*Bemidbar Rabbah, 22, 7.*

Three fine gifts God gave to Israel: Torah, Palestine, and the World-to-Come. All are achieved only through chastisements.

*Berakot, 5.*

God asks: "Has anyone ever given anything to Me before I gave it to him? Has anyone circumcised his son before I granted him a son?"

*Wayyikra Rabbah, 27, 2.*

When a man purchases a pound of meat and the butcher is generous, he grants him an extra ounce for the same price. But God's additional favors are more in quantity and quality than the original reward earned by each man.

*Bereshit Rabbah, 61, 4.*

When a man is beloved of God, He sends him poor men as gifts; if the man aids them, God places upon him a thread of mercy, marking him as beyond the touch of the Angel of Punishment.

*Zohar, i, 104a.*

Happy is the lot of the man who accepts God's gift of a deserving poor man with a pleasant countenance.

*Zohar, ii, 198a.*

A man who has obeyed one commandment is helped by Heaven to obey many commandments.

*Mekilta Beshallah.*

ıf a man wishes to travel a certain road, Heaven guides him to it.

*Makkot, 10.*

Commenting upon the words of the Psalmist, "The voice of the Lord is 'Ko-ah' (powerful)," it is said that God reveals Himself not with His own overwhelming might, but "L'fi Koho Shel Kol Ehad W'ehad"—according to each man's individual power and capacity.

*Midrash Tanhuma, Buber, Jethro, 17.*

## 109. GOD'S GUARDIANSHIP OF ISRAEL

R. Simeon ben Lakish taught the following parable concerning God's guardianship of Israel and His association with Israel; a king fastened a chain to the key of a precious jewel-box in his possession, lest it might be easily mislaid or lost. Even thus did God attach His name "El" to "Israel" to guard against their being lost among the nations of the world.

*Y. Taanit, 11, 6, 65d.*

### THE GREAT SHEPHERD

Hadrian said to R. Joshua: "You are among us as a lamb among seventy wolves. Are we not to be commended for not consuming you?"

R. Joshua replied: "It is not your goodness that saves us, but the fact that we have a great Shepherd as our guardian."

*Tanhuma to Toledot.*

### DEFEATING EDOM'S PLANS

A philosopher said to R. Elashah: "Your Scripture declares that God saith concerning Edom: 'They will build, but I will throw down' (Malachi 1:4). Yet we build and He does not cast down our edifices."

The Rabbi replied: "It is not the physical structures that are intended, but the plans you fashion to destroy us and our faith. These plans God hurls to earth."

*Shoher Tob, 9.*

### THE PATRON

Rab while walking from the Hot Springs at Tiberias was accosted by a Roman official who asked him whence he came. He replied: from a visit to the governor. In the evening when the officer called upon the governor, he inquired regarding his friendship with Jews. "We met a Jew and he affirmed that he had visited you." The governor asked: "And what did you do to him?" "We permitted him to go in peace," was the answer. "You acted rightly," responded the governor. "I like this man's reliance upon my patronage."

Thus we may learn that if faith in a human patron avails, how much the more can we have trust upon God as patron.

*Y. Berakot, 9.*

## 110. THE IMITATION OF GOD

Can a man go behind the Shekinah? The phrase means: Follow the example of the Shekinah. Imitate God.

*Sotah, 14.*

Abba Saul said: I will imitate God. As He is merciful and gracious, I will also be merciful and gracious.

*Mekilta Shirah, 3. See also Shabbat, 133.*

We are the adherents of the King of Kings. What is the duty of the king's entourage? To imitate the king.

*Sifra to Lev. 19:2. ("Be Holy for I am holy.")*

Man, to be Godlike, must be partner with God in this act of creation.

*Shabbat, 10a, 119b.*

Walk in the ways of God; as God is merciful and gracious, so be thou; as God is righteous and just, so be thou; as God is Holy, so be thou!

*Sifre, Ekeb, 85a.*

Man is, in a sense, a creator, and therefore a collaborator with God.

*Shabbat, 10a.*

The judge who renders a just decision is as though he had collaborated with God in the work of creation.

*Shabbat, 10a.*

It is to Abraham, for whose sake, the Rabbis tell us, God created man, and who represented such ideal manhood that all about him called him Prince of God,—it is to Abraham and his spouse that the tribute is paid: "And the souls which they made in Haran."
"What meaneth the Bible with these words?" ask the Rabbis. "Did then Abraham and Sarah make souls?"
"Yes," they answer, "for in bringing men closer and nearer to the Divine, by enlarging, ennobling and uplifting the lives of those about them, they actually became their creators."

*Bereshit Rabbah, 39, 21.*

God, it is said, donned a Tallit like a Reader of the Congregation, and showed Moses the way of prayer, saying to him: "When the Israelites sin against Me, let them copy this example, and I will pardon their sins."

*Rosh ha-Shanah, 17b.*

God is the great exemplar of lovingkindness. The world itself was created solely in lovingkindness (Psalm 89:3). Rabbi Simlai observes: The Pentateuch begins with an act of lovingkindness: God

made garments of skin to clothe the man and his wife; and ends with
another: He buried Moses in the valley. It is in such gracious deeds
that man can and should imitate God, who clothes the naked, visits
the sick, comforts the mourners, and buries the dead.

We learn from this that no one, however dignified his station,
should think himself too good for the humblest offices of human help
and sympathy. In the words of Micah (6:8), "to walk humbly with
thy God," is found the duty of joining the funeral procession, or the
company conducting the bride to the wedding. When such a procession passed his School, Rabbi Judah was accustomed to dismiss his
Disciples, saying: Doing takes precedence over studying.

*Sotah, 14a; Sukkah, 49b; Y. Hagigah, 76c. (Combined).*

## 111. GOD'S JUDGMENT: THE HEAVENLY TRIBUNAL

O Lord, Thou wishest the world to exist, and Thou insistest
upon true judgment!

*Wayyikra Rabbah, 10, beginning.*

Even if thou thinkest that God has justified the wicked and con-
victed the just, remember that He is a "God of faithfulness and without iniquity; just and right is He." (Deut. 32:4)

*Midrash Tehillim, 92, 4.*

In the hour of judgment the Lord sayeth to man: "Oh man, much
trouble have I taken with thee before thou wast born. Much trouble
have I taken with thee after thy birth. Hast thou, however, taken the
trouble to learn what thou must do? Hast thou troubled to perform
in practice that which thou hast learned?"

If the man answers in the affirmative, the Lord sets him near to
Him; if in the negative, the Lord sends the man far from Him. If the
man is found to be good, his parents enjoy a double reward in the
World-to-Come: their own reward and the contemplation of their
son's reward. If the man is found to be evil, his parents do not enjoy
even their own reward because of pity for their erring son.

*Mesikta Hibbut ha-Keber, 5, (paraphrased).*

Rabbi Simai said: "It is written (Psalm 50:4): 'He calleth to the
heavens above, and to the earth, that He may judge His people.' 'He
will call to the heavens above' to bring the soul, 'and to the earth'
to bring the body, and thereafter, 'to judge His people.' "

*Midrash Tannaim, 185.*

The school of Hillel held that at the Last Judgment the religious
and moral mediocrities will not go down to Gehenna, for God graciously shall incline the balance to the good side.

*Tosefta Sanhedrin, 13, 3.*

Beruriah, the noble wife of R. Meir, in suggesting a different reading of the Biblical text, made it offer the lesson: "Not the sinners shall perish from the earth, but the sins." (Psalm 104:35)

*Taanit, 23b.*

Ben Azzai said: "The reward of virtue is virtue, and the punishment of sin is sin."

*Abot, 4, 2.*

The Rabbis envisage God as sitting upon the throne of justice, and only after He is through viewing the world through the eyes of justice does He take His seat upon the throne of love and mercy.

*Rosh ha-Shanah, 17b.*

Even a small bird is not ensnared except by the decree of Heaven; how much the more so a man.

*Y. Shebiit, 9, 1.*

He who does not don the garment of the Torah and the Mitzwot arrives at the Heavenly Tribunal in a state of nakedness.

*Zohar, iv, 174a.*

A man does not hurt his finger unless it is decreed from above.

*Hullin, 7.*

Were there no judgment of God upon the world, men would not have known true faith; moreover they would not trouble themselves to study the Torah and to observe its injunctions.

*Zohar, iv, 178b.*

A man cannot listen to two complainants at once, but God hearkens to the complaints of all his creatures at one time.

*Shemot Rabbah, 21.*

When a soul is judged, it is asked: Have you dealt justly?

*Shabbat. 31.*

In this world a man does what he pleases, but in the World-to-Come he must account for his deeds.

*Kohelet Rabbah, 3, 17.*

Charity and lovingkindness are a powerful defense on the Day of Judgment.

*Tosefta Peah, 1.*

The just are judged by their good inclination; the unjust by their evil inclination.

*Berakot, 61.*

When God judges the world, He judges it according to the merits of the majority of the population.

*Zohar, ii, 194a.*

The judge who acquits the guilty on technicalities, even though these be according to the law, is deemed wicked by the Heavenly Tribunal.

*Zohar Hadash to Ruth, 77b.*

When the world is judged, the judges are brought to the Heavenly Tribunal first.

*Zohar Hadash to Ruth, 71a.*

When God judges the earth, he judges first those who are influential.

*Zohar Hadash to Ruth, 76b.*

The judge who is over-lenient in his judgments will receive harsh judgment by the Heavenly Tribunal.

*Zohar Hadash to Ruth, 76b.*

Each night the soul of the sleeper goes before the Heavenly Tribunal. If it is found worthy, it is returned to the body.

*Zohar, i, 121a.*

Sin thwarts God's purpose of grace. "Whenever I seek to do you good, you, by sinning, enfeeble My supernal power."

*Sifre Deut., par. 319.*

The Rabbis ruled: in some cases a man may not be liable in a human court, but he will be liable in God's Court.

*Baba Metzia, 82b.*

God says: "If by one step I overstep and transgress justice, I should set everything on fire; immediately the whole world would be consumed."

*Tanhuma, Buber, Mishpatim, par. 4.*

In dealing with Adam, God gave the attribute of mercy precedence over the attribute of justice.

*Tanhuma, Buber, Tazria, par. 11.*

Rabbi Eliezer ben Jose ha-Gelili (the Galilean) said: "God's inclination in judgment is always in man's favor. If 999 angels give a bad account of a man, and one only a favorable account, God inclines the balance to the meritorious side; and even if 999 parts of the one angel's report are bad, and only one-thousandth good, God will still do the same."

*Y. Kiddushin, 61d.*

When a king suppresses a rebellion, he slays the innocent with the guilty because he knows not the one from the other. God who knows men's thoughts and the counsel of their hearts and reins, knows who has sinned, and who not, knows the spirit of each individual, and will distinguish the guilty from the guiltless.

*Tanhuma, Buber, Korah, par. 19.*

Rabbi Eliezer ben Jacob said: He who observes a precept secures for himself an advocate (angel), and he who commits a sin procures for himself an accuser.

*Abot, 4, 13.*

## 112. LOVE AND FEAR OF GOD

Love God even though He slay thee; for are we not taught to love God with our very souls? And what does this mean but that we are to love Him even if He takes the soul from us?

*Sifre to Deut., 6, 5.*

Those who serve God from love will be like servants who lay out gardens and delights with which to please their absent lord when he returns.

*Tana d'be Eliyahu, 560.*

He who is learned in the Torah, but hath not the fear of God before his eyes, is like a treasurer who possesses the keys of the inner doors, but lacks the keys of the outer ones. How shall he enter?

*Shabbat, 31a.*

The Rabbis pointed out that the proclamation of the Divine might in the Bible is immediately followed by a declaration of the Divine love.

*Megillah, 31a.*

"And thou shalt love the Lord"—namely, thou shalt make the Lord beloved.

*Yoma, 86.*

The reward of reverence is Torah.

*Shemot Rabbah, 40, 1.*

We read: "Return, O backsliding children." (Jer. 3:14)
And we read: "I will heal their backsliding." (Hosea 14:5)
If Israel repents from love of God, he needs no cure; if from fear, he must first be healed.

*Yoma, 87.*

The lovers of God are of two kinds: some love Him because He gave them wealth, power and length of life. Had they lacked these they might have felt the reverse towards Him. Others love God because He is their beloved Master whether He give them good or evil.

*Introduction to Zohar, 12a.*

Fear Heaven, for everything comes from Heaven.

*Midrash ha-Gadol, 503.*

How does one love the Lord? By encompassing himself with benevolence on every side, by doing benevolence to all without sparing his strength or his property.

*Zohar, v, 267a.*

A man is more feared by outsiders than by his intimates, but the fear of God is more recognized by those who are near to Him.

*Mekilta Beshallah, 8.*

Everything is in the hands of Heaven except the fear of Heaven.

*Berakot, 33.*

Why is God called the King of Glory? Because He distributes glory to those who fear Him.

*Bemidbar Rabbah, 14, 3.*

"Thou shalt love thy God with all thy heart(s)" means with both thine impulses, the good and the evil. "Leb" is singleminded; "lebab," as here, indicates doublemindedness.

*Sifre on Deut., 6, 5.*

"To love the Lord, your God." (Deut. 11:13)

You may be tempted to say that you will learn Torah in order that you may become rich or that you may become Rabbi or that you may acquire a reward. The Scripture, however, says: "To love the Lord, your God." Whatever you do, therefore, do not do except for love.

*Sifre on above verse.*

Rabbi Jose said: "Let thy neighbor's property be as dear to thee as thine own; and address thyself to acquire knowledge of the Law, for it does not come to thee by inheritance; and let all thy deeds be done for the sake of Heaven (i.e., God)."

*Abot, 2, 17.*

The Rabbis teach: "Those who being reviled do not return revilement; those who give no heed to insults; those who act in everything out of love for God, and those who receive affliction with rejoicing, concerning all of them the Scriptures say: 'But they that love Him be as the sun when he goeth forth in his might.' " (Judges 5:31)

*Shabbat, 88b.*

When Beladon, king of Babylon, heard that King Hezekiah of Judaea had recovered his health after being near death, he commanded his secretary to write an epistle of congratulation to Hezekiah. He wrote: "Peace unto King Hezekiah; greetings unto the city of Jerusalem, and respect unto the great God that dwelleth therein."

When Nebuchadnezzer, Beladon's grand-vizier, heard of this, he said: "You called him the great God, yet you mention Him last."

The king gave him permission to intercept the message, and another

epistle was written mentioning God first, then Jerusalem, then Hezekiah. When the Judaeans sinned, it was decided in Heaven to designate Nebuchadnezzer, who had shown respect unto God, to punish
those who had shown disrespect unto Him.

*Sanhedrin, 96.*

He who truly possesses the fear of the Lord deserves to attain
to the love of God.

*Zohar, ii, 216a.*

A robber, according to the Torah, must return the article he has
stolen, but a thief must make double restitution. Why? It is because
the robber demonstrates that he considers the fear of man equal in
importance to the fear of God, but the thief fears man without fearing God.

*Zohar, iii, 16a.*

Fear is the primary element in the service a man should offer to
his Master, namely, he must first show that he fears the Lord. Eventually the man will perform with joy the ordinances of the Lord.

*Zohar, iii, 56a.*

Great is fear in the presence of God, for fear includes humility,
and humility includes Hasiduth, or piety. It will be found that the
man who has the fear of Heaven has every virtue, but he who is not
a God-fearing man has neither humility nor Hasiduth.

*Zohar, iv, 145a.*

Only he who is God-fearing may truly be praised. The Hebrew
word "Beyirat" (in the fear) has the numerical value of 613. It is
an indication that the 613 commandments should be performed by a
man in the fear of God.

*Hakdamah to Tikkune Zohar, 12a.*

The Psalmist assures us that he who is God-fearing will lack for
nothing.

*Hakdamah to Tikkune Zohar, 12a.*

Since fear leads to humility, humility is the greater virtue. Therefore, Moses, who was very humble, considered fear a minor virtue.

*Hakdamah to Tikkune Zohar, 12a.*

If there is no fear there is no wisdom nor learning, for fear is the
storehouse of wisdom, and wisdom is a symbol of the valuables stored
in reverence. Fear secretes wisdom within itself. Fear is the palace
of the King wherein valuables are housed.

*Tikkune Zohar, 31b.*

Fear must precede wisdom; then wisdom will have a place wherein
to abide in security.

*Zohar Hadash, ii, 45b.*

He who observes the commandment to fear the Lord observes all the commandments of the Torah, for fear is the gateway to them all.

*Tikkune Zohar, Hakdamah, 11b.*

There are three forms of fear: some fear God because they are afraid they will lose life and property; some fear the Lord because they are afraid to lose their share in the World-to-Come. These two forms are imperfect. The perfect form is to fear the Lord because he is the Master and the Ruler, and deserves obedience.

*Tikkune Zohar, Hakdamah, 11b.*

He who fears the Lord has proper faith, for he is perfect in the service of Him.

*Zohar, i, 59a.*

The greatest reward in the World-to-Come is reserved for the man who teaches his children how to fear the Lord and how to serve Him in the ways of Torah.

*Zohar, i, 188a.*

Rabbi Akiba said: " 'Thou shalt love the Lord . . . with all thy might' (Deut. 6:5)—in whatever measure He meets out to thee, whether it be the measure of good or the measure of punishment." [1]

*Yalkut, i, 837.*

[1] Rabbi Akiba finds the word "measure," "middah" in "Meodeka,"—"thy might" by dropping the silent "aleph."

## 113. GOD'S LOVE FOR ISRAEL

Though it is written that God loveth justice, the love He bears for His son Israel prevails over His love for justice.

*Zohar, iii, 99b.*

If the children of Israel but knew how much God loves them, they would run to Him with the strength of a lion.

*Zohar, ii, 5b.*

God feeds the world for the sake of Israel.

*Zohar, ii, 152b.*

If a man have a kinsman who is rich, he acknowledges him; if the kinsman be poor, he does not recognize him. This is not true of God, for when the children of Israel are in their lowest estate God calls them brothers and friends.

*Midrash Tehillim, 84, 3.*

A king possessed several uniforms of purple, and he was accustomed to caution his servant to take especial care of one in particular. When the servant asked the reason the king replied: "This is the robe I wore at my coronation."

By the same token God commands His servants to take account of Israel frequently. When asked the reason, God replied: "On the day when I demonstrated My omnipotence at the Red Sea Israel was among the first to recognize My sovereignty."

*Pesikta Rabbati, 10, 11.*

"My beloved is like a gazelle or a young hart" (Song of Songs 2:9). As a gazelle leaps and skips from bush to bush, from covert to covert, from hedge to hedge, so likewise does the Holy One, blessed be He, pass from synagogue to synagogue, and from academy to academy, that He may bless Israel.

*Yalkut Shimeoni, 1070 to the above verse.*

Hillel said in the name of God by way of illustration of the covenant of love between God and Israel: "My feet carry Me to the place which My heart loves. If thou comest to My house I will come to thine; but if thou comest not to My house I will not come to thine."

*Tosefta, Sukkah, 4, 3.*

Rabbi Akiba stressed the image of God in humanity when he said: "Beloved is man, for he is created in God's image, and it was a special token of love that he became conscious of it. Beloved is Israel, for they are called the children of God, and it was a special token of love that they became conscious of it."

*Abot, 3, 18.*

Rabbi Akiba said: "Beloved of God are the children of Israel, for to them was given the instrument (namely, the Torah) wherewith the world was created."

*Abot, 3, 18.*

Come and see how beloved of God are the children of Israel, for wherever they were exiled God went into exile with them.

*Megillah, 29.*

If an unlearned man reads instead of "Weahabta eth Elokeka" "Weayyabta eth Elokeka," namely, instead of "Thou shalt love thy God," the words "Thou shalt hate thy God," God sayeth: "His very error is in Mine eyes a sign of his love."

*Shir ha-Shirim Rabbah, 2, 12.*

## 114. GOD'S MERCIES

The Lord of Mercy does not begin His punishment with the taking away of life.

*Wayyikra Rabbah, 17, 5.*

If a man annoy a human patron overmuch he protests, but God receives a man however much he vex Him.

*Y. Berakot, 9, 1.*

One verse declares: "God is good to all" and another verse says: "God is good to those who trust in Him." This is like a man who owns a fruit-garden. If he irrigates the field he irrigates all the trees, but if he hoes, he hoes only the healthy trees.

*Sanhedrin, 39.*

God judges the nations at night when they perform no evil; and He judges the children of Israel during the day when they perform Mitzwot.

*Abodah Zarah, 3.*

Psalm 145:17 reads: "The Lord is righteous in all His ways," and it continues: "And gracious in all His works," namely, not exacting justice. In the beginning He is righteous, and then gracious.

*Rosh ha-Shanah, 17.*

O give thanks unto the Lord, for He collects an obligation due Him out of a man's goods rather than from his person.

*Pesahim, 118.*

Psalm 57:11 reads: "For Thy mercy is great unto the heavens" and another, Psalm 108:5, reads: "For Thy mercy is great above the heavens." If the performance of good deeds is for the sake of God, His mercy is above the heavens.

*Pesahim, 50.*

A man who wishes to bring evil upon others usually does not disclose his intention, but God reveals it.

*Midrash ha-Gadol, 144.*

Even in His anger, God remembers to send a share of His mercies.

*Pesahim, 87.*

It is written (Psalm 62:13): "Also unto Thee, O Lord, belongeth mercy." And further it is written: "For thou renderest unto every man according to his work." In the beginning God wished to render justice but when He observed that the world could not rest on justice alone, He rendered mercy.

*Rosh ha-Shanah, 17.*

Everything the All-Merciful does is done for the best.

*Berakot, 60.*

When God grants a good crop, He gives it for the living.

*Taanit, 8.*

A man may be conquered by jealousy, but God conquers His own jealousy.

*Midrash Tehillim, 94, 1.*

When God displayed to Moses all the treasuries of merit prepared for the righteous—one for those who give alms, one for those who provide for orphans, and so·on, Moses beheld one large treasury, and inquired as to its owner. God replied: "To the man who has merit I give of his own, and to him who has none I bestow upon without payment, as it is written: 'And I will show favor upon whom I will show favor.'" (Ex. 33:19)

*Tanhuma Buber, Ki-tissa.*

It is thus that God prays: "May it please Me that My mercy may overcome My anger; that all My attributes may be invested with compassion and that I may deal with My children in the attribute of kindness, and that out of regard for them I may omit judgment."

*Berakot, 7a.*

Six and twenty times does the refrain "His mercy endureth for ever" occur in the 136th Psalm, to match the twenty-six generations that lived before the Law was given, but whom God nourished with His grace.

*Pesahim, 118a.*

The liberal Hillelites say that He who is abundant in mercy will turn the scales toward mercy!

*Rosh ha-Shanah, 16b-17a.*

Whatever the All-merciful doeth, He doeth well.

*Berakot, 60b.*

R. Akiba said: "The world is judged by the divine attribute of goodness."

*Abot, 3, 19.*

God was heard praying: "Oh that My attribute of mercy may prevail over My attribute of justice, so that grace alone may be bestowed upon My children on earth."

*Berakot, 7a.*

R. Akiba said that God's love extends to all created in God's image, although the knowledge of it was vouchsafed to Israel alone.

*Abot, 3, 18.*

## 115. GOD—NEAR AND FAR

Let thy God be thy companion.

*Midrash Tehillim to Ps. 104, 1.*

"Behold," said God to Moses, "I will stand before thee there upon the rock in Horeb." (Exod. 17:6)

The Rabbis interpret this to mean: "Wherever thou findest the footprints of men, there I stand before thee."

*Mekilta to Exod., 17, 6.*

"I shall walk before the Lord in the lands of the living" (Psalm 116:9). This means, not only in the privacy of my home, but also amidst the crowded places, even in the market-places, shall I walk before Him.

*Yoma, 71a.*

Man could conceive His abode as the very heavens and yet feel so close to Him that when he prays to Him it is "like a man who talks into the ear of his friend."

*Y. Berakot, chap. 9, 13a.*

Penitents can come near to the Lord in a single moment. Perfect Zaddikim, however, may be compelled to labor many years to come as near.

*Zohar, i, 129b.*

He who prides himself as a disciple of the Sages and is not really learned shall not be admitted into the enclosure of God.

*Baba Batra, 98.*

He on whose account his comrade has been punished is not admitted into the enclosure of God.

*Shabbat, 49.*

When a man smiles at his shadow it smiles back at him. By the same token God is thy shadow; as thou art to Him, so He is to thee.

*Midrash quoted in Shalah.*

He who desires to come nearer to God is helped to do so. He who desires to sanctify himself has holiness spread over him.

*Zohar, iv, 126a.*

Four classes of men will not be received into the Divine Presence: scoffers, liars, hypocrites and those who retail slander.

*Sotah, 42a.*

Seven attributes help to bring a man near to the Throne of Glory, and these are: wisdom, righteousness, judgment, grace, mercy, truth and peace.

*Abot de-Rabbi Nathan, chap. 37.*

## 116. GOD—OMNIPRESENT, OMNISCIENT

Why is God called Makom (Space)? Because He is the space of the universe.

*Bereshit Rabbah, 68, 9.*

A matron said to R. Jose: "My god is greater than thine. When God revealed Himself to Moses, he did not flee, but when my god, the serpent, appeared there, Moses ran away."

The Rabbi replied: "Moses could escape from thy god by retreating a few steps, but where could he have escaped from my God?"

*Shemot Rabbah, 3.*

God appeared to Moses in a despised thorn-bush, not in a carob tree or a fig tree, which men value, in order to teach that there is no place on earth void of the Divine Presence.

*Shemot Rabbah on verse 3, 3.*

"No sin, however done in secrecy and in darkness, can escape the eye of Him who fills heaven and earth. Wherever we are, and in whatever estate, God is present with us."

*Tanhuma Buber, Naso, 14b-15a.*

The various names of God represent difference conceptions: "Elohim" emphasizes the God who dispenses justice; "Jehovah," the God who displays mercy and compassion; "Shaddai," the God of power and might. (The Israelites in Egypt knew God as "El Shaddai," the God who rules the universe, the philosophic or cosmic God.)

*Bereshit Rabbah, 33.*

All expressions concerning the description of God must never be taken literally; they are simply due to the inadequacy of human language, or "to make the ear listen to what it can hear."

*Abot de-R. Nathan, 2.*

A heretic once said sarcastically to Gamaliel II: "Ye say that where ten persons assemble for worship, there the divine majesty (Shekinah) descends upon them; how many such majesties are there?"

To which Gamaliel replied: "Does not the one orb of day send forth a million rays upon the earth? And should not the majesty of God, which is a million times brighter than the sun, be reflected in every spot on earth?"

*Sanhedrin, 39a.*

## WHERE IS GOD?

As the soul fills the body, though no one knows its abode, so God fills the Universe, though no one knows His abode.

A man asked Rabban Gamaliel: "Where is thy God?" He answered: "I do not know." The man continued: "Yet you pray to Him, though you know not where He is?"

R. Gamaliel replied: "Your soul is near to you, yet where is it?"

The man responded: "We do better than you; we behold the idol to which we pray."

The Rabbi retorted: "You may see the idol, but it does not see you. We do not behold God, but He beholds us."

*Shoher Tob, 103.*

The Emperor said to R. Gamaliel: "I know where your God resides, and what He is doing." The Rabbi sighed deeply: "My son is somewhere overseas; can you command that he return to me?"

The Emperor replied: "How can I do this if you do not know where he is?"

R. Gamaliel rejoined: "You, O Emperor, do not know what transpires on earth a short distance away; yet you wish me to believe that you know what transpires in Heaven."

*Sanhedrin, 38.*

On a certain boat were passengers of many different nationalities. A storm threatened to sink the vessel. Each man took into his hand his own particular religious image and offered prayer to it. But the storm only grew in fury.

They turned to a Jewish lad and begged him to pray to his God. As soon as he had completed his prayer, calm ensued.

When they had arrived at the port, all the passengers, except the lad, were about to go on shore to make purchases. They inquired of the boy, and he said: "What do you wish of a despicable creature like myself?"

They answered: "Not you, but we are to be despised. Some of us have their gods in Babylonia; others in Persia; still others, with them on this boat; but none avails in danger. Yet your God is with you wherever you are, and He does what you petition Him to do."

*Y. Berakot, 9.*

A heathen asked R. Joshua b. Karha: "Why did God reveal Himself to Moses in a 'Sneh' (a bush)?"

The Rabbi answered: "To teach thee that the Shekinah is everywhere, even in a wild, lowly bush, like the 'Sneh'."

*Shemot Rabbah, 2.*

Emperor Hadrian once said to Rabbi Joshua: "Why does not your God show Himself?"

"Because," replied the Rabbi, "no human eye can behold Him and live. Remember that the sun is one of the least of His creatures, yet you can look upon it only with the greatest of difficulty."

*Hullin, 60.*

## 117. GOD'S OWNERSHIP OF ALL

God is not like a ship-owner who does not own the cargo. But the universe and the fulness thereof are His.

*Midrash Tehillim, 24, 2.*

We read: "The earth is the Lord's" (Psalm 24:2); and, "But the earth hath He given to the children of men" (Psalm 115:16). How can we explain this? Before one pronounces a benediction for the thing to be enjoyed in the world, he should recognize that all things on earth belong to God. After that "hath He given to the children of men" to be enjoyed by them."

*Berakot, 35.*

From the day that God created the world until the days of Abraham no one called God as "Adon," Master or Lord, until Abraham came and so termed Him.

*Berakot, 7b.*

## 118. GOD'S RELATIONSHIP TO ISRAEL

At the time that you conduct yourselves like sons of God, you are called His sons.

*Kiddushin, 36.*

God said to rebellious Israel in the wilderness: I desire neither your praise nor your grumbling.

*Shemot Rabbah, 25, 7.*

An Israelite who has sinned is still an Israelite.

*Sanhedrin, 21.*

Is then a Jew anywhere an alien? Wherever he goes, his God is with Him.

*Debarim Rabbah, 2, 16.*

According to the nature of mankind, the prosecutor does not become the advocate. But God called Israel "a nation heavy with sin," and He also said of them: "And Thy people are all righteous."

*Shemot Rabbah, 15, 29.*

R. Abin said: "We read: 'And ye shall be "Lamed Yod" (unto Me) a peculiar treasure' (Exodus 19:6). The Lamed is the highest letter; the Yod the lowest. How appropriate is it for the small to cleave to the great!"

*Pesikta Rabbati, 11, 7.*

A prince once asked his shrewish wife to fashion a purple garment for him. During the time she was busy with it, he had peace. When she brought it to him, he exclaimed: "Woe is me!" The princess retorted: "I bring you a fine garment, yet you sigh." The prince answered: "I sigh at the thought that you may now perchance return to your shrewish ways."

By the same token, when Israel continually grumbled, God asked them to build the Tabernacle, that they might thus be too busy to complain. When it was completed, he exclaimed: "Woe is Me! It is finished!" [1]

*Pesikta Rabbati, 5, 9.*

[1] A playful interpretation of the word "Wayyehi," "It Became Woe."

God dealt with Israel even as a mother-hen deals with her chicks. When they are tiny, she feeds and warms them; when they are grown, she tells them: "Go and dig in the earth." When Israel was young, God sent him manna, and illumined his path at night. When he was grown, God told him: "Go and dig in the ground for your food." (Lev. 19:23)

*Wayyikra Rabbah, 25.*

Rabbi Judah ben Ilai said that only when the Children of Israel behaved like sons were they called the sons of God.

Rabbi Meir said: "Whether they are righteous or sinful, they are called the sons of God. We find in the Scripture that they are called foolish sons, untrustworthy sons, vicious sons, but sons notwithstanding."

Kiddushin, 36a.

A philosopher asked R. Gamaliel: "Do you have authority for maintaining that God will redeem you?"

R. Gamaliel answered: "Yes."

"This is an unfounded assertion," rejoined the philosopher. "Does not Hosea say: 'He hath loosed (or withdrawn) himself from them?' (5:6). And can, then, a woman who was loosed by a man, marry the man?" (Deut. 25:9)

R. Gamaliel answered: "Who does the loosening, the man or the woman?"

"The woman," was the response.

"Then what does it avail if God loosed Himself from us? The congregation of Israel is like unto the wife, and God is like unto the husband. And if we have not loosed Him, His loosening is valueless." [1]

Shoher Tob, 10.

[1] The word in Hosea is "Halatz," masculine; in Deuteronomy it is "Halutzah," feminine.

Rabbi Absalom, the Elder, said: "Let me recount a Parable. To what is the matter like? To a man who was angry with his son, and banished him from his home. His friend begged him to restore his son to his house. The father replied: 'Thou asketh of me nothing except on behalf of my son? I am already reconciled with my son.' Thus the Omnipresent said unto Moses: 'Wherefore criest thou unto me?' (Exodus 14:15). Long ago I have become well-disposed unto Israel."

Mekilta Beshallah.

## WHOM DOES GOD CHOOSE?

A matron said to R. Jose: "You are a Chosen People not because you are superior to other peoples, but because God chanced to wish it so."

The Rabbi brought her a basket of figs; she chose the more tasty and ate them.

Rabbi Jose then said: "You know why you choose some figs and reject others. Nevertheless you still assert that God has no reason for making a choice. Did He not choose Israel because He found his deeds of a higher order?"

Bemidbar Rabbah, 3. (Paraphrased.)

## 119. SANCTIFICATION AND PROFANATION OF GOD'S NAME

We read: "Ye shall be holy for I, the Lord your God, am holy." This is equivalent to saying: If ye make yourselves holy, I impute it to you as though you hallowed Me; and if ye do not make yourselves holy, I impute it to you as though ye did not hallow Me.

Can the meaning be: If ye make Me holy, then I am made holy; and if not, I am not made holy? The Scripture declares: "For I am holy," namely, "I abide in My holiness, whether ye hallow Me or not."

Herein do we find an answer to the question: What is meant by Kiddush and Hillul ha-Shem; or since God is by nature holy, how, then, can men hallow or profane Him?

*Sifra on Leviticus, 19, 2.*

Rabbi Johanan ben Berokah said: "If a man profanes the Name of God in secret, he will be requited openly. In the profanation of the Name, there is no distinction of inadvertent and presumptuous."

*Abot, 4, 5.*

When experience showed that the pagan neighbors of the Jews never returned anything which they had found, belonging to a Jew, it was decided in law that a Jew might keep the possession of an idolator which he had found. Some Rabbis, however, decreed that it glorified God's Name to return things found in this way.

Simeon ben Shetah bought a donkey. Under its saddle he discovered a pearl, left there by mistake. He returned it to the Arab who then exclaimed: "Blessed be the God of Israel." The Rabbi's Disciples inquired why he had not kept that which he had found, in accordance with the law. The Rabbi answered: "Am I then a barbarian? His blessing is worth more to me than all the money the pearl might have brought." [1]

*Y. Baba Metzia, 2.*

[1] See my poem in *Joyful Jeremiads*, p. 91, quoted in Raskin's *Anthology of Jewish Poetry*, p. 46.

Some old men bought grain from soldiers, in which they discovered several coins. They returned these to the soldiers, who blessed Israel's God.

Abba Oshaya of Tirea discovered some ornaments belonging to the governor's wife. When he returned them, the matron said: "I beg of you to keep them, since I have many superior to these." The Rabbi declined, saying: "According to the Torah, I must restore that which I have found." The governor's wife blessed the God of Israel who had ordained such a Torah.

R. Samuel bar Susreta chanced to visit Rome, where he found a jewel-box filled with gems. The Empress who had lost them, issued a proclamation: "If the finder brings me the jewel-box within thirty days, he will receive a great reward; if he keeps it longer, he will be punished, when he returns it, for the delay."

R. Samuel kept the gems thirty-one days, and then returned them. When the Empress exclaimed: "Have you not heard my proclamation? Why did you delay more than thirty days?" the Rabbi answered: "I delayed because I wished to show you that I returned the jewel-box not for the reward, nor through fear of you, but solely out of fear of God." The Empress thereupon blessed the God of Israel.

*Y. Baba Metzia, 2.*

Several Sages were seated at the gate of R. Joshua, discussing the reason why Judah merited it that the Royal House of David should descend from him. One said: "Because he confessed his affair with Tamar." Another remarked: "Should, then, a sinner merit not merely forgiveness, but also a great reward? Judah gained merit because he had saved Joseph from being slain."

A third exclaimed: "The saving was an atonement for the sale of Joseph in which Judah took part. But Judah had merit because of his humility; he, only, offered himself as a slave in place of Benjamin. By the same token, Saul merited royalty, for he said: 'My father will be anxious regarding us—my slave and myself.' Thus he placed himself and his slave on a plane of equality."

A fourth Sage declared: "Judah was a surety; hence it was necessary that he offer himself as a slave. But he had merit because the Tribe of Judah was the first to leap into the Red Sea. And it is written: 'Judah became His sanctifier; therefore Israel is his dominion.'" (Psalm 114:2)

*Tosefta Berakot, 4.*

Rabbi Ishmael taught: While other classes of sins are atoned for, according to their heinousness, by repentance, the Day of Atonement, chastisements cumulatively, not all together suffice to atone for the man through whom the Name of God is profaned. Such guilt is wiped out only by the day of death.

*Yoma, 86a.*

Rabbi Hanina remarked to his disciple, Rabbi Eleazar ben Pedat: "Pray, explain which of the two alternatives mentioned in Proverbs 30:9 is worse: 'Lest I be full, and deny, and say: "Who is the Lord?"' or, 'Lest I be poor, and steal, and profane the Name of my God'?"

Rabbi Eleazar replied: "The second is worse. We find that God overlooked idolatry but not the profanation of His Name. 'Go ye, serve every one his idols . . .; but My Holy Name shall ye no more profane.'" (Ezekiel 20:39)[1]

*Wayyikra Rabbah, 22.*

[1] Since most of the students of the Law were poor, any larceny committed by such a student led to the disgrace of the students of the Torah as a body. This was a profanation of the Name of God.

Better that a letter of the Sacred Torah itself be blotted out than that the Divine Name be profaned.

*Yebamot, 79a.*

When Elijah enjoined the priests of Baal to choose one bullock as a sacrifice to Baal while he chose one bullock as a sacrifice to God (I Kings 18:23), the bullock chosen by the priests refused to accompany them. The animal cried aloud: "We are both twins and we grew up together. Why should my brother go to God and I to the Baal?"

Elijah answered the bullock: "Go with them, for thou wilt sanctify God's Name as truly as thy brother."

Nevertheless the bullock refused to go until Elijah led it to the altar of the Baal.

*Bemidbar Rabbah, 23.*

## 120.  SERVICE OF GOD

Whoso serves God from any motive save love is a sordid and useless creature; better had he never been born.

*Berakot, 17a.*

In the ordinary course of the world, a master pays his servant for soiling himself in coarse labors. Not so the Lord. He enjoins us: "Do not make yourselves unclean."

*Bemidbar Rabbah, 10, 1.*

Serve the Lord with joy, for the joy of man draws towards him another joy from above.

*Zohar, ii, 184b.*

Why did God command the Israelite to bore the ear of the Jewish slave who did not wish to go free? (Exodus 21:6). Verily, the ear that heard the words: "To Me shall the sons of Israel be slaves" and yet prefers to be a slave of a man—it shall be bored.

*Kiddushin, 22.*

In reciting the first sentence of the Shema, a man takes upon himself the yoke of the kingdom of Heaven (sovereignty of God), and proceeds in the following to take upon himself the specific commandments.

*Mishnah Berakot, 2, 2.*

Antigonos of Soko said: "Be not like slaves who serve their masters with the expectation of receiving a gratuity; but be like slaves who serve their master without expectation of receiving a gratuity; and let the fear of Heaven be upon you."

*Abot, 1, 3.*

R. Johanan said: "Just as the forty days wherein the spies of Moses sinned before God were turned into forty years of wandering—a year for each day—so by the same token is one day in the year wherein a man serves his Maker well, accounted unto him as if he served Him well the entire year."

Rab Idi was a travelling merchant and could spend only one day in three months at the Academy. The students called him "the one-day student." But when they heard the statement by R. Johanan, their teacher, they grew to respect Rab Idi.

*Hagigah, 5.*


## 121. GOD'S SHEKINAH (DIVINE PRESENCE)

The Shekinah rests only on a man who is brave, wealthy and sensible.

*Shabbat, 92.*

Why do we have the Menorah? Does God then need its light? Nay; the Menorah exists to demonstrate that the Shekinah rests in Israel.

*Shabbat, 22.*

God is the space of the world. What is the world? The Shekinah.

*Zohar, iv, 242a.*

One who transgresses is as if he had removed a garment from the Shekinah; one who observes the commandments is as if he had clothed the Shekinah with a garment.

*Zohar, i, 23b.*

They were exiled to Babylon, the Shekinah with them. They were exiled to Egypt, the Shekinah with them.

*Megillah, 29.*

Because of the merit of Israel's trust in God, they deserved to recite the Song of the Red Sea; and the Shekinah rested upon them. Therefore, if any person should add the Prayer of Redemption to the Eighteen Prayers, the Shekinah will rest upon him.

*Shemot Rabbah, 22.*

There is no space unoccupied by the Shekinah.

*Bemidbar Rabbah, 12, 4.*

At times the universe and its fulness does not contain the glory of God's holiness. At other times, however, He speaks for a man from between the hairs of his head.

*Bereshit Rabbah, 4, 4.*

The scholars who in this world banish sleep from their eyes are rewarded with the splendor of the Shekinah.

*Baba Batra, 10.*

Rabbi Isaac said: "Whenever Israelites prolong their stay in the synagogues and schools, God makes His Presence tarry with them."

*Pesikta Buber, 193a-b.*

Rabbi Eleazar ben Pedat said: "Even after the destruction of the Temple, God's Presence (Shekinah) still abides on the ruined site in accordance with His promise: 'My eyes and My mind will be there perpetually.'" (I Kings 9:3)

*Tanhuma Buber, Shemot, 10.*

R. Hiyya, accompanied by R. Jose, was journeying to Ludd. R. Hiyya said: "If people were aware of the honor paid by God to Jacob when He told him: 'I will go down with thee into Egypt' (Gen. 46:4), they would have greatly honored Jacob's grave."

They met R. Abba, and he said to them: "It is written: 'Who came into Egypt with Jacob' (Ex. 1:1). From this we learn that whenever the children of Israel go into exile, all holiness accompanies them."

*Zohar, ii, 5.*

God addressed Moses from a thornbush to teach us that no place is void of the Shekinah.

*Pesikta Rabbah, 2b.*

In the city of Nehardea in Babylonia there was a synagogue revered as a sacred shrine. Tradition has it that the exiles from Zion after the destruction of the First Temple brought with them some of its stones, and with these they built the synagogue in Nehardea. It was therefore known as the Abode of the Shekinah, and many stories are told of God's visits to it.

Once the blind Rabbi Sheshet was in this synagogue when the Shekinah appeared. The blind and weak Rabbi could not depart from the House quickly enough to satisfy the angels who tormented him. He cried out: "O Lord of the universe, I am so weak and Thou art so mighty. Who of us should yield?"

A voice was heard: "Leave him in peace."

Could any story more truly illustrate the principle that the strong should yield to the weak? Twenty-two times is this tale given in various parts of the Talmud and Midrash.

*Megillah, 29, etc.*

Originally the Presence of God dwelt here below. When Adam sinned, it mounted aloft to the nearest firmament; when Cain sinned, to the second; and so on to the generations of Enosh, of the Flood, of the Dispersion of the Nations (Tower of Babel), and the men of Sodom. Finally the wickedness of the Egyptians in the days of Abraham caused the Shekinah to retreat to the seventh and most remote heaven.

The righteous Patriarchs and their successors in the line of Moses, and ending with him, brought down God's Presence once more through the same seven stages.

*Bereshit Rabbah, 19, 7.*

Rabbi Levi said: "The Tabernacle was like a cave that joins the sea. The sea rushes in and floods the cave. The cave is filled but the sea is in no wise diminished. By the same token, the Tabernacle was filled with the radiance of the Divine Presence, but the world thereby lost nothing of that Presence."

*Shir ha-Shirim Rabbah on verse 3, 10.*

Where God dwelleth there is no sorrow; for doth not Holy Writ declare that "strength and gladness are in His place"?

*Hagigah, 5b.*

God is the place of the universe, but the universe is not His place.

*Midrash Tehillim, to Ps. 90:1.*

## 122. UNITY OF GOD

The Rabbis ask: "And now is not God One? What mean the words: 'In that day God shall be One and His name shall be One'?"

The answer is: "Now God is One, but His names are many. Everyone conceives Him according to his own vision. But in the world that is to be—in that glorious future that is yet to come—not only will God be One; His Name, too, will then be One."

*Pesahim, 50a.*

From Sinai, the Mount of revelation of the only God, there came forth *Sinah,* the hostility of the nations toward the Jew as the banner-bearer of the pure idea of God.

*Shabbat, 89b.*

A Jew is he who opposes every sort of polytheism.

*Megillah, 13a.*

A man should proclaim God's unity with his lips by reciting the Shema. He should feel it in his heart; he should think of it in his mind.

*Zohar, i, 242a.*

Said Rabbi Nathan: "Some theologians argue that a multiple nature of the Godhead may be learned from the phrase: 'Let us make man in our image' (Gen. 1:26). How can they then explain the phrase: 'I will blot out man whom I have created'?" (Gen. 6:7)

If two who build a house are partners, may only one destroy it?

*Introd.. to Tanhuma Buber, 154.*

## 123. GOD'S WILL

Before the Will of God, forsake thine own will, and the will of thy fellow-man.

*Derek Eretz Zuta, 1.*

The Rabbis taught that "the ideal Jew does not say: 'I do not want to eat swine meat'; I want it, I desire it, but I must curb my desire because it is the Will of God—because my people have accepted this prohibition as a rule of discipline."

*Sifra, Kedoshim.*

## 124. GOOD AND EVIL

Repay good with evil.

*Shemot Rabbah, 26, 2.*

There is no absolute good without some evil in its midst.

*Tanhuma, Intr., 9.*

The proverb runs: do no good to an evil man, and evil will not overtake you.

*Bereshit Rabbah, 22, 8.*

Woe unto him who knows not the difference between good and evil.

*Sanhedrin, 103.*

"And of the tree of the knowledge of good and evil, thou shalt not eat of it" (Gen. 2:17). Of the good thou mayest eat; only of the evil thou shalt not eat.

*Zohar Hadash to Ruth, 82b.*

The way of goodness is at the outset a thicket of thorns, but after a little distance it emerges into an open plain; while the way of evil is at first a plain, but presently runs into thorns.

*Sifre on Deut., 11, 6.*

To what may we liken the righteous in this world? To a tree standing entirely in a place of purity, but its branches extending to a place of impurity. The branches are lopped off, and it is entirely in a pure atmosphere. Thus God afflicts the righteous in this world that they may be heirs of the World-to-Come.

And to what may we liken the wicked in this world? To a tree standing entirely in a place of impurity, but with branches extending to a place of purity. The branches are lopped off, and it is entirely in an impure atmosphere. Thus God supplies His abundant goodness to the wicked in this world, that He may overwhelm and thrust them into the lowest depths of misery, as it is said (Prov. 14:12): "There is a way which seemeth right unto a man, but the end thereof are the ways of death."

*Kiddushin, 40b.*

The highest wisdom is goodness. Let not a man study the Law and thrust away his father and mother.

*Berakot, 17a.*

The divine attribute which confers goodness excels the attribute which sends punishment.

*Yoma, 46a.*

## 125. GOOD INTENTIONS

A good intention bringing fruit is added to the good deed.

*Kiddushin, 40.*

Everything follows the intention of the heart.

*Tosefta Yebamot, 2.*

A good intention is accounted as a good deed.

*Zohar, i, 28b.*

Even if a man merely intended to perform a Mitzwah and was prevented from doing so, he is regarded as having performed it.

*Kiddushin, 40.*

A man is not punished for evil which he intends to commit. But for his good deeds he receives reward, not only for what he has done, but also consideration for what he intended to do.

*Zohar, i, 121b.*

Greater is a transgression, said Rab Nahman ben Isaac, with a good intention than a Mitzwah without it.

*Nazir, 23.*

The man intended to improve himself; shall we proceed to fine him?

*Gittin, 54.*

"Good" is the good impulse; "very good" is the human impulse.

*Bereshit Rabbah, 9, 7.*

Whether a man does much or little for the sake of God, it matters not, provided that he directed his heart towards Heaven.

*Menahot, 110a.*

### WITHOUT INTENTION

Once a Hasid forgot a sheaf in his field, and he said to his son: "Go and offer up for me a bullock as a peace-offering, and another as a burnt-offering." The son asked: "Why dost thou rejoice, my father, in this commandment (Deut. 24:19), more than in others?" He replied: "God gave us every commandment in the Torah to fulfil intentionally, but this commandment was given to be performed unintentionally. If we intended to fulfil it, it would not be performing this Mitzwah."

Is it not a matter of logic? If God promises to bless the work of our hands when we perform His commandment without intention on our part, how much the more shall He bless us for performing a commandment which we intend to fulfil!

*Tosefta Peah, 3.*

## But She Is Betrothed

Rab Aha bar Abba came for a visit to his son-in-law Rab Hisda and took his little granddaughter on his lap. Rab Hisda said: "But she is betrothed." Rab Aha replied: "Thou didst wrong to betroth her. Rab said: 'One must not betroth his minor daughter. The father should wait until she is grown, and must ask her if she cares to marry the man whom he has chosen for her.' " Rab Hisda said: "But Samuel warned against caressing a female."

Rab Aha replied: "I agree with the other saying of Samuel: 'All prohibitions of this kind follow the intention.' And since my intention is pure, I may caress her even if she is betrothed."

*Kiddushin, 82.*


## 126. THE GOOD LIFE, ETHICS

If a man walks in the ways of the Lord, but transgresses by accident, every creature below and above helps to conceal it.

*Zohar, iii, 101a.*

When a man steps down from his bed, he should say to himself: "Guard thy feet when thou walkest."

*Zohar, iv, 175b.*

When a man opens his eyes in the morning, he should say to himself: "Thine eyes shall look on the right" (Prov. 4:25). (And the verse continues: "And let thine eyelids look straight before thee.")

*Zohar, i, 191a.*

When the time comes for an accounting of a man's deeds, it is too late to do anything.

*Bereshit Rabbah, 84, 12.*

Judaism is not only ethical, but ethics constitutes its essence, its nature—"its beginning, its middle and its end."

*Midrash Tanhuma, Wayishlah.*

When man appears before the Throne of Judgment, the first question he is asked is not—"Have you believed in God," or, "Have you prayed or performed ritual acts," but "Have you dealt honorably, faithfully in all your dealings with your fellow-man?"

*Shabbat, 31a.*

Every day the good man will seek to realize his moral position; his whole life will be a penitent endeavor. He will strive to keep his garments always white, for who knoweth when the King may summon him to the banquet?

*Shabbat, 153a.*

When the Talmud speaks of Hemirah Da'atah, it does not mean "she changed her religion," but "she changed her way of life."

*Mishnah Ketubot, 7, 6.*

## 127. GOOD TRAITS, CHARACTER

It was said of Rabban Johanan ben Zakkai: he never spoke facetiously; he never walked four ells without Torah or Tefillin; he never slept or took a nap in the House of Study; no one ever came to the House of Study before him, or left after him; he never thought of sacred matters in unclean places; no one ever found him sitting in idle silence, but only sitting and learning. No one else opened the door for his Disciples; and he never uttered anything which he did not hear from his teachers. He never said: "It is time to leave the House of Study," except on the eve of Passover and Yom Kippur, when the meal at home is more important than study. His Disciple, R. Eliezer, imitated his teacher in all these things.

*Sukkah, 27, etc.*

These are the things, the fruit of which a man enjoys in this world, while the principal is secured for him in the World-to-Come: namely, honoring one's parents; deeds of loving-kindness; making peace between a man and his fellow, and the study of the Torah, which is equal to all the others.

*Mishnah Peah, 1, 1.*

Rabbi Johanan adds: Taking in wayfarers, visiting the sick, devoutness in prayer, being early in the School House (Bet ha-Midrash), bringing up sons in the study of the Torah, and judging one's fellow on the side of merit.

*Shabbat, 127a.*

The one great requisite is character.

*Sotah, 27a.*

He who is learned in Scriptures and in the Oral Law, and also has an occupation and good manners does not fall into sin quickly.

*Kiddushin, 40. Mishnah.*

Holiness is a fence to purity; abstinence from jesting is a fence to respect; abstemiousness is a fence to vows; the fear of sin is a fence to humility.

*Abot de-R. Nathan, 26.*

Seven virtues minister before the Throne of Glory: Wisdom, Justice, Righteousness, Kindness, Compassion, Truth and Peace.

*Abot de-R. Nathan, 36, 5.*

It is a good indication of the man's character if his beast is well-fed.

*Sifre Ekeb, 43.*

Shammai's maxim was: "Make thy study a regular thing; say little and do much; and meet every man with a friendly mien."

*Abot, 1, 15.*

Rabbi Phinehas ben Jair said: Heedfulness leads to cleanliness; cleanliness leads to purity; purity to holiness; holiness to humility; humility to the fear of sin; the fear of sin to saintliness; saintliness to the possession of the Holy Spirit; the Holy Spirit to the restoration of the dead; the restoration to life brings a man to Elijah of blessed memory.

*Mishnah Sotah, 9, 9, or 9, 15.*

The Elders of the South were asked by Alexander of Macedon: "Who is wise?" They replied: "He who sees the consequences of every act."

"Who is strong?" "He who subdues his impulses."

"Who is rich?" "He is who is content."

"What should one do in order to live?" "Consider himself as naught."

"What should one do in order to die?" "Consider himself important."

"How can one become popular?" "Ignore politics."

"On the contrary," retorted Alexander. "He should engage in political affairs and improve the lot of the people."

The king left them and eventually arrived in the country of the Amazons. "Are you in fear of me?" he asked them. "Nay," they answered. "You cannot afford to make war upon us. For if you conquer, it will not redound to your honor to have slain women."

He asked them for food, and they brought him loaves of gold. "Is this what you call food in your land?" he asked.

"Nay," they answered, "but bread made of wheat you have in abundance in your own land; you need not have come so far for it."

*Tamid, 31.*

## 128. GOVERNMENT AND OFFICIALDOM

The governor shook my hand, and a smell of rule clung to it.

*Zebahim, 96.*

A kingdom without counsellors is not a kingdom.

*Pirke de R. Eliezer, 3.*

If the son of thy sister is a tax-collector, do not pass him in the street.

*Yoma, 18.*

Let the fear of the government be always upon thee.

*Zebahim, 102.*

A man must respect the government.

*Mekilta Bo.*

He who accepts office in order to profit by it is no better than an adulterer.

*Pesikta Rabbati, Asseret ha-Diberot, 2-4.*

When a man is appointed an official on earth, he becomes a man of evil above.

*Midrash Haser we-Yater, 39.*

Mar Samuel said: "The law of the state is law."

*Nedarim, 28a.*

God said to Moses: "Be respectful to Pharaoh and any king, even when it is My purpose to afflict him with My judgment."

*Shemot Rabbah, 7.*

He who sees a king of Israel should say: "Blessed be He who out of His respect gave a share to those who fear Him." He who sees a non-Jewish king should say: "Blessed be He who giveth a share in His respect to a being of flesh and blood."

*Berakot, 59.*

Rab Sheshet joined a crowd in welcome to the king. A scoffer, who knew that the Rabbi was blind asked him: "Whole vessels are used to draw water, but whither shall broken vessels go?" Rab Sheshet replied: "I shall know as well as you when he comes."
A band of music passed by. The Rabbi said: "The king is not yet here." A cavalcade of mounted men passed. "The king is not yet here." A carriage passed by in silence. "The king is now passing," said the Rabbi. "How did you know that?" he was asked. He answered: "Because an earthly king is like the Heavenly King, of Whom it is written: 'The Lord was not in the wind . . . in the earthquake . . . in the fire . . . and after the fire a still small voice . . . and behold, there came a Voice unto him.'" (I Kings 19:11-13)

*Berakot, 9, 19.*

Be sure that thou prayest for the well-being of the government, for it is respect for authority that saves men from swallowing up each other alive.

*Abot, 3, 2.*

He who rebels against his Sovereign deserves to die.

*Sanhedrin, 49a.*

The rule of kings is a semblance of heaven's rule.

*Berakot, 58a.*

The law of the land is law.

*Baba Kamma, 113a.*

Rabbi Simeon ben Lakish said: "'And behold it was very good' (Gen. 1:4). This is the kingdom of Heaven; this is also the kingdom of earth. Is then the earthly kingdom very good? Yes, for it exacts justice of mankind. As it is said: 'I made the earth and created man upon it.' (Read Edom in place of Adam, man; thus we have, 'I created Rome upon it.')"

*Bereshit Rabbah, 9 near end.*

" 'And Thou makest men like the fishes of the sea' (Hab. 1:14). As it is with the fishes in the sea, the one that is larger swallowing the others, so it is with human kind. Were it not for the fear of the government everyone greater than his fellow would consume him. This is the meaning of the words of Hanina, the Sagan (Prefect) of the priesthood: 'Pray for the welfare of the government, for were it not for the fear of the government, a man would swallow up his neighbor alive.' "

*Abodah Zarah, 4a.*

## 129. TRUE GREATNESS

Great is the man who ignores his own dignity and is not angered at affronts.

*Midrash Gadol u-Gedolah, 15.*

As the vine has large and small clusters of grapes, and the larger cluster hangs down lower than the smaller, so is it among Israel. (The greater the man, the humbler he is.)

*Wayyikra Rabbah, 36, 2.*

The proverb runs: How great that man would be, if he were not so arrogant.

*Kallah Rabbati, 3.*

### WILLING TO ADMIT

R. Hiyya bar Abba asked R. Lazar to intercede for him with the Patriarch Judah on behalf of a letter of recommendation, since he wished to leave Palestine on business. The Patriarch wrote: "Behold, the bearer is a great man. His greatness consists in the fact that he is not ashamed to admit, when asked something he has not learned, that he has not heard this from his teachers. He is our representative and has equal authority with us while away."

*Y. Hagigah, 1.*

## 130. WORLDLY GREATNESS

Greatness seeks out the man who runs away from greatness.

*Erubin, 13.*

Office seeks out the man who runs away from office.

*Tanhuma Wayyikra, 4.*

He who ascends in importance in this world descends by this very token in the World Above.

*Shoher Tob, Jellinek, 5.*

Cleave to the noble, and they will also bow to thee.

*Sifre Debarim, 6.*

The impulses of a man are stronger within him in proportion to his greatness among his fellows.

*Sukkah, 52.*

## 131. RESPECT FOR THE GREAT

He who recognizes greatness in his fellow-man must show him respect.

*Pesahim, 113.*

While a great man lives, the lesser man's fame is not recognized.

*Bereshit Rabbah, 6, 3.*

A great man has said something seemingly illogical: laugh not at it, but try to understand it.

*Berakot, 19.*

## 132. GREEK WISDOM

Go and seek an hour that is neither day nor night, and learn therein the wisdom of the Greeks.

*Menahot, 99.*

## 133. HANUKAH

Rabbi Hanina said: The Tabernacle was finished on the 25th day of Kislev but it was not put together until the 1st of Nisan, so that this might occur in the month of Exodus. And did that day on this account lose its importance? Nay, for the Hasmoneans instituted on it the Dedication of the restored Holy Temple.

*Pesikta Rabbati, Piska, 6.*

Seven Hanukot are inaugurated with lights: the Creation with moonlight (the first moon after Creation appeared on Friday); the Tabernacle and the Two Temples with the Lighting of the Menorah; the festival of the Hasmoneans with the kindling of the Lamps in their temporary receptacles; the Wall of Jerusalem with the Procession of the Lights; and the Millennium, with the Seven-Fold Light of the Sun.

*Pesikta Rabbati, Piska, 2, end, and
commentary of R. David Luria.*

On the 25th of Kislev the eight days of Hanukah begin, and on them no funeral orations may be held. Why is this prohibition? Because a miracle occurred when the Hasmoneans came to kindle the

Temple lights, and one day's supply of ritually pure oil lasted for eight days. But since the season is named Hanukah, Dedication, and the miracle lasted only seven days, why do we not imitate Moses and Solomon who celebrated the festival of Dedication only seven days? Because the Hasmoneans were occupied with the work of restoration for eight days. Why, then, must we observe the second memorial of Hanukah lights, when other miracles were commemorated only by the prohibition against funeral orations? Because the first act of the Restoration was the kindling of the Temple lights. Though the Menorah was not yet restored, seven spears, coated with tin, were used to fashion a temporary Menorah. And why the third Memorial, the chanting of the Hallel? Because the Israelites had a great deliverance from a mighty enemy.

*Megillat Taanit, 9.*

## 134. HAPPINESS AND GLADNESS

Happy is our youth if it leaves no memories in old age of which we are ashamed.

*Sukkah, 53.*

Happy is he who repents while he is in the prime of his strength.

*Abodah Zarah, 19.*

Happy is he whose deeds are more than his learning.

*Eliyahu Rabbah, 17.*

Happy is the man who is supreme over his sins; unhappy is he whose sins are his master.

*Bereshit Rabbah, 22, 6.*

Happy is he who has been reared on Torah, who has labored in Torah and has left the world with a good name.

*Berakot, 17. (See also Ruth Rabbah, 2, 7.)*

Happy are the Zaddikim who turn judgment into mercy.

*Bereshit Rabbah, 33, 3.*

Happy is the man who fortifies himself like a man against his impulses.

*Abodah Zarah, 19.*

Happy is the man who in his hour of death is as pure as he was in his hour of birth.

*Y. Megillah, 1, 9.*

Happy is our old age if it atones for our youth.

*Sukkah, 53.*

Happy is the generation in which the greater give ear to the lesser.

*Rosh ha-Shanah, 25.*

He who is glad today may not be glad tomorrow: he who is sad today may rejoice tomorrow.

*Tanhuma Shemini, 3.*

If a man whose parents are no longer living, invites God to share in his hour of joy, God invites the man's parents to share in the hour of joy, for they are partners with God in their son.

*Zohar, iv, 220a.*

### ELIJAH'S FORMULA FOR HAPPINESS

The Sages said in the name of Elijah, one should always be wise in the fear of the Lord, answer calmly, appease anger, live peacefully with one's father, mother, teacher, neighbor and even with a non-Jew. Father Elijah, of happy and blessed memory, used to say: Heaven and earth testify that to a scholar who studies the Bible and traditions for the sake of God, and who supports himself, the following verse applied: "When thou eatest of the labor of thy hands, happy shalt thou be, and it shall be well with thee."

*Seder Eliyahu Zuta, chap. 15, p. 197.*

## 135. THE HASID (THE PIOUS)

He who hears himself abused, and yet keeps silent is called a Hasid.

*Yalkut to Psalms, 629.*

If an ignorant man is a Hasid, reside not in his vicinity.

*Shabbat, 63.*

If you wish to sanctify yourself, take care even with respect to things that are permitted.

*Yebamot, 20.*

Holiness leads to Hasidut.

*Shekalim, 9.*

He who wishes to be a Hasid must observe the precepts of the Abot (Fathers), the Blessings and the laws of damages.[1]

*Baba Kamma, 30. (Combined.)*

[1] I.e., contained in the tractates: Abot, Berakot, Nezikin.

### APPEASING THE GOVERNOR

A Hasid was reciting the Amidah prayer in a public square, and when the governor passed by, the worshipper gave no heed. The governor was piqued, and after the close of the prayer, he said: "Why didst thou not answer me? If I had pierced thy body with my sword for thy disrespect, no one would have blamed me."

The Hasid replied: "If thou wert standing before the Emperor, and someone, entering, had greeted thee, wouldst thou have answered?"

"Nay," answered the governor. "It is a capital offense for any-one to heed another person if he stands before the Emperor."

"Thou standest before a human king," continued the Rabbi, "who is here today and in his grave tomorrow. Yet thou couldst not reply to another's greeting. How much the less could I acknowledge thy greeting, when I stood before the King of Kings, who is Eternal."

The governor was appeased and left the Hasid in peace.

*Berakot, 32.*

## 136. HATRED, ENMITY

He who hates a man is as if he hated God.

*Pesikta Zutarti Behaaloteka.*

Comrades who do not love each other will leave the world before their time.

*Zohar, ii, 190b.*

Not from the love of Mordecai, but from the hate of Haman.

*Megillah, 16.*

Unmerited hatred is as wicked as idolatry, adultery and murder combined.

*Yoma, 9.*

The Temple was destroyed because of unfounded hatred.

*Yoma, 9.*

If two men claim thy help, and one is thy enemy, help him first.

*Baba Metzia, 32b.*

## 137. THE HEART

The ears and the eyes are the spies which the heart sends forth.

*Zohar, ii, 116a.*

The heart would burn up with desire if the lungs did not cool it with air.

*Tikkune Zohar, 47b.*

Every deed of a man is in his heart. Scripture describes the heart as seeing, understanding, hearing and so forth.

*Tikkune Zohar, 47b.*

The heart is like a nut: it has its shell, namely the unworthy de-sires; and its kernel, namely, its worthy desires. He who breaks the outer shell of unworthy desires, has the broken heart which God desireth.

*Tikkune Zohar, 101a.*

The heart is the Holy of Holies. Yet it contains two chambers, one of healing, and the other of poisonous drugs.

*Tikkune Zohar, T. 70, 173a.*

A man can learn only what his heart desires.

*Abodah Zarah, 19.*

The heart is forgetful.

*Sanhedrin, 35.*

God desires the heart.

*Sanhedrin, 106.*

The heart of a man changes his countenance to good or to evil.

*Bereshit Rabbah, 73.*

Heartache is the most painful of aches.

*Shabbat, 11.*

The tongue is the pen of the heart.

*Shalah, Gate of Letters. Letter Kaph, quoting Rabbis.*

God placed man's heart in the center of his body; it rules his entire body, and through it his life-system circulates.

*Zohar, iv, 161a.*

The Mitzwah handed over to a man's heart[1]—concerning it, Scripture says: "And thou shalt fear the Lord thy God."

*Kiddushin, 32.*

[1] No one else would know whether he observed it or not.

The All-merciful requires but one thing—the heart.

*Sanhedrin, 106b.*

The heart is the home of spiritual emotions. Therefore let no sadness enter therein from the spleen, and no anger from the gall. They (sadness and anger) are as the fire of Gehenna, and to them applies the injunction against kindling a fire on the Sabbath, a symbol of things spiritual.

*Tikkune Zohar, T. 55, 125b.*

## 138. HEAT AND COLD

He who needs the blaze must fan it.

*Midrash Samuel, 9.*

The heat of the late summer is harder to bear than the heat of midsummer.

*Yoma, 29.*

The North wind freezes waters and the South wind melts the ice. (The North lacks the warmth of Torah).

*Zohar, i, 161b.*

It is the way of fire (Torah), that if we stand too near it, it burns; too far away, we grow cold. What shall we do? Take the middle course and be warmed.

*Mekilta to Jethro.*

A river filled with water does not freeze so quickly as a river with little water.[1]

*Zohar, i, 152a.*

[1] The thoroughly-learned will not grow cold to religion like the half-learned.

## 139. HEIRS AND INHERITANCE

A man does not purposely make a faulty will.

*Y. Baba Metzia, 1.*

The words of the dying person are as valid as if they were written down and registered.

*Gittin, 13.*

It is a good deed to fulfil the words of a dying man.

*Taanit, 21.*

### A WILL WITH A RIDDLE

A man died and left a will which no one understood. The three sons asked the help of R. Banaa. He read: "Give my oldest son a barrel of dust, my second son, a barrel of bones, and my youngest son, a barrel of threads." The Rabbi asked: "Did your father leave land, cattle and cloth?" "Yes," was the answer. "Then," said the Rabbi, "The oldest receives the land; the second, the cattle, and the third, the cloth."

*Baba Batra, 143.*

### A CURIOUS CASE

The brother of Mari bar Issak heard that his father had died, and he journeyed from a distant city to collect his share. Mari refused to grant it to him on the plea that he could not recognize him. The brother came to R. Hisda with a complaint, but R. Hisda said: "Mari's plea is justified. Do we not read in Scriptures that Joseph's brothers did not recognize him?"

The plaintiff replied: "But it is only a trick on the part of Mari. Other people in this town recognized me."

"Then let them come here and testify."

"They would do so," replied the brother. "But my brother can inflict injury upon them if they testify against his interests. They are unwilling to come into court."

R. Hisda turned to Mari and said: "It is for you to bring witnesses, long acquainted with your family, to testify that this man is not your brother."

Mari argued: "But that is illegal. The law states that 'he who wishes to secure property out of another's possession must bring the evidence.'"

R. Hisda smiled and said: "I have stated my ruling with respect to persons who threaten others if they fail to act according to their wishes."

Mari continued the argument: "What is the value of my bringing witnesses if you believe they will not testify out of fear of me?"

R. Hisda said: "I do not anticipate that they will do both: abstain from telling the truth, and utter a falsehood. Out of fear of you, they may not testify at all, but they will not perjure themselves."

The witnesses came to court and testified that the claimant was the brother of Mari. The claimant, an educated man, said: "I wish half of the estate as it now is, with all the improvements, since I do not know in what condition Mari received them from my father."

R. Hisda said: "Well spoken, my friend. The Mishnah teaches that if a brother who has taken over an estate does not have the court or witnesses record the condition of the estate before he began to improve it, his other brothers shall share in all the improvements."

*Baba Metzia, 39.*

## THE FINAL THIRD

Once a man, displeased with the conduct of his sons, left a will that all his property should go to Jonathan b. Uzziel. On inheriting the estate, Jonathan sold a third for his own use, gave one-third to holy purposes, and returned one-third to the sons of the deceased. When Shammai heard of this, he rebuked Jonathan for failing to obey the testator's will. But Jonathan replied: "Shammai, if I had a right to sell a third, and to donate a third to holy causes, why have I not the right to do as I please with the final third?"

Shammai exclaimed: "Ben Uzziel has won me over. He is right."

*Baba Batra, 133.*

## MAN AND HIS SONS

If a man wills his property to others and omits his sons, the Sages dislike him.

R. Simeon b. Gamaliel said: "If his sons misbehave themselves and the father cuts them off, he has the blessing of the Sages."

A man left his property to R. Abba b. Memel and wrote in his will, that if his sons conducted themselves well, the Rabbi should give them half, and retain half for himself. But if they misconducted themselves, the Rabbi was to keep the entire estate.

When the father died, the Rabbi gave to the sons half of their father's property. They were unwilling to abide by their father's testament, and sought to nullify it. R. Abba exclaimed: "You are disgraceful sons! Return to me the half I have given you."

*Baba Batra, 133; Y. Baba Batra, 8.*

### Son and Daughter

Samuel said to his Disciple, R. Judah: "Thou sharp one! Always avoid being an accessory to cutting off a son from his heritage, even if the money is to go from a son that has misbehaved to a son of good conduct. And by no means permit a father to take from his son and leave his property to a daughter. The daughter should receive her portion during her father's lifetime."

*Baba Batra, 133.*

### A Wise Will

A wealthy Jew and his slave went to trade in a foreign country. There he sickened and when near to death, commanded a scribe to write down his last will and testament. He dictated these provisions: "To my faithful slave who brings this document I leave all my property. To my only son whom I have left in Judaea I leave a single thing from my possessions according to his choice."

The slave returned with all the wealth of his dead master and showed the will. A Teacher said to the son: "It is a most sagacious will. If your father had left everything to you, the slave would have fled with the wealth. Now he has brought everything safely to you, and you may choose him, according to provision of the will: for what a slave has, belongs to the master."

*Tanhuma Bereshit, Lek Lekah.*

## 140. HOLYDAYS

On a festival a man must make glad his wife and his household.

*Pesahim, 109.*

Why do Israel in Syria keep two days of a Festival (like Shabuot)? Because they failed to keep one day in Palestine.

*Y. Erubin, 3, 9.*

Whenever the Israelites on earth rejoice in the festivals, give praise to the Lord, adorn the table with viands and don fine garments, the angels above inquire: "Why do Israelites pamper themselves so much?" God replies: "They have a distinguished guest with them today."

*Zohar, iii, 94a.*

If God gives to the nations of the world many holidays, they eat, drink and are merry; they troop to the theatres and circuses, and by their talk and actions they cause the Lord much irritation. The people of Israel are not thus. If God gives them holidays, they eat, drink and rejoice; they flock to the synagogues and to the Houses of Study, and they offer praise to God.

*Yalkut Shimeoni, Phinehas, 29.*

A Sectary asked R. Akiba: "Why do you observe the holy-days, when God has said through Isaiah (1:14): 'Your new moons and your festivals My soul hateth'?" R. Akiba replied: "It does not say: 'My holidays' but 'your.' This means holidays instituted by Jeroboam. But the holydays which we observe are not to be abrogated, for they are the holydays of God."

*Tanhuma, Buber, to Phinehas.*

God saith: "If you have spent a pleasant holyday this year, you will spend an equally pleasant holyday the coming year."

*Tanhuma, Bereshit.*

R. Levi said: "When a holyday comes to thee, rejoice and give pleasure to God. How? If the season is a good one, go out to your vineyard and to your grove, that you may behold the profuse growth of your fruits, and rejoice therein."

*Kohelet Rabbah, 7.*

"Half for the Lord and half for yourselves" is the rule for the right observance of all our holy days.

*Pesahim, 68b.*

## 141. HONOR

A man should not say: "I will study in order to attain the degree of Rabbi." He should study for the love of it, and the honor will come in the end as a by-product.

*Nedarim, 62.*

Honor departs when it is sought by the undeserving.[1]

*Midrash Tehillim, 16.*

[1] The title Gaon no longer carries distinction when every Rav claims it.

Not every one who wishes to adopt the name (of being a scholar) is entitled to it.

*Berakot, 16.*

A man protests if his honor is threatened.

*Abot de-R. Nathan, 15.*

Be more careful of thy neighbor's honor than of thine own person.

*Zohar Hadash to Song of Songs, 61a.*

There is a respect which a man receives for himself; and there is a respect received because a man is intimate with another who is respected.

*Hakdamah to Tikkune Zohar, 12a.*

Honors may be increased but not decreased.

*Semahot, 2, 5.*

A man must honor his father-in-law as much as his father.
*Midrash Tehillim, 7, 4.*

Rabbi Eliezer said: "Let the honor of thy fellow be as dear to thee as thine own."
*Abot., 2, 15.*

Rabbi Jose bar Hanina said: "He who honors himself by the disgrace of his fellow has no share in the World-to-Come."
*Bereshit Rabbah, 1, 5.*

Rab Nahman bar Isaac was seated among the young students. Rab Nahman bar Rab Hisda went over to him and said: "Will you not be good enough to take a place more towards the front where I am seated?"

Rab Nahman bar Isaac replied: "The place does not honor the man, but the man honors the place. When the Shekinah was on Mount Sinai no one was allowed to approach the Mount, but when the Shekinah departed, everyone was allowed to ascend it."
*Taanit, 21.*

## WHO SHALL ENTER FIRST?

The family of R. Oshaya and the family of Bar Pazi were frequently guests of the Patriarch. The former would enter first, because R. Oshaya was the greater scholar. Later, when there was a matrimonial connection between the Patriarch and the Bar Pazi family, the latter wished to enter first. Rabbi Ammi was asked, and he said: "The relationship of Bar Pazi placed them on an equal footing with R. Oshaya; therefore the R. Oshaya family should continue to enter first, as was the custom previously.

On another occasion, one family acted as political counselors to the Patriarch, and they entered first at his receptions. Later a family brought forth several scholars, and wished to be allowed to take precedence. R. Johanan decreed that the latter should be granted the right, since a scholar takes rank over a politician.
*Y. Shabbat, 12.*

## 142. HOPE

While there is life there is hope.
*Y. Berakot, 9, 1.*

### THE DESPAIRING

A wealthy man without children complained of his lot, saying: "Of what profit to me are my riches? For what do I labor?" He was advised to make generous donations to the poor, since thus his wealth would avail him after death. The man replied: "Nay, I shall give nothing except to one who despairs of ever seeing a good day in this world."

He sought to discover such a person, but found him not. Once he perceived a poor man, lying on a dunghill in tattered garments. He said to himself: "Surely this man expects no good in this world." But when he spoke with him, the man said: "While there is life, there is hope. God's compassion may descend upon me at any moment. Only the dead expect naught that is good in this world."

The wealthy man went to a cemetery and hid part of his fortune in a grave. It chanced that he lost his wealth and went to the grave to dig out his money. The police captured him, arrested him and brought him before the judge. "Dost thou recognize me?" asked the magistrate. "How should I know a great man like thee?" inquired the prisoner. "I am the poor man who, you thought, had despaired of God," replied the judge. "Thou seest that God remembered me and uplifted my lot."

*Sefer Maasiot l'Rabbi Nissim.*

(Rabbi Nissim lived in North Africa and was a contemporary of the Geonim. His stories are based on Midrashim, not all of which we have in their original form.)

## 143. HOSPITALITY

It is the custom of the world that when a guest arrives, he is given on the first day a calf slaughtered in his honor; on the second day, a sheep, and on the third day, only a fowl.

*Midrash Tehillim, 23, 3.*

Hospitality is greater than a visit to the House of Study; it is greater than welcoming the Shekinah. The hospitable man is rewarded in both worlds.

*Shabbat, 127a.*

There is a Rabbinic legend which tells that when a stranger came to the city of Sodom and asked for hospitality, the Sodomites did not refuse him but forced the stranger to sleep in the bed provided by them. If the bed were too small for him, they would cut off his legs until his body fitted into the bed. If the bed were too large, they would stretch his head and feet, so that even though he lost his life, his body was made to fit.

*Sanhedrin, 109b.*

The Elders shall speak and say: "Our hands have not shed this blood" (Deut. 21:7). By these words it is meant that no one has come to us to whom we refused to give food or escort. Said Rab: "He who escorts his companion four ells even in the city will meet with no mischance."

*Sotah, 45.*

Why was not Micah included among those who have no share in the World-to-Come? Because his bread was available to passers-by.

*Sanhedrin, 103.*

Insist not that a man eat with thee if he does not desire it.

*Hullin, 94.*

### ABRAHAM'S HOSPITALITY

When Job's distress came upon him, he said: "Have I not fed the hungry, given drink to the thirsty and clothed the naked?" (See Chapter 31.)

God replied: "Thy hospitality does not attain Abraham's in greatness. Thou didst sit in thy house and thus thou didst attend the incoming guests. Thou didst ask them regarding the food to which they were accustomed: if one usually ate wheaten bread, thou gavest it to him; if not, thou gavest him oaten. If he was accustomed to meat and wine, thou gavest it to him; otherwise, he received coarse food. Abraham, however, went outside to welcome his guests; he gave them the best bread, meat and wine, even to those who had never enjoyed such good food. In fact, he never inquired from anyone what should be given him; he left on long tables the best viands and drinks, that whosoever wished, might come and drink and eat. 'Good enough for the poor' was not the way of Abraham."

*Abot de-R. Nathan, 7.*

## 144. HOST AND GUEST

The woman recognizes the worth of a guest more than the man.

*Berakot, 10.*

When entering, the host enters first; when leaving, the guest leaves first.

*Derek Eretz Rabbah, 5, end.*

People say: the wine belongs to the host, and the thanks go to the butler.[1]

*Baba Kamma, 92.*

[1] God is the host; man is the butler.

What does the thoughtful guest say: "How much was done for my sake!" What does the thankless guest say: "No trouble was taken for my sake at all. Everything was prepared only for the family."

*Berakot, 58.*

Who is a despicable guest? One who brings along another guest, and one who creates unusual bother.

*Derek Eretz Zuta, 8.*

Woe when the guest banishes the host.

*Wayyikra Rabbah, 7, 7.*

Do everything the host says, except leave.[1]

*Pesahim, 86 (Venice edition).*

[1] This may mean: except to leave one's religion at the bequest of the government.

R. Joshua said: "Everyone should be under thy suspicion as if he were a thief; but always show everyone respect as if he were like Rabban Gamaliel."

R. Joshua was once asked for hospitality late at night. He gave the applicant supper, and led him to a bed beneath the roof. Then he removed the ladder leading to the roof. R. Joshua had placed certain vessels on the roof, which the guest concealed in a shawl. Before it was daylight, he sought to flee with them, but he fell and was injured. R. Joshua found him, took him to a physician and later asked him: "Is this a proper return for my hospitality?" The man remarked: "Could I suspect that you would take away the ladder?" R. Joshua said: "But I had suspicion of you from the first moment you came to me."

*Derek Erets Rabbah, 25; Kallah, 9.*

### AN ACT OF MERCY

"The merciful man doeth good to his own soul" (Proverbs 11:17). This verse applies well to Hillel. When the time for eating arrived, he would bid adieu to his Disciples and walk away hurriedly. His Disciples once escorted him on his way and inquired as to his haste. He said: "I am hastening to perform an act of mercy with a guest in my house."

They asked: "Every day thou hast a guest in thy house?"

He replied: "And this poor soul within me, is it not a guest in the body? Today is here; tomorrow departs."

*Wayyikra Rabbah, 34.*

## 145. HUMANITY AND INHUMANITY

Shall I say: throw a stone at the one who has fallen?

*Kiddushin, 20.*

He who has a claim for money upon his fellow-man and knows that the latter is unable to pay, must not pass by before him constantly.

*Baba Metzia, 75.*

Thou shalt love thy neighbor as thyself: select for him an easy death if he deserves death.

*Pesahim, 75.*

He who is to be executed is given a quart of wine to drink, mixed with frankincense, so that he may lose consciousness.

*Sanhedrin, 43.*

Love all men.

*Abot, 1, 12.*

The Jew is enjoined to do deeds of mercy to those who are not of his brotherhood.

*Gittin, 61a.*

## 146. HUMILITY

My lowliness is my exaltedness.

*Shemot Rabbah, 45, 5.*

O Bush of Moses! Not because thou art tall, but because thou art lowly, did God reveal Himself in thee.

*Shabbat, 67.*

A scholar should be retiring in his deeds and open in his conduct.

*Derek Eretz Zuta, 7.*

This should be the way of the daughters of Israel: talk in a low tone; walk leisurely, and be not prone to giggling.

*Tanhuma, Nosa, 2.*

Why was the law decreed in accordance with the School of Hillel. Because its members were amiable and modest.

*Erubin, 13.*

Run not after rule.

*Pesikta Rabbati, 22.*

If a man should be humble in his own home, how much the more in the House of God.

*Midrash Tehillim, 101, 3.*

A man should be pliable as a reed, and not stiff as a cedar.

*Taanit, 27.*

If a man combats the wave, it overpowers him. If he permits it to roll over him, the wave passes on.

*Pesikta Zutarti Bereshit, 32, 5.*

Why is the letter "Yod" smaller than any other letter? In order to teach thee that he who belittles himself, deserves to inherit the World-to-Come, which was created by virtue of the letter "Yod."

*Otiot de-R. Akiba.*

Be not like the top board above the door which is too high to concern itself with people. Be rather like the bottom board beneath the door upon which everyone treads.

*Abot de-R. Nathan, 26, 6.*

Even if thou art perfect in all virtues, thou art imperfect if thou hast no humility within thee.

*Kallah Rabbati, 3.*

People say: be the first to tell the low thing about thee.

*Baba Kamma, 92.*

He who does not exalt himself will be exalted by Heaven.

*Moed Katon, 28.*

When the Temple stood, a person who offered a burnt-offering received a reward for it. But he who possesses lowliness of spirit, receives a reward as if he had offered every kind of sacrifice.

*Sanhedrin, 43.*

Be very lowly of spirit, for what is the hope of mortals but the grave?

*Abot, 4, 4.*

It is because Moses humbly refrained from looking upon God when He revealed Himself in the flaming bush that he deserved to see Him face to face.

*Tanhuma, 3, 6.*

God is the friend of the man who is humble.

*Zohar, ii, 233b.*

He who is humble in this world is distinguished in the World-to-Come.

*Zohar, iv, 168a.*

Great is humility, for with it Moses, our Teache. was praised. Abraham was humble when he talked with the Hittites; Isaac when he fed the Gerarites; Jacob when he met Esau, and Saul when he was chosen king.

*Midrash Gadol u-Gedolah, 4.*

Hillel was accustomed to say: "My abasement is my exaltation and my exaltation is my abasement."

*Wayyikra Rabbah, 1, 5.*

Take a place in the lecture-room two or three rows behind that to which the order of precedence would entitle you.

*Abot de-R. Nathan, chap. 25.*

## THE TAILOR OF SEPPHORIS

A tailor of Sepphoris, named Justin, presented the Caesar with a fine garment and was invited to visit the palace. His excellent character and unaffected good sense endeared him to the Ruler. When he was about to depart for Palestine, the Emperor asked him his chief desire, and he replied: "To be the duke of Galilee." To his utmost amazement, the Caesar ennobled him and appointed him duke of his native district. When he returned, the people wondered: "Is this Justin, the tailor, or no? If he goes to visit his old premises, we will know that he is Justin." When he visited his old shop, the people recognized him, and could not conceal their astonishment. He remarked: "You are surprised, but I am even more surprised than you."

In like manner, when the nations of the Levantine countries perceived Israel mustered under flags in brigades and regiments, and divided into four armies, they could not hide their astonishment. They said: "Yesterday these were serfs, making bricks out of clay and cement; today they are a most resplendent nation."

Israel answered: "You are surprised, but we are even more surprised."

*Shir ha-Shirim Rabbah, 7.*

### Reproof or Humility

Rabbi Judah ben Rabbi Simeon asked: "What is a more excellent way: to reprove for the sake of Heaven, or to abstain out of humility, which is not for the sake of Heaven. He was told, even in such a case, humility is greater." What is humility not for the sake of Heaven? Rab Huna and Rab Hiyya bar Rab sat before Samuel. Rab Hiyya asked Samuel to order Rab Huna not to give him pain. When Rab Hiyya left, Rab Huna mentioned the misdeeds of Rab Hiyya, wherefor he punished him. This is imperfect humility. Were he truly humble, he would not have made any disclosures.

*Arakin, 16b.*

### Not Granted

Rab said: "For these three things I prayed to Heaven, two of which were granted to me, and one not. I prayed for the wisdom of Rab Huna and for the riches of Rab Hisda, and both these were granted unto me. But the humility and meekness of Rabbah, the son of Rab Huna, for which I also prayed, was not granted."

*Moed Katon, 28a.*

### The Greatest of the Ten Steps

What is the greatest of the ten steps in the ascent of the righteous? Saintliness, as it is said: "Then Thou spakest in vision to Thy saints" (Psalm 89:20). Rabbi Joshua ben Levi said: Humility, for it is said: "The spirit of the Lord God is upon me, to bring good tidings to the humble" (Isaiah 61:1). It is not said: "To the Saints," but "To the humble," whence we learn that humility is the greatest of all virtues.

*Abodah Zarah, 20b.*

## THE EARTHEN JAR

The words of the Torah do not keep in one who is, in his own esteem, like a vessel of silver or of gold; but in one who is in his own esteem, like the lowliest of vessels, an earthenware jar.

*Midrash Tannaim, 42.*

## A WELL-LEARNED LESSON

Rabbi Eleazar ben R. Simeon was returning home from his teacher's residence at Migdal Gerer. He was riding his donkey by the shore of a river, and felt joyful and full of pride because he had learned much Torah. A man accosted him, saying: "Greetings unto thee, Rabbi." The man was very repulsive of countenance, and instead of returning his greetings, the fastidious young Rabbi said: "How ugly thou art! Are all the people of thy town as repulsive as thou?"

The man replied: "I know not, but go and say to the Master Who hath made me: 'How defective a vessel Thou hast fashioned!'"

R. Eleazar realized that he had sinned grievously. He descended from his donkey and threw himself at the man's feet, imploring his pardon. The man said: "I shall not forgive thee until thou heedest my words." The Rabbi walked behind the man until the city of their destination was reached. The people came forth to welcome the Rabbi and greeted him with the words: "Peace be unto thee, Rabbi and Teacher."

The man, however, asked: "Whom do ye call Rabbi and Teacher." And when they told him, he said: "If this be a Rabbi, let there not be many like him in Israel" and he related the incident. The people responded: "Nevertheless, pray forgive him, since he is a scholar, great in Torah." The man replied: "For your sake I will forgive him, provided he does not repeat the offense."

R. Eleazar ben R. Simeon entered the synagogue, and delivered a sermon on the theme: "A man should always be pliable as a reed, and not unyielding as a cedar."[1]

*Taanit, 20.*

[1] I have used the story as the theme of a poem; see *Joyful Jeremiads*, p. 85.

## THE OBEDIENT WIFE

A Babylonian who settled in Palestine married there a woman of little wit. Once he said to her: "Cook for me two lentils," and she obeyed him to the letter. Next day he said: "Cook for me a quart of lentils," and again she obeyed literally. The husband said: "Bring me two 'Butzinin.'" She understood the word not in its Babylonian sense to mean "melons," but in its Palestinian sense, to mean "candles." (In Babylonian dialect candles are "Shragin.") The husband grew angry and said: "Go and break them on the 'Baba.'" By this he meant the door, but she went to the house of a neighbor called Baba ben Butta (a disciple of Shammai), and broke the candles on his head. He was told the reason and he said to the woman: "Thou obeyest thy husband with implicit trust; mayest thou have two children like Baba."

*Nedarim, 66.*

### R. ABBAHU'S HUMILITY

R. Abbahu said: "I considered myself of a humble nature, but when I once saw R. Abba of Acco stand in the pulpit and explain portions of the Halakah and say nothing, though his interpreter gave a reason for the law different from his, then I knew I was not humble."

What do we know of R. Abbahu's humility? Once his interpreter's wife said to his wife: "My husband knows how to deliver an address as well as thine. He merely acts as his interpreter (elaborator) because thy husband is respected by the Governor." R. Abbahu's wife repeated the conversation to her husband, who merely said: "What is the difference to thee, since both of us labor for the honor of God?"

Once the Rabbis wished to appoint R. Abbahu as principal. The latter, however, knew that R. Abba of Acco was afflicted with many debts, and he said to them: "R. Abba is the man you need for the position."

*Sotah, 40.*

### WORDS OF THE LIVING GOD

Said Rab Abba in the name of Samuel: "For three years the Schools of Shammai and Hillel have maintained a controversy, each School asserting that the decision should be given in accordance with its opinion. At last a Voice descended in Jabneh and cried out: "The words of these and these are the words of the Living God, but the decision should follow the School of Hillel."

It was asked: "If the words of both are those of the Living God, why was the decision granted to the School of Hillel?"

The reply was: "Because the members of the School of Hillel are amiable of manner and courteous; they teach the opinions of both, and furthermore, they always give the opinion of their opponents first."

This teaches us that whosoever abases himself, God exalts.

*Erubin, 13.*

### LONG LIFE FOR THE HUMBLE

R. Hanina bar Hama once sat before Rabbi, and when the latter made an error in the recital of a word in a certain verse, R. Hanina publicly corrected him. This displeased Rabbi, since it implied lack of respect for the Patriarchate. He asked: "Who taught thee Scripture so well?" R. Hanina replied: "Rab Hamnuna in Babylonia." Rabbi responded: "Ask him to ordain thee as Hakam."

Before Rabbi died, he asked that R. Hanina be appointed by his son as head of the school. He refused the honor on the plea that Rabbi Offas of the south was older. He heard a certain scholar say: "If Hanina is head, I am next; and if Offas is head, I am next." R. Hanina recalled this, and when Rabbi Offas died, he asked that this scholar succeed, and that he be the third. In his old age he would say: "I know not whether humility has brought me long life or my visit to R. Simeon ben Halafta in Ein Teinah."

*Y. Taanit, 4.*

## INCLINE YOUR HEAD

R. Gamaliel said: "Once I was aboard a ship and I saw another vessel sink. I was greatly stricken by grief, since I knew that R. Akiba was on the wrecked ship. When I landed, however, I found him in the School. He said: 'I seized a piece of wood, and when a wave came, I inclined my head before it.'" When the Sages heard this tale, they said: "We may learn from this story two lessons, firstly, that when the wicked assail you or trouble overtakes you, incline your head and you will be rescued; secondly, we learn the truth of the words of the early Sages, who say: If a husband is known to have drowned in waters with known limits, his widow may remarry if his body is not found. But if he is drowned in waters without known limits, she may not marry. Perhaps he has landed somewhere and cannot communicate with his wife. She remains a married woman until evidence is brought forward that the body has been found."

*Yebamot, 16.*

## GOD AND MAN

God cannot live in the same world with the proud and arrogant man.

Let man always learn from the mind of his Creator, who paid no heed to the other high mountains and peaks, but caused His Presence to rest upon Mount Sinai, which is not difficult to ascend.

His character is not like men's; among men one of exalted station gives heed to one of the same rank, not one far beneath him. But God is exalted, yet He regards the lowly. (Psalm 138:6)

*Sotah, 5a.*

## LET THE GREATER ONE DECIDE

Resh Lakish said: "We read in Numbers (27:5) that when the daughters of Zelophehad claimed their father's inheritance, Moses brought their cause before the Lord. Why did he do this? When the five girls came before the Chief of Ten of their family, he refused to decide, saying: "This is not in our province; go to one who is more important."

They went to the Chief of Fifty, of a Hundred, of a Thousand, of the entire tribe. None wished to decide such a case, and sent them to ever higher authority. The High-Priest Eleazar sent them to

Moses. When Moses beheld that each had paid honor to a higher authority, he thought: "Shall I decide the case and show that I am superior to them all? Nay, I too have a Greater Authority, and He is above me!"

*Tanhuma to Numbers 27:5.*

## 147. HYPOCRISY

It is easier to rule the entire world than to sit before two insincere students of the Torah.

*Abot de-R. Nathan, 25.*

It is like a woman who is in the apartment of her lover, and swears by the life of her husband.

*Tanhuma Emor, 2.*

Prohibit not something to others which you permit to yourself.

*Shemot Rabbah, 25, 8.*

In the World-to-Come Esau the Wicked will don a Tallit and sit with the Zaddikim. Only God Himself will know him for what he really is, and will drag him away.

*Y. Nedarim, 3, 8.*

### THE PHARISEES

There are seven groups of Pharisees: the "shoulder Pharisee" who indulges in ostentatious piety; the "wait-a-bit Pharisee," who when someone has business with him, says: "Wait a little, I must do a good deed"; the "reckoning Pharisee," who when he commits a fault and does a good deed, crosses off one with the other, instead of repenting; the "economizing Pharisee" who asks: "What economy can I practice to spare a little to perform a good deed?" (he should reflect in his own mind); the "show-me-my-fault Pharisee," who says: "Show me what sin I have committed"; the Pharisee of fear, like Job; the Pharisee of love, like Abraham. The last is the only kind dear to God.

*Yer. Sotah, 20c; Sotah, 22b.*

King Jannaeus said to his wife, Salome, on his death-bed: "Fear neither the Pharisees nor the Sadducees. Fear those who are disguised as Pharisees. Their deeds are those of Zimri and they expect the reward like Phineas."

*Sotah, 22.*

Among those who destroy the world are included the foolish Hasid, and the plague of a Pharisee. What is a foolish Hasid? He sees a woman drowning, and remarks: "I must not jump in to save her, lest I see her nakedness."

What is a plague of a Pharisee? He teaches legal tricks. A

widow was spending for her maintenance more money than the heirs, her stepsons, were willing to grant her. They complained to R. Eleazar, who replied: "Perhaps she will accept her Ketubah settlement."

A man who stood by remarked: "Let me explain to you the meaning of the Rabbi. He implied that you should offer your land for sale, and your stepmother in fright will ask for her Ketubah." This was done, and she came to R. Eleazar to demand the payment of her Ketubah. The Rabbi said: "A plague of a Pharisee meddled in this affair." [1]

*Sotah, 22.*

[1] Moore, *Judaism,* ii, 194 gives the following version: Rabbi Joshua ben Hananiah said: "A fool saint, a subtle knave, a woman Pharisee and the plague of Pharisees bring ruin on the world." *Mishnah Sotah,* 3, 4.

What is a subtle knave? One who interprets the law, when applied to himself, in a way to lighten its requirements, but in a more burdensome way for others.

What is the plague of Pharisees? Scholars acting as lawyers who give counsel by which, apparently in strict form of law, the law may be circumvented." *Yer. Sotah,* 19a.

## DECEIT, FLATTERY AND HYPOCRISY

It is forbidden to deceive anyone, Israelite or Gentile.

*Hullin, 94a.*

R. Nathan said: "When the Sages flattered King Agrippa I by crying out to him: 'Thou art our brother,' they made themselves liable to extermination."

*Sotah, 41b.*

To decide a point out of deference to the opinion of a great scholar is a kind of flattery which deserves censure.

*Ketubot, 63b, end.*

Hypocrites are excluded from the presence of God.

*Sotah, 42a.*

R. Eleazar ben Pedat said: "Every man in whom there is hypocrisy brings God's wrath; his prayer is not heard; he is cursed even by infants, and he goes down to Gehenna."

*Sotah, 41b.*

A community in which hypocrisy exists is disgusting, and will go into exile.

*Sotah, 42a.*

## LIKE A HOG

"Why is the Roman Government in Palestine like a hog?"

"Because, after a hog is sated with refuse, it sticks out its paws, and shows that they are like those of a clean animal (cloven-footed). (Lev. 11:7)

Thus is Rome. Rome robs and confiscates, and then opens assizes to try robbers.

There was once a magistrate in Caesarea who sentenced to death robbers and adulterers. Before leaving the bench he was heard to say to the prosecutor: "Last night I robbed and assaulted a woman myself."

*Bereshit Rabbah, 69.*

## THE PURSE

When R. Jannai was asked why even pious Jews were not accustomed to wear their Tefillin all day long, he answered that it was because of the hypocrites. Once a man arrived in a town on Friday afternoon, entered the synagogue and saw a man with Tefillin on his head. He said to himself: "Surely this is an observant person, and I may safely entrust my purse to him until after the Sabbath."

When he later asked the return of the purse, the man denied having received it. The visitor exclaimed: "Not thee, but the Holy Name on thy head have I trusted!" He fell asleep and dreamed that God had sent Elijah to him, instructing him to go to the deceitful man's home for the purse. As a token that her husband had sent him, he was to say that they had eaten Hametz on Passover and a certain dish on Yom Kippur. The wife gave the visitor the purse. When her husband demanded the reason, she repeated the words of the visitor. The husband and wife then said: "Since it has become known that we are impious, let us return to our former ways of open unrighteousness."

*Y. Berakot, 2.*

## 148. IDLENESS

A man can quickly die if he has nothing to do.
*Abot de-R. Nathan, 11.*

Not good eating, but idleness is the cause of sin.
*Esther Rabbah, 7.*

Rabbi Simeon ben Gamaliel said: "If a husband has restrained his wife from doing any work, he should grant her a divorce and pay the Ketubah, for idleness is a cause of insanity."
*Mishnah Ketubot, 5, 5.*

## 149. IMPUDENCE

Impudence is a kingdom without a crown.
*Sanhedrin, 105.*

A man who is impudent shows that he is a sinner.
*Taanit, 7.*

## 150. INCONSISTENCY

I have heard this concerning you: "You uproot trees and then plant them." (You answer a question and then question your answer.)

*Sanhedrin, 30.*

## 151. INDOLENCE AND LAZINESS

He who is indolent in learning cannot stand up in the day of tribulation.

*Berakot, 63.*

How ashamed should the indolent person be that he must learn diligence from the ant.

*Sifre, Haazinu, 306.*

## 152. INSPIRATION (HOLY SPIRIT)

(See God's Shekinah, and Prophecy)

He who learns for the purpose of teaching receives inspiration.

*Wayyikra Rabbah, 35, 7.*

I take as witness unto me Heaven and earth; whether it be Israelite or Gentile; male or female, servant or maid—the Holy Spirit rests upon each, according to the deeds of each.

*Eliyahu Rabbah, 9.*

God does not permit his Shekinah to rest upon anyone except that he be strong, wise, and meek.

*Nedarim, 38.*

## 153. INTEGRITY AND PROBITY

He who holds fast to his word has the approval of the Sages.

*Shebuot, 10 end.*

If a man has no money, he should not bid.

*Baba Metzia, 58.*

One may not sell meat from a dead or mortally wounded beast to a non-Jew, unless he discloses this to him. Otherwise he is guilty of deception.

*Hullin, 94.*

## The Quality of Hasidut (Midat Hasidut)

R. Safra had an article to sell, and was offered five denarii, but wished more. Next day the purchaser came and said: "We have decided to give you your price"; but he refused to accept it. He said: "After you had left, I decided in my heart to give you the merchandise for five denarii; therefore I cannot accept more."

*Sheiltot de Rabbi Aha.*

Rab Gamda gave a few coins to some sailors that they might purchase a curiosity for him. They bought him a monkey. The creature ran away and was captured near a hole of a wall; beneath him there was found a crock filled with gold coins. The sailors gave the treasure to the Rabbi.

*Nedarim, 50.*

The first question that a man will have to answer on the Judgment Day is: "Hast thou been honest in thy business?"

*Shabbat, 31a.*

He who gives false measure is classed with the hypocrite and the blasphemer, whose sin God will never forget.

*Baba Batra, 88a.*

The honest tradesman will be true to his bond. What he has said he will fulfil.

*Baba Matzia, 47b.*

## The Power of a Word

Abba ben Abba was a dealer in silk. Once R. Judah ben Beteirah ordered some silk from him, and Abba laid it aside in his name. But R. Judah found no opportunity to come for the merchandise for a long time. When he finally arrived, R. Abba gave him the very silk he had ordered. R. Judah said: "Why hast thou kept it for me though I did not send thee a deposit?"

R. Abba replied: "Thy word is stronger in my eyes than money."

R. Judah blessed him, asking that he be granted a son as honest in his dealings with his fellow-men as was the Prophet Samuel. Soon R. Abba was vouchsafed a son, who became the great Amora, Samuel.

*Midrash Samuel, 10.*

## The Extra Wine and Oil

Abba Saul ben Batnit dealt in wine and oil. It was his custom to mark down on the barrel the number of measures placed in it, and to cross off what he had sold. At the end of a year he discovered that he had extra wine and oil, because of the foam in the wine, and the fact that oil clung to the sides of the barrel. He took this extra wine and

oil to the treasurer of the donations of the Temple. The latter said:
"By law you may keep it, since the buyers are aware they did not
receive exact measure. But if you do not wish to retain it, sell it and
donate the money for public improvements."

*Betzah, 29.*

## 154. ISRAEL AND ITS MISSION

One empire cometh and another passeth away, but Israel abideth
forever.

*Derek Eretz Zuta, Perek ha-Shalom.*

Israel is likened to the dust and the sand. As nothing can grow
without the dust of the soil, so the nations of the world cannot exist
without Israel, through whom they receive their blessing.

As sand mixed in bread injures the teeth, so those who persecute
Israel suffer for it.

As sand cannot be burned in fire, but turns into glass, so Israel
cannot be consumed in the fire of Gehenna, but emerges stronger from
Purgatory.

*Pesikta Rabbati, 11, 5.*

Israel is likened to a vine: the householders are the branches; the
learned men are the fruit, and the unlearned the leaves.

*Hullin, 92.*

Israel needs only a fence of roses as a protection against inroads.
(A fence of good deeds.)

*Sanhedrin, 37.*

The ladder of Heaven has but three steps: Israel, Torah and God.

*Zohar, iii, 73a.*

Israel is like the heart of humanity. As no one can live if the heart
stops, so humanity cannot exist without Israel.

*Zohar, iv, 221b.*

As the olive tree has its future in the end (namely, the oil), so too
has Israel.

*Menahot, 53.*

Why is Israel like an olive? As the olive gives its oil only by being
crushed, so does Israel repent only through chastisements.

*Menahot, 53.*

Why is Israel like an apple tree? As the apple tree brings forth
fruit before leaves, so the children of Israel promised to do, even
before they heard the Law.

*Shabbat, 88.*

Israel doth not know "L'sh'abar"—what belongeth to the past; therefore, my people doth not consider "L'atid," the demands of the future.

*Sifre Deut., sec. 309, p. 133b.*

If Jews were to disappear, the Torah would disappear and God Himself lose the most effective witness of His presence.

*Cf. Rashi to Ps. 83:6; Midrash Tehillim, p. 185a.*

Israel is to be likened to the stars.[1]

*Shemot Rabbah, 1:3.*

[1] To radiate the light of God about them—that is the function of Israel.

Why is Israel compared to a dove?

All other birds, when tired, rest upon a rock or upon the branch of a tree. Not so the dove. When the dove tires, she does not cease flying; she rests one wing and flies with the other.

*Bereshit Rabbah, 39:10.*

The moon represents Israel, while the sun represents the other mighty powers of the world.

*Bereshit Rabbah, 6, 5.*

Israel is the King's retinue, whose duty it is to look expectantly for the royal commands.

*Sifre and Yalkut to Lev. 19, 1.*

"If ye publish not My divinity to the Gentiles," the Rabbis picture the Supreme as warning Israel, "ye must pay the penalty for your refusal."

*Wayyikra Rabbah, chap. 6.*

God scattered His people over the earth, for only so could the nations be gained for His Service.

*Pesahim, 87b.*

Wherever a Jew enters, there light enters also!

*Shemot Rabbah, 14, 3.*

Even if they are foolish, even if they transgress, even if they are full of blemishes, they are still called "Sons."

*Sifre on Deut., 308.*

Bar Kappara said: "He who calls Jacob by the name *Jacob* and not *Israel* violates a positive command."

Another Rabbi said: "Israel may also be called Jacob, but Jacob must ever be the less important, while the name Israel must ever be this principal distinction."

*Bereshit Rabbah, 88, 5.*

Why is Israel likened to an olive? Because as an olive's oil cannot be mingled with other substances, so Israel cannot be mixed with other peoples.

*Shemot Rabbah, 36, 7.*

As oil does not mix with other liquids, so is it with Israel. As oil always rises to the top of liquids, so, too, does Israel.

*Shir ha-Shirim Rabbah, 1, 3.*

Israel is like a vine. A vine is trodden underfoot, but later its wine is placed on the table of the king. So, too, does Israel, at first oppressed, come to greatness.

*Nedarim, 49.*
*(Wayyikra Rabbah, 36, 2, speaks of the fruit of the vine.)*

As the vine has a watchman above it, so, too, has Israel. As the fruit of the vine is sometimes sweet and sometimes sour, Israel is sometimes happy and sometimes unhappy.

*Wayyikra Rabbah, 36, 2.*

Said Rabbi Simeon ben Lakish: "Israel is like a vine. As the face of him lights up who drinks from the fruit of the vine, so is the face of Israel illumined when he partakes of the words of the Torah."

*Agadat Samuel, 15.*

Rabbi Isaac and Rabbi Judah met a youth, and invited him to pronounce a fitting word. He said: "Why is Israel likened to a vine? Just as the vine cannot receive a grafting from another fruit-tree, Israel cannot receive another divinity, except the Ancient of Days."

*Zohar, i, 238b.*

Why is Israel like sand? As in the sand thou diggest a pit, and in the evening thou findest it filled up, so, too, is it with Israel.

*Pesikta, Buber, 139.*

Why is Israel like glass? Just as wine in a glass can be seen from without, so the true Israelite must be as loyal to God from within as from without.

*Mayyan Ganim, Buber.*

As this palm has but one heart, so Israel.

*Bemidbar Rabbah, 3, 1.*

As the rose is distinguished among the grasses, so is Israel distinguished among the nations.

*Wayyikra Rabbah, 23, 6.*

Why is Israel like a worm? Because the worm's sole strength lies in its mouth. So is it with Israel.

*Zohar, i, 178a.*

As the bee makes for her master whatever she assembles, so are all the good deeds of Israel on behalf of God.

*Debarim Rabbah, 1, 5.*

Why is Israel like a bird? As a bird cannot fly without her wings, Israel can achieve nothing without the Elders (Rabbis).

*Shemot Rabbah, 5, 12.*

Israel is likened in Scripture to the dust and to the stars; when Israel is low, they are even as the dust; when they are exalted, they rise to the stars.

*Megillah, 16a.*

## Like the Moon

The first commandment given to Israel was to know that Nissan should be the head of all the moons (months). Why was this? Because Israel should be like the moon. When Israel is in tribulation, he should look at the moon, which, early in the month, is small, but grows larger and larger. Thus will Israel likewise increase. When Israel has grown wealthy and fat, he should regard the moon, which, after attaining fulness, decreases daily. By this token, Israel's stable and secure position may be diminished. For fourteen days, the moon increases, and after it is full for one day, it decreases for another fourteen days. So it is with Israel. From Abraham to Solomon, he increased in numbers and power for fourteen generations; for fourteen generations, however, from Rehoboam to Zedekiah he decreased.

*Shemot Rabbah to Exodus 12, 2, with comments by Mamigah, 69, ii, 1, in "Mikrae Kodesh."*

## Like Nut-Trees and Nuts

All fruit-trees should be covered at their roots, but the nut-bearing tree should have its roots uncovered. Likewise Israel wins mercy from God when he reveals his sin.

The children play with nuts, and the king does not disdain to eat them. Likewise, when Israel is worthy, princes delight in serving him; but when Israel sins, even children do not hesitate to shower abuses upon him.

The nut-tree is cultivated as long as it bears nuts; likewise God blesses the affairs of householders, only as long as they support the students of Torah.

Fruits are noiseless when one is taken from a bag; but nuts are noisy. Thus, when one Israelite sins, all respond to it.

Fruits become distasteful when they fall into the mire; but a nut can be washed and eaten. Likewise Israel is purified at Yom Kippur, no matter how many their sins.

As room is found within a bag of nuts for peas, so room is found within Israel for proselytes.

Some Israelites are soft of shell; they donate generously for a Mitzwah of their own accord. Some are of medium hardness, and some will not yield, even after much persuasion.

*Pesikta Rabbati, 11, 2.*

There are three classes in Israel: the princes, the servants and the flock in the holy kingdom.

*Zohar, iv, 224b.*

Israel has been called in Scripture: Kings, Zaddikim, Seers, Prophets, Lords of the Torah, Heroes, Hasidim, Intellectuals, Sages and Princes.

*Hakdamah to Tikkune Zohar, 5b.*

Even the conversation of Israel is Torah.

*Midrash Tchillim, 104, 3.*

Abraham is likened to the sun. But spots may be seen upon it. Likewise Ishmael descended from Abraham.

Isaac is likened to the moon. But the moon is not pure light. Likewise Esau was born to Isaac.

Jacob is likened to the stars, wherein no spots are seen. And his sons were all noble.

As a single star may ignite the entire earth if it collides with it, so one Zaddik may bring fire from Heaven, even as Elijah did.

As the stars twinkle, so will Israel twinkle in the Messianic age.

*Pesikta Rabbati, 11, 5.*

As it is impossible for the world to be without air, so also is it impossible for the world to be without Israel.

*Taanit, 3, 2.*

All Israelites are responsible for each other.

*Shebuot, 39.*

All Israelites are brothers.

*Tanhuma Nasso, 3.*

Israel in the present world cannot receive either too much good or too much evil.

*Yebamot, 47.*

Israel in the Diaspora are worshippers of strange gods in purity.

*Tikkune Zohar, T. 66, 136b.*

Israel will never cease to exist.

*Menahot, 53.*

When trouble comes into the world, Israel feels it first; when good comes to the world, Israel feels it first.

*Ekah Rabbah, 2, 3.*

When Israel reaches the lowest depths, he is lifted up.

*Shemot Rabbah, 1, 9.*

Israel was raised little by little to be a great nation, but collapsed all at once.

*Ekah Rabbah, 2, 2.*

### Slander Not Israel

Israel is like a smooth cocoanut-palm tree; he who is inexpert will injure himself if he attempts to climb it.

Even the greatest among Israel have suffered when they lost

patience with Israel. Moses lost patience and exclaimed: "Hear now, ye rebels" (Num. 20:10). His impatience resulted in his smiting the rock instead of speaking to it, as God commanded him to do. As a punishment, God said unto him: "Ye shall not bring this assembly into the land" (verse 12).

Isaiah lost patience, and exclaimed: "And I dwell in the midst of a people of unclean lips" (6:5). What occurred? An angel burned his lips with a glowing stone.

Elijah lost patience, and exclaimed: "The children of Israel have forgotten Thy covenant" (I Kings 19:14). What was the consequence of this outburst? "And Elisha b. Shaphat thou shalt anoint to be prophet in thy stead" (verse 16).

R. Johanan added: "God told Elijah: why inform against Israel? Get thee to Damascus, observe their conduct, and speak against them."

*Yalkut Shimeoni to Numbers, chap. 20.*

## 155. THE CUSTOMS OF ISRAEL

If a law is doubtful in the courts, proceed according to the common law and usage.

*Y. Maaser Sheni, 5, 2, end.*

A court may fine a transgressor against a custom.

*Y. Abodah Zarah, 1, 6.*
*(See also Y. Pesahim, 4, 3.)*

Many a thing depends upon the custom.

*Y. Pesahim, 4, 1.*

### THE BARREL OF NUTS

When a man sold his field, his kinsfolk filled a barrel with nuts, broke it open near a schoolhouse, and called to the children to approach. The children would gather the nuts and cry out: "This man has been cut off from his land." If he repurchased it, a barrel would again be broken open for the children, and while they ate the nuts, they would shout: "This man has returned to his land."

*Y. Kiddushin, 1; Ketubot, 28.*

## 156. ISRAEL'S ENEMIES

If Esau hates Jacob for taking his blessing, why do the Barbarians hate him? [1]

*Midrash Tehillim, 25, 13.*

[1] Esau signifies Rome; the Barbarians all the non-Roman nations.

Those who persecute Israel are unwearying.

*Sanhedrin, 104.*

As the myrtle is sweet to him who smells it, but bitter to him who bites into it, so Israel brings prosperity to the nation which grants them kindness, and depression to the people which afflicts them with evil.

*Esther Rabbah, 6, 5.*

If a man asks thee: Where is thy God? Answer him: He is in the great city of Rome.[1]

*Y. Taanit, 1, 1.*

[1] Rome which persecuted Israel has fallen, but the people of God have survived. In this God's presence is to be seen.

The scourge that smites Israel will meet an evil end.

*Mekilta Beshallah.*

Gog and Magog have the numerical value of 70, namely, the 70 nations.

*Tanhuma, end of Korah.*

As the bee dies once it has stung, so Israel's enemy dies ignominiously once he has smitten him.

*Bereshit Rabbah, 17, 3.*

As everyone treads on dust, so does every nation tread on Israel. But as dust lasts longer than metal, so shall Israel outlast all nations.

*Bereshit Rabbah, 41, 9; Midrash Tehillim, 119, 12.*

The kingdoms of the world are as Asshur; they become enriched through Israel. They are as Mitzraim (Egypt); they oppress Israel. They are as Nineveh; they are beautified through Israel.[1]

*Bereshit Rabbah, 16, 4.*

[1] Asshur in Hebrew has the sound of 'Ashir, rich; Mitzraim, suggests Tzar, persecutor, oppressor. Nineveh suggests Naveh, handsome.

Woe unto us that Ishmael, the son of the servant, rules over Isaac, the son of the mistress. Ishmael persecutes Israel more often than any other nation.[1]

*Zohar, ii, 17a.*

[1] A late excerpt from the Zohar. Ishmael refers to the Mohammedan nations, long after the close of the Talmud.

In his struggle against hostile peoples, what hope has Israel that he will be victorious? If he is loyal to the Torah which he has accepted, he will be triumphant.

*Zohar, ii, 58a.*

Esau wept copiously when Jacob took his blessing from Isaac, and it is these tears which have placed the sons of Jacob in the power of the sons of Esau. When will the exile be ended? When the sons of Jacob will weep as earnestly that they be redeemed from exile.

*Zohar, ii, 12a.*

R. Hiyya said: "We read in Deut. 2:6: 'Ye shall break (or purchase) food of them (Esau) for money.' Why is the term: 'Break' (Tishberu) used instead of the term: 'Purchase'? To teach thee that if thou hast an enemy, break off his hate by feeding him; as it is written: 'If thine enemy is hungry, give him bread to eat' (Prov. 25:21). And if he is needy, give him money."

When R. Jonathan would hear that an influential official had arrived in town, he would provide him with comforts and satisfy his needs, saying: "If an orphan or widow be involved in trouble, he will remember my friendship and give heed to my words in their behalf."

*Y. Abodah Zarah, 2.*

## 157. ISRAEL'S FRIENDS

He who aids Israel is as if he had aided the Shekinah.

*Tanhuma, Wayyehi.*

Moses was the friend of God; Aaron the friend of Israel.

*Zohar, iii, 53b.*

He who defends Israel is uplifted by God.

*Pesikta Buber, Berakah.*

He who loveth My children will rejoice with My children.

*Shemot Rabbah, 18.*

The charity and good deeds which Israel performs in this world bring great peace and raise up strong defenders between them and their Father in Heaven.

*Baba Batra, 10.*

The Archangel Michael is the great patron of Israel. When the Sitra Ahara stands up to prosecute Israel, Michael argues the case and defends Israel. Israel is then acquitted.

*Zohar, ii, 254a.*

God loveth him who loveth Israel. Gideon was neither a Zaddik nor the son of a Zaddik, but when he said to God's angel: "If the Lord be with us, why, then, has all this befallen us?" (Judges 6:13), the Lord said: "Go in this, thy might, and save Israel, from the hand of Midian."

*Zohar, i, 254b.*

## 158. ISRAEL'S FUTURE

In the days to come all Israel will speak one language.

*Otzar Midrashim, 71.*

### When Israel Is Free

Several pieces of fine lumber were lying in muddy ground, and no one paid attention to them. But a skilled cabinet-maker passed by and recognized their worth. He purchased them and wrought them into beautiful furniture. The former owner saw the objects, and said regretfully: "I considered the wood worthless, yet behold what beautiful things have been fashioned from it."

By the same token, Pharaoh and other rulers have forced Israel to live in degradation, and to occupy themselves with low trades. But when they behold the glory and beauty of Israel emancipated, they regret their treatment of him, and are compelled to offer their admiration.

*Introd. to Tanhuma Buber, 135.*

## 159. ISRAEL'S LOYALTY TO GOD

Israel gave three fine gifts to God: modesty, compassion and lovingkindness.

*Y. Sanhedrin, 6, 7.*

A king married a noble girl and wrote her a generous settlement. Once he left her and prolonged his absence a long time. The queen's friends said to her: "He will never return; marry again while you are still young." But she opened her document of settlement and was comforted by his generous promises. Thus the nations say to Israel: "Join our faith. Your Redeemer will not come." But Israel looks into the Torah, and reads God's promises. Then is Israel comforted.

*Pesikta Rabbati, 21, 15.*

Man lends to God in two ways: by gifts to the poor and by generosity on the Sabbath and Festivals.

*Zohar, ii, 25a.*

Israel is likened to sand. As sand may be placed in hot or cold water and will not change, so does Israel change not, though passing through fire and water. As sand is moved from place to place, and is voiceless, so Israel is exiled from place to place without complaint.

*Introd. to Tanhuma Buber, 134.*

Why are the two phrases "And be satisfied" and "Take heed to yourselves" adjoining each other (Deut. 11:15, 16)? Thus spoke Moses: When you are satisfied, take heed to yourselves, lest ye rebel against the Lord. For we find in numerous passages that the sated person grows rebellious.

*Sifre to Num. 11:15-16.*

## BE A JEW!

Rabbi Abba bar Zmina was a tailor. Once he was hired for work in the house of a non-Jew. At dinner time he was given meat, but he refused it. The master of the house said: "If you do not eat it, you will be killed." The tailor replied: "Do what you wish with me, but I shall not eat." The non-Jew smiled, and said: "I will tell you the truth. If you had eaten, I would have felt like killing you. Since you are a Jew, be a Jew! If you are a pagan, act like a pagan."

Rab Manna remarked: "R. Abba was lucky that he did not act upon the law of the Sages, that a Jew need not give up his life to avoid transgressing any law, except incest, murder and idolatry."

*Y. Shebiit, 4.*

## STRICT OBSERVANCE

Hadrian said to R. Joshua ben Hananiah: "I am better than your Master Moses, because a live dog is better than a dead lion." (Eccl. 9:4)

The Rabbi replied: "Moses is an exception to this statement, as I can prove to you. Issue a decree that no fire be lighted tomorrow in Rome."

The decree went forth, and the Caesar and the Rabbi stood on the roof of the palace to watch for smoke. In a few moments they noticed smoke issuing from a chimney. The Caesar investigated and was informed that a patrician felt unwell; and the physician had ordered him to drink warm water.

"See now, O Caesar," commented the Rabbi. "You forbade a fire one day, and yet on a slight pretext, your command was not obeyed. Moses forbade a fire fifty-two times a year, and for many centuries he has been obeyed, except if a life is endangered."

*Kohelet Rabbah to 9, 4.*

The Israelites sinned when they asked Moses at Sinai to speak to them in place of God.

*Shir ha-Shirim Rabbah, 1, 2.*

## 160. LOYALTY TO ISRAEL

Because Moses did not protest when the daughters of Jethro called him an Egyptian, he did not enter the Promised Land. He prayed long and hard: "O Holy Master, if it is decreed by Thee that I shall not enter Canaan in life, at least let my bones be buried there, as are those of Joseph." And the Holy One spoke in reply: "Moses, My son, Joseph acknowledged to his captors that he was a Hebrew lad, but thou gavest thyself out to be an Egyptian."

*Introd. to Tanhuma Buber, 134.*

God instructed Moses to assemble seventy men of the elders of the people, and of his officers whom he knew, saying that He would put His spirit upon them (Num. 11:16). Who were these officers? When Pharaoh decreed that the Children of Israel should make a certain number of bricks daily, he placed over them Hebrew officers. If the number of bricks was less than the quantity stipulated, these officers were held responsible and were punished. Nevertheless they refused to point out the faulty laborers, and submitted rather to a flogging. Therefore when God wished to put His spirit upon seventy Hebrews, he commanded Moses to call together those men who had suffered for the sake of Israel. You may learn from this that whosoever suffers for Israel receives honors, fame, and a portion of the Holy Spirit.

*Bemidbar Rabbah, 15.*


## 161. ISRAEL, UNITED AND DIVIDED

Israel will not be redeemed until all the Children of Israel are united in a single fellowship.

*Tanhuma Nitzabim, 1.*

Be not of many parties; be of one party.

*Sifre Reeh, 96.*

If a man takes in his hands a number of reeds bound together, can he break them? Only if they are separated, each from the other, can they be broken.

*Tanhuma Nitzabim, 1.*

When are "ye standing this day all of you" (Deut. 29:9)? When ye are all of you, of one accord, then ye are standing.

*Yalkut Nitzabim, beginning.*

When an Israelite separates himself from his people in their hour of tribulation, two ministering angels come and say: "He shall not live to see the comforting of Israel."

*Taanit, 11a.*

[1] Another version: If in time of national calamity a man withdraw himself from his kindred and refuse to share in their sorrow, his guardian angel says: "This man has isolated himself from his country in the day of its need; let him not live to see and enjoy the day when God shall restore its prosperity."


## 162. JEALOUSY AND ENVY

The jealousy of scholars increases wisdom.

*Baba Batra, 21.*

Were it not for envy, the world could not stand.

*Midrash Tehillim, 37, 1.*

A sage is jealous of another sage, but not of one unlearned in his subject.

*Abodah Zarah, 55.*

Bad neighbors count a man's income, but not his expenses.
*Pesikta Rabbati, Pes., 31.*
*Tanhuma Buber, Wayyikra, 6.*

## 163. JERUSALEM

God informs Jerusalem that it will be redeemed only with peace.
*Debarim Rabbah, end of chap. 5.*

If a man tells thee: the dispersed have been re-assembled but Jerusalem has not been rebuilt, believe him not.
*Tanhuma Noah, 17.*

He who did not see Jerusalem before its destruction has never in his days seen a beautiful city.
*Sukkah, 48.*

Why are there no sweet fruits in Jerusalem? So that visitors may not say: "We came to eat sweet fruits."
*Pesahim, 8.*

Jerusalem in days to come will ascend higher and higher until she will have reached the Throne of Glory.
*Shir ha-Shirim Rabbah, 7, 5.*

In the future the gates of Jerusalem will reach to Damascus.
*Sifre Debarim, 1.*

Jerusalem in the future will become the capital of the world.
*Shemot Rabbah, 23, 10.*

Jerusalem in the future will become a great light to all the nations.
*Pesikta Rabbati, Piska Kumi Ori.*

In the Jerusalem of the present anyone may enter, but in the Jerusalem of the World-to-Come, only the invited may enter.
*Baba Batra, 75.*

Three are called by the Name of God: Zaddikim, Messiah and Jerusalem.
*Baba Batra, 75.*

When will God build Jerusalem? When He will assemble the dispersed.
*Berakot, 49.*

Ten things will God bring to pass in the future: He will give light; He will cause fresh, curative waters to come forth from Jerusalem; the trees will bear fruit each month; all cities that have been destroyed, including even Sodom, will be rebuilt; Jerusalem will be rebuilt with sapphires; a cow and a bear will graze together; all animals will be domesticated; there will no longer be weeping or death, and everyone will rejoice at all times.

*Shemot Rabbah, 15, 21.*

The Holy One, Blessed be He, hath built a Jerusalem above in the likeness of the one below.

*Zohar, i, 80b.*

When the Holy One, Blessed be He, renews His world, He will build a Jerusalem and lower it down, completely built, from above, an edifice not subject to destruction.

*Zohar, i, 114a; Midrash ha-Neelam.*

The Holy One, Blessed be He, has made an oath that He will not enter the upper Jerusalem until He hath entered the lower.

*Zohar, iii, 15b.*

From the day that Jerusalem was destroyed blessings have been rare and curses frequent in the world.

*Zohar, iii, 74b.*

R. Johanan visited R. Hanina and found him reading aloud Jeremiah 3:17: "At that time they shall call Jerusalem the Throne of the Lord; and all nations shall be gathered into it, to the name of the Lord, to Jerusalem." R. Johanan asked: "Will it hold all nations? Will it be large enough to constitute the Throne of the Lord?"

R. Hanina replied: "God will say unto it: 'Become long, become wide, and receive within thyself all the multitudes who come.' "

*Bereshit Rabbah, 5.*

R. Gamaliel, R. Joshua, R. Eleazar ben Azariah and R. Akiba were entering Rome. Many miles away they heard the tumult of its throngs, and they commenced to weep. R. Akiba, however, laughed; and they said: "We weep because we behold the affluence of Rome compared to the desolation of Jerusalem." R. Akiba answered: "When I see the wealth God grants to those who oppose Him, I think: how much greater wealth will He grant to those who obey Him?"

On another occasion these Sages visited Jerusalem and saw a jackal on the site of the Temple. They wept, but R. Akiba laughed. Again they asked him to explain. He said: "God sent His word through several Prophets. Through some He foretold the desolation of His Holy House, and this very fact we have just witnessed. Through others He foretold the restoration of Jerusalem and the Temple. If we behold the evil prophecies fulfilled, we may rest assured that the favorable prophecies will also come to pass."

*Sifre to Num. 11, 15.*

The Psalmist gives to Jerusalem its ancient name of Salem, its name in the time of Abraham, as it is written (76:3) : "In Salem also is set His tabernacle, and His dwelling-place in Zion." Why was the ancient name revived by the poet? Because in a previous Psalm (68:17), he names the place which God desired for His abode, the Mountain, and this is the name of the place when it was called Salem. It was Abraham who called it a Mountain. The Psalmist tells us that when Jerusalem's most important spot will be the mountain, the Shekinah will return to it.

*Tosefta Berakot, 1.*

## THE DESTRUCTION OF JERUSALEM

When the Holy Temple was being destroyed, Jeremiah awoke Abraham, and the Patriarch wept bitterly, saying: "O Lord, why didst Thou deal more harshly with my sons than with any other nation?" God replied: "Thy sons failed to observe the Torah and she shall testify to it." When the Torah came to bear witness, Abraham said: "My daughter, wilt thou testify against my sons? Dost thou not remember the day when God went around with thee to every nation and they refused to receive thee? Now in their tribulation dost thou wish to testify against those who did receive thee?" The Torah refused to bear witness.

God called the letters of the Torah to testify. The Aleph came and Abraham said to her: "Art thou not ashamed to inform against my sons who, alone of all peoples, accepted the Decalogue which commences with the letter: Aleph?"

The Aleph retreated and the Beth came forward. Abraham said: "Dost thou not remember that my sons received the Torah which begins with the letter Beth?"

The Gimel came, and Abraham said: "With thee begins the word 'Gedilim' (a synonym for Tzitzit), and only my sons performed the commandment to wear thee."

The other letters perceived that Abraham had put the first three to shame, and they did not step forward. Abraham then said: "Why hast Thou not remembered, O Lord, my readiness to surrender to Thee the son Thou gavest me in my hundredth year?" Isaac said: "Why hast Thou not remembered how I stretched forth my throat to my father's knife?" Jacob said: "Why hast Thou not remembered that I was prepared to give my life for my sons, and how I suffered on their account?"

Moses said: "Why hast Thou not remembered my nursing of Israel?"

Rachel said: "I took pity upon my sister Leah, and permitted Jacob to marry her in my stead. I conquered my intense jealousy. Why hast Thou not conquered Thy jealousy of gods that are naught; why hast Thou not pitied them?"

And God replied: "For thy sake, O Rachel, I will have compassion upon Israel."

*Petihtah to Ekah Rabbah.*

### R. Johanan ben Zakkai and Vespasian

R. Johanan beheld the starvation of the people of Jerusalem, and he held a secret conference with the leader of the Zealots. The leader said: "I have lost authority over the Zealots; if I should accept your counsel and advise surrender to them, they would slay me. I suggest that you pretend to sicken and die, and they will permit your casket to leave the city." When the Rabbi was outside the city, he asked to see the Roman commander, Vespasian. He greeted him with the words: "Peace unto you, O Caesar!" Vespasian answered: "Twice do you merit death. You have called me Caesar, though I am but a general; and you come not with a surrender."

The Rabbi replied: "I am confident that God's City will not fall into the hands of one less than the Emperor, and I cannot secure a surrender because of the misguided Zealots.

He was asked in the form of a fable: "If there be a snake in a tower, what should be done?" He said: "A snake-charmer should be brought to draw forth the snake, so that the Tower be not harmed." An Arabian general said: "A better way is to burn the Tower and the snake with it."

R. Johanan said to him: "You are a neighbor of Judea, and yet you advise that Jerusalem be destroyed."

The general responded: "I offered this counsel for your good. As long as the Temple stands, nations will make war against you; when it is destroyed, you will have peace."

Vespasian soon after received word that he had been chosen Emperor. He said to the Rabbi: "I will send my son in my place, but I wish to grant you a favor before I depart." R. Johanan asked three things: that when the walls of Jerusalem should fall, the Western Gate should be left open for four hours that refugees might leave through it; that an Academy be permitted at Jabneh with the House of Hillel in its Presidency; that physicians be sent to R. Zadok who had fasted so long that he could no longer swallow food.

These favors were granted to R. Johanan.

*Gittin, 56, etc.; Ekah Rabbah, 1.*

## 164. JUDGES AND COURTS

He who accuses his comrade before a court is himself first punished.

*Rosh ha-Shanah, 16.*

If there be no officer to enforce the law, of what avail is the judge?
*Tanhuma Shofetim, 2.*

If there is no judgment below, there will be no judgment above.
*Debarim Rabbah, 5, 5.*

If a judge is summoned as a defendant in a civil action, and loses, he is not a worthy judge, for he should not have been guilty of breaking the law he is supposed to know.

*Baba Batra, 58.*

If three persons have a claim of money against one, they may not constitute a court of justice, one as judge and the other two as witnesses.

*Shebuot, 31.*

What mean the words (Prov. 7:26): "For she hath cast down many wounded"? These are incompetent students of the law who render judgments. "Yea, a mighty host are all her slain." These are competent scholars who abstain from giving rulings.

*Abodah Zarah, 19.*

A judge should not stand in judgment over a person whom he likes or dislikes.

*Ketubot, 105.*

What do the words signify: "For your hands are defiled with blood"? (Isaiah 59:3). These are the unjust judges. "And your fingers with iniquity"? These are the clerks of the court. "Your lips have spoken lies"? These are the dishonest advocates.

*Shabbat, 139.*

He who accepts money for acting as judge renders verdicts that are valueless; he who accepts money for testifying renders valueless testimony.

*Berakot, 4, 6. Mishnah.*

What do the words mean: "The Lord hath broken the staff of the wicked?" (Isaiah 14:5). This signifies the judges who support their bailiffs in extortions.

*Shabbat, 139, and Rashi.*

A judge who has made a loan from a man on trial may not sit in judgment over him.

*Sanhedrin, 105.*

If a generation arises in which many tribulations overtake Israel, search the judges of Israel.

*Shabbat, 139.*

A court cannot reverse another court unless it is greater in learning and numbers.

*Eduyot, 1, 5.*

A judge who has not judged with equity has recognized Satan as the ruler of the world.

*Zohar, ii, 117a.*

If a judge is respected, it is evidence that he is a just man, and that the people seek true justice.

*Zohar Hadash, 1, 20a.*

The judge who but for one hour administers justice according to true equity is a partner, as it were, with God in His work of creation.

*Shabbat, 10a.*

The judge who accepts a bribe, however righteous he may otherwise be, will not leave this world with a sane mind.

*Shabbat, 105b.*

A judge will establish the land, if, like a king, he want nothing; but he will ruin it if, like a priest, he receive gifts from the threshing-floor.

*Shabbat, 105b.*

Judges should know that they stand before God, who will exact account of their judgments.

*Sanhedrin, 6b.*

The judge should ever regard himself as if he had had a sword laid upon his thigh, and Gehenna were yawning near him.

*Sanhedrin, 7a.*

When Samuel was crossing a bridge, a man lent him a sustaining hand. "Why so attentive?" queried the Rabbi. "I have a lawsuit before thee." "In that case," said the Rabbi, "thy attention has disqualified me from judging."

*Ketubot, 105a.*

### THE MAGISTRATE'S RESPONSIBILITY

R. Joshua ben Levi said: "If ten learned Rabbis sit at a trial all are responsible, even if one of them is the master, and the others the disciples. The latter must give notice if they believe the decision incorrectly rendered."

*Sanhedrin, 7.*

Rabbi Hanina held court in Sepphoris, and sat alone, to the surprise of R. Johanan and R. Simeon ben Lakish. They thought to themselves: "The aged scholar apparently believes himself incapable of error." One day, however, he summoned them to sit with him, and when they asked the reason, he replied: "In the cases before me until now, I have studied the points at issue hundreds of times, and have seen them decided at least three times. In this case there is a point, however, which I have seen decided only twice before."

*Y. Niddah, chap. 2.*

The magistrate received no fee for sitting. Rab would therefore say: "Of my own free will I go out to a place where I may fall into the danger of deserving heavy punishment. I bring nothing to my house by doing this, like others going into peril. May my return be as sinless as my departure for the court."

R. Samuel bar Nahmani said: "Fear not to judge if your motive be pure, and you follow the evidence."

*Sanhedrin, 7.*

### UNWORTHY MAGISTRATES

The Patriarch Judah II was frequently under the fire of the Sages for exacting unjust revenues to satisfy the greed of the Roman Government in Palestine. The greatest criticism was directed against his appointment of wealthy persons as magistrates in return for their monetary gifts. It was the custom of the magistrates to expound the law publicly on certain days. But frequently they were ignorant of what to say and were forced to rely upon their assistants. A clever orator once applied to them the 19th verse of the second chapter of Habbakuk. He said: "Woe unto him, the patriarch, who saith to one who is like a wooden log: 'Awake,' and to the dumb stone: 'Arise.' Can such as this teach? Behold, it owes its position to the fact that it is overlaid with gold and silver; and there is no breath whatsoever in its midst."

Rabbi Mana said: "Such magistrates deserve no respect. No one need rise when they pass; they should not be considered as Rabbis, and their robe is like the saddle of a donkey."

*Y. Bikkurim, chap. 3.*

### YESTERDAY AND TODAY

A man, victorious in a trial, praised the judge as a wise man; later in another trial, when he was the loser, he abused the judge as a fool. His friends said to him: "Yesterday the judge was wise, but today he has become a fool." The litigant became the butt for jests in the town, and whenever he passed by, the townsfolk would say: "Listen: yesterday wise; today, a fool."

*Tanhuma Mishpatim.*

### SITTING ALONE

Though three judges should sit in a civil case, one judge may sit alone if he is recognized by many as skilled.

R. Abbahu sat alone and held court in an open-air porch. He was asked why he sat alone, and answered: "Not because I consider myself skilled, but because the litigants can see that I sit alone. If nevertheless they still come to me, it is as if they accepted my decision on the same basis as one rendered by three."

R. Tarfon was asked by a butcher if he could sell the meat of a cow whose womb was missing. He declared it should be thrown to the dogs. Later a similar case came before the Sages at Jabneh, and they permitted the meat to be sold to Jews, because the cow was able to live despite this. R. Tarfon, on learning of the decision, said whimsically: "Here goes thy ass, Tarfon." [1] R. Akiba answered: "You are not required to pay the loss, inasmuch as you are a skilled judge, and had the right to pass judgment according to your viewpoint."

Rab said: "A judge who receives the permission of the Exilarch to hold court, is not liable for damages if his decision is faulty."

Rabbah bar Rab Huna deemed himself independent of the Exilarch. He said: "I received my permission to act as judge from my father; he from Rab; and he from Rabbi Judah I."

*Y. Sanhedrin, 1; Sanhedrin, 4, 33.*

[1] To pay the loss.

## FALSE WITNESSES

When R. Huna found that two witnesses gave evidence in identically the same words, he would thoroughly investigate their testimony. But if he found that they told the identical story in different words, he had confidence in them. In the first instance, it was likely that the witnesses were unreliable.

*Y. Sanhedrin, 3.*

## THE OVERHANGING BRANCHES

"Judges and officers shalt thou make thee," namely thou shalt first judge thyself and enforce thy verdict against thyself; then thou shalt judge and enforce the law "in all thy gates" (Deut. 16:18). There must be no defect in judges, and no one must be able to find a complaint against them before they judge others.

R. Hanina b. Eleazar owned a tree the branches of which extended over a neighbor's field. It chanced that a man came to his court asking for a warrant against a man whose tree also extended over his field, and thus prevented the rain and sunshine from nourishing that part of the field. R. Hanina said: "Come tomorrow." At once he commanded that his own tree be chopped off. On the following day he issued the warrant, and the owner of the offending tree came before him. He ordered the man to chop it down. "But your own tree extends over your boundary," the defendant argued.

"Go and take another look at my property," said R. Hanina, "and as you find it, do likewise with your own."

*Tanhuma to Deut. 16:18.*

## THE AUTHORITY OF JUDGES

While a judge may be ordained with authority to limit his decisions to certain cases, he must be fit to judge all cases.

R. Joshua ben Levi ordained his disciples. One of them was blind in one eye. R. Joshua regretfully withheld ordination from him because in certain cases a one-eyed judge cannot sit.

*Y. Hagigah, 1.*

When Rab left for Babylonia, Rabbi gave him permission to answer questions regarding things forbidden and permitted. It was asked: "If he had studied the law, why should he need permission to give answers?" The reply was made: "Because the master must see whether the student can give answers in words that are clearly understood."

Once Rabbi visited a town and saw the wives of the priests knead dough when they were ritually unclean. When asked the reason, they answered: "A young scholar informed us that the water of Betzaim (pools) prevents dough from becoming unclean when it touches something ritually unclean.

Rabbi understood their words to mean that the scholar had said: "The water of Betzim" (eggs). The women misunderstood him because his pronunciation was unclear. He then proclaimed that no one should answer questions of ritual law unless he had received permission from a recognized master.

*Y. Hagigah, 1.; Sanhedrin, 4.*

### According to Circumstances

Rabbi Yannai Saba said: "One judge conducts the trial according to regulations and is rewarded; another does the same, but is punished. Why? The latter judge knows from the evidence that there is no doubt of the defendant's guilt, yet he searches for a flaw in the testimony whereby he may acquit the guilty person. Thereby he breeds contempt for the law and gives the impression that evil may be committed with impunity. There is also a judge who does not conduct the trial according to the law and yet is rewarded. Thus Abba saw a man embrace and kiss a married woman. The pair refused to desist, and Abba summoned officers to arrest them. The man and the woman were punished, as if they had committed adultery, because thus a lesson was taught in a neighborhood where immorality was prevalent."

*Zohar Hadash to Ruth, 77.*

In exceptional cases, the Sanhedrin of twenty-three members has the right to abrogate the law. This is comparable to "martial law."

*Sanhedrin, 45.*

## 165. JUDGES—SANHEDRIN

"If we were in the Sanhedrin, no one would ever suffer capital punishment."

*Mishnah Makkot, 6.*

If an ordinance of the Beth Din is not accepted by the majority, it is not valid.

*Y. Shabbat, 1, 4.*

A scholar known for his humility and popularity would be selected as the local judge whenever there was a vacancy.

The conduct of the judges was carefully scrutinized, and if a vacancy occurred in the Court sitting on the Mount of the Temple, the most suitable one would be summoned to serve.

The conduct of those sitting in the Court of the Temple Mount would be scrutinized, and the best judge would be promoted to the Court sitting within the Temple.

The next promotion was to the Sanhedrin, which sat in the Hall of Gazit. The hours were from early morning till one in the afternoon. On a Sabbath and a Festival, the Sanhedrin sat in the space before the Fort. There they would answer abstract questions, but they would not hold court.

The Sanhedrin was the court of last appeal, and if a lower judge, on receiving their opinion, said: "We must abide by the Sanhedrin's judgment, though I consider it wrong," this was permitted. But if the lower judge counseled obedience to his dissenting opinion, he was arrested and placed on trial.

All judges served for life, unless they resigned or were impeached.

When the authority of the Sanhedrin was weakened, two Schools arose, and it proved difficult to hold court, and to decide the law by majority vote.

*Sanhedrin, 86.*

## 166. JUDGING A FELLOW-MAN

He who judges his fellow-man on the side of merit is himself judged on the side of merit.

*Shabbat, 127.*

Judge a man not according to the words of his mother, but according to the comments of his neighbors.

*Midrash Tehillim, 48, 2.*

Do not attribute the fault within thee to thy fellow-man.

*Baba Metzia, 59.*

Joshua ben Perahiah said: "Take to yourself a master (teacher), and get for yourself a comrade (in studies) ; and judge every man in the most favorable light."

*Abot, 1, 6.*

### In the Scale of Merit

A man from Upper Galilee hired out to a man in the South for a term of three years. On Yom Kippur Eve at the end of the term, the hired man asked for his money. His master said: "I am sorry, but I have neither cash, nor fruit, nor grain, nor land, nor cattle, nor furnishings." The hired man departed without the money due him.

After Sukkot, the Southerner went to Upper Galilee and brought to the hired man not only his money but also many gifts. He said to the worker: "What did you think when I told you I had nothing with which to pay you?"

The man answered: "I thought that in an unguarded moment of anger you had donated all your wealth to the Temple Fund."

"You are right," answered the employer. "I was angry with my son then. Later the Sages annulled my vow. Since you have judged me in the scale of merit, may God judge you likewise."

*Shabbat, 127.*

Hillel invited a guest for a meal at a certain hour. When the time arrived, no meal was brought in. When a half-hour had passed, Hillel's wife brought in the dishes. She explained that after she had prepared everything, a poor young man had entered and said: "I am taking a wife today and have no food in the house." "I gave him all I prepared, and then cooked another meal for you," she continued.

Hillel said: "I did not think ill of thee, dear wife, for making us wait. I knew that thy deeds are always performed for the sake of Heaven."

*Derek Eretz Rabbah, 6.*

Judge not thy neighbor until thou hast put thyself in his place; judge all men charitably.

*Abot, 2, 5.*

## 167. MERCY IN JUSTICE

The world is well conducted by two spinning wheels: one that spins justice, and the other that spins mercy.

*Zohar, iv, 259b.*

Hunger overtakes the world when mercy is not found in justice.

*Zohar, i, 81b.*

There is no true justice unless mercy is part of it.

*Zohar, iv, 146b.*

## 168. JUSTICE AND BRIBERY

Even words may constitute bribery, and they are forbidden.

*Ketubot, 105.*

If bribery blinds the eyes of the wise, how much the more the eyes of the fools.

*Ketubot, 105.*

Rabba said: "Why is bribery so heinous an offense, even if the judge determines it shall not influence him in the least? Because once the judge accepts money, his mind is motivated with kindness for the donor; it becomes as if he had placed himself on trial, and no one can see a demerit in himself."

*Ketubot, 105.*

Mar bar Rab Ashi said: "I cannot try the case of a student of the law, because I love him as myself, and no one can see a fault in himself."

*Shabbat, 119.*

## 169. CORRUPT JUSTICE

Judgment delayed is judgment voided.

*Sanhedrin, 95.*

A judge who listens to one litigant when the other is not present is as if he believed in an idol in addition to the true God.

*Zohar, i, 179b.*

The wicked who take property from one person and give it unjustly to another are not only robbers, but they also compel the Almighty to bring about the restoration of the property to its owner.

*Sanhedrin, 8.*

### Man and Beast

Once the great Alexander visited a king in an outlying corner of the world. The king acted as a magistrate and invited his guest to sit beside him. Two men came before the court. One said: "I have bought a house from this man, and while repairing it, a treasure was found. I offered to return it to him, but he refuses to accept it."

The other said: "I knew nothing of the treasure, and it does not belong to me. Since I sold him the house and the lot, the treasure is his property."

The king said: "Have you a son?" and to the other: "Have you a daughter?" "Yes," was the answer from each. "Then," continued the king, "let them marry and keep the treasure as their dowry."

Alexander smiled, and remarked: "In our country the law is that the king takes unto himself whatever is found."

His host looked at him in astonishment, and replied: "Does the sun shine in your land? Does the rain ripen grain and fruits?"

"Yes," responded Alexander.

"Are there beasts in your land," the king inquired.

"Yes," answered Alexander.

"Then surely, the sun and rain come to your land for the sake of the innocent beasts; not for the sake of unjust men. In our land, however, the sun shines and the rain descends for the sake of men, and the beasts receive their food for our sake."

*Introd. to Tanhuma Buber, 152.*

### CORRUPT MAGISTRATES

Since judges became lovers of the fleshpots. all litigation has become crooked; all moral conduct corrupt, and tranquillity has departed from the earth.

Since the fist of flattery became mighty, judges began to discriminate between litigants; the yoke of man was substituted for the yoke of Heaven.

Since whispering on the bench increased, God's wrath has poured forth, and the Shekinah has departed.

Since judges became partners in business enterprises, bribery and injustice have increased, and prosperity has been turned into depression.

Since judges began to accept favors and to promise favors in return, law and order have been abolished; anarchy and crime have gained the ascendancy; coarse men have risen to power, and noble men have been compelled to conceal themselves, and the government has become more and more infamous.

*Sotah, 28 and 47.*

### WHEN THE JUDGES WERE JUDGED

R. Berechiah narrated the following: A man came to a judge to make complaint that his garment had been stolen. He found it spread on the sofa of the judge.

A man came to a judge to complain that his sprinkler had been stolen. It was found in the garden of the judge.

Orphans came to a judge to demand an accounting from their guardian. They found the guardian closeted with the judge.

A widow came to ask equity from a judge. He ordered her to perform work for him, and then dismissed her with nothing.

Said R. Johanan: "What means the author of Ruth by writing: 'When the judges judged' (1:1). He meant to say: 'When the judges were judged.' If the judge says to the defendant: remove the toothpick from thy teeth (namely, restore the object of a petty larceny), the latter would retort: remove a board from between thine eyes (namely, restore the object of a grand larceny)."

If one says to another: "Thy silver has become dross," he would retort: "Thy wine is mixed with water." (Isaiah 1:22)

*Pesikta de R. Kahana, 15; Ruth Rabbah, 1.*

### THE LAWS OF SODOM

It was the law of Sodom that he who owned a bull or cow took care of the city's cattle one day; but the poor man who had no bull or cow was forced to feed the community herd two days.

A witty orphan, the son of a poor widow, took a knife and slaughtered the cattle he was compelled to feed. He then said: "He who has bulls or cows shall take one hide, and he who has none shall take two."

Another ordinance was that he who entered or left the city by a ferry, was compelled to pay one zuz; he who did not use the ferry, two zuzim.

When a man was drying fruits or vegetables, the passers-by would take something until none was left. If the owner complained, each passer-by would say: "I merely took one piece, and it is worth almost nothing."

A stranger wished to cross the river in order to enter Sodom. Finding a ford, he waded over. The official asked him to pay the sum of the ferry passage. The stranger replied: "But I did not use it." "Then pay two zuzim," was the answer. When he declined, the official struck him and blood flowed from the wound. "Pay me for letting blood from you," he was told, "and double ferry-fare besides." They went to court, and when the judge decided in favor of the official, the stranger promptly struck the judge, till the blood flowed, saying: "Pay to the man of Sodom the money you now owe me for letting your blood."

The vagrancy laws of Sodom forbade the sale or gift of food to an outsider. The Sodomites wished no stranger to come to their city. Once a girl was caught giving food to a poor wanderer. She was deprived of her garments, besmeared with honey, and laid bound on a roof. The bees stung her, and her screams reached Heaven.

*Sanhedrin, 109, condensed.*

## WITHIN THE LAW

Rabbi Johanan said: "Jerusalem was destroyed because the people acted evilly within the law (Baba Metzia, 30b). The following story serves as an illustration: A former apprentice who had become rich was enamored of his master's wife. She returned his love and often visited him by stealth. Once the master needed money and informed his erstwhile apprentice of this. The latter offered to lend him the money and suggested that the master send his wife for it. They remained together for three days, and just as she left her lover, the husband arrived, inquiring for his wife.

"She left me within the hour of her arrival," said the apprentice. "But I have heard a rumor that she has been unfaithful to you."

"What shall I do?" asked the master.

"Divorce her," said the apprentice.

"But her marriage settlement is large, and since it is only a rumor, I must pay it."

"I shall advance you the money," said the apprentice.

As soon as the divorce was effective, the paramour married the woman. Soon he sued his former master for the money, and the latter, being unable to pay it, was compelled to agree to work off his debt by labor. While he waited at the table, his tears trickled down his cheeks and fell into the cups of wine he was serving.

Then it was that the decree was sealed in Heaven that Jerusalem should be destroyed. No actual crime had been committed; it was entirely legal as to procedure, and well within the law, yet it merited a harsher penalty than an actual crime would have brought on. Justice may not be deliberately blind.

*Gittin, 58a.*

## 170. JUSTICE—EXTRA-LEGAL

R. Ishmael ben Jose was walking along the street and met a man carrying a bundle of sticks. He became fatigued and placed the bundle on the ground. Then he asked the Rabbi to help him raise it to his back again. The Rabbi asked: "What is its value?" "Half a zuz," answered the man. "Here is the coin," said the Rabbi. But the man again sought to lift the bundle to his back, and sought the Rabbi's help. Again the Rabbi gave him half a zuz. When the carrier sought to lift it once more, the Rabbi remarked: "I have bought it from you twice; leave it on the street, and some one else will pick it up. I do not give it to you."

It was asked: Is not a Rabbi exempted from this Mitzwah, since he would not carry the load if it were his own? The reply was given: R. Ishmael paid for it, not because he was emboundened by law, but extra-legally.

*Baba Metzia, 30.*

A woman showed a dinar to R. Hiyya and asked him if it was good. He replied in the affirmative. She returned and said: "I cannot succeed in circulating it."

R. Hiyya said to Rab: "Give her another, and write down on my book: 'This is a bad business.' "

*Baba Kamma, 99.*

Rabbah bar Bar Hana hired some porters to carry several barrels of wine to his home. They were careless and broke one of them. In payment he seized their over-garments. They turned to Rab, who ordered Rabbah to make restitution of the garments. Rabbah inquired: "Is this the law?" and Rab replied: "Yes. It is written (Proverbs 2:20): 'that thou mayest walk in the way of good men.' "

The porters thereupon remarked: "We are poor; we have worked all day and we are hungry." Rab commanded Rabbah to pay their hire. Again he protested, asking: "Is this the law?"

Rabbah answered: "Yes. It is written in the same passage: 'and keep the path of the righteous.' "

*Baba Metzia, 83.*

If a governor wishes to punish with death one man in a city, but does not specify the person, whose execution is to serve as an object-lesson, the people of the city may not select the victim, even though the threat is levelled against all. If the ruler points out the victim, the people may surrender him, lest they be slain.

Ulla b. Kisher, on being sentenced to death, ran away to hide himself in the home of R. Joshua b. Levi at Ludd. The governor sent soldiers for him, and threatened to consider all who hid him as rebels. R. Joshua b. Levi went to Ulla and said to him: "Thou wilt be captured under any circumstances. Why cause many to perish on thine account?"

Ulla gave himself up. R. Joshua dreamed that Elijah revealed himself and rebuked him. "Did I not act legally, since he was known and pointed out?" Elijah replied: "It may be legal for common people, but not for the Pious." (Hasidim)

*Bereshit Rabbah, 94.*

If a man returns a loan at the end of the Shemittah year, the lender should say to him: "I release thee." If the borrower says: "Even so, take it," the lender may take it.

Abba bar Martha borrowed money from Rabbah, and, at the end of a Shemittah year, he returned it. Rabbah said: "I release thee." Abba did not know how to act and walked away. Abbaye entered and perceiving that his Master was grieved, he discovered the reason. He went after the borrower and induced him to come again and say: "Even so, take it." The borrower, who really wished to cause no loss to his beloved Master, brightened up and did as he was instructed. Said Abbayi: "He is a student of the Rabbi, and yet he lacked discretion. Even if he did not know the law well, he could have shown reluctance in accepting the money, and this reluctance would have served the purpose."

*Gittin, 37.*

### JUSTICE BEYOND THE MEASURE OF THE LAW

It is a Mitzwah to arbitrate a suit in law rather than to institute it.

*Sanhedrin, 6.*

## 171. JUSTICE—FAIR AND IMPARTIAL

A man is judged only according to his acts at a particular moment.

*Rosh ha-Shanah, 16.*

A court should not be mild to one litigant and harsh to another.

*Ketubot, 46.*

When two litigants would come to R. Huna, and he saw that the defendant, though having a good case, did not know how to bring forth his points well, he would ask him: "Is this what you mean to say?"

*Y. Sanhedrin, 3.*

Rabbi Simeon ben Lakish said: "A lawsuit about a small coin should be esteemed of as much account as a suit of a hundred gold coins."

*Sanhedrin, 8a.*

Rab once boarded with a certain man who treated him with great respect. Several years later he came to Rab to have a lawsuit decided before him. He whispered to Rab: "Dost thou remember how well I treated thee when thou wast my boarder?"

"Yes," replied Rab, "and what is thy business?"

"I came to have a trial before thee."

"I cannot try it for thee, since thou remindest me of thy favors," said Rab.

He instructed Rab Kahana to take the case. The latter observed that the man was proud of his acquaintanceship with Rab, and presumed to be disrespectful to the court. Rab Kahana remarked: "If you behave rightly, it is well; if not, I shall take Rab out of your ear. He cannot help you in this court."

*Sanhedrin, 7.*

The serf of King Yannai killed a man. R. Simeon ben Shetah sent for the King to stand trial. The monarch sent the killer, but R. Simeon summoned the King again, inasmuch as a master is responsible for his serf. The King arrived at court and sat down. R. Simeon declared: "Stand up, O King, as it is written (Deut. 19:17): 'Both the man, between whom the controversy is, shall stand before the Lord . . . and the judges.'"

The King remarked: "Not as you say, but as the other judges say."

The other judges kept their silence. R. Simeon exclaimed: "You permit the fear of man to silence you. May the One who knows your thoughts, deal with you."

Suddenly all of them suffered an attack of paralysis.

From that time on, the rule was adopted that no king should be judged or called as a witness; neither shall he act as a judge, nor have witnesses testify against him.

*Sanhedrin, 101.*

### "A Time to Cast Away"

A merchant and his son, travelling on a ship, left their money with the purser. One day they overheard the officers say: "Let us throw the men overboard and divide their money. We can report their death as due to an accident."

The father pretended to quarrel with his son, then demanded the money from the purser on a pretext, and hurled it overboard, as if he knew not what he did in rage. When they had landed, the merchant summoned the officers into court, and demanded that they make good his loss. "But you threw it overboard yourself," argued the officers.

The judge decreed: "But he did so to save his life and his son's life. Therefore you are responsible and must pay for the loss." The judge acted as Koheleth suggests: "There is a time to cast away." (Eccl. 3:5)

*Kohelet Rabbah to 3, 5.*

### A Harsh Judgment

In Sepphoris, a meat-dealer, notorious for selling unfit meat as ritually fit, fell from a roof while drunk and was killed. Several dogs came and licked his blood. This occurred on a Sabbath, and the people came to Rabbi Hanina, asking permission to move him on the sacred day. He replied: "The Torah tells us to give to the dogs carcasses of dead beasts; he has robbed the dogs of them, and therefore, it is just that they consume his corpse." [1]

*Y. Terumot, 8.*

[1] Two considerations prompted the Rabbi—one was to teach an object lesson to other cheaters who caused hundreds to transgress the Jewish law; the second was to obtain fuller expiation for the sinner following his death and to rescue him from Purgatory.

### Judge Well Thy Fellow-Servant

Rab Joseph taught: "Use good sense in judging him who is a companion with thee in the study of the Torah and the problems of Mitzwot."

Rab Joseph sent a note to Rab Nahman: "The bearer, Rab Ulla, is a companion with us in Torah and Mitzwot, and he has a suit in law before thee."

Rab Nahman thought to himself: "What difference does it make if the plaintiff is a scholar? Can I decide the law otherwise if he is an unlearned man?"

On further thought, however, he understood the following, namely, that he should treat Rab Ulla with great respect and advance his suit. Moreover, if the character of the plaintiff played a role in arriving at a just decision, he would know that Rab Ulla had been recommended to him as a worthy man.

*Shebuot, 30.*

### Without Prejudice

The judge must not say to himself: "This man is poor; and, inasmuch as this rich man is under obligation by the general duty of charity to support him, I will give judgment in his favor, and he will be able to make an honest living."

In the converse case, the judge must not reflect: "This man is rich, this one well connected. Can I see him shamed? How much less put him to shame myself?"

"One is not to be allowed to state his case at length and the other bidden to cut it short; one must not be allowed to be seated in court and the other kept standing, and the like."

*Sifra Kedoshim, Perek, 4.*

### Before Another Court

The judges of the court cannot also act as witnesses in the same court. What shall they do if they have seen a crime? They must go to another court where they do not sit, and testify as laymen.

Rab Huna acted as witness to a certain transaction following which the man engaged in it became involved in a dispute. One of the litigants knew that Rab Huna had witnessed the case and could not testify in his own court. Therefore, he insisted that the dispute be heard in Rab Huna's court, and, when the case came up for consideration, he persistently denied the truth.

Rab Huna was greatly embarrassed and was at a loss how to act, inasmuch as he had never had such an experience before. Rab Samuel ben Isaac, who was present, did not wish to reveal that Rab Huna had forgotten the procedure in such circumstances; therefore, he turned to the man who had lied and said: "You are taking advantage of Rab Huna because you believe it is below his dignity to leave his own court and testify before another judge. But what will be the result if he does exactly that?"

Rab Huna accepted the hint and went to another court.

*Y. Rosh ha-Shanah, 3.*

The Rabbis ask: "Why is the word justice written twice? (Deut. 16:20). To teach us that we must practice justice at all times, whether it be for our profit or for our loss, and towards all men—towards Jews and non-Jews alike!"

*Cf. Sanhedrin, 32b; Tanhuma, Buber to Shofetim, 5 and 7.*

## 172. JUSTICE—SUBMISSION TO

The saying goes: "After you have paid your fine in court, sing a song to yourself and walk away."

*Baba Kamma, 7.*

When litigants came before Rabbi Akiba, he would say to them: "Think ye that ye stand before Akiba ben Joseph? Nay, it is before God that ye stand."

Two litigants came before Rabbi Jose ben Halafta, and asked him to decide their case according to the Torah. He said: "I know not how to decide according to the Torah. The Torah is the truth, and I must decide according to the facts that I hear from you. Will you accept my decision?"

Rabbi Simeon ben Yohai said: "Blessed is God that He has not made me a judge."

*Y. Sanhedrin, 1.*

## 173. JUSTICE—TESTIMONY IN

Three testify, each for the other: God, Israel and Torah.

*Hagigah, 3, (Tosefot).*

It is not said to one who has not seen: "Go and testify that thou hast not seen."

*Niddah, 7.*

The words: "We have not seen," are not considered evidence.

*Eduyot, 2, 2.*

Testimony may be remembered for six years but no longer.

*Ketubot, 20.*

The very stones of a man's home testify against him.

*Zohar, ii, 28a.*

There are three whom God dislikes: he who speaks one way with his mouth, and another way in his heart; he who knows of testimony on behalf of a fellow-man, but does not go forth to present his testimony; he who beholds an immoral act and testifies against it in his role of a single witness.

*Pesahim, 113.*

Testimony which is void in part is void in its entirety.

*Baba Kamma, 73.*

## 174. JUSTICE—WARNING PRECEDING

When a man wishes to revenge himself, he plans his revenge in secret. But when God wishes to punish, he gives warning of His intention several times.

*Zohar, i, 58a.*

He who warns the wicked even if his warning be unheeded has rescued himself from blame, and the wicked will be caught in the snare of his own sins.

*Zohar, i, 68a.*

God does not punish unless He gives warning.

*Yoma, 81.*

There is no penalty unless it is preceded by a warning.

*Sanhedrin, 56.*

A prince owned a garden of fruit and set a watch-dog on guard. The son of the prince's friend entered the garden to steal apples and was severely bitten. Whenever the prince wished to warn the lad, he would say: "Dost thou remember what the dog did to thee?"

In the same fashion, Israel sinned at Rephidim and said: "Is there God among us?"

Amalek came and fought them. Whenever God wished to warn Israel, he would say: "Dost thou remember what Amalek did unto thee?"

*Pesikta Rabbati, 12, 12.*

## 175.  JUSTICE—WITNESSES IN

A man cannot testify in his own favor.

*Ketubot, 27.*

A man cannot accuse himself of being a criminal.

*Yebamot, 25.*

False witnesses are despised even by those who hire them.

*Sanhedrin, 29.*

Dice players and usurers are not admissible as witnesses.

*Rosh ha-Shanah, 22a.*

He who is not instructed either in Scripture, in the Mishnah or in good manners is not qualified to act as a witness.

*Kiddushin, 40b.*

Witnesses should know that they stand before God Who will call them to account.

*Sanhedrin, 6b.*

He who disavows a loan may be accepted as a witness, but he who disowns a deposit on trust is unfit.

*Shebuot, 40b.*

Simeon ben Shetah said: "Fully examine the witnesses; be careful with thy words, lest from them they learn to lie."

*Abot, 1, 9.*

The father of R. Pappa lost a donkey.  After considerable search, he identified his donkey in the lost and found division of the city. He came to Rabbah b. R. Huna and asked for an order returning the donkey.  Rabbah said: "Bring two witnesses to testify that you are an honest man."

When they came, Rabbah, through a slip of the tongue, asked them this question: "Do you know him to be dishonest?"

The witnesses imagined that he had asked them: "Do you know this man to be honest?" and they answered: "Yes."

The claimant smiled and said: "Did you say that you know me to be a dishonest man?"

The witnesses perceived their error, and corrected themselves. Rabbah b. R. Huna also smiled and said: "Surely when a claimant brings witnesses to testify as to his character, he brings favorable witnesses only."

*Baba Metzia, 28.*

"Thou shalt not stand idly by the blood of thy fellow." (Lev. 19:16)

From this may be deduced, among other things, that if a man knows any evidence in favor of the defendant, he is not at liberty to keep silent regarding it, for thus he may become responsible for the man's death. If a man sees another in mortal danger by falling into a river, through an attack by robbers, or some other evil, he is in duty bound not to stand idly by, but must come to his rescue. Moreover, if he sees one man pursuing another to kill or to ravish, he is in duty bound to prevent the commission of the capital crime even by taking the life of the offender.

*Sifra Kedoshim Perek, 4.*

The investigating judge would say to witnesses: "If you have evidence to offer which some one else has seen and mentioned to you, or if you wish to offer as testimony that which a man whom you trust has told you, know that you must desist. This is not like taking money unjustly, for in such a case the mistake can be rectified. In this case, however, if an innocent man is executed his blood will be upon you and the blood of his descendants for all generations. But, if you tell the facts as you know them, you will avoid transgressing the injunction to give evidence in a court of law, and, if you assist in the execution of a murderer or another criminal, you bring security into the world."

*Sanhedrin, 37.*

Simeon ben Shetah saw a man pursue another into a ruin with a sword in his hand. When the Rabbi reached the ruin, the sword in the hand of the pursuer was dripping with blood, while the other man was gasping out his last breath. Simeon said: "Who was the killer—thou or I? But I have not seen the actual murder, and I am only one witness. May He Who knows thy thoughts exact payment from you!"

A snake bit the assailant and he died.

*Sanhedrin, 37.*

## 176. KABALAH—THEOSOPHY

Four Rabbis indulged in theosophy: Rabbi Akiba, Rabbi Elisha ben Abuyah, Simeon ben Azzai, and Simeon ben Zoma. Ben Azzai looked and died; Ben Zoma looked and lost his mind; Elisha Aher cut down the plants of the Torah; only Rabbi Akiba made his exit in safety.

*Hagigah, 14b.*

Everyone who meddles with the following four things, it were better for him had he not come into the world: what is above and what is beneath, what is before and what is after.

*Mishnah, Hagigah, 2, 1.*

The Holy One Blessed Be He has a place reserved for Himself, and its name is "'Mistarim'—Mystery"!

*Hagigah, 5b.*

## 177. KINDNESS—KINDHEARTED

Deeds of loving-kindness are greater than charity.

*Sukkah, 49.*

It is the way of the kind-hearted to run after the poor.

*Shabbat, 104.*

Deeds of kindness are equal in weight to all the commandments.

*Y. Peah, 1, 1.*

Israelites are enjoined to deal kindly with everyone they encounter.

*Midrash Tehillim, 52, 6.*

Comforting the mourner, visiting the sick, and deeds of kindness bring good things into the world.

*Abot de-R. Nathan, 30.*

Men are not forgiven because of their offerings, but because of their Torah and kind deeds.

*Rosh ha-Shanah, 18.*

He who disbelieves in the performance of kind deeds is a disbeliever in that which is fundamental (the belief in God).

*Kohelet Rabbah, 7.*

Israelites are enjoined to sustain with necessities those serfs that are crippled, more than those that are healthy.

*Y. Baba Kamma, 5, 4.*

Virtues such as filial piety, philanthropy, charity, deeds of kindness, have no measure or norm, but are left to the conscience and right feeling of the individual; that is, committed to the heart. Whenever something is thus left to conscience, the Scripture says of it: "And thou shalt revere the Lord, thy God."

*Sifra on Lev., 25, 36; ed., Weiss.*

Whoever gives a small coin to a poor man has six blessings bestowed upon him, and he who speaks a kind word to him realizes eleven blessings in himself. (Isaiah 58:7-8)

*Baba Batra, 9b.*

Almsgiving and deeds of loving-kindness are equal to all the commandments of the Torah, but loving-kindness is greater: almsgiving is exercised towards the living; deeds of loving-kindness towards the living and the dead; almsgiving to the poor, deeds of loving-kindness to the poor and to the rich. Almsgiving is done with a man's money, deeds of loving-kindness either with his money or personally.

*Sukkah, 49b; Tos. Peah, 4, 19.*

## THE KINDNESS OF PEOPLES

Two interpretations are given to the verse: "The kindness of peoples is a sin" (Prov. 14:34). The Rabbis said: "The kind works of non-Jewish people remind God of Israel's sin. If those who did not receive the Torah perform deeds of kindness, how much the more should Israel, who accepted the Torah!"

Rabban Johanan ben Zakkai said: "The kind works of non-Jewish people atone for their sins, even as the sin-offering atones for the sins of Israel." [1]

*Baba Batra, 10; Tanhuma Tissa.*

[1] "Hatat" means either sins or a sin-offering. "Hesed" usually means "kindness," but in this verse it is translated as "reproach."

## THE GATES OF RIGHTEOUSNESS

King David said: "Open to me the gates of righteousness." (Psalm 118:19)

Why did David ask that the "gates" be opened to him, rather than the "gate"?

In the World-to-Come the soul is asked: "What good didst thou perform on behalf of thy fellow-creatures?"

If the soul saith in truth: "I have fed the hungry," they say to him: "This is a gate unto the Lord; he who hath fed the hungry may enter into it."

If he says: "I gave drink to the thirsty; I clothed the naked; I brought up an orphan; I gave charity; I labored in mercy," they say unto him: "This is the gate unto the Lord; he who gave drink unto the thirsty may enter into it"; and the same is true in respect to the other individual deeds.

But David said: "I did all of these things; therefore, open unto me all of the gates."

*Shoher Tob, 118.*

He who studies the Law, but does no works of love, lives without God.

*Abodah Zarah, 17b.*

The beginning and the end thereof (Torah) is the performance of loving-kindness.

*Sotah, 14a.*

He who does not perform deeds of loving-kindness is as one who has no God.

*Abodah Zarah, 17b.*

The whole worth of a benevolent deed lies in the love that inspires it.

*Sukkah, 49b.*

If there is a saving virtue, it is the loving service of men. It saves society, for it is one of the pillars of the world.

*Abot, 1, 2.*

## 178. KINDNESS—TO NEIGHBORS

When the year has been prosperous, people become brotherly toward each other.

*Bereshit Rabbah, 89, 4.*

The owner of the ground that is dug out asks the owner of the mound to sell him the mound to fill his ground. The other declares: "Take it without cost, and thanks be to thee."

*Megillah, 14.*

He who loves his neighbors and lends money to the needy in his need, concerning him it is written: "Thou shalt call and I shall answer."

*Yebamot, 62.*

### AN EXCELLENT LAW

The Rabbis of Nehardea said: "If a field is bought to be sold, it must be sold to the owner of the neighboring field if the latter offers the same price as another. Thus the owner loses nothing and the adjoining owner is the gainer. If a man wishes to buy a field, he must find out from every owner of an adjoining field if he does not wish to use his privilege. If he does not thus inquire, the adjoining owner may take it away and pay back the money to the buyer."

Runia was Rabina's tenant-farmer, and he bought the adjacent field. Rabina protested that Runia was not the owner of his field, and therefore had not the privilege with respect to the adjacent field. Abba said: "People say: 'He who wishes to buy a skin pays the same amount to the owner and to the tanner. Therefore he has the same privilege as you.'"

*Baba Metzia, 108; Baba Batra, 5.*

Rabbi Akiba, in stating the most comprehensive rule in the Torah, cites the classic verse: "Thou shalt love thy neighbor as thyself." (Lev. 19:18)

*Sifra, Kedoshim, 89b.*

"My sons," God is pictured as saying to men, "my sons, do I require aught of you for Myself? No. All I ask of you is that ye love one another."

*Tana d'be Eliyahu, 572.*

## 179. LABOR—LABORERS

Work is more beloved than the merit of the fathers.

*Bereshit Rabbah, 74, 12.*

The merit of work can prevail where the merit of fathers cannot.

*Tanhuma Wayyetze, 13.*

God did not permit His Indwelling Presence (Shekinah) to rest upon Israel until after they had performed labor.

*Abot de-R. Nathan, 11.*

Artisans are not permitted to stand up from their labor when a Sage passes by.

*Kiddushin, 33.*

If a man does not plow in the summer, what will he eat in the winter?

*Midrash Mishle, 6.*

If I do not labor, I shall not eat.

*Bereshit Rabbah, 2, 2.*

Rabbi Joseph turned a mill; Rabbi Sheshet carried logs, extolling a labor that brought sweat to his brow.

*Gittin, 67b.*

Because of the Roman oppression, R. Simeon b. Yohai and his son hid in a cave, and there for many years spent all their days in study and contemplation. One day they came out of the cave and observed people tilling the soil. Turning to his pupils, R. Simeon remarked: "These men neglect eternal life and busy themselves with momentary needs."
Whatever they looked at was immediately destroyed by fire. Thereupon a Heavenly Voice was heard to say to them: "You came out to destroy My world; return to your cave!"

*Shabbat, 33b.*

He who produces for the perpetuation of the world shares in a Divine work.

*Schechter ed. Abot de-R. Nathan, version 2, chap. 21, p. 22b.*

Great is labor, for it brings its master to honor.

*Nedarim, 49b.*

A man should not say: "I shall eat and drink while I may, and Heaven will have compassion upon me." Rather must he work for his sustenance.

*Tanhuma Wayyetze, 13.*

The right of the workingman always has precedence.

*Baba Metzia, 77.*

Whatsoever was created requires the labor of men to enjoy it, as it is written: "Which God has created to be made." (Gen. 2:3)

*Bereshit Rabbah, 11, 7.*
*Wayyikra Rabbah. 11, 7.*

Great is labor! All the prophets engaged in it.

*Midrash Gadol u-Gedolah, 14.*

Great is labor! It warms the doer.

*Gittin, 67.*

Great is labor! It honors the doer.

*Nedarim, 49.*

A breakdown follows hard upon ambition that soars too high. Rest follows labor that fatigues.[1]

*Shene Luhot ha-Berit, 243.*

[1] This is a play on the names for some of the Taamim, used in chanting the Pentateuch: Darga-Tebir; Tirha-Etnah.

### CAUSE NOT THE HIRED MAN TO WAIT

As soon as the day's work was over, Rab Hamnuna would gather his laborers and give them their pay, saying: "Here, take your souls."

If a laborer did not wish to take his money at that time, the Rabbi would insist that he take it. He would say: "Thou canst not deposit with me thy body; how much the more thy soul!"[1]

*Zohar, iii, 85.*

[1] See Deut. 24:15, the Isaac Leeser Translation. The Jewish translation substituted "heart" for the Hebrew "nefesh," "soul."

## 180. LABOR—BLESSINGS IN

If a man works, he is blessed.

*Midrash Tehillim, 23, 3.*

We say to one who has done his work well: "May thy power be increased!"

*Pesikta Rabbati, 19.*

Blessing rests only upon the work of a man's hands.

*Tosefta Berakot, 6.*

A famine of seven years will not injure the artisan.

*Sanhedrin, 29a.*

A man should labor with his two hands and God will surely send him a blessing.

*Tanhuma Wayyetze, 13.*

Greater even than the God-fearing man is he who eats of the fruit of his toil; for Scripture declares him twice-blessed.

*Berakot, 8a.*

Abba Joseph, though a Rabbi, was a builder's labourer. While at his work one day he was accosted by a man who wished to drag him into a theological discussion. The Rabbi refused. "I am a day-labourer," he said, "and cannot leave my work; say quickly what you would and go."

*Shemot Rabbah, 10, 1.*

Beautiful it is when the study of the Torah goes with worldly work; it is a safeguard against sin.

*Abot, ii, 2.*

The Rabbis said: "Do not think that the blessing will be yours even if you stand idle. Oh, no! God's blessings rest only 'on all that thou doest'—on all that thou shalt labor!"

*Sifre, Re'eh, 99b.*

Even though God assured the Patriarch Isaac: "I will bless thee and increase thy seed," Isaac set to work and planted, because he knew that blessings cannot come except through the labor of one's own hands.

*Tosefta Berakot, 7, 8.*

A Rabbi said: "I was once accosted by a man learned in Mishnah, but not in the Scripture. He asked me: 'Why does God prepare food for animals, though they do not work hard to secure it; only man must labor diligently for his bit of bread?' "

"I replied: 'Does not God bless the work of man so that it may bring forth fruit?'

" 'Yes, master, I humbly accept thy explanation. Yet it does not answer my question why man must labor so hard for his food.'

"I replied: 'It is because God has endowed man with reason and wishes him to make use of it. The insane person often acquires his sustenance without labor because he lacks the power of reason. Were man sustained without work, he would spend his time in committing offenses.'

"He then asked me another question: 'Why was a stated time given for the restoration after the First Temple but no stated time has been given for the restoration that is to come?'

"I answered: 'During the time of the First Temple, men worshipped idols but were kind to each other; during the Second Temple, however, each man hated the other without cause.' "

*Tanna de-Bei Eliyahu Rabbah, 14.*

## 181. LABORING FOR WEALTH

Why are men like weasels? A weasel gathers and knows not for what purpose. So it is with men.

*Y. Shabbat, 13, 1.*

There are persons who are chained to gold and silver.

*Shabbat, 54.*

## 182. LABORING FOR WORLDLY PLEASURES

He who strives for pleasures in this world will in all likelihood be deprived of pleasures in the World-to-Come.

*Abot de-R. Nathan, 28, 5.*

There are persons who neglect the Torah and spend all their days in feasting.

*Shabbat, 151.*

## 183. LABORING IN DANGER

Enter not into danger: the gain is little and the loss may be great.

*Y. Terumot, 8, 3.*

Do they say to a man: "Take a loaf and go to Sheol?"

*Sifre Behaaloteka.*

Better is a small measure easily earned than a large amount earned only after hardships.

*Pesahim, 113.*

To the employer of workmen the Rabbis said: "This poor man ascends the highest scaffoldings, climbs the highest trees. For what does he expose himself to such danger if not for the purpose of earning his living? Be careful, therefore, not to oppress him in his wages, for it means his very life."

*Sifre Ki Tetze, sec. 279, p. 123b.*

## 184. LABOR, TRADE, LIVELIHOOD

A man should learn a trade, and God will send him sustenance.
*Kohelet Rabbah, 10, 6.*

And thou shalt choose life—namely, a trade.

*Y. Peah, 1.*

God causes each man to like his own trade.

*Berakot, 43.*

He who has a trade is like a woman who has a husband, and like a vineyard which has a fence.

*Tosefta Kiddushin, 1, 9.*

Greater is he who makes a livelihood from the work of his hands than him who makes his living through his fear of Heaven.[1]

*Berakot, 8.*

[1] Elijah Gaon of Wilna has explained the saying in this way.

A man should teach his sons a clean and easy trade, if at all possible.

*Kiddushin, 82, Mishnah.*

He who does not teach his son an occupation is as one who has taught his son to rob.

*Kiddushin, 29.*

Together with thy knowledge of Torah, acquire a trade.

*Kohelet Rabbah, 9, 7.*

Rabban Gamaliel III, the son of Rabbi, said: "Study, combined with a secular occupation is a fine thing, for the double labor makes sin to be forgotten. All study of the Torah with which no work goes, will in the end come to naught, and bring sin in its train."

*Abot, 2, 2. See Mishnah Kiddushin, 1, 10.*

### The Holy Pair

Rabbi said in the name of the Holy Pair: "Acquire a trade with the Torah." Who are called the Holy Pair? Rabbi Jose ben Meshullam and R. Simeon ben Menasia. They divided the working hours of each day as follows: a third for devotion, a third for learning, and a third for working. Others say: they studied in the winter, and worked in the summer.

*Kohelet Rabbah, 9.*

## 185. UNDIGNIFIED LABOR

Skin a carcass in the market-place, take the fee, and say not: "I am an important man."

*Baba Kamma, 106.*

If thou hast been hired to do work, do what thou art told, even though thou hast distaste for it.

*Yoma, 20.*

Sell thyself over to a work undignified for thee rather than beg favors of men.

*Y. Berakot, 9, 2.*

### The Pagan Priest

Jonathan ben Gershom ben Moses was a priest of the idol set up by the Danites. He was asked: "How does it come about that the grandson of mankind's greatest should be in such a post?" He answered: "I heard from my father that a man should rather occupy himself with a strange service than ask people to aid him." He misunderstood, of course, what he had heard. His father meant that a man should engage in a task undignified in the eyes of his class, but not in strange worship.

How did he serve the idol? When a man slaughtered an animal and wished to have it burned before the idol, he would say: "This idol is not worthy of such an offering; bring some flour and eggs, and I will offer these." When the man brought the offering, he would take of it for himself. Meat slaughtered for an idol was prohibited to him. Once he was asked by a would-be worshipper: "If the idol does not deserve a meat-offering, why does he deserve a flour-offering?" Jonathan replied: "Because I am compelled to make a livelihood." [1]

*Baba Batra, 110.*

[1] This remark is applicable to the case of Jewish apostates engaged in missionary work today.

No labor, however humble, is dishonoring.

*Nedarim, 49b.*

Flay dead cattle on the highway, and do not say: "I am a priest" or "I am a great man, and it is beneath my dignity."

*Pesahim, 113a.*

## 186. LANGUAGES, PEOPLES

There are four languages, of which it can be said: Latin is best for warfare; Greek, for poetry; Persian, for eulogy, and Assyrian, for prayer.

*Y. Megillah, 1, 9.*

A man should address another in the language which the latter understands. He should not use a literary form of speech to an uneducated person, and an uncouth language to the learned.

*Zohar, ii, 80a.*

### NINETY PER CENT

Ninety per cent of vice is found in Alexandria; of wealth, in Rome; of poverty, in Ludd; of sorcery, in Egypt; of foolishness, in Arabia; of health, in Arabia; of personal beauty, in Media; of dirt, in the Orient; of strength, in Babylonia; of heroism, in Judaea; of flattery, in Jerusalem; of beauty, in Jerusalem; of learning, in Palestine; of wisdom, in Palestine; of coarseness, in Elam; of forwardness, in Meishan; of talk, among women; of swarthiness, in Ethiopia; of sleep, among servants.

*Esther Rabbah, 1.*

Rabbi said: "Wherefore the Syriac speech in Babylonia? Either Hebrew or Persian."

*Sotah, 49.*

## 187.  LAW—DISAGREEMENT IN

Disagreements in courts of the law constitute the desolation of the world.

*Derek Eretz Zuta, 9.*

### ROMAN LAW VERSUS PERSIAN

When a person in Jerusalem lost or found anything, he would repair to the local claim station. The finder would call out the article, and the loser, on giving proper identification, would receive it back. After the destruction of the Temple, it was decided to follow this custom in the synagogue.

Later some governors wished to adopt in Palestine the Persian law whereby anything found reverted to the government treasury, and it was decided to call out the articles only among neighbors and friends of the finder.

R. Ammi found a purse containing money. While picking it up, he perceived a man watching him. The Rabbi was afraid that he would be arrested if he did not take the article to the governor. But the man said: "Do not be afraid. I hold not with the Persian, but with the Roman law. If there are no means of identification, the finder may keep the article found."

*Baba Metzia, 28.*

## 188.  LAW OBSERVANCE

If a legislator wishes that the law which he has helped to establish, be observed, he should be the first to observe it.

*Shemot Rabbah, 43, 4.*

As fish die when they are out of the water, so do people die without law and order.

*Abodah Zarah, 3.*

### THE SEVENTH YEAR (SHEMITTAH)

A man came before R. Eliezar ben Zadok, and said: "The people who live in my village dig in my vineyards on the Shemittah, and accept in payment the fruit of my olive trees. Is this according to law?"

"Nay," was the answer.

"Then what shall I do?" asked the man.

"Give the olives to the poor and pay for the digging with cash. No business may be done with fruit grown during the Shemittah year."

When the man left, the Rabbi remarked: "For forty years I have resided here, and I have never met a man so careful with respect to the observance of the law."

*Sukkah, 44.*

The law requires a head as clear as a clear day in the summer.

*Erubin, 65.*

### FRUIT IN THE SHEMITTAH YEAR

"And the Sabbath-produce of the land shall be food for you."

In early days the messengers of the court sat at the city gates, and, when they beheld, during the Shemittah year, a man bringing fruits, they gave him sufficient for three meals and took the remainder for the common storehouse. When the time arrived for each kind of fruit to become ripe, the court sent hired men to pick the fruit. They dried and distributed to each person every Friday sufficient for the week's supply. No private property in the form of produce was recognized during the Shemittah year and the year following, until the new crop was ready.

*Tosefta Shebiit, 7.*

## 189. RULES IN JEWISH LAW

A man cannot be found guilty in his absence.

*Ketubot, 11.*

Silence is equivalent to confession.

*Yebamot, 87.*

The life of the mother takes precedence over the life of the unborn child.

*Ahalot, 7.*

It is permitted to do good on behalf of a minor, but not to injure his interests.

*Tosefta Ketubot, 12.*

A man may not accuse himself of a crime.

*Yebamot, 25.*

If a man pronounces some of his property to be the property of any poor person who can gain control of it, his settlement is not binding. He can change his mind and take his property back; but, if a man gives it to anyone who wishes it, the gift is binding.

*Baba Metzia, 30.*

The hand of him is weakened who changes his mind.

*Baba Metzìa, 76, Mishnah.*

A condition is valid if the maker is able to fulfill it.

*Baba Metzia, 94.*

A man does not lie about that which is certain to be revealed.

*Rosh ha-Shanah, 22.*

An agent cannot make an agent.

*Gittin, 29.*

Warning must precede punishment.

*Yoma, 81.*

A scholar who brings forward a new law before an actual case arises is given attention, but no note is taken of the new law after the case has been closed.[1]

*Yebamot, 77.*

[1] A new law is not retroactive.

Under certain circumstances the court has the right to condemn the property of an individual.

*Yebamot, 89.*

It is permitted to do good to a man without consulting him.

*Ketubot, 11.*

The seduction of a minor female is rape.

*Yebamot, 33.*

Hearsay is of less worth than the evidence of the eye.

*Mekilta Jethro, 19, 9.*

A sale by a drunken man constitutes a sale, and a purchase by him, a purchase. If he has committed a capital crime, he is to suffer death. The rule is that he is equivalent to a sober man in all things.

*Erubin, 65.*

Just as it is forbidden to permit that which is prohibited, so it is forbidden to prohibit that which is permitted.

*Y. Terumot, 5, end.*

## 190. LEADERSHIP

In the place where there is a leader, do not seek to become a leader.

*Berakot, 63.*

In the place where there is no leader, strive to become a leader.

*Berakot, 63.*

Before I was elected to head the court, I would have thrown to the lions anyone who would have suggested to me to become a candidate. After my election, I would throw boiling water on anyone who would suggest that I resign.

*Menahot, 109.*

Like generation, like leader.

*Arakin, 17.*

What can the great ones do if their generation is evil?

*Taanit, 24.*

The acts of the leader are the acts of the nation. If the leader is just, the nation is just; if he is unjust, the nation too is unjust and is punished for the sins of the leader.

*Zohar, ii, 47a.*

Woe to the ship whose captain has been lost.

*Baba Batra, 91.*

A leader who guides Israel with humility shall lead them also in the World-to-Come.

*Sanhedrin, 92.*

Three have surrendered their crown, and thereby have earned the World-to-Come: Jonathan, R. Eleazar b. Azariah, and the Sons of Beteirah.

*Y. Pesahim, 6.*

The Rabbis have said: "Be rather a tail to a lion than the head of a fox."

*Abot, 4:20.*

The Romans, however, said: "Be rather a head to a fox than a tail to a lion."

*Y. Sanhedrin, in 4, 8.*

If the head of the guild runs away, the entire guild likewise runs away.

*Midrash Tehillim, 114, 9.*

What can the great men of the generation accomplish since the public is judged according to the majority?

*Y. Taanit, 3, 5.*

Rabbi Isaac said: "A ruler is not to be appointed unless the community is first consulted."

*Berakot, 55a.*

Over three does God weep daily: over him who is able to study the Torah and does not; over him who is unable to devote his time to Torah and studies it; [1] and over the public leader who is arrogant in his leadership.

*Hagigah, 5.*

[1] Perhaps the explanation of this portion is, as follows: God would like to ease the lot of this person, but He is aware that if he has an abundance of this world's goods he would abandon his studies.

Rabbi Zeira said: "We may learn from the third commandment: 'Thou shalt not take the name of the Lord thy God [1] in vain' this lesson: Thou shalt not take the name of being worthy to become a judge or leader if in truth thou art unworthy."

*Pesikta Rabbati, 22, 4.*

[1] "Elohim" is used here to signify Judge. See Exodus 22:7.

### The Initial Sin

Samuel bar Nahmani said: "It is natural that people should imitate their leaders. If the Patriarch gives permission to do that which is forbidden by the Torah, the chief of the court says to himself: 'If the Patriarch permits this, why should I forbid it?' The Justices say: 'If the chief of the court has given permission, why should we forbid?' And the people say: 'If the Justices have given permission, shall we consider it forbidden?' It is clear that it is the initial sin of the Patriarch which has caused the entire generation to be sinful."

*Debarim Rabbah. 2.*

Rabbah b. Rabba and R. Aha b. Rabba said: "In the entire history of Israel we find only three cases where the greatest influence and the greatest learning were combined in one person: Moses, Rabbi and R. Ashi. This combination resulted in the gift of a monumental work: Moses gave us the Torah; Rabbi, the Mishnah, and Rab Ashi, the Talmud."

*Gittin, 59, paraphrased.*

Woe to high position, for it takes the fear of Heaven from him who occupies it.

*Midrash ha-Gadol, 412.*

### The Alexandrian Temple

When the High Priest, Simeon the Just, died, he designated in his will that his younger son, Onias, should succeed him. Onias declined because his brother, Shimi, was two and a half years older than he. Later, however, he changed his mind. He persuaded his older brother to don a woman's dress and belt, and then said to the Priests: "Behold my brother! When he was accepted by his beloved one, he promised her to don her mantle and girdle at his inauguration as High Priest, and, lo, he has kept his promise."

The Priests fell upon Shimi to slay him, but, when they heard the true facts, they sought rather to slay Onias for the desecration he had committed. Onias escaped to Alexandria and built there an altar. Some say he built it for God; others that he built it for an idol. The Sages said: "How mighty is the desire for rulership! If he who declined the honor acts so wickedly, how much the more one who strives for it!"

*Menahot, 109.*

### An Effective Remedy

R. Hanina b. Papa said: "Blessed is God who chose these two brothers, Moses and Aaron, and created them only to bring Torah and glory to Israel!"

R. Joshua of Shiknin said: "The physicians of Alexandria blended drugs that warmed and cooled, and brewed an effective remedy from them. By the same token the presence of the vigorous Moses and the kind-hearted, humble Aaron served to give to the generation of the wilderness admirable leadership."

*Shir ha-Shirim Rabbah, 4.*

## 191. LEADERSHIP—SHEPHERD AND FLOCK

When the shepherd is enraged at the flock, he blinds the eyes of the bell-wether.

*Baba Kamma, 52.*

When the shepherd blunders along his way, his flock blunders after him.

*Pirke de-R. Eliezer, 42.*

If there is no flock, what shall the shepherd do?

*Yalkut to Pentateuch, 187.*

### THE TEST OF THE RIGHTEOUS

Psalm 11:5 reads: "The Lord trieth the righteous." He tests them while feeding His flocks. David was proved in this fashion. God observed that David first led the young sheep to pasture, so that they might eat tender grass. He then led the older ones to eat the moderately tender blades, and finally he led the mature yearlings to eat the coarse grass.

Saith the Lord: "He who knows so well how to feed the flock deserves to become the shepherd of My flock."

Moses was tried in this way. While tending the flocks of his father-in-law, a kid ran away. Moses followed him until the little creature reached a spring and drank. Moses said: "I did not know that thy thirst prompted thee to run away. Truly thou art tired and I shall carry thee."

Saith the Lord: "Thou hast compassion upon the flock of a man. Come now and become the shepherd of My flock" as it is written: "Now Moses was tending the flock of Jethro . . . and the Angel appeared unto him." (Ex. 3:1)

*Shemot Rabbah, 2.*

## 192. LEADER'S SPAN OF LIFE

The years of him are shortened who runs after leadership.

*Berakot, 55.*

Why did Joseph die before his brothers? Because he was masterful and ruled over them.

*Berakot, 55.*

## 193.  LEGITIMACY AND ILLEGITIMACY IN BIRTH

A man should not marry a pregnant widow or divorcee until after the child is born.

*Yebamot, 36.*

Most bastards are wise and a fool is worse than them.

*Y. Kiddushin, end.*

Even a bastard has a share in the World-to-Come.

*Kohelet Rabbah, 4, 3.*

Silver purifies the bastards.

*Kiddushin, 71.*

A humble bastard is higher than a well-born person who is impudent.

*Sefer Shaashuim, end. (Post-Talmudical).*

A learned bastard takes precedence over an unlearned High Priest.

*Mishnah, Horaiyot, 13.*

Daniel Haita said: "We read: 'And, behold, there are the tears of the oppressed, and they have no comforter.'" (Eccl. 4:1)

"These are the bastards who suffer in many ways through no fault of their own.  Saith God: 'I shall be their Comforter in the World-to-Come.'"

*Kohelet Rabbah, 4, 3; Wayyikra, Rabbah, 32.*

## 194.  LIGHT

Israel is a wick; Torah is oil, and the Shekinah is light.

*Tikkune Zohar, T. 21.*

Place oil within the lamp before it is extinguished.

*Yalkut Psalms, 979.*

Why did Saul deserve royalty?  Because his grandfather had busied himself lighting up the dark passages.

*Tanhuma Tetzaweh.*

Many candles can be kindled from one candle without diminishing it.

*Sifre Behaaloteka, 93.*

Fire was not created during the six days, but at the conclusion of the Sabbath God gave Adam the good sense to rub two stones together to make fire.

*Pesahim, 54.*

A torch in the hands of one who walks alone at night is like one companion; moonlight is like two companions.

*Berakot, 43.*

Seven lights were created before the Universe came into being: the light of Torah; the light of Paradise; the light of Gehenna; the light of the Throne of Glory; the light of the Holy Temple; the light of penitence, and the light of the Messiah.

*Zohar, iii, 31a.*

The wicked are like the man who walks without a torch in the dark night: he stumbles upon a stone and falls. But the righteous are like him who walks in darkness holding a lantern in front of his face: if he comes to a place where he might stumble, he turns aside.

*Pesikta Rabbati, 8, 5.*

### Israel Not God

"Command that they bring unto thee pure olive oil beaten for the light." (Lev. 24:2)

God saith to Moses: "I give you this command, not because I have need of your light, but in order to endow you with merit."

*Bemidbar Rabbah, 6.*

## 195. LOGICAL THINKING

One may be prompted to see the great man and not the logic of the question.

*Baba Metzia, 16.*

The native on earth and the alien in Heaven?[1]

*Erubin, 9.*

[1] Should the alien be more privileged than the native?

He claimed wheat and the other admitted owing barley.

*Baba Kamma, 35.*

### Secondary to Knowledge

Rab Isaac bar Judah used to study under the tutelage of Rami bar Hamma. Later he left him and went to study under Rab Sheshet. Rami met his former pupil, and declared: "It is said when the governor shakes hands with me I receive an aroma of rulership. Did thy going to the more famous teacher make thee like him?"

Rab Isaac replied: "I changed masters for this reason: When I would ask you the law in certain cases, you knew no Tannaitic tradition applicable, but you would answer me according to logic. If later I discovered a Mishnah or Baraita contradicting your reply, your words were nullified. But, when I ask my new master a question, he always knows a Tannaitic tradition germane to the case. If I do find a contradictory tradition, the former does not lose its value, the authority of both being equal."

*Zebahim, 96.*

## THE FIRE OF LOGIC

It was said of Jonathan ben Uzziel, the greatest of Hillel's disciples, that, when he sat and studied the Torah, any bird that flew over his head was consumed by the flames issuing from him.[1]

*Sukkah, 28.*

[1] R. Abraham Zakuto in his "Yuhasin" explains this, as follows: "Every doubt which flew into his mind was consumed in the fire of his logic."

## WITHOUT WITNESSES

A man came into court and demanded the money he had loaned without a receipt to another. The alleged debtor said: "Have I not paid you in the presence of these and these people?"

When called in, however, they denied seeing the transaction. R. Sheshet believed that the man had been revealed as a liar and could not even be sworn in to testify that he had returned the money. Rabbah, however, said to R. Sheshet: "The man is not a liar. Since he was not required by the terms of the loan to return the money in the presence of witnesses, he simply forgot that he had repaid the sum when he and the lender were alone, and therefore he may be sworn in." [1]

*Shebuot, 41.*

[1] Litigants were usually believed without an oath.

## LOGIC IS STRONGER

"Who among the sons of Aaron should blow with the trumpets?" (Num. 10:8)

R. Tarfon said: "Those with a blemish, as well as those without one."

R. Akiba said: "Only those without a blemish may blow with the trumpets."

Said R. Tarfon: "Akiba, I cannot endure this. Thou imaginest rules and they are but chaff. By the health of my sons, I swear that I saw my uncle Simeon blow, though he was lame, having one foot shorter than the other."

R. Akiba replied: "Surely thou must have seen him on Yom Kippur when even the cripples or those with a blemish may blow the Shofar."

R. Tarfon thereupon said: "Holy Temple Service! Thou hast not imagined it. Happy art thou, Abraham, that Akiba is one of thy progeny! I saw this and forgot; Akiba learned by logical thinking and described the correct procedure. He who separates from thee is as if he had separated from life."

*Sifre to Numbers, 10, 8.*

## SELF-INJURY

A man disarranged a woman's hair in the market-place. She complained to R. Akiba, who commanded him to pay the woman a fine of four hundred zuzim.

The man said: "I beg thee to give me time."

This was granted him. The man waited until he saw the woman at the door of her home, and in front of it broke into pieces a vessel containing olive oil. The woman came out, loosened her hair and, wetting her hand, smoothed the oil over it. The man brought witnesses to observe this, and then came to R. Akiba, saying: "Rabbi, shall I give four hundred zuzim to this woman?"

R. Akiba, however, answered: "Your argument is worthless. If a persons wounds himself, though it be a sin, he need pay no fine; but, if some one else inflicts injury upon him, the guilty person must pay a fine."

*Baba Kamma, 90.*

## 196. LOVE

A man should not say: "I will love the learned and hate the unlearned," but rather shall he say: "I will love them all."

*Abot de-R. Nathan, 16.*

Love without admonition is not love.

*Bereshit Rabbah, 54.*

When love was strong, we could lie, as it were, on the edge of a sword; but now, when love is diminished, a bed sixty ells wide is not broad enough for us.

*Sanhedrin, 72.*

"Thou shalt love thy neighbor as thyself." This is the great general rule in Torah.

*Y. Nedarim, 9, 4.*

Before a man marries, his love goes to his parents; after he marries, his love goes to his wife.

*Pirke de-R. Eliezer, 32.*

He who loves without jealousy does not truly love.

*Zohar, iii, 245.*

Love is blind to defects.

*Sanhedrin, 105.*

When two loving souls kiss upon the lips, they are united in love.

*Zohar, ii, 146b.*

Love thy synagogue, so that thou mayest be rewarded daily. Love the House of Study, so that thy children may love to study within it. Love him who admonishes thee, so that thou mayest add to thy wisdom. Love humility, so that thy days may be given thee in full. Love the poor, so that thy children may not become poor. Love to do deeds of kindness, so that thou mayest be saved from death.

*Derek Eretz Zuta, 9.*

Obadiah prophesied that Esau would be punished by the tribes of Joseph. Why? Because Joseph turned the enmity of his brother into love, while Esau turned the love of his brother into hatred. Joseph removed from his heart the sentiment of hate, but Esau retained it.

*Pesikta Rabbati, 13, 3.*

What is the most comprehensive rule in the Torah? Rabbi Akiba said it is: "Love thy neighbor as thyself." (Lev. 19:18)

Ben Azzai said it is: "These are the generations of man; in the day that God created man, in the likeness of God created He him." (Gen. 5:1)

Reverence for the divine image in man is of wider scope than love to our fellow-man.

*Bereshit Rabbah, 24, end.*

## 197. LOVE OF WEALTH

Three were punished with leprosy because they loved possessions, and not the Torah: Noah, Cain and Azariah.

*Otzar Midrashim, 225.*

Many a man loves his riches more than his soul. Instead of utilizing his riches to acquire riches of the soul, namely, Torah and Mitzwot, he uses them to acquire riches of the body, namely, flesh-pots and pleasures.

*Tikkune Zohar, T. 72, p. 186b.*

### THE UNSATISFIED EYE

The great King Alexander asked for admission at the Gate of Paradise.

"Only the righteous may enter here," was the reply.

He then pleaded for a gift, and a piece of human skull with one eye open was thrown to him. Alexander wished to weigh it on his scales, and placed on the balance gold and silver, but the skull was heavier. More gold was added, but to no avail. Acting upon the advice of the Sages, he placed some earth on the eye, and at once the gold became heavier.

"This teaches," they said, "that a human eye is not satisfied with all the gold that exists until it is covered with the earth of the grave."

*Tamid, 31.*

## 198. LUCK

Everything depends upon a lucky star, even the Sefer Torah in the Ark.

*Zohar, iv, 134a.*

Everything depends on luck except Israel.
*Tikkune Zohar, T. 69, 140a.*

According to luck, no man should live over seventy years, but God adds to his years if He so wishes.
*Zohar, i, 257b.*

## 199. MAN—BIRTH AND DEVELOPMENT

There are three partners in man: God, his father and his mother.
*Kiddushin, 30.*

A man's life has three periods: the period when his body develops; the period when his thought develops, and the period when his deeds develop.
*Tikkune Zohar, Tikkun, 19, 67a.*

Man enters and departs from the world with loud outcries.
*Kohelet Rabbah, 5, 14.*

Man enters the world with closed hands, as if to say: "The world is mine." He leaves it with open hands, as if to say: "Behold, I take nothing with me."
*Ibid.*

There is no wicked man who is born into the world into whose future God does not look. He sees whether he is to beget a righteous son, whether he is to save a life, or do a good deed. For these reasons is man born.
*Midrash ha-Neelam, i, 118a.*

R. Akiba finds the highest principle in the words: "Thou shalt love thy neighbor as thy self." [1]
[1] I.e., All men are are born equal. This is more inclusive than neighbor.

Ben Azzai finds an even broader principle in the words: "This is the book of the generations of Adam, in the day that God created man, in the likeness of God made He him." (Gen. 5:1)
*Bereshit Rabbah to Gen. 5:1.*

For two and a half years the schools of Shammai and Hillel argued the question, and finally decided by majority vote that it were better for man not to have been created. Inasmuch, however, as he was created, he must closely scrutinize his doings.
*Erubin, 13.*

### MAN'S SEVEN PERIODS OF LIFE

When a man is a year old, he is like a king: everyone loves and embraces him. At two, he is like a pig, wallowing in his dirt. During his boyhood, he is like a kid: he dances and laughs all day. When he is eighteen, he is like a horse, rejoicing in his youth and strength. When he marries, he is like an ass, carrying a burden. Later, he becomes like a dog, unashamed to ask favors and to beg for a livelihood. In his old age, he is like a monkey: he becomes curious and childish, and no one pays any attention to his words.

*Tanhuma Pekudei.*

## 200. THE GOOD MAN

A good man tastes the goodness of his good deeds.

*Kiddushin, 41.*

A man whose countenance is pleasant may be considered to be God-fearing.

*Sukkah, 49.*

The countenance of the good man reflects the countenance of the Higher Man, and no one in the world dares harm him.

*Zohar, i, 71a.*

Everything depends upon the sort of person a man is.

*Kelim, 17, 11.*

Some of the Rabbis declared that any godly son of Israel exceeds the angels in power and in influence.

*Sanhedrin, 93a.*

Like the Ark of the Covenant, the good man should be golden within as well as without.

*Yoma, 72b.*

The ideal man has the strength of a male and the compassion of a female.

*Zohar, iv, 145b.*

Rabbi Akiba said: "Beloved is man, because he was created in the image of God.

"Beloved are the Israelites, because to them was given the precious Torah; the instrument with which the world was created."

*Abot, 3, 14.*

### EVEN A PORTION

When Rabban Gamaliel read Psalm 15, he would weep. He once said to Rabbi Akiba: "Can there be a man who performs all these injunctions?"

Rabbi Akiba smiled and said: "Rabbi, the Torah enumerates all sorts of unclean reptiles, and declares that whosoever touches them, on their death, would become unclean. But does not one who touches merely a bit of one of these unclean bodies become by this act unclean?

So it is in this matter. He who performs any of these injunctions is a just man."

Rabban Gamaliel responded: "Akiba, thou hast comforted me."

*Shoher Tob, 15.*

R. Akiba said: "He who pleases people pleases God, but he who is unpleasant to people is unpleasant to God. (Cf. Abot, 3, 13.) He who is generous shows his goodness, but he who is ungenerous shows his evil nature."

Ben Azzai said: "He whose bodily strength is weakened through his intense desire to acquire wisdom shows thereby his wisdom. He whose wisdom is weakened through care for his bodily strength shows his folly. He who diminishes his dignity for the sake of acquiring wisdom is wise. He who loses wisdom because he feels it below his dignity to ask when he is in doubt is unwise."

*Tosefta Berakot, 3.*

## 201. MAN—MIND AND THOUGHTS OF

Woe will come to me from my Creator if I hearken to my impulses! Woe will come to me from my impulses if I obey my Creator!

*Berakot, 61.*

A man's very features are influenced by his thoughts and desires. The wise man can discern by looking at a person if his actions are good or bad.

*Zohar Hadash to Song of Songs, 72a.*

All things in the world follow thought.

*Sitre Torah, i, 155a.*

If evil thoughts beset thee, learn Torah and they will leave thee.

*Zohar, i, 222b.*

The power of thinking has two servants: the power of memory and the power of imagination.

*Zohar, iv, 247b.*

Man is inclined to believe that he will be happy to go about this world for many, many years, but, as he goes about it, he finds himself beset by tribulations. They weaken him and he is ready to depart.

*Zohar, iv, 126a.*

The purity of the thought in the heart is recognized by the words on the lips.

*Zohar, v, 295.*

Whatever your heart contains regarding your friend, his heart contains regarding you.

*Sifre Debarim, 1, 27.*

A man does not know what is in the heart of his neighbor.

*Ibid.*

Three things tranquillize the mind of man: a pleasant melody, a pleasant scene and a fragrant odor. Three things broaden the mind of man: a fine house, a handsome wife, and beautiful furniture.

*Berakot, 57b.*

If one beholds crowds of men, he should repeat the eulogy: "Blessed is he who is wise in mysterious things"; for, as the features of no two men are alike, so likewise are the thoughts of no two men alike.

*Tosefta Berakot, 7, 2.*

Rabbi Isaac teaches: "Before a thought is formed in a man's mind, it is already manifest to Thee." "Before an embryo is formed, its thoughts are already manifest to Thee."

*Bereshit Rabbah, 9, 3.*

"There are," said Rab, "three sins from which no man escapes for a single day: letting his imagination play with sin, calculating on prayer [1] (that it will of a certainty bring the desired end), and injurious speech."

*Baba Batra, 164b.*

[1] Rashi: The sin lies in man's presumption that God will grant his request as a compensation due for his praying.

## 202. MAN—PRAISE OF

Do not praise a man if he deserve it not, for thus wilt thou cause him shame.

*Zohar, i, 232b.*

It is not fitting to praise a man to his face.

*Midrash Mishle, 27.*

A little praise of a man may be uttered in his presence, but complete praise in his presence is forbidden.

*Erubin, 18.*

A woman is truly praised, not when her kinsfolk laud her, but when she is lauded by those who envy her.

*Debarim Rabbah, 3, 6.*

Said R. Johanan in the name of R. Eleazar b. R. Simeon: "God has nothing in His World except the Fear of Heaven."
R. Papa chanced to be in Toak, and inquired from his landlady whether a learned man resided in the city. She answered: "There is

a learned man named Samuel, and he is adept in the lore of the Tannaim. May you be like unto him!"

He replied: "Inasmuch as you bless me through him, he must truly be a man who fears the Lord."

*Shabbat, 31; Niddah, 33.*

## 203. MAN'S SOCIAL LIFE

It is hard to live in large cities.

*Ketubot, 110.*

A man should always be sociable among his comrades.

*Ketubot, 17.*

Everyone must contribute to the defense of the city, even the orphans.

*Baba Kamma, 108.*

A man cannot dwell in the same house with a snake (namely, an evil person).

*Yebamot, 112.*

"Woe to the home whose windows open upon darkness!"

*Shemot Rabbah, 14.*

## 204. MAN'S WEAKNESS—MAN'S IMMORTALITY

When Man was created, the Ministering Angels wished to call him holy, but, when they beheld that sleep overcame him, they knew that he was only a mortal creature (mammal).

*Bereshit Rabbah, 8, 10.*

The twelve signs of the Zodiac may be said to represent Man. The white Lamb (Aries), the dark Ox (Taurus), and the Twins (Gemini) remind us that man may walk in light and darkness. The Cancer and Lion (Leo) remind us that man's impulses are at first weak, like the Cancer, and then strong, like the Lion. If man will succumb to worldly pleasures like the Virgin (Virgo), his actions will be weighed on the Balances (Libra). If he is found wanting, he will suffer downfall like the low Scorpion (Scorpio), but, if he repent, he will quickly be relieved with the speed of the Bow (Sagittarius), and will caper like the Kid (Capricornus). He will be purified with the water of the Bucket (Aquarius), and he will inherit bliss like the Fish (Pisces), who are beyond number.

*Pesikta Rabbati, 20, 2.*

Rabbi Simai said: "All heavenly creatures were created from celestial substance; all earthly creatures were created from earthly substance, except man, whose soul is a celestial substance, his body an earthly one. Therefore, if a man keeps the Torah, he is like the creatures above (i.e., immortal in the first case, and mortal in the second case)."

*Sifre on Deut., 32, 2.*

## As Helpless as Flies

The Emperor Antoninus, on his arrival at Caesarea, the capital of the Roman Levant government, sent for Rabbi Judah ha-Nasi. Rabbi took with him his son, Simeon, and his comrade, Rabbi Hanina, the Senior. Young Simeon went out to see the sights of the city, and everything was marvelous in his eyes. He admired especially the soldiers of the Legion in their martial uniform, and the Emperor's tall guardsmen.

"How stuffed are the calves of Esau!" he said to Rabbi Hanina.

"See those flies hovering over the fruits in the market-place?" said Rabbi Hanina. "In the scheme of God's universe all the legions and regiments are of no more value than those flies."

When Rabbi heard of this, he said: "Without God's will they are as helpless as flies."

*Tanhuma Wayesheb.*

## An Everlasting Memorial

When R. Johanan's hour came to die, he wept bitterly, and said: "It is not enough that my sons should have died in their youth, but I shall be punished in the World-to-Come for not having left a son behind me."

His Disciples said: "Are not, we, your Disciples, as sons to thee?"

R. Johanan continued to weep. Then an old man said to him: "Be comforted, O Master! There is a verse (Isaiah 56:4-5) which applies both to thee and to Hezekiah b. Hiyya, who is barren: 'For thus saith the Lord concerning the eunuchs that keep My Sabbaths, and choose the things that please Me, and hold fast to My covenant: Even unto them will I give in My house and within My walls a monument and a memorial, that shall not be cut off.'"

R. Johanan, on hearing this, refrained from tears and blessed the old man.

*Zohar Hadash to Ruth.*

## Only a Man

When Hadrian returned from Palestine, he summoned his wise men, and commanded them to pay him worship as if he were divine. He said: "There is no god whose worshippers have not been subjected to my rule."

A wise man replied: "One does not rebel against a king in his own palace, but from the outside. Depart from the world which is God's palace, and from there rebel against Him."

Another said: "My king, I require your assistance. My ship, laden with freight, has been becalmed three miles out at sea. I beg of you to send a breeze to move it."

"How can I command a wind?" asked Hadrian.

"Then," said the man, "you are lacking in the ability to become God, for He sends His winds at will."

Hadrian entered the chamber of his favorite wife, and told her of this. She said: "You will be recognized as god quickly enough if you return to your Maker that which he has given you in trust."

"And what may that be?" asked Hadrian.

"The breath of life," she answered.

"Will I not then be dead?" continued the Emperor.

"Surely," replied his wife, "but, if you cannot rule the soul within yourself, how can you be anything more than a mere man?"

*Tanhuma Bereshit and Shofetim.*

Rabbi Jose ben Halafta said: "Never did the Presence (that is, God) descend to earth, nor did Moses and Elijah ascend to heaven; for it is written: The heavens are the Lord's heavens, and the earth He has given to the children of men." (Psalm 115, 16)

*Sukkah, 5a.*

Two creatures are blended in man—one intended for this life, the other for the life hereafter.

*Bereshit Rabbah, 8.*

## 205. MAN AND WOMAN

Why is it easier to appease a male than a female? Because a male was created from soft dust, but a female from hard bone.

*Niddah, 31.*

Why is a woman's voice thinner than a man's? Because she was created out of bone and he out of dust.

*Niddah, 31.*

Why does a woman need cosmetics and a man does not? Because dust does not smell, but bone does.

*Bereshit Rabbah, 17, 8.*

A man is more inclined to hospitality than a woman.

*Sifre Shelah, 110.*

A woman recognizes the worth of a guest quicker than a man.

*Berakot, 10.*

### THE RIB OF ADAM

A matron asked Rabbi Jose: "Why did God find it necessary to send a deep sleep upon Adam and remove his rib by stealth to create woman?"

"Do you call it stealth," asked the Rabbi, "when one takes away an ounce and returns a pound?"

"That was not my question," answered the matron. "What I wished to understand is why Adam had to be asleep when Eve was created. Surely God's action would not have brought him pain."

"The reason was," said the Rabbi, "that, had Adam seen the woman in a state of incompletion, he would have been displeased with her."

"You are quite right," said the matron. "And furthermore it required a surprise to call forth his love for her. I once cherished the hope that I might marry the brother of my mother, but he went away and married a woman said to be less charming. Doubtless he knew me too well."

*Bereshit Rabbah, 17.*

## 206. MARTYRDOM

If thou art commanded (by a ruler) to transgress all the commandments of the Torah on penalty of death, transgress all of them except idolatry, incest and the shedding of blood.

*Sanhedrin, 74.*

When Rabbi Akiba heard of the martyrdom of Rabban Simeon ben Gamaliel and R. Ishmael ben Elisha, he said in his funeral discourse: "Brethren in Israel, prepare for troubled times. Were good times destined for us, these two saintly men would have deserved to enjoy them more than any one else."

*Semahot, 8.*

Rabbi Eleazar ben Porta, after his arrest, was asked by the judge: "Why have you taught Torah and why have you been guilty of theft?"

He replied: "If I am a teacher, I am not a thief; if I am a thief, I am not a teacher."

*Abodah Zarah, 18.*

The daughter of R. Hananiah ben Teradion was sentenced to work in a degrading occupation. What was her sin? While walking on a thoroughfare one day, some Romans said: "How beautifully does this girl walk!" Henceforth she began to imitate a woman of the aristocracy in her gait.

*Ibid.*

When Nebuchadnezzar set up the great idol and commanded every nation to pay it homage, Hananiah, Mishael and Azariah, the friends of Daniel, came to champion Israel. Before doing so, they visited the Prophet Ezekiel and told him what they had volunteered to do. The Prophet inquired: "Are you then going to worship the idol?"

They replied: "Nay, we wish to demonstrate to the king that Israel does not forsake his God even though all other nations are obedient to his behest."

The Prophet asked God: "Wilt thou save them from the king's punishment?"

God replied: "Tell them not to anticipate My intervention, but to thee I may say that I may perform a miracle in their behalf."

Ezekiel returned to the three men and said: "You are going to certain death. God will not prevent your being cast into the fiery cauldron."

They replied: "Nevertheless we are prepared to die for Him."
*Shir ha-Shirim Rabbah, 7, 13.*

### PERSECUTIONS OF ISRAEL

Rabbi Nathan said: "There are Israelites who surrender their life for the commandments. Why art thou going forth to be put to death? Because I circumcised my son. Why art thou going forth to be burned? Because I have read in the Torah. Why art thou going forth to be crucified? Because I ate unleavened bread. Why art thou beaten with a scourge? Because I carried the palm branch. 'The wounds I received in the house of my friends' (Zech. 13:6): these wounds cause me to be beloved by my Father who is in Heaven."
*Mekilta, Bahodesh, 6.*

If a man gives himself up to martyrdom in the expectation that a miracle will be wrought for him, no miracle is wrought for him; and, if with no such expectation, a miracle may come to pass in his behalf.
*Sifra, Emor, Perek, 9.*

Rabbi said: "We read: 'For as a man riseth against his neighbor and slayeth him, even so is this matter of a betrothed damsel' (Deut. 22:26). This teaches us that even as one should suffer death rather than slay another, so should a betrothed damsel suffer death rather than commit adultery."

How do we know that a man should rather allow himself to be slain than to slay another? It is a matter of common sense to be killed rather than kill. A man came to Rabba and said: "The owner of my village threatens to kill me if I do not kill another person of whom he wishes to be rid."

Rabba answered: "If there is no way to prevent the village owner from killing thee, thou must let him kill thee rather than kill the other man. Dost thou think that thy blood is redder than his? Perhaps his blood is redder!"
*Pesahim, 25.*

## 207. MASTER AND SERF

He who buys a Jewish serf buys a master for himself.

*Kiddushin, 20.*

### THE OLD SERVANT

An old man dyed his hair black, and came to Rabba and said: "Please take me into thy service."

Rabba answered: "The people of my household suffice for me."

The man thereupon went to Rab Papa bar Samuel, who accepted him as a servant. The aged man washed his hair and then came to his master, saying: "See, I am older than you."

The Rabbi could not ask service from an aged man, and lost the money he had advanced.

*Baba Metzia, 60b.*

### CONSIDERATION FOR SERFS

When a serf dies, the master shall not mourn him as a member of his family, but, when Tabbai died, Rabban Gamaliel accepted consolation of his loss, saying: "Tabbai is different from other serfs." A male serf does not put on Tefillin. Tabbai, however, was permitted to wear Tefillin.

Serfs should not be called "Father" or "Mother" when they are old, but in the house of Rabban Gamaliel the old serfs were thus called because of their fine character.

Samuel, who was a physician, had an occasion to demonstrate to his Disciples the evidence of female maturity. He showed this on the body of a female slave, but paid her for her shame, saying: "They are given us for work, not to be put to shame."

*Berakot, 16, Niddah, 47.*

## 208. MATING—BRIDE AND BRIDEGROOM

A bride who has fine eyes is fine throughout.

*Taanit, 24.*

A groom cannot go under the canopy unless his bride permits him.

*Wayyikra Rabbah, 9, 6.*

When a bridegroom comes to visit his bride, he should accept with happy countenance whatever she does for him.

*Zohar, iv, 224a.*

### Bridal Processions

Rabbi Judah ben Ilai was seated in his School when he saw a small procession pass. "What is that?" he asked.

"It is a bride being led to her home," was the answer.

"Let's leave off our studies," he said, "and join the procession. It is too small now."

Rabbi Tarfon noticed a bridal procession passing by. He called in the bride, and told his wife to shower her with perfumes and other gifts, and accompany her to her new home.

Rabbi Samuel bar Rabbi Isaac would take a bunch of myrtles and dance before the brides. Rabbi Zeira thought this undignified for a scholar. When Rabbi Samuel died, a pillar of fire separated the hearse from the people. They said: "The old man is repaid for his myrtles."

King Agrippa I gave way to a bridal procession on the street, saying: "I wear the crown every day; let the bride have the crown for an hour."

*Ketubot, 17.*

He who does not cheer the bridegroom whose wedding-meal he has enjoyed transgresses against the five voices: the voice of Joy, the voice of Gladness, the voice of the Bridegroom, the voice of the Bride, and the voice of them that shall say "Praise ye the Lord of Hosts." (Jer. 33:11)

*Berakot, 6b.*

### The Bride's Prayer

There once lived a pious man who was childless. He prayed for a son, vowing to invite to his wedding-feast every poor person in the city. A son was eventually born to him, and he gave him the name of Mattaniah, namely, a gift from God. The boy grew up and his wedding-day approach. The father invited all the students of the Torah and all the poor, who together filled six rooms.

God wished to test the bridegroom, and he sent the Angel of Death, in the guise of a man attired in soiled raiment, to beg for a place at the wedding. The bridegroom refused on the plea that all who could be accommodated had been invited. Moreover, the man's garments were objectionable.

In the night the Angel of Death revealed himself, declaring that he was about to take away the bridegroom's soul since he had failed in the test. The bride gave voice to this prayer: "O Lord of the Universe, Thou hast said in Thy Torah that, when a man takes unto himself a wife, he shall bring her cheer for a full year and not leave her. May it be Thy will that my husband live before Thee, and I shall teach him to practice loving-kindness to everyone without discrimination."

Her prayer was heard on High, and the Angel of Death was commanded to leave.

What was the nature of this young woman? Her mother was accustomed to draw cool water from a spring for school children. When she became old, her daughter said: "You need not abandon your good deed. I shall lend you the strength of my arm and carry most of the weight so that you may continue to perform the Mitzwah."

It was this consideration for her mother that made her deserving in the eyes of the Lord.

*Midrash Asseret ha-Dibrot.*

### THE WISE MOTHER'S COUNSEL

A wise woman said to her daughter, who was about to become a bride: "My daughter, if you will respect your husband like a king, he will treat you like a queen. If you will serve him like a slave-girl, he will serve you like a slave. But if you will be too proud to serve him, he will assert his mastership by force and will treat you like a maid-servant. If your husband is about to visit his friends, persuade him to bathe and wear fine raiment. If his friends come to his house, welcome them heartily and set before them more than they can eat, so that they will respect your husband. Watch well your home and all of your husband's possessions. He will be delighted with you, and you will be the crown of his head."

*Menorat ha-Moar quoting a Midrash.*

## 209. CHOOSING A MATE

He who weds his daughter to an old man, and he who gives a wife unto his minor son, commits a wrong.

*Sanhedrin, 76.*

If a man sees that his sons do not care to learn Torah, let him marry his daughter to a Disciple of the Wise.

*Yoma, 71.*

A tall man should not marry a tall woman lest their offspring be abnormally tall.

*Bekorot, 45.*

Mating is as hard as the cleaving of the waters of the Red Sea.[1]

*Sotah, 2.*

[1] See *Joyful Jeremiads,* p. 9; "Marriages Are Made in Heaven."

If there be a male bastard in Israel in one end of the world, and a female bastard in the other, God brings them together and mates them.[1]

*Y. Kiddushin, 3, 12.*

[1] A bastard can marry only a bastard or a proselyte.

It is not wise to take a wife of superior rank—rather go down a step in choosing a wife.

*Yebamot, 63a.*

## GALA DAYS

Rabban Simeon ben Gamaliel related that the 15th of Ab and Yom Kippur used to be gala days in Jerusalem. The young maidens would repair to the vineyard, robed in white garments. It was required that they borrow these, lest maidens without their own should feel humiliated. There they danced gleefully and called out to the onlooking youths: "Choose mates for yourselves!"

The comely ones would call attention to their good looks; those of good family, to their heredity, and those of good character, to their worthiness.

*Taanit, 26b.*

## THE PREDESTINED MATE

King Solomon had a most beautiful daughter, concerning whose fortune he was exceedingly anxious. He prayed that he be shown her intended mate, and it was revealed to him in a dream that her mate was a youth, the poorest of the poor in Israel.

"Let me behold God's ways," thought the King.

He built a palace on an island and erected round about it a high wall. He brought to it his daughter and her servants, left provisions with them, and, locking the gate, departed with the key.

A poor youth was wandering one cold night on a deserted road and lost his way. Observing an open carcass of a large bull, he crept between the ribs for warmth and fell asleep. A huge bird snatched up the carcass, flew away with it and deposited it on the roof of the palace. When the Princess went up to the roof, as was her daily morning custom, she beheld the youth. She commanded that he be bathed and cleansed, and, lo, he was the handsomest youth she had ever seen. She commenced to converse with him, and found him to be cultivated and amiable. The inevitable happened: they fell in love and were married in the presence of the servants. When the King arrived on his periodic visit and beheld his son-in-law, he rejoiced greatly and exclaimed: "Blessed be the Lord!"

*Intro. to Tanhuma Buber, p. 136.*

## THE UNLOVED WIFE

Rabbi Akiba said: "He who marries a woman not suited to him violates five precepts: (1) Thou shalt not avenge; (2) Thou shalt not bear a grudge; (3) Thou shalt not hate thy brother in thy heart; (4) Thou shalt love thy neighbor as thyself; (5) and that thy brother may live with thee. For if he hates her, he wishes she were dead."

*Abot de-Rabbi Nathan, chap. 26.*

## A TASK WORTHY OF GOD

A matron once asked Rabbi Jose ben Halafta: "What has your God been doing since He finished making the world?"

"He has been matching couples in marriage," was the reply, "the daughter of so and so for so and so; so and so's wife for so and so."

The lady declared that she could do as much as that herself; nothing was easier than to couple any number of slaves with as many slave-girls.

"You may think it easy," said Rabbi Jose, "but it is as difficult for God as dividing the Red Sea."

The matron accordingly tried the experiment with a thousand males and as many female slaves, setting them in rows and bidding this man take this woman, etc. The next morning they came to her, one with a broken head, another with gouged-out eyes, a third with a broken leg; one man saying: "I don't want her," and a girl saying: "I don't want him."

Thus was the matron constrained to say that the mating of man and woman was a task not unworthy the intelligence of God.[1]

[1] See my poem in *Joyful Jeremiads*, page 9.

*Pesikta Buber, 11b-12a.*

## 210. MARRIAGE

God creates new worlds constantly. In what way? By causing marriages to take place.

*Zohar, i, 89a.*

A man should not marry a woman with the thought in mind that he may divorce her.

*Yebamot, 37.*

He who weds for money will have delinquent offspring.

*Kiddushin, 70.*

There is no marriage settlement wherein there is no quarrel.

*Shabbat, 130.*

When a soul is sent down from Heaven, it is a combined male and female soul. The male part enters the male child and the female part enters the female. If they are worthy, God causes them to re-unite in marriage. This is true mating.

*Zohar, iii, 43b.*

It is good manners that everyone who partakes of a wedding feast should give a present to the young couple.

*Zohar, i, 149a.*

Marriages are like the dividing of the Red Sea. At the division there was drowning on one side and salvation on the other. At the marriage there is joy on one side and weeping on the other. In Sotah 2a, the word "Bekosharot" (Psalm 68:7) is used with reference to marriages. This word may be divided into two parts: Beki (weeping) and Shirot (songs).

*Zohar, ii, 170b.*

Rabbi Jacob said: "He who has no wife remains without good, without a helper, without joy, without a blessing and without atonement."

Others add: "Without peace (welfare) and without life."

Rabbi Hiyya ben Gamla said: "He is not a whole man, as it is said: 'And He called their (male and female) name Man.'"

Others said: "The unmarried man diminishes the likeness of God."

*Bereshit Rabbah, 17, 2; Yebamot, 62, 63.*

A man who marries may be a true servant of God, since he can concentrate his mind upon desires of the spirit rather than of the emotions.

*Zohar Hadash, i, 5a.*

The Shekinah can rest only upon a married man, because an unmarried man is but half a man, and the Shekinah does not rest upon that which is imperfect.

*Zohar Hadash, iv, 50b.*

A man should trust in his Maker. He should marry and have children so that he may not go alone to the World-to-Come.

*Zohar Hadash, v, 59a.*


## 211. MATING—REQUIREMENTS PRECEDING

A man should build himself a home, plant himself a vineyard and then bring into the home a bride. Fools are they who marry while they have no secure livelihood.

*Zohar Hadash, i, 4b.*

A man who marries and has not the means to support a family is free of Mitzwot like those who have died. They are so busy in the service of their wives that they find no time to engage in the service of God.

*Ibid.*

In olden times the pious Sages were willing to go about hungry, to see their wives and children go hungry, and to devote all their attention to Torah and Mitzwot. God came to their succor and aided them on their way. In our times, however, there are no such sincere scholars, and they must not rely upon the aid of God if they do nothing for themselves. Nowadays no one should marry until his livelihood is secure.

*Ibid.*

## 212. MENTAL CAPACITY

Even the words of Torah were given in a measure fitting each person. The mind of one man has the capacity and aptitude for the Scriptures, another for the Halakot, another for the Aggadah, another for the discussion of the Gemara.

*Yalkut Shimeoni to Isaiah, 281.*

A Rabbi narrates: "I was once accosted by a man who said to me: 'Rabbi, I am entirely unlearned; I do not even know the Pentateuch.'

"I asked him why he did not study, and he replied: 'Because my Father in Heaven did not give me understanding and discernment.'

"I said: 'What is thy occupation?'

" 'I am a fisherman,' he answered.

"And who taught thee to weave nets and to spread them properly for the catch?"

"The fisherman replied: 'Understanding and discernment were given me from Heaven for this purpose.'

"I said: 'If God gave thee understanding wherewith to catch fish, did He not give thee sufficient intelligence to learn His Torah, concerning which He has written: "It is not too hard for thee, neither is it far off. But the Word is very nigh unto thee.' " (Deut. 30:11-14)

"The fisherman began to weep and to sigh. I said to him: 'Be not sad of heart. Other persons have argued like thee, but their occupations betrayed them and brought their arguments to naught. It is never too late to learn.' "

*Seder Eliyahu Zuta, 14.*

## 213. MERITS—DESERTS

Neither poverty nor wealth is gained from a trade, but from merit.

*Kiddushin, 82.*

If they merit it, the Heavens will declare their righteousness; if not, the Heavens will reveal their sins.

*Bereshit Rabbah, 4, 7.*

If a man merits it, his wife is his helpmate; if not, she is his antagonist.

*Yebamot, 63.*

If a man merits it, he will serve; if not, he will be lost.

*Bereshit Rabbah, 67.*

A man does not merit to learn from everybody.

*Abodah Zarah, 13.*

Not everyone merits two tables (scholarship and wealth).

*Berakot, 5.*

If a man merits it, his wife gladdens his life; if not, she desolates it.

*Yoma, 76.*

If you merit it, you will have the hunger of Jacob (for doing good); if not, you will have the satiety of Esau.

*Wayyikra Rabbah, 34, 13.*

If one merits it, the Torah will gladden his heart; if he does not, it acts as a crucible to him.

*Yoma, 72.*

Merit has a principal and interest.

*Kiddushin, 40.*

If one merits it, he receives the desire of his heart, if not, his lips are sealed.

*Erubin, 54.*

If a man merits it, he is told: "Thou art of more importance than the Ministering Angels." If he does not merit it, he is told: "A fly was created before thee in the Creation."

*Bereshit Rabbah, 88.*

Rabbi Simeon b. Lakish said: "If one merits it, the Torah purifies him to life; if not, it smelts him to death."

*Yoma, 72.*

The chief merits are: at a wedding, to cause merriment; among mourners, to keep silent; at a lecture, to listen; at a session, to come early; at teaching, to concentrate; at the fasting, to give charity.

*Berakot, 6.*

Once worms threatened to damage the flax of R. Hiyya. He asked Rabbi's advice, and the latter counseled him to kill a chicken over the water in which the flax was soaking. The worms would smell the blood and disappear.

It was asked: "How does this story agree with the statement that, prior to the coming of Babylonian scholars to Palestine, agriculture failed, but, with their coming, the wine did not sour and the flax did not become spoiled. And chief among those scholars was R. Hiyya and his sons?"

The answer was given that their merit aided in bringing success to others, but not to themselves. As Rab Judah said in the name of Rab: "Daily doth the Daughter of the Voice come forth and saith: 'The entire world is sustained for the sake of My son Hanina bar Dosa, and My son Hanina enjoyeth thereof only a measure of carobs from Friday to Friday.'"

*Hullin, 85.*

## 214. MERITS AND SINS OF THE FATHERS

If a man does no good, he may not depend upon his fathers' goodness.

*Midrash Tehillim, 146, 2.*

The sins of heathen fathers do not exclude their posterity from the Jewish people or from the highest honors the Rabbis could conceive, namely, being Doctors of the Law.

Descendants of Sisera, Sennacherib and Haman became teachers of the Torah.

*Gittin, 57b.*

### RABBI MEIR'S FABLES OF THE FOX AND THE WOLF

The fox met a hungry wolf near the town. He said to him: "Why go hungry when nearby in the town the Jews are preparing so many tasty dishes for the Sabbath? Tell them that you will fetch and carry, and thus you will obtain a share."

The wolf entered the town, and was welcomed with sticks upon his back. He returned to the fox and wished to kill him. The latter, however, said: "The beating you received was for your father's sin. Once he came to help and ate up more than his share."

"Why should I be beaten for my father's sin?" the wolf wished to know.

"Well," said the fox, "it is written: 'The fathers have eaten sour grapes, and the children's teeth are set on edge.'" (Jer. 31:29)

"But I am very hungry," complained the wolf. "I will eat you if you do not find me any food."

"Very well, come with me," said the fox.

They reached a well; the fox stepped into a pail and immediately went down. Holding himself near the surface of the water, the fox said: "There is meat here and cheese. Step into the other pail and you will have plenty to eat."

The wolf looked down, and the reflection of the moon in the water seemed to make the words of the fox credible. He stepped into the pail, and, quick as a shot, the lower pail with the fox in it came up, while the other pail with the wolf went down.

"How will I get up again?" shouted the wolf.

"The owner will raise you up soon enough and you will receive your just deserts. It is written: 'The righteous is delivered out of trouble, and the wicked cometh in his stead.'" (Prov. 11:8)

*Sanhedrin, 38, Rashi.*

## 215. MERRIMENT, JOY, SADNESS

Rejoice in thy lot and enjoy what little thou hast.

*Derek Eretz Zuta, 3.*

He who finishes a tractate should celebrate.

*Pesikta Zutarta to Tzav.*

According to the money, dance.

*Midrash Tehillim, 16, 12.*

A man must make a feast when he circumcises his son.

*Midrash Tehillim, 112, 2.*

There is no joy like the joy of the heart.

*Ben Sirach, 30, 16.*

Kohelet says: "So I commended mirth" (Eccl. 8:15); and he says also of mirth (2:2): "What does it accomplish?" How shall this be explained? If the mirth is at a Mitzwah celebration it is commendable.

*Shabbat, 30.*

The Divine Presence (Shekinah), or the Holy Spirit, does not rest upon a sad heart, but only upon a joyful one.

*Shabbat, 30b.*

He dances and his ear inclines to hear a eulogy for the dead.

*Zohar, iv, 172.*

He who rejoices today may not have cause for merriment tomorrow.

He who is troubled of heart today may have no cause for anxiety tomorrow.

Joy does not await the pleasure of man.

*Tanhuma to Shemini.*

## A JOLLY PAIR

There were two Sectaries, named, respectively, Joy and Gladness.

Said Joy to Gladness "I am better than thou, for the verse saith: 'They shall receive joy and gladness; first joy is mentioned, next gladness.' "

Gladness answered: "I am better than thou, for it is written: 'Gladness and joy for the Jew.' "

Joy said to Gladness: "One day thou wilt become a guide, as it is said: 'Ye shall go forth with gladness.' "

Gladness answered: "One day thou shalt be filled with water, as it is written: 'And ye shall draw waters in joy.' "

Joy said to R. Abbahu: "Some day ye shall draw water for me."

R. Abbahu answered: "If it were written 'for joy' it would be as thou sayest, but 'in joy' means that we shall skin thee, tan thy skin and draw water in it."

*Sukkah, 48b.*

The Divine Spirit rests not upon the sad and the woebegone, but upon those who do their duty and are glad.

*Shabbat, 30b.*

## 216. MESSIAH

The Son of David will not come until the generation will be either all righteous or all wicked.

*Sanhedrin, 98.*

The Son of David will not come until all qualities will be equal in men.

*Ibid.*

A Sage said: "May the curse of heaven fall upon those who calculate the date of the advent of the Messiah, and thus create political and social unrest among the people."

*Sanhedrin, 97b.*

The Son of David will not come until all evil judges will cease out of Israel.

*Shabbat, 139.*

The Son of David will not come until all money will be gone from the purse of man.

*Sanhedrin, 97.*

What is the difference between our times and the Messianic times? Purity and attainment of knowledge.

*Zohar, i, 139a.*

Rabbi Akiba was rebuked by Rabbi Jose, the Galilean, for "profaning the Divine Presence" by teaching that the Messiah occupies a throne alongside of God. (If miracles are to be performed, God alone will perform them. The Messiah's advent will not change the course of nature.)

*Hagigah, 14a.*

### THE EPHRAIMITE MESSIAH

Rabbi Samuel bar Nahmani said: "It is written (Obadiah 1:18): 'And the house of Jacob shall be a fire, and the house of Joseph a flame, and the house of Esau for stubble, and they shall kindle in them, and devour them; and there shall not be any remaining of the house of Esau; for the Lord hath spoken.'

"We learn from this that Esau, namely Rome, would be delivered only into the hand of a descendant of Joseph, the son of Jacob."

*Baba Batra, 123b.*

Rabbi Johanan said: "All the Prophets prophesied (ultimate bliss) only with reference to the Days of the Messiah; but, regarding the World-to-Come (the New World), 'Eye hath not seen a God beside Thee who works for him who waits for Him.'" (Isa. 64:4)

*Sanhedrin, 99a.*

Mar Samuel said: "There is no difference between the present time and the Days of the Messiah, except our subjection to the dominion of the empires."

*Sanhedrin 99a.*

The Son of David will not come until the arrogant cease out of Israel, as it is written: "I will remove from the midst of thee thy proudly exulting ones, . . . and I will leave in the midst of thee an afflicted and poor people, and they shall take refuge in the name of the Lord.' " (Zeph. 3:11, 12)

*Sanhedrin, 98a.*

Rabbi Nathan said: "The vision is yet for the appointed time, and it hurries on to the end and does not deceive. If it delay, wait confidently for it, for it will surely come, and will not delay indefinitely."

*Sanhedrin, 97b.*

Rabbi Joshua ben Levi said: "It is written in Zechariah (9:9): 'Behold, thy king cometh unto thee, . . . lowly, and riding upon an ass'; while Daniel (7:13) says: 'Behold, there came with the clouds of heaven one like unto a son of man.' If Israel were worthy, 'with the clouds of heaven'; if they were not worthy, 'lowly, and riding upon an ass.' "

*Sanhedrin, 98a.*

The juice kept in the grape from the first-grown vine is ancient wisdom which has not yet been revealed.[1]

*Midrash ha-Neelam, i, 135b.*

[1] This is an explanation of the legendary wine to be served at the Messianic Banquet with Leviathan and Wild Bullock. The last two may also be explained in the same way.

### THE MESSIAH'S DONKEY

Shapur I of Persia said to his friend, Samuel: "May I not donate a swift pedigreed horse for the Messiah in place of the ass on which he is to ride?"

Samuel smiled and said: "His ass is a rare one. It will have a hundred colored stripes."

*Sanhedrin, 98a.*

Rabbi Hillel said: "Israel need not look for the advent of Messiah, since Isaiah's prophecy about him was already fulfilled in King Hezekiah!"[1]

*Sanhedrin, 98b.*

[1] Rashi understands Hillel to mean that God alone and not a Messiah would bring about the promised redemption; in other words, that he only denied a personal Messiah but not the coming of the Messianic age. *In loco*, Rab Joseph refutes him by quoting Zechariah 9:9, who lived after Hezekiah. He might have added the other later prophets, Jeremiah, Ezekiel, etc.

Rabbi Johanan said: "Wait for him (the Messiah). When you see the generations of Israel growing smaller, and many troubles coming upon them, then he will appear."

*Sanhedrin, 98a.*

## TODAY IF YE HARKEN

Rabbi Joshua ben Levi dreamed that he saw Elijah at the entrance of R. Simeon b. Yohai's cave. He asked: "When will the Messiah come?"

Elijah replied: "Go thyself and ask him."

"Where will I find him?"

"At the main gate of Rome."

"How will I know him?"

"He sits among the beggars and nurses their wounds. Each one of them will untie every bandage to apply medicine and then rebandage their wounds. He alone unties one wound at a time. He thinks: 'If I am called, I must waste no time.'"

R. Joshua found him, and said: "Greetings unto thee, My Master and Teacher!"

Messiah replied: "Greetings to thee, ben Levi!"

R. Joshua asked: "When will the Master come?"

Messiah answered: "Today."

R. Joshua b. Levi departed. On the following day he again met Elijah, and told him of the conversation. Elijah said: "Since Messiah greeted you and your father, you are sure of a high place in the World-to-Come."

"But he spoke untruthfully," complained R. Joshua. "He said that he would come today, and he has not come."

Elijah answered: "He meant: 'Today, if ye would but hearken to His Voice!'" (Psalm 95:7)[1]

*Sanhedrin, 98.*

[1] See Segal, S. M., *Elijah*, 1935, for stories regarding Elijah.

The Rabbis taught: "The Son of David will not come until Israel despairs of being redeemed."

It was also taught: "The Son of David will come when no one expects him. Three things come unexpectedly: the Messiah, a discovery, and a winning."

*Sanhedrin, 97-99.*

## THE MESSIAH'S ADVENT

Ulla, Rabbah and R. Johanan said: "If the coming of the Messiah depended upon our desire, we would not be living at his advent, for fearsome tribulations will precede him."

A Gentile asked R. Abbahu: "When will the Messiah come?"

He replied: "When darkness will cover the face of the Gentiles."

"Why do you curse us?"

"I do not mean to curse you. I merely repeat for you a verse: 'For, behold, darkness shall cover the earth, and gross darkness the peoples; but upon thee the Lord will arise, and His glory shall be seen upon thee. And nations shall walk at thy light, and kings at the brightness of thy rising.' " (Isaiah 60:2-3)

*Sanhedrin, 97-99.*

### THE VANISHED MESSIAH

R. Judah b. R. Aibu said: "Once a Jew was plowing, and his ox bellowed. An Arab said to him: 'Loosen your plow and free your ox, for the Temple has been destroyed.' A second time the ox bellowed. The Arab said: 'Bind your plow again and harness your ox to it, for the Messiah has been born.' The Jew asked: 'What is his name?' 'Menahem b. Hezekiah.' 'Where was he born?' 'In Bethlehem.' The Jew sold his ox and plow, and bought children's garments to sell for gain. He arrived at Bethlehem. Many women purchased his wares, but the mother of Menahem did not buy. When he inquired the reason, she replied that she had no money. He gave her his goods on credit, but a short time later when he came to collect the debt the mother said: 'Mine was an unfortunate child. He was born when the Temple was destroyed, and after your departure he disappeared and cannot be found.' " [1]

*Y. Berakot, 2.*

[1] This story forms the background for David Pinski's great play, "The Stranger."

### 217. PSEUDO–MESSIAH

In the year 5408 of the Creation of the World, the Rebirth will occur.[1]

*Zohar, i, 139b.*

[1] The massacres of the Jews in Poland in the year 1648 (5408 A.M.) are a contradiction of the Zohar, but they nevertheless prompted Sabbatai Zevi to advance his Messianic pretensions.

### A STAR OUT OF JACOB

We read: "There shall step out a star from Jacob" (Num. 24:17).

Rabbi R. Simeon b. Yohai said: "Rabbi Akiba declared that Bar Koziba is Messiah and should be called Bar Kokba (Bar Koziba—a man from *Koziba;* Bar Kokba—the Son of a Star). When R. Akiba called Bar Koziba, Messiah, R. Johanan b. Torta exclaimed: 'Akiba, grass will grow in thy cheeks before the Son of David comes.' " [1]

*Y. Taanit, 4.*

[1] In I Chronicles 4:22 the spelling is Cozeba.

## THE DOWNFALL OF BAR KOKBA

Bar Kokba had many regiments of brave soldiers in whose valor he trusted. When he went forth to do battle he was accustomed to say: "O Lord, help neither us nor our enemy!"

The saintly R. Eleazar of Modium prayed daily: "Lord, judge us not today."

*Y. Taanit, chap. 4.*

For three and a half years Hadrian besieged Bethar until he grew weary of the effort. A Samaritan came to him and promised that he would cause the fortress to fall. As the saintly Eleazar was praying, the Samaritan went to him and whispered in his ear. He was seized and brought before Bar Kokba. The Samaritan told the leader that he had conspired with the old sage to surrender the city. The Rabbi was summoned and declared that he had neither heard the Samaritan speak to him, nor had he said anything to him. Bar Kokba was incensed and struck the old Rabbi, who fell down and died. Soon Bethar fell and Bar Kokba was slain. Hadrian in his wrath against the defenders of the fortress forbade the burial of the dead. The corpses lay untouched until Hadrian's successor, Antoninus Pius, ordered their burial.

*Y. Taanit, 4.*

## 218. MESSIANIC AGE

Rabbi Judah said: "Unless the children of Israel repent, they will not be delivered, and they do not repent except through tribulations, oppression, exile and lack of a livelihood. The children of Israel will not undertake the Great Repentance until Elijah comes."

*Pirkei de-Rabbi Eliezer, chap. 43.*

Rab said: "The Age-to-Come is not like this age. In the Age-to-Come there is no eating or drinking, no begetting of children, no trading, no jealousy, no hatred and no strife."

*Berakot, 17a.*

In the Age-to-Come there will be no death, no sorrow and no tears.

*Mishnah Moed Katon, 3, 9.*

So horrible did the common conception of the pre-Messianic sufferings become that some of the Rabbis even prayed that the Messiah might not appear in their day.

*Sanhedrin, 98b.*

R. Gamaliel II, the successor to R. Johanan ben Zakkai, transported by his imagination, dwelling upon the supernatural wonders of the new state, said: that women will bear children daily and trees will give forth ripe fruit every day.

*Shabbat, 30b.*

In the Age-to-Come God Himself will purify Israel from all their uncleanness.

*Pesikta Buber, f, 41b.*

## 219. MIRACLES

How many miracles does God perform for man of which man does not know?

*Shemot Rabbah, 24, 1.*

No one should depend upon a miracle to save him. If a miracle has saved him once, he must not depend upon a similar rescue a second time.

*Zohar, i, 111b.*

Every favor which God performs for man is a miracle. Many a miracle remains unnoticed by the recipient of God's favor. Many a time a man is rescued from danger by the space of a nail's breadth.

*Zohar, iv, 200b.*

Ten phenomena were created on the eve of the Sabbath during the twilight: the mouth of the earth that opened up to swallow Korah; the mouth of the well that opened in the rock at the command of Moses; the mouth of the ass of Balaam; the rainbow which demonstrates God's promise not to repeat the flood; the manna; the rod wherewith Moses worked wonders; the worm, Shamir, wherewith stones for the construction of the Temple were split; the shape of the written characters (which appeared on the walls in Belshazzar's palace); the letter (sent by Elijah posthumously to Jehoram); and the Tables of Stone on which the Decalogue was engraved.

*Abot, 5, 6, and commentaries in the Hebrew periodical, Ha-Maggid.*

### The Wings of the Dove

Once the government decreed that the head of him who donned Tefillin should be broken. Elisha wore them on the street, and, when an official ran toward him, Elisha removed his Tefillin and placed them in his hands.

"What have you in your hands?" he was asked.

"A pair of pigeon's wings," he replied.

He opened his hands, and, lo, a pair of wings lay there.

Elisha, says the Gemara, bore in mind the words of the Psalmist (Psalm 68:14): "The wings of the dove are covered with silver." As the dove is protected by her silver wings, so are the children of Israel protected by their Mitzwot.

*Shabbat, 19.*

### IF GRACE BE FORGOTTEN

If one eats and forgets to say grace, he must return to the place of his meal and recite it. Once a Disciple forgot, and, on returning, discovered a valuable article which no one claimed. Another Disciple hastened away without saying grace, intending to say it elsewhere. He walked into a dangerous place and was injured.

Rabbah bar bar Hanah was journeying in a caravan. One day when he had finished eating he forgot to say grace. As he reminded himself, he thought: "If I tell the leader the truth, he will say: 'Recite grace where you are, for, wherever you say grace, it is grace in the eyes of God.' I shall tell them that I have left behind a golden dove."

He did so, and on his path, verily, he found a dove. He exclaimed: "As the dove is protected by its wings, so are the children of Israel protected by their Mitzwot."

*Berakot, 53.*

### THE MIRACLE OF THE ARNON VALLEY

Numbers 21:14-18 contain two short songs. On what occasion were they composed:

The Aggadah declares: "At the boundary between the land of the Amorites and Moab, certain mountains are situated. From one mountain rocks protruded; in the other mountain, opposite the rocks, there were deep caves. Between the two mountains was a deep valley, the Valley of Arnon. When the children of Israel neared this spot, a great number of their enemies concealed themselves in the caves and on the rocks, where they waited for the Israelites to pass through the Valley, intending to fall upon them and slay them. God, however, commanded an earthquake. The mountains bent toward each other and all the enemies of Israel were crushed. Israel marched over the summit of the mountain without suspecting the tragedy below them.

What did God do? When Israel sought a spring of water, they beheld it flow from beneath the center of the mountain filled with blood, weapons and fragments of human limbs. They then understood how God had aided them, and the poets among them composed songs of praise which were recorded in a book entitled *The Wars of the Lord.*

> "Vaheb in Suphah,
> And the valleys of Arnon
> And the slope of the valleys
> That inclineth toward the seat of Ar,
> And leaneth upon the border of Moab."

> "Spring up, O well, sing ye unto it
> The well, which the princes digged,
> Which the nobles of the people delved
> With the sceptre, and with their staves."

*Tanhuma to Num., 21:14.*

### The Story of Nahum Ish Gam Zu

Nahum was an exceedingly pious man who would always say, whatever befell him: "This, also, is for the best (Gam Zu Letobah)." In this way he received his nickname.

It became necessary for the leaders of Palestine to send a gift unto the Roman Emperor. Nahum was chosen as messenger in the expectation that God would grant success to a man so righteous. For the purpose of the gift he was given a jewelled box with gems. At a tavern, while he slept, the inn-keeper emptied his guest's box and filled it with sand. When the Emperor's treasurer opened the casket, it was found to contain sand. Nahum was accused of disrespect for the Emperor and was led forth to execution. Nevertheless Nahum was heard to say: "This, also, is for the best."

God thereupon sent Elijah in the guise of a Roman patrician, who declared: "I have heard there is a tradition among the Jews that when Abraham in his battle against the four kings was short of ammunition and his sword became dull, he threw sand at the enemy, and it smote them like a sword. Let us try this sand; perhaps it has the same property."

The execution was delayed and the sand was tested; the results were admirable. A town which had resisted the Romans was compelled to surrender under the impact of the sand. Nahum was released and his pockets filled with gold. He halted at the same tavern and told the inn-keeper of the gift he had received in exchange for what he had brought. The inn-keeper carried to the palace a wagon-load of sand but, when it was tested, it proved to be no different from any other sand. The inn-keeper was executed for attempting to deceive the Emperor.

*Taanit, 21.*

### R. Hanina b. Dosa Stories

R. Hanina ben Dosa was carrying some salt when rain began to fall. He said in prayer: "Everybody feels pleasant, but Hanina does not." The rain halted. Entering his home, he said: "Everybody feels unpleasant except Hanina." The rain came down once more.

R. Hanina entered his home and discovered his daughter in tears. By mistake she had poured vinegar into the lamp on Sabbath eve. He declared: "May He Who commanded the oil to burn, command also the vinegar to burn." The vinegar burned all day until after Habdalah.

People came to R. Hanina and said: "Your goats are doing damage."

He replied: "If my goats are causing damage, may they be eaten by wolves! If not, may each one bring in a wolf on his horns."

Each goat brought in a wolf.

Once a man left some hens at R. Hanina's door. He set them on their eggs, and, when he had too many chicks, he sold them and purchased goats. When, after considerable time had passed, a man informed him that he had left some hens with him by mistake, R. Hanina gave him the goats. These were the goats who brought in the wolves.

*Taanit, 24.*

## THE RIP VAN WINKLE OF THE TALMUD

Honi ha-Maagal read the verse (Psalm 126:1): "A Song of Ascents. When the Lord brought back those that returned to Zion, we were like unto them that dream." He said: "Is it possible that seventy years should be like a dream? Has anyone ever slept for seventy years?"

One day on the road he saw a man planting a carob tree. He said to him: "A carob tree brings forth no fruit for seventy years. Are you certain that you will live for seventy years?"

The man replied: "Did I find the world empty? As my fathers have planted for me, I am planting for my children."

Honi ate his food and fell asleep on the very spot where he had beheld the planter. A loose rock covered the sleeping man. Later he awakened and he beheld a man gathering the fruit of the carob tree. He said: "Who planted this tree?"

"My grandfather," answered the man.

Honi then understood that he had slept for seventy years. He went to his home and asked for the son of Honi. He was told that the son of Honi had died and that the grandson was now the owner of the house. He disclosed his identity, but no one believed him. He visited the House of Study and heard them say: "Today we understand that Halakah as if Honi were here himself to explain it to us."

But they also refused to believe him, and Honi prayed God to summon him into His Presence.

*Taanit, 23.*

The version in the Jerusalem Talmud runs, as follows: Not the Honi in the days of Simeon ben Shetah slept for seventy years, but a forefather of him by the same name. He fell asleep in a cave in the days of King Zedekiah, just before the destruction of the First Temple, and he awakened just at the dedication of the Second Temple. As he did so, the Temple was lightened by his holiness. He then remarked: "When God returned to Zion, we were as dreamers."

*Y. Taanit, Chap. 3.*

When Alexander of Macedon approached Jerusalem, the Samaritans waited upon him and, describing the loyalty of the Jews to the Persian king, persuaded him to allow them to destroy the city and the Temple.

Simon the Just, on hearing of this, donned his priestly garments and went forth to meet the royal conqueror. When Alexander beheld him, he dismounted and bowed down before him. His general inquired the reason, and Alexander replied: "This man appeared to me in a dream and led me on to victory."

When Alexander learned that the Samaritans had spoken evil of the Holy Man, he gave permission to the Jews to raze the Samaritan Temple. This day was commemorated as the Day of Mount Gerizim, the site of the Samaritan Temple.[1]

*Midrash Lekah Tob to Wayyakhel. Yoma, 69.*
*Megillat Taanit on 25th of Tebet.*

[1] The story has variations in each source.

God is continually working miracles without man's knowing it, in protecting him from unknown evils. But a man should not needlessly expose himself to peril in the expectation that God will miraculously deliver him. God may not do so; and, even if a miracle is wrought for him, the man earns demerit by his presumption.[1]

*Shabbat, 32a.*

[1] Or: having received partial reward for his good deeds by means of his enjoyment of a miracle on his behalf, he receives a diminished reward in Paradise.

### WHATEVER GOD DOES THE RIGHTEOUS CAN DO

What is the meaning of the verse: "The righteous one rules by the fear of the Lord"? This teaches us that whatever God does, the righteous can do. God splits the waters; so did Elijah and Elisha; God withholds the rain; so did Elijah. God brings down the fire; so did Elijah. And as the verse says: "Then the fire of the Lord fell and consumed the burnt offering."

*Debarim Rabbah, 10, 3.*

## 220. MISERS—THE AVARICIOUS

Even birds recognize those who are ungenerous.

*Sotah, 38.*

Birds and fish are not caught in the traps of the ungenerous.[1]

*Midrash Mishle, 1.*

[1] Their bait is poor.

A miser is like a mouse, which lies on coins.

*Sanhedrin, 29.*

Wealthy people frequently are miserly.

*Menahot, 86; Hullin, 46.*

The male fly quarrelled for seven years with his wife, because he sucked the blood of a fat man of Mehuza for seven years and did not invite her to the feast.[1]

*Hullin, 58.*

[1] The Rabbis disliked the miserly residents of Mehuza, the home of Rabba.

At times, an evil spirit is sent to a man because of his sins, and causes him to become a miser. A charity collector visits him, and the spirit objects to his giving. A poor beggar comes to the door; again the spirit protests against the gift of even a mite. If he wishes to enjoy his own money, the spirit intervenes. Hence, all his money is left to be enjoyed by others.

*Zohar, ii, 65a.*

For four reasons does their property pass out of the hands of the avaricious: because they are backward in paying the wages of their hired servants; because they neglect their welfare altogether; because they shift the yoke from themselves and lay the burden upon their neighbors; and because of pride, which is of itself as evil as all the rest put together; whereas of the meek, it is written: "The meek shall inherit the earth." (Psalm 27:11)

*Sukkah, 29b.*

## 221. MITZWOT—LOVE OF

He who loves Mitzwot is not sated with Mitzwot.

*Debarim Rabbah, 2:23.*

Rabbi Eleazar (ben Shammua) said: "The man who fears the Lord, delights greatly in His Commandments." (Psalm 112:1) "In His Commandments, not in the reward of His Commandments."

*Abodah Zarah, 192.*

## 222. MITZWOT—OBSERVANCE OF

Six hundred and thirteen Commandments were transmitted to Moses.

*Makkot, 23.*

Moses taught us six hundred and eleven Mitzwot; the numerical value of the word Torah; and God Himself taught us the first two Commandments in the Decalogue—a total of six hundred and thirteen.

*Pesikta Rabbati, 22:3.*

Mitzwot were given that we may live by them.

*Tosefta Shabbat, 16, end.*

Hast thou already performed all the Mitzwot and only this is left?

*Ekah Rabbah, 1:3.*

I have permitted thee more than I have forbidden thee.

*Wayyikra Rabbah, 22.*

All the Mitzwot, which the Children of Israel perform in this world, come and testify in their favor in the World-to-Come.

*Abodah Zarah, 2.*

He who sits and does not sin is rewarded as if he had performed a Mitzwah.

*Kiddushin, 39.*

May my lot be among those who die as they go forth to perform a Mitzwah.

*Shabbat, 118.*

"This is my God and I will glorify Him" (Ex. 15:2)—glorify Him by observing his Commandments finely: by making a fine Sukkah, a fine synagogue, etc.

*Shabbat, 133.*

If thou hast observed a few Mitzwot, thou wilt end by observing many.

*Shabbat, 133.*

Not the Mishnah is the chief thing, but the practice.

*Sifra Ahare, 18:4.*

The Commandments of the Torah should be performed in a two-fold manner: by the body and by the mind (Kawwanah).

*Zohar, i, 72a.*

Would that they give up discussing Me, and observe instead My Torah!

*Y. Hagigah, 1:7.*

It is better to perform a Mitzwah than to light a candle before God.

*Shemot Rabbah, 37:3.*

God says: "I am Thy watcher; pay Me by observing My ordinances."

*Wayyikra Rabbah, 28:3.*

Every man should perform a Mitzwah in the manner he expects a Sage (a Rabbi) to perform it.

*Pesahim 54, Mishnah.*

Just as a childless man or woman are called barren, so the knowledge of Torah without the observance of its Commandments is called barren. Not the research is the main thing, but the performance; not the theory, but the practice.

*Zohar, iv, 218a.*

What difference does it make to God whether one slaughters the animal at the throat or at the back?
But the Commandments were given to purify the people.

*Tanhuma Shemini, 5.*

We read: "She (namely, Torah) is more precious than rubies, and all things thou canst desire are not to be compared unto her." (Prov. 3:15) Things which thou desirest are not to be compared unto Torah, but Mitzwot desired by God are comparable in importance.

We read further (8:11): "For wisdom is better than rubies, and all things desirable (even by God) are not to be compared unto her." How is this contradiction to be explained? If the Mitzwah can be performed by a person other than the student of Torah, he should not desist from his studies.

*Moed Katan, 9.*

Not every man is able to combine in equal proportions the will and the intention to perform a Mitzwah in perfection. It is for this reason that we pray in the words of the Psalmist (90:17): "And let the graciousness of the Lord be upon us; establish Thou also upon us the work of our hands; Yea, the work of our hands establish Thou it."

*Zohar, ii, 93b.*

He who wishes to prevail for God and His Commandments should not make the endeavor with an empty hand. He should spend on the task according to the substance of his possessions.

*Zohar, ii, 128a.*

The good deeds which a man performs in this world are transformed into threads of light in the other world, and the hosts in Heaven spin them into a garment to clothe him in the After-life.

*Zohar, ii, 229b.*

He who performs Mitzwah extends the boundaries of Heaven.

*Zohar, iii, 113a.*

It is well to spend an extra third to perform a Mitzwah in a more satisfactory manner.

*Baba Kamma, 9.*

Every man should perceive himself as being half good and half evil. By performing one more good act, he becomes a Zaddik; by performing one more evil act, he becomes a man of wickedness.

*Kiddushin, 40.*

Rab said: "Let a man always occupy himself diligently with the study of the Torah and the performance of the Commandments even if it be not for their own sake, for out of performance not for its own sake, comes performance for its own sake."

*Pesahim, 50b.*

### One Mitzwah in Perfection

Rab Nahman prepared a good table for each of the three Sabbath meals. Rab Judah gave his entire mind to his prayer. Rab Huna bar Joshua never went bare-headed. Rab Sheshet never went without Tefillin. Rab Nahman never went without Tzitzit. Abbaye never failed to serve wine when a student had finished a volume. Rabba never retired to slumber without searching for merits among his disciples.

*Shabbat, 117.*

Rabbi Judah ha-Nasi said: "A man should be as careful about a light commandment as about a grave one, since he does not know how they are to be rewarded, nor which has in it for him the issues of life."

*Abot, 2, 1.*

He who does a moral act associates himself with God in His creative work.

*Shabbat, 10a.*

Rabbi Simeon ben Eleazar said: "Greater is he who acts (namely, who is pious) from love than he who acts from fear (of God)."

*Sotah, 31a.*

## 223. MITZWOT—PERFORMANCE IN FEAR AND IN LOVE

A man is respected on High according to the manner in which he performs all positive commandments in fear and in love.[1]

*Tikkune Zohar, T. 70, p. 175b.*

[1] The Kabbalist saying which introduces the benedictions on the performance of a Mitzwah inevitably includes the phrase: "In fear and in love."

Concerning the words: "If they were wise, they would consider this" (Deut. 32, 29), the comment runs: "If Israel would consider the words of the Torah given unto them, no nation or kingdom would have dominion over them. And what does the Torah say to them? "Take upon yourself the yoke of the Kingdom of Heaven, and seek to excel one another in the fear of Heaven; conduct yourselves one toward the other with loving-kindness."

*Sifre on Deut., 32, 29.*

The ritual and ceremonial commandments will be abolished in the future that is to be.

*Niddah, 61b.*

To the statement: "If it (ceremonial observance) has become an empty thing in your life, if it has become meaningless unto you," the Rabbis add: "Know that the fault lies in you, not in it!"

*Y. Peah, chap. 1.*

### UNDERSTANDING THE COMMANDMENTS

Rabbi Simlai said: "Moses gave to Israel six hundred thirteen commandments. David came and comprehended them in eleven. (Psalm 15)

"Isaiah came and comprehended them in six: 'He that walketh righteously, and speaketh uprightly, he that despiseth the gain acquired by oppression, that shaketh out his hands from holding of bribes, that stoppeth his ears from hearing of blood, and shutteth his eyes from looking upon evil, he shall dwell on high.' (Isa. 33:15)

"Micah came and comprehended them in three: 'He has told thee, O man, what is good and what the Lord requireth of thee—only to do justice, to love mercy and to walk humbly with thy God.' (Micah 6:8)

"Isaiah further comprehended them in two: 'Observe justice and do righteousness.' (Isa. 56:1)

"Amos came and comprehended them in one: 'Seek me and live.' " (Amos 5:4)

Another finds the one comprehensive word in Habakkuk: "The righteous man shall live by his faithfulness. (Hab. 2:4)"

*Makkot, 24a.*

From Psalm 111:10: "The first principle of wisdom is the fear (i.e., reverence) of the Lord: all those who do them (the injunctions of God) have good understanding," Rabba deduces: "It is not said: 'who learn them' but 'who do them'; and who do them for their own sake. Whoever does a commandment not for its own sake (from other than a religious motive), it were better for him that he had never been created!"

*Berakot, 17a, below.*

Rabbi Eleazar ben Simeon said: "God has nothing (that He values) in His world save only the fear of Heaven." (What God prizes in men's good works are not the acts themselves, but the religious motive from which they spring.)

*Yalkut Shimeoni on Deut. 10:12.*

Bar Kappara asks: "What short passage is there upon which all the essentials of the Torah depend? 'In all thy ways know (acknowledge) Him, and He will make thy paths straight.' (Prov. 3:6)"

*Berakot, 63a.*

## 224. MITZWOT—REASONS FOR

Why are the reasons for Mitzwot seldom given in the Torah? Because in two cases they were given and Solomon stumbled through this.[1]

*Sanhedrin, 21.*

[1] A king was enjoined not to have too many horses lest he deal with Egypt. Solomon transgressed, and dealt with Egypt. A king should not have many wives, lest they turn his heart to evil. Solomon was guilty of this as well.

We find that the transgression of Jacob's sons in selling Joseph brought it about that Joseph rescued the peoples of several nations from starvation. If their sin availed thus, how much more good did their excellent deeds bring about! What brought about the precept of the half a shekel? The sin of the Golden Calf. If the people's sin resulted in a Mitzwah, how much the more their good deeds.

*Pesikta Rabbati, 10:13.*

Rabbi Johanan ben Zakkai said: "You cannot say, 'These laws appeal to my reason and I shall observe them; those are but futile performances and I do not care to keep them.' We do not know why death makes unclean and why water with the ashes of the red heifer makes clean. It is a decree of the Sovereign King of Kings. God says: 'I have prescribed a statute for you; I have issued a decree to you. You have no right to transgress My decree, for it is written (Num. 19:2): "This is the statute of the law." ' "

*Tanhuma Buber, Hukkat, 26.*

Rab taught that "the Mitzwot were given only for the purpose of disciplining and refining men through their observance."

"What concern is it to God," he continued, "whether the animal is slaughtered in one fashion or another? Know that these laws were given solely as disciplining measures with which to refine those who adhere to them."

*Bereshit Rabbah, 44, 1.*

## 225. MONEY—ITS USE

Three things injure the body: heartache, stomach trouble, and an empty purse, which is the worst.

*Kohelet Rabbah, 7.*

Perform charity and Mitzwot with thy wealth, lest thou fail to do them when thou art without wealth.

*Tanhuma Buber Reeh, 12.*

God is helpful in the home and helpful on the highway.

*Bereshit Rabbah, 16, 2.*

All the members of the body depend upon the heart, and the heart depends upon the purse.

*Y. Terumot, 8, end.*

Why are coins called Zuzim? Because they circulate from hand to hand (zazim).[1]

*Bemidar Rabbah, 22, 8.*

[1] Some say that the word was derived from Zeus, whose image was engraved upon the coin.

He who has the money has the upper hand (in law).

*Baba Metzia, 44, Mishnah.*

I gave thee the money for trade, not to drink liquor with it.

*Baba Kamma, 104.*

People say: "Money is not found for important things, but it is found for unimportant things."

*Hagigah, 5.*

It is the way of God to give riches to a man so that he may assist the needy and perform the commandments. If a man does not act thus and begets pride through his riches, he shall be punished, as it is written: "Riches kept by the owner thereof to his own hurt." (Ecc. 5:12)

*Midrash ha-Neelam, i, 121b.*

Rabbi Simeon ben Yohai visited a friend in Tyre. Before the householder was aware of the visitor's arrival, he said to his servant: "Prepare for the meal a cheaper kind of lentils."

When he observed the guest, he begged him to enter under his roof. Rabbi Simeon noticed with great surprise the rich appointments and costly plate of the dining-room. He said: "And a man who can afford this richness must dine on cheap lentils?"

His host replied: "Rabbi, you and your brothers are respected because of your Torah, but, as for us, if we have no money, who will respect us?"

*Esther Rabbah, 1.*

The Rabbis have taught: "What was engraved on the first coins of Jerusalem? The names, David, or Solomon, on one side; and the words, Jerusalem, the Holy City, on the other side.

"What was engraved on the coins that Abraham circulated? On one side the words, Old Man and Old Woman; on the other side, Young Man and Maiden.

"Joshua circulated coins. They bore the words, Ox, on one side; and Wild-Ox, on the other. (See Deut. 33:17, applicable to Joshua, a descendant of Joseph.)

"David circulated coins. They bore on one side the inscription, A Staff and A Bag; on the other side, Tower.

"Mordecai circulated coins. They bore the words, Sackcloth and Ashes, on one side; and A Golden Crown, on the reverse." [1]

*Baba Kamma, 97; Bereshit Rabbah, 39.*

[1] Most commentators take the above as poetry.


## 226. MOVING

People say: "Moving from house to house brings in its train loss of money; moving from city to city brings loss of health."

*Bereshit Rabbah, 39, 15.*

When a piece of wood is burning and its light is dull, what is done? It is shaken well and its flame becomes bright. Likewise a student frequently becomes bright when moving from one school to another.

*Zohar, iv, 166b.*

## 227. MUNDANE AND SPIRITUAL INTERESTS

Three persons preferred earthly (agricultural) interest to spiritual:
Cain, Noah and Uzziah. This interest proved injurious to them.

*Bereshit Rabbah, 22, 3.*

### THE ORIGIN OF THE ZOHAR

Rabbi Judah ben Ilai, Rabbi Jose ben Halafta and Rabbi Simeon
ben Yohai were sitting together. Rabbi Judah praised the Roman government for the splendid markets, bridges and baths they had erected
in Palestine. Rabbi Jose kept silent. Rabbi Simeon retorted that they
had done so for their own benefit, not for the land's sake.

A disciple incautiously repeated this, and a Roman spy informed
the government. An edict was issued that Rabbi Judah be promoted
to the headship of Jewish assemblies; that Rabbi Jose be banished to
Galilee, and that Rabbi Simeon be executed. Rabbi Simeon and his son,
Rabbi Eleazar, hid in a cave for many years and spent their time there
in mystical studies, laying the foundation for the Zohar and other
works of Kabbalah. When they left the cave, following a change in the
administration of Palestine, they beheld several men engaged in agricultural labor. They exclaimed: "These folk neglect eternal (spiritual)
affairs and trouble themselves with temporal matters."

They then returned to their cave until their minds had grown accustomed to the idea that people should engage in material labor as well
as in spiritual work, and that such is the will of God.

*Shabbat, 33b, paraphrased.*

A landless man is no man; where is his pleasure?

*Yebamot, 63a.*

## 228. MURDER

"Thou shalt not murder."
This means: Thou shalt not cause thy brother's blood to boil with
bitterness because of thine actions.

*Pesikta Rabbati, 25:1.*

He who destroys one soul in Israel is as if he had destroyed the
whole world.

*Sanhedrin, 37, Mishnah.*

Two bandits concealed themselves near a road, and, when an un-
protected person passed by, they would murder him, take his money
away, and hide the corpse in a pit.

Once a caravan passed. Its guide remarked: "This once was a well-
tended road; now grass grows in the middle. Let us investigate."

They found the pit with corpses in it, and, instituting a search, they discovered the bandits. The assassins were seized and eventually executed.

Thus the popular saying was justified: "The end of a thief is the hanging post."

*Wayyikra Rabbah, 23.*

### 229. MUSIC—SONGS

Rabbi Judah said: "In our days the harp (or lyre) had seven strings, as the Psalmist has written: 'By seven daily did I praise Thee.' In the days of the Messiah the harp will have eight, as it is said: 'On the eighth.' (Psalm 6:1) In the World-to-Come, the harp will have ten strings, as it is written (Psalm 33:2): 'With the harp of ten strings sing unto Him.'"

*Pesikta Rabbati, 21, 1.*

When Serah, the daughter of Asher, was sent to bring to Jacob in song the tidings that Joseph still lived, she sang thus:

> "Joseph be-Mitzrayyim
> Yuldu lo al birkayim
> Manasseh we-Ephrayim." [1]

*Midrash ha-Gadol, 672.*

[1] "Joseph in Egypt
Is bringing up on his knees
Manasseh and Ephraim."

What is service with joy? Song.

*Arakin, 11.*

There is no profit in singing a poem to him who cannot understand.

*Petihta Ekah Rabbati, 12.*

The sweetest of poems does not enter into the ears of those troubled in heart.

*Ibid.*

Songs of sailors and shepherds are better than the songs of weavers.

*Sotah, 48.*

The song that pleases the nobles does not please the weavers.

*Yoma, 20.*

He who wishes to chant to God in a loud voice should possess a voice pleasant to others; if not, he should refrain from prayer aloud.

*Zohar, i, 249b.*

Why were the Levites selected to sing in the Temple? Because the name Levi means cleaving. The soul of him who heard their singing at once cleaved to God.

*Zohar, ii, 19a.*

The joy of the heart begets song.

*Zohar, ii, 93a.*

There is a Temple in Heaven that is opened only through song.

*Tikkune Zohar, p. 45a.*

How was Solomon, the wisest man in the world, misled by his wives to the worship of idols? By means of music.

The daughter of Pharaoh, Solomon's favorite wife, brought with her a thousand different kinds of musical instruments, and ordered that they be played for Solomon. "Thus do we play for Osiris, and thus for Ophais." Solomon was charmed and his sense were beguiled.

*Bemidbar Rabbah, 10.*

## 230. NAMES

The majority of Jews in exile had names like Gentiles.

*Gittin, 11.*

Why did Amram call his daughter Miriam? Because with her birth began the bitterness of the exile in Egypt.[1]

*Pesikta Rabbati, 15, 11.*

[1] Miriam means "bitter things."

God, Israel, Jerusalem and Torah have seventy names each.

*Midrash Ha-Gadol, i, 678.*
*Baal Ha-Turim to Numbers, 11:16.*

## 231. NATURE—ITS LAWS

There is no rectangular thing in creation.

*Y. Nedarim, 3, 2.*

The natural laws of the Universe do not change.

*Midrash ha-Neelam, i, 138b.*

Why is the sun called Shemesh? Because it is the Shamash (servant) of the world.

*Midrash Tadshe, 20.*

If thou canst not comprehend the way of the thunder, how canst thou expect to comprehend the way of the Universe?

*Bereshit Rabbah, 12.*

Three things take in profusion and give in profusion: the sea, the earth and the government.

*Wayyikra Rabbah, 4, 2.*

## 232. NINTH OF AB
### (See Also Jerusalem)

In the Days-to-Come God will turn the Ninth of Ab into a day of joy.

*Yalkut Shimeoni Ekah, 998.*

He who fails to mourn over Jerusalem on the Ninth of Ab shall not behold the time of rejoicing.

*Taanit, 30b.*

When God commanded Jeremiah to preach concerning Judah, he exclaimed: "Thou art immodest, my mother, thou art over-richly dressed, and thou art searching for lovers."

The mother of Jeremiah said: "What is this thou sayest, my son?"

He answered: "It is not thee, O mother, not thee, but Jerusalem and Judah that I have in mind." He continued: "O Lord, Thou knowest well that I am but a youth. How can I preach concerning grey-beards?"

God answered: "It is the youth whom I love. When Israel was yet a youthful nation, an unsophisticated people, I then loved him." (Hosea 11:1)

Jeremiah said: "I am likened to a Kohen who is commanded to test the woman whose husband is jealous: before he gives her the bitter drink, he lifts her veil, and, behold, it is his own mother. He exclaims: 'I wished to honor you my whole life, yet now I bring you to shame.'"

*Pesikta Rabbati, 27.*

When the exiled multitude with Jeremiah reached the Euphrates, he took leave of them, and they wept copiously. He said: "I bear witness by Heaven and by earth that if you had but once wept at my prophecy and heeded my words, you would not have been exiled."

*Pesikta Rabbati, 27.*

When Jeremiah returned to Jerusalem he fell asleep in weariness. In his dream he beheld a beautiful woman seated on a hill, dressed in mourning, with hair dishevelled and bitterly weeping. Jeremiah commenced to weep, and approaching her, said: "Thy lot cannot be worse than the lot of our mother, Zion."

And she said: "In truth, I am thy mother, Zion. How could I be comforted?"

Jeremiah said: "Job was smitten and in the end was doubly repaid. So shall it be with thee, O Zion."

*Pesikta Rabbati, 27 end.*

"Hear ye the word of the Lord (Jer. 2:4): If ye hearken, ye shall eat the rich crops which your land has brought forth; if not, others will consume them. If ye hearken, ye shall hear good tidings; if not, evil. If ye hearken, God will be your Father; if not, your Master."

Jeremiah said: "Ye have not obeyed a single commandment. If ye hearken and obey at least the commandment of the Sabbath, ye will not be exiled. But the people refused."

*Pesikta Rabbati, 28.*

A father fashioned some choice pearls into a beautiful necklace, and presented it to his daughter. Later when she disobeyed her father, he took the necklace and tied her hands with it.

Likewise God had twenty-two holy letters, fashioned from them the Torah, and gave it to Israel. When Israel grew disobedient, God took the twenty-two letters and prompted Jeremiah to fashion a lamentation out of them.

*Pesikta Rabbati, 30, 5.*

Elijah was loyal to God, but not to Israel, and he was commanded to surrender his power to Elisha. Jonah was loyal to Israel, but not to God, and his prophetic power was taken from him. But Jeremiah was loyal to both. He declared that Israel was rebellious, but God was harsh, and his prophecy was extended.

*Pesikta Rabbati, 30, 5.*

" 'Comfort ye, comfort ye, My people,' saith your God." (Isaiah 40:1). The prophets were sent to comfort Zion and were not accepted. Zion saith: "Yesterday ye cursed me; how can I believe your words of comfort any more than your words of calamity?"

Then God said: "I shall comfort Zion Myself."

The words: "Comfort ye, My People" may also be interpreted in this fashion: When robbers destroy a vineyard, is not its owner comforted by his friends? "Ye are My vineyard, comfort Me."

*Pesikta Rabbati, 30, 7 and 8.*

## 233. NON-JEWS AND JEWS

What caused Israel to be dispersed among the nations? The friendliness which Israel sought among them.

*Pesahim, 118.*

Whatever robberies non-Jews commit against Jews, they do not consider to be thefts, but acts of justice.

*Bemidbar Rabbah, 10, 2.*

God says: "To Me Israel appears as honest and faithful as doves, but to the nations Israel appears to be as subtle and crooked as serpents."

*Shir ha-Shirim Rabbah, 2.*

If thou hast habituated thy tongue to speak evil of thy brother who is not of thy own nation, thou wilt end by speaking evil of thine own nation.

*Debarim Rabbah, 6, 9.*

Israel said to God: During Sukkoth we offer seventy sacrifices for the welfare of the seventy nations because of our love for them. By right they should return our love. Instead, however, they hate us.

*Tanhuma Phineas, 17.*

"And he (Israel) was a nation there"—they were distinguished as a separate nation in Egypt by their raiment, their speech, their food, etc.

*Pesikta Zutarta Tabo.*

Deeds of mercy are the Gentiles' sin-offering, reconciling them with God.

*Baba Batra, 10b.*

The heathen is thy neighbor, thy brother; to wrong him is a sin.

*Tana d'be Eliyahu, p. 284.*

To cheat a Gentile is even worse than cheating a Jew, for besides being a violation of the moral law, it brings Israel's religion into contempt, and desecrates the name of Israel's God.

*Baba Kama, 113b.*

The Jew is recommended to resort to the aid of Gentiles in administering the affairs of his community.

*Y. Gittin, 5, 9.*

When the Jews prosper, the Gentiles say: "We are your cousins." But when the Jews are in tribulation, the Gentiles add to it.

*Bereshit Rabbah, 37.*

R. Berechiah said: "When Jacob dreamed of the ladder ascending into Heaven, he saw Babylon, Persia, Greece and Rome ascend and fall. Then God said: 'Jacob, ascend thou now.' But Jacob hesitated and asked. 'Will I not fall, O Lord, as they have fallen?' The Lord replied: 'You shall not fall.' Nevertheless, Jacob still disbelieved and was in no hurry to ascend. God then permitted other non-Jewish nations to ascend to power while Israel continued to be the victim of harsh treatment. Jacob then cried out: 'Have I lost for my descendants the chance for all time to ascend?' 'Nay,' answered God, 'in the end your people too will ascend and will not fall.' "

*Pesikta Rabbati, 23.*

"God is Israel's lover; and, when moved by Israel's praises of His Beauty, the nations say: 'We will come with you, as it is written: "Whither has thy lover gone, thou fairest among women?" (Song of Songs 6:1), the Israelites reply: 'You have no part in Him, as it is written: "I am my lover's and My lover is mine" (Song of Songs 6:3).' "

*Sifre Deut. 343 (ed. Friedman, 143a).*

A pagan was distributing charity, and, accosting R. Akiba, said: "I am greater than thee, for I love charity. God loves me in return and places me in a high position."

R. Akiba said: "God loves only Israel and rewards only them in a worthwhile fashion."

The pagan departed, wondering.

Later R. Akiba beheld several athletes competing in a jumping contest. R. Akiba noticed the pagan, who had previously accosted him, and said: "If I jump highest, will I receive the largest prize?"

The pagan answered: "Do you not know that only those may receive a prize who wear the official athlete's badge of the king."

R. Akiba then remarked: "When you left me the other day, you thought that I was unjust. Now you can see that I was right. Circumcision is the badge of God, and he who does not wear it cannot receive a prize even if he does more charity than a Jew."

*Yelamdenu, quoted in Or Zarua.*

Said R. Isaac: A negress met another servant girl while drawing water from the well, and said: "Here is news! My Master intends to divorce his wife. Perchance he will marry me."

"And why do you think he will divorce her?"

"Because she gave him his food with black hands, and he is fastidious."

"Use your intelligence," said her friend. "If your master dislikes his wife for serving him once with black hands, how would he be able to endure you who are black throughout?"

By the same token, the nations say to Israel: "You have sinned and your God will divorce you and marry us instead."

But Israel replies: "If he has disliked us for abandoning His Mitzwot briefly, how much the more will he dislike you who have never accepted His Mitzwot and never performed His precepts."

*Shir ha-Shirim Rabbah, 1.*

A Jew became an intimate friend of a Gentile. When in time the Gentile requested the hand of the Jew's daughter, it was granted him. The girl, however, on learning this, went up to the roof and threw herself down. A Heavenly Voice called out: "Who hath counted the dust of Jacob, or numbered the stock of Israel? Let me die the death of the righteous, and let mine end be like his!" (Num. 23:10)

*Eliyahu Rabbah, 21.*

"Thy body is like a heap of wheat fenced about with lilies" (Song of Songs, 7:3). Why is Israel likened to wheat? As the farmer does not ask his overseer how many heaps of hay, straw, or thorns he has brought into the storehouse, but how many heaps of wheat, so God does not ask for the count of the idol-worshipping nations, but only the number of the Children of Israel.

The grain-stalk and the grain-ear argued that each of them was the more important. When the harvest came, the stalk was burned, but the ears were saved. Thus Israel and the Gentiles argued that each of them is the more important. When the Judgment Day comes, Israel will be saved and the Gentiles will receive their punishment.

*Pesikta Rabbati, 10, 4.*

An old man met Elijah and asked him: "Will there be any non-Jews in the Messianic Era?"

Elijah replied: "Yes, all the nations who have persecuted and done evil unto Israel will behold Israel's rejoicing and then will perish from envy, but those who did not persecute Israel will live throughout the entire Era and labor for Israel. (Isaiah 61:5) And at the conclusion of the Messianic period in the new World-to-Come, then too, they will not share equally with Israel. If the uncircumcised could not eat of the Pascal Lamb with Israel, how much the more logical is it to say that they will not enjoy the Holy of Holies that will then come. A distinct section will be set aside for them apart from Israel."

*Tanna de-Be Eilyahu Rabbah, 22.*

The Rabbis have taught: "For the sake of peaceful intercourse or for the sake of the Torah whose ways are ways of peace, the non-Jewish poor may gather unharvested produce left over in Jewish fields, in the same fashion as the Jewish poor. The non-Jewish poor shall receive food and garments from Jewish charity funds the same as Jews. If the non-Jewish sick have no friends, they should be visited the same as the Jewish sick. If no one claims the body of the non-Jewish dead, they should be buried by Jews, the same as the Jewish dead. When a Jew sees a non-Jew at work in the field, he should greet him with words of blessing, even in the forbidden seventh year when a Jewish worker should be shunned."

*Gittin, 61.*

## 234. NON-JEWS—GENTILES

Even an idolator who studies Torah is like the High Priest.

*Baba Kamma, 38.*

It is forbidden to rob the idolator.

*Y. Baba Metzia, 2, 5.*

Even an idolator can be a Zaddik.

*Bemidbar Rabbah, 8, 2.*

Even a non-Jew who speaks words of wisdom is called a wise man.

*Megillah, 16.*

We should be pleased that the Gentiles enjoy the theater and acquire there an amiable mood. Thus they avoid conversation with each other that leads to fighting.

*Bereshit Rabbah, 80, 1.*

The Gentiles live by the presence among them of thirty just men.

*Hullin, 92.*

The just among the Gentiles are priests of God.

*Eliyahu Zuta, 20.*

The righteous among the Gentiles will have a share in the World-to-Come.

*Yalkut Shimeoni, Prophets, Section 296.*

If they say to thee that there is wisdom among the Gentiles, believe them. But, if they say that there is Torah among them, disbelieve.

*Ekah Rabbati, 2, 13.*

He who befriends the Gentile and brings him to Israel is as if he had given him birth.

*Bereshit Rabbah, 39, 14.*

Said R. Alexanderi: "God saith to the Gentiles: 'Be not afraid to come near Me even if thou hast offended greatly. Have I not accepted in My fold Rahab, the harlot, who married Joshua and had fine descendants? Have I not received Jethro, the Pagan Priest, whose daughter married Moses, our greatest man? Have I not promised that the Messiah will descend from Ruth, the Moabitess?' "

*Pesikta Rabbati, 41, 3.*

Rabbi Jose ben Halafta taught: "In the Time-to-Come (the Messianic Age) the heathen will come to Israel as proselytes."

*Abodah Zara, 3b.*

Rabbi Meir said: " 'Ye shall therefore keep My statutes and My ordinances, which, if a man do, he shall live by them' (Lev. 18:5). It is not said that priests, Levites and Israelites shall live by them, but 'a man'; therefore, even a Gentile."

*Sanhedrin, 59a.*

Rabbi Joshua ben Hananiah said: "It is written (Psalm 9:18): 'The wicked shall return to Sheol, all the Gentiles, who forgot God.' This implies that there are righteous men in the nations of the world (the Gentiles), who have a portion in the World-to-Come."

*Tos. Sanhedrin, 13, 2.*

Diocletian fed hogs near Tiberias. The school-children leaving school would laugh at him and abuse him. As time passed, however, the hog raiser became a soldier in the Roman legion, then a general, and, by a turn of fortune, he was elected Emperor. He resolved to punish the Jews for tormenting him in his youth. On his arrival in Palestine, he stopped at the walled city of Paneas. From there he sent a messenger on Friday afternoon commanding that the Patriarch Rabbi Judah II come to him on Sunday morning. The Patriarch did not know how he could travel from Tiberias and reach Paneas by Sunday morning without desecrating the Sabbath. As luck would have it, a swift equipage passed Tiberias at sunset on Saturday, and the Patriarch took a seat on it. Travelling at a rapid pace all night and all morning, the equipage halted at the Emperor's palace a few moments before noon. The Emperor was impressed by the fortunate coincidence, and said:

"I see that your God has not altogether forsaken you. Is this a reason, however, for tormenting the young Roman?"

The Patriarch answered: "We were guilty of tormenting a feeder of hogs, but we are the most loyal subjects of the Emperor."

The Emperor remarked: "Be careful even of a Roman youngster. He may be destined to become Emperor."

*Bereshit Rabbah, 63.*

Rabbi Jeremiah said: "If you ask whence we learn that even a Gentile who obeys the Torah is like the High Priest, the answer is found in the words: 'Which if a man do, he shall live by them.'

"Again it is said: 'This is the Torah of mankind, Lord God' (II Sam. 7:19);[1] not 'This is the Torah of priests, Levites and lay Israelites,' but 'of mankind.'

"Again, 'Open the gates that a righteous Gentile keeping faithfulness may enter by it' (Psalm 118:20); not 'priests' etc.

"It does not say: 'Rejoice, ye priests, etc., but, 'Rejoice ye righteous, in the Lord' (Psalm 33:11).

"It does not say: 'Do good, O Lord, to the priests,' etc., but: 'Do good, O Lord, to the good.' (Psalm 125:4)

"Hence it follows that even a Gentile who obeys the Torah is like the High Priest."

*Sifra on Lev. 18:5.*

[1] Literal translation of the Hebrew.

God foreknew that the Gentiles would not receive the Torah, but He offered it to them that they might have no ground to impugn His justice. It is not His way to punish without such justification; He does not deal tyrannously with His creatures.

*Pesikta Buber, 200a.*

To rob or defraud a Gentile is worse than to rob an Israelite "on account of the profanation of the Name"—the Israelite lays the wrong to the individual; the Gentile blames the religion.

*Tosefta Baba Kamma, 10, 15.*

Rabbi Johanan said: "Seven laws are binding on the descendants of Noah (Gentiles): establishment of courts of justice; blasphemy prohibition; prohibition of the worship of other gods, of murder, of incest and adultery, of theft and robbery, and of eating the flesh of a living animal before it dies."

*Sanhedrin, 56a.*

"The Lord loveth the righteous" (Psalm 146:8); as He also saith: "I love them that love Me." (Prov. 8:170)

The righteous are not a father's house. Even a Gentile can become a righteous one; as it is said: "Ye that fear the Lord, bless ye the Lord." (Psalm 135:20); not "the house of those who fear the Lord." Of their own accord they offered themselves and loved the Lord; therefore the Lord loves them.

*Bemidbar Rabbah, 8, 2.*

The Torah was given in the desert, given with all publicity in a place to which no one had any claim, lest, if it were given in the land of Israel, the Jews might deny to the Gentiles any part in it.

*Mekilta on Exodus, 19, 2.*

The Torah was given in the desert, in fire and in water, things which are free to all who are born into the world. It was revealed at Sinai, not in one language, but in four (or in seventy)—in Hebrew, Edomic (Roman), Arabic and Aramaic. But the nations refused the Torah because it forbade the sins to which they were by heredity addicted; murder, adultery and robbery.

*Seifre, Dent., Friedman, 14.*

## 235. OATHS

He who responds "Amen" after an oath is as if he had pronounced it.

*Shebuot, 29.*

It is not proper to swear even to the truth.

*Tanhuma Wayyikra, 7.*

That which cannot be destroyed by fire or by water is destroyed by a false oath.

*Shebuot, 39.*

What oath is desirable? If the Evil Impulse is misleading thee away from the performance of a commandment, take an oath that thou wilt perform it.

*Zohar, ii, 91b.*

In a year of famine a man left a gold dinar for safe-keeping with a woman neighbor. She carelessly placed it in a flour box and forgot about it. Later she poured flour into the box and used it to bake bread. One loaf she gave to a poor beggar. Immediately after the beggar's departure the man came for his gold piece. The woman recalled where she had placed it and broke open the loaves, but she did not find the coin. She then understood that it must have been in the loaf she had given away, and she swore: "May a child of mine die if I received any use from the money."

A child, however, did die, since she received a minimum of use in saving the dough in the space of the coin.

*Gittin, 35.*

R. Eliezer said: "Yea is an oath and nay is an oath." [1]

*Shebuot, 36a.*

[1] Your word should be as sacred to you as your oath.

The third commandment prohibits unnecessary swearing. The inhabitants of a certain district were accustomed to swear in God's name when there was no necessity for it, and the district was destroyed.

It also prohibits swearing to a literal truth which is not a real truth. For example, Bar Talmion received for safe-keeping a hundred dinars. When their return was asked, he offered to swear in court that he had already returned the sum. He carried with him a thick cane and asked the plaintiff in court to hold it for him while he uttered the oath. He swore: "All that you gave me, I have returned to you."

The plaintiff was enraged and hurled the cane to the floor. Lo, the cane split and the hundred dinars rolled out from inside.

A third prohibition included in the third commandment is to swear of one's own accord when not ordered to do so in court, even if the oath be altogether truthful. A woman baking bread with a neighbor had in the pocket of her apron two dinars, which fell into the dough unnoticed by anyone. When the woman asked the neighbor if she had seen the money, she jumped up and swore: "May my child die if I saw the coins!"

Her child sickened and died. The other woman brought her a loaf of bread for the first mourning meal, at which one's own food must not be eaten. They broke open the loaf and found the money. It was then declared: "Whether guilty or innocent, do not utter an oath."

*Pesikta Rabbati, piska, 22.*

## 236. OCCUPATIONS

The verse: "And a threefold cord is not quickly broken" (Ecc. 4:12) applies to him who occupies himself with Scripture, with the Oral Law and with practical ways of the world.

*Kiddushin, 40.*

He who does not occupy himself either with the Written Law, the Oral Law or the useful occupations of society is not a civilized man.

*Kiddushin, 41.*

It was a current saying of the Rabbis of Jamnia (Jabneh): "I am a creature (a human being), and my fellow is a creature: my work is in town and his work is in the field; I rise early to do my work, and he to his. As he does not esteem his occupation superior to mine, so I do not esteem mine superior to his. Perhaps you may say that I accomplish much and he little, but we are taught: 'It matters not whether much or little, if only a man directs his mind to heaven.' "

*Berakot, 17a.*

## 237. OPPORTUNITY

While the fire is burning, slice your pumpkin and fry it.

*Sanhedrin, 33.*

If a bone falls to thy share, whether good or bad, pick it up.[1]

*Tikkune Zohar, T. 65.*

[1] Seize your opportunity even though it be small.

The closed door does not open soon.

*Baba Kamma, 80.*

Opportunity falls into the hands of him who is receptive towards it.

*Yalkut to Shemot, 168.*

## 238. ORDINATION—SEMIKAH

### THE RITE OF ORDINATION

Rabbi Aha ben Rabbah asked Rabbi Ashi: "When a student of the Law is ordained, do those who ordain him actually lay their hands upon him?"

Rabbi Ashi replied: "They pronounce him Rabbi and grant him authority to command the payment of fines."

Rab said: "Were it not for Rabbi Judah ben Baba, there would have been no one with authority to levy fines, since only he who has been ordained may ordain another. Once the government forbade ordination on penalty of death to all participants. What did Rabbi Judah ben Baba do? He went to a desolate place and there ordained Rabbi Meir, Rabbi Judah, Rabbi Simeon, Rabbi Jose and Rabbi Eleazar ben Shammua, whom their Master, Rabbi Akiba, had no opportunity to ordain. (Some add Rabbi Nehemiah.) When the enemy became aware of this proceeding, Rabbi Judah ben Baba bade the Rabbis to flee. They asked him: 'What will become of thee?' He answered: 'I am a man of great age, and hope to die for the welfare of Israel.' He was later slain."

*Sanhedrin, 13.*

### RULES FOR ORDINATION

Rabbi Abba said: "Formerly a Master ordained his pupils. Later the practice was instituted that a Master should not ordain without the Patriarch's permission, but the Patriarch might ordain pupils on his own authority. Still later the regulation was adopted that neither the Masters without the Patriarch's authority, nor the Patriarch without the Masters' authority might ordain."

Abbaye asked Rabbi Joseph: "Whence cometh the rule that three Masters are required to ordain?"

The question remained unanswered. Rabbi Joshua ben Levi said: "There is no ordination permitting the levying of fines outside of Palestine."

*Y. Sanhedrin, 1; Sanhedrin, 13-14.*

## ONE OUT OF A THOUSAND

The Midrash, in comment upon the verse: "I have found one man out of a thousand" says: "Such is the way of the world: a thousand enter for the study of the Bible, but only a hundred pass from it to the study of the Mishnah. Ten of these proceed to the study of the Talmud, and only one of the last attains to ordination as Rabbi."

*Kohelet Rabbah to 7, 28.*

## 239. ORNAMENTS

An ornament looks beautiful only on a beautiful body.

*Y. Nedarim, 9.*

The ornament of a man is his Torah; the ornament of Torah is wisdom; the ornament of wisdom is humility; the ornament of humility is fear; the ornament of fear is doing Mitzwot; the ornament of a Mitzwah is modesty in the performance of it.

*Derek Eretz Zuta, 5.*

## 240. ORPHAN

It is a Mitzwah for the orphan to pay his father's debts.

*Ketubot, 91.*

Who does charity all the time? He who adopts an orphan boy and an orphan girl, and marries one to the other.

When it comes to the marriage of an orphan girl, there should be no stint of the money spent from the charity chest, but the girl should have a wedding suitable to her class.

Once before a festival an orphan girl came to Rabbi Ammi and said: "I am about to be married and I have no money for the wedding."

Rabbi Ammi wished to delay her case until after the holyday and give the money in the charity box to the poor for holyday expenses. R. Zeira protested, saying: "If you delay the wedding, perhaps her groom will wed another, and you will cause her to lose her happiness. Rather give her all she needs, and the Lord who has ordered holydays will send other monies for the poor."

*Ketubot, 50; Y. Ketubot, 6.*

## 241. OUTWARDNESS—INWARDNESS

The fool sees but the outer garment of a person; the wise man sees his inner garment—his character.

*Zohar, iv, 152a.*

Our generation sees only the face.

*Sotah, 47.*

A "Talmid Hakam" (student of the Torah) should be like the ark which was plated with pure gold within and without.

Rabba said: "A student who is not inwardly what he is outwardly is no student."

*Yoma, 72b.*

Rabbi Benjamin said: "There are hypocrites of learning. It is supposed by people that they are Biblical and Talmudical scholars, but they are not. They wrap their Tallit about them and have their Tefillin on their head, 'and behold the tears of the oppressed, and they have no comforter.'" (Ecc: 4:1)

*Kohelet Rabbah to 4, 1.*

## 242. OVERGRASPING

He who strives to attain that which is not for him loses that which was intended for him.

*Zohar, iv, 176a.*

If you grasp much, you cannot keep hold of it; if you grasp little, you can hold fast to it.

*Rosh ha-Shanah, 4.*

## 243. PARENTS—HONORING OF

Honor thy father and thy mother after their death even more than during their lifetime.

If a son walks in evil ways, he shows contempt for his departed parents.

*Zohar, iii, 115a.*

A son should lighten the burden of his father and place himself in accord with his will.

*Raia Mehemna, iv, 215b.*

Whether thou hast wealth or not, honor thy parents.

*Y. Peah, 1, 1.*

When a son respects his parents, God accounts it as if the son respected God as well; but, when a son vexes his parents, God saith: "I cannot abide thee."

*Kiddushin, 30.*

A man honors his mother more than his father; therefore, God has placed the father first in the commandment to honor. A man fears his father more than his mother; therefore, the mother is placed first in the commandment to fear.

*Kiddushin, 30 and 31.*

Honor thy father and thy mother, even as thou honorest God; for all three have been partners in thy creation.

*Zohar, iii, 93a.*

Because Esau respected his father, his descendants rule the world.

*Zohar, i, 146b.*

Said R. Nehunya: "What delayed the glory of Jacob? The honoring of Isaac by Esau."

R. Simeon b. Gamaliel said: "When I served my father, I served him in my old garments, but Esau served his father in his finest raiment."

*Pesikta Rabbati, 24 end.*

He who does not sustain his parents testifies to his own illegitimacy.

*Eliyahu Rabbah, 26.*

Rab Joseph, hearing the step of his mother as she entered, would say: "I must stand up, as the Shekinah enters."

*Kiddushin, 31.*

Rab Dimi narrated: "Once Dama ben Netinah, a pagan, was seated in the uniform of a general among the nobles of Rome. His mother tore off his epaulets and spat in his face. He said nothing. His mother's overshoes later fell off; he picked them up and handed them to her."

*Ibid.*

Once the Sanhedrin needed a certain gem for the Temple. They went to buy it from Dama ben Netinah and offered him a hundred dinars. He said: "My father is asleep in my stock-room, and I cannot now wake him."

The emissaries of the Sanhedrin were in haste and offered him more, but he refused. When they came again, he offered them the gem for one hundred dinars, saying: "I will not accept more. Shall I sell for profit the honor I pay my parent?"

*Y. Peah, chap. 1.*

Rab Jacob bar Abbuha asked Abbaye: "When I come from the academy, my father pours me a drink and my mother mixes it. May I accept it?"

Abbaye replied: "You may take it from your mother but not from your father, for he is not only your father but also your teacher in Torah."

*Kiddushin, 31.*

Once a man gave his father several fat chickens. The father asked: "My son, can you afford this?"

The son replied: "Eat, my father, what you are given and ask no questions."

Another man was grinding meal. An official came to enlist a member of the family to perform certain work for the government. The son said: "Do the grinding, my father, and I shall go. Thus will you avoid the discomforts of public labor."

The Sages said: "The first fed his parent well, yet his lot will be in Gehenna. The second made his father perform hard labor, yet his lot will be in Eden."

*Y. Peah, 1.*

R. Tarfon had an aged mother. When she went up to her high bed or came down, he would bend over and she would use his body to make the ascent or descent. When R. Tarfon sickened, his mother said: "Pray for him because he honors me more than enough."

The Sages said: "Even many times this action is not enough."

R. Ishmael's mother complained that her son was not doing her will.

"What is thy will?" she was asked.

"That he let me wash his feet for him."

They told R. Ishmael: "If this be her will, thou must submit to it."

*Kiddushin, 31.*

Rab Assi's aged mother asked for ornaments. He gave them to her. She wished to marry, and he said that he would look for a suitable man. She said: "But I wish a man as handsome as thou."

Thereupon he left her and went to Palestine.

*Kiddushin, 31.*

R. Joshua ben Ilem dreamed that his neighbor in Paradise would be Nanas, the meat-dealer. He visited him to inquire what good deeds he was performing to deserve a high place in Paradise. The dealer said: "I know not, but I have an aged father and mother who are helpless; I give them food and drink, and wash and dress them daily."

The Rabbi said: "I will be happy to have thee as my neighbor in Paradise."

*Midrash quoted in Seder ha-Dorot.*

Dear to God is the honoring of father and mother, for the Scripture employs the same expressions about honoring, revering, or cursing parents, as about honoring, revering, or cursing God. The rewards attached to them are equivalent. It is logical that father, mother and God should be thus joined, for they are, so to speak, partners in bringing the child into life.

*Mekilta de-Rabbi Simeon ben Yohai on Exodus, 20, 12*

When a man honors his father and his mother, God says: "I impute it to you as if I were dwelling among you and you honored Me."

When a man has been spiteful to his father and his mother, God says: "I have done well not to dwell among them, for, if I dwelt among them, they would be spiteful to Me."

*Kiddushin, 30b-31a.*

A man came to a Rabbi and asked him this question: "Why did the early generations live so long?"

The Rabbi replied: "Adam lived nearly a thousand years because God told him that he would die on the day of his sin, and God's day lasts a thousand years. If his son Seth had not lived almost as long, Adam would have had no one to care for him during his declining years, for a grandson usually does not feel bound to support a grandfather. And so it was until Noah came. He was willing to support all his forefathers alive in his time. Therefore, after the Flood, the years of men diminished."

*Tanna de-Be Eliyahu Rabbah, 16.*

A man once overheard his wife admit that one of her two sons was the child of a lover. The husband took this greatly to heart and fell ill. Before he died he informed some friends of his wife's infidelity, and asked that his property be given to his true son only. The friends went to Rabbi Banaah and asked what to do. The Rabbi said: "Let the two sons take canes and beat upon the grave of their father until he appears to them in a dream and tells them which son is truly his own."

The real son refused thus to dishonor the grave of his father, whereas the other was willing to do so. The Rabbi thereupon gave the father's property to the son who had protested against the desecration.

*Baba Batra, 58.*

Rabbi Simeon ben Yohai said: "Great is the honoring of father and mother, for God makes more of it than of honoring Himself. About God, it is written: 'Honor the Lord with thy substance' (Prov. 3:9); if you have substance, you are obligated to do so, and if you have no substance, you are not obligated. But, when it comes to honoring father and mother, whether you have substance or not, 'Honor thy father and thy mother,' even if you have to beg your living from door to door."

*Yer. Peah, 15d, top.*

## 244. PEACE

If there be no quarreling among men, God's judgment does not touch them.

*Zohar, i, 76b.*

"Seek peace and pursue it," namely, seek it in your own place and pursue it in another.

*Y. Peah, 1, 1.*

Blessings do not in the least avail unless peace is included among them.

*Bemidbar Rabbah, 11, 17.*

I beg of you to deal kindly each with the other, so that you may enjoy peace in the government.

*Baba Batra, 90.*

A man should be prudent in fear, and should remember that a soft answer turns away wrath and increases peace.

*Berakot, 17.*

God found no vessel to hold a blessing for Israel, only peace.

*Uktzin, end of Talmud.*

Food and drink may abound, but, if there is no peace, they are as naught.

*Sifra Behukotai.*

Peace is equal to all else.

*Sifra Behukotai.*

Were it not that God determined that there should be peace on earth, the sword and the wild beasts would desolate the world.

*Baraita de-Perek ha-Shalom.*

The Torah enjoins us not to run after a Mitzwah, but to perform it only if it comes to us. With regard to peace, however, it enjoins us to pursue it.

*Bemidbar Rabbah, 19, 27.*

Great is peace! Hateful is quarreling!

*Sifre to Nasso, 2.*

Great is peace; God even changed truth for its sake.

*Yebamot, 65.*

Great is peace; if it abides even among idolators, evil cannot approach them.

*Sifre to Nasso, 42.*

The school of Shammai promulgated their own regulations with reference to many laws of the Torah. The school of Hillel held their own opinions opposite to those of Shammai's disciples. Yet they were friendly each to the other and respected each other's opinions. Their families intermarried, they ate at each other's tables and never sought to mislead one another, as it is written: "Love ye both truth and peace." (Zech. 8:19)

*Tosefta Yebamot, 1, 3.*

Great is peace! All blessings, all favors and all comforts that God brings upon Israel end with peace. In the Shema Evening Service the final words are: "Yea, spread over us the tabernacle of Thy peace." (Singer, p. 114)

The Amidah Service finishes with the words: "Who makest peace." [1]

[1] Singer, p. 95.

The blessing of the Kohanim ends with the phrase: "And give thee peace." (Num. 6:26)

And the Torah is described in the words: "Her paths are peace." (Prov. 3:17)

*Bemidbar Rabbah, 11.*

These things were instituted for the sake of peace and tranquillity: whenever the Torah Scroll is read in the synagogue, the Kohen reads the first portion, the Levite the second, and the Israelite the third. The Erub of the Courtyard should always be left in the yard of the same home, so that there may be no argument. Rabbi Joshua said: "Why do we have an Erub in the courtyard after we already have an Erub in a place which contains several yards? Because it promotes peace between the dwellers in the houses of the yard."

A woman, who disliked her neighbor, sent a little flour by her small son for the Erub which was placed in the home of her neighbor. The latter woman kissed the boy tenderly, and the lad told his mother of it. The mother thought to herself: "She loves me, though I dislike her," and they made peace.

When a rivulet flows from higher to lower ground, the pits of those owning land above should first be filled and then those below for the

Rab Simi said: "Let me irrigate thy land by day and thou wilt have time to teach me after session.

"Agreed," said Abbaye.

Rab Simi played a trick upon the other land-owners. To those on higher ground he said: "Those below should fill their pits first"; to those on lower ground he said the opposite. Thus he quickly filled Abbaye's pits, since they were on middle ground, and after this he opened the dam, allowing the remainder of the water from the rivulet to flow down. When Abbaye heard of this, he refused to eat the fruits of his land during that year.

*Gittin, 59, and Y. Erubin, 3, 7.*

Great is peace! God created no finer virtue in His world.
sake of peace. Rab Simi bar Ashi asked Abbaye to give him special lessons in Torah. Abbaye said: "By day I have my regular teaching, and

*Bemidbar Rabbah, 11, 17.*

after the session I go out to take care of the irrigation of my land."

Great is peace! God enjoined his Holy Name to be erased in the water of bitterness in order that there might be reconciliation between man and wife.

*Bemidbar Rabbah, 11, 16.*

Great is peace! God announced that the redemption of Israel would come through peace.

*Debarim Rabbah, 5, 14.*

Great is peace! Peace is the name of God.
*Bemidbar Rabbah, 11, 18.*

Great is peace! The world cannot conduct itself except with peace.
*Bemidbar Rabbah, 21, 1.*

### Only the Newly-Born Have the Gift of Peace

God does not want to slander His children even when they are sinners. This we know from the cases of Hosea and of Elijah. Elijah (who is identified with Phinehas) was given a covenant of peace at Shittim. But later when Elijah spoke against Israel, that gift was taken from him. He went to the mountain of God in order to implore Moses to intervene in his behalf, that the gift of peace be returned to him. Moses answered: "I cannot do anything for you. You will have to go and visit the newly-born babies in Israel, and they will restore the gift of peace to you."
*Yalkut Hadash, sec. "Elijah," par. 23.*

Beloved is peace! All blessings end with the blessing of peace.
*Debarim Rabbah, 5, 14.*

God made peace between his works and men, between Abraham and fire, between Isaac and the knife, and between Jacob and the Angel (at Jabbok).
*Shir ha-Shirim Rabbah, 3, 20.*

## 245. PEACEMAKING—RECONCILIATION

Do not attempt to pacify a man at the height of his anger.
*Berakot, 7.*

A reconciliation without an explanation that error lay on both sides is not a true reconciliation.
*Bereshit Rabbah, 54, 3.*

He who makes peace in his own home is as if he made peace in all Israel.
*Abot de-R. Nathan, 28, 3.*

Hillel would say: "Be one of the disciples of Aaron, a lover of peace, following after peace, loving mankind, and drawing them to the Torah."
*Abot, 1, 12.*

When Aaron walked on the highway and accosted a man of known wickedness, he would greet him cordially. On the following day, if the man of wickedness wished to perform an evil deed, he thought to himself: "If I meet Aaron again and he greets me so cordially, how will I feel?"

Thus he would be led to abstain from transgression.

When Aaron heard that two people had quarreled, he would go to one and say: "I have just come from a man whom you believe to be your enemy, and what have I seen? He beats at his heart and rends his garments and cries out: 'I have sinned against my neighbor. Woe is me! I am ashamed to look him in the face.'"

He would then do the same thing at the home of the other. Thus, when the two men met, they fell upon each other's neck and embraced each other.

Therefore, when Aaron died, the whole house of Israel wept over him, women as well as men. When Moses died, however, only the men wept. It was said: "So many married couples were reunited after domestic quarrels by Aaron that many thousands of families to whom a son was born after such a reconciliation named the child Aaron in his honor; and at his death eighty thousand persons named Aaron walked in the funeral procession."

*Abot de-R. Nathan, 12; Kallah, 3.*

### NOT FOR THE FOOD

Rabbi gave a banquet in honor of his son, but he forgot to invite Bar Kappara. The latter wrote over the Rabbi's door-post: "Death shall come when thy merriment has ended, and what then will there be to thy merriment?"

When Rabbi read this, and asked who had written it, it was told: "Bar Kappara whom you did not invite."

The following day he gave another banquet, and on this occasion he invited Bar Kappara. When the dishes reached his table, Bar Kappara would embark upon the narration of fables, and the food grew cold. Rabbi noticed that the servants took back the food from this table uneaten and he asked Bar Kappara why he interrupted the meal with his fables. Bar Kappara replied: "To show thee that I rebuked thee yesterday, not because I was eager for your food."

Rabbi begged his pardon and they were reconciled.

Said Abba Bar Kappara to Rabbi: "If thou enjoyest so much prosperity in a world which is not thine for long, how much more shalt thou enjoy in the world which shall be thine forever!"

*Kohelet Rabbah, 1.*

Rabbi Meir, in order to make peace between a man and his wife, allowed a woman to spit in his face in the presence of his disciples. When they protested at his submission to such an indignity, not only to himself but also to the Torah of which he was a teacher, Rabbi Meir replied: "Is it not enough that Meir's honor should be like that of his Creator? If to make peace between a man and his wife the Holy Name, which is written in holiness, may be washed off into the water of bitterness in order to efface jealousy (Num. 5:23), should this not apply all the more to the honor of Meir?"

*Wayyikra Rabbah, 9.*

To banish strife, and to turn enemies into friends, is to show oneself of the disciples of Aaron, the typical peacemaker.

*Abot, 1, 12 (paraphrased).*

A Rabbi once met Elijah in a crowded market-place.

"Master," he asked, "who among this throng are most sure of eternal life?"

The Prophet, in reply, pointed out two men of homely appearance. The Rabbi accosted them.

"What," he asked, "are your special merits?"

"We have none," they answered, "unless it be that when people are in trouble we comfort them, and when they quarrel we make them friends again."

*Taanit, 22a.*

## 246. PERSUASION

He who persuades his brother to perform a good deed is as if he had performed it.

*Sanhedrin, 99.*

Great indeed is the reward of him who causes the sinner to repent and who aids him in his penitence.

*Zohar, ii, 128b.*

Greater is one who prompts a man to do good than one who does it.

*Baba Batra, 9.*

It is more difficult to prompt others to give than to give oneself, and the reward is correspondingly great. "They that turn the many to righteousness (shall shine) as the stars for ever and ever." (Dan. 12:3)

*Baba Batra, 8b.*

### SHALL WE NOT OBEY?

Why were the Canaanites not entirely exiled when Israel conquered the Land of Canaan? Because they did no harm to the spies sent out by Moses. When the spies gave an evil report, the people would not permit Joshua to speak favorably of the Land.

Caleb said: "Listen, my people! Is this all that the son of Amram has done to us?"

The people imagined that he wished to add to the criticism of Moses and became quiet. Caleb then continued: "Did Moses not liberate us from bondage? Did he not divide the sea for us? Did he not bring down manna? If he should tell us: 'Take ladders and climb to the sky, shall we not obey?'"

*Eiyahu Rabbah, 29; Sotah, 35.*

Rabbi Simeon ben Menasya said: " 'Those who cultivate intelligence will shine as the splendor of the firmament, and those who make the many righteous, as the stars forever and aye' (Dan. 12:3). 'Who make the many righteous' means 'who make them love God.' Those who love God are like the sun when it comes out in all its power; greater far are those who make others love Him."

*Midrash Tannaim, pp. 40-1.*
*Sifre Deut. 10 and 47.*

## 247. PASSOVER—PESACH

Rabbi Meir said: "Not only Israel, but God also was redeemed at the Exodus, as it is written: 'Whom Thou didst redeem unto Thee out of Egypt, the nation and his God.' (II Sam. 7:23)"

*Shemot Rabbah to Exodus, 12, 2.*

Why is only half of the Hallel chanted on the six days of Pesach? Because Israel was only half-purified before they received the Torah.

*Raia Mehemna to Emor, 97a.*

### THE SIX DAYS

Between Passover and Shabuot God did unto Israel what he did in the six days of Creation. On the first day He created dry land out of the sea; thus did He do when He turned the Red Sea into dry land. On the second day He created the expanse; thus also did He create the clouds of glory and spread them out over Israel. On the third day He created food-bearing plants; thus for Israel He sent down the manna. On the fourth day He made the great lights, and thus for Israel He made the Pillar of Fire. On the fifth day He created the birds, and for Israel he sent down the quails. On the sixth day He spoke with Adam, and with all Israel He spoke at Sinai.

*Otzar Midrashim, p. 488.*

### THE OMER OFFERING OF PASSOVER

Said R. Abin: "Come and see how much trouble Israel was accustomed to take with the Omer. The messengers of the Bet-Din (Sanhedrin) went out on the day before Passover and tied up the heads of a fistful of grain-stalks of barley, so that it might be easy to cut them down. On the afternoon of the first day of Passover, the people who lived near the barley-field chosen for the Omer would assemble at the field, so that the cutting down might be done in a crowd. When the sun had set, the cutter would cry out: 'Has the sun set?'

" 'Yes,' was the answer.

"This was repeated thrice. Why? Because the Sectaries of Boethus held that the Omer should be cut at sunset on Saturday, not on the first day of Passover. If the sunset of the first day inaugurated the Sabbath, the cutter would say: 'Is today the Sabbath?'

" 'Yes,' was the answer.
" 'Shall I nevertheless cut down the grain-stalks?'
" 'Yes," was the reply.

*Wayyikra Rabbah, 67.*

The moral conduct of the Israelites in Egypt was sufficiently deserving to win their redemption.

*Wayyikra Rabbah Emor.*

The Israelites in Egypt had scrolls in which the redemption was foretold.

*Shemot Rabbah, 5, 18.*

God took the words of the Patriarchs and made them a key to the redemption of their descendants.

*Bereshit Rabbah, 70, 6.*

Said Rabbi Eleazar: "By five things was Israel redeemed from Egypt, and by these very things will they be redeemed in the future: by suffering, by repentance, by the merit of the fathers, by God's compassion, and by the conclusion of the time decreed for their subjection."

*Debarim Rabbah, 2, 14.*

Each one receives a portion of the Pascal Lamb equal to the size of the olive, yet the singing of the Hallel lifts the very roof.

*Pesahim, 85.*

Since God and Israel love each other, why was Israel sent to Egypt to undergo serfdom? R. Haninah said: "It was measure for measure. Before the sons of Israel went into Egypt, we find that the sons of Leah and Rachel disliked the sons of Bilhah and Zilpah and called them sons of serfs. God was distressed at this and cried out: 'Thou, My bride, art altogether noble!' And God said: 'I shall bring all of them down to Egypt and they will all become serfs, and when they are redeemed and celebrate at the Passover meal, they will say: "All of us alike have been serfs unto Pharaoh." ' "

*Pesikta Hadashah on Hadeta in Otzar Midrashim, p. 488.*

When darkness came over Egypt and the assimilators among the Jews found light all about them, they closed their eyes and came to the homes of the Egyptians singing hymns of praise to Egyptian darkness. These are the Jews, who, as the Rabbis tell us, died during the plague of darkness and thus relieved Israel of their shame and dishonor.

*Exodus Rabbah, 14, 3.*

The Rabbis were asked: "Why did God select just these plagues to inflict upon them (in Egypt)?"
They answered: "It was measure for measure!" [1]

*Exodus Rabbah, 9, 9.*

[1] They were but reaping the fruit of their own wicked deeds.

In every generation, it is for the Jew to think that he himself went forth from Egypt.

*Pesahim, 116b.*

On the last days of Passover, the Jew sings the song of Moses; the Rabbis wisely said that song does not only refer to the song that Moses and Israel sang in the past, but also to the song that Israel and his deliverers will sing in the days to come. The Bible does not say: ". . . then Moses *sang*" but ". . . then Moses *will sing*"—and here we find the proof of resurrection in the Torah.

*Sanhedrin, 91b.*

## 248. PHYSICIANS—MEDICINE

The proverb says: "Pay homage to the physician before you need him."

*Y. Taanit, 3, 5.*

If a physician cannot give his patient medicine for his body, he should bring it about that medicine be given him for his soul.

*Zohar, i, 229b.*

Reside not in a town, the mayor of which is the community physician. He will be too busy to attend thee in thy illness.

*Pesahim, 113.*

Things that are sweet are harmful to a wound.

*Baba Kamma, 85.*

The physician must be careful even to a minute grain how he prescribes. He must make no error in a single word, lest he shed the blood of his patient.

*Zohar, v, 299a.*

The proverb says: "The door that is closed to a Mitzwah is open to a physician."

*Shir ha-Shirim Rabbah, 6, 1.*

Acquire not the habit of drugs, and avoid taking medicine if possible even when you are ill.[1]

*Pesahim, 113.*

[1] You may become an addict of drugs. (Rashi)

Asparagus is good both for the heart and the eyes.

*Berakot, 51.*

A physician from afar has a blind eye (namely, the family doctor understands your case better).

*Baba Kamma, 85.*

Can a man live if he takes into his body nothing but harmful drugs?
If a man cannot fully combat the habit of harmful drugs, at least let
him also take healthful ingredients.[1]

*Zohar, iv, 179b.*

[1] He should mix spirituality with worldliness.

The sun has risen and the patient has risen.

*Baba Batra, 16.*

A physician who is himself unwell is usually told: "Cure thyself,
and then cure others."

*Midrash Aggadat Bereshit, 4, 25.*

A physician who takes no fee is worth no fee.

*Baba Kamma, 85.*

A physician must know how rapid are the pulse-beats of his patient.
He must also know to what degree the patient's pulse-beat has risen.[1]

*Zohar, iv, 219a, Raia Mehemna.*

[1] Apparenty the patient's temperature is meant.

### The Apple Wine

Once Rabbi was suffering from a malady of the stomach. He wished
to know whether apple wine made by a non-Jew was permitted him.

R. Ishmael b. Jose said: "Once a non-Jew brought to my father
apple-wine seventy years old."

Rabbi advertised for this, and a non-Jew brought him many bottles
of wine seventy years old. He drank of it and was cured, saying:
"Blessed is the Lord, Who has entrusted His world to such custodians."

*Abodah Zarah, 40.*

Samuel was an experienced physician and taught the science to Mar
Ukba. When Rabbi Yannai was afflicted with pain in his eyes, he sent
a messenger to Mar Ukba, asking for the eye medicine of Mar Samuel.

Mar Ukba answered through the messenger: "I am sending you
some medicine lest you think that I lack sympathy for your pain. But
thus said Samuel: 'To wash the eyes with cold water in the morning,
and to wash the body with warm water in the evening is better for the
eyes than all the medicine in the world.'"

Samuel also said: "After a man has undergone blood-letting, he
shall warm himself before an open fire and guard against a draft."[1]

*Shabbat, 108 and 129.*

[1] Blood-letting was considered a cure for many centuries.

### Against God's Will

R. Ishmael and R. Akiba were walking in Jerusalem and were asked
by a sick person for a remedy. When they told him of this, a man near by
remarked to them: "God has sent sickness, yet you are teaching this
man how to be cured. Are you not working against God's will?"

The Rabbis inquired what the questioner did for a livelihood. He answered that he was a wine-grower. They said: "God created the vine, yet you cut off its fruit."

He answered: "If I do not labor on it, would it bring forth grapes?"

"Thus it is with man," they said. "He must take care of his body if he is to enjoy life. The drugs we recommend are like the fertilizer which you use to strengthen the soil if it becomes weak."

*Midrash Temurah, chap. 2.*

## 249. PIOUS AND IMPIOUS

Even if the impious have no other merit than charitableness, they are deemed worthy thereby and receive the Shekinah.

*Midrash Tehillim, 17, 14.*

Woe unto him who has no courtyard but makes a door for it.[1]

*Yoma, 72.*

[1] One who learns but does not practice.

There are people without even the moisture of a Mitzwah.

*Sanhedrin, 92.*

Who are the pious? Those who consider each day as their last day on earth and repent accordingly.

*Zohar, i, 220a.*

Be not over-pious, lest the others fail to imitate thee even in fundamentals.

*Bemidbar Rabbah, 21, 5.*

### He Knew Them Too Well

A group of hilarious men often chose the vestibule of the synagogue as the place for their unseemly feasts. When the beadle would protest at their conduct, they would pelt him with blows. Once when one of them was sick unto death, he was asked whom he wished to appoint as the guardian of his minor son. He replied: "The beadle of the synagogue."

Did he not have a host of friends? Yes, but he knew them too well to entrust his son to the care of any of them.

*Bereshit Rabbah, 65.*

The Am Ha-Arez, the ignorant man, connot be truly pious. The untaught cannot rightly avoid sin.

*Abot, 2, 6.*

## 250. PLANTS—FRUITS IN PROVERBS

Even one ear of wheat is not exactly like another ear.
*Y. Sanhedrin, 4, 9.*

They say to fruit-bearing trees: "Why do you not make any noise?"
The trees reply: "Our fruits are sufficient advertisement for us."
*Bereshit Rabbah, 16, 3.*

People say: "The quality of the fruit may be recognized by its bloom."
*Berakot, 48.*

A tree is cut down by an ax which is joined to a piece of the tree itself.
*Eliyahu Rabbah, 29.*

Were it not for the leaves the fruit would not ripen.[1]
*Hullin, 92.*

[1] Scholars cannot exist without common laborers who minister to their material needs.

If you reap wheat-stalks before the proper time, even the hay is not good.
*Shir ha-Shirim Rabbah, end.*

People say: "A myrtle which grows among the thorns is still a myrtle."
*Sanhedrin, 44.*

The thin roots of the wheat-stalks bore deep into the ground. The soft roots of a fig tree split the rock.
*Y. Berakot, 9, 2.*

A good tree brings good fruit.
*Shir ha-Shirim Rabbah, 7.*

People are like blades of grass; they sprout and they wither.
*Erubin, 54.*

When iron was mined, the trees began to tremble. It was said to them: "Let none of you combine your wood with iron, and you will not be hewn down."
*Bereshit Rabbah, 5, end.*

When thorns burn, they give out much noise, as if to say: "We too are wood."
*Kohelet Rabbah, 7.*

The grapes pray for leaves, for without leaves there are no grapes.
*Hullin, 92.*

A tree with foliage too heavy casts an unpleasant shade.

*Pesahim, 111.*

Rabba said: "An easy way to know when the Sabbath is near in a village is to watch the plant, Adani. The leaves of this plant incline towards the warmth of the sun: in the morning, they incline towards the east; in the evening, towards the west."

*Shabbat, 35.*

R. Abba, when on the highway, grew weary and dejected. Suddenly a bush of pink roses caught his attention. He smelled the fragrance of the flowers, his soul was revived, and his weariness departed. He said:

"How wondrous is the sweet fragrance! Every living thing feels better because of sweet-smelling plants, and, when we feel dejected at the close of the Sabbath because we lose our Extra-Soul, the fragrant odors (of the Habdalah spices) are a compensation to us."

*Zohar, ii, 20.*

Raba b. R. Hanina owned fruit trees close to the vineyard of R. Joseph. Birds were accustomed to come to the trees for rest and then fly down to the vines and eat the grapes. R. Joseph asked Raba b. R. Hanina to cut down his trees. The latter refused, however, saying: "We have learned that a tree which bears a kab measure of fruit should not be cut down."

Moreover, R. Hanina declared that the days of his son were cut off because he had cut down a fruit tree. He gave permission to R. Joseph to cut down the trees if he so desired.

*Baba Batra, 26.*

## 251. PLEASURE—ENJOYMENT

An enjoyment which comes to a person against his will is no enjoyment.

*Pesahim, 25.*

People say: "Make use of a costly vessel a single day and enjoy it, even if it be taken away tomorrow."

*Berakot, 28.*

The body only has pleasure in some things; the soul only in others.

*Zohar, ii, 258b.*

## 252. POVERTY—THE POOR

God searched for the best gift He might offer Israel, and He found nothing better than poverty.

*Hagigah, 9.*

He who lengthens the life of a poor man has his own life lengthened when his time to die arrives.

*Zohar, iii, 85a.*

Neglect not thine own poor in order to give to others who are poor.

*Zohar, iv, 206a.*

The destitute is likened to the dead. He who saves one from death deserves to be saved from death.

*Zohar, iii, 113b.*

Poverty is more grievous than fifty plagues.

*Baba Batra, 116.*

Poverty is worse than chastisements.

*Shemot Rabbah, 31, 12.*

Before the poor man sees the downfall of the arrogant rich man, his soul leaves him.

*Ekah Rabbah, 3, 7.*

People say: "The poor man is hungry and unaware of it."

*Megillah, 7.*

The poor man offers two sacrifices: the beast and his own fat and blood.

*Zohar, iii, 9b.*

People say: "Poverty is an adornment for Israelites as a crimson ribbon is an adornment for a white horse."

*Hagigah, 9.*

God said: "Thou, man, hast four persons of whom thou must take care: thy son, thy daughter, thy servant, and thy maid. I also have four of whom I must take care: the Levite, the proselyte, the widow, and the orphan. If thou aidest mine, I shall aid thine."

*Otzar Midrashim, p. 493.*

The life of a man is not true life if he does not take care to aid his fellow-man.

*Betzah, 32.*

Take care of the sons of the unlearned and of the poor, for from them the scholars come.

*Sanhedrin, 96; Nedarim, 81 (combined).*

There are men who appear rich on the thoroughfare, but are poor in the home.

*Y. Shebuot, 3, 2.*

If all chastisements were placed on one scale and poverty on the other, they would balance evenly.

*Shemot Rabbah, 31, 12.*

He who is poor in this world will be rich in the World-to-Come.

*Alphabeth of R. Akiba, 22; edit. Jellineck.*

The householder does less for the poor man than the poor man does for the householder.

*Wayyikra Rabbah, 34, 8.*

The eight names of the poor are:
Ani derived from Ane, to afflict.
Ebion derived from Aba, to want.
Misken derived from Masken, impoverished.
Rash derived from Tiwaresh, landless.
Dal derived from Meduldal, empty-handed.
Dak derived from Medukdak, beaten down.
Mak derived from Yamuk, reduced low.
Halek derived from Halok, to wander about.

*Wayyikra Rabbah, Behar.*

Rab Phinehas said: "God said unto David: 'My son, though thou call upon Me many a time to arise, I will not arise. But when do I arise? When thou seest the poor oppressed and the needy sighing, then will I arise.'" (Psalm 12:6)

*Bereshit Rabbah, chap. 75, 1.*

## ZOHAR ITEMS ON THE POOR

Woe unto him against whom the poor man makes complaint to his Heavenly Master, for the poor man is nearest to the King.

*Zohar, ii, 86b.*

He who rages at a poor man is as if he raged against the Shekinah, for the Guardian of the poor is mighty and rules over all. He needs no witnesses and no associate judge. He accepts no bail or surety.

*Ibid.*

The truly poor man is the unlearned man who knows not what Mitzwot to perform. A man's wealth lies in his Torah and Mitzwot.

*Zohar, ii, 93a.*

He who withholds the hire of the poor worker is as if he had snatched the soul of a man and his family. He shortens their lives and his own life will be shortened.

*Zohar, iii, 85a.*

A rich man who is afflicted with sickness is called a poor man; likewise, one who has lost his reason.

*Zohar, v, 273b.*

If a poor man be in debt to God (by reason of his sins) it is not accounted unto him as a debt, for poverty oftentimes misleads a man's reason.

*Zohar Hadash, Wayyikra, 49.*

When a poor man feels his poverty, he quarrels with the Most High. Therefore, he who holds up the hand of the poor man and performs charity in his behalf is as if he had made peace between the poor man and God.

*Zohar Hadash to Ruth, 75b.*

### THE FASTIDIOUS POOR

Abba b. Abba gave to his son, Samuel, several coins to distribute among the poor. When he returned, Samuel said: "I saw one of the poor men drinking old wine."

His father replied: "Here are some more coins to give him. His heart is so bitter he needs old wine to drown his sorrows."

A man once rich became exceptionally poor, and there was no one to care for him. He was taken to a poorhouse and fed excellent food from clay plates. His fastidious soul, however, could not endure this and he became ill. The physician of the institution was summoned and said: "Eat then from the pot, for even rich persons have their food cooked in clay vessels."

A poor man came to R. Nehemiah, who inquired regarding his usual fare. The man replied: "Fat meat and old wine."

"But I have not these to offer you," said the Rabbi. "Will you join me in my dish of lentils?"

The poor man took the dish of lentils, ate from it and fell dead.

R. Nehemiah exclaimed: "Woe unto this man who has caused Nehemiah to kill him. He should not have indulged himself so much when he was rich."

*Y. Peah, 8.*

Let the poor be members of thy household.

*Abot, 1, 5.*

### THE DECEIVING POOR

Samuel in his boyhood went to sit among the poor. He overheard one say to another: "What dishes shall we use today, the golden or the silver ones?"

When he told his father, R. Abba b. Abba, he replied: "We should be thankful that there are cheats among the poor; otherwise we would have no excuse when we find it difficult to answer the plea of a poor man."

R. Johanan and R. Simeon b. Lakish went to bathe in the hot-springs of Tiberias. A poor man accosted them and they said: "We have no money with us, but on our return we shall take you to our home and feed you."

When they returned they found the man dead. They said: "If it was not our merit to aid him in life, we shall at least aid him in death."

When they undressed him, however, a purse with gold fell out.

They said: "Were it not for the swindlers, we would be guilty of a grievous sin every time we did not offer immediate help."

*Y. Peah, 8.*

## The Lowliness of the Poor

We read: "He hath not despised the lowliness of the poor." (Psalm 22:25)

When a rich man and a poor man come before a judge, he usually welcomes the rich man with a smile and turns not his face to the poor. It is not so with God. He doth not despise the lowly poor.

Rab Haggai proclaimed a fast during a drought, and, when he prayed for rain, it came. He said: "It is not because I am worthy to be heard by God that He hath answered me, but because He doth not despise the lowliness of the poor."

*Midrash Tehillim Buber, 22.*

King Agrippa wished to sacrifice one day many free-will offerings, and he instructed the High Priest to sacrifice on that day for no one else. A poor man came to the High Priest and said: "I catch four doves every day; two of them I eat and two I sacrifice. If my daily sacrifice is not offered I shall lose my livelihood."

The Priest proceeded with the sacrifice, and in a dream the king was told: "The poor man's sacrifice was more acceptable than thy thousand bullocks."

*Midrash Tehillim Buber, 22.*

## Poverty Follows the Poor

Rabba said to Rabbah b. Mari: "Whence originated the proverb: 'Poverty follows the poor'?"

Rabbah b. Mari replied: "From the following law: The first fruits were offered by the rich in golden or silver baskets, and the baskets were returned to them. The poor, however, brought their first fruits in wicker baskets, and the baskets were not given back to them."

*Baba Kamma, 92.*

There was once an unlearned man who guaranteed to his daughter-in-law her marriage settlement. His son, R. Huna b. Moses, was a man of great poverty. Abbaye said: "I would offer him this advice: let him divorce his wife so that she may collect the settlement and let him re-marry her."

This advice proved useless, inasmuch as R. Huna b. Moses was a Kohen and could not re-marry his divorced wife. Abbaye said: "For this reason people say: 'Poverty follows the poor.'"

*Baba Batra, 174.*

### Opulence and Distress

R. Joshua ben Levi visited Rome on a wintry day. He observed several statues and monuments covered with valuable tapestries to save them from the cold. Nearby he saw a poor man leaning on a pedestal dressed in a sack used on the back of asses to place below the load. Concerning the monuments he said: "O Lord, where Thou givest, Thou givest in opulence." Concerning the poor man, he said: "And where Thou smitest, Thou smitest heavily."

*Bereshit Rabbah, 33.*

### The Poor Man's Offering

R. Hanina b. Dosa saw many persons bringing to Jerusalem their freewill offerings. He said to himself: "How is it, Hanina, that everyone brings offerings, but thou bringest naught?"

He went to a suburb, took a large stone, cleansed it, chiselled it smoothly, and thought to take it to Jerusalem for use where it was needed. He wished to hire a wagon, but lacked the money required. Suddenly there appeared five persons before him. They agreed to take the stone for a small compensation, provided he also assisted. Before he knew it, they were in Jerusalem. He looked about for his helpers to pay them, but they had vanished. When he related the occurrence to the Sanhedrin, they said: "Verily, it seems to us that God sent angels to help thee."

*Kohelet Rabbah, 1.*

### Poverty is Israel's Crucible

Elijah said to Ben He He and some say to R. Eleazar: "What is the meaning of the verse: 'Behold I have refined thee but not as silver. I have tried thee in the furnace of affliction'?

"God looked around for the best conditions to be afforded Israel and concluded that poverty is the one most fitted to him."

*Hagigah, 9b.*

## 253. PRAYER

All are equal before God in prayer.

*Shemot Rabbah, 21, 4.*

What is the meaning of the words: "But as for me, let my prayer be unto Thee, O Lord, in an acceptable time"? What is an acceptable time? When the congregation prays.

*Berakot, 8.*

He who recites his prayer (Amidah) in a voice heard by others is of a nature unworthy of trust.

*Berakot, 24.*

Amidah is Tefillah.[1]

*Berakot, 6.*

[1] This is the reason for giving to the eighteen benedictions the name "Amidah," particularly among Spanish Jews.

A covenant has been made that the thirteen attributes of the Lord, when recited in prayer, do not return empty.

*Rosh ha-Shanah, 17.*

R. Jose b. Hanina would pray in the morning at sunrise so that he might have upon him the fear of Heaven the entire day.

*Y. Berakot, 4.*

R. Eleazar b. R. Simeon said: "As soon as the sun begins to rise, one should pray, as it is written: 'They shall fear Thee while the sun endureth.' "

*Zohar, i, 178.*

R. Joshua b. Levi said: "In the lands of the East we should turn our face towards the West to pray, as it is written: 'And the host of heaven worshippeth Thee,' and, since the sun comes from the East in the morning, it bows to God towards the West." [1]

*Baba Batra, 25.*

[1] The word "worshippeth" in Hebrew means literally "boweth."

## The Heaven of Prayers

We were taught that R. Jose went to visit R. Simeon in the company of his son. They camped for the night, and, before falling asleep, the boy told his father that he had heard a comment which he liked. R. Jose asked him to repeat it, and the boy said: "We read (I Kings, 8:49): 'Then hear Thou their prayer and their supplication in heaven Thy dwelling-place, and maintain their cause.' Why is it not written 'from heaven' instead of 'in heaven'? Because Metatron, the Archangel, receives the prayers and supplications of Israel and sets them in the place called 'The Heaven, par excellence' and, when God wishes to know that for which Israel prays, He attunes His ear to the Heaven of Prayers and sends forth His compassion."

R. Jose was greatly impressed and blessed his son, that he might become the jewel of his time.

*Zohar Hadash Bereshit.*

Those who live to the North of Jerusalem stand while praying facing the South. Those who live to the South face the North. Those who live at the East face the West, and those who live in the West face the East. Those who dwell in Jerusalem face the site of the Holy Temple. Thus, all the children of Israel face towards a single place in prayer.

A man should not stand on a table, a sofa or a chair, while praying, for there may be no elevation before the Lord. But, if he is old or sick, a man may pray in whatever position he can.

A man should not stand up to pray after completing a profane conversation or a jocular interchange of words, but he should rise for prayer after having completed a wise or learned conversation or discourse.

*Tosefta Berakot, 3.*

### Public Prayer and Private

R. Judah said: "Thus did R. Akiba conduct himself: if he prayed in public, he would hasten with his prayer lest it be a hardship upon the public; but, if he prayed alone, he would pray long with many bowings."

*Berakot, 31.*

R. Jonah would recite the Amidah in the synagogue in a undertone, lest he disturb the others; but, if he prayed at home, he would recite it aloud so that his sons might learn it from hearing him.

*Y. Berakot, 4.*

The school of Shammai said: "When reading the evening Shema, one should incline (or lean) and read as if lying down in bed. When reading it in the morning, one should stand up as if rising from bed, as it is written: 'And shalt talk of them (the Shema verses) . . . when thou liest down and when thou risest up.'"

The school of Hillel said: "One must read the Shema in the evening or in the morning, as he is, namely, sitting, standing or inclining. He should not change his position, as it is written: 'When thou sittest in thine house, and when thou walkest by the way.'"

If this is so, why does it say: "When thou liest down and when thou risest up"? It means at the time of lying down and rising up.

R. Tarfon said: "Once I inclined as the school of Shammai requires, and I nearly fell into danger."

The Sages replied: "Thou didst deserve this since thou hast presumed to contradict the school of Hillel whose opinion is the Law." [1]

*Mishnah Berakot, chap. 1.*

[1] Every Rabbinical code prohibits standing up when saying any part of the Shema.

The Rabbis declared: "See how exalted the Most High is above the world! And yet let a man enter God's House and but whisper a prayer, and the Almighty hearkens, even as a friend into whose ear one pours his secret."

*Y. Berakot, 9, 1.*

"May it be Thy will, O God, that love and peace and brotherliness dwell among us! May our hopes of Heaven be fulfilled! Grant that the good inclination may uphold us. Fill us with the desire to fear Thy name, and do Thou give us our soul's peace. Amen."

*Berakot, 16b.*

"Let not thy prayer be a matter of fixed routine, but heartfelt supplication for mercy at the Divine footstool."

*Mishnah Berakot, 5, 1.*

Only that man's prayer is answered who lifts his hands with his heart in them.

*Taanit, 8a.*

If thou hast prayed, and prayed yet again, it is already declared to thee that thy prayer is heard.

*Midrash Tehillim, 14.*

The essence of every prayer of supplication is that one should be in unison with the divine will, to sum up all the wishes of the heart in the one phrase: "Do that which is good in Thine own eyes, O Lord."

*Berakot, 29b.*

He who prays with the community will have his prayer granted.

*Berakot, 8a.*

Let others rely on the arm of flesh, Israel's weapon is prayer.

*Yalkut to Gen. 27, 22.*

It is said of congregational prayer that through it "Israel lifts his eyes to his Father in heaven."

*Midrash Tehillim to Ps. 121, 1.*

Prayer took the place of the altar, of which R. Johanan ben Zakkai said that it established peace between Israel and his Father in heaven.

*Mekilta Yithro, 2.*

"Address your prayer to the Master of life and not to His Servants; He will hear you in every trouble," said R. Judan.

*Y. Berakot, 9.*

Rabbi Eleazar ben Pedat prayed: "May it be Thy good pleasure, O Lord our God, to cause to dwell in our allotted place love, brotherliness, peace, and fellowship. Enlarge our bounds with Disciples; bring to us a good latter end and everything for which we hope; appoint our portion in Paradise. Establish us by good associates, and by a good impulse in this, Thy world, that, when we arise, we may daily find our heart waiting to revere Thy name; and let the satisfaction of our soul's desire be graciously granted by Thee."

*Berakot, 16b.*

"Unite our hearts, O God, to fear Thy name; keep us far from what Thou hatest; bring us near to what Thou lovest; and deal mercifully with us for Thy name's sake."

*Y. Berakot, 4, 2.*

Rabbi Eliezer ben Hyrcanus composed a short prayer to be recited in a moment of danger: "Do Thy good pleasure in Heaven above, and grant composure of spirit to those who revere Thee below; whatsoever is good in Thy sight, do. Blessed art Thou, O Lord our God, who hearest prayer."

An anonymous prayer runs: "The needs of Thy people Israel are many, and their wit is scant. May it be Thy good pleasure, O Lord our God, to give to each one everything he needs; and mayst Thou supply to each and every person what he requires. Blessed is He who heareth prayer."

*Tos. Berakot, 3, 7; Berakot, 29b.*

In Deut. 11:13, concerning the verse. "To love the Lord and to worship Him with all your heart" we read in Sifre: "To worship Thee." This means prayer. May it not mean literally sacrificial worship? . . . Is there such a thing as worship in the heart? So David says: "Let my prayer be set forth as incense before Thee, the lifting up of my hands as the evening sacrifice." (Psalm 141:2)

*Sifre Deut., 41.*

Rabbi Abbahu said: "Prayer is dearer to God than all good works and than all good sacrifices."

*Tanhuma Buber, Ki Tabo, 1.*

Rabbi Eliezer ben Jacob said: "We learn from the example of Moses that an hour of prayer avails more with God than good works. His life time of good works did not win for him permission to view the Promised Land; but, when he offered prayer, the answer came: 'Go up unto the top of Pisgah.' (Deut. 3:23-27)"

*Sifre Deut., 29.*

Rabbi Meir said: "Let a man's words before God always be few, as it is said: 'Be not rash with thy mouth, and let not thy heart be hasty to utter a word before God; for God is in heaven and thou on earth, therefore let thy words be few!'" (Eccles. 5:1)

*Berakot, 61a.*

## 254. CONCENTRATION IN PRAYER

What is service in the heart? The answer comes "Prayer."

*Taanit, 2.*

He who stands in prayer shall keep his eyes down and his heart upwards.

*Yebamot, 105.*

Prayer without concentration is like a body without a soul.

*Shalah, 249, Tamid, quoting the sages.*

Just as it was necessary that the beast intended for sacrifice be without blemish in order to prove acceptable, so prayer must be without a blemish, namely without foreign thoughts, in order to prove acceptable.

*Zohar Hadash Tikkunim, 108b.*

A man should be like a servant before his master, when he stands up to recite the Eighteen Benedictions. During the first three benedictions, he should be like a servant who extols his master. During the middle ones, he should be like a servant who begs for sustenance. During the last three, he should be like a servant who thanks his master for favors granted, and is about to retire from his presence.

*Zohar, iv, 223a.*

R. Hiyya said: "I have never forced myself to recite the Amidah with mental concentration upon the words, because the mind refuses to be forced. Once I attempted to do so, but my mind rebelled; it gave itself over to thoughts concerning those who might precede me at the audience of the king, the superintendent of the Exilarch or the Exilarch."

*Y. Berakot, 2, 4.*

The words: "And to serve Him with all your heart," mean to concentrate your mind upon your prayer, so that your heart be not divided in the hour of prayer.

*Pesikta Zutarta to Num. 11:13.*

The Rabbis have taught: He who prays must concentrate his heart upon heaven. Abba Saul said: "We find a suggestion of this in the Psalm (10:17): 'Thou wilt direct their heart, Thou wilt cause thine ear to attend.'"

*Berakot, 31.*

R. Eliezer said: "If a man prays only according to the exact text of the prayer and adds nothing from his own mind, his prayer is not proper imploration."

*Berakot, 28.*

If a man does not feel devout, he should refrain from prayer for the time being.

*Berakot, 30b.*

Neither levity nor indolence, neither austerity nor worldliness, must be our mood in prayer, but joy springing from very love of communion.

*Berakot, 31a.*

The Rabbis point to the example of Moses, who, on one occasion prayed for forty days and forty nights, and on another is content with a single sentence: "O Lord, heal her now, I beseech Thee."

*Ibid.*

The older generation of pious ones used to spend an hour in silent devotion before offering their daily prayer, in order to concentrate heart and soul upon their communion with their Father in heaven.

*Berakot, 5, 1.*

R. Aha in the name of R. Jose said: "It is necessary to add new words to the text every time the Amidah is recited."

R. Zeira said: "Every time I did this, I became confused and lost my place."

R. Eleazar was accustomed to recite a new prayer daily, in addition to the set version. R. Abbahu would add a new benediction every day (or substitute his own words for those of one of the Eighteen Benedictions). [1]

*Y. Berakot, 4.*

## A PROPHETIC PRAYER

When a son of Gamaliel II was very ill, the father sent two of his Disciples to Rabbi Hanina ben Dosa that he might beseech God's mercy upon his son. Rabbi Hanina at once ascended to the chamber on the roof and prayed for Gamaliel's son. When he descended, he said to the messenger: "Go, for the fever has left the lad."

They asked: "Are you a prophet?"

He replied: "I am neither a prophet nor the son of a prophet, but I have learned that if my prayer flows freely, I know it is accepted. If not, I know that it is rejected."

The messenger noted down in writing the moment at which he said this. When they arrived at Gamaliel's house, they reported the matter, and he said: "By the divine service! At the very moment, no more and no less, the fever departed from my son, and he asked for a drink of water."

*Berakot, 34b.*

The Eighteen Prayers were regularly said while standing (whence the name "Amidah"). They were recited with a reverent attitude and in an undertone. According to the opinion of some, the eyes should look down (as an aid to "Kawwanah," concentration); others declared that the eyes should be raised; others said: "Eyes down, mind up!"

*Yebamot, 105b.*

---

[1] The best of these additions in time became a fixed part of the text.

## 255. PRAYERS FOR RAIN

### THE PRAYERS OF SIMPLE MEN

Rabbi proclaimed a fast and prayer for rain, but the rain did not arrive. A man, named Ilfa, ascended to the reader's pulpit and began to pray. At once the rain descended.

"What is thy good deed?" he was asked by Rabbi.

"I reside in a poor quarter; I save my money carefully, and buy wine with which to recite the Kiddush and the Habdalah in the synagogue, so that all present may share in the Mitzwah."

Rab prayed in vain for rain. A teacher came to the pulpit, and, as soon as he began, the rain poured down. In reply to Rab's query, he said: "I teach all children alike, whether they be rich or poor. I accept nothing from the poor for tuition; and when a child does not care to learn, I persuade him."

A beggar came to a Rabbi for a donation. The Rabbi said: "Hast thou not heard that thy father's property awaits thee in the hands of the court?"

"Yes," answered the beggar, "but I have heard that it was not acquired in an altogether honest way."

The Rabbi replied: "A man like thee deserveth to be answered when he prays for rain."

A donkey-driver's prayer for rain was speedily granted. When asked his good deed, he said: "Once I hired myself out to drive a woman to the city in my donkey-cart. On the way she told me amid tears that her husband was in prison, and that she lacked the money for his release. I sold my cart, and gave her the money."

*Taanit, 24; Y. Taanit, 1.*

### A DEBT TO GOD

Once rain was delayed in Palestine, and a fast day was proclaimed in Tiberias by R. Hanina and in the South by R. Joshua ben Levi. Rain came down in the South but not in Galilee. The Tiberians said: "R. Joshua knows how to pray aright, but R. Hanina does not." The next season rain was again delayed in Galilee. R. Hanina invited R. Joshua to pray for rain. He did so, but no rain came.

R. Hanina said: "It is not Joshua who is able to bring rain, nor is it myself who am unable. Everything depends upon the good conduct and repentance of the people."

When he left the synagogue and saw the clear sky, his heart became embittered, and the rain poured down. R. Hanina uttered a vow never to pray again for people whose conduct does not deserve God's compassion.

"Who am I to prevent God from collecting His debt?" he said.

*Y. Taanit, 6.*

## God's Spoiled Child

It is told that Honi ha-Meaggel possessed the miraculous power to bring down rain while he stood in a ring (meaggel) he had outlined on the ground. From this he swore not to move till his prayer was answered. Thus he seemed to speak challengingly to God, and would have been excommunicated by Simeon ben Shetah for his irreverence if he had not been so visibly a spoilt child of God.

*Taanit, 23a.*

Hanan ha-Nehba was the son of Honi ha-Meaggel's daughter.

When rain was needed, the Rabbis would send school children to him. They would take hold of his garment and plead: "O Father, send down rain."

Hanan would then speak to God thus: "Lord of the Universe! Send down rain for the sake of those who know not the difference between the Father who can give rain, and the father who can only beg Thee for it."

*Taanit, 23.*

R. Judah II prayed for rain and it did not come. He exclaimed bitterly: "Behold the difference between me and the prophet Samuel." He was overcome by humiliation, and rain came.

R. Papa proclaimed a fast. Feeling weak, he ate a little oatmeal. A man who saw him exclaimed: "Eat another dish and rain will come." Rab Papa was smitten with shame and humiliation, and rain came.

Rab Nahman prayed for rain in vain. He exclaimed: "Take Nahman and cast him to the ground." Rain fell.

Rab Aha prayed for rain without success. A Samaritan said to him: "Squeeze the rain water out of your hat."

R. Aha said: "God will send us a good year, but thou wilt not enjoy it."

Rain descended in abundance, but the Samaritan died.

Rabbi Eliezer's prayer for rain was not answered, but R. Akiba's was. The latter said: "A king had two daughters, one bold and the other modest. When the bold daughter made a demand, he would say: 'Give her what she wishes and let her go.' But when the modest daughter made a request, the king would converse with her for a long time before granting it. Thus it is with Rabbi Eliezer and myself."

Samuel ha-Katon proclaimed a fast day to begin before daylight, but the rain descended before the appointed time.

He said: "Do not consider yourself so good that your wish is granted before you ask. It is like a serf whom his master dislikes. When he comes for something, it is at once given to him so that the master may not look upon him."

On another occasion rain came just at the conclusion of the fast. Samuel said: "It is like a king who is dissatisfied with his serf, and says: 'Let him suffer before I grant his request.'"

*Taanit, 25; Y. Taanit, 3.*

Levi prayed for rain and it came not. He exclaimed: "Lord of the Universe! Behold Thou ascendest to Thy heaven and sittest there in quietude without compassion upon Thy children."

Rain descended, but Levi was punished for his boldness by becoming lame.

R. Hiyya bar Lulianos saw clouds moving toward Moab and Ammon. He said: "O Lord, when Thou didst offer them Thy Torah, they did refuse it; but now Thou sendest rain to them and not to Israel." The rain came down in Palestine.

Rabba chancéd to be in Hagrunia and was asked to pray for rain. He proclaimed a fast to last a day and a night.

The next morning R. Eliezer of Hagrunia said to Rabba: "I dreamed that a voice said to me: 'Good health to the good Rabbi from the good Master, who in His goodness does good to His nation.' "

Rabba said: "Verily now is an acceptable hour before God; let us pray again."

Rain came down.

*Taanit, 24-5.*

Abba Hilkiah was a descendant of Honi ha-Meaggel, and like him frequently brought down rain by his prayer.

Once rain was badly needed, and a pair of Sages went to him. They found him at work in the field, but he did not answer their greeting. On his way home he gathered some kindling wood and placed it with his tools on one shoulder, while on the other he placed his overgarment. He walked barefooted, but, where it was wet, he put on his shoes. When he approached his home, his wife came forth to meet him dressed in all her finery. The wife led the way, Abba followed, and the Rabbis entered after them. He sat down at his scanty meal but did not invite his guests to join. He divided the portions, giving one portion to the older son and two portions to the younger.

When he had finished, he called his wife to the roof. There they prayed for rain. A cloud appeared near the corner where his wife stood. Rain descended and they returned to the house. Now he greeted the Sages and inquired as to the purpose of their coming. On learning that they wished him to pray for rain, he took them to the window, and said: "Behold, the rain is already coming down. Blessed be the Lord who has made it unnecessary for you to ask favors from Abba."

They replied: "But we well know that you have prayed for it. May not we ask you to explain the odd actions which we observed you doing?"

Abba replied: "I did not answer the greetings because I am a day-laborer and did not wish to enter into conversation with you; I placed the overgarment by itself on my other shoulder because it had been loaned to me; I put on my shoes where it was wet lest there be a snake or reptile; my wife met me in her finery lest I be attracted by another woman; she went in first because I did not know you; I did not ask you to join us because I could not spare the food; I gave more to my younger son because he had just come from school; and my wife's prayer was heard first because she prepares food for the poor."

*Taanit, 23.*

R. Eleazar proclaimed thirteen days of fast, but rain did not follow. The people commenced to walk out of the synagogue, and the Rabbi said: "Where are you going? To dig your graves?"

All wept, and rain came down.

*Taanit, 28.*

R. Berechiah proclaimed thirteen fast days, but the rain did not follow, and locusts came and ate up the residue in the fields.

He called every one to the synagogue and said: "Brethren, behold what we do. We do evil with our hands, yet we ask favors of the Lord. Therefore the day on which we hoped our deliverance would come has been turned into a day of yet further calamity. Should you not feel contrition and weep at your sins?"

All the people wept, and the rain poured down.

*Y. Taanit, 2.*

R. Tarfon prayed for rain and it came down before noon.

He said: "Go ye and eat and drink, and come to the synagogue and recite the Great Hallel." (Psalm 136)

How should one give thanks for rain?

He should say: "Blessed be He who is good to the good."

Rab Judah said: "My father Ezekiel would say thus: 'May Thy Name be blessed, exalted and increased in glory for each and every drop which Thou bringest down to us and by which Thou sustainest us.'"

R. Judah of Migdal said: "Myriads and myriads of blessings and thanksgiving we should give to Thy Name for each and every drop of rain, for thus Thou makest gracious payment for those who are in Thy debt."

*Taanit, 26; Y. Berakot, 9.*

## 256. PRAYER—IMPROPER

We may not pray that an overabundance of good be taken away from us.

*Taanit, 22.*

Rabbi said: "It is forbidden us to pray to God that He send death to the wicked. If God had removed from the world the idolatrous Terah before he begat Abraham, there would have been no Israel, no Torah, no Messiah and no Prophets."

*Zohar Hadash, 105.*

To pray for the impossible is disgraceful. It is as if one brought into a shed a hundred measures of corn, and prayed: "May it be Thy will that they become two hundred."

How should one pray? "May Thy blessing enter into the corn, not
Thy curse."

*Tosefta Berakot, 7.*

Rabba once heard a man praying that a certain girl might become
his mate. The Rabbi disapproved of the petition, saying: "If she is the
right one for you, she will not be parted from you; if not, your unanswered prayer might lead you to lose faith in God."

*Moed Katon, 18b (Rashi).*

Rabban Gamaliel visited Rabbi Helbo ben Karua and asked his host
to pray for him.

Rabbi Helbo prayed: "May God grant thee according to thine own
heart." (Psalm 20:4)

Rabbi Huna bar Isaac said: "Only on behalf of a man whose heart
was perfect before His Creator, like Rabban Gamaliel, was such a
prayer proper. On behalf of another man, however, no such prayer
should be offered, for such a man might have it in his heart to steal or
to sin. This would be the right prayer for such a person: 'May the
Lord fulfil all thy petitions.' A man would not petition God to aid him
to commit a transgression."

*Midrash Tehillim, Buber, p. 176.*

## 257. PRAYERS IN AFFLICTION

The heart's cry to God is the highest form of prayer.

*Zohar, ii, 20a.*

The prayer of the afflicted is heard first.

*Zohar, i, 168b.*

The Book of Psalms uses three titles for a prayer: a Prayer of
Moses, a Prayer of David and a Prayer of the Afflicted. The Prayer
of the Afflicted is the most important of the three.

*Zohar, iv, 195a.*

R. Judah bar Nahmani was asked by Rabbi Simeon ben Lakish to
compose prayers for various occasions. He wrote the following:

### Praising the Lord

Thou O Lord art great in all Thy greatness; Thou art mighty
in all strength; Thou revivest the dead by a word; Thou doest
great things unfathomable and wonders uncountable.

### Comforting the Mourners

O my brethren in distress and smitten by this affliction, consider that this is the way of all flesh since time began. Many have
partaken of this bitter cup, and many will yet drink of it, the best

and the worst of men alike. O my brethren, may He who comforts troubled hearts comfort you.

### Appreciation of Those Who Comfort

O my brethren, you perform kind deeds. Sons of those who incline towards deeds of loving kindness, who emulate the kindness shown by Abraham to all mankind. May He who justly rewards render you payment in full.

### A Prayer for the Troubled in Israel

O Master of the World! Redeem, help, save and assist Thy nation from pestilence, the sword; from rapine, blight and drought; from the evil which assails the world. Before we call unto Thee, answer us. Blessed be Thou who canst remove calamity among the peoples.

*Ketubot, 8.*

Rabbi Judah said: "If a man has a patron, when a time of trouble overtakes him, he does not immediately enter into his patron's presence, but comes and stands at the door of his house, and calls one of the servants or a member of his family. The latter brings word to the patron, saying, 'So and so is standing at the entrance of your court.' Perhaps the patron will admit him, perhaps he will make him wait. This is not the way with God. If trouble comes upon a man, he must not cry to Michael or to Gabriel; but let him cry unto Me, and I will answer him forthwith, as the Scripture says, 'Whosoever shall call on the name of the Lord shall be delivered.' " (Joel 3:5—E.V. 2:32)

*Y. Berakot, 13a.*

He who is walking in a place of danger should recite a brief prayer in place of the Eighteen Benedictions. How should he word it?

R. Eliezer said: "Do Thy will in the heavens above, and bestow contentment upon those who fear Thee on earth; and do what is good in Thine eyes. Blessed art Thou who hearest prayer."

R. Jose said: "Hear the voice of the prayer of Thy people Israel, and act speedily in accordance with their entreaty."

R. Eliezar bar Zodak said: "Hear the voice of the cry of . . ."

Others said: "The needs of Thy people are many and their power is limited. May it be Thy will to grant to each one his every need and to everybody everything they lack."

*Tosefta Berakot, 3.*

## 258. PRIVATE PRAYERS

A man should pray that he be safeguarded against misfortune before it is at hand.

*Sanhedrin, 44.*

Nothing can prevent prayer from entering the Gate of Heaven.

*Zohar, i, 24a.*

If a man sees that he has prayed without answer, he should continue praying.

*Berakot, 32.*

The prayer of a sick man for his own recovery avails more than the prayer of another.

*Bereshit Rabba, 53 end.*

Man's awakening on earth below awakens a responsive chord in the realm above.

*Zohar, i, 86b.*

A man should not give up prayer in despair even if a sharp sword be laid at this throat.

*Berakot, 10.*

Before thou prayest that words of Torah enter thy very being, pray that thy sins be forgiven thee.

*Eliyahu Rabbu, 13.*

If it is in a man's power to beseech God's compassion on another individual, it is a sin not to do it, as Samuel says, "Far be it from me that I should sin against the Lord by ceasing to pray for you." (I Samuel, 12:23)

*Berakot, 12b.*

If a man must travel on the highroad, he should pray thrice: the regular prayer, a prayer for safe journey and a prayer for his safe return.

*Zohar, i, 121a; Midrash ha-Neelam.*

Pray and pray again. There will come an hour when thy request will be granted.

*Debarim Rabbah, 2:12.*

If a man stands with his face towards the East, and wishes to petition God for learning, he should turn his face a little towards the South, for the brain is towards the right. If he wishes to pray for riches, he should turn towards the North, for understanding is in the heart which is at the left.

*Zohar, iv, 224a.*

The Holy One seems to be far away, but nothing is nearer than He. Let a man enter the synagogue and pray in an undertone, and God will give ear to his prayer. It is as if a man uttered his thoughts in the ear of his comrade who heard him. Can you have a God nearer than this, who is as near to his creatures as the mouth is to the ear?

*Y. Berakot, 13a.*

Rabba bar R. Huna would don fresh raiment before he went to pray, saying: "It is written: 'Prepare to meet thy God, O Israel.'" (Amos 4:12)

Rabba, on the other hand, would remove his fine garments before he went to pray, saying: "We should be like a serf before our master, not like a man of importance."

R. Kahana, if there were peace in the world, would don his finer garments to pray, but, if there were tribulation in the world, he would remove his finer garments and pray.

*Shabbat, 10.*

R. Eliezer and R. Joshua visited Syria on business. They noticed several children in a certain neighborhood playing at harvesting. The children took some sand and from it they separated a portion for the Terumah (priests' portion) and the Tithe. The Rabbis then understood that this was a Jewish section, and they entered a house. They were welcomed and asked to partake of the meal.

Looking about, they soon observed a strange procedure: every dish was first taken to a small room, and then brought to the table.

On making inquiry, R. Eliezer and R. Joshua were told: "My aged father sits in the little room. He does not leave it because he once vowed to remain there until some Sages came to the house." The Rabbis made themselves known, and summoned the old man. He explained that his son was childless, and therefore he had made the vow in order that his son might diligently look about for Sages to pray for him. This they readily did, and a son was later born to their host. It was Rabbi Judah ben Beteirah.

*Y. Sanhedrin, 7.*

Rabbi Nehunya ben ha-Kanah, a contemporary of Rabban Johanan ben Zakkai, was accustomed, on entering the school, to pray that no occasion of sin or error might occur by his fault; and on leaving it briefly gave thanks that God had appointed his lot in life among those who frequent the synagogue and the school, not the theatre and the circus, nor those that loiter on the street corners.

*Mishnah Berakot, 4, 2.*

## 259. TEARFUL PRAYERS

Never has a tearful prayer been uttered in vain.

*Zohar, i, 132b.*

When a man in affliction sheds tears as he entreats God, his entreaties will be heard.

*Zohar, i, 223a.*

Tears break through the gates and doors of heaven.

*Zohar, ii, 245b.*

Not all tears come before the King. Sullen tears, and tears accompanying the petition for vengeance do not ascend on High. But tears of entreaty and penitence, and tears beseeching relief cleave the very heavens, open the portals and ascend to the King of Kings.

*Zohar Hadash to Ruth, 80a.*

Hannah prayed amid tears: "Thou art the Lord of Hosts, the Lord of two kinds of hosts: those above who are immortal and do not multiply, those below who are mortal and multiply. If I am not to bear children like those above me, let me be immortal like them; but, if I am to die, let me have children like those on earth below."

*Pesikta Rabbati, 44, 4.*

The Rabbis have given a remarkable explanation for the blindness of Isaac. They say: "When Isaac was lying upon the altar ready to be sacrified by his father, according to the command of God, the angels in heaven began to weep and their tears dropped into his eyes and thus blinded him."

*Bereshit Rabbah, 65:5.*

## 260. PREACHERS AND PREACHING

There is a time for long services and long sermons, and a time for short ones.

*Mekilta Beshallah.*

Rabbah would open his discourse with a jest, and let his hearers laugh a little. Then he would become serious.

*Shabbat, 30.*

If a man utters words of Torah in a fashion disagreeable to his hearers, it were better if he refrained from uttering them.

*Shemot Rabbah, 41, 5.*

It is pleasant to ascend the pulpit, but it is difficult to descend.

*Yalkut Shimeoni to Pent., 845.*

Thou preachest beautifully, but is thy practice beautiful?

*Yebamot, 63.*

He who is the first to speak at a public meeting should begin with a kindly word, and he who is the last to speak should end with a kindly word.

*Kohelet Rabbah, 7.*

We read: "Thy lips, O my bride, drop as the honey." (Song of Songs 4:11)
R. Johanan said: "Whosoever preaches or expounds the words of the Torah in public without endeavoring to make his teaching acceptable to his hearers, fails to make himself like a bride who is sweet and

agreeable to her husband on the wedding day. It were better if he did not preach or teach at all."

*Shir ha-Shirim Rabbah to 4, 11.*

There is the preacher of fine words but wicked conduct.

*Hagigah, 14.*

## 261. PRECEDENT

I have not seen Rabbis older than ourselves do this.

*Berakot, 30.*

## 262. PRECIOUS THINGS

Ten things are called precious in the Bible: Torah, Israel, wealth, knowledge, prophecy, understanding, occasional folly, the Zaddikim, loving kindness, and the death of the just.

*Midrash Tehillim, 116, 5.*

Some things stand at the top of the world, and yet people make light of them.

*Berakot, 6.*

One thing obtained with difficulty is more precious in the eyes of a man than a hundred things procured with ease.

*Abot de-Rabbi Nathan, chapter 3.*

When a palace is destroyed, it still retains the name of a palace, but a dunghill remains a dunghill however high it grows.

*Pesikta Buber, 14.*

## 263. PRIDE AND THE PROUD

The proud man is not acceptable even in his own household.

*Baba Batra, 98.*

Absalom was proud of his hair and therefore was hanged by his hair.

*Sotah, 9.*

The Evil Spirit delights in accusing a man of Torah who is full of pride.

*Zohar Hadash, iv, 50b.*

What is the sign of a proud man? He never praises any one.

*Zohar, iv, 193b.*

Pride is a blemish.

*Megillah, 29.*

If a man praises himself, it is a sign that he knows nothing.

*Zohar, iv, 193.*

Poverty is oftentimes a sign of haughtiness in a man.

*Shabbat, 33; Kiddushin, 49.*

Torah is not found among those whose mind is high as the heavens or broad as the sea.

*Erubin, 55.*

He who considers himself greater than his comrade is lower than him.

*Midrash Shemuel, 16.*

One man may not say to another: "My deeds are greater than yours."

*Sotah, 41.*

God says concerning the man of pride: "I and he cannot abide together."

*Sotah, 5.*

### HONORS WHICH INTERFERE

When Rabbi Judah I passed through the city of Simonia, the townspeople asked him to give them a judge and teacher. He gave them Levi bar Sissi.

The people built a platform for him, and asked him to answer their questions while standing on it. But the answers, which he would have known well before, deserted his memory. Recognizing his serious trouble, he arose early in the morning, and rode rapidly in order to intercept the Rabbi.

When Rabbi saw him, he asked with concern: "What have the people of Simonia done to thee?"

Levi bar Sissi answered: "They asked me three questions, but the answers escaped me."

He thereupon repeated the questions, and at this time gave the correct answers.

"If thou knowest the answers so well, why didst thou not give them?" asked Rabbi.

"They placed me upon a platform, and gave me a tall chair. My spirit became conscious of the honor, and the answers escaped me."

"Let this be an example to the Disciples," said Rabbi. "If a man is filled with pride, the Torah escapes him."

*Bereshit Rabbah, 81.*

### THE TREES AND THE SCHOLARS

When God created the trees, they grew higher and higher. They thought, in their pride, that nothing could halt their growth; but the trees lost their arrogance when God placed it in the mind of man to fashion iron and make axes.

The men of learning became overconfident, and did not bewail the destruction of the Holy Temple. They said to themselves: "We are more important than the Temple. We shall lead the world in the spirit of the Torah, and we shall teach the Mitzwot."

Then God prompted the Emperor to prohibit the teaching of the Torah, and to order the execution of the men of learning. They then lost their pride.

*Midrash Eleh Ezkerah.*

## GREATER THAN THE KING

King Solomon received from the Lord a wondrous gift, namely, a silken carpet which flew through the air. The king and his associates would take breakfast in Damascus and supper in Media, carried to and fro on the magic carpet.

Once the king passed an ant-hill. Since he understood the speech of all living creatures, he overheard the queen-ant order the subject-ants to hide from Solomon.

"Why hast thou said this?" the king called down.

"Because I was afraid they might look up to thee, and learn from thee pride in place of humility, diligence and praise for their Maker."

"Let me ask thee a question," Solomon said.

"Take me up to thee, then," answered the queen-ant.

When he took the little creature in his palm, the king asked: "Is there anyone in the world greater than myself?"

"Yes," answered the ant, "I am greater than thee, since God has sent thee to carry me."

*Midrash Wayyosha, end.*

## 264: PROGRESS AND RETROGRESSION

Not all times are equal.[1]

*Tamid, 1.*

The heart of the ancients was open to understanding like the width of a hall; of more recent men, like the width of a room; but our heart is like the eye of a narrow needle.

*Erubin, 50.*

"There were three men who saw destruction—Noah, Daniel and Job. Noah saw a world in existence, saw it destroyed, and again beheld its reconstruction. Daniel saw the glory of the first Temple, witnessed its destruction, but also beheld the building of the second Temple. Job saw the growth, the upbuilding of his home, saw also its ruin, but again beheld its revival and reconstruction."

*Midrash Tanhuma, Noah, 5.*

[1] Compare Ecclesiastes 3:1-8.

## 265. PROPHETS AND PROPHECY

Every prophecy with a lesson for future generations has been published.

*Shir ha-Shirim Rabbah, 4, 22.*

In one respect, prophets were like wives. They were not ashamed to ask God for material maintenance, just as a woman asks it of her husband.

*Shir ha-Shirim Rabbah, 1, 54.*

The men of the Great Synagogue restored the attributes or conceptions of God, by pointing out the defects in the reasoning of Jeremiah and Daniel. The Rabbis ask: "How dared these Prophets contradict that which Moses spoke?"

Rabbi Isaac answered: "Because they knew that God 'Amiti Hu' is the essence of truth; they therefore could not lie to Him!"

*Yoma, 69b.*

The Rabbis said: "Every truth that a prophet will proclaim in any generation he already received from Mt. Sinai, even though he was not personally present at that revelation."

*Shemot Rabbah, chap. 28.*

R. Johanan said: "Since the Temple was destroyed prophecy was taken from the prophets and given to the foolish and to babes."

*Baba Batra, 12b.*

There were as many prophetesses as prophets in Israel.

*Shir ha-Shirim Rabbah, 4, 22.*

The prophecy of Beeri consisted of only two verses, and these were included in the Book of Isaiah.

*Wayyikra Rabbah, 6, 6.*

Compared to Moses, all the prophets were like the moon compared to the sun.

*Zohar, iv, 135b.*

Prophecy is given only to those who are broken of heart.

*Zohar, i, 212a.*

Even the Holy Spirit did not rest upon all the prophets in equal measure. One prophesied to the extent of a book; another in only two verses.

*Yalkut Shimeoni to Isaiah, 281.*

In this world only individuals were prophets. In the World-to-Come, all Israel will be prophets.

*Bemidbar Rabbah, 14, end.*

The prophets had compassion both upon Israel and idolaters.

*Tanhuma Balak, 1.*

A prophet whose native town is not mentioned doubtless came from Jerusalem.

*Petiheta Ekah Rabbah.*

Rabbi Hananiah said: "The Sages are of greater importance than the prophets. It is like a king who sent ambassadors to a province. Concerning one, he sent word that he was not to be trusted without credentials, whereas the other was to be accredited without a token. Who was the greater?

"With respect to a prophet, God says: 'He giveth thee a sign or a token.' (Deut. 13:2)

"With respect to the Sages or Elders, God declares: 'According to the decision which they may say unto thee shalt thou do; thou shalt not depart from the sentence which they may tell thee, to the right or to the left.'" (Deut. 17:11)

*Y. Berakot, 1, 5.*

## 266. PROSELYTE, GER

He who deceives a proselyte is as if he revered idols.

*Midrash Agadah Mishpatim, 22, 15.*

He who turns away a proselyte seeking justice is as if he had turned away the justice of God.

*Hagigah, 5.*

There are three kinds of proselytes: one becomes an Israelite because he loves a Jewess, a second, because he receives Jewish charity, the third, because he reveres the Name of God.

*Yalkut Shimeoni to Pent., 213.*

The old man Jacob was compelled to make entreaty for food and raiment, but the proselyte receives it without asking, because he is beloved of God.

*Bereshit Rabbah, 70, 5.*

Rabbi Nehemiah said: "Those who became proselytes for the love of a Jewess or out of fear of Jews and proselytes for the sake of bettering their lot should not be accepted. Genuine proselytes are those who become Israelites, though there be nothing to gain thereby."

*Yebamot, 24b.*

He who has robbed the alien and has died, receives no forgiveness, for he has profaned the good name of Israel and of God.

*Tosefta Baba Kamma, 10.*

There are three kinds of proselytes: one is like Abraham—he finds the true religion in Judaism; another accepts Judaism through love of a Jewess; the third is like an idolater—he believes that his conversion will benefit him materially.

*Seder Eliyahu Rabbah, 29.*

Proselytes are as difficult for Israel as an ailment of the skin.[1]

*Yebamot, 47b.*

[1] Jews have frequently suffered when it has become known that Gentiles have adopted Judaism.

Sometimes souls mate in the upper world. They create lights, and kindle dark souls with them. The latter are the souls of mortals who have accepted Judaism.

*Zohar, iv, 168a.*

Rabbi Jose ben Halafta said: "A proselyte who embraces Judaism is like a new-born child. God cannot therefore now chastise him for deeds done or duties neglected before his new birth."

*Yebamot, 48b.*

It is said that the stranger who yields himself to the Divine commands is dearer to God even than Israel was at Sinai, for he comes without the constraining terror of thunder and lightning, and voluntarily making himself at one with the Highest, submits to the "yoke of the kingdom of Heaven."

*Tanhuma, 14, 1.*

## AQUILA THE PROSELYTE

Aquila the Proselyte came to Rabbi Eliezer and said: "Is this the love with which God loves the proselyte, that He supplies him with bread and raiment? (Deut. 10:18). Is this all He gives the proselyte? I have many pheasants and many raiments of peacock color, yet even my slaves do not hold them to be of importance." Rabbi Eliezer rebuked Aquila and he departed.

The Proselyte went to Rabbi Joshua, who sought to appease him, saying: "Bread includes spiritual food, and raiment includes the Tallit of the learned doctors. And, when a proselyte was not only rich in material possessions but also in spiritual wealth, the High Priest himself was happy to have him marry his daughter, and he might even see his grandson officiate as the High Priest."

The students said: "Were it not for Rabbi Joshua's patience in dealing with him, Aquila might have returned to paganism." And they said: "He that is slow to anger is better than the mighty."[1]

*Bereshit Rabbah, 70.*

[1] Rabbi Eliezer is called "the Shamutti" in the Talmud. This may mean that he is of the School of Shammai, and, in this story, he imitates Shammai. Another explanation of the term is "the excommunicated"; he was excommunicated for holding fast to his opinions, though the majority decided otherwise.

### Learning Torah

Aquila begged permission from the Emperor Hadrian to be circumcised.

Hadrian was surprised, and said: "Why do you wish to join a barbarian nation that is in subjection?"

"Because I wish to learn the Torah."

"Cannot you learn it without being circumcised?"

"No," answered Aquila. "The Book of Psalms says: 'He declareth His word unto Jacob, His statutes and His ordinances unto Israel. He hath not dealt so with any nation; and as for His ordinances, they have not known them.'" (Psalm 147, 19–20)

*Shemot Rabbah, 30.*

### The Would-Be Proselyte

Timna, the sister of the chief Lotan (Gen. 36:22), admired the family of Isaac and desired to become a proselyte. Isaac did not wish to admit into his immediate family a Horite woman, and he declined her request.

She then went to Eliphaz, the son of Esau, and became his concubine, and her son was Amalek, chief among the enemies of Israel.

Had the patriarch received her into his family, and given her as wife to Jacob, there would have been no Amalek.

*Sanhedrin, 99.*

### The Proselyte's Arguments

When the emperor heard that his kinsman, Aquila, had become a proselyte of Judaism, he dispatched guardsmen to summon him. Aquila entered into discussion with them, and all became proselytes.

Again the emperor sent messengers to summon Aquila with instructions not to converse with him. Aquila said: "Among the Romans an officer of lesser degree holds the lamp before his superior, but, concerning the God of Israel, it is written that he went before Israel to light the way." All became adherents of Judaism.

A third time the emperor sent messengers commanding them not to listen to Aquila's words. Aquila placed his hand over a Mezuzah and smiled broadly.

They asked: "Why dost thou smile?"

He replied: "Among the Romans, the king sits within, and his subjects guard him from without. Of God it is said that His subjects sit within, and He guards them from without." (Psalm 121:8)

All became proselytes. The emperor sent no more messengers to Aquila.

*Kiddushin, 32.*

### THE ASTROLOGER PROSELYTE

R. Huna narrated: "An astrologer who had become a proselyte to Judaism consulted his horoscope before departing on a journey. The reading showed that he would meet with danger, and he was minded to delay his voyage. Then his courage rose within him, and he said to himself: 'Did I not join the nation of Israel because I am convinced that God protects those who believe and trust in Him?'

"He departed on his way, and in a lonely spot encountered some wild beasts. He was about to leave them his donkey, but the beasts ran away.

"Why did the proselyte meet with danger? Because he had consulted the horoscope. Why was he saved? Because he trusted in the Lord."

*Y. Shabbat, 6.*

### ONLY THE WRITTEN LAW

A Gentile asked Shammai to accept him as a proselyte on the condition that he learn the Written Law only. The rabbi refused.

The man then went to Hillel with the same proposal. Hillel had him circumcised, and commenced to teach him the Hebrew alphabet. In the course of time the proselyte was taught the Scriptures and then was told to learn the explanations of the Oral Law.

When he remonstrated, Hillel said: "You trusted me in what I taught you before. Why, then, dost thou not trust me now?"

*Shabbat, 31a, abbreviated.*

When a man comes in these times seeking to become a proselyte, he is asked: "What is your motive in presenting yourself to become a proselyte? Do you not know that in these times the Israelites are afflicted, distressed, downtrodden, torn to pieces, and that suffering is their lot?"

If he answer: "I know; and I am unworthy (to share their sufferings)," they accept him at once, and acquaint him with some of the lighter and some of the weightier commandments; they instruct him regarding the sin he may commit in such matters as picking up the forgotten sheaf, reaping the corner of the field, and the poor tithe. They acquaint him also with the penalties attached to the commandments and with the reward of keeping them. This discourse should not go too much into particulars."

*Yebamot, 46b.*

### THE STRAY GAZELLE

To illustrate God's singular love for proselytes, the Midrash has a parable of a king's affection for a stray gazelle of the desert that had joined itself to his flocks and went in and out with them.

The king said: "Should we not bestow special kindness upon the free animal of the wide plains that has joined us of its own accord?"

In the same way, should we not treat kindly the proselyte who has left his people and his father's house and joined us?

*Bemidbar Rabbah, 8, 2.*

### FOR THE SAKE OF GOD

Rab said: "Even those who become proseyltes from motives of self-interest are proselytes. This is the rule. They are not to be repelled as proselytes are repelled at the outset, but received; and they must have friendly treatment, for perhaps after all they have become proselytes for God's sake."

*Y. Kiddushin, 65b.*

### THE MARTYR PROSELYTE

A certain philosopher who was converted by the constancy of the martyrs, Rabbi Hanina ben Teradion and his wife and daughter, and was sentenced to the same fate, said: "You have told me good news. Tomorrow my portion will be with them in the World-to-Come."

*Sifre Deut., 307.*

Rabbi Nathan used to say: "Do not throw up to your fellow a blemish you have yourself. If you insult a man because he is a proselyte, he can retort: 'The Scripture says: "For ye were aliens."'"

Rabbi Simeon ben Yohai said: "It says: 'And those that love Him are like the sun when it rises in its power.' (Judges 5, 31) Which is greater: he who loves the king, or he whom the king loves? You must say, he whom the king loves. And it is said of God, 'And He loveth a proselyte.'" (Deut. 10:18)

*Mekilta Mishpatim, 18.*

### KEEPING THE DOOR OPEN

Rabbi Simeon ben Yohai said: "Our father Abraham was not circumcised till he was ninety-nine years old. If he had been circumcised at twenty or at thirty, a man could have become a proselyte only at a lower age than twenty or thirty; therefore, God postponed it in his case till he arrived at the age of ninety-nine, in order not to bolt the door in the face of proselytes who come."

*Mekilta Mishpatim, 18.*

### ON ONE FOOT

A foreigner came to Shammai, saying, "Make a proselyte of me, on condition that you teach me the whole of the Torah while I stand on one foot."

Shammai drove him off with a measuring-stick he had in his hand. Thereupon he repaired to Hillel with the same proposition.

Hillel received him as a proselyte and taught him: "What you do not like to have done to you, do not do to your fellow. This is the whole of the Torah; the rest is the explanation of it. Go, learn it."

*Shabbat, 31a.*

When Aquila, the nephew of Emperor Hadrian, desired to become a proselyte to Judaism, he said to the Emperor: "I wish to engage in business. Can you advise me how to buy?"

The Emperor replied: "Go about and see what merchandise is very cheap in the present market, and then buy. It will surely rise in price if you wait long enough."

Aquila departed, and underwent circumcision. When he acquainted his uncle of his deed, the Emperor wished to know who had enjoined him to do this.

"Thou are the man," Aquila replied. "Israel is the cheapest nation today; hence I bought my way into it."

"What will you gain?"

"The ability to learn Torah."

"But why must you circumcise for that?"

Aquila said: "Can any one in your army gain distinction unless he proves his loyalty and readiness to sacrifice himself for you? By the same token, no one can gain distinction in the knowledge of the Torah, unless he shows readiness to shed his blood for God."

*Tanhuma to Mishpatim.*

Rabbi Johanan said: " 'The proselyte shall not lodge without; I will open my doors to the wayfarer.' (Job 31, 32) This is a text proving the rule that proselytes should be held back with the weaker left hand and drawn near with the right. Men should not do like Elisha, who thrust Gehazi away with both hands."

*Y. Sanhedrin, 29b.*

The rabbis say: "If a proselyte takes it upon himself to obey all the words of the Torah except one single commandment, he is not to be received."

*Sifra, Kedoshim, Perek, 8.*

One who brings a foreigner near and makes a proselyte of him is as if he created him.

*Bereshit Rabbah, 39, near end.*

## 267. PROSPERITY

R. Akiba said: "Do not act towards God as other nations act towards their gods. The other nations, when they are prosperous, honor their gods, but when misfortune befalls them, curse their gods. But they who are of Israel should give thanks, whether He bring upon them prosperity or suffering."

*Mekilta to Exodus 20:30.*

## 268. PROVERBS AND FABLES

Let not the parable be light in thine eyes, for through it thou acquirest an insight into the Torah.

*Shir ha-Shirim Rabbah, 1, 8.*

Thou hast entered the city; abide by its customs.

*Bemidbar Rabbah, 48, 14.*

A thread always is found on the tailor.

*Intr. to Tanhuma Buber, 79.*

Throw up a stick into the air, and it will fall to its original place.

*Bereshit Rabbah, 53, end.*

He who loses his coat in a verdict of the court should depart singing. He has suffered no loss.

He who hears an insult and does not mind it is spared a hundred evils.

A thief is not sentenced to death for two or three offenses.

Seven pitfalls do not harm the just man, but one pitfall injures the unjust.

She sleeps and her working bag is light.

I trusted him and he turned against me.

*Sanhedrin, 7.*

Two schoolboys absented themselves from school. One was punished and the other was frightened.

*Bereshit Rabbah, 48, 5.*

Thou hast given bread to a child; let its mother know.

*Bemidbar, R., 19, 20.*

When the idol is smitten, its priests grow terror-stricken.

*Shemot, R., 9, 8.*

If one man says to thee: "Thou art a donkey," do not mind; if two speak thus, purchase a saddle for thyself.

*Bereshit, R., 45, 10.*

In a field where there are mounds, do not tell secrets.

*Bereshit, R., 74, 2.*

Do no good to the wicked man, and no evil will befall thee.

*Bemidbar, R., 18, 18.*

"Go, go," is said to the Nazir. "Turn about, turn about, and do not draw near the vineyard."

*Bemidbarr, 10, 22.*

If thou lackest knowledge, what hast thou acquired? If thou acquirest knowledge, what dost thou lack?

*Bemidbar, R., 19, 3.*

Where the swordsman once hung his weapon, the shepherd now hangs his whip.

*Kohelet, R., 19, 3.*

Better one bird securely bound than a hundred free and flying.

*Kohelet, R., 4, 9.*

He steals the apples and distributes them to the sick.

*Kohelet, R., 4, 9.*

It is not enough that a borrower should lose his own possessions, but he loses also that which is not his own.

*Kohelet, R., 4, 9.*

He who leases one garden eats birds; he who leases many gardens is eaten by birds.

*Kohelet, R., 4, 9.*

He who has been bitten by a snake is frightened by a rope.

*Kohelet, R., 7, 4.*

He who steals kindling wood will be flogged with a log of wood.

*Wayyikra, R., 15, 8.*

If you untie one of the twists of a rope, others become untied.

*Wayyikra, R., 14, 3.*

Cleave to an official, and people will bow down before thee; cleave to a person who is warm, and thou wilt be warm as well.

*Bereshit, 16, 5.*

Do not rear a good pup of a bad dog, or, needless to say, a bad pup of a bad dog.

*Wayyikra, R., 19, 6.*

When prosperity comes to my landlord, I do not share in it; but when depression overtakes him, I must suffer also.

*Petihetah, 24 of Eikah Rabbah.*

The saying has it: "Shila has sinned, but Johanan pays."

*Ruth, R., 1, 4.*

A matron came to a town where no one knew her origin. When they observed her amiable conduct, people said: "Surely she must have come from an excellent family, for her conduct sets an excellent example."

*Zohar, i, 266b.*

A king owned two safes, one full of gold and the other of silver. He placed the latter near him since he used it more.

*Zohar, i, 61b.*

A king possessed a wonderful vessel. He took especial care of it, and admired it greatly. Once his son angered him, and he seized the vessel, and broke it. Akin to this was the burning of the Holy Temple.

*Zohar, i, 61b.*

A king wished to give a banquet for his friend. He first commanded that a feast be served to other officials, and, when they had been served, he called in his friend.

*Zohar, i, 64a.*

A king built hiding places in the city, and later his courtiers rebelled. When they saw themselves outnumbered by the king's loyal guardsmen, the rebels sought to hide themselves.

The king said: "I have built the hiding-places, yet they think they can hide themselves from me there."

*Zohar, i, 68a.*

A bandit chief (Satan) sent out a persuasive member of his company to invite men to visit a place where they might be easily attacked. When the travellers arrive there he is the first to assail them.

*Zohar, i, 111a.*

A king had many armies of brave soldiers. He was informed that a band of robbers was attacking wayfarers, and he sent out against them a small company of men.

When asked why he did not send a strong army, he replied: "Against these enemies, a small company is sufficient."

*Zohar, i, 146a.*

A man dwelt for a long time in a dark place. When he left it he could not bear the light, and was forced to accustom his eyes to it gradually.

*Zohar, i, 170a.*

A king wished to marry his daughter to a friend. He was accustomed to send a message through the princess to the friend. But when the couple were married, he said: "Now I shall speak to him myself."

*Zohar, ii, 22b.*

A son was born to a king, and the ruler sent the child to a village for his upbringing, in order that he might learn the ways of the world. Later he sent the queen for the child, and rejoiced greatly with him. (The Redemption.)

*Zohar, i, 245b.*

A man quarrelled with his wife, and she cursed him. The king chanced to be there, and he said: "Dost thou not know that thou hast spoken evil words before the king?"

*Zohar, ii, 22b.*

A dog brings his master a game-bird. What does he receive? A bone.

*Zohar, ii, 112a.*

A king devised a plan for a palace. He summoned skillful builders, who erected it for him. When it was erected, it was known as the king's palace. What had he given to it? He had contributed an idea.

*Zohar, ii, 161a.*

A man's son fell ill, and the physician prescribed certain foods for the patient.

The man declared: "Let no other food be found in the house." When the son had recovered, every type of food was brought in.

*Zohar, ii, 183b.*

A king invited a beloved guest to visit him.

He said: "Every day, you, my courtiers, concern yourselves with my various needs, but today I wish you to enjoy yourselves with my guest."

*Zohar, iii, 94a.*

A king ordered food to be placed before a guest. Though the king did not eat with the guest, the latter ate the food of the king.

*Zohar, iii, 94b.*

A king gave a banquet for his sons. When the princess entered and asked for a share, the king commanded every son to give her a portion from his plate. Thus the princess had more than any.

*Zohar, 96b.*

Give a little wine to the clown, and he will praise you before the king. If you give him nothing, he will speak evil of you.

*Zohar, iii, 101b.*

Once a shepherd, leading his flock across a brook, saw a wolf approaching. What did he do? He chose a powerful he-goat and set him to fight the wolf. During the fight, he crossed the stream safely with his flock.

*Zohar, iii, 101b.*

If a fool stands before a king, give him a drink of good wine, and tell him of all the mistakes which you have made. He will then praise you before the king, saying that no one in the world is like you.

*Zohar, iii, 102a.*

A man fell in love with a woman who resided in the block of the tanners. If she had not lived there, he would never have entered this evil smelling section; but, since she dwells there, the street seems to him like the street of the perfumers.

*Zohar, iii, 116b.*

A son disobeyed his father, who said: "If I punish him, his pain will bring me pain as well. If I shout at him, he will be shamed. What shall I do? Let me entreat him to do my will."

*Zohar, iv, 203b.*

A skillful tailor cut up some cloth for the king's garment, and gave the pieces to other skilled tailors to fit together properly. Thus did Moses give over the Torah to the Rabbis to fit together appropriately its various pieces.

*Zohar, iv, 254a.*

Some come to the palace to see the royal raiment; some come to look upon the king's countenance; those who are wise come to behold the deeds of the king.

*Tikkune Zohar, T. 22, 95a.*

The beloved of the bride left her and she grew ill. Many physicians were unable to diagnose her illness, but one of them from the city said: "Your beloved is knocking at the door." At once she arose.

*Tikkune Zohar, 146b, T. 68.*

A king, while visiting his garden one summer day, gave orders that the thorns be torn out, but, when he observed budding roses among them, he left the thorns because of the roses. When the flowers grew and were plucked, he ordered that the thorns be removed.

*Zohar Hadash, i, 12b.*

A rich man at a sumptuous meal was asked for food by a beggar, but he gave him nothing.

Later, however, when the rich man had eaten his fill, he commanded his servant to give the poor man a portion of what he had left. Does the rich man deserve any reward?

*Zohar Hadash, i, 24b.*

When the generation of the Flood worshipped idols and the Creator grew sad, two angels came before him, and said: "O Master of the Universe, send us down to earth, and we shall sanctify Thy Name."

When the angels descended, the Evil Impulse generated within them. They coveted the beautiful maidens of earth, and refused to obey the restrictions established by man. Once they beheld a beautiful maiden and became enamoured of her.

"Teach me," she said, "the Holy Name, and I will be yours."

As soon as she had learned the Ineffable Name, she pronounced it, and prayed that she be taken up into heaven.

And God said: "Let her become a star and shine gloriously forever and ever."

The angels married and bore sons whose names were Heave and Hey. Noah preached that God would destroy the sinful earth, and the sons of the angels believed and were sad at heart that their names would be blotted out for the sins of man.

Their father then said: "You need not be anxious regarding this. In the generations to come, your name will not cease from out of the mouths of the laboring people. When they split stones or carry heavy burdens, they will say, 'Heave' and 'Hey!'"

*Yalkut Shimeoni to Gen., 6, 2.*

### A Fable of the Flood

When all living creatures came into Noah's ark, he selected a pair of each kind, and admitted them into the Ark.

Falsehood wished to enter, but, since he did not have a mate, he was refused admittance. When Falsehood saw Injustice (or Deceit) approaching, he said: "Let us join together so that Noah will admit us."

"And what will be my reward?" asked Injustice.

"Whatever reward I collect through my work, you will take."

When every one had left the Ark, Falsehood busied himself gathering prey, and Injustice carried it away.

In reply to Falsehood's complaint, Injustice said: "You may gather into your net everything except me. I insist upon the letter of the agreement."

*Midrash Tehillim, chap. 7.*

Rab Judah of India was fond of narrating fairy tales.

On one occasion, he narrated the following story: "Once upon a time, I chanced to be travelling upon a ship in the Indian Ocean. We beheld a whale swimming about with a sparkling stone in its mouth. A strong swimmer leaped overboard in an attempt to secure the gem. The whale, greatly annoyed, tried to damage the ship.

"Then a huge creature of the sea fell upon him, and killed him. All about us the sea became red. A companion whale seized the gem, applied it to the wound, and the whale revived. Again it wished to overturn the ship; again a monster fell upon him and slew him. This time the monster secured the gem, and hurled it upon the ship.

"Foolishly, we applied the revivifying jewel on some salted fish. The fish came to life again, and jumped into the water, carrying the jewel with them."

*Baba Batra, 74-b.*

## 269. PUBLIC

There is no public in which everyone is rich or everyone is poor.
*Y. Gittin, 3, 7.*

Exclude thyself not from the community.[1]

*Berakot, 49; Abot, 2, 5.*

[1] Share its weal and woe.

The Congregation is immortal. (Ein-ha-tzibbur methim.)
*Temurah, 15b.*

### The Property of All

A man was removing stones from his own to public property. A Hasid noted this and said: "Oh man, why dost thou remove stones from the property of others to thine own?" The man, however, laughed at him.

Time passed. The man sold his field one day, and as he was walking away, he stumbled over some of the stones he had thrown on the roadway. He said to himself: "The Hasid was truly right, when he declared that I was casting stones from the property of others upon mine own." [1]

*Baba Kamma, 50.*

[1] That which belongs to all, belongs to each.

## 270. PUBLIC SERVICE

How can an unlearned man come to merit life? Let him labor for the public welfare.

*Wayyikra Rabbah, 25.*

What shall a man do to be of use in the world if he is not inclined by temperament to be a student? He should devote time to public affairs and to the public welfare.

*Wayyikra Rabbah, 25.*

"And the Lord spoke unto Moses and unto Aaron, and gave them a charge unto the children of Israel." (Exodus 6:13) God said to them: "My sons at times are obstinate; at times of angry mood, and at times, tiresome. With this knowledge accept for yourselves My mission; be prepared for curses and stoning, and your rewards will be ample."

*Shemot Rabbah, 7.*

R. Lazar (Eleazar), an overseer of the poor, once returned to his home and inquired what had occurred during his absence. "Poor persons came here and were fed, and they thanked you heartily."

"This is small reward," he commented.

On another occasion he was informed: "Poor persons were fed here, but they left cursing you." R. Eleazar was elated, and said: "This will bring me a goodly reward."

*Y. Peah, 8.*

Rabban Gamaliel sent for two Disciples, intending to appoint them to a certain office. They refused to come. He sent to them again, saying: "Think ye I am about to give you rulership; nay, it is servitude I am giving you."

*Horaiyot, 10.*

Rabbi returned from the bath and sat down at home to give attention to community tasks. His servant held before him a cup of wine, but he had no time to take it from him. After a while he observed that the servant had fallen asleep. Rabbi remarked: "The servant sleeps sweetly, but we who minister to the public have no time to enjoy sleep. Let it be known that the public servant is compelled to work harder than any other kind of servant."

*Kohelet Rabbah, 5.*

## For Those Who Come After

Honi ha-Meaggel once saw on his travels an old man planting a carob tree. He asked him when he thought the tree would bear fruit. "After seventy years," was the reply.

"Dost thou expect to live seventy years and eat the fruit of thy labor?"

"I did not find the world desolate when I entered it," said the old man, "and as my fathers planted for me before I was born, so do I plant for those who will come after me."

*Taanit, 23a.*

## Learning or Doing

R. Abbahu sent his son Hanina to study at Tiberias. Later he was informed that Hanina was engaging in community work, and he wrote him: "My son, was there no good to be done in Caesarea, thy native town, that I sent you to Tiberias? Was it not decided that learning takes precedence?"

The other Rabbis of Caesarea said: "Learning takes precedence only if there are others to perform works of kindness; but if there is no other, doing comes first."

R. Hiyya bar Abba, Rabbi Assi and Rabbi Ammi once came late to the session of the Academy of Rabbi Eleazar ben Pedat. The latter asked: "Where have you been?"

They replied: "We were busy performing works of kindness."

Rabbi Eleazar ben Pedat asked again: "And were there no other persons to perform this particular labor of clemency?"

The Rabbis answered: "No, for the man to whom we ministered was a stranger."

*Y. Pesahim, 3.*

## Neglecting to Serve

If the man of learning participates in public affairs and serves as a judge or arbitrator, he establishes the land. But if he sits in his home and says to himself: "What have the affairs of society to do with me? Why should I concern myself with the lawsuits of people? Why should I trouble myself with their voices of protest? Let my soul dwell in peace!"—if he does this, he overthrows the world.

When Rabbi Ammi's hour to die was at hand, his nephew found him weeping bitterly. He said: "Uncle and Teacher, why dost thou weep? Is there any Torah which thou hast not learned and taught? Is there any form of kindness which thou hast not practiced? And above all else, thou hast never accepted a public office and hast kept thyself apart from sitting in judgment."

The Rabbi replied: "It is for this very reason that I weep. I was granted the ability to establish equity between disputants in Israel and I have not acted upon it."

*Tanhuma to Mishpatim.*

### Refusing the Honor

R. Assi came to Kiprah and appointed several worthy men to care for communal affairs, but the men refused the honor. He said to them: "The Mishnah enumerates the officials who served in the Temple before its destruction. Among them is mentioned the name of Ben Babai as caretaker of the wicks. Though his labor was lowly, nevertheless he is cited, to his immortal fame, among the higher officials. How much the more will it be with you, whom I have appointed to have charge of the lives of the community!"

*Shekalim, 5.*

R. Haggai was accustomed to appoint his Disciples as bearers of the Scroll of the Torah to the reading-table in the synagogue. Thereby he showed that the Torah they had learned, gained for them the honor.

*Y. Peah, 8.*

The Rabbis commended all acts done for the public good, and among such acts they included the lighting of dark alleys and the keeping of roads in good repair.

*Wayyikra Rabbah, 9.*

## 271. PURIFICATION

Happy are ye, O Children of Israel! Before whom do ye purify yourselves, and who purifies you? Your Father in Heaven.

*Yoma, 85.*

The God-fearing man will be pure, in his inmost chamber, because, though hidden there from the gaze of man, he is still in the company of God, his Judge and his Ideal.

*Betzah, 9a.*

### A Religious Duty

Hillel's Disciples were walking with him on a certain occasion, and when he was about to depart from their company, they inquired: "Whither goest thou?"

He answered: "I go to fulfil a religious duty."

"What duty?"

"To bathe in the bath-house."

"Is this, then, a duty?"

"Ay," replied Hillel. "The statues of kings which are set in theatres and circuses—he who is appointed to care for them cleanses and polishes them. He is sustained for the purpose; and he grows great through intercourse with the great ones of the realm. I, who have been created in the image and likeness of God, how much the more must I keep my body clean and untainted!"

*Wayyikra Rabbah, 34.*

Personal cleanliness is the foundation of spiritual purity; it is the path by which one attains to the Kingdom of Heaven.

*Abodah Zarah, 20b.*

## 272. PURIM

Why is Esther likened to the Morning Star? To tell us that as the Morning Star marks the end of the night, so does Esther mark the end of all miracles.

*Yoma, 29.*

When Esther told Mordecai to proclaim a three-day fast commencing with the Eve of Passover, he asked: "How can we desecrate the Festival?"

She answered: "If there be no Israel in the world, of what avail are the Festivals? If there be no Israel, wherefore the Torah?"

*Midrash Panim Aherim, 2nd Version, 4.*

R. Meir chanced to be in a town of Asia Minor on Purim, and there was at hand no Megillah of Esther in Hebrew. He took some parchment, wrote it out from memory and read it. It was asked: "Is this not against the rule that Scripture may not be read from memory even by one who knows it like Ezra?"

The answer was: "It could not then be helped." Others say that he wrote two copies, one from memory, which he hid, and the other which he copied from the first, in order to meet the requirements of the law.

*Y. Megillah, 4; Tanhuma Buber, Wayyera.*

R. Phinehas narrated this fable: "A lion held a feast for his subjects in a tent fashioned from the skins of lions. They demanded that the fox sing a song, and he said: 'Look about you, O my friends. What is our wish? Only this, that He who permitted us to see the skins of the former, may He permit us to see the skin of the latter.' Likewise, the people of Israel say: 'May He who has permitted us to witness the punishment of the King's two servants permit us also to see the punishment of Haman.'"

*Midrash Abba Gurion.*

### SENDING GIFTS

Rabbah sent to Mari bar Mar on Purim a basket of dates and a plate with sweets. Abbaye remarked: "People will say of thee: when the farmer becomes governor, he forgets to leave behind the grain-box from which he used to feed the cattle. Thou art the Head of the Academy, and yet thou sendest common portions."

Rabbah replied: "Nay, they will say: he cherishes amiable thoughts regarding Mari."

Mari sent back a basket of spices and a box of seasoning. Abbaye said to him: "Rabbah sent sweets to you, but you have sent him bitters in return."

"Nay," replied Mari. "It will be remarked that I believe him to be a well-seasoned sage."

*Megillah, 7. Amplified.*

### THE ARGUMENTS OF HAMAN

Haman said to Ahasuerus: "Sire, thou wilt do well to persecute the Jews. Their taxes are negligible in amount; they have no government to protect their rights; they are unwilling to serve the King on the pretext that it is the Sabbath or Passover; they pretend to be busy with reading the Shema and with prayer whenever they are called upon to labor for the king; and in their prayers, they petition God to destroy the evil ones, namely, ourselves; they open up the Scroll of the Torah, and affirm that we are God's enemies."

*Megillah, 13.*

### THE HABIT OF ANTI-SEMITES

Esther remarked to Ahasuerus: "Thy predecessors had a wise Jew as their counselor, by name, Daniel. Whenever they were perplexed or troubled, he would succeed in assuaging their pain. Why dost thou not do likewise?"

The King answered: "Is there anyone of similar good counsel in the land?"

Esther said: "There is Mordecai, a Jew, who is highly respected for his wisdom."

Mordecai was appointed to sit at the gate of the King, in place of Bigthan and Teresh. When Mordecai superseded them, they said: "Let us kill the King, and everyone will say: when Bigthan and Teresh guarded the King, all was well; as soon, however, as he appointed Mordecai, the King was slain. Jews, they will declare, are not loyal."

*Midrash Panim Aherim, 2.*

## 273. THE PURSUED

Even if a Zaddik persecutes a wicked man, God will seek to aid the persecuted one.

*Wayyikra Rabbah, 27, 5.*

Bring to Me offerings not from those who pursue, but from those who are pursued.

*Wayyikra Rabbah, 27, 5.*

Better to be of the persecuted than of the persecutors.

*Baba Kamma, 93a.*

## 274. QUARRELS

No good results from a quarrel.

*Shemot Rabbah, 30.*

God makes the memory of him to be forgotten who helps to spread a quarrel.

*Bemidbar Rabbah, 18, 4.*

When Jacob was about to lay himself down to sleep upon a rock for a pillow, he found to his surprise that there were twelve rocks where he stood, each bearing the name of one of the tribes in Israel. And the twelve rocks began quarreling amongst themselves. Each said: "On me must the righteous one place his head."

And God caused the twelve rocks to become one—a symbol of the unity of Israel.

*Hullin, 91b.*
*See Rashi to Genesis 28:11.*

Grievous is the sin of quarreling, for it may lead to the shedding of blood.

*Midrash ha-Gadol, 218.*

Most quarrels occur in a home over the lack of necessities.

*Baba Metzia, 59.*

He who disturbs the peace disturbs God, whose Name is Peace.

*Zohar, i, 76a.*

Neither good nor peace comes through a quarrel.

*Sifre Tetze, 86.*

A quarrel is like a stream of water. If it has once opened a way, it becomes a wide path.

*Sanhedrin, 7.*

A home where dissension rules will end in destruction.

*Derek Eretz Zuta, 9.*

People say: when food is lacking in the larder, quarrel knocks at the door.

*Baba Metzia, 59.*

## 275. QUORUM

The reason that ten men are required as a quorum for public worship is stated to be that "wherever ten men gather for prayer the Shekinah is with them."

*Berakot, 6a.*

### 276. RAIN, SUNSHINE, WIND

Great is the period of rain. Even the penny in the purse is blessed by it.

*Taanit, 8.*

Sunshine after a rainfall does as much good as two rains.

*Taanit, 3.*

The rain descends from above, but it is born below.

*Bereshit Rabbah, 12, 11.*

Snow benefits the mountains to the same degree that five rains benefit the plain.

*Taanit, 3.*

The coming down of rain is an event greater than the giving of the Decalogue. The Torah is for Israel only, but rain is for the entire world.

*Midrash Tehillim, 117, 1.*

The miracle of rain is greater than the resurrection of the dead, for resurrection is only for men, whereas rain is for animals as well; resurrection is only for Israelites, rain for the other nations as well; resurrection is only for the righteous, while rain comes down upon the righteous and the wicked alike.

*Berakot, 33a.*

R. Simeon ben Halafta was addicted to corpulence. On a warm day, he sat on a hilltop and said to his daughter: "Pray fan me, and I will give thee a bouquet of sweet-smelling grass." As he spoke, a breeze arose, and the Rabbi said: "How many bouquets does the Master of this breeze deserve!"

*Baba Metzia, 86.*

A Roman asked Rabbi Joshua ben Karha: "When we enjoy a holiday, you do not celebrate it; and when you have a holiday, we do not commemorate it. When do all of us rejoice together at the same time?" The Rabbi answered: "When the rain descends."

*Bereshit Rabbah, 13.*

Rain brings blessings to all: to those engaged in barter or in labor. Rabbi Hiyya bar Abba declares that even the sick feel better after a rain. Some fishermen declare: even fish fatten and weigh more if caught after a heavy rainfall.

*Bereshit Rabbah, 13.*

## 277.  RANSOMING

If a man, his father, his mother and his teacher are captured, and his property suffices not to ransom all of them, who takes precedence? His mother; the man himself; then his teacher, and finally his father.

*Horaiyot, 13.*

### A Holy Ransom

Rabbi Abba once said to Rabbi Eleazar: "Is it true, as I have been taught, that the numbering of holy articles does not remove the blessing from them?"

"It is true," replied R. Eleazar.

"Then why when David took a census of the holy Israelites, were they smitten with a plague?"

"Because even holy men must give a holy ransom for their souls. David ought to have taken the holy shekel from each one of them, and no harm would have befallen them."

*Zohar, ii, 235.*

## 278.  REBUKE AND ADMONITION

A man should learn from God how to rebuke an offender. God out of love first rebukes the sinner in secret. Man should do the same.

*Raia Mehemna, iii, 85b.*

If a scholar is beloved by his fellow-townspeople, in all likelihood it is not because he is a man of superior qualities, but because he does not admonish his comrades.

*Ketubot, 105.*

People say: there is no value in rebuking a man who lacks the sense to differentiate between good and evil.

*Sanhedrin, 103.*

Moses was the appropriate person to rebuke Israel. Had another person done so, they could have retorted: "Should a man who has eaten our bread and drunk our wine, come to rebuke us?" But Moses, who could declare: "I have taken no one's ass nor have I accepted a fee from anyone," could rightly offer rebuke.

*Kohelet Rabbah, 3.*

If a man loves rebuke, he has chosen the right pathway.

*Tamid, 28.*

Love him who rebukes and hate him who praises thee.

*Abot de Rabbi Nathan, 29.*

He who accepts admonition merits blessing.

*Debarim Rabbah, 1, 9.*

Admonition leads to love and peace.

*Sifre Debarim, 2.*

He who is able to rebuke his household and refrains when rebuke is necessary, makes himself liable to penalty for his household's transgressions.

*Shabbat, 54.*

Beautiful are the words of admonition when they issue forth from the mouth of those who practice them.

*Tosefta Yebamot, 8, end.*

When a man transgresses in public, he who wishes to call attention to his offense, should not declare: "You are transgressing," but he should quote the law, rather than point him out as an offender.

*Zohar, iii, 86a.*

He who rebukes his comrade with love, does so in private, so that the offender may not be publicly shamed. But if the rebuke is administered publicly, it is not done with love.

*Zohar, iii, 46a.*

Love which is unaccompanied by rebuke, when it is deserved, is not true love.

*Bereshit Rabbah, 54, 3.*

Johanan ben Nuri furnishes an example of the spirit of love under rebuke: "I call Heaven and earth to witness that more than four or five times Akiba was censured on my account before Rabban Gamaliel because I complained concerning him, and despite this, I know that he loved me the more."

*Sifra on Lev. 19, 17; Arakin, 16b.*

### Rebuke Thy Neighbor and Bear No Sin

Rab said: "He who is able by means of a rebuke to achieve the improvement of his family, yet does not rebuke them, bears their sins. He who refrains from rebuking his townsmen, though he could do so with benefit to them, bears their sins."

Rab Papa said: "The Exilarch bears the sins of all Jewry in the Babylonian Exile, since he has the authority to punish those who presumptuously offend."

Rabbi Nathan said: "From Shiloh to Gereb the distance is only three miles, and the altar-smoke at Shiloh mingled with the smoke of Micah's altar in honor of an image. The Angels wished to interfere in the matter, but God said: 'Let him be. His house is open to wayfarers.' Later, however, when Israel protested against the torture of the concubine at Gibeah and made war against Benjamin, they lost the first battles. God said: 'You offered no vigorous protest against the altar for the image, yet against an injustice to a human being, you forcibly protest. Therefore you shall receive punishment. For had you forcibly destroyed the altar of Micah, you would have shown honor to My name.' "

*Sanhedrin, 103.*

## 279.  REDEMPTION

Nothing reveals more clearly the end of the Exile than what is written: "And ye, the mountains of Israel, ye shall shoot forth your branches, and yield your fruit to My people, Israel; for they are at hand to come." (Ezek. 36:8)

*Sanhedrin, 98.*

If a man tell thee when the End of the Exile will be, believe him not.

*Midrash Tehillim, 9, 2.*

He who despises people, retards the advent of salvation.

*Baraita de-Yeshuah, 247.*

Israel shall not return to their land until they have achieved complete unity.

*Yalkut to Emor, 659.*

As the rose is born only to shed fragrance, so are the Zaddikim born only to redeem Israel.

*Shir ha-Shirim Rabbah, 2, 2.*

If Israel is worthy, the Redemption will be hastened; if not, it will come in its own time.

*Sanhedrin, 98.*

Count up the measure of Israel's poverty and suffering, and hasten to redeem him.

*Yalkut to Tehillim, 802.*

If Israel merits, the Messiah will come in the clouds of the Heavens; if not, he will come riding on an ass.

*Sanhedrin, 98.*

In the time when God will cause us to arise and will take us forth from the Dispersion, He will first open unto us an entrance for a thin thread of light; then for a stronger light, until He will at last prepare great and high entrances open to all sides of the horizon.

*Zohar, i, 170a.*

We read: "The redeemed of the Lord shall return." (Isaiah 51:11) Not the redeemed of Elijah, nor the redeemed of the Messiah, but the redeemed of the Lord.

*Midrash Tehillim, Buber, p. 461, to Psalm 107, 2.*

Great is charity, for it brings the deliverance nearer, as it is said: "Thus saith the Lord: Maintain ye justice and practice charity, for My salvation is near and My loving-kindness is to be revealed." (Isaiah 56:1)

*Baba Batra, 10a.*

Great is repentance, for it brings deliverance nearer, as it is said: "And a redeemer will come to Zion, and unto them that turn from transgression in Jacob." (Isaiah 59:20)

*Yoma, 86b.*

The Disciples asked R. Simeon ben Yohai: "Pray, explain to us what God meant when He said through His Prophet Amos (5:2): 'The Virgin of Israel is fallen; she shall rise no more.'" The Rabbi replied: "In former exiles, Israel rose through their own repentance; but in the present exile, Israel shall not rise again of their own accord. I Myself shall raise up the fallen booth of David."

*Zohar, iii, 6.*

Balaam said that the happy hour of Israel is yet distant (see Numbers 24:17) But all the Hebrew Prophets declared that it is near, depending only upon repentance. And God saith: "For, lo, those that are far shall perish." (Psalm 73:27) He who discourages Israel and makes his redemption to seem distant, shall perish in both worlds.

*Pesikta Rabbati, 42, 3.*

### In a Little While

A man was walking with his small son on a road. After a while, the boy began to complain of fatigue and asked: "When will we reach the city, father?"

"Wait another hour and we will be in the city," was the reply.

A half hour later, the boy again declared: "O father, I am greatly wearied; when will we reach our destination?"

"In a little while now," was the response.

When the lad complained a third time, his father said: "Listen, my son, when you see a cemetery, you will know that we are near the city."

Even so Israel complains: "When will our redemption occur; when will our King and Savior arrive?" And God responds: "My sons, when great afflictions overtake you, be assured of the nearness of the Redemption."

*Introd. to Tanhuma Buber, 134.*

### As Harsh as Haman

R. Eliezer ben Hyrcanus maintained that if Israel did not repent, they would never be delivered, quoting Isaiah 30:15: "By repentance and quietness shall ye be saved."

R. Joshua ben Hananiah remarked: "Really, if Israel remain as they now are, and do not repent, will they never be delivered?"

R. Eliezer responded: "God will raise up over them a king as harsh as Haman, and forthwith they will repent, and they will be delivered. 'It is a time of distress for Jacob, and out of it, he shall be saved.' (Jer. 30:7)"

R. Joshua thereupon quoted Isaiah 52:3: "Ye were sold for nought, and without silver shall ye be delivered."

His position was: whether they do or do not repent, they will be delivered when the time decreed arrives, as it is written: "I, the Lord, in its time, will hasten it." (Isaiah 60:22)

A saying of Rabbi Joshua ben Levi is cited to similar effect: "If ye are worthy, I will hasten it; and if ye are not worthy, 'in its time.'"

*Y. Taanit, 63d; Sanhedrin, 97b-98a.*

## THE MESSAGE FROM THE CAVE

When Rabbi Simeon ben Yohai hid in the cave, the question arose at the Academy: "It is taught that the curses in Leviticus (26:14–41) were fulfilled at the burning of the First Temple, and the curses in Deuteronomy (28:15–68) were fulfilled at the burning of the Second Temple. Why, then, are the curses in Leviticus followed by the good tidings (Lev. 26:42–45), but the curses in Deuteronomy are not followed by words of comfort?"

No one knew a satisfactory reply, and all grieved greatly that their Master could not be reached. One of the Disciples, however, conceived the idea of writing down the question, attaching it to the wings of a pigeon, and loosing it, as if by accident, at the entrance of the cave.

R. Simeon received the message and wrote on the back of the leaf: "The tiding of comfort is suggested in the last verse of the curses in Deuteronomy (verse 68): 'And the Lord shall bring thee back into Egypt.' This means that God will redeem us out of this exile as He redeemed us out of the exile in Egypt.'"

*Zohar Hadash to Tabo.*

## THE UNLIT LANTERN

R. Johanan said: "A man was walking on a road at night, and his lantern went out. He lighted it, but it went out again. Finally he said to himself: 'Why shall I bother with the lantern? I will sit down at the roadside and when the sunlight arrives, I will continue my journey.'

"By the same token, the Children of Israel were enslaved in Egypt, and Moses led them forth; they were enslaved in Babylon, and Zerubabel led them forth; they were enslaved in Persia, and Mordecai led them forth; they were enslaved by Ionia (Greece), and the Maccabees freed them. When they were once more enslaved by Rome, they said: 'O Lord, free us no longer through the intervention of a man; we are weary of the succession of enslavement, freedom and enslavement. Be Thou, O Lord, our Redeemer, not a mortal man. Let not a man lighten us, but do Thou lighten us, as it is written: "For with Thee is the fountain of life; in Thy light, do we see light."' " (Psalm 36:10)

*Midrash Tehillim, to 36:10.*

### DARKNESS AND LIGHT

The verse: "The Lord . . . cast them into another land, as this day" (Deut. 29:27), applies to the Ten Tribes. Rabbi Akiba said: "As this day goes and does not return, so they go and do not return (in the Days of the Messiah)."

Rabbi Eliezer said: "As this day is first dark and then light, so is it with the Ten Tribes. As they were enveloped in darkness, in the future it will be light about them."

Rabbi Simeon ben Yohai said: "If their deeds will be as they are this day, they will not return; otherwise they will return."

*Sanhedrin, 110b.*

### THE INCREASING DAWN

Rabbi Hiyya and Rabbi Simeon ben Halafta were walking before daylight in the Valley of Arbel. They beheld the light of dawn breaking through the darkness.

Rabbi Hiyya remarked: "My friend, behold how the dawn grows stronger and stronger. So shall our Redemption be: at first, a little, then more and more."

*Y. Berakot, 1.*

The Rabbis said that the Redemption of Israel cannot come suddenly, but will come gradually and slowly, just as the sun gradually and slowly rises in the dawn of day."

*Midrash Shoher Tob, 18.*

The Rabbis said: "It was only when the Israelites were almost drowning, when they were submerged in the water up to their very necks, that the waters divided and separated into two massive walls."

*Shemot Rabbah, 21, 9.*

## 280. REMEMBRANCE AND FORGETFULNESS

Remembrance brings action in its train.

*Menahot, 13.*

He who listens to the Rabbis and remembers their words, is like a Rabbi himself.

*Berakot, 47.*

A man can forget in two years what he has learned in twenty.

*Abot de R. Nathan, 24, 6.*

Who is a sage? He who retains his learning.

*Sifre Debarim, 1, 13.*

People do not keep things in mind until they have stumbled in them.

*Shabbat, 120.*

An extraordinary event is remembered by people.

*Hullin, 75.*

That which a person is not obligated to do, he is likely to do without remembering that he has done it.

*Shebuot, 34.*

### DILIGENT STUDY

R. Ishmael narrated: "When I was thirteen years old, I was accustomed to forget what I had learned the previous day. I was heavy of heart and stopped eating and speaking. R. Nehunya ben ha-Kanah took me from my father's house to the Study in the Hall of Gazit and prayed for me. He then remarked to me: 'My prayer has been heard. If thou continuest to study with diligence, I promise that thou shalt remember and know thy learning thoroughly.' And it proved to be so. Daily I gained in knowledge, and I have delved deeply into the inmost secret meanings of the Torah."

"Had I accomplished nothing in the dissemination of Torah more than this one thing," he continued, "that people learn from my example to study with diligence, even though they do not seem to retain in their memory what they have learned, it would be sufficient for me."

*Hekalot, 27.*[1]

[1] Hekalot is a minor Midrash of mystical content.

### AS A GIFT

R. Abbahu said: "For forty days Moses learned the details of the Torah and forgot them as quickly as he learned them. On the fortieth day the Torah was given to him as a gift, and he had no further difficulty in remembering it. By the same token, a diligent student need not despair because he forgets what he has previously learned. In the proper time all of it will be firmly implanted in his memory."

*Y. Horaiyot, 3.*

## 281. REMINDERS AND MEMORIALS

### THE TEMPLE DOORS

When the Hasmoneans restored the Holy Temple, it was found that the Eastern Gate lacked doors. Nicanor volunteered to go to Egypt and bring back from there finely-wrought bronze doors. Returning by ship, a severe storm threatened to break it into pieces. The captain commanded that the ship be lightened, and one of the doors was cast overboard. The storm grew fiercer, and it was ordered that the second door be cast into the sea. Nicanor pleaded to be flung overboard with it. At once the storm grew quiet. When the ship arrived in the port of Acre, the first door was found beneath the keel of the ship.

Years later all the doors were removed and panelled with gold. Nicanor's doors, however, miraculously retained their original beauty of color, and were preserved exactly as they were.[1]

*Yoma, 38.*

[1] The divine favor shown to Nicanor on his journey were commemorated annually on the day when he pleaded to be thrown overboard with the precious cargo. "The Day of Nicanor" was celebrated on the 13th day of Adar; it may, however, have reference to a different Nicanor. See "Megillat Taanit" for that date.

### THE UNNAMED TREE

God does' not permit anything which might serve as a memorial and reminder of a sin committed by an individual or the community. The Torah says: "bull or sheep," not "calf or sheep" in order not to recall the sin of the Golden Calf. God did not reveal, nor will He reveal, the name of the tree, the fruit of which Adam ate with such disastrous consequences, lest whenever men see a tree of this kind, they might think of it as a tree of death."

*Pesikta Buber, 75b-76a.*

People say: if a man has been hanged for a crime, do not say to another member of this family: hang up the fish.

*Baba Metzia, 59.*

### THE FIRST OF JANUARY

The governments of Rome and Egypt waged war against each other for a long time. Once the councils of both countries agreed that the country whose commanding general would, on request, commit suicide by falling on his own sword, would be declared the victor. The Egyptian general refused, but the Roman general consented. His name was Januarius, and the day of his self-sacrifice was celebrated as a "calendus Januarius" and was instituted as the first day of the New Year. The following day was observed as a day of mourning in memory of his death.

*Y. Abodah Zarah, 1.*

## 282. REPENTANCE, PENITENCE

A twinge of conscience in a man's heart is better than all the floggings he may receive.

*Berakot, 7.*

Rabbi Eliezer ben Hyrcanus said: "Repent one day before thy death." His Disciples asked him: "How is it possible for a man to repent one day before his death, since he does not know on what day he shall die?" He replied: "So much the more reason is there that he should repent every day lest he die the next day. Thus will all his days be penitential ones." [1]

*Abot de-Rabbi Nathan, chap. 15.*

[1] See Browning's famous poem.

## CLEANSING THE UTENSILS

We are taught: "Utensils used in cold dishes may be cleansed for the Passover with cold water; those used with warm dishes, may be cleansed with warm water; those used for hot dishes are cleansed by being soaked in hot water; earthenware must be broken."

"In like manner, we may say: those who are righteous in the eyes of God and men, will not feel the heat of Gehenna: they are cleansed of their few sins in a cool atmosphere. Those who were sinners will be purified in a warm atmosphere; they will feel some of the rigors of Gehenna. Those who are wicked will be purified in a hot atmosphere; they will suffer all of the rigors of Gehenna. How will the two last groups save themselves? They should become broken of heart through sincere repentance, even as earthenware becomes ritually clean after being broken."

*Zohar, iv, 289-90.*

"Great is repentance," said Rabbi Jonathan, "for it brings the deliverance, as it is said (Isaiah 59:20): 'A deliverer will come to Zion, and to those who turn from transgression in Jacob.' How is this? A deliverer will come to Zion because of those who turn from transgression in Jacob." [1]

*Yoma, 86b.*

[1] "Repentance unto life is a saving grace, whereby a sinner, out of a true sense of his sins, and apprehension of the mercy of God, doth, with grief and hatred of his sins, turn from them unto God, with full purpose of, and endeavour after, new obedience." This definition, according to Moore (i, 515), although taken from the Westminster Shorter Catechism, completely embodies the rabbinical teaching. Both drew the conception from Jewish Scriptures.

Rabbi Simeon ben Lakish said: "Repentance induced by fear of consequences causes wilful sins to be treated as unwitting. Repentance that springs from a nobler motive—love of God—causes wilful sins to be treated as righteous deeds."

*Yoma, 86b.*

## THE NINE NORMS

The essentially moral character of repentance is exemplified by the "nine norms" of repentance (corresponding to the nine days intervening between New Year's Day and the Day of Atonement), which are found in the nine exhortations God utters in Isaiah 1:16ff.: "Wash you; make you pure; remove the evil of the misdeeds from before My eyes; cease doing evil; learn to do well; seek after justice; relieve the oppressed; do justice to the orphan; take up the cause of the widow."

"What is written after this? 'Come now, let us argue the matter,' saith the Lord. 'If your sins be like scarlet, they shall become white as snow.'"

*Pesikta Rabbati, Friedman edition, 169a.*

If a man repents and goes back to his sins, that is no repentance. If one goes down to take a bath of purification, holding some dead, unclean reptile in his hand, he receives no purification. He must cast away that which he has in his hand; after doing this, he can take his bath and be purified.

*Pesikta Rabbati, chap. 44.*

Rabbi Meir thus interpreted Hosea 14:2: "Return, Israel, to the Lord thy God": "Repent while He is standing in the attitude or attribute of mercy (indicated by the name, the Lord); if you do not, He will be 'your God' (Elohim, the austere judge); repent, that is, before the advocate becomes the accuser."

*Pesikta Buber, p. 146a.*

Rabbi Meir said: "Great is repentance, because for the sake of one who truly repents, the whole world is pardoned; as it is written (Hosea 14:5): 'I will heal their backsliding; I will love them freely, for mine anger is turned away from him.' It is not said: 'from them,' but 'from him.'"

*Yoma, 86b.*

"Great is repentance; for its sake doth God annul His own words. God enjoins (Deut. 24), that if a wife has erred and has been divorced and wedded to another, the first husband may not wed her again. Though Israel, however, worshipped strange gods, He asks their return to Him."

*Pesikta Rabbati, 45, 6.*

"Return, Israel, unto thy God." Return unto Him, half-way, and He will meet thee half-way. Return unto Him with empty hands, and He will dismiss thee with hands full of good. Return unto Him even if thy sins attain the sky, even if they reach thy God in the highest Heavens.

*Pesikta Rabbati, 45, 9.*

A certain Eliezer ben Durdia, a life-long profligate, recommended himself to the favor of Heaven, by one prolonged act of penitence. He placed his head between his knees and did not cease from weeping until his soul departed from him. At the moment of his death a Voice from Heaven came forth and said: "Rabbi Eliezer ben Durdia is appointed to life everlasting." When Judah ha-Nasi heard of this, he wept, and said: "One man wins eternal life after a struggle of years; another finds it within a single hour."

*Abodah Zarah, 17a.*

### Between Us Two Alone

Rabbi Eleazar said: "It is the way of the world, when a man has insulted his fellow in public, and after a time seeks to be reconciled to him, that the other says: 'You insult me publicly, and now you would be reconciled to me between us two alone! Go, bring the men in whose presence you insulted me, and I will be reconciled to you.' But God is not so. A man may stand and rail and blaspheme in the market-place, and the Holy One says: 'Repent between us two alone, and I will receive you.'"

*Pesikta Buber, 163b.*

## THE DYING APOSTATE

Rabbi Meir argued to his former teacher, the apostate, Elisha ben Abuyah, in his last illness, that repentance is possible even in the very last moment of death. Elisha replied: "Would I be received even now?" Meir answered by quoting Psalm 90:3, to which he gave the turn of phrase: "Thou lettest man return even unto crushing," that is to say, until life is crushed out of him,—and sayest: "Repent, ye children of men."

*Kohelet Rabbah, on 7, 8.*

"If a man says to himself: I will sin, and repent (and again), I will sin and repent (and thus escape the consequences), no opportunity is given him to repent. If he says: I will sin, and the Day of Atonement will expiate it, the Day of Atonement does not expiate it."

*Mishnah Yoma, 8, 9.*

Do penance while thou still hast thy full strength.

*Yalkut Shimeoni to Kohelet, 979.*

Not sackcloth and fasting avail, but repentance and good deeds.

*Taanit, 16.*

Zaddikim cannot stand in the place where penitents stand.

*Sanhedrin, 99.*

If a man repents of his evil deeds, and then returns to the same deeds, he has not truly repented.

*Pesikta Rabbati, 44.*

As a rose blooms with its heart turned upward, do penance thus: with your hearts towards the Heavens.

*Midrash Tehillim, 65.*

If you rend your hearts in penitence, it will not be necessary for you to rend your garments for the death of your sons.

*Y. Taanit, 2, 1.*

Why is repentance likened to the sea? As the sea is open at all times, so is the gate of penitence.

*Pesikta Buber, Shubah.*

Repent in the days of thy youth, before thine Evil Impulse grows old, as it is written: "Thou shalt rise up (in repentance) before the (Satan becomes within thee as a) hoary head." (Lev. 19:32)

*Zohar, iv, 227b.*

Repentance in old age is of lesser value, since a man is not tempted to do evil as much as in the years of his youth.

*Tikkune Zohar, T. 69, 155b.*

There is a higher and a lower form of penitence. If a man repents of his evil deeds and ceases to do them again, his is a lower form. If he repents of his evil deeds and then strives to perform good deeds, his penitence is the higher type.

*Zohar, iv, 123a.*

A matron asked R. Jose: "I read in Deuteronomy (10:17) that God will show favor to no person, but in Numbers (6:26), I read that God will show a favorable countenance unto Israel?" The Rabbi replied: "As regards sinners against a fellow-man, God will show no favors, but with respect to offenders against Himself, He will show a face of compassion, if the man repent with a whole heart."

*Otzar Midrashim, p. 494.*

One verse says: "I do not desire the death of the wicked" (Ezek. 33:11), and another verse (I Sam. 2:25) says: "Because the Lord would slay them." If they repent, He does not desire their death.

*Niddah, 70.*

Even a man who has been completely wicked his entire life and repents at the end, is not again reminded of his wickedness.

*Kiddushin, 40.*

Shall he who has eaten garlic and has an unpleasant breath, eat still more garlic and be still more unpleasant?

*Kiddushin, 40.*

Great is repentance. It brings in its train long life, redemption, and a cure for the ills of the world. It reaches the Throne of Glory and annuls evil verdicts against men. By it sins are transformed into virtues.

*Berakot, 32.*

God knew that man would be prone to sin, and He therefore created Repentance before He made man.

*Otzar Midrashim, 494.*

A prince committed a heinous crime, and his friend advised him: "Surely such a crime will be disclosed, and the king will imprison you; he will have you flogged and force you to live on bread and water. Then he will expect you to ask his pardon. Why not do the last thing at the very first? Go, and confess your guilt, and beg his forgiveness at once."

It is thus that Hosea counsels Israel: "Return unto your God at once, and protect yourselves from tribulations and sufferings."

*Pesikta Rabbati, Piska Shubah, 45, 4.*

Rabbi Simeon ben Yohai said: "If a man has been completely righteous all his days and rebels at the end (namely, if he regrets having been righteous), he destroys it all. If a man has been completely wicked all his days and repents at the end (namely, he regrets having been wicked), God receives him.[1]

Kiddushin, 40b.

[1] Based on Ezekiel 33:12. The words in the parentheses are by R. Simeon ben Lakish in explaining the words of the Tanna.

Rabbi Simeon ben Lakish said: "We read: 'The spirit of God was hovering over the face of the waters.' (Gen. 1:2) The spirit of the divine was moved by human repentance, as we read: 'Pour out thine heart like water.'" (Lam. 2:19)

Bereshit Rabbah, 2, 4.

The words of the lover in the Song of Songs (5:2): "Open to me, my sister," are explained thus: God says: "Open to me an entrance no larger than the eye of a needle; and I will open unto you an entrance through which tents and great timbers can pass."

Pesikta Buber, 163b.

An arrow carries the width of a field; but repentance carries to the very throne of God.

Pesikta Buber, 163b.

The gates of petition are sometimes closed; but the gates of repentance are always open.

Bereshit Rabbah, 21, 6.

Rabbi Samuel bar Nahman said: "Repentance is like the sea, in which nothing hinders a man from purifying himself at any time; while prayer may be compared to a bath, access to which may for various reasons be prevented."

Pesikta, ed. Buber, 157a-b.

Manasseh, King of Judah, was one of the greatest sinners in the whole history of mankind. Yet when he called on God in his distress, God made a hole beneath the glorious throne, and heard his supplication. If such a sinner was forgiven, there is no one whose repentance could not be accepted.

Pesikta Buber, 162a-b.

Men asked Wisdom: "What is the doom of the sinner?" It answered: "Evil pursues sinners." (Prov. 13:21) They asked Prophecy the same question, and it answered: "The soul that sins shall die." (Ezek. 18:14) They asked the Law, and it answered: "Let him bring a trespass-offering, and it shall be forgiven him," as it is said: "And it shall be accepted for him to make atonement for him." (Lev. 1:4) They asked God, and He answered: "Let him repent, and it shall be forgiven him." This is the meaning of the text: "Good and righteous is the Lord; therefore will He instruct sinners in the way." (Psalm 25:8)

Pesikta, ed. Buber, f. 158b.<br>Y. Makkot, 31d.

There is more joy in Heaven over one sinner who repenteth than over ninety and nine righteous persons, who need no repentance.

*Sanhedrin, 99a.*

"May it be Thy will, O God, that we return to Thee in perfect penitence, so that we may not be ashamed to meet our fathers in the life to come."

*Y. Berakot, 4, 2.*

Sincere repentance reaches up to the very seat of God; upon it rests the welfare of the world.

*Yoma, 86a.*

Even at the very gate of the nether world wicked men do not return.

*Erubin, 19a.*

"He healeth all who come into the world; to all He crieth, 'Return, ye backsliding children.' None doth He reject; for ever are the gates open to all."

*Mekilta to Exod., 14, 24.*

Repentance makes man a new creature; hitherto, dead through sin, he is fashioned afresh.

*Midrash Tehillim, 18.*

Wait not until death to be justified. "Repent whilst thou art a man."

*Abodah Zarah, 9a.*

The Rabbis declared: "Great is the power of repentance, for, by it deliberate sins are converted into positive virtues."

The Rabbis said that all Jews go to Heaven, because God ever accepts the repentant sinner, and surely every man repents at the moment before death. Even at the gates of Hell one may confess and return to God, and God accepts him in loving mercy.

*Erubin, 19a.*

## REGAINING CONFIDENCE

It was discovered that a certain meat-seller sold unfit meat. Rab Nahman took away his license. The man let his hair and beard grow, and gave the appearance of repentance. Rab Nahman was ready to restore to him his license, but Rabba said: "He may be a hypocrite. How shall we know when to grant him our confidence again? When he goes to a place where he is unknown, and demonstrates that a Mitzwah is more important to him than money, either by returning something which he has found, or by accepting a loss involving a transgression of the law."

*Sanhedrin, 25.*

The touchstone of genuine repentance is that every opportunity being given to repeat the misdeed, the man escapes the snare; for example, in the case of adultery, under identical conditions.

*Yoma, 86b. (Paraphrase.) Moore, i, 510.*

## 283. RESPONSIBILITY AND IRRESPONSIBILITY

A man may not be responsible for his actions in an hour of tribulation and pain.

*Baba Batra, 16.*

### JEPHTHAH'S VOW

Jephthah contracted an evil malady after he had sacrificed his daughter. His limbs dropped off, and it is written (Judges 12:7), "And he was buried in the cities of Gilead." How did he sin? By not calling upon Phinehas, the spiritual leader, to release him from his vow. He said to himself: "I am the Judge of Israel; shall I mar my dignity by calling upon the priest, Phinehas?" Phinehas sinned, also, in this matter, for he said: "I am the High-Priest. Shall I go to an unlearned person to offer unsolicited advice?"

Jephthah was not at fault in the matter of the civil war with the tribe of Ephraim, in which 42,000 fell. He risked his life, and rescued Israel from Ammon and Moab, and the proud Ephraimites rose against him. But Phinehas was to blame for all these slain. If he had intervened, and admonished the Ephraimites, they might have abandoned the uprising. What happened to Phinehas? He no longer received holy inspiration.

This teaches us that if we are able to intervene, but remain indifferent, we are responsible for the consequences.

*Tanna de-Be Eliyahu Rabbah, 11.*

R. Ilai said in the name of R. Eleazar ben R. Simeon: "It is just as much a Mitzwah for a man not to rebuke when he is certain it will do no good, as it is for him to offer rebuke when it will be accepted."

*Yebamot, 65.*

R. Simeon ben Yohai visited the sick in a hospital. One patient suffered greatly, and cried out with blasphemous words. R. Simeon said: "How foolish of thee! Thou hast need to cry unto God for relief, and instead thou blasphemest Him." The sufferer replied: "May God take away my pains from me, and set them upon thee." The Rabbi said: "I have deserved this, for disobeying the words of the Torah and the Sages."

Where is this forbidden in the Scriptures? "Reprove not a scorner, lest he hate thee." (Proverbs 9:8)

What have the Sages said in this matter? "Chastisements cause a man to pass over his own honor and the honor of his Creator." (Erubin 41) "A man is not responsible for his actions while he is suffering." (Baba Batra, 10)

*Abot de-Rabbi Nathan, 41.*

All Israelites are mutually accountable to each other.

*Shebuot, 39a.*

## 284. RESTITUTION

It is the way of the just to make restitution with that which is the object of their sin.

*Shemot Rabbah, 23, 3.*

He who robs the public cannot win full forgiveness through repentance. He knows not to whom he must make restitution.

*Baba Batra, 35.*

## 285. RESURRECTION

In the school of R. Ishmael it was said: "If a glass vessel which is fashioned by the breath of man can be restored again after it is once broken, how much the more can the soul of man be restored, seeing that it has been fashioned by the breath of God!"

*Sanhedrin, 91a.*

"I slay and I make alive; I have wounded and I heal" (Deut. 32:39). From this verse we may learn the doctrine of resurrection. For it cannot be argued that God causes one person to die and another to be born; inasmuch as the words are parallel to the phrase: "I have wounded and I heal." Of necessity He heals the man who was wounded, not him who is unhurt. Thus, also, in the first half of the verse, He makes alive him whom He hath slain.

*Pesahim, 68.*

The accepted view of the Resurrection is that the miracle will be wrought only in Palestine—the people buried outside of the Holy Land will be compelled to pass through subterranean channels until they reach the Land of Israel.

*Ketubot, 111a.*

### THOSE WHO HAVE BEEN

A Sadducee asked Gebiha ben Pesisa: "How can you say that the dead shall revive? Those who live must die; shall then, the dead, come to life?"

He replied: "If those who have never been, arrive in the world, should not those who have been, also appear among us?"

*Sanhedrin, 91.*

## 286. REVENGE

Seek not to take revenge upon the man who has abused thee. Be rather the one who is abused and humble of spirit.

*Derek Eretz Zuta, 2.*

He who returns evil for good, shall not evil go forth from his abode? He who returns evil for evil, acts wrongly. He should have patience, and God will give him help on this account.

*Zohar, i, 201a.*

## 287. REVELATION

The Rabbis declared that to Moses every ordinance was revealed that was to be instituted in after times, however remote, and that the doctrine of any teacher, however obscure he might be, was to be venerated in the same degree as if it had been taught by the Prophets or even by Moses himself.

*Y. Megillah, i, 7.*
*Sifre to Deut., xi, 13.*

Everything that a diligent student—a "Talmud Watik"—will teach in the distant future has already been proclaimed on Mt. Sinai.

*Y. Peah, chap. 2, 17a.*

R. Johanan said: "Every sound of this complete revelation of the truth that came from Sinai, was uttered in seventy languages."

*Shemot Rabbah, 28.*

The Midrash says: "The Truth was always here, but up to now it was not permitted to be revealed."

*Tanhuma, Jethro.*

## 288. REWARD AND PENALTIES

Just as God furnishes the wicked with strength to bear their punishment, so does He furnish the good with strength to bear their rich rewards.

*Sanhedrin, 100.*

There are three groups of men: one declares: "Were we born merely to gaze upon the planets and the stars, it would be sufficient for us." The second declares: "Whatever God has to give us, may He grant us in the future." A third group, like lazy workmen, declares: "Whatever God has in store for us, may He grant to us at once."

*Midrash Tehillim, 8, 6.*

The Saints are punished even for slight offenses, but the wicked only for heinous ones.

*Eliyahu Rabbah, 2.*

The latest bandit is the first one to hang.

*Kohelet Rabbah, 7, 26.*

The robber is hanged in the place of his chief activity.

*Tanhuma Tetzaweh, 7.*

A man is punished after death by the consequences of his own sins.
*Zohar, iv, 177a.*

The servant maid who angers her mistress many times receives her punishment at one time.
*Shabbat, 32.*

God has confused the reward promised to those who perform Mitzwot, so that they may perform them as an act of loyalty to Him.
*Y. Peah, 1, 1.*

The popular saying goes: for two or three offenses a thief is not executed.
*Sanhedrin, 7.*

God has left us this crown that we may be crowned by it.
*Y. Demai, 2, 1.*

He who studies in his native town receives a reward far less than the reward of him who goes elsewhere to study. By the same token, the reward of him who studies in comfort is far less than the reward of him who studies under arduous conditions.
*Shir ha-Shirim Rabbah, 8.*

Four things receive a penalty in this world, but the principal remains in the World-to-Come: Idolatry, Incest, Bloodshed and an Evil Tongue. The last is most pernicious.
*Y. Peah, 1, 1.*

### WHETHER GREAT OR SMALL

When Rabban Simeon ben Gamaliel and Rabbi Ishmael, the High Priest, were sentenced to death, R. Simeon complained aloud: "Woe unto us that we are to be executed as if we were criminals."

R. Ishmael replied: "It shall serve as an expiation for our sins."

"But I know not how I have sinned," said Rabban Simeon.

"There must be instances where some persons of heavy heart have complained against thee," answered the High Priest. "You must have caused persons who came to ask thee for justice to wait until thou wert ready to hear their cases. And the Torah saith: 'If thou afflict him in any wise' (Exod. 22:22). Whether the affliction be great or small, it is a punishable sin."

"I am comforted," exclaimed the Patriarch.
*Abot de-Rabbi Nathan, 38.*

### THE REWARD OF HONESTY

R. Levi narrated that once a man who paid his tithes scrupulously, received an idea from God to transform half his field into a reservoir. When a drought came, he raised a sign saying: "Buy from me a Seah measure of water for the price of two Seaim of wheat, for the Seah of water will bring you in return four Seaim of wheat." As a result of his foresight, he became wealthy.

*Tanhuma to Deut., 14, 22.*

Whenever God gave commands to people which they disobeyed, He commanded spirits to punish them, and from them he received obedience. Adam, Enoch, the Generation of the Flood and the Tower of Babel, and the Sodomites were punished thus. Abraham gave heed to God's commandment, and the Angel of Fertility was commanded to visit Sarah.

*Pesikta Rabbati, 43, 8.*

### The Site of Rome

Said Rabbi Levi: on the day when Solomon wedded the daughter of Pharaoh-Necho, the Archangel Michael descended from Heaven, and struck a large reed into the water. From every side soil clung to it, until it became as a forest. This place became the site of Rome. In the day when Jeroboam fashioned the two Golden Calves, Remus and Romulus came to the site and later founded Rome upon it.

*Shir ha-Shirim Rabbah, 1.*

R. Aha said: "God may be compared to one in charge of a storage-house. If fine goods are stored with him, he returns fine goods; if evil possessions, these are returned accordingly."

*Pesikta Rabbati, 44, 6.*

## FOUR TALES OF MIRACULOUS REWARDS

### The Golden Coins

A Disciple of Rabbi Simeon ben Yohai departed for a foreign country where he grew rich. When he returned, the other Disciples were envious and wished to leave Palestine also. Their Master said: "Come with me; I shall work for you a wonder, and the valley here shall be filled with golden coins. But know ye of a truth, that you will have your reward either in this World or in the Everlasting Life. Make your choice."

### The Pearl on Account

Rabbi Simeon ben Halafta was exceedingly poor. On Passover he saw a great commotion. "People are preparing for the festival," he was told. "Some already have money in their possession, and others secure it from their employers."

"I too will ask for something from my Employer on account," thought Rabbi Simeon.

And, lo, a magnificent pearl appeared before his eyes. He went to Rabbi Judah ha-Nasi and the Rabbi said to him: "Accept a loan of three dinarii and later we shall auction the pearl."

Rabbi Simeon took the money to his wife and told her the story. She remarked: "I do not wish your share in the World-to-Come to be diminished. Give back the loan and return the pearl to your Employer."

Rabbi Judah sent for her and said: "We, his comrades, will endeavour to repay for your husband whatever he received on account. It is better for you to keep the sum and be relieved from poverty."

The pious woman still refused, however, on the plea that every Zaddik can work only for his own reward; he cannot share it with another. Her husband, Rabbi Simeon, thereupon laid down the pearl and at once it disappeared in the air.

### THE MISSING TABLE-LEG

The wife of Rabbi Hanina ben Dosa could not endure her poverty and besought her husband to pray for something on account. A golden table-leg appeared in the room. Later the Rabbi's wife dreamed she was in Paradise. Each Zaddik had a home equipped with furniture of gold. Her husband's table, however, was missing a leg. When the Rabbi's wife awoke she begged that the table-leg be taken back.

### THE FRAGRANT GARMENT

Rabbah bar Abbuha met the Prophet Eliijah and complained that his poverty was a bar to complete concentration upon study. Elijah took him to the Garden of Eden and filled his pocket with leaves. As he was departing the Rabbi heard a voice say: "Rabbi bar Abbaha has already enjoyed his share in Paradise."

At once the Rabbah emptied his pocket. When he was on earth again his garments bore a fragrance of the Garden of Eden, and he sold it for many thousands of dinars. He then distributed the money to his sons-in-law.

*Shemot Rabbah, 52; Ruth Rabbah, 3; Taanit, 25; Baba Metzia, 112.*[1]

[1] Talmudic legends are variously interpreted by the Rabbis. It is generally agreed that all supernatural stories, myths and legends in Rabbinical literature are intended as parables and fables. The disciple of the Gaonim, Rabbi Samuel ha-Nagid advises that the unbelievable in the Talmud and Midrash should not be literally accepted.

### THE DIMINISHING TITHE

A farmer owned a field which produced 1,000 measures of grain. He contributed 100 measures as a tithe, and from the balance he had a comfortable livelihood.

When his son inherited the field, he also contributed 100 measures as tithe for the first year. The second year, however, he gave only 90 measures. The following season, his field produced only 900 measures of grain. Again he gave less tithe than he was bound in duty to give. Again the field produced less in exact proportion. After a few years, his kinsfolk heard that the field produced no more than 100 measures. They attired themselves in white garments and visited him.

The farmer said: "Have you come in holiday attire to rejoice over my evil fortune?"

"Nay, we came to offer you congratulations. Formerly you were the farmer and God was the Kohen (Priest). Now God is become the farmer and you have become the Kohen."

*Shemot Rabbah, 31.*

## The Son of Pure Gold

Once Rabbi Abba declared in a discourse that every one who studies the Torah obtains riches. A young man named Jose took his words to mean material riches. He came to Rabbi Abba saying: "I wish to study in order to obtain these riches."

After a lapse of time, Rabbi Jose wished to know when his wealth would accrue to him. Rabbi Abba was distressed to learn that this excellent student was motivated by ulterior considerations. He said to him: "Continue to study, and if you must have material riches, I shall do my best to give them to you."

A wealthy youth entered the School and asked for Rabbi Abba, saying: "I have inherited great wealth. I appreciate the value of the study of Torah but my mind is not adapted to it. I wish to donate a vessel of pure gold to a fine student on condition that I shall have a share in his Torah." Rabbi Abba summoned Rabbi Jose and said to him: "Here is the first instalment of your riches."

Soon after, Rabbi Jose commenced to perceive the spiritual richness of the Torah, and he wept.

"Why weepest thou?" asked his Master. Rabbi Jose replied, "Because I have sold true for apparent riches."

Rabbi Abba rejoiced in his heart. He recalled the rich youth and said: "The student regrets having accepted your gold. Pray take it back and distribute the money among the needy and orphaned, and it shall be accounted to thee as if thou hadst studied Torah as much as we."

Rabbi Jose was overjoyed to dispense with the "pure gold" (Paz), and he received the name of "Ben Pazi," namely, the "Son of Pure Gold."

*Zohar, part 1, p. 88.*

## Elijah Explains Four Mysteries

Rabbi Joshua ben Levi, the story runs, fasted a long time and prayed that Elijah be revealed to him. Elijah appeared, and in asking the Rabbi his wish, the latter replied: "To accompany you on your journeys throughout the world."

"On one condition," replied Elijah. "You must ask no questions; if you do, I shall leave you at once."

They departed and went on their way until they came to a poor hovel. The owner welcomed them, and offered them hospitality to the best of his means. Before taking leave, Elijah placed his hand on the only cow that his host possessed, and she died on the instant.

They went further and arrived at the home of a wealthy man. At first he refused to admit them, but after persuasion he gave them entrance into his kitchen, without offering them either food or drink. They noticed that one of the walls of his house was being repaired. Before their departure, Elijah placed his hand upon the wall, and lo, it was completely restored.

Eliijah and Rabbi Joshua went further and arrived at a house of study, where some rich people were listening to the discourse. After the discourse, they beheld the wanderers but paid scant attention. They merely ordered the Beadle to give them bread and salt and water. After a moment, Elijah approached them and said: "May ye all become chiefs."

The next morning Elijah and the Rabbi, continuing their travels, arrived at a town where they were accorded a hearty welcome. Elijah blessed the people and said: "May only one of you be a chief."

Rabbi Joshua finally agreed to forego Elijah's company and asked him to explain everything. Elijah responded: "As for the poor man, the death of the cow was in place of his wife's predestined death. As for the rich man, I repaired the wall so that he might not find a treasure hidden there. As for the wealthy students of the Law, many chiefs will bring them to ruin. As for the good men of the city, one chief will bring them prosperity. Thus does God work." [1]

*Maassiot le-Rabbenu Nissim.*

[1] Siegal, *Elijah Legends.*

## THE DESERT AND THE SEA

Rabbi Simeon ben Lakish and two companions in their younger days were robbers. Rabbi Simeon repented and became a man of great piety and learning. His companions, however, held to their evil ways.

It happened that the three died on the same day. Rabbi Simeon was led to Paradise, but his former comrades were taken to Gehenna. They complained: "But we were together in our robberies." They received answer: "But Simeon repented and you did not."

"We are ready, however, to repent now," they said. The answer was given: "He who travels through a desert must take along his food lest he starve. He who travels at sea must carry provisions lest he be hungry. The After-Life is like both the desert and the sea and no provisions can be obtained there."

*Pirke de Rabbi Eliezer, 43.*

## TESTING THE LORD

A boy asked Rabbi Johanan: "Why is it written: 'Tithe shalt thou tithe'?" (Deut. 14:22). He answered: "This means: Tithe in order that thou shalt have an abundance from which to tithe."

The boy remarked, however, "This explanation seems to me merely a guess." Rabbi Johanan answered: "Nay. It is the correct explanation and when thou art a grown man thou mayest test it." The boy was surprised: "Test the Lord! Is this not forbidden in the Torah?"

Rabbi Johanan responded: "Thus said Rabbi Oshaya: 'Test not the Lord except in this instance.' As Malachi (3:10) said: 'Bring ye the whole tithe into the store-house that there may be food in My House, and try Me now herewith, saith the Lord of hosts, to see if I will not open unto you the windows of Heaven, and pour out for you a blessing that there may be more than sufficient.' "

The boy said: "If I had reached in my studies this chapter, would it have been necessary for me to ask thee or thy teacher, Rabbi Oshaya, when the text is so explicit?"

*Taanit, 9.*

## WHY GOD DOES NOT DESTROY IDOLS

Certain philosophers once asked the Jewish elders, when they chanced to be in Rome: "If your God hates idolatry, why does He not destroy the idols?" "And so He would," they replied, "if only such objects were worshipped as the world does not need. But you worship the sun and the moon, the stars and the constellations. Should God destroy the world because of the fools upon it? Nay, the world goes on despite this, but they who transgress must answer for their conduct. According to your philosophy, if one steals wheat and sows it, it should by rights produce no crop. Nevertheless, the world goes on as if no wrong had been done. But they who are guilty will some day smart for their sin."

*Abodah Zarah, 54b.*

"Be not like servants," is the advice of Antigonus of Socko, "who serve the master for the sake of receiving reward; but serve him without the condition of receiving a reward."

*Abot, 1:3.*

## 289. RIGHTEOUSNESS

The Talmud defines the Zadikkim, the truly righteous, saying: "Their money is more precious to them even than their own bodies." This statement is often misunderstood—not that they care for money more than for themselves, but the truly righteous are more painstaking in all matters pertaining to their financial dealings than they are in regard to their own bodily needs; as the Talmud significantly adds: "For they would not permit their hands to touch that which is tainted by stealth or robbery."

*Sotah, 12a; Hullin, 91a.*

### 290. ROBBERY (See Thieves)

Neither the Day of Atonement nor even repentance will suffice to expiate the sin of robbery; full restitution must come first.

*Yoma, 85b.*

To steal, however, with the idea of restitution, even of more than restitution, is a crime.

*Baba Metzia, 61b.*

## 291. ROMAN OFFICIALS

### Be Prepared With Answers

Rabbi Jose ben Judah and Rabbi Judah I were travelling on an unfamiliar road. They saw some Roman official halting passers-by. Said Rabbi Jose: "He will ask us three questions, to which we should give the following three answers:

" 'Who are you?' 'Jews.'

" 'What is your occupation?' 'Merchants.'

" 'Where are you going?' 'To buy wheat from the grainstores of Yabneh.' "

After they had passed the official safely, Rabbi asked: "What gave you the idea to be prepared with answers?"

Rabbi Jose replied: "Jacob's instructions to the messengers he sent to Esau."

*Bereshit Rabbah, 76.*

### The Rabbi in Disguise

Once the Roman Senate planned to adopt a law prohibiting the observance of the Sabbath and the performance of the circumcision rite.

Rabbi Reuben, disguised as a Roman, came before the Senate and said: "You hate the Jewish nation, yet you wish to compel them to become richer by laboring seven days a week instead of six." The Senate voted down the first prohibition.

Rabbi Reuben continued: "You hate the Jewish people, yet you wish to stop them from weakening themselves through the rite of circumcision." This prohibition was also voted down.

*Meilah, 17.*

### Take Not and You Will Give Nothing

Rabbi Judah Nessia (grandson of Rabbi Judah ha-Nasi) complained to Rabbi Simeon ben Lakish that the Roman government demanded too many gifts from him. Said the Rabbi: "Accept no gifts from other persons, and you will not find it necessary to give any."

A woman brought to the Patriarch as a gift, a beautifully wrought dagger. The governor's secretary was present, and a little later the Patriarch received a "request" for a dagger.

An unlearned man said to Rabbi Oshaya: "Will you repeat something good in my name in a public discourse, if I tell it to you?" "Yes," answered the Rabbi.

"All the gifts which the rulers take from Jacob, they will return to the Messiah. As we read: 'The kings of Tarshish and of the Isles shall *return* gifts' (Ps. 72:10). The text reads not 'bring' but 'return'."

"Excellent," exclaimed the Rabbi, "gladly will I repeat this in thy name."

*Bereshit Rabbah, 88.*

## 292. ROSH HA–SHANAH

Adam was created on Rosh ha-Shanah; he stood before His Judgment on the same day; he repented on the same day, and God forgave him.

The Lord said to Adam: "Thus shall it be with thy children. They will stand before Me in judgment on Rosh ha-Shanah, and, if they truly repent, I shall forgive them."

*Zohar, iii, 100b.*

Rabbi Johanan said: "The fate of men of perfection is sealed on Rosh ha-Shanah; they are either to be aided in accumulating more Mitzwot; or they are to enjoy Paradise."

"The fate of men of complete wickedness is also sealed on Rosh ha-Shanah; they are either to receive opportunities to add to their wickedness, or they are to depart for Purgatory."

"The fate of the rank and file of men is left open, however, until Yom Kippur. If they repent, they receive another chance to do good."

*Rosh ha-Shanah, 16b, amplified.*

Rabbi Judah ben Ilai said: "The fate of everything in nature is under judgment on Rosh ha-Shanah, and is sealed on various days: The fate of grain on Passover; the fate of fruit on Shabuot; the fate of water on Sukkot; the fate of man, however, is sealed on Yom Kippur."

*Rosh ha-Shanah, 16a.*

Rabbi Abbahu said: "Sound the Shofar so that God may recall the martyrdom of Isaac, and consider it as if ye too are ready to suffer martyrdom for His sake."

*Rosh ha-Shanah, 16.*

All good things come to Israel through the Shofar. They received the Torah with the sound of the Shofar. They conquered in battle through the blast of the Shofar. They are summoned to repent by the Shofar, and they will be made aware of the Redeemer's advent through the Great Shofar.

*Eliyahu Zuta, 22.*

"Seek ye the Lord, while He may be found; call ye upon Him, while he is near." (Isaiah 55:6)

When is God near? During the Ten Days of Repentance.

*Otzar Midrashim, p. 495.*

On Rosh ha-Shanah we should go about with a subdued spirit; on Yom Kippur with an exalted spirit.

*Rosh ha-Shanah, 26.*

When a man sins during the year, a record of his transgression is inscribed in faint ink. If he repents during the Ten Days of Penitence, the record is erased. If not, it is rewritten in indelible ink.

*Otzar Midrashim, p. 494.*

On Rosh ha-Shanah God's Judgment finds the world undeserving to continue its existence. He then moves from the Throne of Judgment to the Throne of Mercy, and finds the world deserving. Thus on that day it is as if He creates all the world anew.

*Otzar Midrashim, p. 495.*

The most appropriate prophetical portion for Rosh ha-Shanah and Yom Kippur is the second chapter of Joel, especially verse 11:

"Great is the day of the Lord," applies to Rosh ha-Shanah; and "very terrible," applies to Yom Kippur.

*Otzar Midrashim, p. 496.*

The Angels inquire of God: "Why does not Israel chant the Hallel before Thee on Rosh ha-Shanah as on other holydays?" He replies: "The books of life and death are open before Me on Rosh ha-Shanah. Shall I hearken to Psalms of Praise?"

*Arakin, 10.*

A man awaiting trial is usually dejected, and wears sombre garments. Israel, however, is different. On Rosh ha-Shanah the children of Israel dress in holiday attire, and eat a festive-day meal. They are confident of God's mercies.

*Y. Rosh ha-Shanah, 1, 3.*

Rabbi Berechiah said: "It is the Creator's will that on Rosh ha-Shanah the heart of all mankind should be directed to Him in unison.

*Y. Rosh ha-Shanah, 1, 3.*

The sound of "Tekiah" urges us to beg for God's mercies. The sound "Teruah-Shebarim" breaks the enslavement of our heart to desires.

*Sefer ha-Hinuk (post-Talmudical).*

Rabbi Judah bar Nahmani said: "We read: 'God is gone up amidst the sound of the Teruah. He became the Lord amidst the sound of the Shofar' (Ps. 47:6)." The Creator rises up to do justice when he hears the Teruah sound, but when the blasts of the Shofar continue, God is pleased and He takes His seat to dispense mercy.

*Pesikta Buber, 23.*

Rabbi Tahlifa said: "The commandments concerning all sacrifices read: 'And ye shall offer,' but the one concerning sacrifice on Rosh ha-Shanah reads: 'And ye shall make' (Num. 29:2). We should read 'And ye shall be made,' for, after you are dismissed from the Tribunal of Justice above, ye are as freshly created."

*Pesikta Buber, 23.*

Do you ask for God's compassion upon you? Be compassionate then upon your fellow-men. When Job argued stubbornly and unfairly with his friends, he received no pity; but the Lord restored the prosperity of Job when he prayed on behalf of his friends. (Job 42:10)

When did Abraham have a son from Sarah? When he prayed on behalf of Abimelech.[1]

*Pesikta Rabbati, 39.*

[1] We read: "Sarah became pregnant" on Rosh ha-Shanah.

Rabbi Levi said: "God judges the Gentiles in mercy. How? He judges them at night when they are peaceful and do not sin. Why? Because he does not desire to punish even the wicked. Is there a potter who desires that his vessels be broken? But God judges Israel and righteous Gentiles during the daytime when they perform good deeds."

"Why is the Shofar sounded after the Morning Services? In order that the children of Israel may have read the Shema, recited the Amidah, listened to the reading of the Torah, and the preaching of the Rabbi before they stand in judgment."

*Pesikta Rabbati, 41, 3.*

"Sound the Shofar to the God of Jacob." Why not to the God of Abraham or Isaac? Because Abraham and Isaac were satisfied to have the Divine Presence rest upon a mountain and in a field; but Jacob foresaw a House of God as a place fitting for the Shekinah, and, when we assemble on Rosh ha-Shanah in a synagogue, we do so with Jacob's viewpoint.

*Pesikta Rabbati, 40, 2.*

Resh Lakish said: "God saith, 'I desire that the defendants before My tribunal obtain my pardon, for, whenever I am victorious over My creatures, I am the loser, and, when I lose to them, I am the gainer. I was victorious over the generation of the Flood. With what consequence? I lost all the multitude of men. I was vanquished in the generation of the Golden Calf. With what result? I won all the multitudes of men.' "

*Pesikta Rabbati, 41, 1.*

As in the Shofar, the voice goes in at one end, and comes out at the other, so will the words of the accuser enter God's ears and come forth again without leaving any influence.

*Pesikta Rabbati, 41, 6.*

When Isaac was about to be sacrificed, Abraham asked God, who had stayed his hand: "If Thou hast come only to test me, didst Thou not know that I am ready to obey Thee?"

God answered: "Well did I know thy heart but I wished to demonstrate to the peoples the reason why I am friendlier to thee than to them. Moreover, when I judge thy sons each year on Rosh ha-Shanah, I shall remember thy loyalty when they sound the horn of the ram, for the ram was substituted for Isaac."

*Pesikta Rabbati, 41, 6.*

Ten animals were sacrificed on Rosh ha-Shanah to correspond to the ten days of repentance, to the ten sayings by which the world was created, and to the Ten Commandments. At present we say instead: ten verses in the portion of the Musaph Amidah devoted to the sovereignty of God, and ten verses to God's remembrance of all deeds, and ten verses devoted to the Shofar.

*Pesikta Rabbati, 41, 5.*

"It was on Rosh ha-Shanah, in the first hour of that day, that the thought came to God to create Adam, the first human being."

*Wayyikra Rabbah, 29:1.*

In a tradition, we are told that it was on Rosh ha-Shanah that the bondage of the Jewish people ceased in the land of Egypt.

*Rosh ha-Shanah, 11a.*

The Sages said: "And God will say unto Israel—yea, unto humanity, too—'My children, I look upon you as if today, on Rosh ha-Shanah, you have been made for Me anew, as if today I created you— a new being, a new people, a new humanity.'"

*Wayyikra Rabbah, 29:10.*

## 293. RULERS

He who sees the ruler of a State must utter the benediction: "Blessed be God who hath imparted some of His majesty to mortals."

*Berakot, 58a.*

## 294. RUMOR AND REPUTATION

A rumor which has not been upheld in a court is not a reliable rumor.

*Gittin, 89.*

People say: "If you hear the report: 'Thy neighbor has died,' you may believe it. If you hear that your neighbor has become wealthy, you may not believe it."

*Gittin, 30.*

A man's wealth is proved after he dies.

*Moed Katon, 28.*

My work makes me known.

*Bereshit Rabbah, 16, 3.*

People say: "In my own town I am respected because of the name I have made for myself; in another town I am respected for the rich garments which I wear."

*Shabbat, 145.*

## 295. SABBATH

If it is written of God, who never tires, that He rested on the seventh day, how much the more shouldst thou, O man, rest on the Sabbath from thy weariness.

*Pesikta Rabbati, 23, 5.*

Though the days of the week may be coupled in pairs, the seventh day is an odd day. Who shall be its mate? Israel, as it is said: "Remember the Sabbath day to take it unto thee in sanctification," namely, like a bride.

*Pesikta Rabbati, 23, 6.*

Rabbi Yudan said: "According to the ordinary custom of the world, the master tells his servants: 'Work for me six days and one day shall be for yourselves.' God, however, says: 'Work for yourselves six days, and for Me one day.'"

*Pesikta Rabbati, 23, 2.*

Rabbi Tanhuma said: "From what did God rest on the Sabbath? He rested from 'saying.' Thou also shalt rest thyself on the Sabbath from speaking worldly words."

Rabbi Aibo said: "Rest thyself on the Sabbath from thinking mundane thoughts."

*Pesikta Rabbati, 23, 3.*

What was created on the Sabbath day?
Contentment, peace of mind, and physical rest.

*Bereshit Rabbah, 10, 12.*

What is the foretaste of the World-to-Come?
The Sabbath.

*Bereshit Rabbah, 17, 7.*

"Remember" means: The Gentiles should remember that God commanded Israel to keep the Sabbath; they should permit Israel to do so.

"Observe" means that Israel should keep the Sabbath.

On the high seas or in the desert, where you cannot observe the Sabbath entire, remember it as much as you are able.

*Pesikta Rabbati, 23, 1.*

If Israel would properly observe a single Sabbath, the Son of David would come immediately.

*Shemot Rabbah, 25, 16.*

A Gentile may not observe the Sabbath as Jews observe it until he becomes a proselyte.

*Debarim Rabbah, 1, 18.*

This world is like the Eve of the Sabbath, and the next world is like the Sabbath. If one does not prepare for the Sabbath, of what shall he partake?

*Ruth Rabbah, 3, 3.*

"Have I then given thee the Sabbath for thy hurt? Nay, I have given it to thee for thy good."

*Debarim Rabbah, Ekeb.*

One version of the Decalogue reads: "Remember the Sabbath day." The other version reads: "Observe the Sabbath day." Remember it a little while before it arrives, and observe it a little while after it has passed.

*Mekilta to Decalogue.*

He who observes properly one Sabbath is as if he had observed every Sabbath since it was ordained.

*Mekilta Tissa.*

If one is lost in a desert and has forgotten the days of the week, he should count six days and observe the seventh as a Sabbath.

*Shabbat, 69.*

Be not afraid of the Sabbath, but rather of Him who has enjoined the Sabbath.

*Yebamot, 6.*

The Sabbath was committed unto you, not you unto the Sabbath.

*Mekilta on Exodus, 31, 13.*

Rabbi Hanina said: "A joyous spirit should be a rule on the Sabbath day. Only with difficulty was permission granted to console mourners or visit the sick on the Sabbath day."

*Shabbat, 12a-b.*

Rabbi Simeon ben Yohai said: "If Israel should keep two Sabbaths strictly according to rule, they would be delivered forthwith."

*Shabbat, 118b.*

Rabbi Akiba said the following to his son Joshua: "Enter not suddenly into thine own house, and, of course, not into thy neighbor's."

"Make thy Sabbath as a week-day rather than depend for support upon other people."

*Pesahim, 112a.*

A Disciple used to plough with his cow and she became accustomed to rest upon the Sabbath. He grew too poor, however, to keep her, and sold her to a pagan. When the Sabbath came, the cow refused to pull the plough. He came to the Disciple and complained. The Disciple said to his cow: "You may work when your master works."

The creature understood that her former master wished her to work, and she began to pull. The pagan inquired what the Disciple had told her. On receiving the information he said to himself: "If a beast without reason desires to rest on the Sabbath, should I, a reasoning being, do less?" He became a proselyte and was called Rabbi Hanina ben Turta (the Son of a Cow).

*Midrash Asseret ha-Diberot.*

Every man on the Eve of the Sabbath, as he goes from the synagogue to his home, is escorted by two Angels, one of whom is a good angel, and the other an evil. When the man comes home and finds the lamp kindled, the table spread, and the house in order, the Good Angel says: "May the coming Sabbath be even as the present."

To this the Evil Angel is obliged to say: "Amen."

But, if all is in disorder, the Evil Angel says: "May the coming Sabbath be even as the present," and the Good Angel is obliged to say: "Amen" to it.

*Shabbat, 119b.*

R. Simeon ben Menassia said: "A man may profane one Sabbath in order that he may observe many Sabbaths."

*Yoma, 85b.*

"For it is holy unto you" (Exod. 31:14). This means that the Sabbath adds holiness unto Israel.

If it be asked: "Why is that store closed?" The answer is made: "The owner observes the Sabbath."

If it be asked: "Why is that man partaking of his rest?" The answer is: "He observes the Sabbath."

*Mekilta Tissa, Sabbath 1.*

Isaiah (56:2) couples the Sabbath with abstention from evil, in order to teach yourself that he who observes the Sabbath is far from any transgression.

*Mekilta Tissa, Sabbath 1.*

"It is a sign forever." (Exod. 31:17)

These words mean that the Sabbath will never be forsaken by Israel.

If there be a Mitzwah, such as the Sabbath, circumcision, and the study of Torah, for the sake of which Israelites have given up their life, it endures among them. But a Mitzwah for which Israelites do not surrender life, does not endure among them.

*Mekilta Tissa.*

Why is it said in Exodus 20:8: "Remember," and in Deuteronomy 5:12: "Take heed" (Observe)?

Said R. Yudan: "It is like a man who has sent his son with a coin to the store. The boy returns and says he has lost the money. His father punishes him, gives him another coin and says: 'Take heed that thou dost not lose this coin as thou hast lost the other.' Thus is it with Israel. After they had caused Moses to break the Tables with the word 'Remember,' God gave them tables with the word 'Take Heed.'"

*Pesikta Rabbati, Asseret Ha-Diberot.*

One Rabbi declared that the Sabbath was given for delight, namely, for a pleasant time. Another declared that it was given for study. But there is no variance between them. Those who study during the week shall rest and enjoy the Sabbath. Those who do not study during the week, shall do so on the Sabbath.

*Pesikta Rabbati, Asseret Ha-Diberot.*

Moses beheld that the Children of Israel had no rest. He went to Pharaoh and said:

"Ordinarily a serf receives a day of rest in a week, or he dies from exhaustion. Give these serfs their day of rest."

Pharaoh replied: "Order for them a day of rest. What thou sayest is correct."

Moses went forth and ordained that they should rest on the Sabbath day.

*Shemot Rabbah, 1.*

The Torah said: "O Lord, what will become of me when everyone in Israel will be busy with his field and his flock?"

He replied: "I am giving them the Sabbath day and they will devote themselves to thee on that day."

*Midrash.*

In the School of Elijah it was taught:

"'Seven days have been fashioned and he (Israel) has only one of them' (Ps. 139:16). This is the Sabbath day unto Israel. How is this? A man works six days and rests on the seventh, when he enjoys the companionship of his family. Or a man works at forced labor six days and rests on the seventh, when he forgets all his pain. Such is the nature of man: a good day brings forgetfulness of an evil day, and an evil day of a good day."

*Tanna de-Bei Eliyahu, 1.*

"As a lily . . . so is my love." (Song of Songs 2:2)

As a lily is made ready for the Sabbath and Festival table, so is my people Israel being made ready for the coming Redemption.

*Wayyikra Rabbah, 23.*

"I am black but comely" (Song of Songs 1:5) may be interpreted: I am black on working days but I am comely on the Sabbath day.

*Shir ha-Shirim Rabbah, 1.*

The honor of the Sabbath rests in her candles. If thou kindlest the candles of the Sabbath, I will show thee the candles of Zion.

*Yalkut Shimeoni Behaaloteka.*

Rab Tahlifa taught: "A man's income is decreed on Rosh ha-Shanah for the coming year, except that which he spends for the Sabbath, the Yom Tob, and for tuition. If he spends less than it was contemplated on High, they deduct it from his income. If he spends more, they add to it."

*Betzah, 15-16.*

## MYSTICAL THOUGHTS ON THE SABBATH

When the day of the Sabbath arrives, all the Angelic Hosts in the Lower Garden bring up to the Higher Heaven all souls who reside there. They are able to behold the many Holy Hosts moving hither and thither, all rejoicing and eager.

When R. Hamnuna left the river, after his Sabbath-eve bath, he would halt for a moment and say:

"I stopped to behold the joy of the Angels on High."

R. Simeon said: "He who eats in holiness the three Sabbath meals receives perfect faith."

When a festival occurred on a Saturday night, R. Hamnuna did not neglect the third Sabbath meal because of the arriving guest.

R. Abba said: "If Passover occurred on Saturday night, R. Simeon would meditate on the Holy Chariot and say: 'This is the meal of the King, who has come to partake of it.' "

*Zohar, iii, 94-5.*

A Roman asked Rabbi Akiba: "If thy God honoreth the Sabbath day, why doth He permit the rain to descend and the wind to blow?"

The Rabbi answered: "A Jew is permitted to pour water or to blow upon hot dishes in his home on the Sabbath, and the whole universe is the home of God."

Another answer is this: "Only Israel is required to observe the Sabbath day, while the rain and winds are made for all. Thus the manna, which descended for Israel only, did not descend upon the Sabbath."

*Bereshit Rabbah, 11.*

## THE ESSENTIAL INGREDIENT

The Emperor Antoninus lunched with Rabbi Judah ha-Nasi on a Sabbath. Many of the dishes were served cold, but the royal guest ate them with relish. He invited himself again to lunch. As it was on a week-day, the dishes were all hot, and the Emperor enjoyed them less.

He said to his host: "The other lunch was more to my taste."

The Rabbi replied: "This meal lacks an important ingredient."

The Emperor asked: "Why have you not asked for it from my cellars?"

The Rabbi responded: "This ingredient is not in your possession; it is the Sabbath which is lacking. Have you the Sabbath in your stores?"

*Bereshit Rabbah, 11.*

The Emperor once said to Rabbi Joshua ben Hananiah:
"Why does the Sabbath dish give forth so appetizing a fragrance?"
"We Jews have a certain ingredient, which we include within it.
This gives it the pleasing fragrance," answered the Rabbi.
"Let me have some of it for my kitchen," said the Emperor.
"It is of use only to those who keep the Sabbath."

*Shabbat, 119.*

On the Sabbath an "added soul" is given to us, an increased capacity for lofty thoughts and holy yearnings.

*Betzah, 16a.*

The Sabbath is a Queen whose coming changes the humblest home into a palace.

*Shabbat, 119a.*

The Sabbath is a foretaste of heaven, so pure and exalted is the happiness it offers to the careworn spirit.

*Mekilta to Exodus, 31:13.*

The Sabbath is scented with the perfume of Paradise, and as it reaches earth sorrow and sighing flee away, and peace and joy reign supreme.

*Zohar to Vayaphel.*

"Only he who labours on the eve of the Sabbath," said the Rabbis, "shall enjoy the Sabbath."

*Abodah Zarah, 3a.*

When life is in danger it is a duty to violate the Law. The violation is not to be relegated to the Gentile; the greatest in Israel are to share in it, so imperious and sacred is the duty.

*Yoma, 85b.*

Break the Sabbath so that this sick man may live to keep many Sabbaths.

*Yoma, 85b.*

The Sabbath is made coordinate with the whole system of Mosaic law.

*Y. Nedarim, 3, 14(38b).*

"A Psalm: a song of the Sabbath day," refers to the world in which there is Sabbath all the time.

*Mekilta, Ki Tissa, 2.*
*Shabbat, 1.*

## 296. SABBATH—PERMISSIBLE DESECRATION

It is better that the candle of a man should be extinguished on the Sabbath, rather than the candle of God (the soul of the sick person).

*Shabbat, 30.*

The Sabbath was given to you, but you were not given to the Sabbath.

*Betzah, 17.*

Danger to life takes precedence over the sanctity of the Sabbath.

*Shabbat, 75.*

If a battle has commenced previous to the Sabbath, Jews are permitted to continue fighting on the Sabbath, whether in attack or in defense.

*Shabbat, 192.*

To plan for a Mitzwah or for charity is permitted on the Sabbath.

*Shabbat, 15.*

## 297. HONORING THE SABBATH

Thy Sabbath garment should not be like thy week-day garment.

*Shabbat, 113.*

He who takes delight in the Sabbath, receives his heart's desires.

*Shabbat, 118.*

It was related concerning Shammai that he always ate for the sake of the Sabbath. Once he saw a goodly cow and said: "This one shall be for the Sabbath."

The next day he saw a better one, whereupon he slaughtered the first, and kept the second one for the Sabbath.

This was not the case with Hillel, who said: "Blessed be the Lord, who daily gives us of His abundance."

*Betzah, 16.*

R. Hiyya bar Abba said: "Consider this, O Israelite! Thou sanctifiest the Sabbath with eating, drinking, and clean raiment. Thou receivest enjoyment and yet thou also receivest reward from heaven. Thinkest thou that God gave thee the Sabbath for thy discomfort? Thou art wrong. Thou receivest a double profit for Him."

*Midrash quoted in "Oneg Shabbat."*

### THE CAPER-PLANT

A Disciple was walking in his vineyard on a Sabbath. He noticed a breach in the fence, and commenced to plan how he might close it. When he became aware that it was the Sabbath, he exclaimed: "Since I have made plans for it on the Sabbath, I shall ever desist from repairing the breach."

A caper-plant grew up in the breach, and from it the pious man received sustenance all the days of his life.[1]

*Shabbat, 150.*

[1] The flower-buds of the caper-plant are pickled and used as a seasoning.

There was once a man named Joseph, renowned for honoring the Sabbath day. He had a rich neighbor, a Gentile, whose property, according to a fortune-teller's prediction, would eventually revert to Joseph, who honored the Sabbath. To frustrate this prediction, the Gentile disposed of his property, and with the proceeds of the sale purchased a rare and costly jewel, which he affixed to his turban. On crossing a bridge, a gust of wind blew his turban into the river, and a fish swallowed it. This fish, being caught, was brought to a Friday market, and, as luck would have it, it was purchased by Joseph in honor of the coming Sabbath. When the fish was cut up, the jewel was discovered, and Joseph sold it for many purses of gold dinars.

An old man said to him:

"The Sabbath has repaid you in a most generous way all that you have spent on her."

*Shabbat, 119a.*

### THE FATTEST CATTLE

Rabbi Hiyya bar Abba narrated the following:

"I was once a Sabbath guest at the home of a butched in Laodicea. I saw many servants bring in a golden table with silver receptacles, glass decanters, and golden plates. They next brought in every manner of tasty dishes and wines, with many sweetmeats and fruits. I asked the butcher:

"My son, how have you come to deserve such great wealth?"

He answered, "I always leave the fattest cattle for the Sabbath."

I remarked: "Happy art thou to have merited this, and blessed be the Lord, who has rewarded thee."

*Bereshit Rabbah, 11.*

### THE BELOVED GUEST

Rabbah bar Rab Huna chanced to sojourn for the Sabbath at the home of Rabbah bar Rab Nahman. When a large tin of biscuits was brought in, he inquired: "Did you then know that I was going to stop over with you?"

"Nay," they replied, "but the Sabbath is as dear to us as a privileged guest."

Rab Ammi and Rab Assi would leave off learning on Fridays, and would occupy themselves with bringing from the market viands for the Sabbath. They remarked:

"Would we not have done this if Rabbi Johanan happened to visit us?"

*Shabbat, 119.*

### SMOTHERED IN SILK

Rab Huna once went to the Academy wearing a girdle of grass. Said Rab to him: "And where is your silken girdle?"

He answered:

"I had no money to purchase Kiddush wine for the Sabbath; hence I pawned my girdle and bought the wine."

Rab then blessed him, saying: "May it be God's will that you be verily smothered in silk."

Many years later, at the marriage of his son, Rabbah, Rab Huna lay down on the bed to rest. His daughters and daughters-in-law entered and, not noticing him, threw over him their silken garments. When Rab Joseph went to look for him, he found him covered with silk. Thereupon he said:

"In truth, Rab's blessing has been fulfilled."

When Rab heard of it, he said plaintively, "Why did you not have the wit to reply, 'And the same to you, Master.'"

*Megillah, 27b.*

## THE TWO BUNCHES OF MYRTLE

When Rabbi Simeon ben Yohai and his son, Rabbi Eleazar, came out of their cave, where they were hiding from the Roman government, on a Friday afternoon, they saw an old man hurrying along with two bunches of myrtle in his hand.

"What dost thou want with these?" they inquired.

"To smell them in honor of the Sabbath," was the reply.

"Would not one bunch be enough for that purpose?" they remarked.

"Nay. One is in honor of 'Remember the Sabbath day' (Exodus 20:8); and one in honor of 'Observe the Sabbath day' (Deut. 5:12)."

Thereupon Rabbi Simeon remarked to his son: "Behold how the commandments are regarded by Israel!"

*Shabbat, 33b.*

Through the Extra Soul given on the Sabbath, all anxieties and irritations are forgotten, and only joy rules.

*Zohar, ii, 204a.*

In two ways does man lend to God: in donating to the needy and in spending money for the Sabbath and Festivals.

*Zohar, ii, 255a.*

Each one in Israel receives an Extra Soul according to his degree of perfection. If he be a Hasid, his Extra Soul comes from the quality of benevolence. If he be strong in his battle against sin, his Extra Soul comes to him from the quality of strength.

*Raia Mehemna, iv, 242b.*

Ezekiel declares that the future House of God will have the gate of the inner court closed on week-days; but on the Sabbath day it shall be opened (46:1). Why? Because God may not shut His doors in the face of those who have lent to Him, and we are taught: God says to Israel, "Lend for Me and I shall pay."

*Tikkune Zohar, T. 19, p. 61a.*

Three things shall be different unto thee on the Sabbath: the name of the day, since it is called the Sabbath day and not the seventh; the custom of the day, for if thou art accustomed to lighting a fire daily for the morning and evening chill, you are not to light it on the Sabbath; the feeling of the day, for if thou art buried in anxieties every working day, on the Sabbath you may forget them.

*Tikkune Zohar, T. 21, p. 86a.*

When the Sabbath-Bride enters a home, and finds nothing prepared in her honor, the candles not lit, and the table not set, she exclaims: "This is not the home of one in Israel, for it has no holiness."

*Zohar Hadash to Ruth, 84b.*

To the degree that a man gives joy to the Shekinah on the Sabbath, he and his wife receive joy in the World-to-Come.

*Zohar Hadash Tikkunim, 117b.*

### 298. SABBATH LIGHT

The light of a man's countenance on a week-day is not the same as the light of his countenance on the Sabbath.

*Bereshit Rabbah, 11, 2.*

The housewife should kindle the Sabbath candles with a joyous heart and good will, for it is a great privilege accorded to her. It brings her the merit of holy sons, who will be Lights of the World in Torah, and who will increase peace on earth. It also merits her to give long life unto her husband. Therefore she should be careful in the observance of this Mitzwah.

*Zohar, i, 48b.*

The students of the Torah declare that woman caused the Soul of the world, which is its light, to be extinguished; therefore she should kindle the Sabbath light.

*Zohar, i, 48b.*

We read: "For the commandment is a lamp, and the teaching is light" (Prov. 6:23). The Sabbath lamp is the commandment for women, and the learning of Torah is a light unto men. When the wife prepares all that is proper for the Sabbath, and the husband learns or teaches the Torah, both give forth a light.

*Zohar, ii, 166a.*

### THE HOUSE OF THE CARPENTER

Rab Huna often passed the home of Rabbi Abin, the carpenter. He noticed that there was much light in the house on Friday nights. He said to his companions that two great lights in Israel would come forth from this house.

And so it happened. Rabbi Idi bar Abin and Rabbi Hiyya bar Abin made famous the house of the carpenter.

*Shabbat, 23.*

## 299.  SACRIFICES, OFFERINGS

Three tears fell from the Angels upon the knife of Abraham at the sacrifice of Isaac, and made its blade dull.

*Bereshit Rabbah, 56, 7.*

After Abraham had been prevented from actually sacrificing Isaac, he said: "My Lord, Thou knowest that I could have objected to Thy command to sacrifice my son, for Thou hast told me that in him will I have seed for a great nation. Yet I controlled myself and was prepared to obey Thee. Therefore, when my sons are judged by Thee on Rosh ha-Shanah, mayest Thou, also, control Thy justice and be filled with compassion upon them."

*Pesikta Buber, 23.*

All sacrifices, except the offering of thanks, will be abolished in the World-to-Come.

*Tanhuma Emor, 18; Midrash Tehillim, 56, 4.*

According to the Rabbis, Isaac willingly and gladly went with his father to Mount Moriah, to offer up his young life to the God whom he adored. As they were wending their way to perform the command of God, Isaac said to his father: "O Father, I am yet young, and I am fearful lest my body might tremble at the sight of the knife, causing you grief; I am fearful lest the offering shall not be a perfect one, perfect as I should like it to be."

*Bereshit Rabbah, 56:11.*

Whether we bring much or little, it matters not, if only we fix our heart upon our Father in Heaven.

*Berakot, 17a.*

Iron, the weapon of destruction, cannot rear an altar to the God of life and peace.

*Mekilta, Ba-Hodesh, chap. 11.*

Why is the word "soul" mentioned in connection with a flour offering of the poor? God says: "I consider it as if he brought his soul as an offering unto Me."

*Menahot, 104.*

Whosoever sacrifices his evil impulse and confesses it, has honored God.

*Sanhedrin, 43.*

R. Meir was once in a certain city. He was asked: "Why do the Scriptures tell us in some passages that sacrifice is very pleasant unto the Lord; while in others it is said that God dislikes sacrifices?"
He answered: "It depends whether a man's heart is sacrificed at the time he brings the animal sacrifice."

*Baraita Kallah, 8.*

Let no man say within himself: "I will go and do ugly and improper things; then I will bring a bullock, which has a great deal of meat, and offer it as a burnt-offering on the altar, and I shall obtain mercy with Him, and He will accept me in repentance."

*Wayyikra Rabbah, 2, end.*

But let him do good works and study the Torah, and bring but a lean ram . . . and offer it on the altar, and He will be with him in mercy and receive him in repentance.

*Eliyahu Rabbah, Friedman, p. 36.*

The statutory law of bringing sacrifices in atonement for inadvertent transgressions was obligatory on Israel alone. The rest of mankind do not bring sin offerings even for the violation of the commandments of God that were given to them.

*Sifra, on Lev. 4, 2.*

R. Benaiah said: "Thus said God to Israel: 'When I gave to you the omer of manna, I gave an omer to each one of you. But from all of you together, I ask merely one omer, an omer of barley.' "

R. Levi said: "All that God asks of Israel is a recompense for sending them the wind to winnow the grain. His chief assistance He gives without cost."

*Yalkut Shimeoni to Emor.*

## 300. SANCTIFICATION

### Give Every Day to the Supreme

The Bible hallows the lowliest acts—ploughing, sowing, reaping, and the like—and elevates them into a service of God.

*Bemidbar Rabbah, chap. x.*

A hundred religious duties await the Israelite every day.

*Y. Berakot, 9.*

## 301. SCHOLARS AND TEACHERS—HONORING AND SCOFFING

A student who does not stand up before his teacher is wicked.

*Kiddushin, 33.*

An aged scholar, who through no fault of his own, forgets his learning, shall be deemed as holy as the Ark.

*Kiddushin, 33.*

A man's teacher in the Torah stands to him in the place of a parent, and, as his spiritual father, he is entitled to the honor and reverence due to his actual father.

*Sifre on Deut., 6, 7.*

Rabbi Jose the Galilean said: "Who is called an old man? He who has acquired knowledge."

*Kiddushin, 32.*

## EVEN A BOY

R. Judah and R. Isaac met on a road a young boy leading an ass. While they rested, the lad halted near them and listened to their conversation. When R. Isaac had completed a commentary on a Scripture verse, the boy begged his permission to repeat what his father had said in comment upon that very verse.

After he had ended, the Rabbis embraced him and said: "Give back the ass to its owner and meet us at Sepphoris. Thou art too talented to work instead of studying."

When he came to the School at Sepphoris, R. Judah stood up in his honor and called him: "My teacher, Rabbi Jose, from whom I have learned important things."

We may learn from this, that even if a boy is of great learning, we must honor him as if he were an elder.

*Zohar, iii, 39.*

## TO WHOM HONOR IS DUE

During the Patriarchate of Rabban Simeon ben Gamaliel III, the father of Rabbi, Rabbi Nathan was the Chief Justice and Rabbi Meir was the Chief of the Sages. Once the Patriarch observed that both Rabbis were absent from session in the Academy. He said: "I am ordaining that there be instituted various degrees in the respect paid to us three chiefs. When the Patriarch enters, all should arise and wait until he is seated, before they take their seats. When the Chief Justice enters, two rows at each side should arise. When the Chief Sage enters, only one row should arise."

When R. Nathan and R. Meir came in on the following day and observed this innovation, they conspired to ask the Patriarch to expound "Uktzin," the last tractate in the Mishnah, which he had not yet learned.

"If he should admit his ignorance of this tractate, we will declare that he is unworthy of his position."

A Sage overheard this, and, seated near the study of R. Simeon, he expounded the tractate. The following day, when R. Nathan asked the Nassi to expound "Uktzin," he did so, and then commanded that both men be expelled.

R. Meir and R. Nathan took up a place outside and threw written questions into the Academy. Several times no one was able to furnish the answer, and R. Jose complained that the Torah was outside the

Academy. Thereupon both Rabbis were asked to re-enter. R. Nathan begged the Patriarch's pardon, and the latter said: "Your father's position as the Exilarch of Babylonia brought to you the position of Chief Justice, but it is not important enough to make you the Patriarch." R. Meir did not appease the Nasi, and it was decided not to mention his name when a Halakah, taught by him, is quoted, but to declare it to be the opinion of "others."

Once R. Simeon ben Gamaliel taught such a Halakah to his son, Rabbi. The son said: "Who is it from whose fountain we drink and whose name we do not mention?"

"It is one who desired to rob you of your succession," said R. Simeon.

Rabbi retorted: "But he has already died, and his action has done no harm."

His father repeated the Halakah and said: "It was taught in the name of R. Meir."

Rabba remarked: "I am surprised that a meek man like Rabbi did not insist that it be asserted: 'Rabbi Meir said.'"

*Horaiyot, 13.*

If knowledge and wisdom are desirable things, their possessors surely deserve honor at our hands.

*Kiddushin, 33a.*

## EXPOUNDING THE "ETH"

We have learned: "Simeon the Amsonite was accustomed to expound every 'eth' (the accusative term) in the Torah, and to explain why it happened. When he came to the verse: 'Eth the Lord, thy God, thou shalt fear,' he refrained from explaining the 'eth.'"

His Disciples said to him: "Master, what of the 'eths' that thou hast expounded except in this verse?"

He replied: "Just as I shall receive reward for expounding the others, so will I receive reward for not expounding this one."

Then came Rabbi Akiba, who expounded this "eth" also. He said: "It denotes another whom ye shall fear, namely, the Sage."

*Pesahim, 22.*

## MOTHER AND STEPMOTHER

Kahana was scrupulous in his observance of Mitzwot. When he came to the Holy Land, several Jews ridiculed his piety and asked him: "What dost thou hear in heaven?"

His temper got the better of him and he answered: "I have heard that the evil decree against you is already sealed."

It so happened that the scoffers died soon after, and people murmured against Kahana.

He said to himself: "I have come to the Land of Israel in order to serve God better, but here it is maintained on every side that people have died on my account."

He went to Rabbi Johanan and said: "My mother scoffs at me, and my father's wife respects me; with whom shall I remain?"

Said the Rabbi: "With the one who respects you."

Kahana immediately left for Babylonia. Rabbi Johanan was told this and said: "Why did he not come to me for permission to leave me?"

The others said: "His question was by way of asking your permission, and you gave it."

*Y. Berakot, 2.*

### THE MAN OF ABUSE

A rich man of Nehardea entered a butcher shop and demanded instant attention. The dealer said: "I must first attend to the servant of the great Rabbi, Rab Judah bar Ezekiel."

The man retorted: "Who is this Judah bar Ezekiel that I should wait for him?"

Rab Judah heard of this and pronounced the anathema against him. He was told that the wealthy man was accustomed to call people serfs. He caused it to be publicly announced that the wealthy man was himself a descendant of unliberated serfs and that his family was illegitimate.

The man complained to Rab Nahman, the Chief Justice, and a summons was sent to Rab Judah. The latter deemed it beneath his dignity to appear before a younger scholar, but, out of respect for the Exilarch, the father-in-law of R. Nahman, he went.

R. Nahman welcomed the greater Rabbi profusely and commenced to talk with him, making use of unusual and elaborate words.

Rab Judah rebuked him saying: "He who speaks with elaborate words is a haughty person."

A note was brought to R. Nahman from his wife Yalta, not to subject himself to reprimands. R. Nahman asked: "Why have you not flogged the man for abusing you, as Rab was accustomed to do?"

"The anathema will be a sharper lesson for his impudence."

"Why have you announced that he is a serf?"

"My Master, Samuel, taught," answered Rab Judah, "a man calls another man that which he is himself."

The plaintiff appeared and said: "You call me serf? I am a descendant of the Hasmonean kings."

Rab Judah said: "I have heard from Mar Samuel: 'He who claims descent from the Hasmoneans is a serf, since Herod permitted no pretender of that family to live!"

Rab Nahman said: "But we have a law that a Sage cannot bring up a new law after he has done something which is questioned!"

A Sage, Rab Matnah, entered and Rab Judah asked him: "What did Mar Samuel say on this and that occasion?"

Rab Matnah repeated the saying with reference to the Hasmoneans.

The family was then pronounced illegitimate and many divorces took place.

*Kiddushin, 70.*

## The Blind Sage

Rabbi and R. Hiyya came to a town where a blind Sage lived. They visited him, and as they took their departure, the blind Sage remarked: "You came to visit one who is seen and sees not. May you be worthy to visit one who sees and is not seen."

*Hagigah, 5.*

## At Other Times

R. Ilai and R. Jacob bar Zabdai were sitting together and R. Simeon bar Abba passed by. When they arose, R. Simeon said: "Please do not trouble. In the first place, you are Sages and I am merely a comrade, not a Master. Secondly, you were discussing Torah, and the Torah need not arise in the presence of one who studies it on other occasions but not at the moment."

Abbaye held that they acted correctly.

*Kiddushin, 33.*

A Disciple who leaves his Master shall not turn his face away from his Master, but shall go out sidewise, with his profile toward the Master.

*Yoma, 53.*

## The Slap on the Cheek

When R. Zeira came to Palestine he underwent blood-letting and required a meal of good beef to regain his strength. He chanced upon an uncouth butcher who, seeing the newcomer, sought to have fun at his expense. When the Rabbi asked for a pound of beef, he was told that its price was fifty centimes with a slap upon the cheek. The Rabbi was willing to pay up to one hundred centimes in order to be freed from the blow, but the butcher insisted. The Rabbi accepted the slap, and when he encountered several students in the School, he inquired from them the reason for such a custom. They sent for the scoffer but were told that he had suddenly died.

Observing their chagrin, R. Zeira said: "I assure you I had no thought in mind to punish. I believed it was the practice here."

Rabbi Jose came to Tiberias for the baths in the Hot Springs. A scoundrel struck him on the back. The Rabbi said: "Your neck-band is loose."

A police officer happened at the moment to capture a bandit at the entrance to the Hot Springs. When asked: "Who was your accomplice?" the captive replied: "That grinning man there."

The scoundrel was also seized and was later recognized as a murderer. A few hours later when Rabbi Jose left his bath, he beheld his erstwhile assailant with a tight noose about his neck.

*Y. Berakot, 2.*

R. Simeon ben Halafta visited Sepphoris. At the city gate several wild boys halted him and said: "We shall not let you continue until you dance for us."

He protested, pleading old age as an excuse, but in vain. He then commanded them to awaken their father and tell him: "Sin is sweet in the beginning, but bitter in the end."

The father fell at the Rabbi's feet and begged him to be merciful to his foolish sons. R. Simeon consented to overlook the offense of the boys, but nevertheless, the house in which the family lived, soon after fell in ruins.[1]

*Kohelet Rabbah, 3.*

[1] The man had neglected to repair his house, just as he had neglected his sons.

## Grace After Meals

When King Yannai quarrelled with the Sages, and ordered the execution of many for opposing his desire to be both king and High-Priest, no one remained to say Grace. His wife said: "If I bring thee my kinsman, Simeon ben Shetah, wilt thou harm him?" The king promised not to persecute him.

When Simeon arrived, the meal had already ended. Hence he said: "How can I say: 'Blessed be He of whose bounty Yannai and his company have partaken.'"

The king ordered food to be placed before him, and the Rabbi recited Grace properly.

Later the king said to him: "Do you appreciate the honor I have paid you in allowing you to sit next to me?"

The Rabbi replied: "Not you, but my learning has done me honor. Were I unlearned, I should not have been called to sit at the head of the table to say Grace."

The king remarked to his queen: "Seest thou that the Rabbis refuse to give me satisfaction?"

*Berakot, 48.*

## 302. IMPIOUS SCHOLARS

A man should not read and learn and then abuse his parent or teacher.

*Berakot, 17.*

Comrades in Torah who do not love each other betake themselves on a crooked path and cause blemishes in their Torah. For Torah is love, friendship, and truth.

*Zohar, 11, 190b.*

He who learns without the intention of practicing were better not to have been born.

*Y. Shabbat, 1, 2.*

Even as golden vessels that have been damaged may be repaired, so a scholar, who has erred, may become good.

*Hagigah, 15.*

A man who is learned in the Torah but does not fear God is like a treasurer who owns the inner but not the outer keys.

*Shabbat, 31.*

He who says: "I wish only to learn the Torah but not to fulfill it," receives no reward for his studying.

*Yebamot, 109.*

Even if a scholar has sinned, his Torah need not, therefore, be despised.

*Hagigah, 15.*

## STORIES OF ELISHA AHER

### An Ulterior Motive

Said "Aher" (Elisha ben Abuyah) to Rabbi Meir: "Koheleth teaches: 'Better is the end of a thing than the beginning thereof' (7, 8). This means according to your Master, Rabbi Akiba: 'Good is the end of a thing when it is good from its very beginning.'

"Take my own case. My father, Abuyah, was a great man in Jerusalem. At my circumcision every person of importance was present. Rabbi Eliezer and Rabbi Joshua took seats in another room.

"Rabbi Eliezer said: 'While the other guests amuse themselves with music and dancing, let us enjoy ourselves by discussing Torah.'

"Abuyah entered their room, and it seemed to him as if a heavenly flame surrounded them. 'Have you come to burn me out of my house?' he asked.

"'We are only discussing Torah,' they said.

"Abuyah remarked: 'If such be the power of Torah, my son shall become a scholar.'

"Thus did an ulterior motive enter into my education."

*Y. Hagigah, ii.*

### The Mother-Bird and Her Chicks

Some say that the fall of "Aher" resulted from the following: He saw a man ascend a ladder, remove the mother-bird and her chicks, and then descend in safety.

Another man ascended a ladder, freed the mother-bird and took the chicks only, as enjoined in the Torah. On descending, a serpent bit him and he died.

He thought: "The Torah teaches that the second man should have enjoyed long life (Deut. 22–17). Is then the Torah a delusion?"

He did not know that Rabbi Jacob (in some versions, the son of his sister) interpreted it as a reward in the After-Life.

When "Aher" died, his Disciple, Rabbi Meir, said at the bier: "Tarry this night while I am still in this Vale of Tears, which is like unto night; and it shall be in the morning, when I am summoned to the Life Everlasting, which is like the morning; if He the All-Good will redeem thee, let Him redeem, but if He be not willing to redeem thee, then I will redeem thee." (Ruth 3:13)

*Ruth Rabbah, chap. 6.*

### ADVISING THE ENEMY

"Aher" came to hate Torah. When he beheld young students in the School, he would say: "What are you doing here? You would make good tailors, carpenters, builders, and so forth."

Many of them listened to him and renounced their studies.

When the Roman government forced Jews to work on the Sabbath, he would suggest to the officials that which would be a desecration of the Law.

*Y. Hagigah, chap. 2.*

It was asked: "How could Rabbi Meir permit himself to learn from a heretic like Aher?"

Rabbi Meir found a pomegranate; he ate the inside and threw away the shell (peel).

*Hagigah, 15.*

### THE WANDERING SOUL

When "Aher" died, it was revealed to his Disciple, Rabbi Meir, that the Heavenly Court had decided neither to punish him nor to bring him to the enjoyment of Paradise. Rabbi Meir prayed that he be punished as an expiation for his sins.

Rabbi Johanan remarked: "One only was there among us sages who blundered, and yet we seem helpless to rescue him. When my soul is led to Paradise, I shall seize hold of his wandering soul and take it unto Paradise with me."

*Hagigah, 15.*

### THE COVER OF THE SCROLL

Rabbi Meir was asked: "If the Heavenly Tribunal should inquire whom thou wishest first to favor, thy father or thy Master (Elisha ben Abuyah), who will be first in thy sight?"

"My Master," he replied.

"And dost thou believe that thou shalt be obeyed? Hast thou not made a rash promise?"

"Nay," answered Rabbi Meir. "We are taught that when a fire occurs on a Sabbath or a similar day, the cover of the Torah Scroll may be saved with the Scroll. Rabbi Elisha shall be saved for Life Everlasting because his Torah is everlasting."

*Ruth Rabbah, chap. 6.*

In a famine, the daughter of "Aher" asked Rabbi Judah ha-Nasi to sustain her.

He exclaimed: "Is then one of his blood still left?"

She said: "Master, remember his great scholarship."

A flame from heaven descended and licked the chair of Rabbi. Rabbi was touched and said: "If God thus protects the honor of an erring scholar, how much the more that of a righteous one."

How did "Aher" come to fall? He was always fond of Greek songs, and when he would stand up in the School, works of the Minim (Sectaries) would fall from his lap.

*Hagigah, 15.*

## 303. SCHOLARS, MASTERS AND DISCIPLES

If a Disciple sits at a trial, and sees that his Master errs, he must interfere.

*Sanhedrin, 6.*

In one of the Psalms it says: "I hid Thy words in my heart" [1]; and in another [2] it says: "I declared words of righteousness in large assemblies." How is the contradiction to be explained?

When the Master lives, the Disciple conceals his learning; after his demise, he proclaims it in public.

*Erubin, 63.*

[1] Ps. 119:11. "Thy word have I laid up in my heart."
[2] Ps. 40:10. "I have preached righteousness in the great congregation."

Who shall inherit the World-to-Come? He whose teachers are pleased with him.

*Shabbat, 153.*

Let the fear of thy master be unto thee as the fear of Heaven.

*Abot, 4, 12.*

If a Disciple knows that his Teacher is able to answer him, he may ask. Otherwise he may not ask.

*Hullin, 6.*

If you see a student to whom his studies are as hard as iron, it is because his Master has not explained them properly.

*Taanit, 8.*

A man should say to his Teacher: "May thy prayer be heard!"

*Y. Berakot, 4, 3.*

The words of the Master, and the words of the Disciple: to whom shall attention be paid?

*Kiddushin, 42.*

Jose ben Joezer said: "Let thy house be a meeting-place of the learned; sit in the dust at their feet and thirstily drink in their words."

*Abot, 1, 4.*

## Appeasing Rabbi Johanan

Once Rabbi Johanan was walking with Rabbi Jacob bar Idi, and they saw Rabbi Eleazar ben Pedat pass by. The latter did not halt to greet his Master, but went on as if he saw him not.

Rabbi Johanan turned to his companion and said: "Are these then the manners of you Babylonians?"

Rabbi Jacob replied: "Suppose there were an idolatrous temple on this street, would you tell me to take another path?"

"No," said Rabbi Johanan, "why should we pay the idol honor by stepping out of its way?"

"Then, when Rabbi Eleazar did step aside, it meant that he wished to pay you honor. In Babylonia a Disciple does not presume to greet his Master unless the latter summons him."

"But there is another difficulty," said Rabbi Johanan, "he repeats my Halakot, yet fails to say that he has learned them from me."

They passed an ancient House of Study.

Rabbi Jacob said: "In this Bet ha-Midrash, Rabbi Meir was accustomed to hold discourse. When the Halakah was attributed to Rabbi Ishmael, he would mention his name; when it was Rabbi Akiba, he never mentioned the latter's name."

"But every one knew that Rabbi Akiba had been Rabbi Meir's Master, and that he had learned Halakah chiefly from him," retorted Rabbi Johanan.

"By the same token everyone knows that you are the Master of Rabbi Eleazar ben Pedat, and he need not give your name explicitly."

*Y. Berakot, 2.*

All Israel learned Torah from Moses, yet it was his servant who became his successor. This teaches us the importance of rendering service unto the Sages.

*Midrash Lekah Tob, Tissa.*

## The Unknown Corpse

Rabbi Akiba said: "Once I found a corpse in a field. I carried it on my shoulder four miles and buried it in the cemetery. When I came to the Academy and told of this, I was informed that I had sinned grievously at every step because an unidentified corpse must be buried where it is found. I then said to myself: 'I, who intended to perform a good deed, have sinned. How much the more when my intention is not so pure?' I then resolved to minister to the Sages."

*Y. Nazir, 3.*

Others say: "Even one who has read the Written Law and studied the Mishnah is an ignorant man if he has not served the Sages." [1]

*Berakot, 47.*

[1] A man should study under a Master, not from books alone. It was the custom for Disciples to perform small services for their Master, who taught them Halakah and its application to actual cases. Not to serve a Master meant not to study under a Master.

### Rendering Decisions

Rabbi Eliezer said: "A Disciple may not render a decision without his Master's permission if his Master resides within twelve miles."

Abbaye said in the name of Rab Joseph: "He may not decide even the simplest case or issue the simplest ruling."

Rabina said: "He who is both a comrade and a Disciple may issue rulings in a different city from his comrade-Master."

*Wayyikra Rabbah, 20; Erubin, 63.*

### Deferring to the Master

Rabina sat before Rab Ashi, his Master. Near them a Jew tied his ass to a tree, on the Sabbath, against Rabbinical prohibition. Rabina shouted to the man to untie the beast, but the man paid no heed.

He said, "May that man be under the ban."

Rabina then said to Rab Ashi: "In my haste I acted without remembering that you are my Master."

Rab Ashi replied: "You acted rightly. When it is a matter of the profanation of God's name—and rank disobedience to the Rabbis is one of its forms—no deference need be shown to a Master."

*Erubin, 63.*

### For the Children's Sake

A shohet in the city of Rabbah bar Hinena did not appear before the Rabbi to show his knife. Taking this as an insult to his dignity, the Rabbi took away his license. He was told that the shohet had two small children to support. The Rabbi then instructed two of his disciples to examine the knife, and they found it in proper condition. One of them gave a new license to the shohet. The other asked: "Should we not first submit our finding to the Rabbi?"

"He instructed us to learn whether the license may be returned; therefore, we need not trouble him further," was the reply.

*Hullin, 18.*

### Gratitude to Disciples

A sage arrived from Laodicea. Rabbi Eleazar, Rabbi Simeon and Rabbi Johanan ben Beroka came to visit the guest. He said: "It is my duty to thank you for preserving the Torah after I shall be gone. You also should thank your children (Disciples) for maintaining the Torah after you are gone. Moses was great, but if others had not kept the Torah after he had departed, of what use would his greatness have been?"

*Pesikta Zutarta to Deut., 32, 46.*

## 304. SCHOOL, SCHOOLCHILDREN

What stabilizes the world? The voice of the children who study the Torah.

*Hakdamah to Zohar, p. 1b.*

If there are no kids, there are no goats; if there are no goats there are no flocks; if there is no flock, there is no shepherd.[1]

*Y. Sanhedrin, 10, 2.*

[1] We must teach the young Torah.

In the time when the voice of Jacob's children is heard in the Schools of Torah, the hands of Esau do not prevail.

*Bereshit Rabbah, 65, 20.*

Every day an Angel comes down to destroy the world, but when God looks upon the school-children and the students of Torah, His anger is turned into compassion.

*Kallah Rabbati, 2.*

The breath of the children who learn the Torah stabilizes the world. It ascends on High, is crowned with the upper crown, and is appointed to guard the world.

*Zohar, ii, 255b.*

Rab Judah said in the name of Rab: "Blessed be the name of the High-Priest, Joshua ben Gamla, for, were it not for him, Torah might have been forgotten in Israel. Before his time, the duty of teaching was laid upon the fathers; and those who had no fathers or whose fathers could not, or cared not, to teach, did not learn. Joshua ben Gamla instituted schools in every hamlet throughout Palestine.

"The parents would send their sons when they were sixteen or seventeen years old, and if they did not like to study, they would walk out of the School. The High-Priest, therefore, ordained that children should be brought to School at the age of six or seven."

*Baba Batra, 24.*

### THE TOWN WITHOUT SCHOOLMASTERS

"Except the Lord keep the city, the watchman waketh but in vain."
(Psalm 127:1)

Rabbi Judah ha-Nasi II sent out Rabbi Hiyya bar Abba, Rabbi Assi and Rabbi Ammi to learn through an investigation of all the villages and towns of Palestine, whether they had schools.

They came to a place where there was no schoolmaster. They asked the head of the community to summon the town's watchmen. The night watchers were brought into their presence.

"They are no profit to a city," the Rabbis said, "they are only an expense."

"And whom do you call watchmen?" the Rabbis were asked.

"The schoolmasters," they responded. "A town without schools will not be guarded by the Lord."

*Y. Hagigah, 1.*

### Why the Children Come

Two Rabbis, Johanan ben Beroka and Eleazar b. Hisma visited the aged Rabbi Joshua ben Hananiah.

He asked them: "What did you have new in the School today?"

They made an evasive reply, politely implying that they could bring nothing new to so eminent a scholar.

He understood their reticence, however, and pressed his question. "It is impossible," he said, "that there should be a meeting in the School without something new. Who presided?" he asked.

They answered, "Rabbi Eleazar ben Azariah."

"And what did he preach about?"

They, thereupon, told him how Eleazar applied to the congregation the words: " 'Assemble the people, men, women, and children' (Deut. 31:12) : The men come to learn, the women to hear, but why do the children come?"

The answer was: "To acquire a reward for those who bring them."

*Hagigah, 3a-b.*

## 305. SCROLLS OF THE LAW

The Talmud warns against the danger of "taking hold of a Scroll of the Law naked."

*Shabbat, 14a; Megillah, 32a.*

## 306. SECRETS

A man can conceal himself from his enemies but not from his friends.

*Rashi to Psalm, 55, 14.*

He who sins secretly is as if he limited the Omniscience of God.

*Hagigah, 16.*

If a man sins in secret, God takes pity on him. If he repents, God forgives him and forgets his sin. If he does not repent, God causes his transgression to be known in public.

*Zohar, i, 66a.*

Rabbi Berechiah said: "The people of the East (Babylonians?) are exceedingly clever.

"When a man wishes to write a secret to another, he writes the message with the juice of pressed oak-nuts (gall-nuts). The writing is invisible and when the receiver pours over it rosin and copper acid, the writing becomes black and readable, as a result of the mysterious contact with the dried gall-nut juice." [1]

*Y. Shabbat, 12.*

[1] Writers of Sefer-Torahs, Tefillin, Mezuzahs, and the Book of Esther, etc., make ink from these materials; they do not use ordinary ink.

Great is the keeping of a secret. He who reveals a secret oftentimes causes bloodshed.

*Midrash Gadol u-Gedolah, 19.*

If you are told something, do not repeat it unless you are given permission to do so.

*Yoma, 4.*

## 307. SELF

Hillel said: "If I am not for myself, who will be, but if I am only for myself, what am I?"

*Abot, chap. 1.*

## 308. SELF-BLAME

If a man meets with chastisements, let him search out his own deeds; if he finds no wrong in them, let him attribute the reason to his neglect of the Torah.[1]

*Berakot, 5.*

[1] Had he not neglected Torah, he would discover the wrong in his ways.

A man sees every disease of the skin except his own.[1]

*Negaim, 2, 5.*

[1] Popular paraphrase expressing the thought that a man sees all blemishes except his own.

A man sees no fault in himself.

*Shabbat, 119.*

Rab Huna owned four hundred large jars of wine, which went sour on his hands. His colleagues, hearing of his loss, bade him review his conduct.

"Do you suspect me?" he asked.

"Is God to be suspected of injustice?" they replied.

"If anyone has heard anything about me, let him speak out."

"Why does not the Master give cuttings to the wine-dresser as is his right?"

"Is there any of it left for me when he is through? He steals them all."

"People say: 'Steal from the thief and you receive the same treatment.'"

Rab Huna thereupon pledged himself to give the wine-dresser his share of cuttings, and he suffered no loss.

*Berakot, 5b.*

## 309. SELF-DENIAL

Sanctify thyself in the things that are permitted to thee, by denying thyself, that is, something of what is allowed.

*Yebomot, 20a.*

## 310. SELF-ESTEEM

Be not wicked in thine own esteem.

*Abot, 2, 13.*

## 311. SELF-IMPROVEMENT

Cleanse thyself before thou cleansest others.

*Baba Metzia, 107.*

Gatemaker, O see, thine own gate is broken.

*Bereshit Rabbah, 67, 2.*

As the captain of a ship guides it in the best course, guide thou thyself in the best way of performing a Mitzwah.

*Wayyikra Rabbah, 21.*

## 312. SELF-INJURY

He who gives away his property to his sons during his own lifetime buys for himself a master.

*Baba Metzia, 75.*

The steps I was forced to ascend at Bet Biri and Bet Nirash made me old before my time.

*Erubin, 56.*

Who adds to a thing, diminishes it.

*Sanhedrin, 29.*

A man may not weaken his body through much fasting. He might thereby become a public charge and a burden.

*Taanit, 22.*

The spittle, which a man throws upward, will fall upon his own face.

*Kohelet Rabbah, 7, 9.*

He who risks his life needlessly, even for the sake of Torah, will not have his name mentioned when his Halakot are cited.

*Baba Kamma, 61.*

He who takes his own life has no share in the World-to-Come.

*Ascribed to Talmud but not found.*

People say: "The maker of arrows is often slain by the very weapons he fashions."

*Pesahim, 28.*

A man should not hold stubbornly to his own words.

*Eduyot, 1, 4.*

"As an Error Which Proceedeth From a Ruler." (Eccl. 10, 5)

A bone stuck in the throat of the son of Rabbi Joshua ben Levi. The physician who was called belonged to the Sectaries. He recited a verse and removed the bone. When he told the patient what verse he had recited, the latter exclaimed: "I would rather have choked to death." And this very thing occurred to him.[1]

*Kohelet Rabbah, 10.*

[1] The text reads: "One of the followers of Pandera," perhaps "Christian"; if so, the verse was taken from the New Testament.

Antoninus Junior (Codemus), the grandson of Antoninus Senior (Pius), asked Rabbi: "Who of us will die earlier?"

The Rabbi answered: "It will be I."

His Disciples said: "We all pray for your health and yet you speak thus?"

He answered: "My words can neither do harm nor good; when my time comes I will have to go."

Nevertheless, it was believed that he died because of his words.

*Kohelet Rabbah, 10.*

## 313. SELF–PRAISE—BOASTING

A man is permitted to tell who he is in a place where he is unknown.

*Nedarim, 62.*

A single coin in a crock makes much noise, but if the crock is full of coins, it is silent.

*Baba Metzia, 85.*

If thou art so brave, here is a wolf; go out and subdue it.

*Bereshit Rabbah, 87, 3.*

One verse says: "And I thy servant fear the Lord." [1] Another verse says: "Let another praise thee and not thine own mouth." [2]

In a place where a man is known he should not praise himself.

*Nedarim, 62.*

[1] Kings 18:12.
[2] Proverbs 27:2.

## 314. SELF–PRESERVATION

Thine own life comes before the life of thy fellow's.

*Baba Metzia, 62.*

Everything is in the hands of Heaven except the fever and the chill.

*Ketubot, 30.*

Do they say to a man: "Go and sin so that thou mayest merit?"

*Kiddushin, 55.*

Do they say to a man: "Go thou and sin so that thy fellow-man may merit?"

Shabbat, 4.

People say"Do not precede the enemy when thou goest on the road, lest he attack you from behind."

Sanhedrin, 95.

### The Blind Man's Enjoyment of Light

Rabbi Jose said: "We read: 'Thou shalt grope at noon-day, as the blind gropeth in darkness.' (Deut. 28:29) I used to wonder: 'What difference can it make to a blind man whether it be noon-day or night?'

"Once, on a dark night, I met a blind man carrying a torch. I asked him why he carried it, and he answered: 'So that people may see me and save me from obstacles.' "[1]

Megillah, 24.

[1] And since the blind man finds a light to be necessary for his welfare, he, too, should bless the creator of the luminaries (Singer, p. 47).

### Safety First

Rabbi Yannai would not board a ferry until he had examined it as to its safety.

Rabbi Zeira would not pass between trees on a windy day.

Rab and Samuel would not use a short-cut as they had to pass a ruined wall, even though it had stood for many years.

Rabbi Yannai said: "A person should never take chances in a place of danger and depend upon rescue by a miracle. Even if a miracle does occur, his reward in the World-to-Come is thereby lessened."

Shabbat, 32.

What should be done, if one of two wayfarers in the desert has a little water, and the other has none? If one of them should drink all the water, he will be able to survive. If they should divide it, both would die.

Ben Paturi said they should both drink, and die, for it is written: "And thy brother shall live with thee."

Rabbi Akiba replied: "Thy brother shall live with *thee,* namely, thy life takes precedence over his life."

Sifra on Lev. 25, 36 (above verse).

Rabbi Eleazar ben Azariah said: "He who has a mannah (hundred coins) should eat only vegetables. He who has ten mannahs should eat fish for the Sabbath. He who has fifty mannahs should eat meat for the Sabbath. He who has a hundred mannahs may eat fish or meat daily."

Rab said: "It is good counsel and it should be followed."

Rabbi Johanan said: "Rab came from a healthy stock and retained his health by eating vegetables. We are not so vigorous, and if we have money, we should buy food that strengthens."

Rabbi Nahman said: "We should buy strengthening food, even if we must secure it on credit."

*Hullin, 84.*

The motto of Hillel: "If I am not for myself, who is for me? And when I am for myself only, what am I? And if not now, when?" (Abot 1:14) is in the spirit of the commandment: "Thou shalt love thy neighbor as thyself."

A sound morality must take account of our own interest equally with the interest of others.

*Moore, "Judaism," ii, 86.*

### 315.  SELF-SACRIFICE

He who recites the Shema must recall to his mind the crossing of Israel through the waters of the Red Sea.

Why must he think of just that event? Because he who prays must think of the heroic self-sacrifice that our fathers displayed at the shores of the Red Sea, in order to win their freedom from bondage.

*Shemot Rabbah, 22, 4.*

### 316.  SELF-STRENGTHENING, SELF-CONTROL

If two men appeal to thee for aid, one to load, and the other to unload, and thou likest unloading but not loading, do the loading in order to subdue thy inclination.

*Baba Metzia, 32.*

If a man guard himself against transgression once, twice or thrice, God guards him henceforth against transgression.

*Y. Kiddushin, 1, end.*

The eyes and ears of man are not always dependent upon man's will-power; but a man's tongue is always dependent upon his will.

*Zohar, i, 195a.*

If a man makes a harness for his beast, how much the more should he fashion a harness for his impulses, which may prompt him to lead a good or evil life.

*Y. Sanhedrin 10, 1.*

Woe to me from my Creator! Woe to me from my Impulse! [1]

*Berakot, 61.*

[1] The command of the Impulse oftentimes contradicts the injunction of God.

Four things require strength in the observance: Torah, good works, prayer, and social duty.

With respect to the Torah and good works it is written: "Be thou strong and firm, that thou mayest observe to do all the Torah" (Josh. 1:7). In this passage, the word "strong" refers to the Torah, and the word "firm" to good works.

Of prayer it is written: "Wait on the Lord, be strong, and He shall make thy heart firm." (Ps. 27:14)

With respect to social duties it is written: "Be strong, and let us strengthen ourselves for our people, and for the cities of God." (II Samuel 10:12)

*Berakot, 32b.*

## 317. SHABUOT, DECALOGUE, REVELATION

We have seven days of Pesach and seven days of Sukkot, why should we not have seven days of Shabuot? Because Shabuot commemorates the day when all Israel was as one heart in accepting the Torah.

*Zohar, iii, 96a.*

There are 613 letters in the Decalogue, equal to the number of the commandments.

*Bemidbar Rabbah, 13:15.*

A few days before Shabuot, Moses summoned the Elders and said to them: "These are the words which God will soon wish to command. Do you favor adopting them?"

They answered: "Why not? Have not our fathers already adopted these rules of conduct before us? Jacob accepted the Lord as God, and ordered the removal of strange gods. Joseph swore by the life of Pharaoh and not by God; moreover he also prepared a Sabbath table before his brethren. Isaac honored his father and made no protest when led to the sacrifice. Judah opposed the rendering of death to Joseph. Joseph was opposed to adultery. Judah identified before his father the bloody shirt of Joseph and did not lie. Abraham refused the plunder of Sodom. We shall be just as eager to accept God's words as were our fathers."

*Pesikta Hadashah, Otzar Midrashim, p. 489.*

God reveals himself in several guises: when he speaks regarding rewards, His countenance is merry; when He speaks regarding penalties, His face is blanched.

*Pesikta Rabbati, 21:6.*

When the Torah was given, the earth rejoiced, but the heavens wept. It may be likened to a beloved princess given in marriage to a distant prince. The wedding-day is a holiday in the city of the prince but a day of mourning in the city where the princess has grown up.

*Pesikta Rabbati, 20, 1.*

Rabbi Simlai said: "Until the Torah was given, the earth was justly proud: it took God six days in which to complete it. When the Torah was given, however, the earth lost its pride; it took God forty days in which to complete it."

*Pesikta Rabbati, 21:21.*

Rabbi Levi said: "Even as a statue, when visited by a thousand people at one and the same time, seems to gaze upon them all, so did everyone at Sinai feel that God's words were directed to him."

*Pesikta Buber, 110a.*

The human voice can be heard by many, though the human ear can listen attentively to only one voice. As for God, however, He can listen to many voices at one and the same time, and surely His voice can be heard by multitudes.

*Pesikta Rabbati, 21:6.*

The Commandment against murder corresponds to the Commandment that we believe in God, for in God's image has He created man.

The Commandment against adultery corresponds to the one against idolatry; for both are forms of infidelity.

The Commandment against stealing corresponds to the Commandment against perjury, for the first leads to the second.

The Commandment against false testimony corresponds to the Commandment to observe the Sabbath, which was given to us in order that we may testify that God is the Creator.

The Commandment against coveting corresponds to the one enjoining us to honor our parents, for the coveting of one's neighbor's wife results in divorce and prevents children from honoring their parents.

*Pesikta Rabbati, 21, 18.*

We read in Abot 5:1: "With ten sayings the world was created." This number is taken in order to correspond to the Decalogue.

The first saying: "Let there be light," corresponds to the First Commandment; for we remember that God is the Eternal Light.

The second: "Let there be an expanse," reminds us that all heavenly bodies are creatures only.

The third: "Let the waters assemble," reminds us that the water of the sea does not hold lightly the name of God, and does not overflow its bounds.

The fourth: "Let the earth bring forth grass," reminds us of God's bounty to him who honors the Sabbath.

The fifth: "Let there be lights," reminds us of two other lights in the life of man, namely, his father and mother. If he honors them he will walk in light next to the Eternal Light.

The sixth: "Let the waters bring forth fowl, etc.," reminds us that we may slay these creatures for our use, but not men.

The seventh: "Let the earth bring forth creatures after their own kind," reminds us that only beasts may multiply promiscuously, but man must not commit adultery.

The eighth: "Let us make man . . . who shall have dominion," reminds us that man should make use only of that over which he has dominion. He should not steal, however, that over which others have dominion.

The ninth: "I have given . . . every tree on which is the fruit," reminds us that as the tree fulfils its function truly, so should man's lips fulfil their function by speaking the truth.

The tenth: "It is not good that man should be alone," reminds us that just as Adam did not covet another's wife, we also should not covet.

*Pesikta Hadrashah, Otzar Midrashim, p. 491.*

Bring the poor that are cast out to thy house, and thou wilt offer thy choicest first-fruits to God.

*Yalkut, 7.*

When God uttered the first of the ten Divine Words on Sinai, the souls of the people suddenly fled from them. The Torah then rushed back to God and said to Him: "Lord of the World, hast Thou given me to the living or to the dead?"

"To the living, of course!" God replied.

"But they are all dead," the Torah said; "they look as if they were alive, but their souls have fled from them."

*Shemot Rabbah, 39:3.*

### THE ORNAMENTS OF THE BRIDE

Rabbi Simeon said: "No one knows how to fashion the ornaments of the Bride, Torah, like our comrades. The Bride should go to the wedding canopy on Shabuot in pride, with the ornaments we have made for her." And he said to his son Rabbi Eleazar: "Make unto thee a gift for the Bride, who goes to the canopy tomorrow on Shabuot. What is the gift? A new interpretation of Torah."

*Zohar, i, 8.*

"When I gave you My Torah, I said unto you: 'Who would grant that this their heart might remain in them to fear Me?' (Deut. 5:26). You should have replied: 'Mayest Thou, O God, grant this thing,' but ye did not have the sense to say this, and, therefore, ye shall be compelled to ask: 'Who will grant from Zion the salvation of Israel?'" (Ps. 14:7)

*Pesikta Rabbati, 42:4.*

## 318. SHAMEFACEDNESS

Shame leads to fear of sin.

*Nedarim, 20.*

A man who feels shame does not hasten to sin.

*Nedarim, 20.*

It is an excellent sign if a man be modest.

*Nedarim, 20.*

He who transgresses and feels ashamed is forgiven.

*Berakot, 12.*

If a man hath no shamefacedness, it is known that his fathers did not stand at Mount Sinai.

*Nedarim, 20.*

The world was created for the sake of those who are ashamed to do evil.

*Tikkune Zohar, intr. 12b.*

Those who have no shame will not inherit the World-to-Come.

*Zohar Hadash to Song of Songs, 67b.*

## 319. SHAMING AND SHAMED

He who honors himself through the shame of another will have no portion in the World-to-Come.

*Y. Hagigah, 2:1.*

God curses the wicked only with shame.

*Midrash Tehillim, 6:6.*

He who disgraces himself disgraces his family with him.

*Bemidbar Rabbah, 21:3.*

He who is shamed by his own conscience is greater than the one who is shamed by others.

*Taanit, 15.*

It is better for a man to cast himself into a flaming oven than to shame his comrade in public.

*Berakot, 43.*

He who shames his fellow is shamed.

*Mesikta Kallah.*

The shame of him who is shamed by a man of perfection is greater than the shame of him who is shamed by an imperfect man.

*Tosefta Baba Kamma, 9.*

The gift of flesh and blood is little, but their shame is great.

*Y. Berakot, 4:2.*

Why is the Amidah recited in silence? In order not to shame those who confess.

*Sotah, 32.*

He who whitens a comrade's face (by abusing him or shaming him in public) has no share in the World-to-Come.

*Baba Metzia, 59.*

Shame not and you will not be shamed.

*Moed Katon, 9.*

Better that thou shouldst be shamed through thyself than through others.

*Derek Eretz Zuta, 2.*

## ANOTHER'S SHAME

Rab Huna was carrying an axe on his shoulder. Rab Hana bar Hanilai came and sought to carry the tool himself.

Rab Huna remarked: "If thou carriest such a tool for thyself, thou mayest show me respect by taking it on thine own shoulder, but if thou dost not do so for thyself, I do not wish to be honored by another's shame."

*Baba Batra, 22.*

See that thou dost not say: "Inasmuch as I have been despised, my comrades shall be despised with me; inasmuch as I have been cursed, my comrades shall be cursed with me."

Rabbi Tanhuma said: "If thou dost this, reflect whom thou dost despise for 'In the image of God He made him.' "

*Bereshit Rabbah, 24:7.*

## THE UNAUTHORIZED PERSON

Once Rabban Gamaliel addressed the members of his court: "Select from your number six persons to come up at sunrise to my attic to discuss whether the year shall have an additional month."

In the morning he found seven beside him. He inquired: "Who came up though not selected?"

Samuel ha-Katon arose and said: "I came in to learn, not to take part."

An inquiry showed that Samuel had been selected. He said the contrary in order to protect the unauthorized person from confusion.

This teaches us that it is better to delay a Mitzwah than to bring shame upon any one.

*Sanhedrin, 11.*

## 320. SHIP

"For with wise advice thou shalt make thy war." [1] Commenting on this verse, and playing upon the root of the word "advice" [2]—which means in Hebrew "a sailor"—Rabbi Johanan has interpreted the verse as referring to the art of the helmsman, the pilot or the captain of a ship. "For," says Rabbi Johanan, "a man should ever be at the helm, like the captain on the ship, on the lookout how good may best be achieved and accomplished!"

*Wayyikra Rabbah, 21:4.*

[1] Proverbs 24:6.
[2] Tabulah, "advice," is derived from the same root as Hobel, a "sailor."

## 321. SICKNESS AND HEALTH

No man in the world is free from pain.

*Yalkut Shimeoni to Ekeb, 850.*

If a subject sin against his ruler, a blacksmith is commanded to fashion chains, in which the ruler imprisons the sinner. When a man, however, sins against the Lord, his limbs become his fetters. (Through disease.)

*Midrash Tadshe, 16.*

Uncleanness of the body brings illnesses of the skin; of the garments, madness; of the head, blindness.

*Nedarim, 81.*

He who has a sick person in his home should go to a Hakam (a Sage) and the latter should pray for his recovery.

*Baba Batra, 116.*

Every ache, but not a headache!

*Shabbat, 11.*

When there are no longer pauses between the heart-beats, the soul departs.

*Zohar, iv, 219a.*

Every sickness and every weakness comes from the liver. Every strength, joy, and peace, needed by the sick, come from the heart. It is pure of all impurities, and from it issues also good and health for the sick.

*Zohar, iv, 225a.*

Three things weaken the strength of man: Fear, trouble, and sin.

*Gittin, 70b.*

The Rabbis have taught: "If there be an epidemic in the city, rest thy feet in thine own home and venture not in the street."

When there was an epidemic in Mehuza, Rabba would order his windows to be stuffed up, as it is written: "For death is come up into our windows." (Jer. 9:20)

*Baba Kamma, 60.*

When visiting the sick on a week-day, say: "May the All-Compassionate remember thee and give thee health."

On a Sabbath day, when you enter: "Take good health unto thee"; when you depart, say: "It is the Sabbath, and we may not offer tearful entreaties. Be assured that your recovery will arrive speedily. Have confidence in the great mercies of God and spend the Holy day in peace of mind."

*Shabbat, 12.*

## VISITING THE SICK

Rab Helbo became ill and Rab Kahana announced the fact in the synagogue; yet no one came to visit the patient.

Rab Kahana said: "Give ear, my friends. Once a Disciple of Rabbi Akiba became ill and no one visited him. Rabbi Akiba, however, entered the sick man's room, arranged that it be swept and cleansed, placed the pillow in order, and the like. All this assisted the recovery of the Disciple.

"He exclaimed: 'O Master, thou has revived me.'

"When Rabbi Akiba departed he said: 'Whosoever neglects to visit a friendless, sick person is as if he shed his blood.' "

Raba followed this custom: On the first day of his sickness he gave orders that he be left in quiet. On the second day, he would command that it be called out on the street: "Raba is ill."

He said: "Let those who hate me, rejoice, and God will turn away His anger from me. Those who love me will pray in my behalf."

*Nedarim, 40.*

Zunin met Rabbi Akiba and said: "Rabbi, there is a thing that perplexes me greatly. Scores of sick and ailing people come and testify: 'We have worshipped in this or that temple of an idol and we have been cured.' "

Rabbi Akiba replied: "I shall explain it to you by a parable. In a certain town there lived a trustworthy and reliable person. He owned a strong safe, and people would deposit with him their valuables, without either witness or a receipt. Once a man came with witnesses for his deposit. He followed this routine many times, but on one occasion, he brought no witnesses.

"The wife of the man of trust said to him: 'Let us teach this fellow a lesson since he mistrusts us, and when he asks for his deposit, deny that we have received it.'

"Her husband answered: 'Because this man does not act correctly, shall I also act falsely?'

"So it is with sicknesses. When God sends them He places a limited time upon them. Should these ailments betray their mission and not depart from their victims when their time is passed, merely because these persons have acted unwisely or mistakenly? And in the Torah (Deut. 28:59) sicknesses are described as 'Neemanim,' or things that are trustworthy." [1]

*Abodah Zarah, 54.*

[1] The word "Neemanim" is translated both by Leeser and the Jewish Translation to mean "of long continuance." "Neemanim," however, means literally those that are trustworthy.

Rabbi Hanina and Rabbi Nathan said: "Ninety-nine out of a hundred persons die from fever, and one dies a natural death."

Rabbi Ishmael ben Rabbi Jose said: "The cold stones on which we sat in our youth caused us disorders in our old age."

Rabbi Jonah told his Disciples never to sit on the outer steps of the Schools, since they were certain to be cold.

When Rabbi Joseph felt chilly he would work in a mill to warm himself.

Rabbi Sheshet, in such a case, would drag logs, saying: "Great is labor; it warms up the laborer."

*Y. Shabbat, 14. 3.*

## PROTECTION AGAINST COLD

Antoninus Caesar asked Rabbi to bless him.

Rabbi said: "May you be preserved from a chill!"

"That is nothing," retorted the Emperor, "an extra garment drives away a chill."

Rabbi then blessed him, saying: "May you be preserved from fever."

"That is a true blessing," exclaimed the Emperor.

*Wayyikra Rabbah, 16; Y. Betza, 1; Gittin, 67.*

Why do diseases of the skin assail a person?

Moses teaches that they come from slander. When Miriam slandered him she was affected by leprosy. (Num. 12:10)

Isaiah teaches that they come because of immorality. When the daughters of Zion dressed indecently, they lapsed into evil ways and contracted diseases of the skin. (3:17)

The Zohar teaches that, just as the one who speaks evil contracts skin maladies, by the same token, he who does not utter gracious words of admonition, if he be respected, contracts diseases of the skin.

*Zohar, iii, 45, etc.*

Visiting the sick is a deed of kindness.

*Baba Metzia, 30.*

He who visits the sick prolongs their life.

*Nedarim. 39.*

## 322. SIGNS

He who properly observes the four signs: the sign of the circumcision, the sign of the Tefillin, the sign of the Sabbath, and the sign of the Festivals, light emanates from him, and the beings above and below reverence him.

*Tikkune Zohar, T. 22, p. 96a.*

## 323. SILENCE

At times he who keeps silence receives reward. At times he who speaks receives reward.

*Zebahim, 115.*

One verse declares that God was revealed in a great tumult; another declares that God was revealed in a still small voice. When God speaks, all Nature is silent.

*Sifre to Nasso, end.*

Silence is restful. It gives rest to the heart, the lungs, the larynx, the tongue, the lips and the mouth.

*Zohar, iv, 173a.*

If a speech is worth one sela, silence is worth two.

*Megillah, 18.*

If silence be good for wise men, how much better must it be for fools!

*Pesahim, 98b.*

For every evil, silence is the best remedy.

*Megillah, 182.*

Silence is as good as agreement.

*Yebamot, 87a.*

Rabbi Simeon ben Gamaliel said: "I have been brought up all my life among the wise and I have never found anything of more benefit to man than silence."

*Abot, i, 17.*

Rabbi Akiba said: "The fence of wisdom is silence."

*Abot, iii, 17.*

Hadrian was present at a debate of the Sophists on the theme: "Is speech or silence more to be preferred?"

The advocate of "Speech" commenced to argue: "How would the commerce and social intercourse of the world persist without the interchange of words?"

The adversary of "Speech" wished to state his argument, but the other man struck him on the mouth.

"Why didst thou strike him?" inquired the Emperor.

"Because he wishes to use that which is mine to argue on behalf of his own."

When the wise men tell thee that silence is good for men, they do not mean that thou shouldst be dumb and not open thy lips. They mean that thou shouldst keep silent when other people quarrel, and thou shouldst utter no slander.

*Yalkut Shimeoni to Num. 12:1.*

## 324. SILENCE UNDER ABUSE

When two quarrel, he who yields first displays the nobler nature.

*Ketubot, 71b.*

The One Who Lives Forever shall perform justice on behalf of him who keeps silent, though he have a just complaint against his fellow.

*Gittin, 7.*

If evil words are spoken concerning thee, give no answer.

*Derek Erets Zuta, 1.*

People say: "He who hears himself abused and is silent will be preserved from many abuses."

*Sanhedrin, 71.*

## 325. SIMILES, WORD-PICTURES

There is no smoke without a fire.

*Zohar, i, 70.*

Dost thou wish to hold the rope by both ends?

*Wayyikra Rabbah, 10.*

The well may be disliked as a place of danger, but its water is greatly desired.

*Wayyikra Rabbah, 7.*

Offer not pearls for sale to those who deal in vegetables and onions.

*Tanhuma, Behukotai, 3.*

I would speak my opinion if I did not fear to place my head among the lions.

*Y. Shabbat, 1:5.*

If I had not removed for thee the pieces of clay, how wouldst thou have found the pearl?

*Yebamot, 92.*

Thou hast dived into deep water and hast brought up in thy hand only a piece of clay.[1]

*Baba Kamma, 91.*

[1] The labor was difficult and the result small.

A pearl is a pearl anywhere. If it be lost, it is lost only to its owner.
*Megillah, 15.*

A precious pearl (important law) was in your hands and you wished to prevent my knowledge of it.
*Hagigah, 3.*

The stone fell on the pitcher? Woe to the pitcher. The pitcher fell on the stone? Woe to the pitcher.
*Esther Rabbah, 7:10.*

He did not find his hands or feet in the Academy.
*Yebamot, 77.*

It is as hard as rock to extract from them a penny.
*Sifre Haazinu, 32:14.*

Like the staff of a blind man, he blundered into this.
*Y. Terumot, 5:1.*

Was then the belt loosened? [1]
*Pesikta Buber, 8.*

[1] Was then the law abrogated?

The barrel of wine was clear, but you have stirred it up. [1]
*Bereshit Rabbah, 80, end.*

[1] This refers to Torah discussion, which has been confused.

Woe to the dough which its baker admits is bad.
*Bemidbar Rabbah, 13.*

## 326. SIN, SINLESSNESS

Say not to a man: "Go and sin in order that thou mayest acquire a merit."
*Tosefta Hallah, 1.*

No man sins for someone else.
*Baba Metzia, 8.*

He who destroys a thing of use is guilty of a transgression.
*Midrash Aggadah Shofetim.*

Even a transgression is good in its season, if it be performed for the sake of God.
*Kohelet Rabbah, 3:2.*

If a man has not sinned during the majority of his years, he will not sin. [1]
*Yoma, 38.*

[1] During thirty-six years?

Whoso sins in secret thrusts away the Divine presence.
*Kiddushin, 31a.*

Remember three things, if thou wouldst not sin—the all-seeing Eye, the all-hearing Ear, the Recording Hand.

*Abot, 2, 1.*

Even though he has sinned, he remains a Jew.

*Sanhedrin, 44a.*

To cause another to sin is even worse than to slay him; it is to compass his death not only in this world but in the next.

*Bemidbar Rabbah, 21.*

Four classes of men will never see God's face—the scoffer, the liar, the slanderer, the hypocrite.

*Sotah, 42a.*

The greater the personality, the more severely will God call him to account for the smallest trespass, for God desires to be "sanctified" by His righteous ones.

*Yebamot, 121b.*

No one is to be called holy until death has put an end to his struggle with the ever-lurking tempter within, and he lies in the earth with the victor's crown of peace upon his brow.

*Midrash Tehillim to Ps. 16, 2.*

Keep far from a minor sin lest it cause thee to commit a greater.

*Abot de R. Nathan, 2.*

He who has had an opportunity to offend, and refrained, has accomplished a great Mitzwah.

*Shir ha-Shirim Rabbah, 4.*

A transgression hardens the heart.

*Yoma, 39.*

If a certain sin has crossed a man's path three times, and he has not transgressed, he will never transgress through it.

*Yoma, 38.*

If a transgression has tempted a man and he has not succumbed, he has performed a great Mitzwah.

*Shir ha-Shirim Rabbah, 4.*

There are people of subtle mind who, nevertheless, behave like beasts.

*Hullin, 5.*

No man goes to a married woman for an evil purpose, unless he has lost his senses.

*Bemidbar Rabbah, 9:6.*

Every sin of a man is engraved upon his bones.

*Kallah Rabbati, 3.*

When a man commits the same offense twice, it seems to him already permissible.

*Yoma, 86.*

He who sins is mere clay; had he cared for his divine soul, he would not have sinned and shamed it.

*Midrash ha-Neelam, i, 121a.*

When sins are light, they whiten like snow. When sins are heavy, they whiten like wool.

*Y. Shabbat, 9:3, end.*

Akabiah ben Mehalalel said: "I would rather be called a fool all my days, than sin for a single moment before God."

*Mishnah Eduyot, 5:6.*

Rabbi Akiba said: "At the beginning, sin is like a thread of a spider's web; but in the end, it becomes like the cable of a ship."

*Bereshit Rabbah, 22:6.*

The question was asked: "If a man wishes to give financial aid to his friend, and the latter refuses to accept a gift, is it permissible for the former to steal something from his friend in order to gain the opportunity to repay him two-fold?"

"Or if a man finds that his friend is careless of money and often leaves it in a place where a dishonest man may take it, is it permissible to take the money and hide it for a few days, in order to teach him a lesson?"

The answer in both cases is in the negative.

*Tanhuma, Noah, 4.*

Rabbi Simeon ben Yohai said, to illustrate the truth that no man can sin for himself alone: "A number of men were seated in a boat, when one of them took an auger and began boring a hole beneath him.

"His comrades exclaimed: 'What are you doing there?'

"He replied: 'What concern is it of yours? Am I not boring a hole beneath my own place?'

"They replied: 'Surely it is our business, for the water will swamp the boat and us with it.' "

*Wayyikra Rabbah, 4:6.*

The disciples of Rabbi Johanan ben Zakkai once asked their Master: "Why does the Law prescribe that the thief pay two-fold and more, but that the robber pay only what he has taken by violence?"

"Because," replied the Rabbi, "the robber has demonstrated that he is as little afraid of man, as he is of God; but the thief, who takes by stealth shows that he is in fear of man but not of God."

Rabbi Meir related a fable he had heard in the name of Rabban Gamaliel: "There were two weddings in a city. To one, a great many people were invited, but the governor was omitted; to the other, only the near relatives were invited and the governor left out. Whose conduct showed disrespect to the governor?

"The man who invited many people."

*Tanhuma, Noah, 4.*

The righteous reproach Adam, saying, "Thou art the cause of our death."

He replies: "I was guilty of one sin, but there is not a person among you, who is not guilty of many iniquities."

*Tanhuma Buber, Hukkat, 39.*

## 327. SIN DRAWS SIN

If thou hast been dishonest, thou wilt, as a consequence, deny, thou wilt tell an untruth, and thou wilt swear falsely.

*Sifra Kedoshim.*

The first step in transgression is the evil thought; the second, scoffing; the third, pride; the fourth, outrage; the fifth, idleness; the sixth, hatred; and the seventh, an evil eye.

*Derek Eretz Zuta, chap. 6.*

He who transgresses a light commandment will end in violating the weightier one. If he neglect "Thou shalt love thy neighbor as thyself" (Lev. 19:18), he will soon transgress the commandment, "Thou shalt not hate thy brother in thy heart" (Lev. 19:17) and "Thou shalt not avenge nor bear a grudge against the children of thy people" (Lev. 19:18); these resulting in transgressing "And thy brother shall live with thee" (Lev. 25:36), will lead to the shedding of blood.

*Sifre Deut., 187.*

Rabbi Judah ha-Nasi said: "He who has fulfilled one Mitzwah for its own sake, and not in prospect of reward, should not rejoice over this duty by itself, for in the end it brings many Mitzwot in its train; nor should a sinner grieve over the sin by itself, for a duty draws a duty after it, and a transgression a transgression."

*Sifre on Numbers, 15:30, 112.*

Simeon ben Azzai said: "If a man of his own accord resolves to hearken to the commands of God, he will be helped to do so without his own endeavor. If he resolves to ignore them, he will be made to do so when he does not wish to. We read: 'If it concerneth the scorners, He scorneth them, but unto the humble He giveth grace.'"

*Mekilta on Exodus, 15:26.*

## 328. SINNER'S BETTER NATURE

Many of the wicked in Israel drew near to the learning of Torah, and, as a consequence, became pious and good.

*Abot de R. Nathan, 2, end.*

### THE KEY TO PARADISE

There was once a man of wickedness who never donated to charity and who was thoroughly impious. He fell sick and believed that the end of his days was nigh. His son asked him why he ate nothing. The sick man asked for an egg, and, as it was given to him, a hungry beggar knocked at the door. The sick man ordered the egg to be given him. A few days later, he died and was buried.

On the first anniversary of his death, the elder son dreamed that his father came to him and he asked: "Father, what is your fortune in the next world where you abide?"

The father replied: "My son, do charity for the needy, if you desire the assurance of a pleasant existence in the World-to-Come. The single egg, which I gave to the hungry beggar against all the inclinations and habits of a lifetime, sufficed to draw down the balance in my favor, and to grant me entrance into Paradise."

*Midrash, quoted in "Meil Zedakah."*

We may learn some good trait from the worst of creatures, whether a human being or an animal.

Even Jezebel, the worst woman in the Bible, performed deeds of kindness. Her palace was near the center of the city and when a bridegroom would pass, she would go out, clap her hands, and sing a merry tune. When a funeral passed by, she would smite her palms, chant mournfully, and accompany the procession.

What was her reward? When she was killed by Jehu, and the dogs fed on her, only the skull, the hands, and the feet, were unconsumed and were left to be buried.

*Pirke de-Rabbi Eliezer, 17.*

### A GOOD OMEN

In the neighborhood of Rabbi Zeira, there lived several robbers with whom the Rabbi associated on terms of friendship and respect. The other Rabbis deplored Rabbi Zeira's attitude, but he declared that by his ways he might prompt them to improve their conduct.

The brigands believed that the Rabbi's friendship was a good omen. Therefore, when he died, they grew afraid, made restitution, and did penance.

*Sanhedrin. 37a.*

## THE CAPTIVE'S BLESSING

Rabbi Issi was captured by several bandits. When word reached the School, Rabbi Jonathan found that the local police would not effect his rescue, since the bandit forces were very strong.

Rabbi Simeon ben Lakish said: "I shall go out to them, and either kill some of their number, or be killed, to teach them that Jews are not defenseless. Or both of us will return alive."

Rabbi Simeon succeeded in inspiring fear and respect in the bandits and they permitted Rabbi Issi and himself to depart.

Rabbi Simeon said: "If you will visit Rabbi Johanan at Tiberias, he will bless you for releasing us."

When they came, Rabbi Johanan said: "May God do to you what you wished to do to Rabbi Issi!"

A few days later the brigands were captured in ambuscade and were executed.

Previous to this, these very brigands had a queen, who ruled over their city. Once they captured Zeer bar Hanina, and Rabbi Immi and Rabbi Samuel visited the city to ask for his ransom.

The queen said: "Only a miracle can save his life. He has spied upon us and deserves death."

At that very moment a messenger entered and said: "O Queen, thy brother has been captured and slain."

The queen's heart was softened by her grief and she released Zeer bar Hanina.

*Y. Terumot, 8.*

We read: "And he (Isaac) smelled the smell of his (Jacob's) raiment." (Gen. 27:27)

We should read not "Begadov," his raiment, but "Bogdov," his traitors. Even the traitors in Jacob have the smell of a field, which the Lord hath blessed.

It is told that when the Syrians were ready to desecrate the Temple, they were afraid to do so, but called out: "Whosoever of the Jews will enter and begin the spoliation of the Temple, may have whatever he will bring forth!"

Jose Meshita entered and brought forth the Menorah.

The Syrians declared: "This is not for an individual to keep as spoil. Go in again and take what you desire."

He refused. They wished to free him from taxes for three years, but still he declined. They grew incensed and tortured him, but he merely said: "I deserve this agony because I have spited my Creator."

Another instance is that of Jakom Ish Zerorot, a nephew of Jose b. Joezer Ish Zeredah. He was a Hellenizing apostate, and, when his uncle was being led to execution for studying the Torah, he rode up on a magnificent horse, though it was the Sabbath, and said: "You have led an exemplary life and have obeyed your Master, yet you will ride on the gallows and I ride on a noble horse."

Jose ben Joezer replied: "If the Almighty wills it that those who do His will be treated thus, how much will He punish those who do not fulfill His will?"

These words entered into Jakom, like the venom of a snake. He committed suicide by hurling himself from a rock upon a sword, and then casting himself into a fire, with a strangling cord about his neck.

Jose ben Joezer fell into a coma, and exclaimed: "My nephew has preceded me into Paradise by a few moments."

*Yalkut Shimeoni to Gen. 27:27.*

Rabbi Johanan said: "God Himself expresses His delight and admiration for an unmarried man who lives in a large city and does not sin; for a poor man who returns to the owner an object he has found; for a rich man who gives a tithe to charity anonymously."

Rab Saphra was a bachelor in a large city, and he was overjoyed when he heard these words.

Rabba said to him: "Not one like thee is meant, but those who are like Rabbi Hanina and Rabbi Oshaya. They were shoemakers in Palestine, and, when called upon to make shoes for women of evil repute, would not lift their eyes above their feet. These women would swear thus: 'By the life of the holy Rabbis of Palestine.' "

*Pesahim, 113.*

Rabbi Akiba's disciples were overtaken on a road by a band of robbers, who demanded to know their destination.

"To Acco," was their reply, but, when they arrived at Chezib, they went no further.

"Who are you?" inquired the bandits.

"The disciples of Rabbi Akiba," was the reply.

Upon hearing this, the robbers exclaimed: "Blessed are Rabbi Akiba and his disciples, for no man can ever do them harm."

*Abodah Zarah, 26b.*

One day, Rabbi Johanan, on entering the Academy, seemed very absent-minded. Rabbi Simeon ben Lakish asked him several questions in Torah, but received no answer.

Rabbi Simeon inquired the reason, and Rabbi Johanan replied: "Some brigands set upon me and took away my purse; all thinking depends upon the heart, and the heart depends upon the purse."

Rabbi Simeon ben Lakish, after inquiry, discovered the hiding-place of the brigands. He went to them and roundly berated them for robbing the Rabbi.

They responded: "If it was Rabbi Johanan, we shall return half the amount."

Rabbi Simeon ben Lakish retorted: "No. By your lives, you shall return the whole sum."

The brigands, thereupon, returned all they had taken from Rabbi Johanan.[1]

*Y. Terumot, 8.*

[1] It is hard to understand why the Rabbi did not inform against them to the government, unless he did not wish to send Jews, even wicked ones, to their death.

## 329. SINNER'S FOLLY

To what may a sinner be likened?
To one who beholds open handcuffs and places his hands into them.
*Y. Nedarim, 9:1.*

Even in the hour of tribulation, the man of wickedness is impudent, and remains wicked.
*Zohar, i, 106b.*

Such is the way of everyone who does evil: when he sees evil approaching him, he is terrified for the moment, but immediately after, he returns to his wickedness.
*Zohar, i, 110b.*

## 330. NO REPULSION OF SINNERS

Even when thy left hand repulses, thy right hand should still draw sinners near.
*Sotah, 47.*

If thou keepest far those who are far, thou wilt in the end keep away those who are near.
*Bemidbar Rabbah, 8:4.*

Frankincense has an evil odor, and yet it is included among the ingredients of the incense. This teaches us that thou shalt not hesitate to include sinners in Israel among the congregation that worships.
*Keritot 6 and Rashi to Tissa (Exod. 30:34).*

It is a good deed to pray that the wicked should return to beneficent ways.
*Midrash ha-Neelam, i, 105a.*

It is forbidden to pray that a wicked man should die. Had Terah died while he worshipped idols, Abraham would not have come into the world.
*Midrash ha-Neelam, i, 105a.*

Rabbi Meir was sorely vexed by some neighbors, and fervently prayed that God take them from the earth. His wife, Beruriah, however, reasoned with her husband thus: "It is not written: 'Let sinners cease from the earth' (Ps. 104:35), but it is written: 'Let sin cease to be and the wicked will be no more.' Pray, therefore, on their behalf, that they may be led to repentance and those who are wicked will be evil no more."
*Berakot, 9b.*

## 331. SINCERITY

It is not external rites that win forgiveness, but inward sincerity.
*Taanit, 16a.*

It matters not whether a man gives little or much, if only his heart goes out with it to his Father in Heaven.
*Berakot, 17a.*

Beware of giving God merely a share of thy heart.
*Siphre to Deut. 6, 5.*

The essence of goodness is good intent.
*Megillah, 20a.*

## 332. SLAVES

The Sages tell us that there were Jews whose hearts and souls became so enslaved that they did not want to be set free. When Moses brought them the good news of God's intention to liberate them, they said to him: "God decreed that we must be slaves for four hundred years, and our time is not yet up."
*Shemot Rabbah, 15, 1.*

## 333. SOLITUDE

He who journeys on the highway without companionship shall lead his thoughts to dwell upon the Torah.
*Erubin, 54.*

## 334. SOUL, SPIRIT

Know that God is pure and that the soul He gave thee is pure.
*Niddah, 30.*

"And the man became a living soul." This teaches us that we should make vital the soul, which God has given unto us.
*Taanit, 22.*

It benefits a soul more to suffer than to rejoice, as it is written: "Vexation is better than laughter." (Eccl. 7:3)
*Zohar, iv, 232b; Raia Mehemna.*

A transgression extinguishes a Mitzwah, but not Torah. The Mitzwah and the soul are called a lamp. If a man quenches the light of a Mitzwah, the lamp of his soul may likewise be quenched.
*Raia Mehemna, iii, 28b.*

Two types of garment were given to the soul: the body and the light of knowledge. The latter is called the garment of the Rabbanan.

*Zohar, i, 264a.*

When God sends down His daughter, the pure soul, to labor in this world within the body, let us pray that we may return her to her Father, when her time is over, free from sin.

*Zohar, iii, 97a.*

Rabbi Abba bar Kahana said: "When one loses his life by the hand of men, his place in the World-After-Death (Sheol) is not prepared for him, and he must sit in an outer Sheol. Thus the murderer compels God to cause his soul to lose its final repose."

*Pesikta Rabbati, 25:1.*

The spirit became pregnant and brought forth wisdom.

*Shemot Rabbah, 15:22.*

Rabbi Tanhuma said: "A man's soul informs the Recording Angel of his every deed. It is like a nobleman, who has married the daughter of his king. Frequently the king admonishes him: 'Thus and thus hast thou done.'

"The nobleman asks the courtiers: 'Who among you has informed against me?'

"They laugh at him, 'Art thou not wedded to the royal princess?'

"By the same token, man is wedded to the soul, who is the daughter of God and informs Him of all secret deeds."

*Pesikta Rabbati, 8:2.*

The soul consists of three parts: power of life, power of endurance, and the power of higher feeling.

*Zohar, i, 81a.*

A man's soul testifies during the night whatsoever he does during the day.

*Zohar, i, 92b.*

When God finds pleasure in a person's soul, he weakens his body so that the soul may rule him more easily.

*Zohar, i, 140b.*

The soul, like the body, has a father and mother.

*Zohar, ii, 12a.*

When a man is born, he receives a soul linked with the Ophanim. If he is worthy, his soul is joined with the Havyot; if he is still more worthy, his soul is connected with the Throne of Glory.[1]

*Zohar, ii, 94b.*

[1] Ezekiel 1.

When referring to a single human soul, Rabbi Nehemiah said: "God esteems man equal in value to the entire creation."

*Abot de-R. Nathan, 31.*

"Just as God permeates the world and carries it, unseen yet seeing all, enthroned within as the Only One, the Perfect, and the Pure, yet never to be reached or found out; so the soul penetrates and carries the body, as the *one* pure and luminous being which sees and holds all things, while itself unseen and unreached."

*Berakot, 10a.*

Among the Zaddikim, the Nefesh joins the Ruah, the Ruah joins the Neshamah, the Neshamah joins God.

Thus is man's soul bound in the bundle of life with the Lord his God. (1 Sam. 25:29)

*Zohar, iii, 71b.*

We are taught that he who adds to his expenses for the sake of the Sabbath is himself the recipient of things added. What is the thing added? It is the Neshamah Yeteirah, the special soul.

And he who does not add to his expenses for the sake of the Sabbath is as if he diminished the Sabbath; his soul shall likewise be diminished.

*Tikkune Zohar, T. 19, 61a.*

The Neshamah is father to the spirit and mother to the body.

*Zohar Hadash to Ruth, 75b.*

When the hour of death is at hand, the soul is greatly terrified, and refuses to leave the body.

Then the Shekinah appears to it and beckons. The soul, then, touched with an irresistible longing to cleave unto the Shekinah, will, by its own choice, depart from the body.

*Zohar, iii, 8.*

The all-pervading presence of God in the world is like the soul of man. As the soul fills the body, so God fills His world. The soul sustains the body—God sustains the world; the soul outlasts the decrepit body—God outlasts the world; the soul is one only in the body—God is one only in the world; like God, the soul sees, but is not seen; it is pure; it never sleeps, etc.

*Wayyikra Rabbah, 4:8.*

In Rabbinic phrase the human soul is a tiny lamp kindled from the Divine torch; it is the "vital spark of heavenly flame."

*Berakot, 10a.*

Two men jointly committed the same offense against the king, the one a simple villager, the other a man reared in the palace. The king released the villager, but pronounced sentence against the other.

When his courtiers inquired the reason, he replied: "I released the villager because he was ignorant of the laws of the government; but the courtier, who has been with me continually, knows these laws thoroughly. Hence I pronounce judgment against him."

The body is a villager, fashioned out of the dust of the earth, but the soul is a courtier from on High.

*Tanhuma Buber, Wayyikra, 11.*

## 335. THE STRONG AND THE WEAK

When the weaker man is on top, he is victorious over the strong man beneath.[1]

*Tanhuma Wayyikra, 7.*

[1] The strong man is the Evil Impulse.

As the larger among fish swallow the smaller, so among men.

*Abodah Zarah, 4.*

There are five weak things that are a source of terror to the strong: the mosquito is a terror to the lion; the gnat to the elephant; the fly to the scorpion; the flycatcher to the eagle; and the stickle-back is a terror to the Leviathan.

*Shabbat, 77b.*

## 336. SUFFICIENCY

Sufficient unto the hour is its tribulation.

*Berakot, 9.*

When the measure is full and one adds to it, even that which was in it before, falls out.

*Tosefta Shabbat, 1.*

Of eight things a little is good and much is evil: travel, mating, wealth, work, wine, sleep, hot drinks and medicine.

*Gittin, 70.*

Three things are good in a little measure and evil in large: yeast, salt and hesitation.

*Berakot, 34.*

## 337. SUKKOT, SHEMINI ATZERET

Said R. Levi: "He who observes the precept of the Sukkah in this world will be rescued by God from all loss and damage."

*Otzar Midrashim, p. 493.*

### THE ROMANS IN THE SUKKAH

On the Judgment Day God calls out: "Let him who has a share in My Torah come and receive his reward."

The Romans enter and declare, that by building roads and baths, they have made it easier for Israel to study Torah.

God, however, says: "For your own profit only have you labored. You have persecuted students of the Law."

The Romans answer: "Let us practise the Torah now."

But God replies: "Go and sit in the Sukkah."

The day will be hot and the Romans will angrily abandon the Sukkah, foregoing their reward.

*Otzar Midrashim, p. 493.*

We read: "I will wash my hands in innocency; so will I compass Thine Altar, O Lord, that I may make the voice of thanksgiving be heard and tell of all Thy wondrous works." (Ps. 26:67)

I will take in innocency my Lulab, not take it by force without paying for it; and I will compass Thine Altar, O Lord, with the four Minim (the four species); that I may publish with a loud voice a thanksgiving, and relate all Thy wondrous works by chanting the Hallel, which applies both to the past and future favors of God.[1]

*Pesikta Buber, p. 181b.*

[1] The Psalmist uses the word "Kappai," which may mean either "my hands" or "my Lulabs"; Lulabs-Kappot in Lev. 23:40.

Just as one cannot fulfill his duty on Sukkot unless all four Minim are held together, by the same token Israel cannot be redeemed unless all Israelites hold together.

*Yalkut, 188a.*

The palm branch is like the spine; the myrtle is like the eye; the willow is like the mouth; and the Etrog is like the heart. With all thy limbs praise God.

*Yalkut, 188b.*

R. Eliezer bar Maros said: "Why do we go to live in a Sukkah after Yom Kippur? Because it may be that banishment was decreed against us for an atonement, and we fulfill the decree by voluntary banishment to a Sukkah."

*Yalkut, 188b.*

On Shemini Atzeret God saith: "Ye shall have a shutting off." (Num. 29:35) But on Pesach God saith: "Shall be a shutting off to the Lord." (Deut. 16:8)

Why these different expressions?

God saith to Israel: "On Pesach shut Me off from giving rain unto the land of Israel,[1] but on Shemini Atzeret I shall shut you off, by my rains, from walking in My outdoors."

*Yalkut Hadash, 188b.*

[1] Rain is injurious after Pesach in Palestine. See I Samuel, 12:17.

### THE THREE LETTERS

Rab said: "It is like a king, who has called his servants and courtiers to a banquet, and is in a joyful mood.

"The queen suggests to them: 'Now that the king's mood is so favorable, appeal to him for your needs.'

"Likewise the Torah, on the joyful feast of Sukkot, suggests to us a prayer for water by a superfluous letter 'Mem' in the word 'vnish-kehem' instead of 'vniskah'; by a superfluous letter 'Yod' in the word 'unesakeiha,' instead of 'vniskah'; and another 'Mem' in 'kemishpatam' instead of 'kemishpat.'

"The three letters spell 'mayim,' or water.

"When the Israelites did not accept this suggestion, God commanded them to remain another day in Festivity and to pray for rain." [1]

*Yalkut Hadash, p. 106.*

[1] The Hebrew word "Atzeret" may be translated: solemn assembly, keeping back, shutting off, etc. . . . ; it is the same as "Atzirah"

Said R. Levi: "If a man prays on Sukkot with a stolen Lulab, he is likened to a robber, who despoils travelers at the crossroads. An officer happened to pass by, and was likewise robbed. Later the officer hears that the robber has been imprisoned and seeks him out.

"He says: 'Return what you have stolen from me and I will defend you.'

"The robber says: 'The only thing I have of yours is this small rug.'

"When the thief is asked at the trial if he has any witnesses in his defense, he answers: 'This officer will defend me.'

"When the officer is asked what he knows in the thief's favor, he replies: 'Here is the small rug, which he has returned to me from my property, which he plundered.'

"The people said: 'The advocate has turned accuser.' "

*Pesikta Buber, 182.*

God says to Israel: "My sons, reside in the Sukkah for seven days so that ye may remember the miracles, which I did for you in the desert. Moreover, I deserve this at your hands, for I gave you Sukkot in which to dwell amid the desert.

"I also say! Take unto you the Lulab and wave it before Me. I have deserved this at your hands, for I have caused the mountains to shake before you; and in the future, I shall also cause the mountains and the hills to caper and to sing before you."

*Yalkut Emor, Pesikta Buber, p. 189a.*

"And ye shall take unto yourselves on the first day, the fruit of the tree Hadar, branches of palm-trees, and the boughs of the myrtle-tree, and willows of the brook." (Lev. 23:40)

Why is it called "the first day"?

God saith: "I forgave your sins on Yom Kippur, and now, when I see that you are erecting the Sukkah, and taking up the four Minim, I shall begin a new account with you, and credit you with these Mitzwot."

R. Berechiah said: "For the merit of your taking the four Minim on the First day, I will reveal Myself unto you; I shall punish Esau who was born first, and I shall erect the first in importance of holy houses; and I shall bring to you the one concerning whom Isaiah said: 'The First to Zion will he be beholden, and to Jerusalem will I give the one that bringeth good tidings.' "

*Pesikta Buber, pp. 183, 185.*

### EACH FOR THE OTHER

The Etrog has a fragrance and a taste symbolic of those in Israel who possess an abundance of Torah and Mitzwot.

The fruit of the palm has no fragrance, but has taste, symbolic of those scholars who perform only a few kind deeds.

The myrtle has a fragrance, but no taste, symbolic of kindly persons who are unlearned.

The willow has neither taste nor fragrance, symbolic of those who are neither learned nor kind.

God says: "It is impossible for Me to destroy them, but let them all be united, and let each atone for the other."

*Yalkut Emor, Pesikta Buber, p. 185.*

### ALL ARE NEEDED

There are four things taken up on Sukkot. Two of them: the palm and the Etrog, bear fruit; the two others: the myrtle and the willow, bear no edible fruit. But all of them are needed to observe the Commandment.

In a like manner, when Israel fasts and prays for God's aid in the hour of calamity, those who study the Torah and observe the Commandments, and those who are unlearned and fail to observe the Commandments, must all unite in prayer and fasting, if they wish God to answer them.

*Menahot, 27a.*

"Thou hast done more for the Gentile nation, Thou hast done more, O Lord. Hast Thou been glorified by them? Therefore, Thou hast put far from thee the Gentiles of all ends of the earth." (Isaiah 26:15)

Thou hast given much power to Pharaoh. Has he not denied Thee? Thou hast given might to Sennacherib. Did he not insult Thee? Thou didst make Nebuchadnezzar powerful. Did he not say: "No one can 'deliver you out of my hand'?" (Daniel 3:15)

But Thou didst give victory, peace, and salvation to David, Solomon, and Daniel, and all of them blessed Thee. Bring, then, near to Thee, those who love Thy nearness, and keep distant those who are far.

When Thou grantest a son unto a Gentile, he remains uncircumcised and vexes Thee in his temple. But when Thou givest a son unto an Israelite, he circumcises him, as a sign of Thy covenant; when he grows up, he takes him into the synagogue to bless Thee.

Thou givest holidays to the Gentiles. What do they do? They eat, drink, jest, go to the theatres and circuses, and they vex Thee by their words and their deeds.

Thou gavest holidays to Israel. They, too, eat and drink, and are joyful, but they go to the synagogues to pray much, and to thank Thee.

Therefore it is written: "On the eighth day, a solemn, holy day shall YE have." (Num. 29:35)

*Pesikta Buber, p. 190.*

R. Alexanderi said: "To what may Shemini Atzeret be likened?

"To a king, whose sons entertained the sons of visiting nobles the entire week. When the visitors left, the king said: 'Now let us prepare an intimate meal for ourselves only.'

"So, on Sukkot, Israel was commanded to offer seventy bullocks for the atonement of the seventy Gentile nations; but on Shemini Atzeret, God enjoined only one bullock for the sake of Israel."

*Pesikta Buber, p. 193.*

God gives an agricultural reason for the three festivals, in order that it may be said: "Just as you prove by sowing that you trust in Me that I shall cause the seed to produce manifold increase, you should sow good deeds in this world, and have confidence in Me, that I shall cause the seed of kindness and of obedience, to increase manifold for you, that ye may reap in the World-to-Come, and in the Age of the Messiah. And as you enjoy a holiday when you reap and gather in the produce, so will you enjoy great reward in Paradise, when you reap what you have sown in the field of benevolence." [1]

*Mikrae Kodesh, p. 109.*

[1] This item is post-Talmudical.

### RULES FOR REJOICING

Scripture enjoins us to rejoice on the feast of Sukkot three times; on the feast of Shabuot, only once; and on the feast of Pesach, not even once. Why?

Because on Pesach, neither wheat nor fruit are yet ripe, and men know not how the harvest will transpire. On Shabuot, the wheat harvest has been gathered, and we may rejoice in part, but the fruit and the increase of the flocks and herds have not yet arrived. On Sukkot, when everything has been gathered, we may thrice be blessed.

Another reason why we find no injunction to rejoice on Pesach, is because the Egyptians were drowned on Pesach, and it is written: "Rejoice not when thine enemy falleth." (Prov. 24:17)

*Yalkut Shimeoni to Emor, 23.*
*Pesikta Buber, p. 189a.*

### THE EXTRA DAY

As the solemn assembly of Pesach is fifty days after the beginning of the feast, this solemn assembly of the Eighth Day should also be fifty days after the first day of Sukkot. But it is celebrated immediately after Sukkot. Why?

R. Joshua ben Levi said: "It may be likened to a king with many sons, some married in distant places, others in nearby. When those who live nearby wished to come, they came; and when they wished to go, they departed; and their father gave his consent. Why was this? Because the way was short and the sons could come and go whenever they wished.

"But those who lived at a distance, when they came and later wished to depart, their father would continue to urge upon them to delay their departure one day. At Pesach time they can come again in dry weather, but after Sukkot the rainy season commences and the roads are muddy.

"Therefore, God hath said: 'While they are here, let them have an extra day of solemn assembly.'"

*Yalkut Shimeoni Phinehas, 29.*

### The Holy Guests in the Sukkah

The verse says: "Ye shall dwell in booths," and continues, "All shall dwell in booths." (Lev. 23:42)

R. Abba said: "The first part applies to the Holy Guests, and the second to all of Israel."

As for the Holy Guests, when Rab Humnuna Saba entered the Sukkah, he would stand at the door on the inside and say: "Let us invite the Holy Guests." He then made ready the courses, stood up, recited the Kiddush and continued: "Be seated, O Guests of Truth, be seated."

He then lifted up his hands and said: "Gracious is our lot; gracious is the lot of Israel; gracious is the lot of mankind, who have been privileged in this; gracious is the lot of the righteous in this world and in the World-to-Come." [1]

*Zohar, iii, 103.*

[1] The Holy Guests are supposed to be Abraham, Isaac, Jacob, Joseph, Moses, Aaron, and David. In the Diaspora, Solomon was also listed, as the chief guest on the eighth day. Every one is represented by a deserving poor man as guest.

### The Escaped Prisoner

A prisoner of war, who had been made a slave, succeeded in escaping from his master. Though he was free in body the moment he escaped, he was not free from anxiety and fear until he reached a distant place, where his master could not recapture him.

By the same token, Israel was freed on Pesach, which is called "the season of our freedom," but he did not feel free from anxiety of pursuit and sustenance until he reached His father and received His hospitality. And to demonstrate his feeling of true freedom, he takes up his residence in a flimsy hut, not in a stockade or a fortified camp. Then he rejoices in his freedom, and for this reason, Sukkot is called "the season of our rejoicing."

*Mikrae Kodesh, 151-2.*
*A post-Talmudical item.*

## THE OFFERING OF BULLOCKS

On the first day of Sukkot, thirteen bullocks were sacrificed; on the second—twelve; on the third—eleven; on the fourth—ten; on the fifth—nine; on the sixth—eight; on the seventh—seven; a total of seventy. On Shemini Atzeret, only one bullock was sacrificed.

The seventy were brought to atone for the seventy nations of the world, and the one, for the nation of Israel.

Why were less sacrificed every succeeding day? To show that the number of the nations persecuting Israel will become less and less, if his sins shall grow less.

*Zohar, iv, 476.*

## THE VICTOR'S DECORATION

Rabbi Abin said: "Why did God enjoin us to take the palm branch and the Etrog on Sukkot? It is like two men who appeared before the king in judgment. The actual trial is held in secret. How do we know who receives the king's approval? If we see one of them depart with a palm branch in one hand and beautiful fruit in another, we know that he was won.

"Likewise, we Jews, with the Nations of the world, go before God on Rosh ha-Shanah and Yom Kippur, that our actions may be judged.

"How do we know who wins the approval of the King of Kings?

"Those whom He hath enjoined to take up the palm branch and the Etrog."

*Pesikta Buber, p. 180, 1st ed.*

Rabbi Joshua ben Levi interpreted the ceremony of drawing water on the Feast of Tabernacles:

"Why was it called the place of drawing? Because from it they draw the Holy Spirit (prophetic inspiration), according to Isaiah 12:3: 'Ye shall draw with joy from the fountains of salvation.' "

*Y. Sukkah, 55a.*

He who has never seen the rejoicing at the water-drawing, has never seen true rejoicing in his life.

*Mishnah Sukkah, 5:1.*

R. Johanan said: "We wave the Lulab to the four sides of the horizon, upwards and downwards, to demonstrate God's Omnipresence."

R. Jose b. Hanina said: "We pray thereby that no heated winds and no over-heavy rainfall may damage our crops."

*Sukkah, 37b.*

## THE JOY OF THE WATER-DRAWING

If Hillel observed the Israelites in a mood of frivolity rejoicing in the joy of the drawing of water, he would say: "We are assembled here for what purpose? Does God need our praises if they be rendered in this mood? Has He not angels without number to praise Him?"

But if he beheld the Israelites rejoicing in an earnest mood, he would say: "If we are not here to sing God's praise, who else could please Him as much? Does He not enjoy our praises more than the praise of His Heavenly Hosts?"

*Y. Sukkah, 5.*

## FOURTEEN MEALS

R. Eliezer said: "A Jew should eat fourteen meals in the Sukkah."

King Agrippa's secretary objected, saying: "But I cannot eat more than once a day."

R. Eliezer said: "Every day you eat many appetizers for your own sake, cannot you eat an extra appetizer at a time different from your regular meal, for the sake of God?"

*Sukkah, 27.*

## 338. SUKKOT-DIVINE GLORY

One Rabbi says we must take "Sukkot Mamash" literally to refer to actual huts in which the Jews dwelt and found protection in the sun-beaten desert.

Another sage, Rabbi Eliezer, interprets the word figuratively. . . . He says "Sukkot" means "Anene Kabod"—"Clouds of Divine Glory." The Jews were saved in the desert, because they dwelt in the protecting clouds of God's glory.[1]

*Sukkah, 11b.*

[1] According to R. Eliezer, the actual hut commanded to sit in is in memory of the divine clouds.

The Sages tell us that there were seven such clouds of Divine Glory, which enveloped the hosts of Israel and which served as their protecting shields.

"Four of the clouds surrounded the Israelite on all sides of him, one on the east, one on the west, one on the north and one on the south." These four clouds protected him against the constant attacks of the enemies who came from all sides, and who were ever eager to destroy him. Their efforts were of no avail, for, behold, they could not penetrate the Divine protection of God's glory.

"There was a fifth cloud that accompanied him in his journey," say the Rabbis. "It covered his head." The rays of the desert sun would have scorched him. But God placed this cloud above him to shield him from the burning heat of the sun.

"And then there was a sixth cloud—that went before him,"—that paved and illumined the path on which he should go. He could not stand still. He had to march forward. But what path should he take? This cloud God sent before the people of Israel to guide them, to lead them, that they should not stumble, but march ever onward toward the desired goal.

"And finally," say the Rabbis, "there was a seventh cloud—that went after him." For in the long and dreary march many fell by the wayside. They had not the strength, either physical or spiritual, to endure the hardships of the journey. What should be done with these weaklings? Should they be left to die in the desert? God, therefore, sent this seventh cloud of His Divine Glory, to lift the fallen, to help the weary, to carry, if need be, those who could no longer stand on their feet.

*Bemidbar Rabbah, i, 2; Mekilta, Tanhuma, etc.*

## 339. SURGERY

The dead flesh in the living body does not feel the lancet.

*Shabbat, 13.*

The life of one man may not be sacrificed to save the life of another man.

*Ahalot, 7.*

## 340. SUSTENANCE (PARNASSAH)

No man knows by what he will earn his living.

*Pesahim, 54.*

On a week-day man receives his food through an intermediary, but on the Sabbath, through God.

*Tikkune Zohar, T. 21, p. 72b.*

He who has created the day has also created sustenance for it.

*Mekilta, Beshallah, Wa-Yisu, 2.*

Those who breathlessly run after a livelihood, rarely overtake it.

*Shabbat, 32.*

The bit of bread, which a man places in his mouth, is a more difficult thing than the deliverance of Israel.

*Pesahim, 118a.*

Rabbi Eleazar ben Pedat said: "The Scripture places provision for man's needs in the same catagory with deliverance; even as provision comes each day, so man's deliverance."

Rabbi Samuel bar Nahman said: "It is greater than deliverance, for deliverance comes by the hand of an angel—'the angel who delivers me from every evil' (Gen. 48:16)—but provision for man's needs comes from the hand of God Himself, who opens His hand and satisfies the desire of every being. (Ps. 145:16)."

Rabbi Joshua ben Levi declared: "This constant provision was no less a wonder than the cleaving of the Red Sea."

*Bereshit Rabbah, 20:9.*

The bread which Jacob prayed for was Torah, and the raiment he asked for was the Tallit, the prayer shawl.

*Bereshit Rabbah, chap. 70.*

## 341. SWORD

The Rabbis, commenting on the words: "He placed at the east of the Garden of Eden the Cherubim and the flaming sword" say: "At the east of the Garden of Eden—at the very spot where stood the Cherubim with the flaming sword—there was the Gehenna created."[1]

*Bereshit Rabbah, 21, 13.*

[1] It is the Sword, flashing before our eyes, which keeps us in a world that is a Gehenna instead of a Garden of Eden where God had planned man to be.

The Sages said that "God sent down from the heavens the Book and the Sword and said to His children on earth: 'You shall have to choose one or the other. Either the Book or the Sword. If you choose the Book you must reject the Sword; if you choose the Sword the Book will be destroyed.' "

*Wayyikra Rabbah, 35, 5.*

If you are a man of the Sword, then you cannot lay claim to be a man of the Book; if you are a man of the Book, you will not be a man of the Sword.

*Abodah Zarah, 17b.*

## 342. SYNAGOGUE

He who does not enter a synagogue in this world will not enter a synagogue in the World-to-Come.

*Y. Berakot, 5:1.*

A synagogue retains its holiness even after it has been desolated.

*Megillah, 28.*

What mean the words: "Lord, Thou hast been our dwelling-place in all generations?" (Ps. 90:1)
These are the synagogues and the Houses of Study.

*Megillah, 29.*

The God of Abraham shall aid him who has a steady place for his worship.

*Berakot, 6.*

No synagogue should be demolished until a new synagogue is ready.

*Megillah, 26.*

As the heart skips from place to place, so does God skip from synagogue to synagogue. (Cf. Song of Songs)

*Pesikta Rabbati, Behodesh ha-Shebii.*

The Rabbis have taught: "No levity shall occur within a synagogue, and no profane use shall be made of it. No eating is permissible, no powdering or beautifying oneself, no walking back and forth for exercise, no entering to avoid discomfort caused by the sun or rain. Neither is it to be used as an arcade to shorten one's way."

*Megillah, 28.*

Woe to him who converses in the synagogue; he shows us that he does not belong there; he diminishes the faith; he has no share in the God of Israel; he proves that he has no God.

*Zohar, i, 256a.*

He who comes to the synagogue early and leaves late merits a goodly portion; the Shekinah regards him among the Just.

*Zohar, i, 256a.*

A synagogue should be finely built and comfortably furnished. The synagogue below represents the synagogue on High.

*Raia Mehemna, ii, 59a.*

He who enters a synagogue, dons neither Tefillin nor Tzitzit, and says: "I will worship toward Thy holy temple in the fear of Thee," prompts God to say: "He is uttering a falsehood; where is his reverence?"

*Zohar, v, 265a.*

The Sanctuary on earth must aspire to resemble the Sanctuary in Heaven.

*Tanhuma, Pekude, chap. 2.*

"And every great house he burned with fire." (II Kings 25:9)

Rabbi Johanan said: "This means the synagogues, the places where they magnify prayer."

Rabbi Joshua ben Levi said: "This means the schools, the places where they magnify the Torah." He also said: "The building occupied by a synagogue may be transformed into a School, but not contrariwise, since this would be a descent."

*Megillah, 27a.*

## THE SINCERE WORSHIPPER

A man renowned for his physical prowess came to the synagogue and recited the few responses he knew in an exceedingly loud voice.

When asked the reason, he replied: "I cannot serve God by learning the Scriptures or the Mishnah; I am quite unlearned, but I am able to serve Him thus. Shall I not calm my soul's longing for Him as best I can?"

His manner of worship disturbed the decorum of the services, but he received great reward: he became a high official and prospered greatly.

*Tanna Debei Eliyahu Rabbah, 13.*

### The Alexandrian Synagogue

He who has not seen the synagogue at Alexandria, has not seen the glory of Israel. The congregation did not sit together, without plan, but in guilds: the goldsmiths in one section; the silversmiths in another, each group separate from its fellows. When a poor craftsman entered, he took his seat among the members of his guild who maintained him and assisted him in obtaining employment.

*Sukkah, 51b.*

The Rabbis warned that a city, in which the houses tower above the synagogue, is doomed and must meet destruction.

*Shabbat, 11a.*

## 343. TABERNACLE

### Ark of the Covenant

The Sages asked: "Why is it that of the Tabernacle of Moses we read that the faces of the Cherubim were turned one to another, whereas of the Temple of Solomon we read that the Cherubim turned their faces inward—hidden toward the ark?"

The answer was: "The former typifies Israel's fulfilling the will of God, while the latter shows what happens when Israel fails to fulfil God's will."

*Baba Batra, 99a.*

The clasps of brass that held the ancient tabernacle together resembled the stars in the heavens.

*Shemot Rabbah, 35:6.*

When all the materials of the tabernacle and its appurtenances had been got together, the Israelites tried in vain to set it up. They then asked Moses to set it up, but he was unable to do so. He then turned to God and said: "I do not know how to set it up."

"Try again," God replied, "and before long you will find that the tabernacle will set itself up, as it were."

*Tanhuma on Exod., 39, 33.*

Not only did the Israelites carry the Ark on their journey in the wilderness, but the Ark carried its bearers.

*Sotah, 35a.*

## 344. TALE-BEARING, SLANDER, EVIL SPEECH

R. Phinehas said: "Daily does the accuser come before God and say: 'Where is the love of Israel for Thee? They swear falsely by Thy name, and they utter slander.'

"And God in His love for Israel replies: 'Hast thou seen another nation full of Torah and Mitzwot like Israel? Is there another nation so charitable, so fond of studying, and so eager to bring glory to My name on earth?' "

*Otzar Midrashim, p. 491.*

On the Day of Judgment God asks the Nations: "Why have you dealt harshly with Israel?"

They reply: "Those among them came to us, and each Jew spoke slanderously of his fellow-Jew."

*Bereshit Rabbah, 20.*

He who slanders piles up offenses as high as the sky, and deserves to be stoned.

*Arakin, 15.*

He who informs against a man in secret has no share in the World-to-Come.

*Pirke de-R. Eliezer, 53.*

Hot coals, which are cooled on the outside, grow cool within, but gossip and slander, even if cooled outwardly, do not cool inwardly.

*Y. Peah, 1:1.*

People say: "That which a child speaks he has heard from his father or mother."

*Sukkah, end.*

This is the way of gossipers: They commence with praise and end with derogation.

*Tanhuma Shelah, 9.*

Greater is the sin of the evil tongue than the sin of idolatry.

*Midrash Gadol u-Gedolah, 18.*

Why does the offering of a leper consist of birds?

He has sinned by gossiping (like Miriam), hence he must bring a sacrifice of gossiping birds.

*Arakin, 16.*

If a man changes his lodging, ill words are spoken concerning him and his host.

*Arakin, 16.*

Even if all the words of slander are not accepted as true, half of them are accepted.

*Bereshit Rabbah, 56:4.*

He who slanders, who listens to slander, and who testifies falsely, deserves to be thrown to the dogs.

*Pesahim, 118.*

Slander is worse than the weapons of war: the latter damage from near, the former from afar.

*Y. Peah, 1:1.*

The evil decree against Israel in the Wilderness was sealed only because of the sin of slander.

*Arakin, 15, Mishnah.*

Even if thou hast appeased him whom thou hast slandered, thy sin rankles within him.

*Bereshit Rabbah, 98:19.*

If thou speakest evil of Esau, thou wilt in the end speak evil of thy fellow-Israelite.

*Tanhuma Buber Pekude.*

God accepts repentance for all sins, except the sin of imposing a bad name upon another.

*Zohar, iii, 53a.*

Even the greatest Zaddik is harshly punished, if he speaks evil of Israel.

*Zohar Hadash, i, 23a.*

Rabbi Johanan said: "God addressed the tongue as follows: 'All the members of the body are erect, but you are recumbent; all are without, but you are within. I have also surrounded you with two walls, one of bone and one of flesh. "What else shall be given unto thee, or what shall be added unto thee, O thou slanderous tongue." ' " (Ps. 120:3)

*Arakin, 15b.*

Slander injures three persons: the slanderer, the recipient of the slander, and the person slandered.

*Arakin, 15b.*

The animals will one day remonstrate with the serpent and say: "The lion treads upon his prey and devours it; the wolf tears and eats it. What profit hast thou in biting?"
The serpent will reply: "I am no worse than a slanderer."

*Taanit, 8a.*

Rabban Gamaliel commanded his slave, Tobi, to buy the best edible in the market. The slave brought home a tongue.
The next day Rabban Gamaliel commanded him to buy the worst thing in the market, and again Tobi brought home a tongue.
When asked for an explanation, the wise slave replied: "There is nothing better than a good tongue, and nothing worse than an evil tongue."

*Wayyikra Rabbah, 33.*

"Death and life are in the power of the tongue." (Prov. 18:21)
If a man employs his tongue to learn Torah and to please the Lord, he acquires everlasting life. If he uses it to carry slanders and to speak evil, he earns death in the World-to-Come.

*Tanhuma Buber to Metzora.*

The Rabbis were opposed to the publication of the minority opinion. They declared: "When a judge leaves the courtroom, he should not say: 'I voted for acquittal, but what can I do when the majority voted for conviction?' This is equivalent to tale-bearing."

*Sanhedrin, 31.*

Rabbi Johanan quoted a saying of Rabbi Simeon ben Yohai that injurious words constitute a greater wrong than monetary injury. The former affect a man's person, the other his profit. Financial harm can be repaired, personal harm cannot.

*Baba Metzia, 58b (includes the sayings of several rabbis).*

Rabbi Yannai heard a man on the street crying aloud: "Who desires life? Who desires life?"

He invited the man to enter, but the man declined, saying: "It is not for thee and for those like thee, that I am making my round."

When the Rabbi insisted, the man entered and showed the Rabbi in his Psalter: "Who is the man that desireth life, and loveth days, that he may see good therein? Keep thy tongue from evil, and thy lips from speaking guile. Depart from evil and do good; seek peace and pursue it." (37:13)

*Wayyikra Rabbah, 16.*

### A SLIP OF THE TONGUE

A king contracted an unusual malady and the physicians recommended an unusual remedy, namely, the milk of a lioness. To obtain this milk, a wise man placed ten kids near a lion's den. Standing somewhat apart, he threw a kid into the den, and repeated this procedure until, on the tenth day, the lioness having become friendly, he found it safe to draw some of her milk into a small vessel.

The courageous man departed, and, when night arrived, he camped under a tree. He dreamed that a quarrel arose between his limbs.

The feet said: "We are the most important; had we not walked, the man could not have secured the milk."

The hands said: "Nay. It was we who drew the milk."

The eyes said: "Without us he could not have found his way."

The heart said: "Had I not counselled him, the rest of you would have had nothing to do."

The tongue said: "Without my words man is helpless."

The others, however, exclaimed: "Be silent, thou boneless, blind thing!"

The tongue, indignant, retorted: "I shall show you this very day that I am your master."

When the man finally entered the palace, the king asked him: "Have you brought it?"

"Yes, your Majesty," replied the man, "I have brought you the milk of a she-dog."

The king was greatly enraged and ordered that the man be hanged.

All the limbs began to tremble and the tongue said: "If I save you, will you recognize me as your master?"

"Yes," they answered in reply.

The man then spoke up: "A slip of the tongue has created a misunderstanding. Take me back, I beg you, to the king."

The man was able to prove that he had brought, in truth, the milk of a lioness. The king drank it and was cured. The man received a reward and henceforth he controlled his tongue.

*Midrash Tehillim Buber, 39.*

### THE INCURABLE AILMENT

A man had three daughters, all of good appearance but each with a defect: one was lazy, the second a kleptomaniac, the third was fond of slander.

A friend proposed that the daughters marry his sons, and promised that he would cure them of their faults.

He placed the lazy daughter in charge of many servants, and she had nothing requiring time or effort. He gave his keys to the thieving maiden, and told her to take whatever she wished at any time; she therefore had no reason to take anything in secret. As for the gossiper, he would ask her for her criticism, even before she began to speak words of slander.

When their father arrived, the first daughter said to him: "I can be as lazy as I wish, and I am happy here."

The second said: "I can take whatever I wish and I am happy."

The third one, however, said: "My father-in-law makes love to me."

She alone was not happy; she had no opportunity to speak slander.

*Midrash Assereth ha-Diberot.*

### THE DOUBLE-MOUTHED

In a certain city there was a shortage of salt. The owners of donkeys agreed to go together to a nearby town and purchase salt for re-sale in the city market.

One owner, however, had no intention, from the first, to keep the agreement. He said to the others: "I must finish some ploughing. Wait for the morrow."

They agreed. He went to his wife and said in a whisper. "When I call out to you for the yoke, bring me the saddle; when I ask for the water-bottle, bring me the sack."

Thus his comrades were deceived into believing that he went out to plough. In reality, he went out to the nearby town and bought a sack of salt. When he returned, the others demanded an explanation.

He said: "Had we gone together, we would have come back with much salt, and could sell only at a moderate price; now I shall be able to sell at a high price, and shall not compete with you tomorrow."

Such is the argument, which the double-mouthed employ. Unless a yoke be a saddle, and a water-flask a sack, they cannot make a livelihood.

*Midrash Tehillim, 12.*

### INDIRECT SLANDER

It was the custom of the Roman government to conscript people in the cities of Palestine to perform work for the administration. Once the officials overlooked a man by the name of Bar Hobetz. The others were angry and cried out: "Let us eat Hobetz" (a kind of cheese dish). The official was thus given a reminder and sent for Bar Hobetz.

R. Johanan, however, declared: "This is a form of indirect slander."

On another occasion, a certain Johanan was overlooked. A man cried out: "I hear that R. Johanan is ill. Shall we visit him after work?" The authorities then sent for the missing Johanan.

R. Simeon ben Lakish said: "This is slander intermixed with righteous duty."

Rab Dimi said: "Speak not words of praise for another, lest from words of praise thou wilt eventually tend to defame him."

*Y. Peah, 1.*

### SLANDER VERSUS WARNING

The Tosafot explain that sometimes a man must warn his comrades against those of evil repute, and must be aware of them himself.

Several Galileans suspected of a murder besought R. Tarfon to hide them.

He said: "If I hide you, I become an accessory after the fact, if you are captured and the suspicion is verified. Therefore I must refuse my assistance. Go and conceal yourselves."

While a man should not accept a rumor as certain and disseminate it, he should nevertheless assume that it may be true. He must guard himself and warn others who may be injured, if the rumor be proved a fact.

*Niddah, 61, and Tosafot.*

R. Abbahu and R. Simeon ben Lakish visited Caesarea.

R. Abbahu said: "Why enter so evil a city; its inhabitants are guilty of profaning and blaspheming God?"

R. Simeon descended from his donkey and, picking up some gravel, threw it into the mouth of R. Abbahu.

"Why have you done this?" exclaimed R. Abbahu.

"To teach you," said R. Simeon, "that God dislikes men who slander Israel, as it is written: 'Look not upon me that I am swarthy.' " (Song of Songs 1:6)

*Shir ha-Shirim, Rabbah, 1.*

A good man of evil speech the Rabbis aptly likened to a palace built next to a tannery; the one defect destroys all his grandeur.

*Shabbat, 56b.*

Why have fingers been made flexible? So that we may stop our ears with them when evil is being spoken.

*Ketubot, 5b.*

## 345. TALK—MANNER OF

Futile words weary a man.

*Kohelet Rabbah, 1.*

A man's mouth reveals his character.

*Zohar, iv, 187a.*

Rub thy lips one against the other and be not in a hurry to answer.

*Abodah Zarah, 35.*

The speech of a man should always be clean and his words polite.

*Pesahim, 3.*

As a fish is caught at its throat, so are men caught by their words.

*Bereshit Rabbah, 97:3.*

Some speak with their eyes, some with their hands, some with the shaking of their head, some with the movement of their body, and some with their feet.

*Tikkune Zohar, T. 70, 177b.*

He who guards his lips and tongue is worthy to be clothed with the spirit of holiness.

*Zohar, iv, 183b.*

Do not intrude upon the speech of thy fellow-man while he is still talking.

*Sifre Bahaaloteka.*

People say: "A woman knits while she talks."

*Megillah, 14.*

He who is vulger of speech descends to the deepest region of Gehenna.

*Shabbat, 33.*

Even as it is a man's duty to speak what is acceptable, it is his duty to refrain from speaking the unacceptable.

*Yebamot, 65.*

Speak not before one who is wiser.

*Derek Eretz Zuta, 2.*

Cause not thyself to bow to thine own words (do not make thy words thy master by speaking unthinkingly).

*Derek Eretz Zuta, 2.*

## 346. TALMID HAKAM, RABBI

An elder who chances to sin is not removed but is told: "Honor thyself and sit at home." (Resign?)

*Y. Moed Katon, 3:1.*

A learned man is better than a prophet.

*Baba Batra, 12.*

If a Sage dies, everyone is his kinsman, and should mourn for him.

*Shabbat, 105.*

The prayer of a scholar who studies under handicaps is answered.

*Sotah, 49.*

A disciple of the scholars should not be like a dish without salt, but should be pleasant to all.

*Kallah Rabbati, 3.*

He who is learned and God-fearing is like a Master, whose tools are in his hand.

*Abot de-R. Nathan, 22:1.*

Sages are higher than prophets, for prophecy does not abide with a man continuously. Wisdom, however, remains with the Sage at all times.

*Zohar, ii, 6b.*

A scholar who is not the same inwardly as he is outwardly is an abomination.

*Yoma, 72.*

A carcass is better than a scholar without common sense.

*Wayyikra Rabbah, i, 15.*

A scholar who has studied and abandoned his learning cannot hope for a share in the World-to-Come.

*Abot de-R. Nathan, 36.*

If a scholar engages in business and is not too successful, it is a good omen for him. God loves his learning and does not wish to enrich him.

*Midrash Shemuel, 29.*

If two scholars living in one city do not agree concerning Halakah, one dies, and the other is exiled.

*Sotah, 49.*

Two scholars who dislike each other shall not sit together as judges at a trial.

*Sanhedrin, 29.*

A Disciple of the Sages may live only in a city with these ten things: a court, a police department, a charity organization, a synagogue, a bath, a physician, a surgeon, a druggist, a writer, and a school-teacher.[1]

*Sanhedrin, 17.*

[1] Slightly paraphrased.

We should read not: "The daughters of Jerusalem," but the "builders of Jerusalem." (Bonot instead of Banot).[1]

*Shir ha-Shirim Rabbah, 1:5.*

[1] See Singer, p. 176 for an analogy.

Reside not in a town, whose mayor is a Disciple of the Wise. He will have no time to attend to municipal affairs, being occupied with his studies.

*Pesahim, 112.*

As the bride is anointed with twenty-four kinds of cosmetics, so should the Disciple of the Sages be acquainted with the twenty-four books of the Bible.

*Shemot Rabbah, 41:5.*

A pseudo-sage is like a donkey that carries a load of books.

*Zohar Hadash, Tikkun, 70.*

Who is a Disciple of the Sages?
He who considers his studies more important than his business.

*Kohelet Rabbah, 7.*

Humility and lowliness of spirit mark the manner of the Disciples of the Sages.

*Kallah Rabbati, 3.*

Why is Torah like a piece of wood?
As a small piece of wood kindles the log, so a minor scholar sharpens the mind of the greater.

*Taanit, 7.*

Even the profane talk of a Disciple of the Sages needs to be studied.

*Sukkah, 21.*

A scholar on whose garment a soiled spot is found is deserving of censure.

*Shabbat, 114.*

As with perfume, any one who desires may be made fragrant by it, so the scholar should be willing to teach any one who desires to profit by his learning. In such a case, his learning will be retained by him.

*Erubin, 54.*

Why is a scholar like the nut?
Even as a nut has four skins, the scholar has four virtues: Wisdom, understanding, knowledge, and common sense.

*Eliyahu Rabbah, 18.*

A scholar who has abandoned the study of the Torah is like a bird which has abandoned its nest.

*Hagigah, 9.*

As the kernel of a nut is not despised, even though the shell be marred, so it is with the scholar.

*Hagigah, 15.*

If a man, his son, and grandson, are scholars, the Torah will not cease among his descendants.

*Baba Metzia, 85.*

Who is learned?
He who is never at a loss when he is asked a question.
Who is wise?
He who respects his teacher.
Who has understanding?
He who reads everything and knows more than his own subject.

*Zohar, ii, 201a.*

A scholar must possess the following fifteen qualifications:
1. Correct behavior on entering the Academy.
2. Correct behavior on leaving.
3. Humility while taking his seat.
4. Prudence in his reverence.
5. Open-mindedness in his knowledge.
6. Wisdom in his conduct.
7. Receptiveness of mood.
8. The capacity for remembering.
9. The willingness to serve his teacher.
10. Regularity of attendance at the Academy.
11. The habit of asking questions only on the subject of the discussion.
12. The habit of answering according to the rule.
13. The ability to add his own observation on every chapter told.
14. The readiness to travel if necessary, to find a teacher who can increase his learning.
15. The ability to learn in order to teach and to practise.[1]

*Derek Eretz Zuta, 3, end.*

[1] Version and translation of J. D. Eisenstein in a letter to S. Spitz. The printed version is faulty and has not the fifteen stated.

Six things are a disgrace to an educated person:
1. To walk on the street perfumed.
2. To walk alone by night.
3. To wear old clouted shoes.
4. To talk with a woman overlong in the street.
5. To sit at table with illiterate men.
6. To be late at the synagogue.

*Berakot, 43b.*

Rabbi Simeon ben Lakish said: "Just as the bride is modest and chaste, so should the scholar be modest and free from every kind of tain or reproach."

*Shir ha-Shirim Rabbah to 4:11.*

We read: "As the tents of Kedar" (Song of Songs 1:5). As the tents of the Ishmaelites are ugly without and comely within, by the same token, the Disciples of the Sages, though apparently lacking in beauty, are nevertheless filled with Scripture, Mishnah, Talmud, Halakah, and Haggadot.

*Shemot Rabbah, 23.*

### 347. TALMUD

R. Bannayah said: "We read: 'For by wise counsel canst thou conduct thy war.' (Prov. 24:6) When thou wishest to conduct with wisdom thy discussions and debates on the Torah, acquaint thyself thoroughly with the Mishnah. If thou wilt enter into it deeply, the door of either the Halakah or the Aggadah will open easily to thee."

R. Eleazar in the name of R. Joshua b. Levi said: "An iron post is the Mishnah."

*Pesikta Buber, p. 176a.*

In the darkness of exile hath God refreshed me, namely, He gave us the Talmud of Babylonia.[1]

*Sanhedrin, 24.*

[1] According to a Hasidic comment on Lamentations 3:6, which reads: "He hath made me to dwell in dark places."

He who learns Halakot daily is assured of the World-to-Come.

*Niddah, end.*

Are then the sayings of the Midrash to be accepted as obligatory?
Nevertheless, search out the truths they contain and receive thy reward.[1]

*Y. Nazir, 7:2.*

[1] Applicable to anti-Semitic critics of the Aggadic and Midrashic sayings, who put forth every saying as obligatory law.

Those who interpret the implications of Scripture say: "If you would learn to know Him at whose word the world came into being, learn Aggadah, for thus you will come to know the Holy One and cleave to His ways."

*Sifre on Deut. 11:22.*

He who learns Aggadah from a book does not forget it quickly.

*Y. Berakot, 5:1.*

R. Abbahu and R. Hiyya ben Abba came to the same town at the same time. R. Hiyya gave an exposition of Halakah, while R. Abbahu delivered an Aggadic discourse. Thereupon all the people left R. Hiyya and came to R. Abbahu. R. Hiyya was greatly discouraged, but R. Abbahu said to him: "I will tell thee a parable. Two men once entered the same town, the one offering for sale precious stones and pearls, the other, tinsel. To whom do you think people crowd? Is it not to him who sells the tinsel, which they can afford to purchase?" [1]

*Sotah, 40a.*

[1] See *Joyful Jeremiads*, p. 95.

He who loves the study of God's words will not be satisfied with the Written Torah, but will go on to the Mishnah and the Talmud.

*Wayyikra Rabbah, 22:1.*

We read: "The Lord spoke with you faces to faces." (Deut. 5:4)
The passage does not read "pan to pan," face to face, but "panim le-panim," faces to faces. This teaches there are four faces or kinds of Torah: Scripture, Mishnah, Halakah, and Aggadah.

*Sopherim, 16.*

The Rabbis have taught: "Those who study only Scripture are scholars of degree, but not of high degree. Those who study also the Mishnah are scholars of higher degree. Those who study Talmud also are scholars of the highest degree."

*Baba Metzia, 33.*

When men learn subjects of Torah, four various countenances may be observed: if the student has a sombre aspect, he is learning the Scriptures; if his countenance is neither serious nor frivolous, he is learning the Mishnah; if he seems to be interested, he is reasoning in Halakah; and if his face be merry, he is occupied with Aggadah.

*Pesikta Rabbati, 21:6.*

Aggadot attract a man's heart like wine.

*Sifre on Deut. 32:14.*

## 348.  TALMUD—INTERPRETATION OF

Beware that thou takest not literally those words of the Sages of the Talmud, for this would be degrading to the sacred doctrine, and would sometimes contradict it. Seek rather the hidden sense; and if thou canst not find the kernel, let the shell alone, and confess: "I cannot understand this!"

*Maimonides.*

One man can find new meanings in the Torah, which another man cannot find.

*The Will of R. Eliezer.*

Let me expound well the statement which I have made, so that men in coming generations shall not ridicule it.

*Shabbat, 75.*

Frequently questions or objections, which men might raise to something in God's conduct of affairs in the world, are put into the mouth of the angels, to give God, so to speak, occasion to explain or justify His ways—(a transparent homiletical device, which modern writers have not always recognized).

*Bereshit, Rabbah, 8:3.*
*Shabbat, 88b, etc.*

### THE OWNER OF THE STOREHOUSE

A vacancy occurred in the position of Head of the Academy, and the students found it difficult to decide upon a successor. Some preferred Rab Joseph for his remarkable store of knowledge regarding tradition; others preferred Rabbah, for his amazing ability to elucidate. The former was called "Sinai" and the latter "Grinder of Mountains."

The students decided to ask counsel of the Academy in Palestine. The reply came: "All must come to the owner of the storehouse for food."

On another occasion, a small circle of distinguished scholars wished one of their number to preside. They said: "Let each one recite some new Halakah, and he who cannot be overruled shall preside." Abbaye was victorious. Among this circle were Rab Zeira and Rabbah bar Matnah. The former was acute and easily discerned difficulties in a new Halakah. The mind of the latter was slower, but he persisted in the explanation of a Halakah until he found its true application. Who was the more important? No answer could be given.

*Horaiyot, 14.*

R. Ivia Saba asked R. Huna: "Is it permissible on a festival to slaughter an animal, in which a Jew and a non-Jew are partners?"

"Yes," said R. Huna.

"Why, then, is it forbidden to slaughter free-will offerings, part of which are offered on the Altar, and part are eaten by him who makes the offering?"

R. Huna laughingly said: "Look, a crow has flown by!"

His son, Rabbah, heard this facetious reply with astonishment.

His father remarked: "Today I delivered a sermon and drank some wine after it, and he wishes me to give him an impromptu answer to a difficult question!"

*Betzah, 21.*

Said R. Ammi: "In the matter of judgment, give the seat of honor to him who is most learned; in social etiquette, give the seat of honor to him who is oldest."

*Baba Batra, 120.*

### THE MASTER OR THE TEACHER

Rabbi introduced R. Hama to R. Ishmael b. R. Jose, saying that he was an admirable scholar.

R. Ishmael said to R. Hama: "Please inquire of me and I will explain the matter to thee."

R. Hama inquired regarding the correct law in a certain case.

R. Ishmael said: "Shall I state Rabbi's opinion, or my father's?"

"Rabbi's," said R. Hama.

"But my father, R. Jose, was the Teacher of Rabbi. How does it come then, that a scholar like thee prefers the opinion of the Disciple against the opinion of the teacher?"

R. Hama said: "At present Rabbi is the President of the Academy, and discusses all matters relating to Halakah with many Rabbis. In this way, he becomes more learned than his former teachers, and gives sounder opinions in legal matters."

*Niddah, 14.*

A Rabbi wished to relate a gem of Torah in the form of an allegory. Some thought that he had uttered a jest. For example, he related that an egg fell down and drowned sixty towns. The men who enjoy jokes explain that the Rabbi wrote down the words "Sixty towns" and placed the paper on a table. A chicken jumped up and laid an egg there; it broke and erased the words. This is incorrect. The Rabbi would not utter jests with reference to the Talmud. These words have a serious meaning, and it lies with the skilled in the Torah to explain it.

*Zohar, iv, 216a.*

## 349. TALMUDIC PERSONALITIES—LIVES OF

"And there arose no prophet like Moses." But a Sage like him did arise, namely, Rabbi Akiba.

*Yalkut Reubeni Berakah.*

With Ben Zoma, preaching perished; with Ben Azzai, diligence died; with R. Eliezer b. Hyrcanus, the Torah was concealed; with R. Eleazar b. Azariah, the ornament of wisdom disappeared; with R. Judah ha-Nasi, humility and the fear of sin ceased; with R. Hanina b. Dosa, men of marvelous deeds were no more; with R. Joshua b. Hananiah, counsel and thinking were lost; with R. Jose, understanding ended; with R. Jose the Lesser, piety ceased; with R. Ishmael b. Pabi, the glamor of the priesthood was finished; with R. Meir, the makers of the proverbs ceased; with R. Gamaliel respect for the Torah, purity and abstemiousness ended.

*M. Sotah, 49; Y. Sotah, 9, 4.*

For this (namely, a ridiculous question) R. Jeremiah was expelled from the House of Study.

*Baba Batra, 23.*

For this, R. Jeremiah was readmitted into the House of Study.

*Baba Batra, 165.*

### HILLEL THE PERSISTENT

It is told that Hillel supported himself and his family by daily labor, and out of his wages of half a dinar a day, he paid half to the janitor of the School.

One day he earned nothing, and, since the janitor would not allow him to enter without the customary fee, Hillel climbed up, fastened himself, and sat on the window sill, "that he might hear the words of Shemaiah and Abtalion."

In this position, he was found next morning, buried in snow, and nearly frozen to death.

*Yoma, 35b.*

R. Johanan b. Zakkai said: "R. Eliezer b. Hyrcanus is like a plastered cistern, which loses not a drop; or like a tarred vessel, which keeps its wine well.

"Happy was the mother of R. Joshua b. Hananiah, that she bore him. She earnestly prayed that her son would become a Sage, and from his earliest youth, she sent him to the School, that his ears might be filled with Torah, and Torah alone.

"R. Jose ha-Kohen was a Hasid in his generation. He never gave anything he wrote to a non-Jew, lest it be transported on the Sabbath.

"R. Simeon b. Nathaniel stood in fear of sin and was likened to a deep furrow, which holds its water.

"R. Eliezer b. Arak was like a spring flowing with ever-sustained vigor. He was also likened to an overflowing river."

*Abot, 2:11, Abot de-R. Nathan, 14.*

### R. Gamaliel and His Colleagues

A student came to R. Joshua and asked: "Is the evening Amidah prayer obligatory or optional?"

"Optional," was the reply.

He went to R. Gamaliel with the same question and was told that the evening prayer is a duty.

"But," protested the student, "R. Joshua said it was optional."

"Wait," said R. Gamaliel, "until the scholars have arrived in the School."

When they had come, the student placed his question again: R. Gamaliel said: "The evening prayer is a duty. Is there anyone who speaks to the contrary?"

R. Joshua said: "No."

"But," said R. Gamaliel, "I was told that you had declared it to be optional. Stand on thy feet and let the witness testify that you disagree with the head of the School."

R. Joshua remained standing for a long time, while R. Gamaliel continued his discourse.

The scholars were indignant at the autocratic conduct of R. Gamaliel, and called upon the interpreter, R. Hutzpit, to cease his interpretation of the lecture.

They held a conference and said: "R. Gamaliel is too prone to torment R. Joshua. Let us depose him and place another in his stead. But whom shall we elect? R. Joshua is the cause, R. Akiba, as the son of a proselyte, has no merit of the fathers. Let us elect R. Eleazar ben Azariah; he is wise and rich, he can win respect from the government, and he is the tenth generation from Ezra."

The scholars visited R. Eleazar and asked if he were willing to become the chief of the School.

He answered: "Let me first take counsel with my wife."

She said to him: "Perhaps they may become reconciled with R. Gamaliel, and depose you."

R. Eleazar replied: "People say: 'A man enjoys the use of a fine article for a single day, even if he knows he will lose it the next day.'"

"But," protested his wife, "your beard is not gray."

Instantly a miracle occurred and R. Eleazar's beard became white. Therefore, he said: "I am as a man of seventy." (Passover Haggadah, etc.)

When he became chief, he abolished the post of doorman at the Academy, and insisted that new benches be introduced.

R. Gamaliel had ordered that any student whose inside was not like his outside should not be permitted to enter. R. Gamaliel grew conscience-stricken, and, in a dream, heard the words: "They are like white logs full of smoke." But the words were merely to quieten his conscience.

We are taught Eduyot was composed on that day, and wherever we have the expression "in that day," the item was taught on the day R. Eleazar ben Azariah assumed the chairmanship of the Academy. Every doubtful Halakah was clarified on that day, and R. Gamaliel did not absent himself even for a single hour.

On that day, Judah, a convert of Ammon, asked in the Academy: "May I wed a Jewish maiden?"

R. Gamaliel held it was forbidden by the Torah. R. Joshua held the prohibition to be effective no longer, since it applied to the true Ammonites, and not to settlers from other people; it is well known that the kings of Assyria made it a rule to displace conquered peoples with other peoples, and to colonize the exiles in remote lands.

The question was put to vote, and the majority held with R. Joshua.

"If the matter stands thus, that I, not Joshua, failed to agree with the majority, then I was wrong in forcing a minority opinion upon him," said R. Gamaliel to himself. "I shall visit him and appease him."

When he came to the humble dwelling of R. Joshua, he said: "From the walls of thy home, I perceive that thou art a smith."

"Woe to the generation, of which thou art the leader; woe to the ship, of which thou art the captain; for thou didst never show interest in the affairs of the scholars, nor in the manner of their livelihood," responded R. Joshua.

R. Gamaliel said: "Be reconciled with me, for the sake of the House of Hillel."

And R. Joshua declared him forgiven.

R. Joshua thereupon resolved to restore R. Gamaliel to the presidency. He went to the conference of the scholars and said: "It were better that the son of the president preside again."

R. Akiba answered: "We deposed him because of thee, but, if you ask us to : :store him, we shall do so."

This procedure was henceforth followed: R. Gamaliel presided for two weeks, and R. Elea zar for the third week. Hence we find the expression: "Whose week was it?"

The student who asked the question concerning the evening prayer was Rabbi Simeon ben Yohai.

*Berakot, 27.*

## The Runaway Rabbi

When Rabbi Eliezer was twenty-two years of age, he abandoned his work as a farmer in his father's field, and ran away to study under Rabbi Johanan ben Zakkai. In the course of time, his father, Hyrcanus, discovered his whereabouts and came to the school. He drew up a will, in which he disinherited his runaway son.

Rabbi Johanan understood the father's object in coming, and bade Rabbi Eliezer deliver an exposition of the law. So racy and cogent were his observations that Rabban Johanan rose and styled him his own Master, and thanked him in the name of the rest for the instruction he had afforded them.

Then Hyrcanus said: "Instead of disinheriting Eliezer, I wish to make him my sole heir."

Rabbi Eliezer refused to accept more than his rightful share.

*Abot de-Rabbi Nathan, chap. 6.*

## Even as a Tender of Sheep

R. Dosa b. Harkinas was the oldest Rabbi in the generation of R. Akiba. Once, the Sages heard that the son of Harkinas permitted the brother of a man, who had died childless, to marry the dead man's wife, even though the dead man's other wife was his daughter, or his own wife's sister.

The Sages were greatly distressed, as this marriage was incestuous according to the School of Hillel, and the offspring would be illegitimate. They visited the old Rabbi, whose eyesight was grievously impaired from age. He welcomed them with great enthusiasm and told them stories of their childhood. They then asked his opinion in the particular case, and he answered that such a marriage surely was incestuous, and it had been deemed so since time immemorial.

The Sages told the old Rabbi what they had heard, and he said: "That was my brother Jonathan. He is very sharp and clings to his false teaching."

The Sages expressed a wish to visit the brother, and hear his side. R. Dosa sent a message to R. Jonathan informing him that the Sages of Israel planned to visit him.

When they arrived, R. Jonathan began to expound the reasons for his opinion, but, his expositions were so involved, they could not follow him, and commenced to grow sleepy.

R. Jonathan sent a message to his brother: "Thou hast written that thou sendest me the Sages of Israel, but I find that they still ought to attend a school."

The Sages departed, but R. Akiba lingered. R. Jonathan again labored to explain his position, but R. Akiba could not understand him; neither was he able to answer his host's queries.

R. Jonathan exclaimed: "Art thou the Akiba renowned wherever Torah is studied? Thou hast the name, but in reality thou hast not attained any more true knowledge of Torah than a tender of cattle."

R. Akiba humbly retorted: "Not even as a tender of sheep."

*Y. Yebamot, 1.*

## THE HASTY VOW

In his youth, Rabbi Akiba was a shepherd in the employ of a wealthy inhabitant of Jerusalem, Kalba Shabua. His employer's daughter, Rachel, fell in love with him. When they were married, her father disowned her, and the young couple lived in abject poverty. Rachel recognized her husband's great abilities, and persuaded him to leave her, to study under the great teachers, Rabbi Eliezer ben Hyrcanus, and Rabbi Joshua ben Hananiah.

As he journeyed by himself, Akiba began to harbor misgivings as to the wisdom of his decision. A waterfall arrested his attention, and he noted that the water, by its continual dripping, was wearing away the solid rock. "May not the Torah," he reasoned, "work its way into my hard and stony heart in the same way?"

His native ability soon began to make itself known, and he became famous as a scholar. Accompanied by many of his disciples, he returned to his wife. At the door, he overheard Rachel say to her neighbor: "I am not at all sorry that my husband is away at his studies. If needs be, I should be entirely willing to have him remain away another long period to enlarge his knowledge."

R. Akiba, hearing this, did not enter, but returned to the School. When he was ready to open his own Academy, he returned again.

The whole population came out to welcome him, among them his wife, dressed in humble attire. She pushed her way forward to greet him, but the Disciples sought to prevent her. R. Akiba, however, took her in his arms and said: "All the knowledge of Torah, which you and I have acquired, is due to the self-sacrifice of my wife."

Kalba Shabua thereupon said to Akiba: "When you were an ignorant shepherd, I vowed that you would not enjoy one penny of my property. If I had known, however, that you were destined to become an illustrious scholar, I should never have uttered such a vow."

The vow was then nullified on the ground that it was made through an error of judgment, and R. Akiba received a large endowment for his Academy.

*Ketubot, 63a, condensed.*

### The Endowment of Rabbi Akiba's Academy

R. Akiba was accustomed to gather bundles of wood daily, selling half and using half.

His neighbors declared: "Akiba, thou almost overcomest us by the smoke of thy torch. Sell us the other half of thy wood as well, and buy oil for a lamp."

Akiba replied: "Three uses do I have for my wood: It gives light at night, it gives me warmth, and I use some of it for a pillow."

At the end of many years R. Akiba grew rich, and was able to maintain a large School. For six reasons did he grow wealthy:

1. From what his father-in-law gave him.

2. From discovering the lucky mascot of a ship, in which gold was hidden.

3. From the chest of a ship sold him for a small amount by a sailor, which was found to contain considerable gold, hidden beneath some ragged cloths.

4. From a rich matron, who loaned him money for his School, and who accepted as sureties, God and the sea. When the loan matured, R. Akiba was ill. The matron went to the shore of the sea, and at that very instant, the waves cast upon the beach, a chest filled with jewels and gold pieces. The matron took what was due her, and donated the remainder to the Rabbi.

5. From the wife of the Roman governor, Turnus Rufus. The governor enjoyed discussing religion with R. Akiba, but was always vanquished in argument. His beautiful wife was enamoured of the wise Sage, and, when her husband died, she became a proselyte and married R. Akiba, giving him a large sum for the Academy.

6. From the will of Ketia bar Shalom, an aristocratic Roman who adopted Judaism in secret. He was the senator, who took his own life, so that the senate might lay aside the anti-Jewish legislation, which it was then discussing. In his will, the Roman gave half his property to R. Akiba.

*Abot de-R. Nathan, 6; Nedarim, 50.*

Once Rabbi Akiba was delayed, and on his arrival, took a seat outside the School, in order not to disturb the students.

A question was asked in Halakah, and the reply was made: "The Halakah is outside."

A second time they said: "The Torah is outside."

A third time they said: "Akiba is outside."

All the students arose, and Rabbi Akiba was summoned.

For thirteen years R. Akiba sat at the feet of R. Eliezer and R. Joshua, unnoticed by either of them. When he made his first argument in favor of R. Joshua, the latter cried out to R. Eliezer: "Is this not the people whom thou hast despised? Go out there, I pray, and do battle with them." (Judges 9:38)

*Shir ha-Shirim Rabbah, 1.*
*Y. Pesahim, 6.*

## The Burial of Rabbi Akiba

When Hadrian commanded that R. Akiba be tortured to death because he taught Torah, it was the time for the reading of the Shema. In torment R. Akiba recited the Shema, and his disciples said: "Is it obligatory in the hour of death?"

He replied: "I have always explained the verse: 'To love God with all thy soul,' to mean, 'Even if He takes thy soul.' Shall I cease to love God, when He has given me the opportunity to fulfill my own explanation?"

Again he recited the first verse of the Shema, and his soul took its departure at the word "One."

A Voice descended from heaven and said: "Happy art thou, Akiba, thy body is pure and thy soul is pure. It has left thy body in purity with the testimony of God's unity. Thou shalt surely have a goodly share in the World-to-Come."

On that very night, Elijah, the Prophet, came to R. Joshua the Garsi, R. Akiba's servant, and asked him to accompany him; and, lo, they found the prison doors open, and the warden asleep. They took up the holy body of Akiba, and the road was light for them; the angels on High wept.

Near Caesarea they descended thrice and ascended six flights and there they found a cave, where they laid down the body of the martyr. R. Joshua, the Garsi, saw space at hand for another body. He asked Elijah concerning it, and received the reply: "This is for the former wife of Turnus Rufus."

*Otzar Midrashim, p. 447.*

## The Aching Tooth

Once Rabbi said: "I am prepared to do what people ask me, but I am not ready to go to the length of the sons of Beteirah, who voluntarily relinquished the Patriarchate to my forefather, Hillel. I am a great believer in family nobility, and, if Rab Huna, the Exilarch, should ever visit Palestine, I would yield precedence to him, because his family is of nobler descent than mine."

Rabbi Hiyya said: "The Exilarch, in truth, has come."

Rabbi's countenance grew pale, and R. Hiyya amended his statement saying: "It is the coffin of the Exilarch, which has arrived for interment in the Holy Land."

Rabbi said to him: "Go outside and see who is looking for thee."

R. Hiyya found no one outside and understood from this occurrence that Rabbi was angry with him. He, therefore, resolved to remain away from his presence for a month. During this month he taught his nephew, Rab, the rules of the Torah, and in this way, he helped to bring knowledge of the Torah to Babylonia.

Rabbi dreamed that R. Hiyya came to him, pressed his hand on an aching tooth, and thereby cured it.

When the month had ended, R. Hiyya returned to the School, and inquired regarding Rabbi's toothache.

Rabbi said: "Ever since thou didst place thy hand upon it, it has pained no longer."

R. Hiyya denied doing this, and Rabbi then understood that God had sent his messenger in the guise of R. Hiyya to cure him.

Henceforth Rabbi paid great respect to R. Hiyya.

*Bereshit Rabbah, 33 and 100.*

### THE GLORY OF R. HIYYA

R. Zeira dreamed that he ascended to the Garden of Eden, and beheld his Master, R. Jose ben Hanina. The light blinded him and he could see no other Zaddik.

He asked R. Jose: "Who is thy neighbor, teacher and master?"

"R. Johanan," was the answer.

"And to whom is he near?"

"My father, R. Hanina."

"And his neighbor?"

"R. Hiyya."

"But should not the great teacher R. Johanan be placed near that other great teacher, R. Hiyya?"

"Nay, he could not abide in such glory." And he continued, "Great Rabbis desired to see the glory of R. Hiyya, but it blinded them. Once his comrade, R. Joshua ben Levi, wished to see the glory of R. Hiyya, but it was not vouchsafed to him. He said: 'Have I learned less Torah than R. Hiyya?' The answer was given: 'Yea, thou hast learned as much, but thou didst not teach as much. Thou didst leave thy native town to learn; he departed in order to teach.'"

*Kohelet Rabbah, 9.*

Once a Jew came to Rab and said: "A neighbor of mine, a Jew, has done me a wrong. May I show some robbers where he keeps his hay?"

Rab replied: "Beware of this, for it would be as if thou thyself had despoiled him."

The man said: "Nevertheless, I shall do so. I must revenge myself."

Rab Kahana, who sat nearby, hurled himself upon the man, and in the ensuing fight, the man fell down and broke his head.

Rab said: "I do not blame thee, since thy only wish was to punish him for his disrespect to God and to the Torah. Heretofore the Greeks (Byzantines) ruled here, and they cared not if blood was shed. Now the Persians, however, are the rulers and they will make trouble for thee. Go to Palestine, but promise me not to question R. Johanan's teachings for seven years, so that thou mayest become acquainted with his manner of arriving at a decision."

When Rab Kahana arrived at the School, he found R. Simeon ben Lakish propounding what R. Johanan had taught earlier in the day. Rab Kahana questioned him, and, when the Rabbi was unable to furnish a suitable reply, though knowing that the decision was correct, the newcomer furnished the proper answer to his own questions.

R. Simeon went to R. Johanan and said: "I advise thee to prepare for your lecture tomorrow most thoroughly. A lion has come from Babylonia, who knows how to place queries in such a manner that it is difficult to find a reply."

True to his promise, R. Kahana listened in silence and did not question R. Johanan. When he entered, he was given a place in the first row, but since he failed to say anything when the Master pronounced a decision, he was asked to go back a row, until he sat in the very last row.

R. Kahana exclaimed: "I consider the humiliation of being put back seven rows the equivalent of seven years."

He then asked the Master to commence his lecture anew. Every time he placed a question and no answer was forthcoming, R. Kahana was advanced a row. Finally the cushion was removed from under R. Johanan, until he was forced to sit on the ground, and R. Kahana was again in the first row.

R. Johanan inquired from him regarding all his doubts, and the guest answered them all.

R. Johanan remarked: "Of a surety, the Torah is with the Babylonians, and not with us."

*Baba Kamma, 117.*

### Rab Huna's Habits

Rabba asked Reforem bar Papa to relate some reminiscences about Rab Huna.

Reforem said: "I do not recall much regarding his younger days, but I can relate to you some of his admirable doings in his later years.

"Whenever there was a windy day, R. Huna would order out his gilded carriage and ride throughout the city. If he noticed any cracks in a house, he would order it demolished as dangerous. The rich had to rebuild their houses themselves, but the poor received money from him for rebuilding.

"Late in the afternoon on Sabbath-Eve, he would go to the vegetable market and would buy up all good stuff left over and order it thrown into the river. He would do this in order that the growers might suffer no loss and would have no reason for not coming to market on Fridays with plenty of vegetables. He would not distribute the goods to the poor, because they would come to depend upon this free distribution, and, if everything should be sold, they would have nothing for the Sabbath meals.

"When sitting at a meal, he would have the door opened, and would invite everyone in need of food to share in his meal."

Rabba remarked: "I am able to do the same with the exception of inviting all comers to participate in my meal: too many would come."

*Taanit, 20.*

## 350. TAXES AND EXCISE

He who cheats the customs authorities is comparable to an idolater.

*Semahot, 2:9.*

## 351. TEACHERS AND TEACHING

David said: "O Lord, many groups of Zaddikim shall be admitted into Thy presence. Which one of them is most beloved before Thee?"

God answereth: "The teachers of the youth, who perform their work in sincerity and with joy, shall sit at My right hand." [1]

*Pesikta Buber, p. 180a.*

[1] A paraphrase of Psalm 16:11.

It is written: "She openeth her mouth with wisdom, and the Torah of kindness is on her tongue." (Prov. 31:26)

Is there any Torah that is not all kindness?

If a man teaches his wisdom to others, it is the Torah of kindness.

*Sukkah, 49.*

Rabbi Jose ben Halafta said: "There is nothing more futile than to learn and not to teach."

*Kohelet Rabbah, 5, 9.*

If thou hast learned much Torah, do not hold fast to it for thyself, but teach it to others, for thereunto wast thou created.

*Abot, 2:8, according to explanation of Rabbi A. Heyman.*
*But see translation of Singer, 2:9, p. 188.*

He who teaches his grandson is as if he had received his teaching from Mount Sinai.

*Kiddushin, 30.*

He who teaches his neighbor's son will deserve to sit in the Heavenly Academy.

*Baba Metzia, 85.*

He who teaches his neighbor's son is as if he had created him.

*Sanhedrin, 19.*

He who learns receives but one-fifth of the reward of him who teaches.

*Midrash Shir ha-Shirim, edition of Dr. Greenhut.*

He who learns and does not teach is like a myrtle which grows in the desert: no one receives enjoyment from it.

He who learns and teaches in a place where there are no teachers is like a myrtle in the desert: it is greatly appreciated.

*Rosh ha-Shanah, 23.*

We read: "Let thy springs (of Torah) be dispersed abroad" (Prov. 5:16) and, "Let them be only thine own." (Prov. 5:17)

If the scholar is competent, he should disseminate his teaching.

*Taanit, 7.*

He who teaches the son of an unlearned man can make void a decree, even if it comes from God.

*Baba Metzia, 85.*

Rabbi Eliezer ben Hyrcanus said: "He who teaches his daughter Torah is as if he taught her frivolity."

Ben Azzai, however, said: "A man is bound to teach his daughter Torah." [1]

*M. Sotah, 3:4.*

[1] A compromise has been effected in the practice of teaching girls the Bible and the laws obligatory upon them, but they rarely study the Oral Law.

We read: "My doctrine shall drop as the rain, my speech shall distil as the dew." (Deut. 32:2)

If a teacher is incompetent, his words seem to the pupils as harsh as falling rain. If he is competent, his teaching is distilled gently like dew.

*Taanit, 7.*

Rab Abba, the father of Samuel, found his son weeping.

"Why do you weep?" he asked.

"My teacher struck me," the boy replied.

"Why did he strike you?"

"Because I fed his child without washing my hands before."

"Why did you not wash?"

The boy replied: "Should I wash my hands if the child eats?"

"You are right, my son," said Rab Abba; "a teacher, who does not know thoroughly the regulations, should not presume to strike another for a neglect of them."

*Hullin, 107.*

### UNMARRIED TEACHERS

R. Jose bar Hanan narrated the following: "Once as I walked on the road, I beheld a distinguished personage in costly garments approaching me. I fell back in agitation and thought: perhaps he is an angel.

"As I grew quiet I ran after him and said: 'Rabbi, what is thy name?'

"He answered: 'Isaac ben Huna is my name.'

" 'Art thou a scholar in the Mishnah or the Aggadah?'

" 'In neither,' he replied.

" 'What then may thy occupation be?'

" 'I have none.'

" 'Has God then fashioned a human being who does no work whatsoever?'

" 'I teach children,' he replied.

" 'And art thou married?'

" 'No,' he answered.

" 'Be cursed, then, thou rogue,' I said; 'such as thou go to homes to teach, and mislead the matrons of the household.' "

Unmarried teachers, our Sages tell us, are arrogant in their hearts as kings, and their minds are like those of children. To greet them is to greet an idolater; he who respects them, inherits Gehenna; and he who says on their death: Blessed be the Righteous Judge, shall have no share in the World-to-Come.

*Pirke de-Rabbenu ha-Kodosh, 7.*

It was taught: "A scholar should not take up his abode in a town in which there is not, among other requisites of civilization, an elementary teacher."

*Sanhedrin, 17b.*

### THE PERSIAN PROSELYTE

A Persian came to Rab and said: "Will you teach me the Torah?" He agreed and showed him the letter "aleph."

The Persian said: "How will you prove to me that this is an aleph?"

He went to Samuel and tried the same argument on him.

Samuel pulled his ear, and the Persian exclaimed: "O, my ear! my ear!"

"And how will you prove to me that this is your ear?"

"Everyone knows that this is my ear."

"By the same token everyone knows that this is an aleph," was the teacher's reply.

The Persian laughed and became a proselyte.

*Kohelet Rabbah, 7.*

### THE PATIENT TEACHER

Rabbi Perida had a pupil with whom he found it necessary to rehearse a lesson many, many times before the latter comprehended it.

One day the Rabbi was hurriedly called away to perform a charitable act. Before he departed, however, he repeated the lesson at hand the usual number of times, but, on this occasion, his pupil failed to learn it.

"Why is it, my son," asked Rabbi Perida, "that the repetitions this time have been thrown away?"

The pupil replied: "Because, Master, my mind was so preoccupied with the summons you received to discharge another duty."

"Well, then," said the Rabbi, "let us begin again."

And he repeated the lesson again the usual number of times.

Rabbi Perida was rewarded with a long life.

*Erubin, 54b.*

## 352. METHODS OF TEACHING

Teach mnemonics by symbolic signs, and explain by the method of parallels (or analogies).

*Erubin, 21.*

A teacher should teach by a short method.

*Pesahim, 3.*

### RULES FOR TEACHING

Raba said: "If there are more than twenty-five children in a class for elementary instruction, an assistant should be appointed.

"If there are fifty children in a class, two competent instructors should be in charge."

Rab Dimi said: "A teacher who teaches less than his fellow-instructors should be dismissed. The other teachers will become more diligent both out of fear of dismissal, and out of gratitude.

"If a teacher is to be appointed, preference should be given to him who teaches thoroughly, not to him who teaches much material superficially; for an error once learned is difficult to unlearn."

*Baba Batra, 21a.*

R. Judah ha-Nasi said: "To what may R. Tarfon be likened? To a pile of nuts: if you take out one, all the others tumble down upon each other. By the same token, if a student came to study unto him, he taught him Scriptures, Mishnah, Midrash, Halakot, and Aggadot.

"R. Akiba is like a storehouse with various goods. He is like a workman, who receives his wage in produce. He throws into a sack some wheat, barley, beans and lentils. When he reaches home, he assorts each kind of produce separately. By the same token, R. Akiba assorted each type of Torah learning separately, and taught it thus.

"R. Eleazar b. Azariah is like a peddler's basket: the peddler takes his basket about town and is able to furnish whatever his customers ask. By the same token R. Eleazar was able to answer in any subject concerning which his disciples asked.

"R. Johanan b. Nuri is like a basket of Halakot.

"R. Jose, the Galilean, knew how to select acceptable Halakot without seeming to be haughty, and he taught them to all Israel."

*Abot de-R. Nathan, 18.*

## 353. TEMPLE—MORIAH—SITE OF

### (*See Bet ha-Mikdash*)

The Rabbis ask: "Whence came the light that God first created?"

The answer is: "On the spot where the future Temple was to be built, there the first light was created!"

*Bereshit Rabbah, 3:4.*

The Rabbis said that the Shekinah dwelt only in the First Temple which was built by the efforts of the Jews themselves, "but did not dwell in the Second Temple, which was built not by the efforts of the Jews themselves, but with the help and aid of the Persians." [1]

*Yoma, 9b, 10a.*

[1] If the Shekinah—God's blessing—is to rest on a Jewish Palestine, Palestine must be won by Jewish work, Jewish efforts, Jewish self-sacrifice, Jewish heroism!

"Where is the land of Moriah?" the Sages asked.

Rabbi Hiyya, deriving the word Moriah from "Horo-oh"—teaching—interprets the land of Moriah as referring to the place whence goeth forth the teaching, the study of God's law.

Rabbi Yannai, deriving the word Moriah from "Yirah"—fear—interprets the land of Moriah as referring to the place whence fear—the fear of and reverence of God—goeth forth to the world.

Rabbi Simeon ben Yohai, deriving the word Moriah from "Mor"—the incense of sacrifice—interprets the land of Moriah to be the place directly beneath the Heavenly Altar of Sacrifice.

*Bereshit Rabbah, 60:9.*

## 354. TEMPORARY AND PERMANENT HOMES

Snatch and eat; snatch and drink; for this world is like a wedding.

*Erubin, 54.*

This world is thy inn; the World-to-Come is thy home.

*Moed Katon, 9.*

## 355. TEMPTATION, TEMPTER

Rabbi Simeon ben Yohai said: "One who causes another to sin does a worse thing to him than one who kills him. For he who kills him only puts him out of this world; while he who causes him to sin puts him out of this world and the World-to-Come as well."

*Sifre on Deut., 23:8.*

Place no temptation in the path of the honest man; and the same is all the more true for the dishonest.

*Tanhuma Buber Wayishlah, 2.*

No man should lead himself into temptation.

*Sanhedrin, 107.*

A man may lead his neighbor from out of the ways of life into the ways of death, but God leads a man into the ways of life.

*Menahot, 99.*

A man should not say: "May the All-Merciful keep me far from sin," but he should say: "May the All-Merciful keep sin (the opportunity of sin) far from me."

*Midrash Tehillim, 103:13.*

## 356. TEFILLIN, TZITZIT, MEZUZAH

On the festivals and on the intermediate days it is forbidden to remove the Tefillin of the Lord of the Universe, and to put on the material Tefillin.

*Zohar Hadash to Shir ha-Shirim, 64b.*

God says to Israel: "Write my name, Shaddai, on the door-post of thy house, and while thou sittest inside, I shall sit outside to guard thee."

*Zohar, ii, 36a.*

R. Simeon said: "If you have been guilty of many transgressions. perform many precepts accordingly. If you have been guilty of the seven things which are an abomination to the spirit of God (Prov. 6:16–18), present to Him an antidote for them:

"For haughty eyes—the Tefillin between thine eyes; for a tongue of falsehood—teach Torah unto thy sons; for hands that shed innocent blood (shaming a fellowman)—the Tefillin of the hand; for a heart that contriveth plans of injustice—let the words of Torah be in your heart; for feet that hasten to run after evil—run after Mizwot; for a false witness that eagerly uttereth lies—'be ye My witnesses' (Isaiah 43:10) ; for him that scattereth abroad discord among brethren—seek peace and security."

*Pesikta Buber, 176.*

Why has God commanded that a blue thread be inserted in the fringes?
Because it reminds us of Heaven.

*Sotah, 17.*

R. Bibi said: "Take not the name of the Lord in vain."
"Do not wear Tefillin and then go about transgressing with the Divine name on thy forehead."

*Pesikta Rabbati, 22:5.*

In this world, the four paragraphs of the Pentateuch contained in the Tefillin, should be in this order: "Consecrate," "And when He will bring thee," "Hear," "And when it shall come to pass that you will hearken."
In the World-to-Come, the order will be: "Consecrate," "And when," the second "And when," and "Hear." [1]

*Zohar, iv, 258a to Phineas.*

[1] Many Hasidim wear two pairs of Tefillin, one with the paragraphs in the first order; one with the second order—called the Tefillin according to Rabbenu Tam (died 1170). The first is according to Rashi and Maimonides. This passage of the Zohar seems to be a compromise between the two opinions.

No Tefillin should be worn on the intermediate days of the festivals. It is like a king, who gave to his beloved servant a counterpart of his seal, but, on holidays, he gave him the seal itself.

If the servant had covered up the original with the copy, would it not show disrespect on his part towards the king? [1]

*Zohar Hadash to Song of Songs, 64b.*

[1] Hasidim follow this prohibition, but not their opponents. Both holy days and Tefillin are signs or seals.

The paragraph regarding Tzitzit is included in the Shema, but is missing in the Mezuzah. How is this omission rectified?

A man must robe himself in the Tallit with the Tzitzit. Then is his home complete, and he is rescued from injury and plague.

*Zohar, iii, 300b.*

The blue in the Tzitzit represents Justice; the white represents Mercy.

When is man ready to read the Shema, and to receive the Kingdom of Heaven? When he can distinguish between blue and white, between Justice and Mercy.

*Zohar, iv, 175a.*

The four fringes of the Tzitzit are the four witnesses of the truth of the King.

*Zohar, iv, 175b.*

## A True Gift

The Persian king, Arteban, once visited the Emperor Marcus Aurelius Antoninus when the latter was in Syria. The Emperor introduced to him his friend, the Patriarch Rabbi Judah I.

The king sent to Rabbi a priceless gem as a gift, and Rabbi presented to him in return a Mezuzah.

When the King met Rabbi he said: "I sent you a costly gift, but thou hast given me in return a gift worth a small coin."

Rabbi replied: "The portion of the Torah inscribed upon it is of more worth than all valuables. Moreover, your gift must be kept safe by me, whereas my gift will keep you safe, as it is written: 'When thou liest down, it shall watch over thee.'" (Prov. 6:22)

*Bereshit Rabbah, 35.*

## Evading the Mitzwah

An angel found R. Ketina wrapped in a thin blanket.

He said: "Ketina, Ketina, in summer-time I find thee in a blanket; in winter-time, in a shawl with round corners. What will become of the Mitzwah of Tzitzit?"

R. Ketina answered: "But I am not transgressing any law. I am merely wearing garments, which the law does not require to have Tzitzit at its corners."

The angel said: "If there is a calamity in the world, a man is punished for evading the performance of a Mitzwah, even if it be done in a lawful manner."

*Menahot, 41.*

R. Eliezer said: "Israel declared before the Lord: 'We wish to labor in the Torah day and night, but we have no time.'

"And God replied: 'Observe the precept of Tefillin, and it shall be accounted unto you as if you had labored in the Torah day and night.' "

R. Johanan said: "The above statement is given clearly in the Torah itself: 'And it shall be for a sign unto thee upon thy hand, and for a memorial between thine eyes, that the law of thy Lord may be in thy mouth.' " (Exod. 13:9)[1]

*Midrash Tehillim, 1.*

[1] And, therefore, R. Eliezer's statement is superfluous.

## 357. THANKSGIVING

In the days to come, all prayers will be abolished except prayers of thanksgiving.

*Wayyikra Rabbah, 9:7.*

R. Phinehas said: "In the days to come, all voluntary sacrifices will be abolished, except those of thanksgiving."

R. Judah in the name of Rab said: "Four should offer thanksgiving prayers: Those who have landed safely after a sea-voyage; those who have returned from desert travel; those who have recovered from a serious illness; and those who have been liberated from prison." (See Ps. 107)

*Berakot, 54b.*

Rab Judah, after recovering from illness, was visited by Rab Hanan of Bagdad and other Rabbis.

They said: "Blessed be the Compassionate One, who gave thee to us, and not to the earth."

He said: "Amen." Then he said to them: "My response is sufficient to fulfill the duty of thanksgiving."

*Berakot, 54.*

## 358. THEFT, ROBBERY

It is worse to rob the dead than to rob the living.

*Semahot, 9.*

A partner in robbery is also a robber.

*Y. Sanhedrin, 1:2.*

A man cannot assemble riches from theft.

*Midrash Aseret ha-Diberot.*

He who steals from an idolater will end by stealing from an Israelite.

*Eliyahu Rabbah, 28.*

If you take what is not thine, what is thine will be taken from thee.

*Kallah Rabbati, 5.*

All thievery depends upon the receiver.

*Wayyikra Rabbah, 6:2.*

People say: "Steal from a thief and you will acquire the taste."

*Berakot, 5.*

The thief becomes law-abiding when he can steal no more.

*Sanhedrin, 22.*

It is a more grievous sin to rob men than God.

*Baba Batra, 88.*

He who steals is as if he shed blood and revered idols.

*Semahot, 2:1.*

People say: "Even the thief calls upon God at the entrance he has dug out into the place he wishes to rob."

*Berakot, 63.*

Do not steal back your property from a thief, lest you likewise appear to be a thief.

*Y. Sanhedrin, 8:3.*

Come and see how great is the sin of violence (robbery)!
The Generation of the Flood transgressed every law, yet the decree of destriction was issued only because of the violence of which they were guilty.

*Sanhedrin, 108.*

Why does the Torah say that he who has stolen a beast, slaughtered it, and sold the meat, should be fined four or five times its value?
Because he has become rooted in offending.

*Baba Kamma, 68.*

He whose hands are smeared in robbery will call upon God but will not be heard.

*Shemot Rabbah, 22:3.*

He who robs his fellow of a pennyworth is as if he took his life.

*Baba Kamma, 119.*

How can a man bless God over bread, which he has made from stolen flour?
His blessing would be a curse.

*Baba Kamma, 94.*

If I am an armed bandit, I am not a scholar; if I am a scholar, I am not a bandit.

*Abodah Zarah, 17.*

He who does not handle property entrusted to him according to the wishes of its owner, is called a robber.

*Baba Metzia, 78.*

If the mouse were not guilty, how would it be found in the hole?
(Contrast to the famous saying: Not the mouse is the thief but the
hole.)

*Gittin, 45.*

## My Brother Kitob

R. Levi told this story:

In a southern town, an evil innkeeper would persuade his patrons to
dress before daylight, saying that he wished to accompany them on
their way and thereby spare them travel in the heat of the day. Once
on their journey, he would lead them to a band of brigands, who would
rob them, and on returning to the inn, divide the spoils with the inn-
keeper.

Once R. Meir chanced to stay at the inn. The landlord coveted his
ass and goods, and tried to persuade him to leave before sunrise.

R. Meir said: "I am awaiting my brother, Kitob; he is to meet me
here."

The innkeeper went out several times to see if Kitob had arrived.

When daylight came, R. Meir ascended his donkey and prepared
to depart.

"Where is thy brother, Kitob?" he was asked by the disappointed
partner of the thieves.

"The light of day," was the Rabbi's response. "It is written: 'And
God saw the light, ki-tov: it is "good".'"

*Bereshit Rabbah, 92.*

## Vinegar, the Son of Wine

Following a wave of crimes, the chief of the police received orders
to seize all thieves.

Rabbi Eleazar ben Rabbi Simeon went to him and said: "Let me
teach you to safeguard against arresting innocent persons, whose actions seem suspicious: At ten o'clock in the morning, if you perceive a
person with a wine cup in his hand, acting as if he had had no sleep,
investigate him. If he is a student, a night-laborer, or the like, he is
innocent; if not, he has spent the night in revelry."

The chief reported this counsel to the governor, who promptly
appointed the Rabbi as police head.

Rabbi Joshua ben Karha said to him: "Thou vinegar, the son of
wine! How long wilt thou give over to execution the people of our
God?"

"But I am weeding out the thorns from the vineyard," was Rabbi
Eleazar's excuse.

"Leave it to the Owner of the vineyard," he was told, "to weed out
His thorns himself."

*Baba Metzia, 83b.*

## The Buried Purse

A merchant came to a town to buy goods, and, on hearing that a bargain-sale would soon take place, resolved to wait. In the interval, he sought out a deserted lot, and buried there his purse.

When he returned to claim it, it was gone. In great distress, he looked about him, and saw a hole in the wall near the road. He understood then that the owner of the property beyond the wall had chanced to watch him when he buried the purse.

He visited the man and said: "I hear that thou art gifted with wisdom. Please give me counsel. I brought with me two purses: one with five hundred guldens, the other with eight hundred. I buried the smaller purse in a secret place. Shall I do likewise with the larger, or shall I entrust it to a reliable person?"

"My advice," said the thief, "is to bury the second where you buried the first, until you need it."

The thief thought to himself: "If he does not find the first purse, he will not bury the second."

Therefore, he returned the purse to the spot, where it had been buried, and the merchant, watching from a distance, later recovered it.

*Midrash Aseret ha-Diberot.*

## Closing the Weasel-Holes

A magistrate was accustomed to imprison receivers of stolen goods, and to release the thieves. He heard the people grumbling and ordered that every grumbler should come to the courtyard.

When they had arrived, he distributed portions of meat among a few weasels. The weasels hastened away with them to their hiding-places in the ground.

A little later, he commanded that the holes of the weasels be stopped up, and again distributed meat to the same weasels. When the little animals saw that they had no place to keep their meat safely, they brought it back.

"See then, my friends," remarked the judge, "if the thieves have no place to dispose of their stolen wares, they will not steal."

*Wayyikra Rabbah, 6.*

## His Son's Property

Rabbi Hanina invited R. Jonathan into his fruit-garden, and treated him to ripe figs. On leaving, the guest noticed a tree bearing exceptionally fine white figs. His host noticed him gazing at the figs and said: "This tree belongs to my son. I have no right to rob my own son, even when I know he would not object."

*Y. Baba Batra, 2.*

### THE SPIRIT AND THE LETTER OF THE LAW

R. Zeira, while walking with R. Haggai, passed a man with a load of wood.

R. Zeira said: "Bring me, I beg you, a sliver of wood to cleanse my teeth."

At once, however, he called R. Haggai back and said: "Do not do this. If every one took but a sliver, the man's livelihood would be gone."

Was R. Zeira unreasonably scrupulous in this instance?

Nay. Being a famous person, it was incumbent on him, through his actions, to teach the spirit of our Creator's laws, even though no objection could be found to the letter thereof.

*Y. Demai, 3.*

### STEALING THE MIND

Said Samuel: "The Commandment 'Do not steal' includes the prohibition against stealing a man's mind with misleading words. No one may steal a person's mind, not even a pagan's.

"No one may sell meat to a pagan that is unfit for a Jew, unless he first tells him why a Jew may not eat it." Rab Isaac bar Joseph said: "We must not tell the pagans a deliberate falsehood, but if they do not ask, we are not required to specify why the meat may not be eaten by a Jew. Therefore, a place may be set aside in a butcher's market, with the announcement: 'Meat for non-Jews.' This is not stealing the mind of the buyers."

Thus Mar Zutra went from Sikra to Mehuza, and Rabba and Rab Saphra went to Sikra.

When they met, Mar Zutra said: "Why did you take so much trouble to meet me?"

Rab Saphra said: "You deserve the inconvenience, but this time we did not know of your coming; we merely went on our business."

Later Rabba remarked: "Why did you make this explanation?"

"But I did not wish to mislead him," said Rab Saphra.

Rabba replied: "He would have misled himself."

*Hullin, 94.*

### THE STOLEN BEAKER

No man shall put his hand out to steal, for he will surely betray himself by his actions.

Once when Mar Zutra, the Hasid, sojourned at an inn, one of the guests stole the innkeeper's silver beaker. Mar Zutra watched the actions of the guests. He saw a man wash his hands and wipe them on the robe of another who was not present.

Mar Zutra advised the landlord to search through this man's effects, and lo, the beaker was discovered.

He said: "He who does not care for the property of another is not an honest man."

*Baba Metzia, 23.*

He who steals words of Torah has acquired merit for himself.

*Midrash Lekah Tob, Mishpatim, 22:3.*

### FOOD FOR THE FAINT

Rabbi Judah and R. Jose were walking when suddenly R. Judah grew faint, and his eyesight was affected. A shepherd passed by and R. Jose snatched a sweet cake from his basket.

R. Jose said: "On your account I was forced to deprive a shepherd of a portion of his meal."

Later, when they neared the city, R. Jose became faint. The townspeople hurried to them with cakes and honey.

Later R. Judah said: "On my account, only one was deprived of food, but, on your account, the people of an entire town were forced to deprive themselves."

*Yoma, 83.*

## 359. THRIFT AND SPENDTHRIFT

A man should not place all his money in one corner.

*Bereshit Rabbah, 76:3.*

He who has inherited much and desires to lose his inheritance should clothe himself in linen and use glassware.[1]

*Baba Metzia, 29.*

[1] Glassware was very expensive.

A penny added to a penny creates in the end a large sum.

*Sotah, 9.*

The improvident man who refuses to live within his means, and seeks to be supported by charity, must not be helped.

*Ketubot, 67b.*

## 360. TOOLS

A carpenter who has no tools is not a carpenter.[1]

*Shemot Rabbah, 40:1.*

[1] This also refers to a Rabbi and his books.

A man is not an artisan, if he lacks tools.

*Midrash Temurah.*

R. Johanan ben Zakkai said: "A scholar who is God-fearing is like an artisan who has his tools in his hand."

*Abot de-R. Nathan, 22.*

### 361. TORAH

The Torah is like a goad because it serves to guide the students on their way.

*Hagigah, 3.*

As the bee gives honey to its owner, but its bite is poison to a stranger, so the words of Torah are life for Israel, but poison for idolaters.

*Debarim Rabbah, 1, 5.*

Sell thy field which was created in six days to acquire Torah which was received after forty days.

*Tanhuma Tissa, 19.*

Why may the Torah be likened to a breast? Just as a suckling babe always finds the milk of the breast pleasing, so the scholar always finds savor in the Torah.

*Erubin, 54.*

Even matters which in Torah seem as fruitless as thorns, are in reality of the highest significance.

*Shir ha-Shirim Rabbah, 1.*

He who abolishes one thing in the Torah is as if he had burned it.

*Ruth Rabbah, 2.*

The Torah was given portion by portion.

*Gittin, 60.*

The Torah is likened unto a good woman.

*Yebamot, 63.*

What mean the words: "The earth feared and was still" (Ps. 76:9)? Before Israel accepted the Torah, the earth feared; after they accepted the Torah, it was still. For the earth could not exist if no nation had accepted the Torah.

*Shabbat, 88.*

Why are the words of Torah like fire? A fire is built by many logs and the words of Torah survive only through many minds.

*Taanit, 7.*

What mean the words: "Gold and glass cannot equal it (Job 28:7)"? These are the words of Torah which are as difficult to acquire as golden vessels, and as easy to lose as glassware.

*Hagigah, 15.*

As waters cover the nakedness of the sea bottom, so Torah covers the nakedness of Israel.

*Midrash Tehillim, 41, 18.*

His soul is guarded who guards the Torah.

*Menahot, 99.*

Torah leads to diligence.

*Abodah Zarah, 20.*

A man should bear the yoke of the burden of the Torah like an ass and an ox.

*Abodah Zarah, 5.*

Better that a letter of the Torah be torn out than that the Name of God be profaned, or the Torah be forgotten.

*Temurah, 14.*

The Torah was not given to angels.

*Berakot, 25.*

The Torah is as greatly beloved by its students as on the day it was given.

*Berakot, 63.*

The Torah commences with kindness and ends with kindness.

*Sotah, 14.*

The Torah is like two paths, one of fire and one of ice. It is best to walk in the middle course.

*Y. Hagigah, 2, 1.*

Why are men like fish? As fish die out of water, so men die without the Torah and the Mitzwot.

*Abodah Zarah, 3.*

Is then fatherhood in the Torah, namely, Can Torah be inherited?

*Tosefta Baba Metzia, 3.*

The scholars in Babylonia form blossoms and flowers for the Torah.

*Shabbat, 145.*

The Torah is likened to salt; the Mishnah to peppers, and the Gemara to spices. The Torah is likened to water; the Mishnah to wine, and the Gemara to spiced wine.

*Soferim, 14.*

Words of the Torah are forgotten only if the mind is inattentive.

*Taanit, 7.*

In this world the coin of Torah does not circulate, but in the World-to-Come only Torah will be desired.

*Shoher Tob in Bet Midrash, 4, 99.*

Kindness says to Torah: Thou art beautiful only if I beautify thee. Thou art like unto a beautiful woman who needs a maid-servant to watch over her beauty.

*Hakdamah to Halakot Gedolot.*

Words of Torah need each other. What one passage locks up, the other discloses.

*Bemidbar Rabbah. 19. 27.*

Only Torah serves to purify a man.

*Zohar, iii, 80b.*

To him who masters it the Torah is a life-giving drug; to him who fails to master it, the Torah is a drug of death.

*Yoma, 72.*

Were it not for the Torah, the world would not stand.

*Nedarim, 32.*

A broken body will find solace in the Torah.

*Zohar, iv, 160b.*

Words of Torah are not lasting except in him who is lowly of spirit.

*Taanit, 7.*

Before the Scroll of the Torah all men are as the poor.

*Baba Batra, 43.*

Torah is Peace.

*Zohar, iv, 176b.*

The older the words of the Torah grow within a man, the better he understands them.

*Sifre Ekeb, 48.*

Whenever a man studies words of the Torah, he is certain to find a meaning in them.

*Erubin, 54.*

Let not the words of Torah be an obligation unto thee; at the same time, however, thou must not free thyself of them.

*Menahot, 99.*

Words of Torah may be sparing in one passage, though they are abundant in another.

*Y. Rosh ha-Shanah, 3, 5.*

Rabbah bar Bar Hana said: "Why are the words of Torah likened unto fire (Jer. 23:29)? It is to teach that, as the fire from a single piece of wood does not give forth heat, so the Torah of a single student likewise does not give forth warmth."

*Taanit, 7.*

Rab Hanina bar Idi said: "Why is the Torah likened to water (Isa. 55:1)? It is to teach that, as one who is thirsty is not too lazy to seek water, so a disciple who has the thirst for knowledge does not hesitate to seek out a teacher."

*Taanit, 7.*

Rab Hisda said: "To learn Torah, it is best to go to one teacher; to discuss it, it is better to go to several teachers. The many different explanations will help to give you understanding."

*Abodah Zara, 19.*

Rab said: "Even the seemingly simple speech of the learned man contains within it excellent lessons in Torah."

*Sukkah, 21.*

Rabbi Jose said: "Torah is clearer at night than in the daytime, for the explanations of the Written Torah make up Oral Torah, and the Oral Torah belongs to the night."

*Zohar, iii, 23.*

R. Hanina bar Idi said: "Why are the words of the Torah likened unto water (Isa. 55:1)? The answer is, as follows: Just as water forsakes a high place and travels to a low place, thus the words of Torah find a resting-place only in a man of lowly spirit."

R. Oshaya said: "Why are the words of the Torah likened to water, wine and milk (Isa. 55:1)? The answer is, as follows: Just as these liquids are kept only in the simplest of vessels, so the words are preserved only in the man of humble spirit."

*Taanit, 7a.*

### The Ugly Vessel

The Emperor's daughter once said to R. Joshua ben Hananiah: "Ho, Glorious Wisdom in an ugly vessel!"

He replied: "Why does thy father keep wine in an earthen pitcher?"

"How else should we keep it?" asked the Emperor's daughter.

"People of your rank," said the Rabbi, "should keep their wine in vessels of gold or silver."

The Emperor's daughter persuaded her father to transfer the wine from earthen to gold and silver vessels. The wine, however, turned sour. The Emperor summoned the Rabbi and inquired why he had given such poor counsel.

R. Joshua answered: "I did so to show to thy daughter that wisdom like wine is best kept in a plain vessel."

"But," continued the Emperor's daughter, "are there not handsome scholars as well?"

"Yes," answered the Rabbi, "but they would have been greater scholars had they been unhandsome."

*Taanit, 7a.*

Heaven and Earth have measures (limit of time and space), but the Torah has none.

*Bereshit Rabbah, 10, 1.*

No other Moses will come and bring another Torah, for there is no Torah left in Heaven.

*Debarim Rabbah, 8, 6.*

Of the seven things which were created before the creation of the world, the Torah is first and repentance the second.

*Pesahim, 54b.*

Said Rabbi Benaiah: "The world and everything in it were created solely for the sake of the Torah, as it is said: 'The Lord founded the earth for the sake of Wisdom.'" (Prov. 3:19)

*Bereshit Rabbah, 1, 1 (beginning).*

The Sages said: "He who says he has only Torah, know then that Afilu Torah En Lo, even Torah he does not possess." [1]

*Yebamot, 109b.*

[1] He who is merely interested in the study of the Torah but has no intention of practising it, receives no reward for his study.

In justice it could be said: "Turn it and turn it, for everything is found therein!"

*Abot, 5, 22.*

"The words of the Torah are fruitful and multiply!"

*Hagigah, 3b.*

"Would that they forgot Me but kept My Torah!"

*Ekah Rabbah, Proem.*

Hillel, when about to summarize the whole Torah in one phrase, said: "What is distasteful to thee do not unto others."

*Shabbat, 31a.*

R. Ishmael said: "The Torah speaks in the language of men."
R. Akiba, on the other hand, said: "The Torah does not speak in the language of men."
Both views are in reality the truth. The Torah speaks to the Jew in the language of men—in the language that men of the earliest generations could understand. It wanted the human mind to discover new truths for itself, and to penetrate deeper into the mysteries of life. It wanted men to enjoy this adventure of the human mind and spirit. But the Bible also spoke "not in the language of men," but in a mystical language in which could be found hidden the hints, the suggestions of all truths to be discovered in all the years to come.

*Arakin, 11a; Levinthal, "Judaism," pp. 85-6.*

"The Torah, because it is more highly prized than everything, was created before everything, as it is said: 'The Lord created me as the beginning of His way.'" (Prov. 8:22)

*Sifre to Deut., 11, 10.*

## TORAH IS THE BEST SEHORAH (MERCHANDISE)

A scholar on board a ship with many other merchants was asked: "What merchandise have you?"
He answered them: "The best merchandise in the world."
They looked in the hold of the ship, but, finding nothing but what they themselves had on board, they laughed at him. The ship was wrecked and all of its freight was lost. The merchants barely escaped

with their lives, and finally reached a strange port. The scholar sought out the local synagogue and asked permission to deliver a discourse. When it was seen that he was a greater scholar than anyone in the city, he was appointed head of the School, and was given a worthy stipend. When the scholar departed from the synagogue, the most important men of the community accompanied him. The impoverished merchants came to him and begged him for aid. He secured for them their passage money home, and they said to him: "You were right. Our merchandise has been lost, but yours remains (endures)."

*Tanhuma to Terumah.*

Rabbi Oshaya Rabbah said: "The Torah says: 'I was an architect's apparatus for God.' As a rule an earthly king who is building a palace does not build it according to his own ideas, but according to those of an architect; and the architect does not build it out of his head, but has parchments or tablets to know how he shall make the rooms and the openings. Likewise, God looked into the Torah and created the world."

*Bereshit Rabbah, 1, 1.*

### A New Torah

Rabbi Abba said: "It is written: 'Thou shalt not make unto thee an image' (Ex. 20:4). This includes also the injunction: 'Thou shalt not make unto thee a new Torah which thou hast not learned from thy teacher, and knowest not to be correct. For I, the Lord thy God, am a jealous God, and I am ready to exact payment from thee in the World-to-Come.' "[1]

*Zohar Hadash, chap. 7.*

[1] The author of the Zohar Hadash may have had in mind the New Testament and the Koran. In the same fashion that an image is an imitation of God, so the new Scriptures are supposed to be an imitation of the Torah.

### 362. TORAH AND HEAVEN

The road to Heaven bears signposts based upon the Torah. Those who study the Torah will therefore be able to find their way to Heaven.

*Zohar, i, 175b.*

A new word of Torah which comes from the mouth of a man ascends heavenward and adds to the Crown of God.

*Hakdamah to Zohar, 1b.*

### The "Good" and the Three

"And she (mother of Moses) saw that he was good." (Ex. 2:2)

The Rabbis said: "Let the Good (Moses) receive the Good (Torah) from the Good (God) for the Good (Israel).

"Let the Third (Moses was the third child) receive the Three (Scripture has the Torah, Prophets and Writings) on the Third (month since the Exodus) for the sons of the Three (Patriarchs)."

*Menahot, 53, etc.*

## 363. TORAH—AND ITS ANNULMENT

Sometimes the annulment of the Torah is the establishment of the Torah.

*Menahot, 99.*

"It is time for the Lord to work; they have made void Thy Law." (Ps. 119:126)

It is obligatory to suspend the law, when, by doing so, religion will benefit. Another interpretation of the verse is: "It is obligatory to make a fence around the law when it is neglected."

*Gittin, 60.*


## 364. TORAH—DISCOURSES AND DISCUSSION

A man may not discourse on the Torah in public unless he has rehearsed his discourse three or four times.

*Tanhuma Jethro, 6.*

He who arranges comes before him who discusses.[1]

*Y. Horaiyot, 3, 5.*

[1] Master in an orderly way the laws before you commence to discuss them.

Worldly arguments usually end in quarrels and injuries, but arguments concerning the Torah usually end in mutual respect and love.

*Zohar, ii, 56a.*

Because of his very acuteness he overlooked the point.

*Erubin, 90.*

Because of thy haste in study thou hast given in argument a Halakah inappropriate to the subject.

*Shabbat, 130.*


## 365. TORAH—DUTY TO STUDY

In the School of Rabbi Ishmael it was taught that the obligation to study the Torah is not like a debt which a man can discharge by paying a fixed amount and be done with it; it is an abiding duty from which no one has authority to release himself.

*Menahot, 99b, end.*

R. Eleazar b. Harsom at harvest time chanced to pass a village which he owned. The overseer pressed him into service to do a day's work as a menial, the Rabbi being unknown to him. When the Rabbi pleaded that he was on his way to a nearby School, the overseer swore by the life of his master, R. Eleazar, that he must finish the task before departing. The Rabbi did so, and thereupon left for the School. R. Eleazar did not consider his great wealth as an excuse for neglecting the study of Torah.

*Yoma, 35b.*

### 366. TORAH—FENCE ABOUT

"Go around, go around," is said to a Nazirite (who may not drink wine). "Do not go near the vineyard."

*Shabbat, 13.*

If there is no vineyard, why is there the fence?

*Mekilta Bo.*

Make not a fence more expensive (more important) than the thing that is fenced.

*Bereshit Rabbah, 19, 3.*

The boundaries (namely, the regulations) formed by the early leaders may not be thrown down.

*Shabbat, 85.*

"Fenced with lilies" occurs in the Song of Songs (7, 3). Can these words be understood in their plain meaning? Does a man ever fence around his wheat-fields with lilies? These words must be understood symbolically, as follows: The life of Israel is fenced with the precepts of the Torah.

*Pesikta Rabbati, 10, 3.*

The Sages said: "Keep a man far removed from transgression."

*Mishnah Berakot, 1, 1.*

The men of the Great Synagogue said: "Be deliberate in giving judgment. Raise up many disciples and make a barrier about the Law."

*Abot, 1, 1.*

Rabbi Nathan said: "Read not: 'It is time for the Lord to do something (because) they have made void Thy Law' (Psalm 119:126); but, 'It is time to do something for the Lord (when) they have made void Thy Law.'"

*Mishnah Berakot, 9, 5.*

Rabban Simeon ben Gamaliel said: "A decree is not to be imposed on the public unless the majority are able to abide by it."

*Horaiyot, 3b.*

### 367. TORAH AND SCHOLARS—IMPROPER USE OF

He who speaks words of Torah opposite to those he has learned from his teacher is as if he had made for himself an image.

*Zohar, ii, 87a.*

He who makes use of the crown of the Torah shall pass away. This refers to one who employs a man who has studied the Halakot as a servant.

*Megillah, 28.*

## ACCEPT NO SERVICE FROM A SAGE

While a disciple may do small services for his master, a master may not accept actual service from a sage who is not his disciple. The following story is an illustration.

R. Simeon ben Lakish, while walking, reached a pool of muddy water. A man picked up the Rabbi and carried him across. On the way over, the Rabbi asked the man: "Hast thou studied Torah?"

"Yes," was the reply. "I have learned four orders in the Mishnah."

"Thou hast plowed thy way through four mountains and yet thou carriest me thus. Drop me at once into the water," said Resh Lakish.

The man said: "I am still a disciple compared to thee, and I wish to hear wisdom from thee."

Thereupon the Rabbi taught him a new Halakah, thus receiving the right to accept his service.

Ulla said: "Had the sage whom R. Simeon ben Lakish encountered taught four orders, he could not have accepted his services."

*Megillah, 29.*

"Do not make the Torah a crown wherewith to magnify thyself, or a spade wherewith to dig."

Hillel was accustomed to say: "He who utilizes for his own ends the crown of the Torah which he has learned passes away. Lo, thou hast learned: 'Everyone who makes a profit out of the words of the Torah drives his life out of the world.' "

*Abot, 4, 5 (in Singer, 4, 7).*

Knowledge must be pursued for its own sake. "The Crown" must not be used for sordid ends.

*Abot, 1, 13.*

## 368. TORAH—LABORING IN

If a man tell thee: "I have labored in Torah and have not mastered it," believe him not.

*Megillah, 6.*

If a man have a son who labors in Torah, God will be filled with compassion for him.

*Bereshit Rabbah, 63.*

All men are created to labor; happy is he who labors in the Torah.

*Sanhedrin, 99.*

A place has been left for me to labor in it (the Torah).

*Hullin, 7.*

He who makes himself a slave to the Torah is a free-man in the World-to-Come.

*Baba Metzia, 85.*

He who labors in the Torah may be certain that if he issues a decree others will enforce it.

*Wayyikra Rabbah, 31, 4.*

Builders are those disciples of the Sages who occupy themselves all their years in upbuilding the world.

*Shabbat, 114.*

If a man does not follow after Torah, Torah does not follow after him.

*Midrash Mishle, 2.*

A man who does not labor to acquire knowledge deserves no compassion.

*Sanhedrin, 92.*

If thou seest that Israel neglects the study of the Torah, stand up and strengthen thyself in it; thou wilt receive the reward of thine endeavour.

*Y. Berakot, end.*

If you wish to be charitable, select for your beneficence those who labor in the Torah.

*Kohelet Rabbah, 11, 1.*

Those who toil in the Torah occupy the highest rank. In the lower grade stand the prophets, and lowest in order are those who give directions through the Holy Spirit.

*Zohar, iii, 35a.*

He who toils in Torah needs no sacrifice to atone for his sins, for Torah is more valuable than sacrifice.

*Zohar, iii, 35a.*

R. Eleazar was accustomed to say: "The Torah is my field. It is my duty to plow it, to sow, to irrigate it, before I may reap. Workers in the fields arise with the sun and carry loads of fertilizer for the soil; shall I not do the same thing in my own field?"

*Shir ha-Shirim Rabbah, 1 (paraphrased).*

R. Samuel bar Nahmani said: "The Torah is my weapon. If I labor diligently to keep my weapon sharp and bright, it will be of benefit to me; if I neglect it, of what profit is it to me?"

*Pesikta Buber, 12 (paraphrased).*

R. Sidor said: "Once there was a student who memorized the Mesikta Makshirin in six months, but he did not labor at discovering the reasons for the rules and their application. A disciple of R. Simai inquired of him regarding a matter in the Mesikta, and he knew not how to make use of his learning. The inquirer remarked: 'It is as if he had never entered the portal of Torah.'"

*Y. Shabbat, 7.*

## 369. TORAH—LOVE FOR

He who loves Torah is never satisfied with Torah.

*Debarim Rabbah, 2, 23.*

### In Full Measure

R. Johanan and R. Hiyya bar Abba, while walking from Tiberias to Sepphoris, passed a field. R. Johanan remarked: "This field once belonged to me, but I sold it to support myself while I was studying Torah."

Further on the journey, R. Johanan made the same remark.

R. Hiyya remarked: "Why did you not leave yourself a little property for your old age?"

R. Johanan replied: "I sold that which was given to man after six days and bought what was given to man after forty days."

When R. Johanan died, the people declared concerning him: "If a man should give all the substance of his house on behalf of love in the measure that R. Johanan loveth the Torah, he would be utterly condemned." [1]

[1] Cf. Song of Songs, 8:7.

*Pesikta de-Rabbi Kahana, 28.*

The Sage said: "It is not thy duty to complete the work, but neither art thou free to desist from it."

*Abot, 2, 21.*

R. Jonathan said: "False is grace and vain is beauty, but a woman who feareth the Lord, she shall be praised." (Prov. 31:30)

"Grace is deceitful"—this applies to the generation of Moses. "Vain is beauty"—this refers to the generation of Hezekiah. "She shall be praised"—this refers to the generation of R. Judah ben Ilai.

Why is this? Because in the generations of Moses and Hezekiah Torah was studied amid prosperity, but in R. Judah's time six disciples had only one garment to wrap about them, and they studied amid dire need.

*Sanhedrin, 20.*

### The Source of Illumination

A pagan beheld R. Judah ben Ilai's face when it was illumined. He remarked: "Thou art either a usurer, or one who raises swine, or thou must drink too much wine."

R. Judah replied: "I am none of the three, and even the four cups which I am in duty bound to drink at Passover bring pain to my head until Shebuot. My face is illumined because I find joy in Torah."

*Kohelet Rabbah, 8.*

R. Abbahu returned from a journey with his face illumined. A student inquired: "Hast thou discovered a treasure?"

"Yes," replied the Rabbi, "I have discovered an ancient Tosefta."

*Nedarim, 49.*

### THE BEST MERCHANDISE

Ilfa and R. Johanan studied together. They spent their money and were in great distress. Ilfa proposed that they abandon study and engage in business, saying: "Let us fulfill in ourselves the promise: 'Howbeit, there shall be no needy among you.' " (Deut. 15:4)

R. Johanan remarked: "I prefer to live on what is given to me by good people, in order to continue my studies. I prefer to fulfill in myself the opposite promise: 'For the poor shall never cease out of the land.' " (Deut. 15:11)

When Ilfa returned to the study, he learned that his former comrade had been appointed Principal of the Academy. He was told: "Had you remained, you would have been appointed."

Thus R. Johanan had both increased knowledge and gained a position with high emolument. Torah is in truth the best merchandise.

*Taanit, 21, with addition.*

A man should not say: "I will study the Scriptures in order that I may be called a learned man. I will study tradition in order that I may become an elder and sit in the advanced Yeshibah"; but rather: "I will learn out of love, and honor will come to me in the end."

*Nedarim, 62a.*

## 370. TORAH—MANNER OF ACQUIRING

The Torah remains only with him who is prepared to slay himself for its sake. What does this signify? He is content to remain poor for the sake of learning, inasmuch as the poor man is accounted as dead.

*Zohar, ii, 158b: c, 279a.*

Torah requires neither comfort nor merchandising, but only study by day and by night.

*Zohar, iii, 9a.*

### THE YOKE UPON HIM

A student visited a Rabbi and said: "I am most eager for knowledge and covet a desire to know Torah well, but it does not come to pass."

The Rabbi replied: "My son, a man does not become worthy to acquire Torah unless he gives his life in its behalf; unless he dispenses with all comforts and pleasures while he strives to attain it. He must be like an ox who permits his master to place a yoke upon him, and who labors for his master without sparing his strength."

*Eliyahu Rabbah, 21.*

### FOREGOING COMFORTS

Rabban Johanan ben Zakkai had five disciples. When he died, they remained at Jabneh. Later one of them, R. Eleazar ben Arak, with his wife, went to Emmaeus to take the cure, since the water there was

healthful, and the climate pleasant. Inasmuch as he was the greatest
of the sages, he expected his comrades to move to Emmaus likewise,
in order to be with him. But they had no opportunity to do so for a
long time. R. Eleazar wished to return to Jabneh, but his wife protested, saying: "Dost thou need their instruction, or do they need
thine?"

"They need mine," he replied.

His wife continued: "Then thou shouldst remain here where the
climate benefits thy health."

Because R. Eleazar placed his health above participation in discussions of the Torah, he forgot nearly all he had learned. When finally
the Sages found an opportunity to visit him, he was unable to answer a
simple question.

We may learn from this that, unless the greatest scholar is prepared
to sacrifice his comforts in order to learn Torah, he forgets what he has
learned.

*Kohelet Rabbah, 7, amplified.*

## 371. TORAH—NEGLECT OF STUDY

In olden times a man was willing to pay a mannah of silver in order
to receive instruction in a new theme of the Torah. Nowadays, if people
are willing to give a young man a mannah of silver to learn Torah, no
youth is interested or inclines his ear to the suggestion.

*Zohar, ii, 176a.*

The Torah says: "If thou forsakest me a single day I shall forsake
thee two days."

*Y. Berakot, end.*

He who knows how to labor in Torah and does not do so is subjected
to a life of tribulation and misfortune.

*Zohar, i, 242b.*

No one is so poor as he who is ignorant of the Torah and its commandments, for this is all that can be considered as wealth.

*Zohar, ii, 93a.*

He who does not study Torah lives in a world of darkness and his
soul is drawn to the bright flame of Gehenna.

*Zohar, i, 185a.*

He who does not study Torah lacks the Holy Soul which is created
when the lips move in the study of the Torah.

*Hakdamah to Zohar, 12b.*

He who neglects the study of Torah has neglected God, for Torah
is one of the supreme manifestations of God.

*Zohar, iii, 13b.*

## Misapplied Gifts

Rabbi Jose of Meona once spoke thus: "We read: 'Hear this, O ye priests, and attend, ye House of Israel, and give ear, O House of the king, for unto you pertaineth the judgment.' (Hosea 5:1)

"God asks the priests: 'Why have you not labored in Torah? Have I not ordained twenty-four kinds of gifts for you?'

"The priests make answer: 'We have received none of them.'

"God continues: 'Ye House of Israel, why have you not given to the priests the gifts ordained for them?'

"They make answer: 'The House of the Nassi has taken all of them.'

"God then declares to the House of Nassi: 'The neglect of the Torah is due to you, and you will be judged on this account.'"

This came to the ears of Rabbi Judah Nessia, and he was greatly enraged. R. Simeon ben Lakish visited him and said: "The Roman governor receives with a smile criticism directed against him which he hears at the theatre or on the lips of a clown at the circus; yet you become enraged when one merely repeats a Biblical verse and applies it to you."

*Bereshit Rabbah, 80.*


## 372. TORAH—SEARCH FOR

He who toils in Torah and discovers in it new meanings that are true contributes new Torah which is treasured by the congregation of Israel.

*Zohar, i, 243a.*


## The Function of Stories

The Torah consists of a body, namely, the commandments, and of a garment, namely, the stories. The Torah is like wine and requires a vessel. For this reason there are stories in the Torah. The Sages search out both the wine and the body; they are not satisfied either with the vessel or the garment alone.

*Zohar, iv, 152a.*


## 373. TORAH—RESPECT AND DISRESPECT FOR

He who despises the Torah is himself despised.

*Bemidbar Rabbah, 8, 3.*

A reader in the Torah was leaning his body against the post of the Bimah. R. Samuel b. Nahmani protested, saying: "As it was given in fear and awe, so shall it be read."

*Tanhuma Buber, Wayyera.*

Torah does not rise for her son. If a disciple is studying and his teacher passes, he need not rise. His teacher who is not at the moment studying Torah is only the son of the Torah, but the disciple who is engaged in study is Torah itself.

*Y. Bikkurim, 3, 3.*

The sixth person called up to the reading of the Torah on Sabbath is regarded as the most honored.

*Zohar, iv, 164b.*

When do the unlearned lose their respect for Torah? In the hour when the learned are guilty of disrespect for it.

*Ruth Rabbah, 1.*

### THOSE WHO DESPISE

Who is signified in the phrase: "Because he hath despised the word of the Lord" (Numb. 15:31)?

He who speaks words of Torah in an unclean place; also he who is a scoffer.

R. Joseph said: "This signifies one who says: 'What did the Rabbis do for us? They study merely for their own benefit.'"

Rabba said: "This signifies, for example, Benjamin, the physician, who declares: 'Of what use are the Rabbis? They do not permit the eating of a crow, nor do they forbid the eating of a dove.' When a case from the physician's home with reference to doubtful Kashrut was laid before the Rabbi, he smilingly said to the inquirers: 'Do you not now see that you are awaiting my decision as to whether I shall permit you the crow or forbid you the dove?'"

*Y. Sanhedrin, 6; Sanhedrin, 99.*

A pagan wished to ridicule the ceremonies of Judaism. Knowing that a non-Jew may not eat of the paschal lamb, he disguised himself as a Jew and partook of it. He came to R. Judah ben Beteirah, who lived outside of Palestine and was not required to go to Jerusalem for the Passover feast, and said to him: "Your Torah reads that no stranger shall eat of it, yet I partook of the best."

The Rabbi replied: "And have they given you a share from the fat portion of the tail?"

"No," answered the pagan.

"Then ask for it next year," continued the Rabbi.

When the pagan did so, they said to him: "But this portion belongs to the altar! Who has taught you to ask for it?"

The man replied: "R. Judah ben Beteirah."

They investigated and discovered that he was a pagan. He was heavily fined for ridiculing the Jewish religion.

*Pesahim, 4.*

## 374. TORAH AND ITS STUDENTS

He whose occupation is the study of Torah is a free-man in both Worlds.

*Zohar, i, 132a.*

The good city depends upon the men who study Torah, and not upon the men who possess power and wealth.

*Zohar, i, 151a.*

A student of Torah is like a seed planted within a fertile lump of earth: if it sprouts, it grows.

*Taanit, 4.*

One student is sharpened by a fellow-student.

*Bereshit Rabbah, 69, 2.*

The voice of the student of the Torah is a ladder on which the Angels ascend and descend.

*Zohar, iv, 230b; Raia Mehemna.*

He who studies Torah is not a withered tree, but a tree planted by streams of water.

*Zohar, iv, 202a.*

If he be a worthy disciple, bring to him when he is thirsty, living water (Torah).

*Taanit, 7.*

If he be a worthy disciple, let thy words of Torah flow forth from thy lips; if not, let them be reserved for thyself only.

*Taanit, 7.*

He who withholds a Halakah from a disciple is as one who has robbed him of his father's heritage.

*Sanhedrin. 91.*

Why are students of the Torah in the habit of shaking their bodies to and fro while studying? Because the Torah is like a flame which never remains still.

*Zohar, iv, 218b.*

Much have I learned from my teacher; more from my comrades, and most from my disciples.

*Taanit, 7.*

"There shall not be in thee a childless man," that is to say, a man without disciples; "and a barren one," that is to say, one whose prayer gains no fruition.

*Berakot, 44.*

## SYNAGOGUES OR STUDIES?

Rab Hisda said: "It is written: 'The Lord loveth the gates of Zion more than all the dwellings of Jacob' (Psalm 87:2) This signifies: 'The Lord loveth more the gates distinguished by learning than all the synagogues in Jacob.'"

*Berakot, 8.*

Rabbi Hama bar Hanina and R. Oshaya, the Elder, were walking past the synagogues in Lud. R. Hama said: "How much money have my fathers devoted to these edifices!"

R. Oshaya replied: "How many souls have they caused to be lost here! Think of all the people who could have studied Torah if they had received support from thy fathers!

*Y. Shekalim, 515.*

R. Abin built new doors for the great synagogue. When he met R. Mani, he exclaimed: "See what I have done!"

R. Mani replied: "It is written: 'For Israel hath forgotten his Maker and buildeth palaces' (Hosea 8:14). Think of the many students thou couldst support with the money thou hast spent on these doors!"

*Y. Shekalim, 515.*

## 375. TORAH AND ITS STUDY

A man should study and perform Mitzwot even with an ulterior motive, for in the end he will do so for the sake of the Lord.

*Pesahim, 50.*

When a man has been buried, the first question addressed to him in the World-to-Come is: "Have you studied the Torah?"

*Midrash ha-Neelam, i, 127b.*

May my lot be among those who request that the session be opened at the academy, not among those who request that the session be adjourned.

*Shabbat, 118.*

He who merely studies at stated times breaks the covenant.

*Y. Berakot, 9.*

If we are to be so thorough, we may not be able to learn.

*Erubin, 48.*

Learn your Mishnah, and then attend the academy.

*Keritot, 6.*

To study the Torah is more important than to honor parents.

*Megillah, 16.*

The study of Torah is granted only to those who obtain sustenance without labor, like those who eat the manna or partake of the Terumah.
*Mekilta Beshallah, 17.*

He who exalts himself over his knowledge of Torah ends by being abashed; he who abases himself for the sake of learning Torah ends by being exalted.
*Abot de-R. Nathan, 11, 2.*

A matron asked R. Jose: "Why is the letter 'Lamed' higher than all others?"
He replied: "It is the herald saying 'Lamed!' (learn), and a herald is stationed on a high place."
*Pesikta Rabbati, 22, 2.*

He who must observe the law is required to learn the law.
*Yebamot, 109.*

In the future the nobles of Judah shall learn Torah in the theatres and circuses of Rome.
*Megillah, 6.*

A man should learn Torah at the place [1] which his heart desires most.
*Abodah Zarah, 19.*

[1] Or, in the subject.

When a man departs from the Halakah to study the Scriptures, he no longer has peace of mind.
*Hagigah, 10.*

### Elijah Studied Constantly

R. Samuel, the son of Emi, says: "The words of the Torah should be studied mornings and evenings, and this is the proof of it: Elijah, his memory be blessed, would study the Torah mornings and evenings, while the ravens supplied him with bread and meat, as the verse says: 'And the ravens brought him bread and meat in the evening, and he drank the waters of the brook.' "
*Midrash Samuel, 5, 2.*

When a person studies the Torah during the night, a thread of kindness is spread out for him during the day.
*Zohar, i, 194b.*

Those who learn for the sake of learning find the Torah sweet; those who learn for ulterior purposes find it bitter.
*Zohar, iv, 229b.*

He who studies and does not repeat his lessons is as one who plants and does not enjoy the fruit.
*Sanhedrin, 99.*

A man should first learn Torah and then undertake research in it.
*Berakot, 63.*

Be not afraid of a work which has no end (such as learning Torah).
*Abot de-R. Nathan, 27, 3.*

He who learns by himself is very inferior to one who learns from a teacher.
*Ketubot, 111.*

He who suffers hunger in this world on account of his devotion to the study of Torah shall be sated in the World-to-Come.
*Sanhedrin, 110.*

Rabbi Simeon ben Yohai said: "To occupy oneself exclusively with the study of Scriptures is a way, but not the true way."
*Y. Shabbat, 15c.*

"Doing depends upon learning, not learning upon doing."
At a conference of Rabbis at Lydda, the question was propounded: "Is study the greater thing, or doing?"
The decision was unanimous in favor of study, on the ground that study leads to doing.
*Kiddushin, 40b.*

Rabbi Meir advised: "Be not much engaged in business, and busy yourself with the Torah, and be lowly in spirit before every man. If you give yourself a vacation from study, you will find many reasons for wasting your time; but, if you study industriously, He has a great reward to give you."
*Abot, 4, 10.*

### RAISING THE VOICE

Beruriah, the wife of Rabbi Meir, noticed a student studying in silence. She declared: "We read: 'Ordered in all things and sure' (II Samuel, 23:5). If the Torah is studied properly with all thy faculties, it is sure to be remembered."

Samuel said to Rab Judah: "Shinenna (diligent student), open thy mouth and read, open they mouth and learn, so that thou mayest live long and remember well."
*Erubin, 54.*

### THE POOR, THE RICH AND THE WICKED

When the poor man, the rich man and the wicked stand in Judgment, the poor man will be asked: "Why have you not learned and obeyed the Torah?"

If he says: "I was forced to earn a livelihood," he is asked: "Art thou poorer than Hillel, who studied amid the direst poverty?"

If the rich man, in answer to the same question, says: "I was too concerned with my many affairs of business," he is told: "Art thou richer than Rabbi Eliezer ben Harsom, who owned a thousand villages but left the management to others that he might study day and night?"

If the wicked man in reply declares: "My passion was over-strong within me," they say to him: "Was it stronger within thee than within the lonely youth, Joseph, the son of Jacob? If one mortal can conquer the circumstances of his life and attain goodness, others can do so, for Joseph was human like his fellow-beings."

*Yoma, 35.*

## 376. TORAH—TRADITIONAL, ORAL LAW

The Torah was given to Moses chiefly in writing, a small portion in oral form.

*Gittin, 60.*

Torah that is not a tradition is not Torah.

*Y. Shabbit, 19, 6.*

As the sea has little waves between the large ones, so the Torah has many details of Oral Law affecting commandments of the Written Law.

*Shekalim, 6, 1.*

Two Torahs were given to Israel—one in written and one in oral form.

*Sifra Behukotai.*

He who abides by the precepts of the Sages is called modest and holy.

*Yebamot, 20; Niddah, 12.*

When the wall of the vineyard fell, the vineyard was destroyed.[1]
*Abot de-R. Nathan, 24.*

[1] The Traditional Law is the wall.

When Moses received the Oral Law, he asked permission to write it down. God replied: "A time will come when the Gentiles will translate the written Torah and say: 'We are the true Israel, we are the true sons of God.' And then Israel will say: 'We are the keepers of God's secret Law, and the people to whom God has entrusted His Tradition are his true sons.' "

*Pesikta Rabbati, Piska, 5.*

Moses was amazed when it was vouchsafed to him to listen to Rabbi Akiba [1] discovering in his laws meanings of which he had never thought.

*Menahot, 29b.*

[1] See below.

When Moses received his first revelation from God, he received at the same time the power to look into the future. He observed the Sanhedrin discussing the Torah, and he beheld R. Akiba discover within it new laws without number. Moses stepped backwards, saying: "I cannot accept Thy mission, O Lord, for I do not understand what I hear and see."

The angels came and turned his face toward other Sanhedrin courts. He heard them say: "Whence comes this Law? It is a tradition received from Moses at Sinai."

Moses then became calm, and said: "I accept my mission and I shall go."

*Midrash Abkir in Yalkut to Exodus, 3.*

It is believed that "the Holy One Blessed Be He entered into a covenant with Israel only by virtue of the Oral Tradition."

*Gittin, 60b.*

A Rabbi narrated: "While travelling, a man met me and continued on the way with me. He said: 'Rabbi, it is my belief that only the Torah was given on Mount Sinai, but not the Mishnah.'

"I replied: 'Nay, my son, both were given to Moses on Mount Sinai. Are you open to reason?'

" 'Yes,' he answered.

"I said: 'When you recite a definite number of benedictions in the Amidah, is the number inscribed in the Torah? When you hold Services, is the procedure definitely inscribed in the Torah? In every Mitzwah you must refer to the Traditional Law concerning the manner of its performance. Therefore, the Traditional or Oral Law must have originated at Mount Sinai.' "

*Eliyahu Zuta, 2.*

The Biblical words, "An eye for an eye" were understood in the light of the interpretation put into them by the Oral Tradition, that the accused was obligated to pay the money value of the injured eye or limb.

*Baba Kamma, 84a.*

## 377. TORAH—TREE OF LIFE

If thou studiest Torah, thou art joined to the Tree of Life. If thou dost not study Torah, thou art joined to the Tree of Death.

*Zohar, i, 152b.*

When Torah is studied by mortals, the Tree of Life remains on earth. If ever a time should come when the Torah is no longer studied, the Tree of Life will depart and leave behind it a world that is dead.

*Zohar, i, 151a.*

The Torah gives life to him who makes use of its light.

*Ketubot, 111.*

The laws of the Torah were given that men should live by them, not that they should die by them.

*Abodah Zarah, 27b.*

When a passenger on the deck of a ship falls into the sea, the captain throws to him a line, crying: "Grasp it firmly and slacken not thy hold upon it at the peril of thy life!"

By the same token, amid the troubled seas of his earthly voyage, man should cling to the precepts of Torah and thereby remain attached to God. For thus he may truly live.

*Tanhuma Buber to Numbers, p. 74.*

The Law of God perpetually in man's mind guides him on his way, guards him in his sleep and converses with him when he wakes; it guides him through this world, guards him in the hour of death; it will be with him when he awakes in the days of the Messiah, and it will converse with him in the World-to-Come.

*Sifre Deut., 34, after Prov. 6, 22.*

Rabbi Eleazar ben Pedat said: "One should not travel in the company of an ignorant man, for it is said: 'For it is thy life and the length of thy days' (Deut. 30:20). The unlearned man has no surety for his own life (since he has no desire to study the Law which would prolong his life); how much less then will he regard the life of his neighbor?"

*Pesahim, 49b.*

### THE FOX AND THE FISHES

Papus ben Judah one day found Rabbi Akiba teaching the Torah in public, though this was prohibited by the Roman government.

"Art thou not afraid of the government?" inquired Papus.

"I will tell you a parable," replied the Rabbi. "Once while walking beside the river, a fox saw some fishes darting distractedly to and fro in the stream. 'From what, pray, are you fleeing?' the fox inquired.

"'From the nets,' they replied.

"'Why, then,' rejoined the fox, 'do you not try the dry land with me, where you and I can live together?'

"'Surely,' exclaimed the fishes, 'thou art not he of whom we have heard so much as the most cunning of animals. If we have cause to fear where it is natural for us to live, how much more reason have we to do so where we needs must die!'

"Just so," continued Akiba, "is it with us who study the Torah, in which it is written: 'For that is thy life, and the length of thy days' (Deut. 30:20); for, if we suffer while we study the Torah, how much more shall we suffer if we neglect it!"

*Berakot, 61b.*

### 378. TORAH—TRUTH OF

A matron said to Rabbi Jose: "How was it possible for a youth of seventeen like Joseph, when approached by Zelikah,[1] to resist the allurement of a beautiful young woman? This seems to me unnatural."

[1] Wife of Potiphar.

The Rabbi took out a Greek Pentateuch and read to her the story of Reuben and the story of Judah. He remarked: "You see from these that the Torah did not hide the fact when the passions were not resisted. You must, therefore, believe the Torah when it said that Joseph did resist, difficult though it was."

*Bereshit Rabbah, 87.*

## 379. TRADESMAN—HONEST

Once the tradesman has made up his mind to take a certain price for his goods, he may not raise it if he has the chance.

*Kiddushin, 30b.*

Nor may the tradesman demand twice the amount of his debt, in order that he may the more easily recover the true amount.

*Shebuot, 31a.*

Overreaching of every sort the tradesman should abominate. His lightest word, his yea and his nay, should be righteous.

*Sifra, 36.*

## 380. TRANSGRESSION (See Sin)

Transgression defiles even when it is unintentional; for it taints the soul—the soul that has lived in Heaven.

*Tanhuma, 4, 2.*

He that transgresses, though it be in secret, thrusts God away from him.

*Hagigah, 16a.*

## 381. TRAVEL

### The Road of God

When a man travels a road, let him make it the road of God, and let him invite God to be his companion.

*Zohar, iii, 87b.*

Elijah said to Rab Salla, the Hasid: "Grow not angry and thou wilt not sin; abstain from drunkenness and thou wilt not transgress. When thou leavest on a journey, pray to Thy Maker, and then take thy departure."

*Berakot, 29.*

When Rabbi Meir saw a man go on a journey alone, he would say: "Greetings to thee, O Thou who courtest death." When he saw two walking forth, he would say: "Greetings to you, O ye who court quarrels." If he saw three departing, he would say: "Greetings, O men of peace."

*Kohelet Rabbah, 4.*

## The Proper Season

R. Nathan, brother of R. Hiyya bar Abba, was about to embark upon a sea journey in the closing days of summer. He asked his brother to offer prayer for his safe travel. R. Hiyya replied: "If you wish to travel safely, do not sail in the season of winds and rains. If you halt to bind your Lulab, for Sukkot, remain there until the weather becomes clear."

*Kohelet Rabbah, 3.*

R. Joshua, the son of R. Tanhum ben R. Hiyya, wished to sail from an Asia Minor port in the days between Sukkot and Hanukah. A matron warned him: "Is it wise to sail in these days?" He gave no heed. His father appeared to him in a dream, saying: "If you sail, the deep will be your grave." R. Joshua ignored this warning also. The ship sank and he with it.

*Y. Berakot, 3.*

R. Jose ben Jose was travelling on a boat and saw a passenger tie a rope about his waist with the intention of bathing. The Rabbi forbade him to do so. The man protested: "But I wish to eat and I am unclean." The Rabbi replied: "Eat as you are, but do not bathe." When they reached port, R. Jose said: "Until now you were permitted to eat without cleansing yourself. But here you must first immerse before eating."

*Y. Berakot, 3.*

## 382. TREES

A golden vine was stationed outside the gates of the Sanctuary. Rabbi Aha said that when King Solomon built the Temple, he fashioned and designed within the sacred walls all types of trees. As soon as the golden vine outside the gates brought forth its fruit, the trees within the Temple walls produced their beautiful fruit.

*Y. Yoma, 4, 4.*

## 383. TRESPASSING

Rabbi Yannai's tree extended over the public road. When it was called to his attention that the branches interfered with the passing of the camels, he ordered that it be chopped down.

*Baba Batra, 60.*

R. Jonathan's tree sent its branches into the field of a Roman. He commanded that it be chopped down.

*Y. Baba Batra, 2.*

Rabbah b. R. Huna owned a number of trees on a river shore. Certain boatmen came to him and asked him to chop them down so that they might have a landing place. He refused, however, to do so, saying: "Above my property and below are trees belonging to a government official. If he should chop down his trees, you will have a landing place on this side of the river. But if he should refuse, would you take the trouble to squeeze your way into the empty place in the middle? Would you not rather continue to the opposite shore?"

*Baba Metzia, 108.*

Rabbi Simeon ben Yohai and his son, Eleazar, visited Rabbi Phinehas ben Jair. The host was delighted and invited Rabbi Eleazar to make a few remarks. The latter responded, saying: "We find that the death of Aaron's two eldest sons was due to the fact that they presumed to offer incense before the Lord, a duty belonging solely to their father. By the same token, if I should expound Torah in the presence of such great authorities as my host and my father, I, too, would be guilty of trespassing upon the rights of my elders, and would deserve punishment."

*Zohar, iii, 59.*

## 384. TRIBULATION AND SUFFERING

He whose merits outbalance his demerits receives tribulations in this world in order to achieve complete bliss in the World-to-Come.

*Kiddushin, 39.*

Israel does not turn to good without chastisement.

*Menahot, 53.*

Bodily sufferings purge away sin.

*Berakot, 5a.*

He who suffers will not see purgatory.

*Erubin, 41b.*

If they had tortured Hananiah, Mishael, and Azariah, they would have bowed to the idol, for torture is worse than death.

*Ketubot, 33.*

Three have a great share in chastisements: the Patriarchs, the generation which witnessed the persecution of Israel's faith, and the King Messiah.

*Midrash Tehillim, 16, 4.*

Tribulation brings satiety to a man, and he feels no desire to eat.

*Midrash Tehillim, 42, 3.*

Grievous is it for the strong man who must ask the aid of the weaker; for the generation led by a woman; for the living man who asks death; and for the seeing man who must request aid from the blind.

*Midrash Tehillim, 22, 20.*

There is no tribulation which overtakes a man without some benefit to others.

*Bereshit Rabbah, 38, 10.*

As salt sweetens meat, so do chastisements sweeten man's every sin.

*Berakot, 5.*

"On the day of prosperity be joyful; but on the day of adversity, consider." [1] (Eccl. 7, 14)

R. Abba b. Kahana said: "When the day of adversity is at hand, consider how to perform deeds of repentance, so that adversity may depart from you."

R. Tanhum b. Hiyya said: "In the day of prosperity, share thy comrade's prosperity, and on the day of adversity, consider how to aid him."

R. Aha said: "If thou wilt make thy day in this world a good day by virtue of learning and the performance of good, it will happen on the Judgment Day that thou shalt gaze upon the punishment then meted out, but thou shalt not be numbered among the punished."

*Pesikta, Buber, p. 191.*

[1] "Consider" can also mean "gaze upon."

R. Simeon ben Lakish said: "The term covenant is used in connection with salt (Lev. 2:13), and in connection with the curses (Deut. 28:69). From this we may learn that just as salt removes the impurities from meat, seasons and sweetens it, even so do sufferings penetrate and purify the human body."

*Berakot, 5a.*

R. Jose ben Judah said: "Precious to God are chastisements, for the Glory of God lights upon those to whom chastisements come, as it is said: 'The Lord thy God (in person) chastises thee.' (Deut. 8:5)."

*Sifre Deut., 32.*

Why is Israel likened unto an olive? Because as the olive does not yield its oil until it is pressed, so the people of Israel do not repent until they are afflicted.

*Menahot, 53b.*

When Rabbi Eliezer ben Hyrcanus was sick, four Rabbis visited him. Three of them praised him to his face, saying that he was of more worth to Israel than the rain, the sun, and parents. For these are of use only in this world, whereas a great teacher is of value in the World-to-Come.

Rabbi Akiba said: "O Master, how good are chastisements for a man!" He was asked to explain his words. He said: "We find that Hezekiah instructed every child of Judah in the Law and in godliness. Did he then forget his own son, Manasseh, who proved to be so wicked? Nay, he taught him more than the others, but instruction does not always avail to keep a man on the pathway of goodness. And what caused Manasseh to repent and return to God? Chastisements—as it is related in II Chronicles 33:11-13. From this thou art to learn the value of affliction."

*Sanhedrin, 101a.*

Rabbi Akiba said: "A man should rejoice in chastisements more than in good fortune; for if a man lives in good fortune all his life, his sin is not remitted. How is it remitted? Through chastisements."

Rabbi Nehemiah said: "Precious are sufferings; for as sacrifices atone, so do sufferings atone. They are an even better atonement than sacrifices, for sacrifices are of a man's property, but sufferings touch his very person."

*Sifre Deut., 32.*

The Rabbis represent God as saying to man: "With thy very wounds will I heal thee."

*Wayyikra Rabbah, 28.*

Those whom God afflicts bear His name.

*Midrash Tehillim to Ps. 94:1.*

Let men rejoice in suffering, for "whom the Lord loveth He chasteneth"—chasteneth and purifieth in this life.

*Sifre to Deut., 4, 5.*

If thou desirest life, hope for affliction.

*Midrash Tehillim to Ps. 16:11.*

## 385. TRUSTWORTHINESS

He who is trustworthy brings God's blessings through his deeds.

*Shemot Rabbah, 51.*

He who steals men's confidence is chief among thieves.

*Mekilta Mishpatim.*

Be a good and trustworthy man.

*Berakot, 16.*

Even when Jerusalem stumbled, men of trustworthiness were to be found in her midst.

*Shabbat, 119.*

## 386. TRUTH AND FALSEHOOD

Truth is heavy; therefore few wear it.

*Midrash Samuel on Abot, 4.*

People say: "The liar narrates that in Media he saw a camel dance on a pail."

*Yebamot, 45.*

What is the origin of the saying: "Falsehood hath no feet?" It lies is the story of the serpent. He was the first to tell a falsehood, and was cursed to go upon his belly.

*Tikkune Zohar, T. 22, p. 97a.*

Everything has been created by God, except falsehood.

*Eliyahu Zuta, 3.*

The seal of God is truth.

*Shabbat, 55.*

Let thy ears hear, what thy mouth speaketh.

*Y. Berakot, 2, 4.*

There is no salvation in falsehood.

*Ruth Rabbah, 5, 13.*

Nowadays falsehood stands erect and truth lies prostrate on the ground.

*Zohar, ii, 188.*

All lies are forbidden unless they are spoken for the sake of making peace.

*Baraita Perek ha-Shalom.*

This is the penalty for the liar: even when he tells the truth, no one believes him.

*Sanhedrin, 89b.*

No man should talk one way with his lips and think another way in his heart.

*Baba Metzia, 49.*

Truth is hard to impart, but falsehood stands behind the ear.

*Yalkut Shimeoni to Pentateuch, 3.*

The Prophets know that God is fond of truth, and they do not flatter Him.

*Y. Berakot, 7, 3.*

If you hear it said: "Your friend has died," believe! "That he has become wealthy," do not believe!

*Gittin, 30.*

God hates the man who says one thing with his mouth and another with his mind.

*Pesahim, 113b.*

A liar is excluded from the presence of the Shekinah.

*Sotah, 42a.*

Rabbi Jose ben Judah said: "Let your 'Yes' be honest and your 'No' be honest."

*Baba Metzia, 49a.*

Teach thy tongue to say: "I do not know," lest thou invent something and be trapped.

*Berakot, 4a.*

Stealing a man's thought (deception) is the worst form of theft.
*Tos. Baba Kamma, 7, 8.*

## TRUTH PREVENTS CRIMES

A young man came into the presence of Simeon ben Shetah and said: "I find it difficult to control my evil inclinations. What shall I do?"

Simeon replied: "Swear to me that you will always tell the truth. Thus you will be cured." The youth uttered the vow, but wondered at the lightness of Simeon's injunction.

Once, however, he entered a neighbor's home in her absence and stole her valuables. A few moments later he bethought himself: "If all the neighbors are questioned, I will be included, and I swore to tell the truth." He hastened to restore the stolen goods, and then appreciated the wisdom of Simeon's counsel.

*Midrash ha-Katzer in Rab Pealim.*

## THE KOHEN IN THE VINEYARD

Rabbi Simeon ben Lakish saw a man working in a vineyard in the seventh year. He said to him: "I know that thou art a Kohen. How is it that thou workest during the prohibited season?"

The man answered: "I merely am trimming the vines because I need the wood to tie my olive-press."

The Rabbi said: "Thy heart knows whether it is to bind or to loosen." [1]

*Sanhedrin, 25.*

[1] R. Simeon's reply became a popular proverb . . . A Kohen is usually learned in the Law and cannot plead ignorance as an excuse.

## PROTECTION AGAINST FALSE JUDGMENT

When two disputants come before the judge, one richly, the other poorly dressed, the judge should instruct the rich man to don a poor garment. Thus the other litigant will not feel that the judge is giving credence to a man of importance rather than to himself.

The poor man oftentimes becomes confused before the judge, and does not present his case effectively. The judge should guard against this possibility.

*Shebuot, 31.*

## THE DECEIVER DECEIVED

When Jacob perceived that his bride was Leah, he exclaimed angrily: "Thou deceiver, and daughter of a deceiver! Several times I called thee Rachel and thou didst make answer."

Leah responded: "Thy father called to thee: 'Art thou my son Esau?' And thou didst make answer!"

*Bereshit Rabbah, 70.*

### 387. UNDERSTANDING, INTELLIGENCE, KNOWLEDGE

He who has understanding has everything.

*Nedarim, 41.*

If thou hast acquired understanding, thou lackest naught. If thou hast no understanding, what hast thou?[1]

*Nedarim, 41.*

[1] Or knowledge.

Without understanding, the world cannot stand.

*Otiot de R. Akiba, Beth.*

Great is understanding! It is for understanding that we first pray in the Amidah.[1]

*Berakot, 33.*

[1] Singer, p. 114.

A man who has gold, but no knowledge—what has he?

*Kohelet Rabbah, 1, 6.*

A man should first learn much, and then seek to understand it profoundly.

*Shabbat, 63.*

Three things broaden the mind: a fine dwelling, a fine woman, and fine furnishings.

*Berakot, 57.*

A man cannot understand Torah unless he has stumbled in it.

*Gittin, 43.*

He who understands the why and wherefore of what he learns does not forget it quickly.

*Y. Berakot, 5, 1.*

If you understand the old lessons, you will understand the new.

*Berakot, 40.*


### 388. UNHAPPINESS

All the days of a poor man's life are unhappy. Who is this poor man? He who is delicate; he who is compassionate; he who has little intelligence; he who is hungry for learning.

*Baba Batra, 145. (Paraphrased.)*

There are three types of men whose life is not worth living: he who must eat at another's table; he whose wife rules over him, and he whose body is racked by pain.

*Betzah, 32.*

There are three types of men whose life is not worth living: he who is prone to rage; he who is too soft-hearted, and he who is too fastidious.

*Pesahim, 113.*

### The Greater Punishment

A Jew became tired of life and wrote to Hadrian: "If thou hatest the circumcised, why dost thou not persecute the Ishmaelites? If thou hatest those who keep the Sabbath, why dost thou not persecute the Samaritans? It is not religion, but hatred of Israel that moves thee. May the God of Israel repay thee for this!"

Hadrian sent for the Jew and said: "Thou deservest death, but I am eager to know why thou courtest it."

The Jew replied: "Because I hoped thou wouldst save my soul from three worries."

"And what are they?" asked the Emperor.

"My soul wishes food and cannot obtain it; my wife and my child also are in want."

"Let him go," commanded the cruel ruler. "Life will be a greater punishment for him than death."

*Kohelet Rabbah, 2.*

## 389. UNIVERSALISM, UNIVERSALITY

### Family Disputes

A pagan asked Rabbi Joshua ben Karha this question: "You profess to adopt the ruling of the majority with respect to your Law. We are the majority. Why do you not adopt our religion?"

Rabbi Joshua said: "Have you sons?"

"Yes," answered the pagan. "But I am tormented by their conduct. When we sit at a meal, each one says grace in the name of a different divinity, and they quarrel among themselves because of this."

"Well," answered the Rabbi. "Suppose you decide among your own family the religion you are to accept, and afterwards come to us."

*Wayyikra Rabbah, 4.*

Every benediction to Him as "the Lord our God" must add "King of the Universe" to emphasize the universality of the Deity.

*Cf. Berakot, 40b.*

When God resolved to create Adam, the father of the human race, he took the dust from which man was made, not from Palestine, mark you, the land of the Jew; not from Jerusalem, the Holy City; not from Zion, the site of the Holy Temple; but He took a little earth from every corner of the globe, from East and West, from North and South. Why? The Rabbis answered: "So that in the future no nation shall say, from my earth was Adam created; so that no people may say, we are greater, we are worthier than our neighbor, for Adam had his birth here."

*Sanhedrin, 38a.*

## 390. UNIVERSE

God fills the universe just as the soul fills the body of man.

*Berakot, 10a.*

Abraham was absorbed by the vastness, the orderliness of the universe. Studying the skies, he thought at first that the sun must be the power to regulate it, and to direct it all. But evening came, and again looking at the skies he saw that the sun had disappeared. Perhaps the moon, he then thought, was this directing force. But again, on the morrow, he observed that the moon was no more and that the sun had again taken its place. Thus contemplating the cosmos, he came to the conclusion that there must be a Power higher and above all these powers visible to the eye, who rules and guides the order of the universe.

*Ma'aseh Abraham, pp. 27-29.*

"He is One; the only God of all the universe! But He is also our God, in the sense that a unique, a special relationship has been created by Israel and God to accept Him as its ideal of the holy life!"

*Sifre Deut., p. 73a.*

R. Isaac said that the Bible should really have begun with the 12th chapter of Exodus, where it tells of the first Mizwah or duty of the Israelite, and not with the story of creation; but that God does so for the specific purpose of proving the Jew's right to inherit Canaan, since all the world is God's and God can assign portions of it to whomsoever He wills.

*Rashi to Genesis, 1:1; cf. also Genesis Rabbah, 1:3.*

"With what does God occupy Himself at night?" it is asked:
The teacher answers: "He rides on the wings of one of His swift Cherubs and visits the eighteen thousand worlds that are His."

*Abodah Zarah, 3b.*

## 391. USURY (INTEREST)

Usury is like slow-working poison.

*Shemot Rabbah, 31, 6.*

Is it not enough that the poor man is poor? Must thou also, O lender of money, seek to exact interest from him? [1]

*Shemot Rabbah, 31, 12.*

[1] If he must borrow to pay taxes, he would therefore be forced to pay a double tax.

### PUMPKINS LARGE AND SMALL

"Take thou no interest or increase." (Lev. 25, 36)
Rab Kahana entered the Academy while Rab was completing his discourse. He heard Rab mention the word "pumpkins" several times,

and asked the other Disciples regarding it. They answered: "Thus spoke Rab: 'If a man goes to a gardener and wishes to buy small pumpkins for a zuz, and the gardener says: "wait until later and I will give you just as many large pumpkins for your zuz," the buyer may accept the proposition only if there are already large pumpkins in the garden. But if they are all still small, he is forbidden to accept the larger size later under the market price.' "

*Baba Metzia, 64.*

Mark the blind folly of the usurer. If a man were to call him a scoundrel he would fight him to the death. And yet he takes pen, ink and paper, and in the presence of witnesses solemnly writes himself down a rogue, and a denier of Israel's God.

*Baba Metzia, 71a.*

The usurer breaks all the commandments; his sin is as flagrant as murder.

*Shemot Rabbah, 31.*

If a man borrow of another, and merely because he is his debtor, greets him in the street, he does a wrong act. He is guilty of paying usury in words.

*Baba Metzia, 75b.*

Usury is like the bite of a poisoned snake; it is a small thing in itself, but its deadly effects are far-reaching.

*Shemot Rabbah, 31.*

Far better that a man should take a small sum and trade with it, and earn his bread with difficulty, than get rich by money-lending. There is a taint clinging to the trade which no one who values comeliness and dignity of life will ignore.

*Wayyikra, Rabbah, 3.*

## 392. THE VOICE

"God's voice at Sinai was heard in all languages."

*Shabbat, 88b.*

Rabbah bar Rab Huna said: "A householder should give his orders to hirelings in a gentle voice. This will assure obedience."

*Shabbat, 94.*

Three voices gladden the heart: the voice of the Torah, the voice of rain, and the voice of coins.

*Otzar Midrashin, p. 168.*
*Midrash Hupat Eliyahu.*

Every word and every outgoing of a voice occupies a space within the Universe, and the Lord utilizes it as He wishes.

*Zohar, ii, 100b.*

When the last Prophets, Haggai, Zechariah and Malachi died, the Holy Spirit ceased out of Israel. But nevertheless it was granted Israel to hear communications from God by means of a Voice (Bat Kol).

*Tosefta Sotah, 13, 2.*

Hiyya, the nephew of Rabbi Eleazar ha-Kappar possessed a fine voice. Whenever he chanced to be in his uncle's synagogue, the Rabbi would say: "Go to the Ammud (the Reader's Desk), my son, and honor the Lord with the gift He has presented unto Thee." [1]

*Pesikta de Rabbi Kahana, 11.*

[1] Lead the prayers.

### THE HANDS OF ESAU

"The voice is the voice of Jacob, and the hands are the hands of Esau." (Gen. 27, 22)

Said Rabbi Berechiah: "When the voice of the Jews is occupied with profane learning or complaints, the hands of Esau are strong against them. But when the voice of the Jews utters words of Torah and prayer, the hands of Esau have no power against them."

*Bereshit Rabbah, 65.*

The Echo of the Voice [1] said: "The dicta of both the schools of Hillel and Shammai are words of the living God, but that of the school of Hillel is the norm (Halakah)."

*Y. Berakot, 3b.*

[1] Bat Kol.

A ram has but one voice while alive, and seven after he is dead. How is this so? His horns make two trumpets; his hip-bones two pipes; his skin can be extended into a drum; his large intestines can yield strings for the lyre, and the smaller cords for the harp.

*Mishnah Kinnim, 3, 6.*

R. Jose narrated: I was once walking by myself, and I entered a ruin in Jerusalem to offer prayer within it. Elijah of Blessed Memory appeared and waited for me at the entrance. When I had finished and was about to depart, he greeted me and said: "My son, why hast thou entered this ruin?"

"To pray," I responded.

"Why hast thou not prayed on the road," he asked.

"Because I feared that passers-by would disturb me."

Elijah answered: "Thou shouldst have offered a short prayer."

Thus did I learn three things from him: one should not enter a ruin (since it is dangerous and suspicious); one may pray on a road; he who prays on a road may offer a short prayer.

Elijah inquired from me: "Hast thou heard aught?"

I replied: "I heard an Echo of a Voice, moaning like a dove, and saying: 'Woe is Me that I have destroyed My House, burned My Temple and exiled My People.'" [1]

*Berakot, 3.*

[1] The Bat Kol, or the Daughter of the Voice, is symbolized as a dove, comparable to the form which the Holy Ghost takes in the New Testament.

### GOD'S YEARNING

Why did God bring Israel into the extremity of danger at the Red Sea before He rescued him? Because He longed to hear Israel's prayer.

R. Joshua ben Levi said: "To what is this to be compared? To a king traveling on the highway, to whom a princess cried out: 'I pray thee, deliver me out of the hands of these brigands!' The king obeyed and rescued her. Later he sought to make her his wife. He yearned to hear her sweet accents again, but she was silent. What did the king do? He hired the brigands to set upon the princess, that she might cry out, and he might hear her voice. He then hastened to her side, saying: 'This is what I have yearned for: to hear thy beloved voice.'"

"Israel in Egypt cried unto God and He delivered them. And He wished to hear their voice again, but they kept silent. What did God do? He incited Pharaoh to pursue them. At once Israel cried unto the Lord. In that hour God said: 'For this I have been seeking: to hear your voice once more, as it is written (Song of Songs 2:14): "My dove in the clefts of the rock, let Me hear thy voice." Thy voice is the same voice which I first heard in Egypt.'"

*Shemot Rabbah, 21, 5.*

## 393. VOWS

He who utters a vow places a burden about his neck.

*Y. Nedarim, 9, 1.*

Ben Sirach said: "Before thou makest a vow, think well, lest thou mislead thyself."

*Tanhuma Wayyishlah, 8.*

The making of vows is the portal to folly.

*Kallah Rabbati, 5.*

### THE DETAILS OF A VOW

A man came to R. Judah ben Shalom. The Rabbi asked him: "And what was it that you swore not to do?"

"I swore to make no profit," answered the man.

The Rabbi said: "How can a person in his right mind swear to such a thing?"

The man finally confessed that he intended to make no gambling profits.

The Rabbi exclaimed: "Blessed be those Sages who required that the details of an oath be explained." He refused, of course, to void such a vow.

*Y. Nedarim, 5.*

## Settlement in Full

A man vowed that his wife would enjoy nothing from his property. Her marriage settlement was 400 dinars. He came to R. Akiba and was instructed to divorce her and pay her settlement.

The man said: "My father left 800 dinars. My brother received 400 dinars, and I 400. Will it not be enough if I give her 200 and keep 200 for myself?"

R. Akiba said: "Even if thou must sell the hair on thy head, thou shalt pay her the settlement in full."

"If I had known that," answered the man, "I should not have made the vow."

R. Akiba then voided the vow.

*Nedarim, 65.*

## Annulment of Vows

How do we know it is possible to void a vow or an oath? We learn this from the passage: "He shall not break his word" (Numbers 30:3). He shall not break it, but others may break it for him. But they must be convinced that he has made the vow without appreciating all its consequences, and that, had he been mindful of them, he would not have uttered the vow.

*Pesikta Zutarti to Num. 30:3.*

A man came to R. Huna to ask that his vow be annulled. R. Huna inquired: "Is thy heart still agreeable to your vow?" "No," answered the man, and the Rabbi voided it.

A man came to Rabbah b. R. Huna who inquired: "If ten people had tried to pacify thee when thou madest the vow, wouldst thou still have made it?" When the man answered: "No," the Rabbi voided the vow.

A woman vowed that her daughter should enjoy nothing which belonged to her. Later she regretted this oath and came to R. Johanan, who inquired: "If thou hadst known that thy neighbors would say: 'the girl must be wicked if her mother shuts the door against her, wouldst thou have vowed?'" When the mother answered: "No," the Rabbi voided the vow.

Rab Sehorah came to R. Nahman, who inquired: "Wouldst thou have vowed if thou knewest that this and that would result?" "Yes," answered Rab Sehorah. R. Nahman tried several arguments in vain; in each instance, Rab Sehorah foresaw every consequence when he vowed. Finally R. Nahman said: "If thou hadst thought of everything, why bother me now?"

Rab Sehorah replied: "Rabbi (Judah ha-Nasi) teaches us that the right course is that which a man feels to be honorable to himself and which also brings him honor from man. (Abot, 2:1) Therefore since thou believest that I have troubled thee for nothing, I have not followed the right course, an outcome of which I did not think when I made the vow."

R. Nahman was then able to void the oath for him.

R. Ishmael b. R. Jose made a vow and wished to have it annulled. He went to the Sages, but they could think of no outcome which he had not foreseen. Finally a laundryman, seeing the Sages troubled, struck the Rabbi. "This I did not foresee," said R. Ishmael, and the vow was voided for him.

*Nedarim, 21-22.*

### CINDERELLA

A man grew tired of his ugly wife and vowed that she should enjoy nothing of his property until she showed him something fine in herself. Such a vow necessitates an immediate divorce. The husband regretted his hastiness, and sought the counsel of R. Ishmael b. Jose.

The Rabbi asked him: "Is her head fine?"

"It is round," replied the husband.

"Is her hair fine?"

"It is like strands of flax."

"Are her eyes fine?"

"They are watery."

"Are her ears fine?"

"They are like cauliflowers."

"Is her nose fine?"

"It is flat."

"Are her lips fine?"

"They are thick."

"Is her throat fine?"

"It is sunken."

"Are her feet fine?"

"They are as wide as those of a goose."

"Is her name fine?"

"Her name," said the husband, "is Cinderella."

"Aha," said the Rabbi. "Her name fits her finely. She is full of cinders (defects) and her name is Cinderella."

Thereupon the husband's rash vow was annulled.

*Nedarim, 65.*

### THE BEAUTY OF JEWISH MAIDENS

A man uttered a vow against his wife who was his sister's daughter. She was taken to R. Ishmael who ordered a gold tooth for one that was missing, and arranged that beauty experts make her more handsome.

Her husband was called in and was asked: "Did you vow against so beautiful a woman?" "No." R. Ishmael voided his vow, and said: "The daughters of Israel are beautiful, but poverty destroys their looks." When R. Ishmael died, the daughters of Israel mourned him, and paraphrased the Biblical words (II Samuel 1:24), thus: "Ye daughters of Israel, weep over R. Ishmael."

*Nedarim, 65.*

### Penalty for Bad Manners

Simeon ben Antiperes held open house, but the strange rumor reached the Sages that he beat his guests before permitting them to depart. Rabban Johanan ben Zakkai asked for a volunteer to investigate, and R. Joshua bravely accepted the challenge.

He arrived at the home of Simeon and received accommodations: an excellent meal, a clean bed and bath. A discussion regarding Torah completed his satisfaction, though he continued to wonder when the beating would be forthcoming.

When he was about to depart, the host courteously accompanied his guest a short distance. Since everything was in the best of taste, Rabbi Joshua wondered what report he might make of his experiences. As the host bade him farewell, the Rabbi plucked up sufficient courage to ask: "How is it that others have been beaten but I have been spared?"

Simeon answered: "Thou, Rabbi, art a man of wisdom after mine own heart. Thou hast breeding and good manners. As for the others, however, when I give them food, they vow by the Torah that they will have none of it, yet after a while, they eat voraciously. Have I done wrong in beating them to teach them that vows must not be made and broken immediately?"

R. Joshua replied: "Thou gavest them their just deserts. Next time give them forty stripes of thy own, and forty more for the Sages who sent me."

R. Joshua returned to the Sages and mirthfully related the result of his investigation.

*Derek Eretz Rabbah, 6.*


### The Effect of Prohibition

R. Jeremiah made a vow not to drink strong wine, but later had it annulled. Nevertheless he refused to drink it even afterwards. His Disciples discussed this action of their Master, and one of them explained it thus: R. Jeremiah intended to abstain from strong wine, but when he made a pledge, the prohibition served to awaken within him the desire to drink. After he had voided it, he no longer felt the urge.

*Y. Nedarim, 9.*


### Mentioning God's Name

R. Assi said: "When God's Name is mentioned in a vow, it cannot be annulled. One reason is that the vow is thus made too strong to be nullified. Another is that the vower must be taught not to use God's Name lightly."

R. Kahana visited R. Joseph, who invited him to partake of refreshments. The guest exclaimed: "By the Master of the World, I shall eat nothing."

R. Joseph said: "Surely you can eat nothing now, since you have mentioned the Name of God."

*Nedarim, 22.*

## 394. WASHING THE HANDS

Rab Dimi told the following story: Failure to wash the hands before eating once caused a man to eat swine's flesh, and failure to wash them after eating prompted another to commit murder.

During a period of religious persecution a Jewish tavern-keeper served both permitted and forbidden foods. If a man washed his hands and said grace, he served him permitted foods; if not, he gave him swine's flesh. Once a Jew entered and in his haste neglected to wash his hands and say grace. When he paid his bill, he complained at its size.

"But you ate swine's flesh and it is more costly."

"But I am a Jew. Why did you serve me pork?"

"Because," said the tavern-keeper, "since you did not wash your hands and say grace, I took you for a Gentile."

A man ate pea soup and failed to wash his hands afterwards. A swindler met him on the street, went to his house and said to the housewife: "Your husband sent me for his diamond ring. As an identification, he asked me to say that you have just had pea soup at your meal." When the husband learned that his wife had given the rogue the ring, he killed her in anger.

*Hullin, 106.*

When R. Akiba was in prison, his Disciple, R. Joshua ha-Garsi attended to his needs. Once when the attendant brought water, the jailer said: "What need is there for so much water. Perhaps you wish to soften the wall and bore a hole through it to escape!" He spilled out half the water.

When R. Joshua came to R. Akiba, the latter exclaimed: "Why have you delayed? Do you not know that I am an aged man, and that my life depends upon your prompt service?"

R. Joshua told him of the occurrence. R. Akiba then asked for water with which to wash his hands. "But there is not enough," said R. Joshua, "for drinking purposes!"

"Better it is that I should die from thirst," said R. Akiba, "than that I should transgress the law of the Sages."

He would touch no food until he had washed his hands.

*Erubin, 21.*

## 395. WELCOME

He who welcomes his fellow-man is as one who welcomes the Shekinah.

*Y. Erubin, 5, 1.*

He who receives his fellow-man with a pleasant countenance, even though he gives him nothing, is as one who has given him all possible gifts.

*Abot de-R. Nathan, 13.*

Leah went forth to greet Jacob and she is buried with him. Rachel did not go out to greet him, and she is buried in a different place.

*Zohar, i, 223a.*

Welcoming a wayfarer is an essential part of hospitality.

*Zohar Hadash, i, 25a.*

## 396. WIDOWER

The widower lives in a darkened world.

*Sanhedrin, 22a.*

## 397. WINE—DRUNKARDS

When a man drinks wine, his body begins to function lazily and his mind is befuddled. When wine enters, reason departs, and secret thoughts are revealed.

*Tanhuma to Shemini.*

Rab Judah said in the name of Samuel, that if a judge drank a glass of wine, he should give no decision on that day.

*Erubin, 64.*

Rabbah bar Rab Huna said: "If a man drinks wine and feels that he can speak rationally if called upon by the ruler, he should not offer prayer. But if he is called on, and prays, the prayer is acceptable. If he drinks so much, however, that he cannot speak rationally before a ruler, his prayer is worthless."

*Erubin, 64.*

If you wish to keep your affairs secret, drink no wine. For wine causes the voice to be uplifted and secrets to be revealed.

*Zohar, iv, 177b.*

Two things cannot go hand in hand: drinking wine and serving the Lord prayerfully and with learning.

*Zohar Hadash, i, 22b.*

No good comes from wine.

*Bemidbar Rabbah, 10, 8.*

Where there is wine, there is no sense.

*Bemidbar Rabbah, 10, 8.*

The good wine and the good waters have been the misfortune of the Ten Tribes.[1]

*Shabbat, 147.*

[1] They partook overmuch of enjoyments and forsook the spirit.

In a place where there is no wine, drugs are needed.

*Baba Batra, 58.*

Wine was created only for the purpose of comforting mourners, and of rewarding the wicked for their good deeds.

*Erubin, 65.*

Where thou findest wine, there wilt thou find stumbling.

*Tanhuma Noah, 21.*

Wine reddens the face of the wicked in this world, and whitens it in the next.

*Sanhedrin, 70.*

Drink not wine whose numerical value in Hebrew is 70, and thou wilt not be summoned to appear before the Seventy (the Sanhedrin).

*Tanhuma, Buber, Shemini, 5.*

The drunkard keeps his eye on the tankard and the wine seller on his purse.

*Tanhuma Shemini, 6.*

## THE ORIGIN OF VITICULTURE

Once while Noah was hard at work, breaking up the ground for a vineyard, Satan drew near and inquired what he was doing.

On ascertaining that the Patriarch was about to cultivate the grape, he at once volunteered to assist him in his task. He began to fertilize the soil with the blood of a lamb, a lion, a pig and a monkey.

"Now," said Satan, when his work was done, "If a man drinks one glass of the juice of the grape, he is as meek and gentle as the lamb; if he drinks two glasses, he becomes bold and fearless as the lion; if he drinks three glasses, he grows as foul and beastly as the pig; and if he drinks four glasses, he loses his senses, dances, and talks nonsense like a monkey."

*Tanhuma, Noah, to Gen. 9:20.*

## EVEN IN THE CEMETERY

An aged drunkard would sell pieces of his household goods in order to buy wine. Once his sons, while the old man was still insensible with wine, took him to the cemetery and left him there, thinking that a fright might effect a cure.

A caravan passed by with a load of wine in leather bottles. Suddenly a tumult was heard, arising in the city, and they decided to unload their goods, leaving them behind to investigate. The old man awoke, saw a leather wine bottle at his head, promptly drained it, and went to sleep again. When his sons came for him, they found the bottle at his mouth, and said: "If God sees fit to provide him with drink even in the cemetery, what can we be expected to do?"

*Wayyikra Rabbah, 12.*

### After Hours

"Who hath wounds without cause? They that tarry late at the wine." (Proverbs 23:29)  A man was in the habit of drinking twelve pints of wine daily.  Once he had only eleven and could not fall asleep. He awakened the wine seller and begged admittance.  "It is after hours and the police will punish me," he replied.

"Then do this," said the drunkard.  "There is a small hole in the door; place the mouth of the bottle to the hole, and I will drink."

When the city watchmen passed by, they mistook him for a thief and beat him soundly before he had an opportunity to explain.  He then said: "How closely does the verse in Proverbs apply to me!"

*Wayyikra Rabbah, 12.*

### "Where Did You Obtain It?"

A man loved wine above all else in life.  Frequently he would drink so much that he would tumble into the gutter, and small boys would throw pebbles at him and make sport of him.

His son begged him to do his drinking in the house, and promised to give him all he craved.  When going for his father's wine, the son beheld a drunkard lying in the gutter with boys surrounding him.  He called his father to witness the sight, thinking thereby to shame him. But the father went over to the drunkard, shook him vigorously until he awakened from his torpor, and bending an ear, he inquired: "Pray tell me, friend, where did you obtain the wine which made you so thoroughly drunk?"

When the son expressed his disdain, the father said: "Believe me, my son, wine is my very life and Paradise."

*Tanhuma, Shemini.*

## 398.  WIT AND WISDOM

What wisdom places as a crown for her head, humility places as a sole for her feet.

*Y. Shabbat, 1, 13.*

The end and aim of wisdom is repentance and good deeds.

*Berakot, 17.*

What shall a man do to become wise?  Let him study much and trade little.

*Niddah, 70.*

And Solomon became wiser than all men, even than idiots.

*Source unknown. Often quoted as a Midrash.*

Excellent is wisdom when associated with an inheritance.

*Kohlet Rabbah, 7, 11.*

The wisdom of Elisha was of more avail than all the wars of Joram.

*Eliyahu Rabbah, 6.*

Every drop that goes forth from Paradise carries with it a drop of wisdom.

*Zohar, i, 125a.*

A wise man should also learn a little concerning subjects of unwisdom. He will then appreciate his wisdom more.

*Zohar, iii, 47b.*

Great is the wisdom which brings a man to the Fear of Heaven.

*Midrash ha-Gadol, 454.*

There is no Torah without wisdom, and no wisdom without Torah; both are one.

*Zohar, iii, 81a.*

He who increases wisdom increases dissatisfaction, and he who increases knowledge increases affliction.

*Kohelet Rabbah, 1 end.*

In the year 1840 (5600 Anno Mundi), the Gates of Wisdom will open above, the Springs of Wisdom will flow below, and the world will prepare for the Millennium. It is like a Jew who prepares on the afternoon of the sixth day of the week for the Sabbath.[1]

*Zohar, i, 118a.*

[1] This has been interpreted to refer to the beginning of the age of inventions.

A king was pleased with a courtier, and invited him to ask an honor for himself. The wise courtier thought: "If I ask for a governorship, I shall have no opportunity for still higher honors." He therefore said: "Since you have singled me out for honor, I presume to ask for the hand of your daughter." In the same fashion Solomon thought: "If I ask for wealth I shall have nothing else." Hence he asked for God's Daughter—Wisdom.

*Pesikta Rabbati, 14, 7.*

The unwise man declares that wisdom is above his head. Not so the wise man who says: "One human hand has grasped it." Why not I? It is like a jewel hanging high, which with wisdom can be reached.

*Shir ha-Shirim Rabbah, 5, 8.*

Great is sagacity; greater still are knowledge and understanding.

*Shemot Rabbah, 41, 3.*

Some men increase wisdom to their benefit—others to their loss.

*Kohelet Rabbah, 1, 39.*

### The Sagacious Heir

A merchant of Jerusalem was near death in a strange city. He summoned his host and said to him: "When my son comes from Jerusalem to claim my property, compel him to show you his sagacity in three ways before you deliver it to him."

The son learned of his father's death and came to the city. To his chagrin no one would tell him where his late father's host resided. What did he do? He beheld a man selling wood and hired him to take wood to the man whose house he was seeking. By following him he found the house.

He introduced himself and was invited to a meal. A dish with five birds was brought in, and the guest was invited to divide the food. He gave one to his host and hostess, one to his two sons, one to his two daughters, and kept two for himself. They said nothing, and at the evening meal again asked him to divide a fowl which was brought to the table. The guest gave the head to the host, the inwards to the hostess, to the sons a leg apiece, and to the daughters a wing apiece; for himself he kept the body of the chicken. He was then asked: "Do you divide in this fashion at Jerusalem?"

He replied: "I divided correctly. At lunch my host and hostess and one bird make three; so do a single bird and two sons, and one bird and two daughters. Likewise I and two birds make three. At dinner I gave the head to the head of the house; the inwards quite fittingly to the mother; to the daughters the wings, since they marry and leave the house; to the sons the legs, since they are the support of the home. I took the body myself, since it looks like a boat. It was in a boat that I came to the city."

The host praised the son's sagacity and conveyed to him the inheritance.

*Ekah Rabbah, 1.*

### A Fable of a Snake

An unusual pair of litigants appeared in the court of the wise king: a man with a long serpent coiled about his throat.

"This man has robbed me of my treasure," spoke the serpent to Solomon. "I wish to do as the Torah gives me license to do: 'Thou shalt bruise his heel' (Gen. 3:15)."

"Remove thyself from his neck, then, and I will judge between you," replied the king.[1]

When the man was asked to relate his version of the facts, he stated that as he passed the snake in a field, the latter begged a drink from a pitcher of milk he bore on his shoulder. As a reward he promised to show the man a treasure under a rock.

The King-Judge then replied: "He wishes to kill thee as the Torah giveth him leave to do. Do thou, then, what the Lord giveth thee the right to do: 'He shall bruise thy head.' "[1]

*Tanhuma, Buber, Introd., p. 157.*

[1] Slightly paraphrased.

### The Clever Lad

An Athenian gave a boy in Jerusalem a copper coin and said: "Buy me that which I will eat plentifully and take with me on the road." The boy brought to him salt.

An Athenian came to a Jerusalem tailor with a broken metal vessel and asked him to sew it together. The tailor took some sand and said: "Make me some thread out of this, and I will do what you wish."

An Athenian gave money to a Jerusalem lad and commanded him to buy cheeses and eggs. When he had brought them, the man said: "Tell me which cheese comes from the milk of a black cow and which from a white cow." The lad answered: "You are older; tell me first which eggs are from a white hen, and which from a black."

*Ekah Rabbah, 1.*

### Wise Replies

R. Joshua b. Hananiah related the following tale: Once I walked on a path through a field. A girl stopped me and said: "Are you not trespassing on this field?" I replied: "But I see a path through it." She answered: "Yes, it has been made by other trespassers like yourself."

I walked further and came to the crossroads. I asked a boy: "Which is the way to town?" He answered: "This to the right is near and far; the other is far and near." I took the right road and found the way blocked by fruit gardens with fences. I returned and asked the boy why he had misled me. He answered: "Why did you not take heed of my directions? Did I not say that to the right the road was near and far?"

I went still further and beheld a child carrying a dish covered with a cloth. When I inquired what he was carrying, the lad answered: "If my mother had wished everyone to know, she would not have covered it."

I continued on my way and entered the town. I found a girl drawing water from a well and asked her for a drink. She said: "Here is water for thee and for thy donkey." When I had finished drinking, I said: "Daughter, thou hast done as did Rebekah." "But thou hast not done as did Eliezer," she retorted.

*Erubin, 53; Ekah Rabbah, 1.*

### The Stolen Money

Three men came to Jerusalem on Friday near sundown. They selected a safe place and left their money there. One of them, however returned to the place on the Sabbath and hid the money elsewhere. When they came for it, and found it not, they accused each the other, and finally sought a hearing before King Solomon. The wise monarch heard their case and then said: "I perceive that you are men of intelligence. Please help me in another case before I decide yours."

"A foreign king told me this story: a girl promised herself in marriage to a youth; later, however, she fell in love with another, and asked the first youth to release her for a money consideration. The youth declined the money but released her from her promise. On her return from him she was kidnapped by an old man who insisted that she remain with him. She replied. 'The youth who had a claim upon me would not separate me from my beloved; how much the more shouldst thou, an old man, restrain thyself?' He consented to release her and also refused her money. Who of the three acted in most praise-worthy fashion?"

One man said: "The girl who would not break a promise." The other: "the youth who would not take her against her desire and re-fused her money." The third said: "the old man, for if he troubled himself to kidnap her, why did he not at least retain her money?"

Solomon thereupon said to the third man: "Thou art the thief. If even the mention of money prompted you to think how foolish it was to surrender it, how much the more when you had the opportunity actually to take it!" He cast the thief into prison until he had made restitution.

*Midrash Asseret ha-Diberot.*

### COINS AMID THE HONEY

During the reign of King Saul a widow wished to leave Gilboa in order to be rid of an unwelcome suitor among the monarch's friends. She placed her money in vessels filled with honey and covered the coins with it, leaving the jars with a neighbor for safe-keeping. One day by mistake one of her vessels was opened and the gold-pieces were dis-covered beneath the layer of honey. The neighbor emptied the widow's jars and filled them with honey. When the owner returned, she re-ceived her vessels, but the money was missing. She went to King Saul and to his court, but without success, since she had no witnesses to testify that she had placed the gold-pieces in the vessels. The young David, however, sought permission to investigate the matter further. He took witnesses with him to make note when the vessels were identi-fied by the widow and her neighbor as the jars in question. He then emptied all the vessels, broke them into bits, and lo, two gold pieces remained clinging to the bottom of one of the jars. "Go and return the rest of the money," commanded David and it was done.

*A Midrash.*

### WISDOM FOR THE WISE

A matron asked R. Jose ben Halafta: "Why is it written that God gives wisdom unto the wise? Should it not be said: 'He giveth wis-dom unto the fools' ?"

R. Jose replied: "Suppose a rich man and a poor man came to thee to borrow money. To whom wouldst thou lend it?"

"The rich man," was the answer.

"Why?" asked the Rabbi.

"Because if he lost the money in his venture, he would be able to repay the loan from his other possessions."

"It is the same with God," said the Rabbi. "If He gives His wisdom to the wise, they will use it in worthy ways; but if He gives it to fools, they will use it in the ways of folly."

*Tanhuma to Wayyakhel.*

## SOLOMON'S COUNSEL

Three brothers sojourned with King Solomon in order to learn wisdom. He appointed them as courtiers but gave them no special instruction. They thereupon resolved to return home and entered the King's presence to bid him farewell. The ruler said: "For your service you may choose either a hundred gold pieces each, or three good counsels from me." They selected the money and left. Later the youngest changed his mind, and said to his brothers: "We came to learn wisdom, but we depart merely with money. Let us return the money and receive the wisdom instead." The two brothers refused to exchange a hundred pieces of gold for three suggestions of wisdom.

The youngest one, however, left them and returned to the King, saying: "I came to thee not for gold but for instruction. Take back, I beg thee, the money and impart to me your wisdom."

The King said "First, let me advise you: on the road commence your travel with the dawn and halt with the sunset. Second: if you approach a river when it is full, wait until the water recedes. Third: tell not your secret to any woman, not even your wife."

The youth left the King and by hard riding soon overtook his brothers. They inquired what he had learned, but he did not tell them. At sunset they came to a shady spot near a spring. The youngest counselled them to halt for the night, but the others said: "we can travel five miles more before it is too dark," and they declined to stop. The youngest halted, assembled branches, built a shelter for himself and his beast, and built a fire against the increasing cold. In the night a snowstorm took place. The two brothers had journeyed on until it was too dark to look for wood, and they had frozen to death in the storm. The following day the youngest brother came upon their bodies, and, in great sorrow, buried them.

The melting snow filled the river, and when he reached a river, usually narrow, but now swollen from the floods, he halted and made no attempt to ford it. Other travelers were not so wise, and were drowned as a consequence. When the river was normal, he crossed it, collected the wealth of the drowned men, continued on his journey till he reached his home, and prospered greatly henceforth. His wife was eager to learn the secret of his wealth, but he refused to tell her. When Solomon heard of these happenings, he said: "Verily wisdom is better than gold."

*Jellinek: Bet ha-Midrash.*

## INEXHAUSTIBLE WISDOM

We are told that God took a portion of the spirit of Moses and imparted it to the Seventy Elders. Does this infer that Moses lost a part of his wisdom? No. It is like a candle which kindles others and loses nothing. Rabban Johanan ben Zakkai compares it to a fly which, immersing itself in the sea, takes almost nothing away from it. R. Akiba compares it to the Etrog which loses nothing of its fragrance because one has smelled it.

*Sifre to Num., 11:17. Shir ha-Shirim Rabbah, 1; Sopherim, 16.*

### 399.  WIVES AND HUSBANDS

That man's life is indeed enriched who is wedded to a virtuous woman.

*Shabbat, 25b.*

Whatever blessing dwells in the house comes from her (the wife).

*Baba Metzia, 59a.*

Among the necessary qualifications of a good wife are a gentle temper, tact, modesty, industry.

*Sotah, 3b.*

He who loves his wife as himself, and honours her more than himself—to him the Scriptural promise is uttered: "Thou shalt know that thy tent is in peace."

*Yebamot, 62b.*

Thy wife has been given to thee in order that thou mayest realize with her life's great plan; she is not thine to vex or grieve. Vex her not, for God notes her tears.

*Ketubot, 61a.*

He who puts away the wife of his youth, for him God's very altar weeps.

*Sanhedrin, 22a.*

The Bible, speaking of the Jewish kings, says: "He shall not multiply horses to himself . . . neither shall he multiply wives to himself, that his heart turn not away, neither shall he greatly multiply to himself silver and gold."

When King Solomon studied these words, he said: "Why did God prohibit this indulgence? Is it not only because of the danger 'lest his heart be turned'? I will take unto myself many wives, and yet show God that my heart will not be turned from its sense of duty."

Just then the letter "Yod," the first letter of the word "Yarbeh," ascended before the throne of God and pleaded before Him: "See, Solomon is annihilating me!"

God answered: "Solomon and a thousand like him may be wiped from the face of the earth, but no one shall dare to destroy you!"

*Shemot Rabbah, 6, 1.*

A wife is the joy of a man's heart.

*Shabbat, 152.*

When the husband is blessed, his wife is also blessed thereby.

*Zohar, 233a.*

He who looks for the earnings of his wife sees never a sign of blessing.

*Pesahim, 50.*

He who awaits his wife's death in order to inherit her possessions will be buried by her.

*Tosefta Sotah, 5.*

Every man receives the wife he deserves.

*Sotah, 2.*

A man without a wife lives without good, without help, without joy, without blessing and without forgiveness.

*Kohelet Rabbah, 9, 7.*

The blessing of the Lord is found only where there is a happy communion of man and woman.

*Zohar, i, 55b.*

A husband usually thinks: I can walk about in a frayed and shabby garment, but my wife must have fine clothes.

*Y. Ketubot, 6, 5.*

Rather than order me to make peace with my wife, command my wife to obey me, says the man.

*Bemidbar Rabbah, 21, 2.*

People say: If thy wife is low of stature, bend down to consult her.

*Baba Metzia, 59.*

Who is the poor man whose days are filled with misery? He who must live with an evil-natured wife.

*Sanhedrin, 110.*

Give me all evils, but not an evil wife.

*Shabbat, 11.*

A woman barren for a few years may ask the court to compel her husband to divorce her. She may say: "Do I not need a support in my old age and a hand to bury me, in case I am left a widow?"

*Yebamot, 65.*

Sometimes a man listens to his wife with profit, and sometimes with loss.

*Debarim Rabbah, 4, 4.*

A man should eat less than he can afford, and should honor his wife and children more than he can afford.

*Hullin, 84.*

There is a substitute for everything except for the wife of one's youth.

*Sanhedrin, 22.*

Multitudes marry and are happy, but some individuals stumble.

*Bemidbar Rabbah, 9, 4.*

A man should be careful not to irritate his wife and cause her to weep.

*Baba Metzia, 59.*

A man should be careful of his wife's honor.

*Baba Metzia, 59.*

A man can find contentment only in his first wife.

*Yebamot, 63.*

The married man receives a double blessing from God: one for himself, and one for his wife.

*Zohar, i, 233b.*

A woman who in this world has been twice married will in the World-to-Come go to the first husband.

*Zohar, i, 21b.*

A married man may not leave his home without his wife's consent.

*Zohar, i, 79a.*

When a man marries a second wife after his first wife's death, he then remembers how good his first wife was.

*Berakot, 32.*

Deserving of a curse is the wife who does not beautify herself for her husband. Deserving of a curse is a woman who beautifies herself for a strange man. Deserving of a curse is a scholar who does not feel himself beautified by the glory of the Torah.

*Shaare Teshubah, 4, by Hai Gaon, quoting Shekalim.*

If a man and wife are worthy, the Shekinah abides among them; if not, a fire will consume them.

*Sotah, 17.*

When the wandering son goes about in torn shoes, he is reminded of his home. When the young wife hears abuse from the lips of her mate, she is reminded of her honeymoon days.

*Ekah Rabbah, 1, 34.*

If a man come to the House of Study and no honor is paid to him, he should not relate this to his wife on his return home. She, too, will lose respect for him. This will be his only gain from bearing tales.

*Abot de-R. Nathan, 7.*

### WOMAN'S POWER

A pious couple lived together for ten years, and having no children, were divorced. The man married an impious woman and she transformed him into a man of wickedness. The pious woman married a man of wickedness and she transformed him into a man of goodness.

The Sages declare: "Woman determines man's behaviour."

**Bereshit Rabbah, 17.**

### THE SHREWISH WIFE

Rabbi Hiyya had a shrewish wife. Once when he was presenting her with a gift wrapped in a cloth, his nephew and Disciple, Rab, exclaimed: "And you do this, though she plagues you so?" Rabbi Hiyya answered: "All that we can expect of them is that they bring up our children and preserve us from sin."

*Yebamot, 63a, end.*

A wife who receives love gives love in return; if she receives anger, she returns anger in equal measure.

*Zohar, iv, 259b.*

A woman is like a candle kindled from another. As two candles give forth the same light, so is the light of the husband and the wife the same.

*Zohar, iv, 167a.*

A woman is like the cup of blessing: if one has tasted it, it becomes faulty.

*Raia Mehemna, iii, 89b.*

He who wins a wise woman by his own worth, has won the chief victory in life.

*Zohar, iii, 52a.*

A man's jealousy for his wife proves his love for her, and demonstrates thereby that he looks with admiration at no other woman.

*Zohar, i, 115b.*

The chief influence transforming a man's house into his home is his wife. The Shekinah will not forsake his house if his wife keeps it according to the ways of Israel.

*Zohar, i, 50a.*

### THE WATERS OF BITTERNESS (NUMBERS 5:24)

There were twin sisters, one of whom was unfaithful to her husband. The latter became suspicious and asked the High Priest to command his wife to drink the water of bitterness at the Temple. When the unfaithful woman received the summons, she confessed her defilement to her sister, saying she feared to drink. The twin sister offered to go in her place. She drank the water and no ill effects resulted. When she returned home and put off her sister's clothes, the guilty one kissed her. At the instant the odor of the water entered into her, and she dropped dead.

*Bemidbar Rabbah, 9.*

### THE TWO WIVES

Rab said: The wife of On, the son of Peleth, saved her husband's life, and the wife of Korah caused his death. In Numbers 16:1, we read that both were mentioned in the conspiracy, but no punishment for On is recorded. When On told his wife of the plan, she said: "Be not a fool and refrain from intrusion into a matter which concerns you not. What matters it to you whether Moses or Korah is leader? In either case you will be a subordinate." She sat down at the threshold with hair in disarray, and no one wished to enter her home while she was in this dishevelled state. In the meantime the rebellion took place and ended.

Korah's wife, however, said to her husband: "See how Moses deals with you. He himself is like a king; his brother is the High-Priest, and his nephews are associate priests. All honors he allots to his own family." With such talk she incited Korah to rebel against the authority of Moses, and this led to his death.

*Sanhedrin, 110.*

### EFFACING THE HOLY NAME

Rabbi Meir was accustomed to hold discourses on Friday evenings. A certain woman attended these discourses frequently and returned home after the lamp had been extinguished. Her husband, a churlish fellow, demanded to know where she had been. When she replied that she had attended a lecture, the husband cried: "Get thee out the house, and do not return until thou hast spat into the eye of the speaker."

The wife departed from the house and remained with a neighbor. The following Friday evening, she and her friend went together to hear the discourse of Rabbi Meir. The latter had heard of the disagreement, and, calling her into his presence, he said: "My eye gives me pain. Spit into it, and it will be relieved." After considerable persuasion, the woman did so, and thereupon left for her home.

R. Meir's Disciples asked him: "Is it proper to lower the dignity of the Torah in such a fashion?" The Rabbi replied: "Surely it is correct that Meir should not insist upon more dignity than does His Maker. When a husband becomes jealous God permits His Holy Name to be effaced in the water, in order to make peace between the man and his wife."

*Wayyikra Rabbah, 9.*

### THE THING MOST DESIRED

Rab Idi told this story: a husband and a wife lived together for ten years, but were without children. They asked Rabbi Simeon ben Yohai to divorce them. The Rabbi, however, noted that they were still in love, and regretted the action they contemplated. He said to them: "As your lives were joined together at a feast, be disjoined, also, at a feast." The couple invited many friends, and the festivities were like those of a wedding. When the guests had left, the husband said: "You may take with you to your father's house anything you most desire in my house." When the husband had fallen asleep, the wife commanded her servants to carry him gently to her father's home. In the morning he awoke and cried out: "Where am I?"

The woman answered: "In my father's house."

"What am I doing here?" he inquired.

"Well-beloved, you are the thing I most desire in your house, and, by your promise, I am entitled to keep you."

They returned to the Rabbi, who blessed them, offering prayer that God might remember them. The following year Rabbi Simeon officiated at the circumcision of their son.

*Shir ha-shirim Rabbah, chapter 1.*

### THE WIVES OF ISHMAEL

Three years had passed since the day that Abraham had sent Ishmael away. He longed to see him, and sought out his camp in the pasture-country of Paran. When Abraham came to his son's tent, he found Ishmael absent from home. He asked Ishmael's wife for a little water, but the ill-natured woman refused to give it to him. Abraham said: "When thy husband returns, pray tell him that an old man from Philistia came to visit him, and not finding him at home, offered this advice: 'the pegs of your tent should be changed.'"

Ishmael understood this allusion to his wicked wife and divorced her. He wedded another woman, named Fatima.

The following year Abraham again wished to visit his son, and again found him away from home. Without waiting for a request, Fatima offered him hospitality, and urged him to partake of food and drink. Abraham said: "When thy husband returns, tell him: 'his pegs are excellent and he should retain them.'"

Ishmael thanked his gracious wife, and blessed the Lord who had sent him so admirable a mate.

*Yalkut Shimeoni, 95.*

### THE LAST ROBBER

Once a man engaged in robbery by night, keeping his family in luxury as a consequence. The wife of a neighbor complained to her husband: "What ill-luck is mine that I am married to you. The man across the way keeps his family in every comfort."

The husband replied: "But rumor has it that he is a thief. Do you wish me to become like him?"

The wife answered: "I care not what your occupation is, provided you give me the luxuries I crave."

Being enamored of his wife, the husband begged his neighbor to allow him to participate in his next enterprise. The police were informed and laid a trap for him. The experienced robber succeeded in escaping the snare, but the novice was captured and hanged.

Hence people say: "the last robber to join the band is the first to be hanged."

*Kohelet Rabbah, 7.*

### 400. WIVES AND HUSBANDS—DIVORCED

When a divorced man marries a divorced woman, there are four natures with which to contend.

*Pesahim, 112.*

Rabbi Eleazar ben Pedat said: "The very altar drops tears on every one who divorces the wife of his youth."

*Gittin, 90b.*

## LOST LOVE

A married woman was publicly kissed by a lover. The story came to the attention of R. Jose who commanded that she be divorced, and that no marriage settlement be paid her.

Her kinsfolk protested, saying that she had lost her wits and knew not what she did.

The Rabbi said: "Bring to me her Ketubah, and let it be read."

The Ketubah was found to contain a clause to the effect that if the wife came to hate her husband and disliked looking at him, she should receive but half the settlement. The Rabbi decided that if she were still in love with her husband, she would not permit another man to kiss her lips, and he therefore told the husband to give her half the settlement portion.

*Y. Ketubot, 7.*

## THE PAIN OF THE SOUL

Rabbi Jose, the Galilean, married his sister's daughter. She proved to be a woman of a contrary disposition, and did not hesitate to show him disrespect in the presence of his Disciples.

Once Rabbi Eleazar ben Azariah visited the School of Rabbi Jose. When meal-time arrived, Rabbi Jose invited his guest to dine with him. His wife showed her displeasure and said: "I have prepared only a dish of turnips, not having expected a guest." When the guest declared that he would be satisfied with this, the woman shamefacedly admitted that she had really prepared a meal of fried birds. When the two Rabbis returned to the School, Rabbi Eleazar counselled Rabbi Jose to divorce his wife, and made him a gift of money to pay for her settlement portion.

The woman accepted the divorce, and married a town-watchman. Later her husband was blinded in an accident, and she was compelled to lead him from house to house asking donations. She refused, however, to visit the house of her former husband.

One day when the collection was discouragingly small, the blind man insisted that she visit Rabbi Jose as well. When she declined, her husband beat her. Rabbi Jose heard her cries, and learning of the argument, he secured for them a small house, and provided for them henceforth all their necessaries.

Nevertheless the woman was heard to say: "It was easier for me to bear the blows of my husband than to accept the charity of Rabbi Jose. The first only injured my body, but the latter touched the very soul within me."

*Y. Ketubot, chapter 11.*

## 401. WIVES OF SCHOLARS

The wives of scholars are frequently compelled to forego their sleep by virtue of their husbands' prolonged study. Thus they gain a portion in the World-to-Come.

*Ketubot, 62.*

### WORTHY OF TRUST

The wife of R. Amram, the Hasid, offered to sell to R. Huna b. Manyumi true blue thread for the Tzitzit. He inquired from the Sages if he might repose confidence in the woman inasmuch as so much unreliable material was sold. The words of Samuel were quoted to him: "The wife of a colleague is to be trusted as much as a colleague himself."

The serf of Levi was selling watermelon. After the demise of Levi, R. Johanan was asked whether the serf might be trusted to use a Kasher knife with which to cut the melon. R. Johanan answered: "The serf of a comrade is to be trusted as much as a comrade."

*Abodah Zarah, 39.*

## 402. WOMEN

God has endowed women with a special sense of wisdom which man lacks.

*Niddah, 45.*

The custom of women is Torah.

*Y. Pesahim, 4, 1.*

We read: "He will bless the House of Israel" (Psalm 115:12), namely, the women. "He will bless the House of Aaron," namely, their women. "He will bless them that fear the Lord," namely the men. and because of these, the women and children, too, are blessed.

*Zohar, iv, 117b.*

A shrewish woman is like a disease of the skin. (Both are easiest to bear when they are not touched.)

*Yebamot, 63.*

Everything derives from the woman.

*Bereshit Rabbah, 17, 7.*

A woman would rather live in a pleasant home than eat fat calves.

*Esther Rabbah, 3.*

Even more than the man wishes to wed, the woman wishes to be wedded.

*Yebamot, 113.*

He who weds a woman of piety has observed the entire Torah.

*Yalkut to Ruth, 606.*

A woman's weapons are always with her. (Tears, smiles, etc.)

*Yebamot, 115.*

A woman loves a poor young man more than a rich old man.

*Ruth Rabbah, 6, 4.*

A woman loves ornaments better than the finest viands.

*Midrash ha-Gadol, 469.*

The scholars of Israel have always labored diligently for the welfare of the daughters of Israel.

*Ketubot, 2.*

It is not seemly for a woman to sit in idleness.

*Y. Ketubot, 5, 6.*

It is not seemly for a woman to beg from door to door.

*Ketubot, 67.*

A woman takes precedence over a man in being provided with clothing from the Charity Chest, and in being ransomed.

*Horaiyot, 4, 6.*

Before you labor to aid women of folly, aid women of wisdom.

*Niddah, 53.*

### THE CONQUEST OF PASSION

An unchaste woman had an assignation with a student of the Law. She visited the School and beheld him presiding over many fellow-students, and lecturing on the Law with great zeal and enthusiasm. When he came to her, she said: "I watched you today in the School. If you could but subdue your passions, yours will be a great destiny in this world, and you will have an abundant portion in the World-to-Come. Why sacrifice these for momentary satisfaction?"

The student was impressed by her words and left her. The conduct of the woman also improved henceforth and she became a God-fearing person. A Voice said to her: "Thou wilt have a goodly share in Paradise."

*Tanna debei Eliyahu Zuta, 22.*

### TEMPTATION

Rabbi Mattithiah ben Haresh was exceedingly handsome, and once Satan received permission to tempt him. He visited him in the guise of a very beautiful young woman, who sought to allure him. The Rabbi snatched a nail, placed it in the flame and blinded his eyes with it. The Angel Raphael was sent to heal him, but the Rabbi refused to accept healing. Then God Himself assured the pious man that he would not again be tempted. Then the Rabbi consented to be healed.

*Midrash Abkir in Yalkut to Wayyehi.*

### RECEIVING THE TITHE

When the tithe for the poor was being distributed, the women received their share first, since it is more distressing for them to receive relief.

Rabba said: "If a case in court came before me in which one of the litigants was a woman, I would always advance the hearing of that case, since it is more disagreeable for a woman to be in court than a man.

*Yebamot, 100.*

A woman of sixty runs after music like a girl of six.

*Moed Katon, 9b.*

### 403. GOOD WOMEN

Israel is always redeemed for the sake of the pious women of the generation.

*Yalkut Shimeoni Ruth, 606.*

There is no end to the goodness of a good woman, nor is there any end to the wickedness of an evil woman.

*Midrash Tehillim, 53.*

The Rabbis have taught: "A virgin who prays continually, a widow who visits her neighbors too frequently, and an immature student who gives decisions in the law—these are the destroyers of the world."

Rabbi Johanan said: "My experience has shown me that we may learn true fear of sin from a chaste virgin, and true zeal for the performance of a Mitzwah from a widow." He once heard a maiden thus pray: "Lord of the Universe, Thou hast created Paradise for those who obey their good impulse, and Gehenna for those who follow their evil desires. I beg of Thee that no one be cast into Gehenna on my account."

On another occasion, he observed a widow, whom he knew to reside at a distance, visiting his place of worship for prayer. He asked her: "Is there no synagogue nearer your home?"

She answered: "Yes, Rabbi, but the more trouble I take, the greater my reward will be."

*Sotah, 22.*

### THE GOOD WOMEN IN THE BIBLE

Twenty-three good women in Israel and nine in other nations are mentioned in the Bible.

1. Sarah; 2. Rebekah; 3. Rachel; 4. Leah; 5. Jochebed; 6. Miriam; 7. Deborah; 8. the wife of Manoah; 9. Hannah; 10. Abigail; 11. the woman of Tekoah; 12. the widow whom Elijah helped; 13. the Shunamite; 14. Ruldah; 15. Naomi; 16. Jehosheba; 17. the wife of one of the prophets aided by Elisha; 18. Esther; 19-23. the five daughters of Zelophehad.

Those of other nations were: 1. Hagar; 2. Osenath; 3. Zipporah; 4. Shiphrah; 5. Puah; 6. Bathia, who brought up Moses; 7. Rahab; 8. Ruth; 9. Jael.

*Midrash Tadshe, 21.*

## 404. WORDS—DEFINITION OF

Why is God called "Makom"? Because He is to be found wherever Zaddikim stand.[1]

*Bereshit Rabbah, 68-9.*

[1] "Kum" means "stand."

"Teiko" means: "The question is still standing" or "the question is still in its sheath uncovered." [1]

*Tishbi by Elijah Bahur.*

[1] Arukand Maarik.

Why do we find the name "Urim and Tumim?" "Urim" means "Light up their words"; "Tumim" means "Fulfil their words."

*Yoma, 73.*

When we find the word "Adam" in Scripture, it means "Man"; "Adam and animal," it means a man who is as senseless as an animal. "Ish" or "Geber" signifies "a wise man"; "Enosh" means "a foolish man."

*Midrash Tehillim, 9, 16.*

What is the definition of "Ebion"? "The poor man who is not ashamed to ask."

*Baba Metzia, 111.*

The inhabitants of Galilee were careless in their pronunciation. Once a Galilean came to Judea and called out: "Who has amar for sale?"

The Judeans laughed at him, and answered: "Thou foolish Galilean, how are we to understand what thou wishest? Is it 'hamar' (ass) to ride on, 'hemar' (wine) to drink, 'amar' (wool) for a garment, or 'imar' (a sheep) to slaughter?"

*Erubin, 53.*

## 405. THE POWER OF WORDS

The punishment meted out to him who speaks evil words is also meted out to him who has an opportunity to utter good words but does not speak them.

*Zohar, iii, 46b.*

A word once spoken ascends to Heaven, and prepares for the speaker good or evil as his portion in the World-to-Come.

*Zohar, iii, 31b.*

No man should treat lightly the speech of another man. We find that Moses listened attentively to the words of Jethro.

*Zohar, ii, 68b, Tosefta.*

These words neither help nor hurt my arguments.

*Y. Taanit, 2, 12.*

## Be Careful of Your Words

Because Antigonus of Soko remarked that we must not serve God with the expectation of a reward, sects arose in Israel, for words may act like poisonous waters and poison the mind of listeners.

All of the Disciples of Antigonus did not understand the meaning of his words. Some of them thought: "If it were true that there is life after death and a resurrection, our Master would not have reminded us to expect no reward. Is it logical to tell workers that they will not be compensated for their labors?"

When the Sectaries beheld that the Pharisees cared little for the enjoyments of the world, they said: "We truly pity them. In this life they torment themselves, and after death they shall have nothing as recompense."

*Abot de-R. Nathan, 5, paraphrased.*

## 406. WORDS—AS INITIALS AND NUMBERS

ADaM has the initials of Efer (ashes), Dam (blood), Marah (gall).

*Sotah, 5.*

The first letter of the alphabet is "Aleph." These are the initials of the words: "Emet Lemad Pika"; "make the mouth habituated to speak the truth."

*Otiot de Rabbi Akiba, 1.*

YaH and the word SheMI have the numerical value of 365; this is the number of the negative Mitzwot.

YaH and the word ZiKRI have the value of 248; and this is the number of positive commandments. All Mitzwot are bound up with God's name.

*Zohar, iii, 110b.*

We find that Moses was unable to understand three command-ments: concerning the Menorah, the New Moon and the Shekel Temple-tax. God showed him a fiery Menorah, a fiery Shekel, and the sprouting Moon, and said to Moses: "See and do." He also told Moses: "The initials of thy name will remind thee of these three things: M-enorah, S-hekel and H-aHodesh spell MoSheH."

*Raia Mehemna, ii, 157b.*

We learn in Erubin 13 that R. Meir's name was originally R. Nehorai. Why was the name changed from the Aramaic form to the Hebrew form of the word: Meir, "The Light-giver"?

It may be because four marginal notes were discovered in his private Bible and their initials, Mem, Aleph, Iod and Resh, spell Mair, pronounced Meir.

The notes are, as follows:

1. And it was very good—and death was very good. Death is Mawet.

2. "And He clothed them in garments of skins ('Or)—and He clothed them in garments of light (Or)." Aleph substituted.

3. "And the sons (Bnei) of Dan was Hushim—and the son (Ben) of Dan was Hushim. He omitted the Iod or Yud.

4. The burden of Domah—the burden of Romah. He changed a Resh for Dalet, so as to apply the prophecy to Rome.

*An explanation by Rabbi A. Heyman.*

Ben Azzai was requested to say something on the subject of the Book of Lamentations. He said: "Israel was not exiled until he denied the Aleph, the One God; the Yod, the Ten Commandments; the Kaph, the circumcision which was ordered on the 20th generation since Adam; the He, the five books of the Torah. Therefore, does the Book of Lamentations begin with the letters Aleph, Yod, Kaph and He.[1]

*Ekah Rabbah, 1.*

[1] Aleph has the numerical value of 1. Yod has the numerical value of 10 Kaph has the numerical value of 20. He has the numerical value of 5.

## 407. WORK, WORKMAN

R. Simeon suggests that nothing shall stand in the way of continuous study of God's word. As for the daily needs of life, do not worry! "When Israel acts according to the wish of God, his work will be performed by others."

*Sifre Ekeb, p. 80b.*

The unfaithful workman is a robber. He does God's work deceitfully.

*Baba Metzia, 78a.*

## 408. THE WORLD

The center of the world is exactly where you stand.

*Bekorot, 8.*

God is the space of the universe, but the space of God is far vaster than the universe.

*Tikkune Zohar, T. 42, 121b.*

The world is like a ladder—some ascend and some descend.

*Tanhuma Matot, 9.*

The world is shaped like a ball.

*Y. Abodah Zorah, 3, 1.*

The earth revolves in a circle like a ball; always a part is above and a part is below. The natives of different origins have different colors of the skin, according to their respective climates. There is a portion of the world where it is daylight, while it is night in the opposite region.

There is a place where at a certain season it is only daylight and not night.

*Zohar, iii, 10a.*

The world is like the oval of the eye. The white is the sea which surrounds the dry land; the black is the dry land. The pupil is the city of Jerusalem, and the face within it is the Holy Temple.

*Derek Eretz Zuta, 9.*

Each man should say: "The world was created for my sake."

*Sanhedrin, 37, Mishnah.*

The world exists for the sake of him who sacrifices his soul for the benefit of the world.

*Zohar, iii, 29a.*

Rabban Simeon ben Gamaliel said: "The world is sustained by three things: Justice, Truth and Peace."

*Abot, 1, 18.*

The Emperor Hadrian asked Aquila: "Pray, tell me what sustains the life of the earth?"

Aquila replied: "The breath of life. If a cord were placed about the neck of a living person, and you would pull from one side and I from the other, what would happen? No limb would be injured, but the life would vanish."

*Tanhuma Bereshit.*

Simeon, the Righteous, said: "The world rests on three pillars: on the Torah, on the cultus, and on works of charity," or "on the knowledge of divine revelation, the worship of God, and deeds of loving-kindness to men."

*Abot, 1, 2.*

## 409. WORLDLY ENJOYMENTS

This world can be enjoyed in its perfection only by either a perfect Zaddik or a thoroughly wicked man.

*Berakot, 61.*

One man cannot seize that which has been prepared for another.

*Yoma, 38.*

## 410. WORRY

Hillel said: "The more property, the more anxiety; the more wives, the more superstition; the more slaves, the more robbery."

*Abot, 2, 7.*

When a man has no anxiety regarding money, he loves company; when he is worried, however, he cannot tolerate company.

*Bereshit Rabbah, 91, 5.*

Let no worry enter thy heart, for worry hath killed man after man

*Sanhedrin, 100.*

A sigh breaks half the body.

*Berakot, 58.*

## 411. WORTHINESS

Rabbi Judah bar Shalum told of a king's son who was anxious that every one should know that he was a prince. "Oh, my father," he once cried, "let the people know that I am the king's son."

"Would you have the people know that you are my son?" asked the king; "then don my regal robe and put on my kingly crown and let the people see with what grace and honor you wear them."

*Debarim Rabbah, 7, 10.*

## 412. WRONG ASPIRATIONS—WRONG AMBITIONS

The Rabbis have taught: "We learn from the penalty meted out unto the suspected wife that he who desires what he should not have, does not secure what he wishes and loses what he has. The same lesson may be learned from the fate of the following: 'Cain, who wished the same approval from God as Abel received, though he did not labor to deserve it; Korah, who wished the priesthood; Balaam, who was prepared to curse Israel for money and lost his inspiration from God; Doeg and Ahitophel, who were envious of David and lost their high positions; Gehazi, who lost his holy position in his desire for money from Naaman; Absalom, who lost his life in attempting to anticipate his succession to the throne; Adonijah, who lost his life by reason of his desire for the royal widow, Abishag; Uzziah, who wished to take unto himself the priestly duty and became a leper; Haman, who lost his life because he wished even Mordecai to bow to him.'"

*Sotah, 10.*

### THE OVER-AMBITIOUS

Two very wise men, Balaam and Ahitophel, were very ambitious and failed. Two very strong men, Samson and Goliath, were very ambitious and failed. Two very rich men, Korah and Haman, were over-ambitious and failed. The tribes of Reuben, Gad and half of Menasseh were rich in cattle and flocks; they were over-ambitious in regard to acquiring Transjordania. They were the first to taste exile.

*Bemidbar Rabbah, 22.*

An ancient adage says: "Many an old ass carries a load of hides from young foals."

When Moses and Aaron led the people of Israel into the desert, the two ambitious sons of Aaron, Nadab and Abihu, said to one another: "When the aged leaders shall pass away, we shall take over the leadership."

But God said: "Let us first see who buries whom."

*Sanhedrin, 52.*

## 413. YOM KIPPUR

### The Old Man

"And there shall not be any man in the Tabernacle of the congregation when he goeth in to make an atonement in the holy place." (Lev. 16:17)

How can we reconcile this with the story told by the High Priest, Simon the Just? Once on a Yom Kippur, Simon said: "This year I shall die."

His friends asked: "How do you know?"

He answered: "Every Yom Kippur an old man, dressed in white, has entered the Holy of Holies and departed from it with me. Today, however, he entered with me but did not leave."

Rabbi Abbahu said: "It was not a man, but God Himself, in the guise of an old man."

It was further asked: "Why does not the verse add after the words "Any man"—"beside the High Priest"?

Rabbi Simon answered: "The High Priest was like unto an angel, and his face was burning like a flame."

*Pesikta Buber, pp. 177–8.*

Psalm 27 may be said to apply to Rosh ha-Shanah and Yom Kippur: "The Lord is my light" means Rosh ha-Shanah; "And my salvation" means Yom Kippur; And on these days I am unafraid of my enemies, namely, my evil inclinations and passions. For I have been privileged to come into the Holy Place and that gives me assurance that I shall triumph in the war they make against me.

*Pesikta Buber, p. 176a (modernized).*

### With This Thing

Rabbi Yudan said: We read (Lev. 16:3): "With ZOT (this thing) will Aaron enter the Holy Place on Yom Kippur to atone for Israel."

With what thing? With the merit of the Mitzwot which are introduced by the word "Zot". These are: Torah (Deut. 4:44), Circumcision (Gen. 7:10), Sabbath (Isaiah 56:2), Jerusalem (e.g. with the Mitzwot applicable only to Jerusalem, Ezekiel 5:5), the sons of Jacob (Genesis 49:28), Judah (Deut. 33:7), Israel (Song of Songs 7:8), Terumah (Exodus 25:3), Tithes (Malachi 3:10).

*Pesikta Buber, p. 176b.*

### Desiring the Forbidden

The man who led the he-goat to Azazel was permitted to partake of food and drink. Huts with food and water were prepared for his benefit at several stop-over points, yet it never happened that the man took advantage of this permission. Why, then, did they prepare the food year after year? Because the Yetzer Ha-Ra (the Evil Impulse) desires most that which is forbidden.

Rabbi Mani visited Rabbi Haggai on Yom Kippur because the latter was feeling weak. Rabbi Haggai said: "I am very thirsty."

Rabbi Mani remarked: "Here is water; take it and drink."

He then left and returned an hour later. "Have you quenched your thirst?"

"I did not drink," said Rabbi Haggai, "because, since you gave me permission, my thirst left me."

At the conclusion of the additional prayer for Yom Kippur (Musaf), Rabbi Aha would say: "All of you who have small children, go home and feed them even if they do not ask for food."

*Yoma, 66; Y. Yoma, 6.*

### The Interpreter

Rab Shela was lecturing on Temple procedure during Yom Kippur. The interpreter became ill, and Rab, who had just come to Babylonia from Palestine, and was still unknown, volunteered to serve as interpreter. Rab Shela read the Mishnah in Yoma, that before the calling of Geber at sunrise, the Temple spaces were filled with men. Rab interpreted the phrase to mean: "Calling of the loud-voiced herald."

Rab Shela said: " 'Geber' means a rooster."

Rab replied: "In our region we have a folk-saying: 'The song beloved by the patrons of music was sung before the rabble and they booed it down.' I translated 'Geber' before Rabbi Hiyya to mean 'herald' and he was satisfied. Thou art a lesser man and art dissatisfied."

"Art thou Rab?" asked Rab Shela.

"Yes," he answered.

"Then thou art too important to serve as an interpreter."

"Nay," Rab replied, "if a man once hires himself out, he must do any kind of work demanded of him. Furthermore, it would demean the quality of the sacred lecture to have it interpreted by one who is unlearned."

*Yoma, 20.*

When the Sanctuary fell there fell with it the wall of iron that had severed Israel from his God.

*Berakot, 32b.*

### The High Priest's Prayer

On Yom Kippur in the Holy of Holies the following prayer is offered:

"May it be Thy Will, O Lord, that the coming year shall have sufficient dew, rain and shade; may it be a year of good-will, of blessing, of abundance, of a rich harvest, of good exchange of goods. May no one in Israel find it necessary to accept favors from another Israelite; may no one in Israel show mastery over another Israelite. Mayest Thou not incline Thine ear when travelers on the highway pray for dry weather.

Mayest Thou have compassion on those who dwell in the low country, that neither sand-dunes nor cloud-bursts make their homes their graves." [1]

*Wayyikra Rabbah, 17.*

[1] During the existence of the Temple, there were no fixed prayers with exact wording. The prayers could be varied so long as they contained the proper idea. Variants of the above prayer exist.

### THE ORIGIN OF YOM KIPPUR

After the Ten Commandments were given to Israel on Shabuot, Moses ascended Mount Sinai and remained there forty days to receive the Tablets. He descended on the 17th of Tamuz, and broke the Tablets because the people worshipped the Golden Calf. For forty days Moses set up his tent beyond the camp of Israel, and the people mourned. On the 1st day of Elul, Moses ascended the mountain again to receive the second Tablets. During this period the Hebrews fasted daily from sunrise to sunset. On the fortieth day they fasted from sunset to sunset. This day was the 10th of Tishri. The Hebrews wept when they went forth to meet Moses in the morning; and he wept when he beheld their repentance. Then God said: "Your repentance is accepted, and this day will remain the Day of Atonement throughout all generations."

*Tanna Eliyahu Zuta, 4.*

### THE MISCHIEVOUS BABYLONIANS

The he-goat for Azazel was taken out by a priest to be cast over the precipice. Rabbi Jose remarked that he had been told that a Rabbi from Sepphoris, the Rabbi's native town, once took out the goat. At first the Babylonian Jews would tear the hair of the man taking out the goat, and they would say: "Begone, thou carrier of our many sins; tarry not."

For this reason it was found necessary to build a ladder from a high window, so that the man might escape thus. When Rabbi Jose heard of his country-men's [1] misbehaviour, he felt ashamed. Rabbi Judah wished to console him, and said: "It was really the Jews of Alexandria who misbehaved, but the Palestinian Jews disliked the Babylonian Jews and spread the rumor that the latter were guilty."

When this came to the ears of the Alexandrians, they indignantly denied the charge.

*Yoma, 6, paraphrased.*

[1] R. Isaac Halevi in "Dorot Ha-Rishonim" denies that R. Jose was a Babylonian. He felt ashamed, because the Babylonian Jews were scholars and pious men.

### THE TWO GOATS

Why were there two goats, one a sacrifice on the altar, and one a sacrifice on the rock to Azazel? The goats represent Esau and Jacob, or the righteous and the wicked. Both were born in the same home; both were brought up in goodness. Yet one chose to labor for God, and the other against God.

"Az" means "impudent"; "Azal" means "departed". If Israel is impudent and disobedient, he shall be forced to take his departure into lands of exile.[1]

*Abrabanel, Ahare.*

[1] We include this late item, because it gives a good explanation of this mysterious rite.

### 414. ANCIENT SERMONS ON YOM KIPPUR

"For thou hast stumbled through thy iniquity." (Hosea 14:2)
Rabbi Simi said: "We may use the simile of a large rock which fell into the middle of the highway where people stumbled over it. The governor said: 'Let each one of you bring a hammer, and, when you pass by, break off a piece. When it is thus crushed, I shall cause it to be removed.' By the same token, God also saith: 'An Evil Impulse is a vast stumbling-stone. Let each one of you break off a piece by means of repentance, and resolve not to obey it. When the Evil Impulse is sufficiently crushed, I shall in the days-to-come remove Satan from your midst.'" (Ezekiel 36:26)

*Pesikta Shubah, Buber, p. 165a.*

Rabbi Isaac commented upon the verse: "Adding one to another to find out the account." (Eccl. 7:27) Every tribulation which comes to man adds up to pay his account to God.

*Pesikta Buber, p. 165a.*

God saith to Israel: "My sons, I have tried arduously to aid you in your conduct, but it has not availed. I set chastisements upon you; I rebuked you; I warned you; I exiled you; I took away your wealth; yet it proved in vain. I sought to promise you blessings if you improved; I sought to be patient with you; I commanded you; I sent messengers unto you; I blessed you; I cursed you; I sent terror and panic upon you; I placed on you the fear of violent death and violated graves, and of Gehenna. Yet you gave no heed. You did not regret your conduct, though it brought to pass the burning of the Holy Temple and the profanation of My Name. What will you do on the Day of Accounting?" (Isaiah 10:3)

*Pesikta Hadashah to Yom Kippur in Otzar Midrashim, p. 407.*

"He who sins with his eyes will suffer from weakened eyes. He who offends with his ears shall hear abuse of himself. He who transgresses with his mouth shall find his words unheard. He who transgresses with counsel shall lose the power of good counsel in his own affairs. He who transgresses with thought shall find his life seems unendurable. He who transgresses with his tongue shall suffer chastisements. He who transgresses with his hands shall lose his honors. He who transgresses with his heart shall be filled with anxieties. He who transgresses with his feet shall find his years shortened. He who transgresses with his Evil Impulse shall behold his Impulse testify against him. The fate of the scoffer shall be sealed to evil. The companion of the wicked is driven from the world. The flatterer of the wicked enrages the Lord; the deceiver will suffer injury. The traducer curses his Maker. He who laughs at Mitzwot will receive no compassion. He who ridicules scholars will find no cure; he who caricatures the poor will die in poverty. Observe, O man, all these things and abstain from sin. Hast thou not seen many rich become poor; many strong become weak; many wise, stumble by their wisdom; many young who have not lived to maturity? It is within your power to resist temptation, but, if you have become a victim of your tempter, sin no more, return to the Lord and ask his forgiveness. Be assured that your repentance will reach the Throne of God and your days will be lengthened on earth."

*Otzar Midrashim, p. 497.*

Koheleth says that he who enjoys worldly pleasures should not offend, for he must in the end render an account. (See Eccl. 11:9.)

Rabbi Hiyya said: "It is like a man who runs away from being questioned by an official of the law. He is counselled not to run too far, lest he find it difficult to return when the matter quiets down.

Rabbi Simeon ben Halafta said: "It is like a swimmer who is cautioned not to swim too far from shore. Thus he cannot avoid the hardship of returning."

Rabbi Hanina ben Papa said: "It is like him who has evaded customs duties many times. When discovered he is forced not only to pay the duties for this single instance, but he is commanded to pay for previous evasions as well.

Rabbi Levi said: "It is like a caged bird who is looked upon with envy by a free bird, and is told: 'Thou seest my food but not my fate.' "

Rabbi Tanhum said: "It is like a mischievous lad who orders a meal at a tavern. He refuses to pay and is brought to court."

*Pesikta Shubah, Buber, p. 164.*

Rabbi Eliezer said: "We read: 'Oh Thou God who art for Israel like unto a purifying water.' (Jer. 14:18) [1] 'Since it is customary that an impure person go to the water for purification, therefore, saith God, come unto my House to be cleansed on Yom Kippur. But if thou art unable to come to the House of Prayer, pray in thy garden, in thy home, or in thy bed. If thou art unable to speak, speak in your heart (Ps. 4:5), but, whatever the circumstances, return unto Me.' "

*Pesikta Shubah, Buber, p. 158a.*

[1] Mikweh means "hope" and "purifying vessel of water."

Rabbi Jose said: "He who repents is regarded by God as if he went up to Jerusalem and offered sacrifices to Him." (Psalm 51, 19:21)

Rabbi Alexanderi said: "A man hates to use broken vessels, but God loves them." (Psalm 34:19)

*Pesikta Shubah, Buber, 158.*

Said Rabbi Jose: "Open to Me, My sister." (Song of Songs, 5:2) [1]

[1] Me and my refer to God according to interpretation.

God saith: "Open to Me an entrance the width of a needle's eye, and I shall open to you an entrance through which tents and wagons can pass."

Rabbi Tanhum said: "You may repent during the trembling of an eye. Tremble and know that I am God." (Psalm 46:11)

Rabbi Levi said: "If Israel truly repented for a single day, they would be redeemed, as it is written: 'Yea, this day, if he will hearken to His Voice.'" (Psalm 95:7)

Rabbi Judah bar Simon said: "It is written: 'Return, O Israel, unto thy God, (Hosea 14:2), even if thou hast denied God.'"

Rabbi Eliezer said: "If a man insults a comrade in public and wishes to appease him, he is told: 'You have insulted me in public. Go and bring unto my presence those who have heard the insult and offer your apology before them.' It is not so with God. A man may blaspheme in the market-place; yet God saith to him: 'Seek My pardon between ourselves and I shall accept thy petition.'"

*Pesikta Shubah, Buber, p. 163b.*

When the fate of Israel is about to be sealed on Yom Kippur, Satan saith: "Are there not enough criminals and wicked men among Israel? Why should they of all nations deserve atonement on this day?" God replies: "Their sins and their Mitzwot are of equal weight, but the blood of their martyrs inclines their fate towards mercy."

*Pesikta Rabbati, 46, 2, and comment.*

Abbaye said: "Thou shalt love thy God and make Him beloved. How? Show people by your example how to demonstrate love for God. Study Torah in public, honor men of learning in public, speak in a gentle manner, deal with people faithfully. What will people say concerning you? They will say: 'Happy is the man who has learned Torah; happy is the father of the learned man; happy is the teacher of the scholarly person. Behold how admirable are the actions of him who has learned Torah; how perfect are his ways.'

"What will God say concerning you? 'My servant art thou, O Israelite, in whom I take pride.'" (Isaiah 59:3)

*Otzar Midrashim, p. 498.*

Rabbi Phinehas said: "Good and upright is the Lord. Therefore He pointeth out to sinners the right way." (Psalm 25:8)

"Why is He good? Because He is upright. Why is He upright? Because He is good. And because of both attributes, He longs for repentance."

Rabbi Isaac said: "But whoso confesseth and forsaketh them shall obtain mercy" (Proverbs 28:13). "This means: 'Whoso confesseth with the intention of forsaking his sins shall surely receive mercy.'"

*Pesikta Shubah, Buber, p. 158-9*

A man of perfect righteousness shall enjoy happiness in both worlds; a completely evil man shall be unhappy in both worlds. But a Zaddik who is not perfect may enjoy only the next world and suffer in this world as a purification. The wicked man who prospers is the one who is not completely evil. Many such persons accumulate riches and forget God, but will cherish the happy thought that their children will have no need to immerse themselves in worldliness because of the wealth they will inherit. It may also be that when they have reached their goal, they will return unto God and sin no more.

*Otzar Midrashim, p. 498.*

## 415. YOM KIPPUR—FORGIVENESS ON

Things between thee and God are forgiven on Yom Kippur. Things between thee and thy fellow-man are not forgiven thee, until he has forgiven thee.

*Sifra to Ahare.*

Satan accuses the Jews every day of the year except on the Day of Atonement.

*Yoma, 20a.*

### Satan's Report

When Satan is ready to take his departure from the Lord on Yom Kippur, God tells him: "It will not avail you to tempt and inform against Israel on this day. But, if you wish to see what they are doing, you may visit them."

When Satan returns to God, he reports: "The Israelites are all fasting and are dressed in white like the Ministering Angels."

God then locks up Satan and proclaims: "I have forgiven!"

*Midrash Tehillim, 27.*

### Without Guile

People congratulated a friend who had been cleared of a crime. Another friend, however, remarked: "Congratulate me rather who have never been on trial."

By the same token, David says: "Happy is he whose transgression is forgiven" (Psalm 32:1). And God responds: "Nay, happy is he unto whom the Lord imputeth not iniquity, and in whose spirit there is no guile." (Psalm 32:2)

*Pesikta Rabbati, 46, 3.*

If a man says: I shall sin and repent, he is not given an opportunity to repent.

If a man says: I shall sin and Yom Kippur will atone, it does not atone.

Sins between God and man are atoned by Yom Kippur.

Sins between man and man are not forgiven on Yom Kippur until the offender has appeased him who is offended.

*Yoma, Mishnah, 5, 9.*

### The Great Fish

There is a legend that once a huge fish was brought to the market on the eve of Yom Kippur. There were only two customers for this fish: the governor's servant, and a Jewish tailor. Each bid against the other until the price was twelve dinars, when the governor's servant withdrew from the bidding in favor of the tailor. When the governor learned of this, he sent for the tailor.

"Why dost thou, a tailor, buy a fish worth twelve dinars?" he inquired.

"Because we have a day on which all the sins of the entire year are forgiven. Shall I not honor the day when it comes?"

The tailor returned to his home, and, on opening the fish, discovered within a large pearl. He became a wealthy man.

*Bereshit Rabbah, 11.*

## 416. YOUTH

The deeds of a man in his youth blacken his face in his old age.

*Shabbat, 152.*

Happy is the man who has acquired Torah in his youth.

*Midrash Mishle, 5.*

If you do not bend the twig of a vine when it is young, you cannot bend it when it hardens.

*Midrash Mishle, 22.*

If thou has not desired the lessons of Torah in thy youth, how shalt thou attain them in thy old age?

*Abot de-R. Nathan, 24, 4.*

Learning becomes part of the very blood of him who learns in his youth.

*Abot de-R. Nathan, 24.*

### A MINOR'S ACTS

Giddul bar Menashia asked Rabba: "May our teacher inform us how the law considers a girl fourteen years and a day old who understands the principles of trade and barter?"

Rabba replied: "If she understands the rules of barter, her purchases and sales are legal."

Why a girl? Because the case involved a girl.

*Baba Batra, 155.*

A minor left a will and died. Dependent relatives went before the Sages, and argued that a minor could not make a will. Persons who benefited asserted that the dead testator was not a minor. The first claimants wished to have the body exhumed and examined, but the Sages refused to order this.

*Baba Batra, 155.*

A minor sold his field and then changed his mind. His relatives counselled him to eat dates in court and to throw the stones in front of him. He came to Rabba and did so. Thereupon Rabba issued a decision, saying that he might change his mind since he was a fool. The purchaser of the field went to the boy, however, and said: "Listen, the court-writer wishes to overcharge you. When he asks you for a zuz to write the decision, complain to Rabba that only a zuz is demanded for writing the long Book of Esther, and the court-writer wishes a zuz for only a few lines."

The boy did as he was told, and thereupon Rabba tore up the verdict of the court. His relatives said to Rabba: "It was the purchaser who advised him to make this complaint."

Rabba answered: "A boy who can act upon advice when he reasons it out to be beneficial to himself is no fool. As to his throwing date stones in front of the court, this was merely bad manners."

*Baba Batra, 155.*

## 417. ZADDIK

A good Zaddik is good to God and good to people.
*Kiddushin, 40.*

The world never has less than thirty-six Zaddikim who welcome the Shekinah daily.[1]
*Sukkah, 45.*

[1] Many folk-tales are based on this.

Why is the word " 'Eter" [1] used to denote the prayer of the Zaddikim? Because as the 'Eter or hay-fork, turns over the hay, so does the Zaddik's prayer turn the will of God from justice to mercy.
*Sukkah, 14.*

[1] Genesis 25:21.

The Zaddikim say little and do much.
*Hullin, 7.*

God tests only the Zaddikim.
*Bereshit Rabbah, 34, 2.*

The Zaddikim says little and do much.
*Baba Metzia, 87.*

The more honors the Zaddikim receive, the more humble they become.
*Pesikta Zutarti to Bemidbar.*

The world is sustained by the merit of the Zaddikim, but the Zaddikim are not sustained by their own merit.
*Berakot, 17.*

God beheld that the Zaddikim are extremely few. He planted them in each generation.
*Yoma, 38.*

The prayer of the Zaddikim turns God's nature from anger to compassion.
*Yebamot, 64.*

The soul of one Zaddik has the weight (importance) of the entire world.

*Sanhedrin, 103.*

If the householder is a Zaddik, the members of his household are also Zaddikim.

*Pesikta Rabbati, Beyom ha-Shemini.*

Before God causes the sun of one Zaddik to set, he causes the sun of another to rise.

*Kohelet Rabbah, 1.*

Even if a decree has issued from God, the Zaddik can annul it.

*Shabbat, 63.*

The way of Zaddikim on the road is thus: when he travels, light accompanies him; when he travels, Torah accompanies him.

*Zohar Hadash to Ruth, 77b.*

A Zaddik does not depart from this world until another Zaddik like him has come into it.

*Yoma, 38.*

The earth is supported on one pillar, the name of which is Zaddik.

*Zohar, ii, 116a.*

Each Zaddik has a world for himself: it is his body, and it is called "Little World."

*Tikkune Zohar, T. 69, p. 140b.*

"I rule over man," says God. "Who rules over Me? The Zaddik. I decree and he annuls."

*Moed Katon, 16.*

For the sake of one righteous man the whole world is preserved in existence, as it is written: "The righteous man is an everlasting foundation." (Or, the Zaddik is the foundation of the world.) (Proverbs 10:25)

*Yoma, 38b.*

You will not often find a man who loves one of the same calling. The scholar, however, loves one of his calling. And God loves one of His calling, as it is said: "The Lord is righteous; He loves righteousness." (Psalm 11:7)

*Midrash Tehillim on above verse.*

The true Zaddik is not like Noah, who heard of the doom of the world and did not pray for the doomed; but like Abraham, who heard of the doom of Sodom and immediately prayed for its inhabitants.

*Zohar, i, 254b.*

Why is a Zaddik likened to a palm-tree? As a palm-tree when cut down will not have in its place another palm-tree for a long-time, so a Zaddik when cut down leaves no equal in his place for a long time.[1]

*Zohar, i, 82a.*

[1] This does not contradict the statement in Yoma, 38 (above), for the succeeding Zaddik may be a lesser personality.

How can a Zaddik be distinguished? By the existence of the wicked.
*Zohar, ii, 20b.*

The man who walks in the ways of the Lord eats his bread and drinks his wine in the joy of his heart.
*Zohar, ii, 29a.*

The world stands upon the chiefs of the people. If they are meritorious, good attends the world and good attends the people.
*Zohar, ii, 36b.*

The worthy man should follow the guilty man and aid him to remove all uncleanliness, to subdue the Sitra Ahara, and to cure his soul. Thus will it be accounted to the man of merit as if he had begotten the man of guilt.
*Zohar, ii, 128b.*

All the merits of the Zaddik are engraved upon his limbs.
*Raia Mehemna, iii, 16b.*

The Zaddik who cleaves in love to the Higher King with all his soul, as he should, receives rulership over the world; whatsoever he decrees with reference to the world is fulfilled.
*Zohar, iii, 68a.*

Sometimes a Zaddik is summoned by death before he has completed the garment of holiness wherewith to clothe himself in the Other World. What does God do? He completes the garment by utilizing the good deeds of the wicked. The wicked help to prepare the garment and the Zaddik clothes himself with it.[1]
*Zohar, iii, 101a.*

[1] The merits of the wicked are thus increased in worth.

When God wishes to send healing to the world in pain, he sends it to the Zaddik, and for his sake the world also profits.
*Zohar, iv, 218a.*

A Zaddik frequently pays his debts to God in this world. This is why so many Zaddikim suffer penalty and sickness.
*Zohar, iv, 231a.*

The highest chamber on High is allotted to those whose love God reciprocates.
*Zohar, v, 267b.*

God wishes to honor the Zaddik more than he wishes honor for Himself.
*Zohar, v, 288a.*

Moses is spread out in all generations and in every Zaddik.
*Tikkune, Zohar, T., 69, p. 140b.*

When one is called "Man" in the Bible, he is a great man in his generation, able to stand up for himself and others.
*Zohar Hadash to Ruth, 77b.*

God does not decree that a man should be a Zaddik and a good man but, if his father's desire has been to raise up his son as a Zaddik, God brings the gracious thought to fulfilment.

*Zohar Hadash, Tikkunim, 121b.*

### THE UNLEARNED ZADDIK

Rabbi Yannai once met a distinguished-looking man, whom he took to be a "Talmid Hakam" (Disciple of the Wise, namely a Rabbi). He invited him to join in a meal, after which he started to discuss a Biblical topic with him. But the man knew neither Mishnah, Aggadah, or any Talmudical subject. Rabbi Yannai asked his guest to recite grace, but even this the man could not do. The Rabbi became angry, and said: "Are you able to repeat after me what I say"

"Yes," answered the man.

"Then say after me: "A dog ate Yannai's bread.' "

The guest seized hold of the Rabbi, and said: "I demand my inheritance."

"What do you mean?" asked Rabbi Yannai.

"I heard a school-boy recite: 'Moses commanded us the Torah, an inheritance of the congregation of Jacob' (Deut. 33:4). He did not say: 'an inheritance of Yannai' but of all Jacob."

The Rabbi then asked his guest: "Have you any values outside of learning?"

"I believe I have," replied the man. "I never repeat slander, and I always endeavour to pacify those who quarrel."

The Rabbi begged the pardon of his guest, saying: "How could I have called, even by implication, a man of such admirable character, 'a dog'? Indeed I am heartily sorry."

*Wayyikra Rabbah, 9.*

### DROUGHT IN JUDAEA

On the occasion of a drought in Judæa, people reported to Rabbi Abbahu that they knew a man whose prayers for rain were infallible. His popular name was "Five Sins."

Rabbi Abbahu interviewed him and inquired regarding the origin of his name. He said: "My work is among the women of ill-fame. I clean the theatre, I carry the vessels to the bath, I amuse the bathers with my jokes, and I play the flute."

"But," said the Rabbi, "you must have done some good thing in your life, if God hears your prayer."

The man replied: "Once as I was sweeping the theatre, I saw a woman standing between the pillars weeping bitterly. I learned from her that her husband was a prisoner. She could purchase his freedom only by sacrificing her honor, since she had no money to redeem him. Thereupon I sold all my possessions and gave her the money to ransom her husband."

On hearing these words, Rabbi Abbahu exclaimed: "Thou art truly a man fit to pray for us in this hour of tribulation."

*Y. Taanit, 1, 2.*

### GREETINGS FROM HEAVEN

Three persons received greetings from the Heavenly Yeshibah (Academy on High), during the age of Rabba: Abba, the Bleeder, daily; Abbaye, each Friday; and Rabba, on the Eve of Yom Kippur. Abbaye envied Abba, and Rabba envied Abbaye.

Abbaye was told: "Thou canst not do what Abba does. When he bleeds a female, he does so through a hole in the door, in order that he may not look at her bared arm. He has a box into which people throw his fee if they have the money; otherwise they leave without payment. He does not see who pays and who does not. He takes no fee from the student and gives him coins with which to eat well and regain his strength."

Abbaye wished to test him, and sent two Disciples to his house. Abba welcomed them, and, when night fell, he laid over their beds costly woolen blankets. In the morning, they took the blankets and waited for him at the next corner. Abba appeared, they asked him: "How much are these worth?"

He told them how much he had paid for similar blankets.

They inquired: "Will you buy these from us?"

When he had agreed to buy them from them, the Disciples informed the Rabbi that they were merely testing his character, and offered to return the blankets. Abba said: "No, I shall pay you for them, as if I were a stranger to you, for, when I saw you leave with them, I thought you needed the money in haste to ransom captives, and I vowed these blankets to charity. Give the money rather to a worthy cause."

Rabba in his turn was told: "Be not envious, for thy merit protects the city."

*Taanit, 21.*

## 418. ZION

Ulla said: "Our Redemption will come only through freewill gifts; as Isaiah said (1, 27): 'Zion shall be redeemed with justice and they that return of her with charity (or righteousness).'"

*Shabbat, 139a*

The Sages declare: "Out of Zion was the creation of dry land begun; as it is said: 'The Lord has spoken and called the earth . . . out of Zion the perfection of beauty' (Psalm 50:1, 2). Out of Zion was perfected the best part of the world, namely dry land."

*Yoma, 54b.*

Of Zion it shall be said: "This man and that was born in her." (Psalm 87:5, 6)

Rabbi Measha said: "Whether one was born in Zion or looks forward to see Zion, the Lord shall number both in the roster of the peoples."

*Ketubot, 75a.*

R. Johanan said: "In the Days-to-Come God will grant to each

Zaddik residing in Zion several canopies, as it is written in Isaiah 4:5. It is asked: 'Why is smoke needed?' To cause discomfort to the eyes of those who looked with disfavor upon the scholars.

"And why is fire needed? To make it impossible for the lesser Zaddik to see the more glorious canopies of the greater Zaddik, and thus to prevent the bitterness of jealousy."

R. Eleazar said: "The Zaddikim in the future shall be called holy, just as God is called; as it is written: 'He that is left in Zion . . . shall be called holy.' " (Isa. 4:3)

*Baba Batra, 75a-b.*

But Zion said: "The Lord hath forsaken me, and the Lord hath forgotten me." (Isaiah 49:14)

Rabbi Simeon ben Lakish said: "God answered: 'I have created in the expanse twelve Zodiac constellations; under each Zodiac I have set up thirty divisions of stars; in each division there are thirty legions; in each legion thirty regiments; in each regiment thirty companies. . . . Each one consists of 365 millions of stars, and all were formed by Me for thy sake only, and yet thou sayest that I have forgotten thee.' "

*Berakot, 32b.*

Rabbi Johanan said: "In the Days-to-Come, the houses (descendants) of the Zaddikim will be restored to fame; as we read: 'They that trust in the Lord are as Mount Zion' (Psalm 125:1). Just as Mount Zion will be restored to its former glory, so the houses of Zaddikim."

*Berakot, 58b.*

R. Johanan said: "The glory that the Israelites acquired when they accepted the Torah was taken away when they sinned by the adoration of the Golden Calf; and it will be restored to them when they will ascend to Zion; as it is written (Isaiah 35:10): 'And the ransomed of the Lord shall return, and Some with singing unto Zion, and the everlasting joy shall be upon their heads.' The joy which they received in the beginning of their national life and which should have lasted forever shall be upon their heads."

*Shabbat, 88.*

"No one inquireth concerning Zion." This teaches us that inquiry should be made regarding Zion.

*Rosh ha-Shanah, 30.*

Every good blessing and comfort that God intends for Israel shall come only from Zion.

*Wayyikra Rabbah, 24:4.*

Resh Lakish said: "We find verses which tell us that joy, blessing, Torah, the salvation of Israel, life, help and the blowing of the Shofar announcing the Redemption of Zion, and so forth, will all come from Zion."

*Pesikta Rabbati, 42:2.*

Out of Zion the beauty of the world hath been, and shall yet be perfected.

*Yoma, 54b.*

# Bibliography

STANDARD EDITIONS OF TALMUDIC-MIDRASHIC LITERATURE

*Talmud Babli,* Romm, Wilna, 1922. Munich Ms. published by Strack in 1910.
*Yerushalmi,* Romm, Wilna, 1922.
*Mishnah,* Romm, Wilna, 1922. Also edition of W. H. Loewe, Cambridge, 1883.
*Tosefta,* Zuckermandel, Tel Aviv, 1937. Also Romm edition, Wilna, 1922.
*Mekilta,* I. H. Weiss, Vienna, 1885. Also M. Friedmann, Vienna, 1870.
*Sifra,* I. H. Weiss, Vienna, 1862.
*Sifre,* M. Friedmann, Vienna, 1864. Also L. Finkelstein, on Deuteronomy, Breslau, 1935–1936, and S. Horowitz, Sifre Numbers, Breslau, 1917.
*Abot de Rabbi Nathan,* S. Schechter, Vienna, 1886.
*Mekilta de Rabbi Simeon ben Yohai,* D. Hoffman, Frankfurt, 1905.
*Sifre Zuta,* S. Horovitz, Leipsic, 1917 (supplement to Sifre Numbers).
*Midrash Tannaim,* D. Hoffman, Frankfurt, 1908.
*Midrash Bereshit Rabbah,* J. Theodor, Berlin, 1912 (completed by C. Albeck, 1932).
*Midrash Rabbah,* Romm, Wilna, 1921.
*Midrash Tehillim,* S. Buber, Wilna, 1891.
*Midrash Mishle,* S. Buber, Wilna, 1893.
*Pesikta,* S. Buber, Lyck, 1868.
*Pesikta Rabbati,* M. Friedmann, Vienna, 1880.
*Tanna debe Eliyahu,* M. Friedmann, Vienna, 1900–3. Also Warsaw edition, 1880.
*Tanhuma,* S. Buber, Wilna, 1885. Also other versions in any edition.
*Megillat Taanit,* Romm, Wilna, 1925. Also H. Lichtenstein, HUCA 8 and 9.
*Yalkut Shimeoni,* I. Goldman, Warsaw, 1876.
*Zohar,* I. Goldman, Warsaw, 1878.
*Bet ha-Midrash,* A. Jellinek, Leipsic and Vienna, 1853–1877.
*Otzar Midrashim,* J. D. Eisenstein, New York, 1915.
*Sefer ha-Likkutim,* E. Gruenhut, Jerusalem, 1898–1903.
*Otzar Midrashim, Bate Midrashot* and *Leket Midrashim,* Wertheimer, ˙Jerusalem, 1897–1914.
*Agudat Aggadot* and *Bet Eked ha-Aggadot,* Horowitz, Frankfurt, 1881.
*Seder Olam Rabbah,* B. Ratner, Wilna, 1894. Also A. Marx, Berlin, 1903.
*Minor Maseketat,* M. Higger, various volumes, New York.

WRITINGS IN ENGLISH ON THE TALMUD, MIDRASH, KABBALAH, ETC.

Articles in the *Jewish Encyclopaedia* and in all other encyclopaedias.
Abelson, J., *Immanence of God in Rabbinic Literature,* London, 1912.
Abelson, J., *Jewish Mysticism,* London, 1913.
Abrahams, Israel, *Studies in Pharisaism and the Gospels,* 2 volumes, Cambridge, 1917–1924.
Belkin, S., *The Alexandrian Halakah,* Philadelphia, 1936.
Baron, S. W., *Social and Religious History of the Jews,* New York, 1937, 3 vols.

Bevan, E. R. and Singer, C., *The Legacy of Israel,* Oxford, 1927.

Bialik, C. N., *Halakah and Agaddah;* English by J. L. Siegel, New York, 1923.

Bloch, J. S., *Israel and the Nations,* Berlin, 1927.

Bokser, B. Z., *Pharisaic Judaism in Transition,* New York, 1935.

Buechler, A., *Studies in Sin and Atonement in Rabbinical Literature,* Oxford, 1929.

Charles, R. H., *Apocrypha and Pseudepigrapha of the Old Testament,* London (Oxford), 1913.

Cohen, A., *Everyman's Talmud,* London, 1932.

Cohen, A., *Babylonian Talmud, Tractate Berakot,* in English, Cambridge, 1921.

Cohen, A., *Ancient Jewish Proverbs,* London, 1911.

Cohen, Henry, *Six Hundred Talmudic Sayings,* Cincinnati, 1894.

Cohn, Joseph, *Flowers of the Midrash,* Yonkers, 1912.

Cohon, Beryl D., *Ethics of the Rabbis,* Boston, 1932.

Dalman, G., *Jesus in Talmud, Midrash, Zohar and Synagogue,* Cambridge, 1893.

Darmesteter, A., *The Talmud,* Philadelphia, 1896.

Delitzsch, *Jewish Artisan Life,* New York, 1883.

Deutsch, Emmanuel, *The Talmud,* Philadelphia, 1895.

Eisenstein, J. D., *The Tales of Rabbah bar bar Hannah,* New York, 1937.

*Encyclopedia of Jewish Knowledge* by Jacob de Haas, New York, 1934.

Feldman, A., *Parables and Similes of the Rabbis,* Cambridge, 1924.

Finkelstein, L., *Akiba,* New York, 1936.

Finkelstein, L., *The Pharisees,* 2 volumes, Philadelphia, 1938.

Fleg, E. and Samuel, M., *The Jewish Anthology,* New York, 1925.

Franck, A., *The Kabbalah,* New York, 1926.

Friedlander, Gerald, *Rabbinic Philosophy and Ethics,* London, 1912.

Friedlander, Gerald, *Laws and Customs of Israel,* 4 vols., London, 1921.

Friedlander, Gerald, *Pirke de Rabbi Eliezer in English,* London, 1916.

Friedlander, Gerald, *Jewish Sources of the Sermon on the Mount,* London, 1911.

Friedlander, L., *Past and Present,* Cincinnati, 1910.

Friedlander, M., *Jewish Religion,* London, 1900.

Gaster, M., *The Exempla of the Rabbis,* London, 1924.

Geiger, Abraham, *Judaism and Its History,* New York, 1865.

Gewurtz, E., *Beautiful Thoughts of the Ancient Hebrews,* New York, 1924.

Ginzberg, Louis, *Legends of the Jews,* 7 volumes, Philadelphia, 1909–1937.

Ginzberg, Louis, *A Commentary on The Talmud of Jerusalem,* New York, 1941.

Ginzburg, C. D., *The Kabbalah,* London, 1920.

Goldin, H. E., *The Book of Legends,* New York, 1929.

Gollancz, H., *Midrash of the Ten Jewish Martyrs in English,* London, 1908.

Gollancz, H., *Pedagogics of the Talmud,* London, 1924.

Gorfinkle, J. I., *Sayings of the Jewish Fathers,* New York, 1913.

Greenup, A. W., *Taanit Yerushalmi in English,* London, 1918.

Harris, M. H., *Hebraic Literature,* New York, 1935.

Hasting's *Encyclopedia of Religion and Ethics,* 12 volumes, New York, 1908–1922.

Herford, R. T., *Christianity in Talmud and Midrash,* London, 1903.

Mielziner, M., *Jewish Law of Marriage and Divorce,* New York, 1901.
Mielziner, M., *Introduction to the Talmud,* new edition, New York, 1925.
*Mishnah,* English translation by H. Danby, Oxford, 1933.
Montague, E. R., *Tales from the Talmud,* Edinburgh, 1906.
Montefiore, C. G., *Rabbinic Literature and Gospel Teaching,* London, 1930.
Montefiore, C. G. and Loewe, J. H., *Rabbinic Anthology,* London, 1938.
Moore, G. F., *Judaism,* 3 volumes, Cambridge, 1927–1930.
Morantz, D., *Talmudic Tales,* Kansas City, 1936.
Newman, J., *Agricultural Life of Babylonian Jews,* London, 1932.
Newman, L. I. and Spitz, S., *Hasidic Anthology,* New York, 1934.
Oesterley, W. O. E., *Tractate Shabbat in English,* London, 1927.
Oesterley, W. O. E., *Tractate Abot in English,* London, 1919.
Oesterley, W. O. E., *Jewish Doctrine of Mediation,* London, 1915.
Oesterley, W. O. E., *Gospel Parables in Light of Jewish Background,* New York, 1936.
Oesterley, W. O. E. and Box, G. E., *The Literature of Rabbinical and Medieval Judaism,* London, 1920.
Oesterley, W. O. E., *Religion and Worship of the Synagogue,* London, 1911.
Peters, M. C., *Wit and Wisdom of the Talmud,* New York, 1901 and 1930.
Porter, F. C., *Jewish Doctrine of Sin or Yezer ha-Ra,* New York, 1901.
Rabinowitz, J., *Mishnah Megillah in English,* Oxford, 1931.
Raisin, J. S., *Twice-Told Talmud Tales,* New York, 1929.
Rapoport, S., *Tales and Maxims from the Midrash,* London, 1907.
Rapoport, S., *Stories and Sayings from the Talmud,* London, 1912.
Reisenstein, J., *Rabbinic Wisdom,* Cincinnati, 1921.
Remy, Nahida, *Prayer in Bible and Talmud,* New York, 1910.
Rodkinson, M. L., *The History of the Talmud,* New York, 1903.
Sachar, A. L., *A History of the Jews,* New York, 1930.
Schechter, S., "The Talmud," *Hastings Dictionary of the Bible,* volume 5.
Schechter, S., *Some Aspects of Rabbinic Theology,* New York, 1910.
Schwab, M., *Berakot of the Palestinian Talmud in English,* London, 1886.
Silver, Abba Hillel, *Messianic Speculation in Israel,* New York, 1927.
Silver, M., *Ethics of Judaism,* New York, 1938.
Sperling, H., *The Zohar in English,* 5 vols., London, 1931–1934.
Strack, H. L., *Introduction to Talmud and Midrash,* Philadelphia, 1931.
*Talmud,* Abridged, English Translation, 10 volumes by M. L. Rodkinson, Boston, 1918.
*Talmud,* Babylonian, English, 24 volumes by I. Epstein, London, 1935–39.
Taylor, C., *Sayings of the Jewish Fathers,* Cambridge, 1877 and 1897.
Trachtenberg, J., *Jewish Magic and Superstition,* New York, 1939.
Trachtenberg, J., *The Devil and the Jews,* New Haven, 1943.
Waite, A. E., *The Holy Kabbalah,* New York, 1929.
Waite, A. E., *The Book of Formation,* London, 1923.
Weiss, L., *Talmudic and Other Legends,* 1888.
Wise, I. M., *The Origin of Christianity,* Cincinnati, 1868.
Yahuda, J., *Life and Law According to Hebrew Thought,* Oxford, 1932.
Zeitlin, S., *Megillat Taanit as a Source,* Philadelphia, 1922.
Zeitlin, S., *History of the Second Jewish Commonwealth,* Philadelphia, 1933.
Zeitlin, S., *The Pharisees and their Opponents,* New York, 1939.

# BIBLIOGRAPHY 569

Herford, R. T., *The Pharisees,* London, 1924.
Herford, R. T., *Ethics of the Fathers,* New York, 1930.
Hershon, P. I., *Treasures of the Talmud,* London, 1882.
Hershon, P. I., *Genesis With a Talmudic Commentary,* London, 1883.
Herzog, I., *Main Institutions of Jewish Law, 2* volumes, London, 1936.
Higger, M., *Jewish Utopia in Rabbinic Literature,* New York, 1932.
Higger, M., *Tractate Derek Eertz with Tosefta, in English,* New York, 1935.
Hirsch, S. A., *The Kabbalists and Other Essays,* London, 1922.
Hoexter, J. and Jung, M., *Source Book of Jewish History and Literature,* London, 1938.
Hurwitz, Hyman, *Hebrew Tales,* New York, 1917.
Isaacs, A. S., *Stories from the Rabbis of the Talmud,* New York, 1911.
Jastrow, M., *A Dictionary of the Talmud,* London, 1926.
Joseph, Morris, *Judaism as Creed and Life,* London, 1910.
Jung, Leo, *Jewish Library,* 3 series, New York, 1928–1934.
Kadushin, J. L., *Jewish Code of Jurisprudence,* 4 vols., Boston, 1921.
Kadushin, M., *Organic Thinking in Rabbinic Thought,* New York, 1938.
Kalisch, I., *A Sketch of the Talmud and a Book of Creation,* New York, 1877.
Kaplan, Julius, *Redaction of the Babylonian Talmud,* New York, 1936.
Kaplan, M. M., *Meaning of God in Modern Jewish Religion,* New York, 1937.
Kaplan, M. M., *Judaism as a Civilization,* New York, 1934.
Kaplan, M. M., *Judaism in Transition,* New York, 1936.
Karpeles, G., *Jewish Literature,* Philadelphia, 1895.
Kastein, J., *History and Destiny of the Jews,* New York, 1934.
Kauvar, H., *Pirke Abot Comments.*
Klausner, Joseph, *Jesus of Nazareth* (English by H. Danby), New York, 1929.
Klausner, Joseph, *From Jesus to Paul* (English by Wm. F. Steinspring), New York, 1943.
Kohler, K., *Jewish Theology,* New York, 1918.
Kohler, K., *Heaven and Hell,* New York, 1923.
Kohut, Alexander, *Ethics of the Fathers,* New York, 1885.
Lauterbach, J. Z., *Critical Text and English Translation of the Mekilta,* 3 vols., Philadelphia, 1931–1935.
Lauterbach, J. Z., *Midrash and Mishnah,* New York, 1916.
Levias, Caspar, *Grammar of the Aramaic Idiom,* Cincinnati, 1900.
Levinthal, I. H., *Judaism,* New York, 1935.
Levinthal, I. H., "Jewish Law of Agency," *JQR,* xiii, 117–191, New York, 1923.
Lucas, Alice, *Talmudic Legends,* London, 1908.
Macintosh, W., *Gleanings from the Talmud,* London, 1905.
Malter, H., *Treatise Taanit of the Talmud Babli,* Philadelphia, 1928.
Mann, Jacob, *Text and Studies in Jewish History and Literature,* 2 vols., Cincinnati, 1931–1935.
Margolis and Marx, *A History of the Jewish People,* Philadelphia, 1927.
Margolis, M. L., *Manual of the Aramaic Language of the Talmud,* Munich, 1910.
*Midrash Rabbah,* English Translation, 10 volumes by Friedman and Simon, London, 1936.
Mielziner, M., *Institution of Slavery Among Ancient Hebrews,* Cincinnati, 1894.